Establishing and Evaluating Digital Ethos and Online Credibility

Moe Folk
Kutztown University of Pennsylvania, USA

Shawn Apostel
Bellarmine University, USA

A volume in the Advances in Linguistics and
Communication Studies (ALCS) Book Series

www.igi-global.com

Published in the United States of America by
IGI Global
Information Science Reference (an imprint of IGI Global)
701 E. Chocolate Avenue
Hershey PA, USA 17033
Tel: 717-533-8845
Fax: 717-533-8661
E-mail: cust@igi-global.com
Web site: http://www.igi-global.com

Library of Congress Cataloging-in-Publication Data

Names: Folk, Moe, 1972- editor. | Apostel, Shawn, 1971- editor.
Title: Establishing and evaluating digital ethos and online credibility / Moe
    Folk and Shawn Apostel, editors.
Description: Hershey : Information Science Reference, [2017] | Series:
    Advances in linguistics and communication studies | Includes
    bibliographical references and index.
Identifiers: LCCN 2016037306| ISBN 9781522510727 (hardcover) | ISBN
    9781522510734 (ebook)
Subjects: LCSH: Information technology--Moral and ethical aspects. | Mass
    media--Moral and ethical aspects. | Digital media--Evaluation. |
    Electronic information resources--Evaluation. | Trust.
Classification: LCC HM851 .E768 2017 | DDC 302.23/1--dc23 LC record available at https://lccn.loc.gov/2016037306

This book is published in the IGI Global book series Advances in Linguistics and Communication Studies (ALCS) (ISSN: 2372-109X; eISSN: 2372-1111).

British Cataloguing in Publication Data
A Cataloguing in Publication record for this book is available from the British Library.

For electronic access to this publication, please contact: eresources@igi-global.com.

Advances in Linguistics and Communication Studies (ALCS) Book Series

Abigail G. Scheg
Western Governors University, USA

ISSN:2372-109X
EISSN:2372-1111

MISSION

The scope of language and communication is constantly changing as society evolves, new modes of communication are developed through technological advancement, and novel words enter our lexicon as the result of cultural change. Understanding how we communicate and use language is crucial in all industries and updated research is necessary in order to promote further knowledge in this field.

The **Advances in Linguistics and Communication Studies (ALCS)** book series presents the latest research in diverse topics relating to language and communication. Interdisciplinary in its coverage, ALCS presents comprehensive research on the use of language and communication in various industries including business, education, government, and healthcare.

COVERAGE

- Interpersonal Communication
- Discourse Analysis
- Non-Verbal Communication
- Language and Identity
- Media and Public Communications
- Language acquisition
- Semantics
- Sociolinguistics
- Computational Linguistics
- Computer-Mediated Communication

IGI Global is currently accepting manuscripts for publication within this series. To submit a proposal for a volume in this series, please contact our Acquisition Editors at Acquisitions@igi-global.com or visit: http://www.igi-global.com/publish/.

Titles in this Series

For a list of additional titles in this series, please visit: www.igi-global.com

Computational and Cognitive Approaches to Narratology
Takashi Ogata (Iwate Prefectural University, Japan) and Taisuke Akimoto (The University of Electoro-Communications, Japan)
Information Science Reference • copyright 2016 • 467pp • H/C (ISBN: 9781522504320) • US $215.00 (our price)

Analyzing Language and Humor in Online Communication
Rotimi Taiwo (Obafemi Awolowo University, Nigeria) Akinola Odebunmi (University of Ibadan, Nigeria) and Akin Adetunji (Emmanuel Alayande College of Education, Nigeria)
Information Science Reference • copyright 2016 • 324pp • H/C (ISBN: 9781522503385) • US $185.00 (our price)

Discourse Analysis as a Tool for Understanding Gender Identity, Representation, and Equality
Nazmunnessa Mahtab (University of Dhaka, Bangladesh) Sara Parker (John Moores University, UK) Farah Kabir (Action Aid, Bangladesh) Tania Haque (University of Dhaka, Bangladesh) Aditi Sabur (University of Dhaka, Bangladesh) and Abu Saleh Mohammad Sowad (University of Dhaka, Bangladesh)
Information Science Reference • copyright 2016 • 323pp • H/C (ISBN: 9781522502258) • US $185.00 (our price)

Revealing Gender Inequalities and Perceptions in South Asian Countries through Discourse Analysis
Nazmunnessa Mahtab (University of Dhaka, Bangladesh) Sara Parker (John Moores University, UK) Farah Kabir (Action Aid, Bangladesh) Tania Haque (University of Dhaka, Bangladesh) Aditi Sabur (University of Dhaka, Bangladesh) and Abu Saleh Mohammad Sowad (University of Dhaka, Bangladesh)
Information Science Reference • copyright 2016 • 286pp • H/C (ISBN: 9781522502791) • US $185.00 (our price)

Interdisciplinary Perspectives on Contemporary Conflict Resolution
Paulo Novais (University of Minho, Portugal) and Davide Carneiro (University of Minho, Portugal)
Information Science Reference • copyright 2016 • 363pp • H/C (ISBN: 9781522502456) • US $185.00 (our price)

Handbook of Research on Effective Communication, Leadership, and Conflict Resolution
Anthony H. Normore (California State University Dominguez Hills, USA & International Academy of Public safety, USA) Larry W. Long (Illinois State University, USA & International Academy of Public Safety, USA) and Mitch Javidi (North Carolina State University, USA & International Academy of Public Safety, USA)
Information Science Reference • copyright 2016 • 733pp • H/C (ISBN: 9781466699700) • US $315.00 (our price)

Handbook of Research on Cross-Cultural Approaches to Language and Literacy Development
Patriann Smith (University of Illinois at Urbana-Champaign, USA) and Alex Kumi-Yeboah (University at Albany–State University of New York, USA)
Information Science Reference • copyright 2015 • 567pp • H/C (ISBN: 9781466686687) • US $305.00 (our price)

www.igi-global.com

701 E. Chocolate Ave., Hershey, PA 17033
Order online at www.igi-global.com or call 717-533-8845 x100
To place a standing order for titles released in this series, contact: cust@igi-global.com
Mon-Fri 8:00 am - 5:00 pm (est) or fax 24 hours a day 717-533-8661

Nathan Rodriguez, *University of Wisconsin – Stevens Point, USA*

Sean Sadri, *Old Dominion University, USA*

Thomas A. Salek, *University of Wisconsin – Milwaukee, USA*

Erika M. Sparby, *Northern Illinois University, USA*

Table of Contents

Section 1
Evaluating and Gathering Research

Section 2
Evaluating Digital Ethos and Online Credibility in Medical Contexts

Section 3
Addressing Anonymity in Digital Realms

Section 4
Reconciling Individual and Group Ethos

Detailed Table of Contents

Section 1
Evaluating and Gathering Research

This section offers a variety of methods for evaluating and conducting online research, focusing on the problems involved in finding trustworthy information. The chapters in this section focus on evaluating scientific arguments, connecting with information experts, cultivating a beneficial digital ethos in research documents, and evaluating what is often hidden—how websites use our data for research purposes.

Chapter 1

Determining the credibility of statistical research has traditionally been done through peer-reviewed journal publications. With the recent increase in research shared in online forums comes emerging challenges for authors sharing results and for readers determining if research is valid. This chapter introduces a heuristic for evaluating the credibility of statistics based on methods used to counteract claims made in The Bell Curve. The approaches gleaned from this case are then updated for online environments and demonstrated using contemporary online debates about climate change science and skepticism. The heuristic for evaluating credibility of statistical arguments online is useful for readers and as a guide for authors adapting their research for online publication and debate.

This chapter argues that as the online informational landscape continues to expand, shortcuts to source credibility evaluation, in particular the revered checklist approach, falls short of its intended goal, and this method cannot replace the acquisition of a more formally acquired and comprehensive information literacy skill set. By examining the current standard of checklist criteria, the authors identify problems with this approach. Such shortcuts are not necessarily effective for online source credibility assessment, and the authors contend that in cases of high-stakes informational needs, they cannot adequately replace the expertise of information professionals, nor displace the need for proper and continuous information literacy education.

Chapter 3

This chapter aims at presenting and discussing credible online recruitment eliciting techniques targeting scientific purposes adjusted to the digital age. Based on several illustrations conducted by the author within the framework of both quantitative and qualitative inquiries, this chapter critically explores the digital ethos in three main challenges faced when dealing with online recruitment for scientific purposes: entering the normality of the everyday life, entering the idiosyncrasy of multicultural lives, and entering the chaos of busy lives. By the end, a toolbox for establishing and evaluating (dis)credibility within online recruitment strategies is presented. Moreover, it is argued that success of data collection at the present time in online environments seems to rely as ever on internal factors of the communication process vis-à-vis e-mail content, design and related strategies.

Chapter 4

Exchanging information online often involves a degree of assessing the credibility and reliability of websites, which include the authors, sources, and content. This chapter argues for an additional assessment category: evaluating privacy and/or data use statements of websites because of the underlying ideologies, methods of tracking technologies used to collect data, and the need for comprehension of what website terms and conditions mean for the average person. This chapter provides a rhetorical framework as suggested guidelines to follow when evaluating privacy and/or data use statements of websites.

Section 2
Evaluating Digital Ethos and Online Credibility in Medical Contexts

Because the number of people who desire access to heath information continues to grow (and the amount of health information available to those people continues to grow as well), this section offers advice for assessing the credibility of online health information. Considering that many people around the world lack access to adequate health care but can easily access online health information, this section offers a range of advice that is very important for a wide audience to consider.

Chapter 5

The proliferation of medical information online, without physicians or peer reviewers as gatekeepers, has made e-health an important focus for credibility research. Web 2.0, enabling lay users to contribute content, has complicated patients' challenge of deciding who to trust. To help inspire trust, an e-health website must convey a credible ethos in its homepage and other pages that constitute a user's first impression of a site. This chapter compares the visual and textual ethos strategies of three major e-health sites that represent a continuum from informational to interactive: a government site, a commercial site, and a patient social networking site. The findings reveal a variety of features, such as scientific imagery, privacy seals, and video of patient stories, that can ultimately contribute to an ethos based in expertise and/or in community. This study has implications for the design and evaluation of trustworthy e-health communication.

Andrew W. Cole, Waukesha County Technical College, USA
Thomas A. Salek, University of Wisconsin-Stevens Point, USA

This chapter approaches online ethos rhetorically to argue that professional medical sources (e.g., practitioners, organizations) must overcome a rhetorically constituted kakoethos in order to influence online health information seekers. Professional medical source kakoethos is established through a lack of identified, authentic personal experience with specific medical conditions, and health information message content that focuses exclusively on the science behind the condition. Conversely, lay health information sources fashion ethos through identifying personal experience with specific medical conditions, and employing emotionally supportive messages. The result is an online health rhetoric appearing credible and authentic. Rhetorically crafting a parasocial connection to online health information seekers may offer a means for professional medical sources to overcome the kakoethos established through lack of personal experience.

Lluïsa Llamero, Blanquerna-Ramon Llull University, Spain

This chapter reflects on the process of truth representation in different topics of human knowledge to reach an understanding of differences in online credibility assessment. The author argues that new cultural trends for legitimizing second-hand information –as wisdom of crowds, self-sufficiency or gatewatching– may cause friction with symbolic cultural factors and social structures settled by historical processes. This makes the evaluation of credibility an issue under negotiation. Analysis of qualitative data into the areas of health, economy and tourism allow to propose a processual theoretical model of credibility assessment.

Nathan Rodriguez, University of Wisconsin – Stevens Point, USA

This chapter adopts a case study approach to examine the echo chamber effect online. Individuals cobble together personalized newsfeeds by active choice and those choices are often accompanied by subtle manipulations in social media and online search engine algorithms that may shape and constrain the parameters of information on a given topic. In this chapter, the author studied vaccine-hesitant discourse in an online forum over a five-year period. Those conversations exhibited characteristics of what would be considered an echo chamber. The implications of this case study suggest that the echo chamber within the realm of vaccination can lead individuals toward content and information of dubious veracity, with significant implications for public health.

Section 3
Addressing Anonymity in Digital Realms

Much advice on evaluating online information hinges on determining the author of a source, then making judgments about the credibility of that author's credentials. However, a vast amount of the digital information we encounter has no discernible author, much less an author whose background and credentials are readily available for evaluation. This section examines the benefits and drawbacks of anonymity with regard to establishing digital credibility, and it offers strategies for assessing information on sites where anonymity reigns.

Chapter 9

The chapter explores the complex emergent feminist ethos in two virtual spaces created by the San Francisco chapter of AWSA—the Arab Women's Solidarity Association International, an Arab women's activist group. First, the chapter discusses ethos and identity construction in cyberspace. Second, the chapter analyzes AWSA's cyber discourses to uncover the characteristics of its feminist ethos and the opportunities allowed or lost for authenticity and the role of anonymity in constructing its feminist ethos. Third, the chapter questions whether anonymity allows for the critical examination of the discourses and ideologies of the powerful in addition to the creation of a sustainable counter-hegemonic discourse or whether it heightens the threat of homogeneity and streamlining in cyberspace. The chapter, in its conclusion, calls for a critical investigation of the potential of the digital domain to challenge the concentration of power in virtual spaces and uncover frameworks through which revolutionary discourses can be sustained and disseminated.

Chapter 10

Information credibility is difficult to ascertain online, especially when identity is obscured. Yet increasingly, individuals ascertain credibility of emerging information in such contexts, including in the midst of crises. The authors, using data from reddit, examine the influence of potentially credibility cues in a pseudonymous context, investigating not both general effects and whether cues affecting credibility perceptions maintain their effects during crises. Findings include a positive relationship between commenter reputation and perceived credibility in non-crises; a positive relationship between perceived credibility and the use of persuasive appeals relating to one's character or experiences during crisis; and a positive relationship between perceived credibility and the use of a link during crisis. The authors explore how reddit's structure impacts credibility perception, describe how persuasion is operationalized, and elaborate a typology of highly credible comments. Through this study, the authors contribute to both credibility research and crisis informatics.

This chapter explores the issue of credibility in online dating. 200 posts to a website called eDateReview. com were inductively analyzed. Examination of these posts revealed that online daters negotiate the potential for selective self-presentation by developing strategies for evaluating the credibility of online dating profiles which builds on established theories of self-presentation in online spaces. These strategies include determining the credibility of the dating sites themselves, assessing the credibility of online profiles, and the demonization of dishonesty to establish norms. Implications and future research are discussed.

Chapter 12

Digital media has seen a proliferation of Third-Party Review Sites (TPRS) that encourage the public to comment and reflect on their interactions and experiences with a retailer, brand, or company. Sites like Yelp build massive audiences based on their credibility as authentic, accurate, external reviewers. This study looks at how the co-opting of TPRS pages by advocates and protesters influences public perceptions of credibility on these sites. Specifically, it explores the public's reaction to Yelp as a digital space of protest after the death of Cecil the Lion at the hands of a Minnesota dentist. Through focus groups, this study identifies that TPRS audiences look for consistency in reviews to determine credibility; the public sees advocacy as harming the credibility of the overall site; current events play a role in the interpretation of TPRS; and the intentions of users is key to building a reputation as credible in digital media.

Section 4
Reconciling Individual and Group Ethos

This section examines the different impacts that individual ethos can have on how we access, assess, share, and build online information. The chapters in this section all focus on different digital sites and genres, but each one sheds light on the importance of negotiating the relationship between individual and group ethos by illustrating the specific benefits and drawbacks of acknowledging—or effacing— individual ethos in different contexts.

Chapter 13

As human interaction increasingly shifts to on-line environments, the age-old challenge of determining communicators' credibility becomes all the more important and challenging. The absence of nonverbal behaviors adds to this challenge, though "rich media" attempt to compensate for this traditional lacuna within mediated interpersonal communication. The present study seeks to empirically understand how the ability and necessity of trust and credibility are built, maintained, and depreciated in online environments, using the on-line "Couchsurfing" travel environment as a worthy sample. In this environment, both hosts and guests must determine whether the other is a viable candidate for free housing, even though they have typically never met face-to-face, or even spoken via phone. Results show participants relying on information found in members' request messages and references, both when accepting and rejecting requests, with a lack of reliance placed on photos and other textual profile information.

Chapter 14

Jonathan S. Carter, University of Nebraska – Lincoln, USA

Traditionally, the artistic proofs center on the individual rhetor as the locusof ethos. However, as communication becomes internetworked, rhetorical phenomena increasingly circulate independent of traditional rhetors. This absence transfers ethos onto textual assemblages that often function as agents in their own right. This transfer of ethos is particularly apparent in memes, where fragmented images constructed across divergent networked media come together to form a single agentic text. Therefore, this chapter argues that a theory of modal ethos is important to understand this artistic proof's role in a networked media ecology. Through a modal analysis of the meme Scumbag Steve, this chapter argues that the modal construction of the meme gives it a unique point of view, complete with narrative history, affective representation, and social expertise—in short, its very own ethos. This allows networked participants to evoke the meme in controversies ranging from NSA wiretapping to the Ukraine Crisis, demanding new forms of political judgment.

Chapter 15

Sean R. Sadri, Old Dominion University, USA

The evolution of online media has brought forth a new age of fandom online for sport enthusiasts with access to hundreds of new sports articles daily. This chapter touches on the perceived credibility of the modern sports article and provides evidence from scholarly studies, including the author's own sports credibility study. The study examines how article source, medium, fan identification, and user comment tone can all impact the credibility of a sports article. Study participants were randomly assigned to read a sports article in 1 of 12 stimuli groups. The article source was indicated to have appeared on a mainstream sports website, a sports blog, a social networking site, or a wire service as well as with positive comments, negative comments, or without comments. Analysis revealed that fan identification level was an important factor in credibility ratings as highly identified fans found the article to be significantly more credible than low identification fans as a whole. The study implications and factors influencing the credibility of an online sports article are explored.

Chapter 16

Alison A. Lukowski, Christian Brothers University, USA
Erika M. Sparby, Northern Illinois University, USA

This chapter is concerned with women's mis- or underrepresentation in knowledge creation, particularly when it comes to their bodies. In this chapter, the authors examine how Wikipedia's generic regulations determine that women's often experiential ethos is unwelcome on the site. Thus, women are often unable to construct knowledge on the "Breastfeeding" entry; their epistemological methods are ignored or banned by other contributors. This chapter also examines six breastfeeding-focused mommyblogs, proposing blogs as an alternative genre that welcomes women's ethos. However, the authors also recognize that such blogs are not a perfect epistemological paradigm. The chapter closes with an examination of the implications of this work for academic collaboration across fields and for women's agency.

Foreword

LOCATING ETHOS, CREDIBILITY, AND POWER IN THE (DIGITAL) RHETORICAL TRADITION

In its earliest incarnation, ethos resulted from the "good man speaking well," according to the Roman rhetorician Quintilian (2001). Certainly, this definition is a product of its historical moment, one in which the rhetorical situation typically represented a masculine public sphere relying upon oral discourse in political and judicial contexts. Whether in print or speech, this definition held for nearly two millennia, privileging a particularly narrow view of argument that positioned ethos within the public persona of the writer or speaker, an embodied phenomenon that even numerous textbooks in our contemporary moment continue to uphold as they stress critical reading, writing and listening strategies to detect the ways rhetoricians gain and maintain credibility with audiences. Yet those Greek and Roman rhetoricians could not have envisioned the extent to which ethos and credibility would circulate so pervasively in a digital era of ubiquitous information access and equally ubiquitous information overload. Indeed, one user's online trash is another's online treasure and, unlike the conception of ethos reserved for the canonical speakers and writers we often consume in graduate seminars on rhetorical history, ethos, like Foucault's (1978) concept of power, is everywhere. Ethos circulates within both social and news media spaces from Facebook to the *New York Times*, within online resources that include Google and Wikipedia, and, ever more increasingly, within the algorithms behind those spaces that track our movements and present us with information in ways that hail us as audiences. These tools garner ethos and credibility by providing today's Web 2.0 audiences what they want to see and hear, or what they think we need to hear about which news source to read, which political pundit to believe or not, and which link to click.

Moe Folk and Shawn Apostel superbly captured this dynamic landscape in their first edited volume, *Online Credibility and Digital Ethos: Evaluating Computer-Mediated Communication* (2013), a collection featuring both national and international scholars who situate the topic in theories of design and arrangement, ideologies and epistemologies of information access, contexts that range from digital scholarly publishing to popular news media and games, and tools as diverse as weblogs, LinkedIn, and Wikipedia. What became clear through this first compilation is that not only does our understanding of ethos shift and evolve at a pace similar to the digital rhetorical contexts in which online personae flourish but also that our corresponding operational definitions of credibility must move beyond the face to face, the alphabetic, the monolingual/modal, and the heteronormative.

Given the fact that digital technology advances more rapidly than the print-based publishing processes that academics are compelled to rely upon to circulate scholarship about such technology, it makes sense to say, ala the late novelist Jacqueline Susann (1973), that "once is not enough." Indeed, within this landscape of online information exchange, the three years since the publication of Folk and Apostel's first volume approximates an epoch. And while those initial conversations nevertheless maintain their currency, it's even more vital to extend the dialogue, bridging the gap between the academy and the larger culture by conducting further critical analyses of the spaces occupied by our students and ourselves. With that thought in mind, Folk's and Apostel's *Establishing and Evaluating Digital Ethos and Online Credibility* represents an equally diverse sequel in its emphasis on the latest genres and tools of identity formation, to the online dating profile to the ever-pervasive meme, not to mention its sustained attention to international perspectives on social media space, with contributors from Canada, Egypt, France, Spain, and Turkey. Although this collection does as much as the first in its focus on the what's and why's of online credibility and ethos, it moves its readers forward in its focus on both process and product, using a broad but helpful array of theoretical, methodological, pedagogical, and ethical frameworks.

Moreover, these essays strongly suggest that ethos is a multiliterate process (Selber, 2004), for while many students and citizens possess functional literacies in that they know how to use various communication tools, their ability to critically read and ethically produce content is another matter. Many of the essays provide strong guidance in this regard through their own rhetorical example as well as through specific strategies for individual and classroom adoption so that researchers and teachers benefit equally. In this sense, the collection as a whole represents a powerful call to action, as it is explicit in its presumption that the numerous non-academic settings in which both ethos and credibility circulate are ones that must be studied in academic settings by both teachers and students. And as some contributors suggest, our traditional ways of understanding credibility need to be updated. For Jill R. Kavanaugh and Bartlomiej A. Lenart, this includes that standard emphasis on student information literacy training. Given the rise of open access and anonymous posting, our definitions of authorship, peer review, and ultimately credibility are what needs to be reevaluated. Yet, even as we apply more flexible criteria to assess credibility in an era of Web 2.0, another assumption subject to reevaluation is our ability as citizens to access reliable, objective information in mainstream news media, something we take for granted in the United States, yet is of great concern for international journalists and the diverse communities they serve. Ceren Sözeri provides a powerful case study of Turkish news organizations' efforts to sustain impartiality, immediacy, and transparency, relying on interviews with both mainstream and independent media journalists as they discuss strategies to maintain a culture of trust in reporting. Admittedly, trust is an increasingly difficult standard measure for Western media outlets as well.

Academics who study and teach ethos and credibility online and off will learn that these concepts are not only rhetorical and technological but also cultural, subject to assumptions and limitations about who does what, where, and how. For instance, Alison A. Lukowski and Ericka M. Sparby make visible the challenges women have in establishing ethos in blog- and wiki-based settings and the epistemological values in digital space that prohibit and discount women's experiential knowledge, even on topics of motherhood and breastfeeding. These hierarchies also extend to other types of health and wellness spaces, something Abigail Baake articulates in her analysis of medical information sites like WebMD and the need for better balance between physician expertise and patient experience.

Such discussions document the ways in which ethos and credibility are reinscribed in many virtual contexts as individual, and often male-dominated, rather than the result of a collective, activist, and even feminist partnership. Contributor Samaa Gamie applies a feminist analysis to the ethos of the Arab Women's Solidarity Association, and the ability of these collective digital discourses to "challenge patriarchy and the concentration of power in virtual spaces." For Gamie and others, such co-constructions of ethos are dynamic and span time, text, and space, something Wendi Sierra and Douglas Eyman also address in their analysis of a newer game, Elder Scrolls Online. As Sierra and Eyman note, because gaming spaces rely on external sources for knowledge building and credibility, they challenge classical assumptions about a stabilized sense of ethos solely in the persona of the rhetor. While ethos and credibility may be more difficult to pinpoint in such spaces, the websites we visit and the search engines we utilize have their own agency, using surveillance software to track our activities and use those activities to appeal to us. As a result, as Estee Beck and others in this collection imply, today's rhetorical education should not be so very far removed from the classical emphasis on the ethical personae, but should shift that ethical standard from the individual to the site itself and its inherently value-laden rhetorical practices. Despite Selber's useful triangulation of functional, critical, and rhetorical multiliteracies, a literate education should emphasize the ethical as well, helping citizens better interrogate the policies and practices of the spaces we use, and that undoubtedly use us.

Rhetorical tools and situations may have evolved since the times of Plato, Aristotle, Cicero, and Quintilian, but *Establishing and Evaluating Digital Ethos and Online Credibility* proves that the credibility of people, information, and space is thriving online. Ethos, rather than being a lost art of persuasion, is like writing itself, remediated (Bolter, 2001) and circulating in virtual space. This remediation mandates ongoing analysis that undoubtedly sustains and reshapes the rhetorical tradition as it continues into the digital age, an era where a hashtag, a meme, or a like has as much power to reflect and shape cultural values as a political speech or a news article. Folk and Apostel's collection admirably fulfills this analytical goal and will undoubtedly serve as a multidisciplinary resource for global scholars and educators working along the axes of literacy, communication, and technology studies.

Kristine L. Blair
Youngstown State University, USA

REFERENCES

Bolter, J. D. (1991). *Writing space: The computer, hypertext, and the history of writing*. Hillsdale, NJ: Lawrence Erlbaum.

Folk, M., & Apostel, S. (2013). *Online credibility and digital ethos: Evaluating computer-mediated communication*. Hershey, PA: IGI Global.

Foucault, M. (1978). *The history of sexuality*. New York: Pantheon Books.

Quintilian, , & Russell, D. A. (2001). *The orator's education*. Cambridge, MA: Harvard University Press.

Selber, S. A. (2004). *Multiliteracies for a digital age*. Carbondale, IL: Southern Illinois University Press.

Susann, J. (1973). *Once is not enough*. New York: Bantam.

Preface

Eleven years ago, as Ph.D. students at Michigan Technological University, the editors of this collection found themselves frustrated by the "easy to memorize" lists students were offered to inoculate themselves from the dangers of false information. The list excluded many sites we found helpful on a day-to-day basis. As soon as the first article we wrote on the subject, "First Phase Information Literacy on a Fourth Generation Website: An Argument for a New Approach to Website Evaluation Criteria," was published, the rise of Web 2.0 and social media began to take shape, and the simple checklist approach that had been ubiquitous, as we had predicted, soon revealed itself to be woefully inadequate. Thus began the first of many publications in which we explored the complex negotiations that take place when someone searches for information online, culminating in *Online Credibility and Digital Ethos: Evaluating Computer-Mediated Communication* (2012), which featured the work of 21 scholars from around the globe who examined a range of digital genres in order to shed light on the issue.

Fast-forward a few years, and what was true in 2012 is even more true now: The near-ubiquity of smartphones, tablets, and laptops, provides easy access to acquiring and publishing online information anywhere, anytime; however, with advances in information technology, new challenges arise for content providers in establishing credibility and for students, researchers, and consumers in developing effective ways of evaluating online credibility. For example, students and instructors in writing classes across the world face challenges in creating research projects that did not exist even a decade ago. These issues are not just affecting American universities; therefore, this book addresses an international audience by offering approaches to evaluating the credibility of digital sources, including specific advice that can be gleaned from popular websites and techniques useful for a wide variety of digital genres.

An international audience will find this book useful for a variety of academic disciplines because students continue to utilize online sources in their research. Information literacy specialists will find the chapters useful because each chapter focuses on a particular type of source. Journalists and educators in the field of Mass Communication and Library Sciences will find the book useful in establishing protocol for approaching a wide variety of sources. Cultural Studies researchers will find the information invaluable for evaluating and conducting online research. Web designers and writers could use this book to establish a more credible online presence. However, we feel that while a broad segment of graduate students and academics could utilize certain chapters to establish a method for determining the credibility of a source for research purposes, a main audience will be writing instructors who assign papers and projects that require extensive research. In addition, a variety of digital sites that many people visit regularly are explored thoroughly in case studies throughout this book, and strategies for assessing health and science sites, whose use is important to a wide swath of the planet, are also included.

Section 1, "Evaluating and Gathering Research," offers a variety of methods for evaluating and conducting online research, focusing on the problems involved in finding trustworthy information. The chapters in this section focus on evaluating scientific arguments, connecting with information experts, cultivating a beneficial digital ethos in research documents, and evaluating what is often hidden—how websites use our data for research purposes.

In "Telling the Quants from the Quacks: Evaluating Statistical Arguments in Debates Online," Candice Lanius of Rensselaer Polytechnic Institute, USA, transcends generic digital evaluation frameworks to provide a robust framework for assessing the quality of science information. She focuses on how statistics are used to present scientific data on climate change websites, and her work provides a valuable tool for constructing web evaluation strategies aimed at websites with a specific focus. We feel this chapter offers an important model for future researchers to follow going forward because the field needs more specific models that target particular types of information and audiences.

In "No Shortcuts to Credibility Evaluation: The Importance of Expertise and Information," Jill R. Kavanaugh of the Center on Media and Child Health at Boston Children's Hospital and Bartlomiej A. Lenart of the University of Alberta, Canada, further demonstrate the limitations of the generic checklist approach in an age of diverse information sources. They argue that we are overwhelmed by the vast amount of information at our fingertips, and the best way to deal with that deluge is to embrace information experts. They argue that even experts in their own fields would benefit from more exposure to information experts in order to keep pace with their fields efficiently; as a result, they advocate for information literacy instruction being handled by embedded librarians, and they examine a novel case of embedded librarianship in a hospital that can serve as a model for other institutions and corporations.

In "Knockin' on Digital Doors: Dealing with Online [Dis]Credit in an Era of Digital Scientific," Rosalina Pisco Costa of the University of Évora, Portugal, offers ways for researchers to increase their online ethos for the purposes of recruiting study participants online. She focuses on digital documents designed to recruit participants for both quantitative and qualitative purposes, paying particular attention to techniques that allow researchers to connect with others by entering through the context of everyday life, the chaos of busy lives, and the diversity of multicultural lives. Her advice in designing these documents, particular emails, is applicable not only to social science researchers but also all those who need to establish online contacts through "cold" digital communication.

Can we evaluate what we don't see (or refuse to look at)? In "Who Is Tracking You? A Rhetorical Framework for Evaluating Surveillance & Privacy," Estee Beck, of The University of Texas at Arlington, USA, tackles the issue of website policies regarding the tracking and sharing of user data. Beck argues that we must add a wholly unique aspect to current digital evaluation criteria: a website's privacy and/ or data use statement. Thus, instead of merely ignoring or instantly clicking "I agree" like so many users, Beck argues that these privacy statements should be of paramount concern when evaluating digital credibility because they alone truly reflect the ethos of a site's creator.

Section 2, "Digital Ethos and Online Credibility in Medical Contexts," addresses the increasing numbers of people who desire access to quality online health care information by offering advice for assessing a source's ethos. As many people around the world may not have the physical proximity to, or the resources to visit, a quality health care provider, this section provides suggestions intended to help people navigate that environment. Conversely, the information may also be useful to health care providers who hope to communicate with patients online.

In "Ethos in E-Health: From Informational to Interactive Websites," Abigail Bakke of Minnesota State University, Mankato, USA, examines three different types of e-health sites— government, corporate, and patient-driven—and argues that e-health information is perceived as most credible when it is rooted in both traditional medical expertise *and* the patient community. She demonstrates that medical sites that do not include patients' voices are viewed as untrustworthy, and her work makes many important points for consumers and designers of e-health information.

In "Adopting a Parasocial Connection to Overcome Professional Kakoethos in Online Health Information," Andrew W. Cole of Waukesha County Technical College, USA, and Thomas A. Salek of University of Wisconsin-Milwaukee, USA, demonstrate that laypersons seeking e-health information are more apt to trust sources that include people sharing their personal medical stories instead of professional medical sources that privilege subjective science information and lack authentic personal experience with medical conditions. Coupled with Abigail Bakke's chapter mentioned above, Cole and Salek help to further the importance of rhetorical identification for health information seekers and designers hoping to establish trust.

In "The Social Determinants in the Process of Credibility Assessment and the Influence of Topic Areas," Lluïsa Llamero of Ramon Llull University, Spain, reflects on how truth is represented in different areas of human knowledge, including health. She contrasts traditional medical expertise rooted in symbolic cultural factors with the second-hand information patients feel more comfortable accessing. Through the analysis of qualitative data from health and other areas, she proposes a processual theoretical model of credibility assessment that has wide application.

In "Credible to Whom? The Curse of the Echo Chamber," Nathan Rodriguez of the University of Wisconsin-Stevens Point, USA, examines issues with online health information seekers who become trapped inside circles of like-minded people. Rodriquez demonstrates the damage that this echo chamber can cause to public health by looking at vaccine-hesitant discourse and how it perpetuates its digital ethos in its own spaces, as well as others. His chapter offers beneficial insights that can apply to a host of other controversial topics that are debated online.

Section 3, "Addressing Anonymity in Digital Realms," tackles the problem of unattributed digital content. Much advice on evaluating online information hinges on determining the author of a source, then making judgments about the credibility of that author's credentials. However, a vast amount of the digital information we encounter has no discernible author, much less an author whose background and credentials are readily available for evaluation. This section examines the benefits and drawbacks of anonymity with regard to establishing digital credibility, and it offers strategies for assessing information on sites where anonymity reigns.

In "Ethos Construction, Identification, and Authenticity in the Discourses of AWSA: The Arab Women's Solidarity Association International," Samaa Gamie of Lincoln University, USA, explores the affordances and constraints of anonymity on liberatory and revolutionary discourses by analyzing two iterations of an invitation-only international feminist website. In this case, anonymity had to be granted to users because lives were potentially at stake, and Gamie examines how anonymity impacts a site's ethos by altering authenticity. Ultimately, Gamie questions whether anonymity allows for the critical examination of the hegemonic and the construction of suitable digital counter-discourse by thoroughly analyzing the ethos surrounding both AWSA website iterations.

In "Credibility and Crisis in Pseudonymous Communities," Sarah Lefkowith of the University of Oxford, United Kingdom, focuses on how reddit users respond to emerging crises. All reddit users are anonymous, which makes assessing credibility in a crisis extremely complex because some users may, for example, post to the site stating they are involved with the crisis, yet many readers are unsure whether to trust them or not. Lefkowith conducted an extensive case study of crisis communication on reddit, and her results offer not only incredibly useful techniques for assessing and cultivating credibility on reddit, but also broader precepts that help to address anonymity on other sites.

In "Don't Tell Us You're Handsome...Post Your Great Photo and Let It Stand": Creating and Enforcing Credibility in Online Dating, Shana Kopaczewski of Indiana State University, USA, examines the role anonymity plays in online dating. Through an analysis of more than 200 exchanges on one dating website, she asserts that credibility in online dating is determined by how the website structures and shares its profiles, and she argues that users establish the norms of credibility by demonizing dishonesty. This chapter provides helpful techniques for consumers and producers of user-generated content.

In "Revenge of Cecil the Lion: Credibility in Third-Party Review Sites," Alison N. Novak of Rowan University, USA, analyzes the effects of co-opting third-party review sites in order to promulgate personal agendas and causes for which the sites were not originally intended. She focuses on analyzing how advocates co-opted Yelp after Dr. Walter Palmer killed Cecil the lion and altered the ethos of site, which has important ethos ramifications for sites that allow user-generated reviews and other content.

Section 4, "Reconciling Individual and Group Ethos," examines the different impacts that individual ethos can have on how we access, assess, share, and build online information. The chapters in this section all focus on different digital sites and genres, but each one sheds light on the importance of negotiating the relationship between individual and group ethos by illustrating the specific benefits and drawbacks of acknowledging—or effacing—individual ethos in different contexts.

In "Surf's Up: Communicative Aspects of Online Trust-Building Among Couchsurfing Hosts," Maura Cherney of the University of Wisconsin-Milwaukee, USA, Daniel Cochese Davis of Illinois State University, USA, and Sandra Metts of Illinois State University, USA, focus on discerning how trust is formed through digital environments. Through their analysis of communication between couchsurfing guests and hosts, they argue that the most important credibility cues occurred in request messages and references, with less reliance placed on photos and textual profile information. Their findings are significant for a wide swath of digital realms where people connect to buy, sell, share, and trade; in addition, their findings are important for those who maintain static websites that incorporate Web 2.0 elements—such as many universities.

In "Modal Ethos: Scumbag Steve and the Establishing of Ethos in Memetic Agents," Jonathan S. Carter of the University of Nebraska-Lincoln, USA, provides a close analysis of one of the world's most famous memes to show the intricate ways in which ethos attaches to memes. Carter argues that memes become their own powerful agents of ethos, which allows networked participants to evoke the meme in a range of contexts that are often quite removed from the meme's original intended meaning. This chapter represents another powerful means of challenging the checklist approach, which relies on relatively static conceptions of meaning and ethos that memes transcend.

In "The Rise of the Modern Sports Article: Examining the Factors That Can Influence the Credibility of Online Sports News," Sean Sadri, Old Dominion University, USA, shares research that demonstrates the impact of individual ethos on consuming different types of online content. Through an analysis of fans exposed to different sports articles, Sadri shows how individual ethos helps to determine how different styles, sources, levels of fan identification, and antagonistic comments are perceived by the reader. Additionally, this study demonstrates how different kinds of digital content connect with readers (or not). This chapter offers a valuable rhetorical lesson in illustrating the effect that motivated ethos has on connecting with audiences and achieving purpose in the digital age.

In "Breastfeeding, Authority, and Genre: Women's Ethos in Wikipedia and Blogs," Allison A. Lukowski of Christian Brothers University, USA, and Erika M. Sparby of Northern Illinois University,

USA, argue that sites discussing breastfeeding tend to ignore personal narrative in favor of quantifiable data. While this data may help physicians, it does little to inform the women who struggle with the challenges mothers face when breastfeeding. By examining how sites such as Wikipedia enforce generic gatekeeping practices that limit ethos appeals, the chapter makes an important argument that sites should follow inclusive practices that harness divergent information styles because doing so is important for their audience and therefore increases credibility.

While there are a handful of academic articles and popular books on select topics listed above (e.g., *Building Online Credibility* by Anonymous, *Ultimate Guide to Building Online Credibility for Infopreneurs* by Partha Sarkel, and *Persuasion On-Line and Communicability: The Destruction of Credibility in the Virtual Community and Cognitive Models* by Francisco V. Cipolla-Ficarra), this collection is unique in that it offers theoretical, qualitative, and quantitative research on the topic from a variety of angles, a wide range of disciplines, and with a global perspective. Multiple online sources are discussed in depth, as well as a wide variety of approaches to establishing and evaluating online credibility. As the amount of online information proliferates, the number of digital genres used to carry meaning grows as well; as a result, the issues surrounding digital ethos and online credibility grow more complex and demonstrate the need for this and future books addressing these important issues. The strategies and ideas this book provide will help its audience make sense of the complexity found within current digital realms and also create a strong base for future research.

Acknowledgment

We would like to thank Cindy Selfe for initially encouraging us to explore this topic back in 2004. Since that time, we have been lucky enough to examine the complex issues revolving around digital ethos and online credibility with talented scholars from all over the world, and we hope to continue doing so in the future.

We would also like to thank all of the authors and reviewers for their contributions to this project. Many people gave generously of their time and prioritized their commitment to this book, despite having many other commitments to juggle as well.

Finally, we would also like to thank our families for their patience and support as we worked on this book.

Moe Folk
Kutztown University of Pennsylvania, USA

Shawn Apostel
Bellarmine University, USA

Section 1
Evaluating and Gathering Research

This section offers a variety of methods for evaluating and conducting online research, focusing on the problems involved in finding trustworthy information. The chapters in this section focus on evaluating scientific arguments, connecting with information experts, cultivating a beneficial digital ethos in research documents, and evaluating what is often hidden—how websites use our data for research purposes.

Chapter 1
Telling the Quants from the Quacks:
Evaluating Statistical Arguments in Debates Online

Candice Lanius
Rensselaer Polytechnic Institute, USA

ABSTRACT

Determining the credibility of statistical research has traditionally been done through peer-reviewed journal publications. With the recent increase in research shared in online forums comes emerging challenges for authors sharing results and for readers determining if research is valid. This chapter introduces a heuristic for evaluating the credibility of statistics based on methods used to counteract claims made in The Bell Curve. The approaches gleaned from this case are then updated for online environments and demonstrated using contemporary online debates about climate change science and skepticism. The heuristic for evaluating credibility of statistical arguments online is useful for readers and as a guide for authors adapting their research for online publication and debate.

INTRODUCTION

Numbers have been described many times as a universal language. With their ubiquity and precision, the use of numbers allows information to travel quickly through different communities. However, numerical communications rely on taken-for-granted structures of practice that give numbers their credibility and legitimacy. Traditional validity strategies, the strategies that demonstrate research is credible and empirically grounded, include triangulation (the use of multiple types of evidence), a basis in previous research, and peer-review (Creswell, 2009, p. 191). For research shared online, however, there are frequently no guarantees for the provenance of information being shared, and the speed at which information is generated has increased ten-fold, leaving less time for review and correction (Terras & Ramsay, 2012). As a result, questionable information is shared by readers when it is expressed numerically and therefore appears credible. There are also researchers who have done the hard work, performing time-consuming

DOI: 10.4018/978-1-5225-1072-7.ch001

research, who run the risk of their work being ignored if they do not share it online in a way that attracts the attention of readers. Telling the "quants," those with legitimate claims to expertise and knowledge in data, from the "quacks," those who make claims that are not supported by research or experience, has become incredibly difficult with computer-mediated communication.

This chapter addresses new challenges for authors in establishing authority—and for readers in determining credibility—when quantification and statistical methods are used in online debates. Whether the statistical arguments are in the form of original results or paraphrased from other primary sources, the stakes are high. With the Internet being a facilitator for education, communication, and political argument, it is crucial that authors have the tools to share their work persuasively and for readers to have the literacy necessary to evaluate research critically. The online debate over the credibility of statistical methods in climate change is one crucial case: Each side appears to use reliable rhetoric and evidence to justify their position. How are lay audiences to know which side is correct? How should scientists explain their work online so that it is perceived as authoritative? To answer these questions, this chapter introduces a heuristic developed from the controversial debate centered on *The Bell Curve*, Herrnstein and Murray's (1994)*New York Times* bestseller. This heuristic is based on the critical responses to Herrnstein and Murray's research and is adapted to the exigencies of online communication. The method is demonstrated using the popular climate change websites *Watts Up With That? The World's Most Viewed Site on Global Warming and Climate Change* and *Skeptical Science: Getting Skeptical about Global Warming Skepticism*. The proposed heuristic helps readers sort the "quants" from the "quacks" while simultaneously providing a guide to authors for gaining the attention and respect of their online audience.

LITERATURE REVIEW

Credible Statistics

There is a lack of contemporary literature on the relationship between statistical evidence and online credibility. While there are numerous resources on digital ethos, they tend to be content-agnostic, and statistics and research design require specialized approaches to evaluate their credibility. At the same time, the online environment complicates many traditional approaches to trusting statistics. Two well-known analogue resources on statistics and credibility are Best's (2001)*Damned Lies and Statistics* and Huff's (1954)*How to Lie with Statistics*. Best covered the two primary causes for bad statistics:

1.   The use of bad data and dubious interpretations, and
2.   The "mangling" of statistics once they are being used by secondary sources (2001, p. 5).

However, his advice for thinking critically about statistics only covers basic, descriptive statistics such as percentages and averages. While critical approaches for basic statistics are important, they cannot help the reader with inferential statistics and the complex reasoning needed to understand research design. This chapter addresses the gap by considering critical approaches to inferential statistics while building from Best's (2001) observation, "We think of statistics as facts that we discover, not as numbers we create. But, of course, statistics do not exist independently; people have to create them" (pp. 160-1). Best recommended that a critical reader ask questions about a statistic's origin, focus on definitions, measurement, and sampling, and attend to how claims can be misleading or make inappropriate comparisons.

Huff's book remains relevant as a guide for "self-defense" against the use of statistics to deceive (1954, p. 9). Huff advised the reader to be suspicious of figures that are "surprisingly precise," especially when researchers have no means to measure the phenomena accurately due to a lack of instrumentation or a biased sampling technique. Throughout *How to Lie with Statistics*, Huff also warned against relying on numbers without accompanying technical detail, such as how the average was calculated, what the magnitude of difference is, or what alternative explanations are possible yet excluded. One poignant point from Huff: "If you can't prove what you want to prove, demonstrate something else and pretend that they are the same thing" (p. 74). He continued, "[D]espite its mathematical base, statistics is as much an art as it is a science. A great many manipulations and even distortions are possible within the bounds of propriety" (p. 120). Statistics always involve moments of interpretation and assumptions by the researcher. In the presence of unavoidable distortions, Huff suggested looking for biases, both conscious and unconscious, to assess the credibility of an argument.

Digital Ethos

While Best and Huff discussed credibility and statistics broadly, the demands of modern technology require additional techniques for establishing the credibility of statistical arguments. Classical rhetorical theory described ethos as the audience's belief or trust in a speaker's authority (Warnick, 2004). To establish ethos, rhetoric teaches strategies for sharing the speaker's qualifications. Traditionally, this would include espousing the rhetor's education and good character (extrinsic ethos) or the use of linguistic flourishes and technical vocabulary (intrinsic ethos). In Aristotle's time, 4th century C.E., these strategies were used to convince a jury that the speaker was knowledgeable, a virtuous citizen, and motivated by good intentions. The setting, however, drastically changes how ethos is created and perceived by an audience. Rather than speaking face-to-face in a public arena, modern Internet users are disconnected from their audience. Yet credibility online is essential to social and political life because the Internet continues to be a space to share and collect information. In online settings where the speaker can be anonymous, extrinsic ethos is less decisive because the audience evaluates the argument based on website or textual features rather than formal credentials (Fogg, 2003). To counteract the separation of networked communication, users will use the extrinsic ethos of others; Warnick (2004) described this as intertextuality, where texts are parasitic, borrowing ethos from others on the web.

Depending on the social space, users will use different elements to evaluate credibility. Warnick (2004) emphasized that any method for understanding digital ethos must be reader-oriented (p. 259). Ethos and credibility are not "yes" or "no" propositions; instead, readers attribute credibility along a sliding scale. Any concept of credibility must include the speaker or author's position in relation to the information being conveyed and the intended audience. In many online communities, there is a range of audiences who require different types of ethos. One type is related to the means of transmission—online communication—and is a form of cultural ethos. It is developed when an author follows the norms for using a specific platform. Scientific ethos, alternatively, is more stable and includes institutional affiliation and the peer-review system. Warnick warned that this combination of field-dependent rhetorical requirements and field-independent formal criteria make the creation of guidelines difficult: Rules for evaluating ethos "cannot be generic and universally applied but instead must be sensitive to the context and the user's purpose" (Warnick, 2004, p. 264). Credibility and ethos exist in a subjective space: what makes a text suspicious to one reader will reaffirm its credibility in the eyes of another reader. However, the subjective nature of the audience's evaluation does not make credibility and ethos impenetrable.

Evaluation Heuristics

A heuristic designed to evaluate the credibility of online sources can be effective, but it must be sensitive to individual, subjective experiences. Wichowski and Kohl (2013) argued an evaluation test is an effective way to teach students and early career scholars the critical thinking skills and basic literacy to evaluate online sources. In their work, Wichowski and Kohl adapted the currency, relevance, authority, accuracy, and purpose (CRAAP) test to evaluate blogs. They described digital ethos as fluid and "progressive," changing to fit evolving cultural norms. The use of slang is a mark of credibility online and is used to construct an identity—a digital ethos—with an audience. Their test is a checklist that "provides signposts to remind researchers what kinds of elements they should be locating and evaluating" (p. 245). While an excellent starting point, the CRAAP test is content-agnostic. My proposed heuristic takes the complex set of responses to *The Bell Curve* and distills them into a manageable program for understanding and evaluating the credibility of online statistical arguments specifically.

Rhetoricians of science have created a sophisticated method for dealing with competing layers of ethos, such as someone invoking both cultural and scientific credibility to persuade their audience. Constantinides (2001) argued that Aristotle's concept of ethos is specific to political actors, where other speaking situations require different performances (p. 61). An earlier scholar, Prelli, proposed a set of *topoi* of scientific reasonableness based on the normative conditions of science. *Topoi*, roughly translated as topics, are the tools available to a speaker for establishing ethos by creating strong statements. For scientific discourse, these norms or *topoi* are universalism, communality, disinterestedness, and organized skepticism. Scientific speakers who discuss how their research is objective and emphasize that they are motivated by the pursuit of knowledge would be perceived as credible. The counternorms to these four are particularism, solitariness, interestedness, and organized dogmatism (Constantinides, 2001, p. 63). Constantinides found that these competing sets of norms can exist in popular science texts simultaneously, especially because the counternorms are part of popular culture. To understand how these norms, which are diametrically opposed, can co-exist in scientific communications, Constantinides introduced a theory of "surface" versus "deep structure" (p. 71). Effective communications will have a stylish surface that is personal and contextual while the deep structure, the argument, follows the requirements of scientific communication; in this way the norms and counternorms "balance fair-mindedness and thicken the concept of social status" (p. 71). Online, that means that authors, bloggers, or posters can use strong language, argue from a shared position, take credit for their work, and apply it in specific settings (the counternorms of scientific communication), and yet also be credible due to the deep structure of their scientific argument. As Constantinides put it, "The social norms and counternorms of science can be used as either heuristic tools for inventing scientific discourse or as interpretive tools for the analysis of textual features" (p. 64). When evaluating online statistical arguments, the gold standard for credibility is when the style and performance are balanced with strong, underlying evidence and reason.

METHOD: *THE BELL CURVE*

Statistics are much more than the single number used to summarize results. The creation of these numbers involves a detailed process of defining target data, setting research questions, collecting data, improving its quality, performing an analysis, and the generation of explanations for the results (Creswell, 2009). While common usage refers to statistics as simple numbers, there is a complicated process to achieving valid numerical representations for complex research settings. In online social communities, summary statistics are invoked as evidence in conversation, and it is important to trace the origin of these numbers to determine the "quants" from the "quacks." Quants are individuals who maintain the standards of scientific reasoning while successfully communicating their analysis and argument; quacks, on the other hand, are individuals who, through ulterior motives or ignorance, manipulate scientific research and statistical analysis to support their dogma. The heuristic introduced in this chapter provides a way for lay audiences to develop critical literacy for the statistical evidence invoked in online communication by addressing statistics as a process, not an objective number to be trusted at face value.

The proposed heuristic is generated from a careful reading of *The Bell Curve*, a 1994 study that used the appearance of sound scientific theories and statistical analysis to convince the American public that a difference in average intelligence quotient score (IQ) exists between races. In 1995, twenty leading American intellectuals replied with a collection of essays showing the racial bias and scientific flaws rampant in the original study. My method takes the experts' wisdom, consolidates their responses into a practical approach, and demonstrates how the average, lay audience member can be more critical in the face of statistical "quacks" by applying a critical heuristic.

Herrnstein and Murray's (1994) *The Bell Curve* argued that racial differences explain why certain ethnicities are clustered at the top and bottom of the American class system. Murray, a political scientist, and Herrnstein, a psychologist, provided scientific research to support conservative social policies with the theory of hereditary meritocracy (that immutable genetic differences determine success in life) (Goleman, 1994). In the book, Herrnstein and Murray used psychometric methods on data collected by the *National Longitudinal Survey of Youth* (*NLSY*). The authors explained that low IQ creates "socially undesirable" behaviors and outcomes such as poverty, high school dropouts, and crime. The authors correlated low IQ to an increased probability of unemployment, general "idleness," and injury. They argue that "intelligence and its correlates—maturity, farsightedness, and personal competence—are important in keeping a person employed" (Herrnstein & Murray, 1994, p. 165). They also tackle the family unit, claiming "the more intelligent get married at higher rates than the less intelligent" (p. 179). The most controversial section of the book deals with ethnic groups and IQ. Herrnstein and Murray argued that there is a noticeable "black/ white differential" in IQ scores of 15 points. By arguing that more blacks of low intelligence produce greater numbers of offspring, they claimed America's average IQ score was dropping. They argued that America's social funding is wasted on an immutable fact: IQ differentials cannot change. Instead, they argued that money should be directed towards "gifted" students and that affirmative action should end immediately (p. 551).

In response, a group of scholars from a range of fields published *The Bell Curve Wars* (1995), a collection of essays showing how Herrnstein and Murray's statistical tome was "quackery," lacking the credibility and sophistication of social scientific projects. The essays in the volume used different approaches to reveal the shaky foundations of *The Bell Curve's* scientific claims and faulty policy recommendations. Lind (1995), Kaus (1995), and Lemann (1997) performed discourse analysis of the media coverage of the book to uncover the social anxieties and historical concerns the book addressed. Gould, a historian of science, traced the basic research used to explain Herrnstein and Murray's conclusions, showing that modern science has debunked phrenology and racialized categories (two key parts of their method). Hacker and Sowell uncovered moments where the mathematical statistics are manipulated and misleading due to the omission of key details such as correlation coefficients. Nisbett (1995) and Gardner (1995) explored the rhetorical techniques used to undermine opposing viewpoints, and Fischer (1996) and Jones (1995) revealed the book's false mythology and poorly researched historical examples.

Rosen and Lane traced the project's funding to *The Pioneer Fund,* a disreputable eugenics political organization. Ultimately, Ramos showed the terrible economic and social consequences of Herrnstein and Murray's plan to end affirmative action and reinstitute segregation. This group of scholars used their fields' critical methods to uncover the political motivations and biases of the research project, and their work provides a practical blue print for approaching data projects in order to uncover their constituent motivations, ideologies, biases, and silences.

To adapt *The Bell Curve Wars* methods to statistical arguments *online* requires the additional consideration of certainty behind claims and the level of explanation provided with the results. Because the Internet has constantly emerging genre expectations, it is urgent that claims do not overstate their evidentiary support. Additionally, having extra explanation available for a diverse audience will make a document credible. The heuristic is laid out in detail in Table 1.

Table 1. Ways to evaluate credibility in statistical arguments online

Category	Definition	Method of Discovery
Discourse	The academic or public conversation the research is situated within.	Search for the topic and find sources with known ideological biases or motivations. For academic conversations, find the publisher or university providing institutional authority and check for the institution's age, mission statement, and founders to uncover underlying viewpoints and potential biases.
Science	The basic theory and observations that connect data to research conclusions.	Determine the underlying theory that is used to support the conclusions, usually marked by a reference to a peer-reviewed journal article. Check the publication date to see if it is up-to-date and that the discipline is appropriate to the topic.
Mathematical Statistics	The technical aspects of the research are correct.	Find the statistical approach being used (e.g. linear regression) in an instructional manual, referred textbook, or exemplary journal article. Note the required steps for a robust analysis shown in the textbook or article and compare them to the content being evaluated.
Rhetoric	The language and structure used to make the research persuasive.	Evaluate the language choice, argument structure, and persuasive elements (such as emotional appeals) and determine if the text is persuasive to its intended audience.
History	The accurate and complete depiction of historical examples.	When a historical example is used, check with a secondary source for accuracy of details. It might be prudent to find additional information on a time period to ensure that the example is not decontextualized and other valuable factors are included.
Economics	How the research is funded.	Find the institutional affiliation for the research, any funding agency, private grants, or self-funding will direct attention to the motivations behind the research.
Cartography	How the visual elements are used.	Evaluate the aesthetic elements and how they emphasize certain meanings while diminishing others.
Consequences	The policy outcomes and effects of the research conclusions.	Find the recommendations for action and determine if the level of evidence presented matches the scale of action. Be cautious of expensive, time consuming, or system-wide policy changes; also screen for potential adverse effects.
Claims	The magnitude and certainty of claims correspond to the study's evidence.	Check that the claims are appropriately limited by the size and scope of the original research design. A small sample size (e.g. 25 people) of a target population (e.g. college students) does not support claims about all of humanity.
Additional Explanation	A broad explanation of technical content based on the expanded audience for online debates.	Determine the types of literacy needed to understand the research. The author should provide extra documentation or explanation to explain the material to a broad audience.

THE HEURISTIC IN ACTION: CLIMATE CHANGE DEBATES

The ten approaches to determining the credibility of statistical arguments online can be demonstrated using a comparison of texts from climate change believers and climate change skeptics. The case was selected to demonstrate the heuristic because of the importance of climate change to the future of humanity. With such high stakes, voters must have the critical skills to determine the "quants" from the "quacks," and this overview can provide pointers for communicators to improve their message. The climate change debate online also represents a complex of arguments and rhetorical ploys that are rich terrain for discussion: The two websites included were selected for their age, breadth of coverage, and high traffic volume.

On one side of the issue is *Skeptical Science,* a website dedicated to explaining peer review science to a broad audience (*About Skeptical Science*, 2015). It was created by Cook, a PhD student and climate communication fellow for the *Global Change Institute* (GCI) of the University of Queensland in Australia. The GCI focuses on developing solutions to challenges that emerge from a rapidly changing climate such as population growth and movement and ecosystem drift. In a bid for extrinsic ethos, the site has published Cook's publication record, including college textbooks and a paper on "Quantifying the Consensus on Anthropogenic Global Warming in the Scientific Literature."

On the other side, *Watts Up with That* is edited by American retiree Watts and provides "news and commentary on puzzling things in life, nature, science, weather, climate change, [and] technology" (*About,* 2015). The about page is written in first person from Watts's perspective, explaining that he started the blog after a 25-year career as a television meteorologist. Watts handles his qualifications to be editor for the site by stating, "While I'm not a degreed climate scientist, I'll point out that neither is Al Gore, and his specialty is presentation also. And that's part of what this blog is about: presentation of weather and climate data in a form the public can understand and discuss" (*About,* 2015). The science news site has grown to twelve contributors and nine moderators since its inception in 2006. Credibility is dependent on the context where it is being evaluated, and the international scope of the climate change debate introduces complexity into how formal qualifications are evaluated.

In the following sections, I will provide a definition for each category of the heuristic, discuss a method for discovery, and demonstrate the approach on the climate change websites. Ultimately, I provide an evaluation of either side's status as a "quant" versus a "quack."

Discourse

Discourse captures the academic and public conversations that the argument is situated within and determines the context for evaluation because each community has its own standards for credibility and authority. While some controversial issues can appear new at first glance, they are frequently connected to older issues and social anxieties (Lind, 1995). For example, new technologies tend to be met with a classical dystopian versus utopian argument over how the technology will change our world: "robots will take jobs from people" or "artificial intelligence will come to rule over humanity." This is an argument that appears in different guises throughout history. One way to uncover how a text is connected to a larger discourse is to look at the values that are invoked in the text, such as civic virtues or economic principles. Another important feature of discourse is how it changes the grounds for debate: one side will stress the values and evidence that support their policy claims while the other focuses on their position. This chosen ground emerges in the discourse. For example, in America's "culture wars"—the 1990's contest between traditional conservative social values and progressive liberal ones—the conservative side relied on arguments that emerged from family traditions, connections to the past, and (frequently) religious practices. The liberal position, on the other hand, argued from a place that valued change, modernity, and independence. These two positions appear in a range of debates such as public school curricula, immigration reform, secular and religious freedoms, and global warming. One common practice in controversial debates is to maneuver the opposition into a weaker position where their criticism becomes evidence of bad faith in the debate, usually when they do not reply directly to the values invoked by the original position (Kaus, 1995).

Another feature of discourse is the role that news media play in shaping the overarching narrative for debate. While traditional media's impact in shaping the narrative may be reduced in the face of fragmented new media, there are still common practices that shape debates across platforms. News sites tend to provide equal airtime to opposing sides, despite the actual merits of either side. Controversy and disagreement bring the attention of audiences better than consensus and educational information. Giving time to controversial authors to discuss their ideas lends them credibility as being within the realm of possible scientific knowledge (Lemann, 1997). Identifying the discourse will help in understanding how the audience evaluates the credibility of the argument.

Skeptical aims to be a universal communication site with content available and translated into twenty-three different languages; they also provide "intermediate" and "advanced" tabs on their climate change myths to allow the reader to toggle between a simplified or detailed explanation of the situation (Cook, 2009). *Skeptical* makes two broad claims about their mission. The first is that they provide a holistic view, the "broader picture," which forgives small errors because the vast weight of scientific evidence proves climate change. The second claim is that disbelief in human-made global warming is a political choice, not a scientific one: Skeptical strives to "[remove] the politics from the debate" (*About Skeptical Science*, 2015).

WUWT, alternatively, argues that systematic errors invalidate the whole enterprise. Their primary claim about climate science is that the data used to generate the models is not reliable. The "Climategate" emails are mustered as proof of poor data quality, showing the "back room" dealings that were necessary to clean and homogenize the data sets before they were analyzed (Watts, 2012). Climategate (*WUWT's* term) or the CRU email hack (*Skeptical's* term) happened in November 2009. Several servers at the University of East Anglia were breached and emails between climate scientists were leaked online. One side sees the sometimes sarcastic and blunt conversations as proof of an academic conspiracy to inflate global temperatures while the other side views this as normal, work-day rhetoric with all of the data manipulations justified by peer-review. *Watts* also contends that climate science is politically motivated, frequently citing an anti-capitalist ideology. Recent support by the Catholic Church is also offered as proof that climate change science is more of a "dogma" and "religion" than a valid scientific endeavor (Watts, #AGU, 2015). From their perspective, Church support of climate change scientists lessens their credibility.

Science

The basic science that connects data to conclusions is vital for establishing authority in statistical arguments. Since a large portion of statistical methods are designed to reveal correlational relationships, the statistical analysis alone cannot prove or reveal causation. For that, researchers must turn to phenomenological theories. For example, a pharmaceutical trial can demonstrate correlation between a medication or treatment regimen and a therapeutic effect, but a chemist or biologist will explain the underlying mechanism that causes the change using basic science research. The same is true for the statistical models necessary to demonstrate climate change. Each side has differing scientific explanations for the associations revealed by the models, with ramifications for the consequences depending on which causal force is selected.

While the principles of disinterestedness and objectivity are part of the scientific method, as human actors, there will be unavoidable cultural motivation behind the choice and interpretation of statistical methods (Gould, 1995). Gould warned against two common assumptions made in sociological research. First, researchers concretize abstract concepts into stable features. The intelligence quotient (IQ), for example, is a constantly changing scale used to approximate the distribution of human intelligence, yet people speak about IQ as if it is an immutable part of their identity. Another common assumption is that complexity and variation are outliers, and outliers can be judged morally. Those at the high end of a distribution are admired while those at the low end are vilified. Gould cautions against these literal interpretations of statistics into social theory. Social Darwinism for many years was a solipsistic loop because social theory fed into the analysis, which fed into the social theory. Social Darwinism applied the evolutionary mechanisms of natural selection and survival of the fittest to human hierarchies and retroactively justified class systems with valid scientific basis.

To uncover the underlying scientific theory that informs a causal explanation, look for citations to scholarship intended to justify "A" causes "B"; check both the date of the research and its relevance to the topic at hand. For some online debates, the structure will not be as formal, but the scientific justification will be stated as a causal explanation or implied in the text. In some popular, pseudo-scientific information, the author will invoke "common sense" as the link between two items. As an example, "anti-vaxxers," those parents who are opposed to immunizing their children, often show correlational studies between receiving vaccinations and autoimmune and neurological disorders. One common feature of their argument is a list of the ingredients that are used in the production of vaccines, notably mercury and formaldehyde. They claim that these poisons are causing the medical problems. As an argument from "common sense," the ingredient list is compelling and frightening, but it ignores the fact that these compounds are used in production and are present in harmless quantities in the final vaccine. The "vaccines as poison" theory does not provide a sound scientific explanation for side effects.

The scientific theories behind climate modeling are varied. *Skeptical* relies on the greenhouse gasses theory of climate change: Throughout geological (deep) history, as the rate of CO2 and methane gas in the atmosphere has increased or decreased, the global temperature has increased or decreased (*What does past climate change*, 2015). When the change was rapid, the effects were dire for both flora and fauna, leading to numerous mass extinctions. *Skeptical* shows that recent, massive increases in CO2 and methane gases are a result of humans. They argue that these high rates are going to cause a drastic climate change over a short period of time that could lead to another mass extinction.

WUWT agrees that CO2 and methane gases alter the global temperature; however, it argues that there are alternative, non-human causes of climate change and that the rate of change is much less drastic than currently reported. While there are many potential non-human causes of climate change that *WUWT* offers, a few are the thermostat hypothesis and influence from cosmic radiation. The thermostat hypothesis posits the earth as a giant heat engine, and when heat is collected from the sun at the tropics, thunderstorms and cloud coverage help dissipate that heat north and south where it is released into space at the poles (Eschenbach, 2009). According to the thermostat hypothesis, the earth shifts global temperatures regularly in a 6% range, and thunderstorms help moderate this balanced cycle. In our current state, changes in cosmic rays and shifts in landmass over the poles explain the natural increase in temperature, but the mechanisms will continue to maintain a global balance. Watts (2011) cited a CERN experiment that showed the effect of cosmic rays on cloud seeds. According to the CLOUD experiment, cosmic rays affect "cloud condensation nuclei in the Earth's atmosphere." Watts extrapolated that this will have an effect on global climate since clouds are the primary source of variation in climate temperatures (Watts, 2011). The two websites use expertise differently. *Skeptical* is quoting the science and scientists who interpret their own research to explain the earth's climate; *WUWT* is quoting the science to counter the interpretation of the original scientists.

Mathematical Statistics

Technical details ensure an analysis is accurate and appropriate. There are several steps where different choices can be made during an analysis, and these must be justified. The best way to look for mistakes is to find a well-known and respected manual or peer-reviewed journal with the same method explained in detail for comparison. If there are no mistakes or errors, the mathematical statistics might still be misused to justify bad arguments by misleading the audience or claiming a higher degree of certainty than the test can provide. The reader should be wary of the deliberate omission of content that is standard in reporting results. For example, in longitudinal regression analysis, analysts should show the variation of data points surrounding the regression curve so the viewer can quickly grasp the degree of variance in the data set. A lack of information such as the scatter plot could mislead them into believing there is a higher degree of correlation and confidence in the analysis than is warranted. While the omission of details is not technically incorrect, the lack of explanation and detail can mislead a popular audience.

Sowell (1995), an economist, also explained that an analysis can be manipulated by selecting opportunistic categories and not showing the full range of comparisons: "when any factor differs as much from A_1 to A_2 as it does from A_2 to B_2, how can one conclude that this factor is due to the difference between A in general and B in general?" (1995, p. 76). Such manipulations are instances of mathematical precision disguising bias. Another way an analysis can be biased is in the selection of variables. To perform a regression analysis, the analyst selects one outcome they wish to predict and dependent variables in order to see which variable has a large effect. If the analyst selects a set of predictor variables that have a multicollinearity effect (exerting the same type of correlational relationship on the outcome), this can make the effect size look stronger than it is in reality. The procedures may be suspect not for their lack of mathematical precision, but rather because the data placed into the models and the interpretation of model outcomes are dubiously connected to scientific theory.

Mathematical statistics are the technical core behind the climate change debate. Without the ability to model or predict the climate, no one would have a basis for changing policies. While there is very little debate around the proven computational methods involved in modeling, both sides focus on the data quality and parameter assumptions that are necessary inputs to climate modeling. Wayne (2007), writing for *Skeptical*, defended the basis of modeling on two fronts. First, Wayne differentiated between predicting events and estimating trends. Many criticisms of modeling are that they miss events (such as a cold, snowy winter) and therefore cannot be correct. However, climate modeling is designed to estimate trends over a three-decade period, not to provide discrete weather forecasts. Second, there are criticisms that models are not tested, so they cannot be considered valid. Wayne explains the process of *hindcasting*, where models are compared against a sub-section of the full data set to test their accuracy. For a justification of the parameter assumptions used in modeling, the site suggests a NASA science brief written by Schmidt (2007). The physics for climate modeling can be divided into three categories: fundamental principles, approximated continuous events, and empirically known physics that are naturally variable. The fundamental principles include equations for energy, momentum, and mass, and the approximated events include radiation transfer. These are relatively stable phenomena, whereas the empirically known physics introduce an element of emergent surprise such as the eruption of a volcano. The models are steadily improving as the scientific community's understanding of physics improves, yet there will always be an unavoidable amount of variability and chance.

WUWT focuses on parameter variability and the need to update climate models as a marker of poor accuracy and politically driven science. One primary criticism is that the global climate is too complex to model; a recent study shows that nine current climate models cannot account for a period of "weak" El Niños (the periodic warming of the Pacific ocean) from 3,000 to 5,000 years ago (Watts, *Study*, 2015). While the original investigator suggested this could be used to improve the models, *WUWT* argued this is a reason to discount climate models. Additionally, data quality and data adjustments are questioned. For data quality, Watts pointed out that the temperature station locations have an effect on measurement precision (*Watts at #AGU15*, 2015). Several photographs are included to show the historical site of temperature stations in grassy fields followed by after photos of the same stations now resting over parking lots. Watts, presenting his research at the American Geophysical Union in 2015, argued that "NOAA's climate network shows a lower 30-year temperature trend when high quality temperature stations unperturbed by urbanization are considered" (Watts, *Press Release,* 2015). Beyond data quality, *WUWT* suggests that data adjustments assume positive trends, so corrections are masking natural cooling effects in the climate. An oft-cited piece of evidence for this comes from the Climategate hack, where code from a climate study was released online. Shephard (in Nelson, 2012), a programmer, shared his perception of the code:

Skimming through the often spaghetti-like code, the number of programs which subject the data to a mixed-bag of transformative and filtering routines is simply staggering. Granted, many of these "alterations" run from benign smoothing algorithms (e.g., omitting rogue outliers) to moderate infilling mechanisms... But many others fall into the precarious range between highly questionable (removing MXD data which demonstrate poor correlations with local temperature) to downright fraudulent. (n.p.)

Corrective procedures to increase data quality are standard practices in the sciences, yet here they are used as evidence of fraud and questionable research ethics. As a de-contextualization of research practices, this is a persuasive piece of evidence against climate change scientists. However, once re-contextualized and placed in a peer-review system, these practices become normalized and are judged as ethical by the community of scientists.

Rhetoric

Rhetoric is a significant part of statistical arguments to understand how the author's language choices create a persuasive text for the reader. A purely technical document with dry prose will bore the reader while a document with excessive hyperbole and flowery metaphor might drive the reader away. The balance between Constantinides' (2001) "surface" style and scientific "deep structure" is meaningful for understanding persuasion and also assessing credibility. Rhetoric is part of surface style. A text can draw from a range of popular language and contemporary discussions and still maintain its scientific objectivity in the structure of its arguments. However, there are some rhetorical practices to avoid. One is the creation of a veil of obscurity by overloading the reader with a large number of references: quantity does not mean it is of good quality (Nisbett, 1995, p. 36). Another tactic is what psychologist Gardner (1995) described as "scholarly brinkmanship", where the author leads the reader to an unsupported conclusion without explicitly stating it (p. 26). The reader grasps the idea, and the author is not required to provide evidence for the overextended argument. A critical reader should also be suspicious of attempts to compliment the audience; pandering and undue praise are attempts to prime the reader to accept the text. Next, there are rhetorical techniques used to highlight certain ideas while undermining opposing perspectives. This is done by introducing both sides of an issue yet only treating one side to a "kitchen-sink barrage of objections that have the effect of minimizing their significance" (Kaus, 1995, p. 133). Concentrating on the rhetorical appeals emergent in the text assists in understanding the way the text accrues meaning with its audience.

Both *Skeptical* and *WUWT* tend to use a mixture of language that implies an authoritative reporter sharing a balanced view while also offering posts that use colloquialisms and humor to straw man the other side. For example, this December *Skeptical* posted a series entitled "The Ghosts of Climate Past, Present and Future," a modern re-telling of Charles Dicken's *A Christmas Carol* that imagines the narrative with modern technology and in light of climate change. Another example is the page on "Does Cold Weather Disprove Global Warming?" The author used direct and technical language in the rebuttal, but the myth is phrased in a way to cast aspersions on the other side, quoting the opposition as saying "It's freaking cold!" (Meador, 2009). This simple phrase functions as a stand-in for the argument that colder weather casts doubt on current predictions and subtly lowers the valuation of the opposing side's argument.

WUWT, while banning all profanity on the site, still mocks individuals they consider non-critical believers. One sarcastic post shows a picture of the Korean peninsula during Earth hour and declares, "Earth hour in North Korea a stunning success" (Watts, 2010). If the climate change "agenda" is successful, we will all be living in the complete dark year round. The other side is also treated to heavy hyperbole in Calder's (in Watts, 2011) assessment of the CLOUD experiment:

Although they never said so, the High Priests of the Inconvenient Truth... always knew that Svensmark's cosmic ray hypothesis was the principal threat to their sketchy and poorly modelled notions of self-amplifying action of greenhouse gases. ...Svensmark put the alarmist predictions at risk – and with them the billions of dollars flowing from anxious governments into the global warming enterprise. (n.p.)

The tactic of using in-group rhetoric to describe the other side's viewpoint and goals while simultaneously appearing reasonable and measured in assessments of one's own viewpoint crosses both sides. Arguably, it is a successful strategy for attracting sympathetic audiences before creating a buffer between the opposing arguments.

History

History provides examples and case studies for statistical analysis. Historical examples can direct our attention to certain issues while disguising others. One way that history can be poorly used is if pertinent case studies that counteract the author's argument are squashed (Gardner, 1995; Fischer, 1996). If examples are presented without exceptions, this is usually a smoothing out of history that strategically minimizes alternative arguments. Historian Jones described this form of a-historical analysis as building a "mythology" in place of real history (1995, p. 92).

Skeptical tends to use deep history to support climate change theories. These include the collection of ice cores from glaciers where ancient air bubbles are trapped. By melting the cores in a vacuum, the air is released and can be measured for the amount of CO_2 present. Through this process, the amount of greenhouse gases at certain depths are compared to known temperatures to understand the relationship between the two. Another use of historical materials is paleogeographical reconstructions which show that "at certain periods in the past, often lasting for tens of millions of years, the distribution of flora and fauna in the fossil record showed that warmth-loving species had enjoyed a much greater latitudinal range than they do at the present day… [and] carbon dioxide levels had indeed been much higher at these times" (Mason, 2013). These approaches to sampling and comparing fossils to chemical traces allow for an understanding of how the Earth's climate has changed over time.

WUWT uses recent history in its rebuttal to climate change models. In one instance, Ball (2015) criticized an IPCC study—that warmer temperatures today will create storms of greater intensity—by pointing out historic examples of harsh storms that occurred during periods of general cooling. The historic storms are reconstructed using anthropological records such as ship logs and town annotations from the 16th century to today. Another *WUWT* essay by Endlich (2013) took a similar approach by using historical coast lines to show that sea levels have both risen and fallen in the course of human history: "The Battle of Ostia in 849, depicted in a painting attributed to Raphael, shows sea levels high enough for warships to assemble at the mouth of the Tiber. However, today this modern-day tourist destination is two miles up-river from the mouth of the Tiber." The painting is used as proof that sea levels were higher in the Roman Warm Period. These collective examples are intended to undermine media concerns about extreme weather patterns today.

Economics

Economics are generally a serious consideration for uncovering explicit biases in statistical arguments; the party funding the research is invested in the outcome, and it is easier to provide a result that is amenable to their long-term goals than one which is inconvenient. A favorable result may be generated intentionally, or it could be a form of accidental bias due to subtle pressures on the researcher. Occasionally, biased interpretations are not obvious in the text or in public information. In these cases, it can be valuable to follow the money to trace the origin of data used in research projects (Naureckas, 1995; Rosen & Lane, 1995).

For the sites *Skeptical* and *WUWT*, funding is through donations, with much of the efforts by writers and moderators done as volunteer labor (*About, 2015*). The primary research presented on both sites comes from nationally funded research laboratories or government agencies. One notable exception is Watts' *Surfacestations.org*, which is an example of collective, citizen science. The project seeks to review the validity of measurements taken from different climate stations around the United States and relies upon volunteers to cover the hundreds of sites around the country: "Given such a massive failure of bureaucracy to perform something so simple as taking some photographs and making some measurements and notes of a few to a few dozen weather stations in each state, it seemed that a grass roots network of volunteers could easily accomplish this task" (*Surface Stations*, 2009). The two sites make competing claims for credibility based on funding. Skeptical argues that government-funded scientific research is the true standard for expertise and that the efforts of deniers are at best amateurish and at worst intentionally ignorant. *WUWT*, on the other hand, feels that government funded researchers are interpreting their results based on the goals of current governments. They argue that the citizen science of interested volunteers is not institutionally funded and is therefore not biased.

Cartography

Cartography, the study of the role charts and maps play in the generation of meaning, involves an understanding of human perception, aesthetics, and the material being represented. Images, charts, and maps can play a significant role in anchoring statistical arguments. Grey (1999), a rhetorician, tackled the interpretation of visual aesthetics by describing some implications of a normal (bell) curve. Grey described the normal curve as a "visual imperative that resists egalitarian principles" and "moral complexity" (p. 320). The act of reading the curve from left to right creates a sense of linear progression, with the people falling on the left side (lower tail) viewed as deficient. The curve also creates a false sense of competition. As a closed system, the normal curve implies that progression towards the right requires the higher ranked individuals fall. Other visual features, such as color, can also highlight meaning.

Both climate change websites use a mixture of images to maintain interest along with reproducing the charts and graphs from primary sources. *Skeptical* uses a thermometer to list the "Most Used Climate Myths and What the Science Really sSays..." along with the menu items "newcomers, start here" and "the big picture" superimposed over line graphs with sharply increasing green lines. These features underline the site's claim to share peer-reviewed research to a broad audience. The implements are symbolically bolstering the validity of the text. The banner image features penguins walking away from one another while glancing over their shoulders to see a small green plant popping through the ice. The penguins provide a glib reminder of the stakes of rapid climate change, which the site argues will lead to glacial melts and a massive change in the flora and fauna around the world. *WUWT*, as a WordPress site, has simple menu icons, but it does provide a banner image featuring the earth from high atmospheric levels. The deep blue of space slowly blends into the blue line of the horizon where a large cloud formation obscures the surface below. This perspective has symbolic weight, placing the site's perspective above the earth, in an omniscient view. Arguably, this perspective also places the site's claims above political or ideological bias; *WUWT* is "above it all". For both sites, the reproduction of original charts, graphs, and maps emphasizes the value of the scientific method for both. Both support the scientific method; *WUWT*, however, thinks that climate science is poor science due to rough data, data manipulation, and politicized interpretation. Watt's project *Surface Stations* uses a map of the United States and charts showing temperature readings over time to anchor the data that his team and volunteers collected.

In addition to these individual artistic elements, the websites' overall appearance and navigability can impact how readers and users evaluate credibility. *Skeptical* has created the appearance of a reference text with pinned lists of important articles that address common myths. *WUWT*, on the other hand, functions more as a current events or news blog, with the uppermost posts reflecting timely issues. These strategies emphasize different types of information and contribute to highlighting different issues. *Skeptical's* mission is to show the consistent nature of climate change science while *WUWT* is dedicated to showing political manipulations as they happen, so the examples scrolling back in time fit with their communication goals.

Consequences

The consequences of suggested policies are also considered in evaluating the credibility of the source. The policy recommendations should be feasible and reflect the risks and costs associated with the study. To phrase this another way, a small risk does not justify a massive expenditure of costs. Two main problems with suggested policy changes are perverse effects and self-fulfilling problems. Perverse effects happen when a policy makes a minor change to the target problem while causing major issues in other areas (Ramos, 1995). Self-fulfilling policy recommendations are those that create the problem they claim to solve. Attending to the policy recommendations reveals how attenuated a text is to a functional system.

In the case of global climate change, both the risks and costs are very high. *Skeptical* outlines the steadily increasing harms from rising temperatures which include decreased fresh water supply, poor agriculture, deaths due to heat waves, spread of disease, flooding and the disappearance of coast lines, the extinction of plants and animals, damage to public infrastructure, risk of human conflict, and natural disasters (Painting, 2007). To prevent these consequences, *Skeptical* fully supports the efforts of international treaties like the 2015 Paris Agreement to reduce carbon emissions. *WUWT*, on the other hand, has two major problems with the Paris Agreement. For them, the treaty is guaranteed to cause economic damage, and they are not convinced of the risks of climate change. They argue that green policies result from an unbalanced risk assessment that destroys jobs (Watts, *Green war on jobs*, 2015). The second major problem is doubt that green policies will achieve the desired result, leading to a high economic cost to implement carbon reduction policies without any clear effect on the environment.

Claims and Additional Explanation

Statistical appropriateness, while often mistaken for a label of veracity, is actually a technical consideration divorced from the empirical realm. An analysis can be statistically appropriate—meaning it follows the conventions of the discipline, uses proper sampling techniques, fulfills the mathematical assumptions, and is performed without computational error—and yet still not be "true." There are two potential problems to be cautious of when making and evaluating claims using statistical evidence. The first is that many authors overstate certainty: statistics are based on measuring and controlling chance and therefore always have some uncertainty built in. This is why confidence intervals are a necessary part of reporting results. It is important to never overstate the certainty or magnitude of the results because scientists must preserve room for modification in the face of new evidence.

Skeptical is balancing between maintaining a space to update research while also arguing that climate change science has reached a consensus. Depending on the page and author, the site balances between these two poles of assurance and space for change. The magnitude of the problem is also carefully couched in "if-then" statements. For example, the site never says. Tthere will be a cataclysmic event in the next 100 years"; rather, it frames the outcomes in light of an increase in temperature. *WUWT* argues that climate scientists both overstate their certainty in results and are too confident in the magnitude of the problem. They critique the models and data to show weaknesses in the climate scientist's approach while providing examples of how climate change is not as severe as current consensus reports. However, the site has a tendency to use preliminary results, such as the CERN seed cloud experiment, to make arguments about the environment when the results were observed in a laboratory setting (Watts, 2011). This is an example of magnifying the results to apply them in a setting that is not warranted by the initial experimental parameters. While the use of claims differs, both the technical details and scientific explanations are generally well elaborated for both sites. The primary divergence emerges from the interpretation of inputs and outputs.

DISCUSSION

The values that we use to evaluate credibility are based on both individual and shared aspects. The heuristic introduced in this chapter is useful in helping readers of all levels determine credibility markers and then evaluate those against their own values and provide evidence for that evaluation. Constantinides (2011) proposed that two layers be used to evaluate a text's persuasive potential. Adopting her theory to this case, the most effective website must capture both "surface style," a form of cultural ethos, and yet maintain its "deep structure," the standards for scientific credibility. After applying the heuristic, the *Skeptical* community emerges as a more credible source of information on climate change: They are the quants. For scientific credibility, *Skeptical* relies on the original interpretation of scientists and shares a broad range of scientific resources all directing attention to the "big picture" of climate change. The site also successfully defends the core norms of scientific practice by discussing climate modeling as a process that is continually being improved through community peer review. While creating a strong cultural ethos with some hyperbole and sarcasm, *Skeptical* carefully uses approachable language and avoids overtly political statements.

WUWT has a complicated ethos that is partially scientific and partially political. The website attempts to bridge the two speaking positions by providing scientific evidence for conservative political arguments at the cost of their scientific ethos: They are the quacks. Many of the site's overarching frameworks are tenuous, such as the claim that nearly all climate scientists around the globe share identical political motivations or that errors and mistakes spoil the entire enterprise. The decision to re-interpret results but not quote scientists directly supports the political argument well, but that is not a scientific practice. Additionally, this "cherry picking" of scientific evidence contradicts the political stance that scientific research cannot be trusted writ large because of private and government funding agencies. The claim that "scientists are mistaken and politically biased" is inconsistent with quoting those scientific studies that are convenient for the political argument. Additionally, *WUWT* offers criticisms that do not match the scale of climate science. For example, the use of a single oil painting to argue about sea levels is ridiculous when contrasted with the physical evidence provided by geological studies of ice cores. There are also other inconsistencies that weaken the site's "deep structure," such as the barrage of arguments related to economics. The politically motivated conclusion that carbon emission control policies are a bad idea is reached with several arguments:

1. The rate and magnitude of global warming is overstated,
2. Global warming is not human-made, so there is no need to intervene,
3. Global warming might be caused by humans, but the proposed policies will not change the warming trend, and
4. There are too many unknowns in climate modeling, so do not make policy changes.

This range of arguments may work in a political arena where the audience only needs to pick one to affirm the conclusion, but in a scientific space, this is abhorrent practice. These arguments cannot all be true, and by claiming all four, *WUWT* undercuts its authority to speak on scientific matters.

In contrasting the two sites, *Skeptical's* multi-lingual options give it a veneer of international universalism that again upholds scientific values. *WUWT*, on the other hand, is written solely in English, which further highlights its political motivations to influence American environmental policy. Despite emerging as the more credible source of these two websites, *Skeptical* could still improve its ethos. To improve the balance between culturally appealing stylistic flourishes and the more somber scientific arguments, *Skeptical* could explicitly tag the fiction and editorialized content, such as the retelling of Dicken's "A Christmas Carol" with global warming effects, and remove the hyperbole from scientific reporting. This allows them to connect with their audience on a cultural level without undercutting the disinterested, objective structure of their scientific arguments.

CONCLUSION

There are numerous potential cases for application of this heuristic. Many can be found listed on *ProCon. org*, a website dedicated to discussing controversial issues. Any controversial subject that is debated online using statistical evidence can be evaluated using the ten categories. The anti-vaccination movement, briefly mentioned as an example earlier, is one case where the community does not have a strong scientific ethos, yet they continue to have traction online because they address the anxieties parents have about modern technologies and their children. Several online debates revolve around crime and law enforcement statistics: whether the issue is gun control laws or police "stop and frisk" policies, this heuristic can be used to evaluate the credibility of the source and the validity of their arguments. Political polling figures are another space where this heuristic could be applied to show whose analysis and numbers are to be trusted.

The ten approaches discussed in this chapter are foundational when assessing the credibility of online sources that rely on quantification and statistical methods. Statistical methods are the foundation of a great deal of modern science and establish that a result is not possible from chance alone. When statistical results are posted online, however, the results can be technically correct, but be built on poor research design or aggrandized claims. Both the author and reader should be cognizant of common technical mistakes related to statistics. Errors can reveal an imperfect knowledge of the methods being used, but they could also disqualify valid research for a superficial mistake. Even if the evidence is presented without technical flaw, many statistical arguments are based on interpretation. By critically evaluating the discourse, science, rhetoric, history, economics, cartography, consequences, claims, and explanations provided by online sources, it becomes clear which source has a higher degree of credibility. While the audiences of *Skeptical* and *WUWT* vary, *Skeptical* has achieved a higher degree of digital credibility by constructing a stronger scientific ethos. *WUWT* has a strong political ethos that harms their credibility to speak authoritatively on climate change science. By understanding the role of technical accuracy and claim management, authors can write authoritative and persuasive online arguments using statistical methods. Likewise, readers can quickly differentiate the "quants" from the "quacks."

REFERENCES

About. (2015). *Watts Up With That?* Retrieved December 1, 2015, from http://wattsupwiththat.com/about-wuwt/about2

About Skeptical Science. (2015). *About Skeptical Science*. Retrieved December 1, 2015, from http://www.skepticalscience.com/about.shtml

AEI. (2015). *Charles Murray*. Retrieved December 1, 2015, from https://www.aei.org/scholar/charles-murray

Ball, T. (2015). *How does the IPCC explain the severe storms of history?* Retrieved December 1, 2015, from http://wattsupwiththat.com/2015/08/19/how-does-the-ipcc-explain-the-severe-storms-of- history

Best, J. (2001). *Damned lies and statistics: Untangling numbers from the media, politicians, and activists*. Berkeley, CA: University of California Press.

Best, J. (2004). *More damned lies and statistics: How numbers confuse public issues*. Berkeley, CA: University of California Press.

Constantinides, H. (2001). The duality of scientific ethos: Deep and surface structures. *The Quarterly Journal of Speech*, *87*(1), 61–72. doi:10.1080/00335630109384318

Cook, J. (2009). *What do the 'climategate' hacked CRU emails tell us?* Retrieved December 1, 2015, from http://www.skepticalscience.com/Climategate-CRU-emails-hacked-intermediate.htm

Creswell, J. W. (2009). *Research design: Qualitative, quantitative, and mixed method approaches*. Los Angeles, CA: SAGE Publications, Inc.

Endlich, R. W. (2013). *History falsifies climate alarmist sea level claims*. Retrieved December 1, 2015, from http://wattsupwiththat.com/2013/12/02/history-falsifies-climate-alarmist-sea-level-claims

Eschenbach, W. (2009). *The thermostat hypothesis*. Retrieved December 1, 2015, from http://wattsupwiththat.com/2009/06/14/the-thermostat-hypothesis

Fischer, C. S. (1996). *Inequality by design: Cracking the bell curve myth*. Princeton, NJ: Princeton University Press.

Fogg, B. J. (2003, April). *Prominence-interpretation theory: Explaining how people assess credibility online*. Paper presented at CHI 2003. Ft. Lauderdale, FL. doi:10.1145/765891.765951

Fraser, S. (Ed.). (1995). *The bell curve wars: Race, intelligence, and the future of America*. New York, NY: Basic Books.

Gardner, H. (1995). Cracking open the IQ box. In The bell curve wars: Race, intelligence, and the future of America (pp. 23-35). New York, NY: Basic Books.

Goleman, D. (1994, September 16). Richard Herrnstein, 64, dies; backed nature over nurture. *The New York Times*.

Gould, S. J. (1995). Curveball. In S. Fraser (Ed.), *The bell curve wars: Race, intelligence, and the future of America* (pp. 11–22). New York, NY: Basic Books.

Grey, S. (1999). The statistical war on equality: Visions of American virtuosity in the bell curve. *The Quarterly Journal of Speech, 85*(3), 303–329. doi:10.1080/00335639909384263

Hacker, A. (1995). Caste, crime, and precocity. In S. Fraser (Ed.), *The bell curve wars: Race, intelligence, and the future of America* (pp. 97–108). New York, NY: Basic Books.

Herrnstein, R. J., & Murray, C. (1994). *The bell curve: Intelligence and class structure in American life.* New York, NY: Free Press.

Huff, D., & Geis, I. (1954). *How to lie with statistics.* New York, NY: W.W. Norton & Company, Inc.

Jones, J. (1995). Back to the future with *The Bell Curve*: Jim Crow, slavery, and g. In S. Fraser (Ed.), *The bell curve wars: Race, intelligence, and the future of America* (pp. 80–93). New York, NY: Basic Books.

Judis, J. B. (1995). Hearts of darkness. In S. Fraser (Ed.), *The bell curve wars: Race, intelligence, and the future of America* (pp. 124–129). New York, NY: Basic Books.

Kaus, M. (1995). The "it-matters-little" gambit. In S. Fraser (Ed.), *The bell curve wars: Race, intelligence, and the future of America* (pp. 130–138). New York, NY: Basic Books.

Lemann, N. (1997, January 8). *The bell curve flattened.* Slate.

Lind, M. (1995). Brave new right. In S. Fraser (Ed.), *The bell curve wars: Race, intelligence, and the future of America* (pp. 172–178). New York, NY: Basic Books.

Mason, J. (2013). *The history of climate science.* Retrieved December 1, 2015, from http://www.skepticalscience.com/history-climate-science.html

Meador, J. (2009). *Does cold weather disprove global warming?* Retrieved December 1, 2015, from http://www.skepticalscience.com/global-warming-cold-weather.htm

Naureckas, J. (1995, January 1). Racism resurgent: How media let the bell curve's pseudo-science define the agenda on race. *FAIR Extra!*.

Nelson, T. (2012). *In case you missed it, on CRU's source code: "In fact, all data between 1930 and 1994 are subject to "correction".* Retrieved December 1, 2015, from http://tomnelson.blogspot.com/2012/01/in-case-you-missed-it-on-cru-source.html

Nisbett, R. (1995). Race, IQ, and scientism. In S. Fraser (Ed.), *The bell curve wars: Race, intelligence, and the future of America* (pp. 36–57). New York, NY: Basic Books.

Painting, R. (2007). *Positives and negatives of global warming.* Retrieved December 1, 2015, from http://www.skepticalscience.com/global-warming-positives-negatives-intermediate.htm

Patterson, O. (1995). For whom the bell curves. In S. Fraser (Ed.), *The bell curve wars: Race, intelligence, and the future of America* (pp. 187–214). New York, NY: Basic Books.

Ramos, D. (1995). Paradise miscalculated. In S. Fraser (Ed.), *The bell curve wars: Race, intelligence, and the future of America* (pp. 62–69). New York, NY: Basic Books.

Rosen, J., & Lane, C. (1995). The sources of *The Bell Curve*. In S. Fraser (Ed.), *The bell curve wars: Race, intelligence, and the future of America* (pp. 58–61). New York, NY: Basic Books.

Schmidt, G. A. (2007, January). The physics of climate modeling. *Physics Today*, *60*(1), 72–73. doi:10.1063/1.2709569

Sowell, T. (1995). Ethnicity and IQ. In S. Fraser (Ed.), *The bell curve wars: Race, intelligence, and the future of America* (pp. 70–79). New York, NY: Basic Books.

Surface Stations. (2009). *About.* Retrieved December 1, 2015, from http://surfacestations.org/about.htm

Terras, M. M., & Ramsay, J. (2012). The five central psychological challenges facing effective mobile learning. *British Journal of Educational Technology*, *43*(5), 820–832. doi:10.1111/j.1467-8535.2012.01362.x

Warnick, B. (2004). Online ethos: Source credibility in an "authorless" environment. *The American Behavioral Scientist*, *48*(2), 256–265. doi:10.1177/0002764204267273

Watts, A. (2010). *Earth hour in North Korea a stunning success.* Retrieved December 1, 2015, from http://wattsupwiththat.com/2010/03/27/earth-hour-in-north-korea-a-stunning-success

Watts, A. (2011). *Breaking news – CERN experiment confirms cosmic rays influence cloud seeds.* Retrieved December 1, 2015, from http://wattsupwiththat.com/2011/08/24/breaking-news-cern-experiment-confirms-cosmic-rays-influence-climate-change

Watts, A. (2012). *Over 250 noteworthy climategate 2.0 emails.* Retrieved December 1, 2015, from http://wattsupwiththat.com/2012/01/06/250-plus-noteworthy-climategate-2-0-emails

Watts, A. (2015a). *#AGU15 religion and climate change addressed.* Retrieved December 15, 2015 from, http://wattsupwiththat.com/2015/12/15/agu15-religion-and-climate-change-addressed

Watts, A. (2015b). *Green war on jobs: Britain's last deep coal-mine closes.* Retrieved December 21, 2015, from http://wattsupwiththat.com/2015/12/21/green-war-on-jobs-britains-last-deep-coal-mine-closes

Watts, A. (2015c). *Press release – Watts at #AGU the quality of temperature station siting matters for temperature trends.* Retrieved December 15, 2015, from http://wattsupwiththat.com/2015/12/17/press-release-agu15-the-quality-of-temperature-station-siting-matters-for-temperature-trends

Watts, A. (2015d). *Study: Current climate models misrepresent El Niño.* Retrieved December 15, 2015, from http://wattsupwiththat.com/2015/12/15/study-current-climate-models-misrepresent-el-nino

Wayne, G. P. (2007). *How reliable are climate models?* Retrieved December 1, 2015, from http://www.skepticalscience.com/climate-models.htm

What does past climate change tell us about global warming ? (2015). Skeptical Science. Retrieved December 1, 2015, from http://www.skepticalscience.com/climate-change-little-ice-age- medieval-warm-period.htm

Wichowski, D. W., & Kohl, L. E. (2013). Establishing credibility in the information jungle: Blogs, microblogs, and the CRAAP test. In M. Folk & S. Apostel (Eds.), *Online credibility and digital ethos: Evaluating computer-mediated communication* (pp. 229–251). Hershey, PA: IGI Global. doi:10.4018/978-1-4666-2663-8.ch013

KEY TERMS AND DEFINITIONS

Anthropogenic Climate Change: The warming trend of the earth as a result of man-made greenhouse gases.

Heuristic: A method or strategy based on practical experience for learning, discovery, and completing a target task.

Hindcasting: The practice of saving a sub-set of the data to test after a model has been created; e.g. using weather data from 1900 to 2000 to build a model then testing the model with data from 2000 to 2015.

Multicollinearity: Two predictor variables have a similar, positive or negative, effect on the variable of interest, which can mean the same causal force is being measured twice.

Quacks: Individuals who, through ulterior motives or ignorance, manipulate scientific research and statistical analyses to support their dogma.

Quants: Individuals who maintain the norms of scientific reason while successfully communicating their research and analyses.

Statistical Appropriateness: The principle that there are numerous models which are appropriate according to established methods, so the final selection must be justified by the researcher.

Topoi: Translated as topics, *topoi* function as categories for inventing or composing arguments.

Chapter 2
No Shortcuts to Credibility Evaluation:
The Importance of Expertise and Information Literacy

Jill R. Kavanaugh
Center on Media and Child Health at Boston Children's Hospital, USA

Bartlomiej A. Lenart
University of Alberta, Canada

ABSTRACT

This chapter argues that as the online informational landscape continues to expand, shortcuts to source credibility evaluation, in particular the revered checklist approach, falls short of its intended goal, and this method cannot replace the acquisition of a more formally acquired and comprehensive information literacy skill set. By examining the current standard of checklist criteria, the authors identify problems with this approach. Such shortcuts are not necessarily effective for online source credibility assessment, and the authors contend that in cases of high-stakes informational needs, they cannot adequately replace the expertise of information professionals, nor displace the need for proper and continuous information literacy education.

INTRODUCTION

While even Aristotle recognized the value of credible information and the problem of source credibility evaluation, the Internet era has made possible an information revolution that brings new urgency to the question of how to promote information literacy. Living in a world as digital citizens, there is no choice but to navigate and reevaluate this ever growing information landscape; however, as predatory sources set informational snares, the navigation of our vast informational world is becoming increasingly difficult without a robust credibility assessment toolkit at our disposal.

DOI: 10.4018/978-1-5225-1072-7.ch002

This chapter argues that as the informational landscape continues to expand, shortcuts to source credibility assessment designed to aid information seekers in dependably judging the credibility of a source or the content of a website cannot replace the acquisition of a more comprehensive set of information literacy competencies, especially since source credibility evaluation is just one of the several interrelated components of information literacy. Not all content requires thorough evaluation; in fact, research shows that information seekers do not assess source credibility for all content equally, and source credibility evaluation is most crucial during searches for high-stakes information, where misinformation can be most damaging, as, for example, when sifting through sources offering health-related content. The authors contend that shortcuts are not effective for online source credibility assessment, and shortcuts such as checklists cannot adequately replace the expertise of information professionals, nor displace the need for comprehensive lifelong information literacy education.

BACKGROUND: CONCEPTUALIZING CREDIBILITY

In the context of information quality, credibility is often understood in terms of the believability of some information in virtue of the perceived trustworthiness of its source (Hovland, Janis, & Kelley, 1963). Miriam J. Metzger (2007) argued that credibility is "a multifaceted concept with two primary dimensions: expertise and trustworthiness" (p. 2078).

Source trustworthiness, however, when not conjoined with expertise (see Ericsson et al. [1993] for an account of expertise acquisition), need not be a necessary component of credibility. From an epistemological perspective:

One need not demonstrate trustworthiness to secure credibility. One can, for example, secure it externally, by providing evidence that one has reason for being truthful even though the reason functions independently of one's goodwill. One can say to another: "I know that you don't trust me, but you nonetheless have reason to believe what I say; if what I say is false, I will suffer the consequences. (Strudler, 2009, p. 142)

What this suggests is that, logically speaking, the relation between Metzger's two primary dimensions of credibility places expertise at the center of the concept of credibility, with trustworthiness as an emergent property realized in the presence of expertise. Unfortunately, research has shown that credibility is not always evaluated in this manner, which is part of the bigger problem. In fact, studies have found that people are rarely conscientious enough to expend the required energy to evaluate the source credibility of the information they find online (Flanagin & Metzger, 2000; Scholz-Crane, 1998).

Such things as website design and the perceived character, rather than expertise, of the source play into the trust and persuasion of the average information seeker. Although such studies have been conducted in the context of online credibility, this is not a new phenomenon by any means. The ancient Greek philosopher Aristotle, for example, in his *Rhetoric*, pointed to three means of persuasion, *ethos*, *pathos*, and *logos* (McKeon, 1941, p. I.3, 1358a1337ff), which, in our context, can be understood as three sources of credibility evaluation. *Ethos* pertains to the perceived character of the speaker, *pathos* to the emotional state of the receiver, and *logos* to the logical organization of the content or the argument itself.

The first form of persuasion is accomplished merely "whenever the speech is held in such a way as to render the speaker worthy of credence. If the speaker appears to be credible, the audience will form the second-order judgment that propositions put forward by the credible speaker are true or acceptable" (Rapp, 2010, Section 5). It is worth noting that this has nothing to do with the content of the information being conveyed, and some propose that information receivers are more likely to be persuaded when the source merely presents itself as credible (Hovland et al., 1963).

In our contemporary context, this is the kind of persuasion one might expect individuals with the appropriate credentials to wield. Unfortunately, that is not always the way information seekers evaluate source credibility. Source familiarity appears to have a similar, and in some cases an even greater, epistemic pull as credentials and expertise. This source familiarity phenomenon is exemplified by the persuasive power famous public figures can often brandish when they voice opinions or make pronouncements on matters that lie beyond their own expertise, such as, for example, aligning themselves with scientific stances on such issues as climate change or commenting on political debates. Perhaps even more disturbingly, as Wathen and Burkell (2002) pointed out, good web design can have a similar persuasive effect on the information seeker.

Aristotle's second means of persuasion focuses on the information receiver's inner states during the course of acquiring information, and "[t]he success of the persuasive efforts depends on the emotional dispositions of the audience; for we do not judge in the same way when we grieve and rejoice or when we are friendly and hostile. Thus, the orator has to arouse emotions exactly because emotions have the power to modify our judgments" (Rapp, 2010, Section 5). Wathen and Burkell's (2002) model of user online information credibility evaluation, for example, factored in the user's cognitive states at the time of information retrieval.

Aristotle's third means of persuasion is arguably the best strategy for ascertaining the credibility of a source. The evaluation of the argument itself is often a good way of judging whether the information being acquired is persuasive; thus, "[w]e persuade by the argument itself when we demonstrate or seem to demonstrate that something is the case" (Rapp, 2010, Section 5). The evaluation of the content of information requires the greatest amount of effort because it will often include cross-referencing and fact-checking. The third mode of credibility evaluation is most reliant on the expertise dimension of Metzger's definition of credibility, and plays a central role in the recommendations at the end of this chapter. This chapter's recommendations will also incorporate Wathen and Burkell's (2002) three-pronged model of credibility assessment:

1. Surface characteristics and appearance of a website,
2. Usability and interface design, and
3. Cognitive states of the user (including prior knowledge).

Parts (1) and (2) correspond to Aristotle's notion of *ethos* as a tool of persuasion while (3) touches on both *pathos* and *logos* insofar as the cognitive states of the information seeker include prior knowledge, which is linked to his or her level of expertise or familiarity with the subject matter being searched and evaluated for validity, soundness, and consistency (Wathen & Burkell, 2002). Unfortunately, most common user practices reveal that information seekers seldom engage in the latter form of evaluation. Regardless of how in-depth (or not) the average user assesses information, it is important to note that "the environment may have changed the ways in which users create ethos and identity, but what readers look for in a credible source has remained essentially the same since ancient times" (Frobish, 2013, p. 18).

THE EVALUATION CHECKLIST AS A COMMON SHORTCUT TO DETERMINING ONLINE CREDIBILITY

Contemporary scholars and information professionals have struggled with the question of online credibility evaluation for years, as illustrated in research such as Miriam J. Metzger's (2007) seminal review of online credibility; Thomas J. Johnson and Barbara K. Kaye's (1998) early work comparing the perception of credibility in online versus print sources; Sarah Blakeslee's (2004) use of an innovative acronym for the CRAAP test; and B.J. Fogg's (Fogg et al., 2001) work with the Stanford Persuasive Tech Lab determining what aspects of websites lend themselves to more credibility. A common thread running through all of the aforementioned research is the fact that the use of the checklist approach remains a constant shortcut in the determination of credibility (although the checklist has had its detractors; see Meola 2004; Apostel & Folk, 2005). The checklist approach can be traced back to Jim Kapoun (1998), who proposed to base web evaluation on five criteria used for print evaluation. The purpose of developing a checklist, according to Kapoun, was to accommodate student proclivity for speed rather than accuracy when evaluating sources. He wrote:

To develop this model I had to first acknowledge that most students today tend to conduct research with speed rather than accuracy and rarely evaluate resources. So the criteria I present must be digestible and almost transparent to the student. In other words, the student must be trained to evaluate a Web document like second nature. (Kapoun, 1998, p. 522)

The typical credibility checklist provides researchers with a list of questions they should ask about their online source. Kapoun listed five generally accepted criteria that should appear on a credibility checklist: accuracy, authority, objectivity, currency, and coverage. Many versions of Kapoun's credibility checklist exist in abundance online because many university libraries, writing centers, and individual departments provide variations of the checklist, encouraging researchers to tally whether their source meets enough of the so-called desirable criteria and creating scoring systems to help information seekers evaluate a website quickly and easily. Unfortunately, just as this approach to credibility evaluation persists, so do the problems with each of the accepted checklist criteria.

Accuracy

Accuracy is "the degree to which a Web site is free from errors, whether the information can be verified offline, and the reliability of the information on the site" (Metzger, 2007, p. 2079). Kapoun cautioned about being aware of the purpose of the document and understanding the distinction between author and Webmaster (p. 522). According to the University of Pittsburgh's (2015)*Evaluating Web Resources* checklist (itself adapted from Kapoun's original criteria), researchers should ask some of the following questions:

- Is this information coming from an educational institution (.edu), a company (.com), the government (.gov), or an organization (.org)?
- Is the information free from error?
- Is it purposely misleading?

Many evaluation checklists encourage researchers to determine accuracy based on a website's URL, often emphasizing the website's top-level domain (such as whether the website ends in a .edu, .com, or .gov). This rule persists from the relatively early days of the Internet, when initially only seven top-level domains (TLDs) existed. As domain names become scarcer due to the continual amounts of information being posted online, the concept of determining a website's accuracy by its TLD is becoming antiquated. According to the Internet Assigned Numbers Authority, there are over 1000 TLDs as of 2015—many of which remain unknown to the general public (Internet Corporation for Assigned Names and Numbers (ICANN), 2015). Scholars may view websites ending in uncommon TLDs with a more skeptical eye and discredit them without fairly reviewing the content, thereby disqualifying potentially credible and salient information.

One telling example of unfounded mistrust of a website's credibility as a result of an unusual URL is the Center on Media and Child Health (CMCH). CMCH is an evidence-based research group at Boston Children's Hospital, which provides a myriad of tools, tip sheets, advice, and other resources on the Center's website, http://cmch.tv. By the time the Center was established in 2003, many of the desired domain names were already claimed, and the team made the decision to use cmch.tv as their primary URL. Since then, the Center has had many inquiries into why the .tv TLD was chosen, especially since .tv is typically used for video content sites. If the Center had been able to choose .org, like its parent organization Boston Children's Hospital, it would have perhaps been given more credence. Conversely, relying on a more recognized TLD does not always meet the presumption of accuracy. For example, many university students, staff, and faculty can share information on university-hosted web space, providing the illusion that if the resource exists on a site ending in .edu, it is automatically accurate.

Another one of the major issues with questioning the accuracy of a website, such as whether it is free from error or provides misleading content, is whether it is possible for burgeoning researchers to truly comprehend the level of accuracy provided. The Dunning-Kruger effect (Kruger & Dunning, 1999) is a cognitive bias that can be applied to evaluating accuracy: unskilled individuals may remain unaware that they are unskilled, and those with a higher level of skill may underrate their own knowledge. From an information literacy perspective (Gross, Latham, & Armstrong, 2012), the Dunning-Kruger effect can contribute to the inability of individuals to accurately evaluate and assess the need, value, and relevance of information. More importantly, it suggests that less-skilled individuals are likely to be unaware of the degree to which they are accurately assessing the quality of the information they collect, while those with higher levels of information literacy are likely to underestimate their ability to determine the credibility of a source. As a result, determining the accuracy of a website may not always be a simple task due to our own biases and knowledge levels.

Authority

Authority is determined "by noting who authored the site and whether contact information is provided for that person or organization, what the author's credentials, qualifications, and affiliations are, and whether the Web site is recommended by a trusted source" (Metzger, 2007, p. 2079). According to the University of California at Berkeley Library (UC Berkeley, 2012), questions researchers should ask in regard to authority include:

- Who wrote the page?
- What are the author's credentials on this subject?

The idea of being able to identify the author is deemed a necessity in many credibility checklists, but it raises the issue as to whether anonymity can be credible. Social networking sites are often some of the most difficult sources to assess for credibility because many individuals using these outlets are doing so anonymously. One study (Thomson et al., 2012) found that over 70% of tweets using the #fukushima hashtag during the Fukushima Daiichi nuclear power plant disaster in Japan were citing highly credible sources, despite the anonymity of many of the Twitter accounts. During the Arab Spring revolution, anonymous social media accounts on Twitter, Facebook, and YouTube were essential to distributing information and staging demonstrations (Howard et al., 2011; Gamie, 2013). As a result, discrediting certain online sources due to a lack of clear authorship requires more critical thinking about the context in which the anonymous sources provide the information, as well as reasons for the anonymity itself.

Another persistent problem is the notion of authority itself, and how that authority can be abused. In some research, it may be difficult to determine who should be listed as an author, depending on the type of expertise that author lends to the project, and in larger research projects, it becomes more difficult to identify fair attribution (Smith & Williams-Jones, 2012). Related to this issue is the problem known as *guested* authorship (sometimes referred to as *gifted* authorship), which occurs when an individual who did not contribute to the article in a meaningful way is listed as an author (Schofferman, Wetzel, & Bono, 2015). Conversely, *ghosted* authorship occurs when an individual contributes significantly to the article, but is not listed as an author (Schofferman et al., 2015). The practice of gifting or guesting hurts the integrity of rigorous scientific research, but as research shows, it is a common convention (Street, Rogers, Israel, & Braunack-Mayer, 2010). While publishers, journal editors, and even governing authorities have their own policies for attributing authorship in scholarly works, research shows that the field is far from regulated. For example, while the International Committee of Medical Journal Editors (ICMJE) recommendations exist in order to standardize authorship guidelines in the area of biomedical journals, research shows that many journals are in fact not adhering to the ICMJE requirements (Bosch, Pericas, Hernandez, & Torrents, 2012).

Objectivity

Objectivity "involves identifying the purpose of the site and whether the information provided is fact or opinion, which also includes understanding whether there might be commercial intent [see Kapoun 1998] or a conflict of interest on the part of the source, as well as the nature of relationships between linked information sources" (Metzger, 2007, p. 2079). According to Cornell University's (2015)*Evaluating Web Pages: Questions to Consider*, questions related to objectivity include:

- What goals/objectives does this page meet?
- How detailed is the information?
- What opinions (if any) are expressed by the author?

Identifying objectivity and bias is another area that may not be easily discerned from a checklist of questions. Many online resources claim to provide information that is grounded in science; however, these claims require substantiation. One study found that not all research methodologies are considered equal, and terms like research-based, evidence-based, and recommended practice are not necessarily standardized (Test, Kemp-Inman, Diegelmann, Hitt, & Bethune, 2015).

The question of credibility is also important when considering the establishment of foundations for the evaluation of more innovative and less established sources, especially with the dramatic and continual shift in available technologies and sources of information. YouTube, for example, has emerged as a source of information utilized by reputable organizations. Unfortunately, health-related organizations that release educational videos do not, in fact, see a higher engagement, despite their high level of credibility (Desai et al., 2013).

Moreover, user biases will undoubtedly impact the user's ability to critically examine an online source with an objective eye; individuals are twice as likely to select information that is already in line with their preexisting beliefs (Hart et al., 2009). This lack of objectivity can be particularly dangerous in the health sciences realm, where websites with strong agendas attempt to prove their validity. A recent example is the anti-vaccination debate; one study found that when individuals were provided with statistical information about vaccine-adverse events, their opinions were swayed by reading less credible narratives online (Haase, Betsch, & Renkewitz, 2015).

Currency

Currency is one of the more straightforward criteria on many website evaluation checklists, and refers to "whether the information is up to date" (Metzger, 2007, p. 2079). According to the Queen's University (2001)*Evaluating Web Sources* checklist, researchers should ask:

- Is there a date of publication or last update?
- Is the page maintained on a regular basis?
- Is the information considered current for your topic/research?

While a website's currency can often be determined simply by looking for a publication date, this checklist criterion lacks the integration of critical thinking skills except in specific circumstances. The problem of article retraction can affect how credible the information may be, even if the website has been recently updated. Research from as early as 1990 identified that retracted journal articles often continue to be cited (Pfeifer & Snodgrass, 1990), and more recent research shows that article retractions have increased (Wager & Williams, 2011). If an author of a website is unaware that an article has been retracted, they may be inadvertently sharing outdated information on their recently updated websites. As "authors, editors, reviewers, and librarians are all involved, a multi-faceted approach will be required to address the problem of continued use of invalid data and ideas" (Pfeifer & Snodgrass, 1990, p. 1422).

Coverage

Coverage is "the comprehensiveness or depth of the information provided on the site" (Metzger, 2007, p. 2079). According to the *6 Criteria for Websites* checklist provided by Dalhousie University (2015), questions should include:

- Does the site claim to be selective or comprehensive?
- Are the topics explored in depth?

One problem with the idea of coverage is that a lack of time may prevent a researcher from exploring a resource in greater depth. In particular, research has established that in the field of medicine, health sciences professionals often rely solely on a journal article's abstract instead of the full text in order to make decisions, mostly due to a lack of time and a need for a concise summary (Saint et al., 2000). While structured abstracts can be useful, they are not always available, and research shows that quality issues continue to exist in certain types of article abstracts (Mbuagbaw et al., 2014). Time, especially in medical research, is always going to be of the essence. As a result, instructing researchers to use in-depth online resources such as full journal articles as opposed to abstracts may not be a practical or useful criterion for determining credibility.

Notes on the Peer Review Process

Another major component of the checklist approach, which may be interwoven into any one of the five previously discussed criteria, is whether the article has been peer reviewed. The peer-reviewed journal article is often seen as the gold standard for credibility; however, issues with the peer-review process (as with the checklist approach) persist.

To begin, there has been an increase in predatory open access publishers offering journals with lax publishing guidelines, and differentiating between legitimate and non-legitimate journals is becoming increasingly difficult. While Beall's List of Potential, Possible, or Probable Predatory Scholarly Open-Access Publishers attempts to curate a list of publishers to avoid (Beall, 2015), this is still a relatively new domain for researchers outside of the information sciences realm, although awareness is growing, especially as well-publicized hoax papers continue to pass the peer review process (Gasparyan, Yessirkepov, Diyanova, & Kitas, 2015).

Moreover, different methods of the peer-review process may in fact diminish an article's credibility. In particular, the single-blind peer review, where reviewers are made aware of the identities of the authors whose work they are reviewing, is still unfortunately prevalent in academic journals. The single-blind peer review is seen by some as the worst type of review (Manchikanti, Kaye, Boswell, & Hirsch, 2015) because reviewers required to use these less-than-optimal peer review methods must ensure that they provide honest critiques, regardless of whether the author is well-established or a junior investigator (Bickham, Kavanaugh, & Rich, In press).

Additionally, some disciplines place a high value on non-peer reviewed resources, whereas others do not. For example, systematic reviews, where all clinical evidence (relevant to the review question) is appraised and synthesized, are considered to be examples of some of the highest levels of evidence; the Cochrane Handbook for Systematic Reviews of Interventions (2011) emphasizes the importance of the inclusion of grey literature such as research reports, white papers, and other documents typically not published through traditional avenues into its methodology—and grey literature does not often go through the peer review process. Many existing credibility checklists continue to eschew any research that is not peer reviewed, without taking into consideration the importance of this type of work, especially in quickly evolving fields such as media and technology. The University of British Columbia's *Evaluating Information Sources* site (2015) strongly emphasizes the importance of using peer-reviewed sources, which may lead some researchers to avoid using grey literature; however, research suggests that grey literature adds to the credibility of systematic reviews (Mahood, Van Eerd, & Irvin, 2014). Many reputable organizations, such as the Pew Research Center and the Henry J. Kaiser Family Foundation, self-publish, and several databases exist for the purpose of locating grey literature.

The first problem with the checklist approach, then, is that it is designed by information professionals as a conceptual crutch for the informationally uninitiated (see Kapoun 1998); nevertheless, in order to offer the evaluative support such aids promise, the knowledge and experience of the information experts who design these devices must somehow be distilled into a list or whatever simplified evaluative tool is produced. Unfortunately for the informationally uninitiated user, the simplified and distilled advice, which, as is the case with checklists, often comes in the form of rules of thumb, and is therefore devoid of the contextual nuances to be effectively utilized across the expanse of web-based sources. While checklists are designed to be used independently by the average user, they can never fully address the complex problem of determining credibility, and, as is evidenced by research, users unsurprisingly utilize them inefficiently (see Flanagin & Metzger, 2000; Gunther, 1992; Meola, 2004).

The second problem with such evaluative devices is that although the rules of thumb do contain sound advice, they are merely rules of thumb, which cannot generate the kind of confidence in one's source credibility evaluation as one ought to expect. The worry here is twofold. First, not all highly credible sources will necessarily be current, have a listed author, or be peer reviewed. In cases where author anonymity is imperative due to a hostile political climate, for instance, all three signs of credibility may well be missing as the author will choose to remain unlisted, no peer review process will likely occur, and the release of information may well be considerably delayed. For example, Samaa Gamie (2013) argued that anonymity played a powerful role in activist digital discourses during the youth movement that initiated the Egyptian Revolution because anonymity was necessary for credibility in that context. The second worry with such evaluative devices is that fraudulent and predatory information disseminators can camouflage their content with the aid of those devices themselves by ensuring that the manner in which information is presented passes as credible by following the very rules of thumb meant to help make the credibility evaluation.

Fraudulent sites do not even have to engage in original research in order to reap the benefits of copying successful strategies because such research is regularly conducted and published. For example, Knight, et al. (2013) provided guidelines for using social networking to build online credibility by engaging in audience analysis, maintaining a continual online presence, building immediacy or close relationships, etc.; Tai and Zhang (2013) examined the key defining features of the most successful blog sites and bloggers in China; while Wichowski and Kohl (2013) discussed the CRAAP test in relation to the establishment of online credibility of blogs and microblogs. In fact, a web search for tips on how to make one's website more credible opens a floodgate to opinions and self-published blogs, articles, and books drawing on the massive efforts of researchers discussing the evaluation of online credibility. Every piece of advice that occurs on most evaluation checklists, then, is also being absorbed and utilized by those who aim to build online credibility, whether for noble or malicious reasons, meaning that important research into source credibility evaluation is itself being utilized by some in a manner that perpetuates the problem.

SOURCE CREDIBILITY EVALUATION

The evaluation of source credibility is a complicated psychological process, which, as extensive research indicates, people are generally not very diligent in executing even with the aid of a checklist (see Eysenbach & Köhler, 2002; Flanagin & Metzger, 2000; Gunther, 1992; Lucassen & Maarten-Schraagen, 2012; Meola, 2004; Metzger, Flanagin, & Medders, 2010; Scholz-Crane, 1998; Taylor & Dalal, 2014; Taylor 2015), arguably due to the inadequacy inherent in the checklist approach. One salient question that needs addressing pertains to the factors that make a source credible. This is often the starting point for the development of the various techniques of credibility assessment published by university libraries or writing centers. There are, however, two problems with many of these techniques:

1.   People seldom use them effectively and diligently, and
2.   As we have already explored above, none of them is adequate at properly judging the credibility of the source or content.

Regarding the first problem, one study of American undergraduate students asked them about their personal web-surfing habits and found that

Respondents reported verifying the information they obtained via the Internet only "rarely" to "occasionally"...People scored highest on those verification behaviors that are easy to perform and require their opinion (e.g., considering whether information is current and complete) and lowest on the verification behaviors that are difficult to perform and require their action (e.g., verifying the qualifications or credentials of the author). (Flanagin & Metzger, 2000, p. 531)

Of course, not every user query merits the same scrutiny, nor the same amount of time and energy expended on source credibility evaluation. Information seekers need not be very diligent at evaluating content when the informational stakes are low, such as, for example, when sifting through gossip columns or other low stakes entertainment news. Source credibility evaluation, however, plays a much more salient role when stakes are high. Unsurprisingly, Flanagin and Metzger (2000) found that

... verification behaviors varied depending on the type of information sought. Reference information was verified more rigorously than either commercial or entertainment information and news information was verified more stringently than entertainment information as well. However, reference and news information were verified equally rigorously. The same held true for news and commercial information and for commercial and entertainment information. Overall, these findings indicate that when misinformation is least damaging (e.g., entertainment) it is verified least rigorously, and information where accuracy may be more important (e.g., reference and news information) is verified significantly more. (pp. 531-532)

Flanagin and Metzger's findings support Albert C. Gunther's (1992) theory that more salient information is verified more rigorously while less vital information is less diligently assessed. Gunther wrote: "The findings are consistent with the prediction that high involvement prompts not only more scrutiny but more biased scrutiny of media content and therefore increases likelihood that a person will take a skeptical view of the source of that content" (p. 161). Gunther continued by pointing toward the notion of expertise already mentioned above: "Of course, high-involvement people often do know more about an issue or group than their less involved counterparts, and therefore some portion of perceived distortion in news coverage may consist of the real errors or omissions that people with such expertise accurately discern" (p. 161).

Credibility evaluation is a complex process, which, as research has shown, is quite easily manipulated, especially with the onset of digitization and the ready availability of information online. While credible sources can utilize various methods of persuasion, including the establishment of proper credentials by emphasizing their expertise in a certain field or noting their affiliation with credible institutions, the information seeker is also exposed to less credible, and even fraudulent, sources that can also exert an epistemic pull on their audience in various ways, such as, among others:

1. Affiliating themselves with credible institutional authorities such as universities or government agencies;
2. Presenting trusted credentials such as academic ranks or other professional titles;
3. Utilizing familiar public personalities in the delivery of content;
4. Mimicking professional web design or incorporating professional jargon with the hopes of legitimizing otherwise unverified information; or
5. Targeting individuals who are epistemically predisposed to accepting some information at face value due to certain emotional states by taking advantage of the motivational dimension of relevance, which may resonate with a targeted group of information seekers (see Cosijn & Ingwersen, 2000; Saracevic, 1975; 1996 for discussions of affective/motivational relevance in the context of information retrieval).

EXPERTISE AND INFORMATION LITERACY

Carol Kuhlthau's (1987, 2004) insightful consideration of the information seeker's emotional dichotomy between uncertainty and control of information seeking behavior is closely related to Aristotle's notion of *pathos*, which is the information seeker's inner experience during the course of information acquisition. Kuhlthau argued that information seekers face an inherent uncertainty in the information seeking process. Part of becoming an information literate user, then, involves the mastery of this inherent uncertainty. Credibility evaluation, which is inseparably entangled with information literacy, cannot rely on the checklist approach to information literacy, but must involve a certain level of proficiency in critical thinking and problem solving skills. Christina Doyle (1994) wrote:

Research into cognitive processes has shown clearly that personal experience, the discovery of meaning, and the discerning of connections, are necessary conditions for successful learning. Students learn best when they connect new experiences with older ones, and then extend the connection to new possibilities. This requires thinking! As students prepare for the 21st century, the traditional basic courses in reading, mathematics, and writing need to be coupled with communication, critical thinking, and problem solving skills. (Costa, 1985). Information literacy is the platform upon which these skills can stand, consisting as it does of knowledge of resources and tools of access, skillful search strategies, and appropriate techniques of processing information (Kuhlthau, 1987). (p. 45)

Information literacy education is the best tool for proper source credibility evaluation since one's capacity to evaluate source credibility proficiently is proportionally related to one's information literacy skills, which involve, as Doyle (1994) argued, communication, critical thinking, and problem solving skills. Proficiency in information literacy, however, is a process that cannot be distilled into a credibility evaluation shortcut, such as a checklist, because it takes time to form the expertise that is the result of the interaction between theoretical knowledge and practice (or experience).

This does not entail that all information seekers should become information professionals or information literacy experts. The employment of search strategies like the list approach, however, is also not the answer, especially since research has consistently shown that information seekers do not properly utilize such devices. Nevertheless, the problem is not insoluble, as there already are information professionals at hand to help guide users in their searches, as well as provide users with information literacy education (where more of the latter is always a good thing). Librarians, then, provide an invaluable service, both in helping information seekers search for credible information, as well as educating users on how to become more critical information seekers, thereby increasing their proficiency in source credibility evaluation.

SOLUTIONS AND RECOMMENDATIONS

Although, as is evidenced by the vast amount of literature on the issue of credibility, information professionals are diligently working to help prepare information seekers for the complexity of today's information-driven world, no dependable shortcut to source credibility evaluation has been proposed. The most dependable means of credibility evaluation will always be grounded in expertise, both in the form of subject matter knowledge and information literacy more generally. Of course, not every person can be an expert on every subject, but every person should have access to an authoritative, credible source when browsing through a vast amount of content—information literacy is the necessary skill required for discerning that source. Therefore, the authors contend that the Internet age demands that digital citizens acquire an adequate, though not necessarily an expert, level of proficiency in navigating the plethora of sources disseminating information. There will be circumstances in which information literacy cannot be acquired, whether due to time or budgetary constraints; in such cases, the best solution is to either embed an expert into an organization (if possible), or to make use of those experts available to the general public.

Recommendation 1: Embedded Librarianship

Even experts in their respective fields find it difficult to keep up with the rapid changes in their own fields, apart from their particular specializations, thus necessitating the employment of the skill sets possessed by information professionals in order to help them navigate the ever-expanding informational landscape. The authors offer an example, as a case in point, of The Center on Media and Child Health, and argue that the Center's information organizational structure can serve as a model of the kind of social collaboration of experts and information seekers (who may well be experts in some fields, but novices or amateurs in others) that the rapidly expanding—and continuously changing—information landscape demands of the digital citizens who inhabit it and depend on it for social, economic, and civic reasons.

The Center on Media and Child Health (CMCH) is a grant-funded research center within the Division of Adolescent and Young Adult Medicine at Boston Children's Hospital. The mission of CMCH is to educate and empower children and those who care for them to create and consume media in ways that optimize children's health and development. The Center fulfills this mission through three distinct, yet interconnected realms:

1. Investigation, in which the team conducts original research to understand the positive and negative effects of media on health;
2. Translation, which involves synthesizing and disseminating research as useful and practical tools for parents and other stakeholders; and
3. Innovation, which involves using media to develop creative interventions for health.

This small interdisciplinary research team consists of a pediatrician, social scientist, content strategist, program coordinators, and other associated personnel, all of whom collaborate using their specific expertise and their diverse backgrounds, which cultivates ingenuity, innovation, and creativity—all salient factors in conducting and publishing research.

Since the Center's inception in 2003, the founder has employed a full-time embedded librarian, a position held by three different individuals over the past 12 years (and currently held by one of the co-authors). Shumaker (2012) outlined the roles of the embedded librarian as follows:

Embedded librarianship is a distinctive innovation that moves the librarians out of libraries and creates a new model of library and information work. It emphasizes the importance of forming a strong working relationship between the librarian and a group or team of people who need the librarian's information expertise. As the relationship develops, the librarian's knowledge and understanding of the group's work and objectives grow, which leads in turn to greater alertness to the information and knowledge needs of the group. (p. 4)

The Librarian assists with every project at the Center, providing a myriad of support, including performing literature searches, providing citation management services, monitoring emerging research, and co-writing content for research papers and other resources. The CMCH team, although small, produces a vast amount of informational resources and other products, and each team member is engrossed in several concurrent projects. As a result of high demand and low time availability, each team member relies on the embedded librarian to use her expertise as an information professional in order to assist the team in any way possible. The embedded librarian is thus more involved in the research process, having a deeper impact on the research and stronger relationships with the team than traditional, non-embedded librarians (Carlson & Kneale, 2011).

As the organizational structure of CMCH suggests, nothing can actually replace the value of highly trained professionals, and only information literacy and the acquisition of expertise are truly dependable enablers of the most effective credibility evaluation strategies. Lifelong learning is no longer merely a professional requirement; the average information seekers, in virtue of their digital citizenship, must engage in constant and progressive acquisition of an ever-growing information literacy skill set.

With the abundance of literature and resources being published on a daily basis, it is impractical to carry the burden of source credibility evaluation for all, and especially the vitally important information queries. Thus, where the acquisition of expertise is impossible and the process of information literacy education incomplete or insufficient given the gravity of the information seeker's query, consultation with information professionals is a strategy to which information seekers should have access. As the Center on Media and Child Health example indicates, even experts in their field employ the services of information professionals.

As the information profession continues to redefine itself in the context of emerging and evolving technologies and information needs, the value of, and the demand for, embedded and subject specialist librarians will increase. This is already evident in the aforementioned organizational structure of CMCH, and this trend can be traced throughout Canada (Dennett et al., 2014) and the United Kingdom (Vassilakaki et al., 2015). One way of ensuring that new professionals and potential employers become aware of this emerging trend is for library schools to offer courses dedicated to embedded librarianship and encourage practicum and internship partnerships in such non-traditional library settings.

While research centers like CMCH employ dedicated librarians, the average user has access to the same professional services through institutions like libraries and other publicly funded agencies. In most cases, this access, though readily available in local libraries and online, is underused, a tendency that can be remedied by more visible advertising of library services in general and implementing information literacy education through primary and secondary schooling. Information literacy education, though it does not offer any shortcuts to source credibility evaluation, is, the authors argue, the best means of ensuring adequate user credibility assessment, but it also requires a shift in how students are introduced to, and encouraged to utilize, the services librarians offer. While many universities do provide an introduction to information literacy as part of a core university course, this is far from sufficient training for students who will be expected to evaluate sources for their own independent research.

There is not, however, a need for librarians to embed more exclusively within classrooms or departments than they already do; subject librarians already liaise with departments and faculty. What is needed is a more consistent and continuous relationship between subject librarians and teaching faculty. One way of achieving this is by collaborating on shared learning outcomes that focus on a department's particular area of study in the context of information literacy skills most pertinent to that particular department. Active recruitment of subject specialists to fill the roles of subject librarians would be tremendously helpful in achieving such collaboration. Moreover, faculty are much more likely to collaborate fruitfully with librarians who share some level of expertise in their subject matter; faculty in the department of philosophy, for example, are much more likely to seek out the services of a librarian who is also a philosopher. Continued collaboration between faculty and subject librarians is not only beneficial to student learning, but is also instrumental to the development of information literacy, which, as the second recommendation suggests, is the key to competent source credibility evaluation.

Recommendation 2: Information Literacy and Source Credibility Evaluation

Information literacy is a difficult term to define, partly because its application is context sensitive and partly because this complex set of competencies is continually adapting to emerging and evolving informational media. Generally speaking, information literacy is a set of competencies that allow individuals to recognize when information is needed and what information is needed, and enables an individual to locate, evaluate, and effectively utilize the required information. Breivik and Jones (1993) explained that information literate individuals "become sophisticated users of [informational] resources and technologies as they:

1. Gather needed information from all sources;
2. Test the validity of information as it remains constant and as it changes from discipline to discipline;
3. Place information into various contexts that ultimately will yield its pertinent meaning;
4. Remain skeptical about information and discriminate fact from truth" (p. 26).

Source credibility evaluation, then, is one of the constitutive competencies of information literacy.

Although the concept of information literacy as a set of fundamental competencies must certainly be applicable to any information context where the seeking, locating, evaluating, and utilizing of information is necessary, the term itself was coined by Paul Zurkowski in 1974 and contextualized within the modern work environment where information has enormous utility. Zurkowski explained that "[p]eople trained in the application of information resources to their work can be called information literates... [having] learned techniques and skills for utilizing the wide range of information tools as well as primary sources in moulding information-solutions to their problems" (p. 6).

The need to introduce the formal concept of information literacy arose within the context of the emergence of a workforce reliant on information, and, with the further evolution of information technologies, the concept inevitably grew in complexity and breadth of applicability. Rather than understanding the term as solely a workplace competency, the emerging technological social infrastructure shifted the understanding of the term from merely being a workplace competency to a much wider context where information literacy serves as the foundation for lifelong learning (Demo, 1986).

Shirley Behrens (1994) stated that in 1982, "*Time* magazine chose the computer as Machine of the Year, and, inspired by the feature, Forest Horton [1983] considered the potential role that computers had as a resource in an information age. [Horton] referred to *Time*'s consciousness-raising of the computer's problem-solving capabilities as computer literacy...[h]e went on to explain, however, that information literacy extended beyond computer literacy" (p. 317). Behrens adds that "[i]nformation literacy had become a major issue in librarianship, since the profession saw in it a way that its members could make a contribution toward a society of lifelong learners" (Behrens, 1994, p. 317)

As is becoming evident from the history of the term, the concept of information literacy has been evolving in parallel with the emergence of information technologies. Information literacy today, however, bears little resemblance to Zurkowski's definition of the term or the traditional model utilized within the library context, which concentrated on user education aimed at the acquisition of library skills and bibliographic instruction. The evolution of our understanding of what information literacy entails has also shifted approaches to teaching the complex and continually growing skill set; the approach has been shifting from a focus on instruction pertaining to information seeking tools to teaching information competencies (Špiranec & Zorica, 2010). Kuhlthau (1999) captured the evolving concept of information literacy when she wrote, "Information literacy incorporates both library skills and information skills, but adds the critical component of understanding the process of learning in information-rich environments. Information literacy extends library skills beyond the use of discrete skills and strategies to the ability to use complex information from a variety of sources to develop meaning or solve problems" (p. 11).

Being information literate, then, no longer implies the mere ability to use information tools, but rather entails the competency to critically evaluate information needs, sources, and uses. Critical thinking skills, in turn, ground the various competencies constitutive of information literacy; moreover, critical thinking skills are, in fact, central to Aristotle's third means of persuasion, *logos* (the evaluation of the argument itself), which, as already argued above, is the best strategy for ascertaining the credibility of a source.

Sadly, students are not leaving school with an adequately developed critical thinking skill set, which, unsurprisingly, results in very low information literacy competencies. Research suggests that post-secondary students are information illiterate upon entry (Gross & Latham, 2007). What this means is that students do not begin to receive information literacy education until their undergraduate studies (and even then, many undergraduates slip through the cracks), and those who do not attend university seldom receive information literacy education at all.

Although some research suggests that the critical thinking skills necessary for information literacy depend on the cognitive development levels of senior undergraduate students (Jackson, 2008), this certainly does not mean that information literacy should be taught only in graduate school. In fact, other research supports the claim that information literacy education benefits junior undergraduate students (see Selegean, Thomas, & Richman, 1983; Ren, 2000; Wang, 2006).

Moreover, the philosopher Matthew Lipman, after leaving his professorship at Columbia University to found the Institute for the Advancement of Philosophy for Children in 1974, developed successful strategies to engage children (from K-12) in critical thinking through classic problems in philosophy. The general consensus in philosophy, going as far back as Plato, was that children were cognitively ill equipped to comprehend philosophical problems, partly due to the lack of critical thinking skills required for the engagement with abstract philosophical concepts. Nevertheless, Lipman's program was successful and subsequently spawned various adaptations (see Wartenberg, 2014; Lewis & Chandley, 2012; Lipman, Sharp, & Oscanyon, 1985) and is currently being introduced into school districts as part of a wider demand for critical thinking initiatives.

Because critical thinking skills are foundational for information literacy competencies, the development of such skills in the general population is instrumental to the development of an information literate society. This sort of training must not be initiated in adulthood, but rather should be integrated into both primary and secondary educational curricula (and beyond) because, as Thomas (2004) argued, "unless youngsters are taught and also expected to appraise critically the resources they find on the Internet and pursue research questions rather than fact-finding tasks, the potential for inspiring the development of higher-order thinking skills represented by the activity of Internet-based searching will remain largely unrealized" (p. 136).

A strong foundation in critical thinking skills is no longer merely useful for some professions, but rather is a necessary competency of every digital citizen. Checklists and other rules of thumb will become obsolete at an increasing rate and "students will need to evaluate information in more nuanced ways than they are currently taught at most colleges and universities. Information literacy needs to be increasingly focused on teaching evaluative skills to students, skills that go well beyond determining whether or not something is peer-reviewed" (Farkas, 2012, p. 90). Critical thinking skills and, by extension, Aristotle's third means of persuasion, are the best strategies for ensuring competent source credibility evaluation that will continue to develop with the emergence of new information technologies and the evolution of the information infrastructure itself.

Source credibility evaluation is a constitutive competency possessed by information literate individuals; just as there are no shortcuts to information literacy education, so there are no shortcuts to source credibility evaluation. A strong grounding in critical thinking skills (including an understanding that there is a difference between various sources of information) starting at a young age and continuing through to adulthood is the best way of ensuring that digital citizens have the tools to navigate a continuously evolving informational landscape.

Information literacy education, then, is perhaps the best means of ensuring consistently dependable source credibility evaluation. While not everyone is, or can be, an expert in a given field of inquiry, just as not everyone is, or can be, an expert in information organization and evaluation, only some need to be experts in order for credible, authoritative information to be available. Fortunately, information professionals, who are in possession of, among other skills, expertise in information literacy, which is essential to dependable source credibility evaluation, are readily available, both in person and online, to help connect information seekers with expert sources and provide information literacy education.

FUTURE RESEARCH DIRECTIONS

One idea only briefly touched upon in this chapter is the effect of visual web design on credibility. Much of the research evaluating the more physical human-computer interaction aspects lags behind what is currently in use. Within the last several years, there has been a massive shift from full browser-based web design to a more mobile-friendly responsive design, leaving little room for aesthetic variations. Some content services have moved strictly to a mobile app interface, and early questions posited regarding web design impact, such as how links were presented, whether ads were present, and how fast a website loads, are no longer valid; however, questions pertaining to responsive design, the overall shift to smaller screens, and how this affects credibility judgments will need to be explored. This shift was further emphasized during Google's 2015 algorithm change (Makino, 2015), which rewarded websites that have fully responsive designs with higher rankings in their results. Websites with non-responsive designs but that possess otherwise credible content will essentially be ignored by the search engine giant, leading to questions regarding the role of advancing technology in credibility evaluations.

Another important area requiring more attention is the role of embedded librarians in research-based organizations. While research exists on embedded librarianship, it often does not pertain to how their expertise is utilized throughout all portions of the research process. As more librarians become subject specialists, the lines between librarian and researcher may blur, and librarians may develop more intricate skills. While outside of the scope of this chapter, librarian advocacy remains an important and controversial topic, one that ought to continue to be addressed in future research.

CONCLUSION

Although this chapter identifies problems with the checklist approach, the authors do so not in an attempt to discredit the rigorous work that has gone into creating such checklists, but more so to highlight the growing need for information literacy education and for expertise in the form of highly trained information professionals. Academic institutions need to emphasize information literacy skills in their curricula, research organizations need to consider employing or consulting information literacy experts, and information seekers in general must continually add to their credibility evaluation toolkits via a lifelong engagement in information literacy education.

Not all sources require the same level of credibility assessment. Where the stakes are low, information seekers need not worry about consulting checklists as they evaluate the credibility of the source. In fact, research suggests (Flanagin & Metzger, 2000; Gunther, 1992) that information seekers do not actually care about credibility where low risk information, such as entertainment, for example, is concerned. Where the stakes are higher, as in reference or news, information literacy education has an immensely greater utility than shortcut strategies can ever have. In cases where the stakes are arguably the highest, such as when seeking health-related information, expertise plays a crucial functional role in credibility evaluation, making expert consultation the best evaluative strategy (whether in the form of a health care practitioner or an information professional capable of navigating health care literature). Where the stakes are high, shortcuts are undesirable; where the stakes are low, shortcuts are unnecessary.

ACKNOWLEDGMENT

The authors would like to thank Dr. Ali Shiri for his guidance on this chapter.

REFERENCES

Apostel, S., & Folk, M. (2005). *First phase in-formation literacy on a fourth generation Web site: An argument for a new approach to Web site evaluation criteria. Computers & Composition Online, Spring 2005.* Retrieved March 10, 2016 from http://www2.bgsu.edu/departments/english/cconline/apostelfolk/c_and_c_online_apostel_folk/

Beall, J. (2015). *Potential, possible, or probable predatory scholarly open-access publishers.* Retrieved December 1, 2015, from http://scholarlyoa.com/publishers/

Behrens, S. J. (1994). A conceptual analysis and historical overview of Information Literacy. *College & Research Libraries, 55*(4), 309–322. doi:10.5860/crl_55_04_309

Berkeley, U. C. (2012). *Evaluating web pages: Techniques to apply & questions to ask.* Retrieved December 1, 2015, from http://www.lib.berkeley.edu/TeachingLib/Guides/Internet/Evaluate.html

Bickham, D. S., Kavanaugh, J. R., & Rich, M. (2016). Media effects as health research: How pediatricians have changed the study of media and child development. *Journal of Children and Media, 10*(2), 191–199. doi:10.1080/17482798.2015.1127842

Blakeslee, S. (2004). The CRAAP test. *LOEX Quarterly, 31*(3), 4.

Bosch, X., Pericas, J. M., Hernandez, C., & Torrents, A. (2012). A comparison of authorship policies at top-ranked peer-reviewed biomedical journals. *Archives of Internal Medicine, 172*(1), 70–72. doi:10.1001/archinternmed.2011.600 PMID:22232152

Breivik, P. S., & Jones, D. L. (1993). Information Literacy: Liberal education for the Information Age. *Liberal Education, 79*(1), 24–29.

Carlson, J., & Kneale, R. (2011). Embedded librarianship in the research context: Navigating new waters. *College & Research Libraries News, 72*(3), 167–170.

Cornell University. (2015). *Evaluating web pages: Questions to consider.* Retrieved December 1, 2015, from http://guides.library.cornell.edu/evaluating_Web_pages

Cosijn, E., & Ingwersen, P. (2000). Dimensions of relevance. *Information Processing & Management, 36*(4), 533–550. doi:10.1016/S0306-4573(99)00072-2

Dalhousie University. (2015). *6 criteria for websites.* Retrieved December 1, 2015, from https://libraries.dal.ca/using_the_library/evaluating_web_resources/6_criteria_for_websites.html

Demo, W. (1986). The idea of "information literacy" in the age of high-tech. Tompkins Cortland Community College. Retrieved from http://files.eric.ed.gov/fulltext/ED282537.pdf

Dennett, L., Chatterley, T., Greyson, D., & Surette, S. (2014). Research Embedded Health Librarianship: The Canadian Landscape. *Journal of the Canadian Health Libraries Association/Journal de l'Association des bibliothèques de la santé du Canada, 34*(2), 61-68.

Desai, T., Shariff, A., Dhingra, V., Minhas, D., Eure, M., & Kats, M. (2013). Is content really king? An objective analysis of the public's response to medical videos on Youtube. *PLoS ONE, 8*(12), e82469. doi:10.1371/journal.pone.0082469 PMID:24367517

Doyle, C. S. (1994). *Information literacy in an information society: A concept for the information age.* Syracuse, NY: ERIC Clearinghouse on Information & Technology.

Ericsson, K. A., Krampe, R. T., & Tesch-Römer, C. (1993). The role of deliberate practice in the acquisition of expert performance. *Psychological Review, 100*(3), 363–406. doi:10.1037/0033-295X.100.3.363

Eysenbach, G., & Köhler, C. (2002). How do consumers search for and appraise health information on the world wide web? Qualitative study using focus groups, usability tests, and in-depth interviews. *BMJ (Clinical Research Ed.), 324*(7337), 573–577. doi:10.1136/bmj.324.7337.573 PMID:11884321

Farkas, M. (2012). Participatory technologies, pedagogy 2.0 and information literacy. *Library Hi Tech, 30*(1), 82–94. doi:10.1108/07378831211213229

Flanagin, A. J., & Metzger, M. J. (2000). Perceptions of internet information credibility. *Journalism & Mass Communication Quarterly, 77*(3), 515–540. doi:10.1177/107769900007700304

Fogg, B., Marshall, J., Laraki, O., Osipovich, A., Varma, C., Fang, N., & Swani, P. et al. (2001). What makes web sites credible?: A report on a large quantitative study. In *Proceedings of the SIGCHI Conference on Human Factors in Computing Systems*. doi:10.1145/365024.365037

Frobish, T. S. (2013). On Pixels, Perceptions, and Personae: Toward a Model of Online Ethos. In M. Folk & S. Apostel (Eds.), *Online Credibility and Digital Ethos: Evaluating Computer-Mediated Communication* (pp. 1–23). Hershey, PA: Information Science Reference; doi:10.4018/978-1-4666-2663-8.ch001

Gamie, S. (2013). The cyber-propelled Egyptian revolution and the de/construction of ethos. In M. Folk & S. Apostel (Eds.), *Online Credibility and Digital Ethos: Evaluating Computer-Mediated Communication* (pp. 316–330). Hershey, PA: IGI Global. doi:10.4018/978-1-4666-2663-8.ch018

Gasparyan, A. Y., Yessirkepov, M., Diyanova, S. N., & Kitas, G. D. (2015). Publishing ethics and predatory practices: A dilemma for all stakeholders of science communication. *Journal of Korean Medical Science, 30*(8), 1010–1016. doi:10.3346/jkms.2015.30.8.1010 PMID:26240476

Gross, M., & Latham, D. (2007). Attaining information literacy: An investigation of the relationship between skill level, self-estimates of skill, and library anxiety. *Library & Information Science Research, 29*(3), 332–353. doi:10.1016/j.lisr.2007.04.012

Gross, M., Latham, D., & Armstrong, B. (2012). Improving below-proficient information literacy skills: Designing an evidence-based educational intervention. *College Teaching, 60*(3), 104–111. doi:10.1080/87567555.2011.645257

Gunther, A. C. (1992). Biased press or biased public? Attitudes toward media coverage of social groups. *Public Opinion Quarterly, 56*(2), 147–167. doi:10.1086/269308

Haase, N., Betsch, C., & Renkewitz, F. (2015). Source credibility and the biasing effect of narrative information on the perception of vaccination risks. *Journal of Health Communication*, *20*(8), 920–929. doi:10.1080/10810730.2015.1018605 PMID:26065492

Hart, W., Albarracín, D., Eagly, A. H., Brechan, I., Lindberg, M. J., & Merrill, L. (2009). Feeling validated versus being correct: A meta-analysis of selective exposure to information. *Psychological Bulletin*, *135*(4), 555–588. doi:10.1037/a0015701 PMID:19586162

Higgins, J., & Green, S. (Eds.). (2011). *Cochrane handbook for systematic reviews of interventions version* (5.1.0 ed.). The Cochrane Collaboration.

Horton, F. W. (1983). Information literacy vs. computer literacy. *Bulletin of the American Society for Information Science*, *9*, 14–18.

Hovland, C. I., Janis, I. L., & Kelley, H. H. (1963). Communication and persuasion. In Psychological studies of opinion change. New Haven, CT: Academic Press.

Howard, P. N., Duffy, A., Freelon, D., Hussain, M. M., Mari, W., & Mazaid, M. (2011). *Opening closed regimes: What was the role of social media during the Arab spring?* Available at SSRN 2595096

Internet Corporation for Assigned Names and Numbers (ICANN). (2015). *IANA - root zone database*. Retrieved December 1, 2015, from http://www.iana.org/domains/root/db

Jackson, R. (2008). Information literacy and its relationship to cognitive development and reflective judgment. *New Directions for Teaching and Learning*, *114*(114), 47–61. doi:10.1002/tl.316

Johnson, T. J., & Kaye, B. K. (1998). Cruising is believing?: Comparing internet and traditional sources on media credibility measures. *Journalism & Mass Communication Quarterly*, *75*(2), 325–340. doi:10.1177/107769909807500208

Kapoun, J. (1998). Teaching undergrads WEB evaluation: A guide for library instruction. *College & Research Libraries News*, *59*(7), 522–523.

Knight, M. L., Knight, R. A., Goben, A., & Dobbs, A. W. (2013). Theory and Application: Using social networking to build online credibility. In M. Folk & S. Apostel (Eds.), *Online Credibility and Digital Ethos: Evaluating Computer-Mediated Communication* (pp. 285–301). Hershey, PA: IGI Global. doi:10.4018/978-1-4666-2663-8.ch016

Kruger, J., & Dunning, D. (1999). Unskilled and unaware of it: How difficulties in recognizing one's own incompetence lead to inflated self-assessments. *Journal of Personality and Social Psychology*, *77*(6), 1121–1134. doi:10.1037/0022-3514.77.6.1121 PMID:10626367

Kuhlthau, C. (1987). Information skills: Tools for learning. *School Library Media Quarterly*, *16*, 22–28.

Kuhlthau, C. (2004). Seeking meaning: A process approach to library and information services (2nd ed.). Westport, CT: Libraries Unlimited.

Kuhlthau, C. C. (1999). Literacy and learning for the information age. In B. K. Stripling (Ed.), *Learning and libraries in an information age: Principles and practice*. Englewood, CO: Libraries Unlimited.

Lewis, L., & Chandley, N. (Eds.). (2012). *Philosophy for children through the secondary curriculum.* New York, NY: Continuum.

Lipman, M., Sharp, A. M., & Oscanyon, F. S. (1985). *Philosophy in the classroom.* Philadelphia, PA: Temple University Press.

Lucassen, T., & Maarten-Schraagen, J. (2012). Propensity to trust and the influence of source and medium cues in credibility evaluation. *Journal of Information Science, 38*(6), 566–577. doi:10.1177/0165551512459921

Mahood, Q., Van Eerd, D., & Irvin, E. (2014). Searching for grey literature for systematic reviews: Challenges and benefits. *Research Synthesis Methods, 5*(3), 221–234. doi:10.1002/jrsm.1106 PMID:26052848

Makino, T., Jung, C., & Phan, D. (2015, February 26). *Finding more mobile-friendly search results.* Retrieved May 10, 2016, from https://webmasters.googleblog.com/2015/02/finding-more-mobile-friendly-search.html

Manchikanti, L., Kaye, A. D., Boswell, M. V., & Hirsch, J. A. (2015). Medical journal peer review: Process and bias. *Pain Physician, 18*(1), E1–e14. PMID:25675064

Mbuagbaw, L., Thabane, M., Vanniyasingam, T., Debono, V. B., Kosa, S., Zhang, S., & Thabane, L. et al. (2014). Improvement in the quality of abstracts in major clinical journals since consort extension for abstracts: A systematic review. *Contemporary Clinical Trials, 38*(2), 245–250. doi:10.1016/j.cct.2014.05.012 PMID:24861557

McKeon, R. (1941). The basic works of Aristotle. *The Journal of Philosophy, 38*(20), 553. doi:10.2307/2017332

Meola, M. (2004). Chucking the checklist: A contextual approach to teaching undergraduates web-site evaluation. portal. *Libraries and the Academy, 4*(3), 331–344. doi:10.1353/pla.2004.0055

Metzger, M. J. (2007). Making sense of credibility on the web: Models for evaluating online information and recommendations for future research. *Journal of the American Society for Information Science and Technology, 58*(13), 2078–2091. doi:10.1002/asi.20672

Metzger, M. J., Flanagin, A., & Medders, R. B. (2010). Social and heuristic approaches to credibility evaluation online. *Journal of Communication, 60*(3), 413–439. doi:10.1111/j.1460-2466.2010.01488.x

Pfeifer, M. P., & Snodgrass, G. L. (1990). The continued use of retracted, invalid scientific literature. *Journal of the American Medical Association, 263*(10), 1420–1423. doi:10.1001/jama.1990.03440100140020 PMID:2406475

Queens University. (2011). *Evaluating web sources.* Retrieved December 1, 2015, from http://library.queensu.ca/inforef/tutorials/qcat/evalint.htm

Rapp, C. (2010). *Aristotle's rhetoric.* Stanford Encyclopedia of Philosophy. Retrieved December 1, 2015, from http://plato.stanford.edu/archives/spr2010/entries/aristotle-rhetoric/

Ren, W. H. (2000). Library instruction and college student self-efficacy in electronic information searching. *Journal of Academic Librarianship, 26*(5), 323–328. doi:10.1016/S0099-1333(00)00138-5

Saint, S., Christakis, D. A., Saha, S., Elmore, J. G., Welsh, D. E., Baker, P., & Koepsell, T. D. (2000). Journal reading habits of internists. *Journal of General Internal Medicine*, *15*(12), 881–884. doi:10.1046/j.1525-1497.2000.00202.x PMID:11119185

Saracevic, T. (1975). Relevance: A review of and a framework for the thinking on the notion in information science. *Journal of the American Society for Information Science*, *26*(6), 321–343. doi:10.1002/asi.4630260604

Saracevic, T. (1996). Relevance reconsidered. In *Proceedings of the Second Conference on Conceptions of Library and Information Science.*

Schofferman, J., Wetzel, F. T., & Bono, C. (2015). Ghost and guest authors: You can't always trust who you read. *Pain Medicine*, *16*(3), 416–420. doi:10.1111/pme.12579 PMID:25338945

Scholz-Crane, A. (1998). Evaluating the future: A preliminary study of the process of how undergraduate students evaluate web sources.RSR: Reference Services Review, 26, 53-60.

Selegean, J. C., Thomas, M. L., & Richman, M. L. (1983). Long-range effectiveness of library use instruction. *College & Research Libraries*, *44*(6), 476–480. doi:10.5860/crl_44_06_476

Shumaker, D. (2012). *The embedded librarian: Innovative strategies for taking knowledge where it's needed.* Medford, NJ: Information Today, Inc.

Smith, E., & Williams-Jones, B. (2012). Authorship and responsibility in health sciences research: A review of procedures for fairly allocating authorship in multi-author studies. *Science and Engineering Ethics*, *18*(2), 199–212. doi:10.1007/s11948-011-9263-5 PMID:21312000

Špiranec, S., & Zorica, M. B. (2010). Information Literacy 2.0: Hype or discourse refinement? *The Journal of Documentation*, *66*(1), 140–153. doi:10.1108/00220411011016407

Street, J. M., Rogers, W. A., Israel, M., & Braunack-Mayer, A. J. (2010). Credit where credit is due? Regulation, research integrity and the attribution of authorship in the health sciences. *Social Science & Medicine*, *70*(9), 1458–1465. doi:10.1016/j.socscimed.2010.01.013 PMID:20172638

Strudler, A. (2009). Deception and trust. In C. Martin (Ed.), *The philosophy of deception* (pp. 139–152). Oxford, UK: Oxford University Press. doi:10.1093/acprof:oso/9780195327939.003.0009

Tai, Z., & Zhang, Y. (2013). Online identity formation and digital ethos building in the Chinese blogosphere. In M. Folk & S. Apostel (Eds.), *Online Credibility and Digital Ethos: Evaluating Computer-Mediated Communication* (pp. 269–284). Hershey, PA: IGI Global. doi:10.4018/978-1-4666-2663-8.ch015

Taylor, A., & Dalal, H. A. (2014). Information literacy standards and the world wide web: Results from a student survey on evaluation of internet information sources. *Information Research: An International Electronic Journal*, *19*(4), 1–33.

Taylor, J. (2015). An examination of how student journalists seek information and evaluate online sources during the newsgathering process. *New Media & Society*, *17*(8), 1277–1298. doi:10.1177/1461444814523079

Test, D. W., Kemp-Inman, A., Diegelmann, K., Hitt, S. B., & Bethune, L. (2015). Are online sources for identifying evidence-based practices trustworthy? An evaluation. *Exceptional Children*, *82*(1), 58–80. doi:10.1177/0014402915585477

The University of British Columbia. (2015). *Evaluating information sources*. Retrieved December 1, 2015, from http://help.library.ubc.ca/evaluating-and-citing-sources/evaluating-information-sources/

Thomas, N. P. (2004). *Information Literacy and information skills instruction: Applying research to practice in the school library media center*. Westport, CT: Libraries Unlimited.

Thomson, R., Ito, N., Suda, H., Lin, F., Liu, Y., Hayasaka, R., & Wang, Z. et al. (2012). Trusting tweets: The fukushima disaster and information source credibility on twitter. In *Proceedings of the 9th International ISCRAM Conference*.

University of Pittsburgh. (2015). *Evaluating web resources*. Retrieved December 1, 2015, from http://www.library.pitt.edu/evaluating-web-resources

Vassilakaki, E., & Moniarou-Papaconstantinou, V. (2015). A systematic literature review informing library and information professionals' emerging roles. *New Library World*, *116*(1/2), 37–66. doi:10.1108/NLW-05-2014-0060

Wager, E., & Williams, P. (2011). Why and how do journals retract articles? An analysis of Medline retractions 1988–2008. *Journal of Medical Ethics*, *37*(9), 567–570. doi:10.1136/jme.2010.040964 PMID:21486985

Wang, R. (2006). The lasting impact of a library credit course. *Libraries and the Academy*, *6*(1), 79–92. doi:10.1353/pla.2006.0013

Wartenberg, T. E. (2014). *Big ideas for little kids: Teaching philosophy through children's literature* (2nd ed.). New York, NY: Rowman & Littlefield.

Wathen, C. N., & Burkell, J. (2002). Believe it or not: Factors influencing credibility on the web. *Journal of the American Society for Information Science and Technology*, *53*(2), 134–144. doi:10.1002/asi.10016

Wichowski, D. E., & Kohl, L. E. (2013). Establishing credibility in the information jungle: Blogs, microblogs, and the CRAAP test. In M. Folk & S. Apostel (Eds.), *Online Credibility and Digital Ethos: Evaluating Computer-Mediated Communication* (pp. 229–251). Hershey, PA: IGI Global.

Zurkowski, P. G. (1974). The information service environment relationships and priorities. Washington, DC: National Commission on Libraries and Information Science. Retrieved from http://files.eric.ed.gov/fulltext/ED100391.pdf

KEY TERMS AND DEFINITIONS

Epistemology: A branch of philosophy that studies the nature, scope, origins, and limits of human knowledge.

Grey Literature: Various research reports, white papers, issue briefs, conference proceedings, and other non-peer-reviewed documents, typically not published through traditional avenues.

ICMJE: The International Committee of Medical Journal Editors is a working group of selected biomedical journal editors. This group created the Recommendations for the Conduct, Reporting, Editing and Publication of Scholarly Work in Medical Journals.

Information Literacy: A set of competencies enabling the effective location, evaluation, and utility of information.

Information Professional: An individual, such as a librarian, with a specialized skill set and expertise in collecting, organizing, describing, storing, preserving, and disseminating information packets in both physical and digital formats.

Peer Review: The process in which a research article is evaluated by other professionals in the same field.

Systematic Review: A methodology in which all clinical evidence (relevant to the review question) is appraised and synthesized.

Chapter 3
Knockin' on Digital Doors:
Dealing with Online [Dis]Credit in an Era of Digital Scientific Inquiry

Rosalina Pisco Costa
University of Évora, Portugal

ABSTRACT

This chapter aims at presenting and discussing credible online recruitment eliciting techniques targeting scientific purposes adjusted to the digital age. Based on several illustrations conducted by the author within the framework of both quantitative and qualitative inquiries, this chapter critically explores the digital ethos in three main challenges faced when dealing with online recruitment for scientific purposes: entering the normality of the everyday life, entering the idiosyncrasy of multicultural lives, and entering the chaos of busy lives. By the end, a toolbox for establishing and evaluating (dis)credibility within online recruitment strategies is presented. Moreover, it is argued that success of data collection at the present time in online environments seems to rely as ever on internal factors of the communication process vis-à-vis e-mail content, design and related strategies.

INTRODUCTION

The near-ubiquity of a permanent online existence, made possible through the generalized use of smartphones, tablets, and laptops, is evolving together with the increasing availability of free Wi-Fi access, not only in traditional areas such as military centers, computing environments, universities, commercial organizations, business centers, and highly trafficked cosmopolitan spots, is now found in the most diverse urban spaces, shopping malls, public transportation, and many private homes. This realization led the scientific community, particularly in the field of the social sciences, to look at the World Wide Web as a powerful alternative (or as a supplement) to personal recruitment for research purposes, metaphorically referred to as "knocking on doors."

As the younger generation is "born digital" and the use of the Internet in their daily lives is often perceived as a trivial and easy task, social researchers have, naturally, used the Internet to carry out their research projects (Gilbert, 2001; Punch, 2014). Despite the fact that even in the "net generation,"

DOI: 10.4018/978-1-5225-1072-7.ch003

the modes of accessing, using, and making sense of the Internet are not homogenous so much as they are socially shaped (Hargittai, 2010), the World Wide Web greatly expands the possibility of easily and rapidly accessing big data, reaching geographically dispersed groups of respondents, and locating samples to address rare topics (Couper, 2005; Fielding, Lee & Blank, 2008). Although recruiting for scientific purposes apparently has never been easier, recruitment now faces new challenges due to the absence of face-to-face interaction. Online, scientists have to compete with numerous advertisers, marketers, and swindlers of all kinds who overload individual mailboxes with hundreds of messages seducing the reader to open an email, follow a link, and, ultimately, do what they originally expected them to do, which might cause users harm or at least make them wary of any unknown or unsolicited digital communications in the future.

To be sure, most social scientists do not have extensive experience in digital connection and recruitment. Traditionally, recruitment for scientific purposes was based essentially in person-to-person communication, which, in turn, was anchored on external factors such as the credibility of the organizing or funding institution (usually a university or research center) or the researcher or team reputation; today, successful data collection in online environments still relies on person-to-person communication, but the process now entails different means of connection such as e-mail and attention to different strategies such as visual design.

Within this backdrop, this chapter aims to present and discuss credible social scientific online recruitment techniques adjusted to the digital age. In the background, the chapter starts by discussing how the Internet is affecting inquiry in social sciences. Afterwards, based on research conducted by the author within the framework of both quantitative and qualitative inquiries recently carried out at the University of Évora, Portugal, the chapter critically explores the many challenges faced when recruiting research participants online in an era of digital scientific inquiry. Metaphorically, online recruitment can be seen as "knocking on digital doors"[1], an action that will be successful if individuals – potential participants – assign credibility to the attempt. In three different sections, the article explores three areas of the online environment where this assessment is particularly demanding: within the normality of the everyday life, when dealing with the idiosyncrasy of multicultural lives, and, finally, when finding time in the chaos of busy lives. At the end of presenting arguments for best practices, a toolbox for establishing and evaluating credibility within online recruitment strategies is presented. The chapter ends with the presentation of future research directions and concludes by arguing that successful data collection in present online environments relies on internal factors of the communication process, namely e-mail content, design, and related strategies.

BACKGROUND: HOW DOES THE INTERNET AFFECT SOCIAL SCIENCE INQUIRY?

Traditionally, recruitment for scientific research was based essentially in person-to-person communication, which, in turn, was anchored on external factors such as the credibility of the organizing or funding institution, usually a university or research center, or the researcher or team reputation (Patton, 2002; Schostak, 2006).

In recent times, the Internet serves both as a location for social research and as a tool for conducting it (Fielding, Lee & Blank, 2008). Regarding this last aspect, the computer-based global information and communication system is changing the way social research is conducted because it facilitates data collection "by making contact and interaction with informants quicker, cheaper and easier." (Punch, 2014, p. 280). Moreover, many individuals, particularly young researchers or potential participants, are often perceived as digital natives because they were born and raised in the digital era and, to them, using the Internet as a research tool seems a "natural" way of collecting data. As Punch (2014) also put it, "The capacity to observe so many, doing so much and in so many different ways makes the Internet an extremely attractive yet challenging research tool for social researchers" (p. 281).

Nonetheless, using the World Wide Web to undertake research is not free from pitfalls, as there is a false expectation that the Internet provides a homogeneous landscape. One of the most recent and interesting theoretical debates across the social sciences is related to digital divides. Beyond official efforts and discourses to portray equal, massive access to the Internet and digital inclusion, empirical evidence shows that individuals' appropriation of the Internet is far from homogeneous or uniform. Among individuals, particularly children and teenagers, social distinctions (still) strongly shape their relation to, and involvement with, the digital. Moreover, increased access to the Internet remains a privilege of wealthier families and children whose parents have the highest educational and digital literacy levels (Buckingham, 2008; Livingstone and Helsper, 2007; Lee, 2008). Specifically, al access is not equal because there is a tremendous variance among Internet users based on many factors including the primary uses of it (e.g., working, chatting, gaming, tagging, commenting); the profile of the users (e.g., gender, class, race, and education); the proficiency of the computing users (e.g., more or less keyboard skill); the machines used (e.g., more or less technologically advanced equipment); the operating systems (e.g., Microsoft Windows, Apple's Mac OS, or the open source operating system Linux); the type of relationship established between the transmitter and receiver (e.g., many-to-many or one-to-many) and the type of interaction (e.g., one-way versus two-way); the timing of people's communications and interactions (e.g., synchronous versus asynchronous); modes of access (e.g., free versus restricted), and many other dimensions establish important differences pervasive to the uses and meanings associated with the Internet (Fielding, Lee & Blank, 2008; Denscombe, 1998; Denzin & Lincoln, 2000; Gaiser & Schreiner, 2009).

Despite these challenges, digital inquiry gradually attracts more interest and growth because the Internet affords so many opportunities for collecting data without the need for traveling or being physically present. Surveys conducted online constitute a striking example. It is now easier than ever before to conduct a survey that could attract a large and meaningful audience, but there are disadvantages of using digital data collection such as the low response rates of the target audience or the distrust regarding anonymity, which can diminish the motivation to participate (Bryman, 2008; Hewson, 2003). Moreover, some platforms, particularly the free ones, allow one single participant to answer multiple times. However, the use of email offers a radically cheaper and faster delivery and return of the self-administrated questionnaire than the conventional postal service. This way, it is possible to reach a wide audience quickly and cheaply, receive responses around the clock, and automatically load responses into an analytical package with no need to enter data manually. In addition to saving time and money, it is possible to access geographically and physically diverse groups, including those with physical or psychological impairments, in completely new and revolutionary ways (Fielding, Lee & Blank, 2008; Gaiser & Schreiner, 2009).

At first sight, the Internet is replacing "traditional" techniques of data collection, namely surveys, interviews, ethnography and documentary analysis. Regarding the interview technique, Valerie Janesick advocated in 1998 that "Interviewing has taken on a new tone recently with Internet inquiry and interviewing individuals virtually, that is, on the Internet and on websites. As a result, many are wondering what will happen to the tried-and-true, face-to-face interview." (p. 99). The doubts of Janesick, dating back to 1998, no longer make sense nowadays as the "traditional" techniques of data collection are not at risk of disappearing. Surveys, interviews and focus groups, ethnography (netnography), documentary analysis, and even experiments can all be carried out (and are, in fact, being carried out) online in compliance with the scientific protocols and demands (Flick, 2015; Hooley, Wellens, & Marriott, 2012; Hughes, 2012; Salmons, 2010).

Specifically, surveys constitute a very well-known technique for empirical research in the social sciences, and they have revealed the plasticity necessary to take advantage of the advances of technology: First, they adapted to the telephone, then they adapted to the Internet. In online environments, one can distinguish between server-side surveys and client-side surveys. The first is far more common nowadays—instead of sending an email to the machine of potential respondents over the Internet, either embedded in the body of an email message or attached to the email as a downloadable document, the Internet survey is made executable on a web-server (Couper, 2005; Gaiser & Schreiner, 2009). Accordingly, at the basis of such recruitment strategy is an email that is used to send a URL link to the website where the survey is hosted and to request that the recipient visit the website and complete the questionnaire. Advances in software, including free and open source options over the past decade, turned the design and administration of the web-based (server-side) survey into a very easy, user-friendly task that provides an efficient means of collecting quantitative data using a standardized tool designed to attract a high respondent rate[2].

Given all these changes, this chapter argues that despite the relocation to the virtual world and the digital form of many inquiry procedures, inquiry into the digital age still contains the basics of methodological research procedures. Additionally, many of the issues of conventional social research methods continue to apply in the virtual venue with each of these requiring some adaptations to ensure that data collection and analysis are both as effective and credible as possible.

KNOCKIN' ON DIGITAL DOORS: CHALLENGES IN DEALING WITH ONLINE RECRUITMENT

It is important to capitalize on the potential of the Internet for collecting data and to help in the recruitment of participants, yet researchers need to be aware of some of the pitfalls they might face when entering online environment. The Internet may appear to promise high respondent rates; however, online recruiting is not always as easy as it first may seem (Fielding, Lee & Blank, 2008; Gaiser & Schreiner, 2009).

On the one hand, there are lots of publicity campaigns using emails containing links to a survey or a link to a particular website. Internet users are a constant target for these campaigns, which subsequently raise many suspicions on the users' part about even the most serious and strictly scientific contact. On the other hand, the Internet itself has also developed into a mainstream means of buying and selling a wide range of products, services, and ideologies. In short, the Internet has developed from a very specialized medium for a particular set of specialists into a widespread service that is used across society, not only regarding the different dimensions of social life that it addresses (communication, consumption, leisure, religion, politics, etc.) but also the age range—everyone from children to senior citizens. This means that social scientists operating online compete with several other actors, each one trying to catch the attention, time, and action of the user—or consumer—participant.

In cyberspace, tips and rules abound as to how to behave, write, and comment online. Such advice, usually referred to as "netiquette," is significant and often recommended to researchers (Eynon et al., 2008; Kimmel, 1988). In this chapter, it is argued that following some "netiquette" rules is important, though not sufficient enough for establishing and evaluating the online credibility of recruitment emails within scientific research. As many actors compete for a potential respondent's scarce attention resources—their interests, motivations, or simply just lack of time may take precedence, how can researchers attract respondents in such a fuzzy environment?

In answering this question, it is important to properly craft the instruments, with particular attention being paid to designing the initial approach for potential respondents. This task is particularly demanding because the Internet, especially email strategies, remove a personal presence from the contact by reducing the amount of communication modes. However, despite the absence of an actual person with a specific appearance, facial expression, tone of voice, eye contact, and body language to supplement and create meanings, email does not have to be a sterile exchange. Instead, this means that the absence of co-presence requires more effort by the researcher in crafting the email. As Punch (2014) advised: "When the social pressure of personal contact is missing, participants tend to feel less compelled to agree and more at ease should they decide to pull out of the study" (p. 294). To compensate, researchers have to create a richer environment by accentuating the tools they have at their disposal, primarily text and image in the case of email-based approaches.

Moreover, as online research is often based on an asynchronous approach, the respondent runs the risk of data delay and losing "the impulse response" (Gaiser & Schreiner, 2009). In fact, the asynchronous nature of email postings makes it easier for a participant "simply not to respond"; consequently, "Social researchers need to pay particular attention to the development of trusting research relationships online" (Gilbert, 2001, p. 305). Establishing and evaluating digital ethos and online credibility is, thus, a key topic when researching in (with) the Internet. On the one hand, researchers must develop ways of establishing credibility online; on the other, Internet users should be aware of ways of evaluating online credibility.

The literature review on this topic strengthens the idea that the future seems to be the time-space where online trust relations matters more than ever. As (apparently) it has never been easier to access specific information on the web, the researcher must develop new skills in building online trust relations (see Folk & Apostel, 2013). Particularly when seeking recruiting participants to take part in data collection procedures, credibility cannot be based exclusively in a rhetoric of credibility. Despite being necessary, such a rhetoric is made visible by a set of best practices that the scientist must adopt. Nonetheless, such practices are not defined, adapted, and pursued alone, rather, they rely on a certain communal ethos. It is in this context that it makes sense to bring to light the concept of ethos as "a dwelling place" (Hyde, 2004). Based on concluded studies, the next section showcases adjusted recommendations and advice regarding the formation and understanding of digital ethos.

ENHANCING CREDIBILITY WITHIN ONLINE RECRUITMENT STRATEGIES

In order to discuss solutions and recommendations in dealing with the issues, controversies, and problems presented earlier, this section explores the many challenges faced when dealing with online recruitment for research purposes in social sciences. Based upon previous research carried out by the author, the next pages present and detail strategies used to enhance credibility within the online recruitment procedures in the framework of both quantitative and qualitative inquiries as main design strategies (Miles & Huberman, 1994; Neuman, 2011). Specifically, this section explores three broad areas of the online environment where evaluating credibility is particularly demanding: within the normality of the everyday life, when dealing with the idiosyncrasy of targeted multicultural lives and audiences, and, finally, in finding a time when the individuals are willing to collaborate in the chaos of busy lives. Moreover, it is argued that researchers have the responsibility to enhance the credibility associated with online recruitment strategies because they have ample time to reflect and construct, write, and, if necessary, reconsider and rewrite the message choosing the best words. Writing for potential respondents should, therefore, be as demanding as writing for social scientists (Becker, 1986).

Entering the Normality of the Everyday Life

For the purposes of exploring the challenge of entering into the normality of an everyday life for research purposes, this section draws on previous research developed in 2015 that provided an exploratory analysis of students' representations of the effects of distance from the family home on academic performance (DISTANCE)[3]. This study was driven by the key idea that the transition from secondary to higher education may be a challenging time for students. Students must adjust to a new social environment, different pedagogical and learning approaches, increased autonomy, and more responsibility, and there is no uniform way of adjusting. In particular, there is some evidence that the distance between the university and the family residence has, on average, a negative effect on the academic performance, particularly noted on male students. However, the empirical evidence on the causes for this effect is scant and mostly indirect.

This example is interesting and worthwhile to explore because it benefits from the experience of conducting a study using server-side surveys to investigate the determinants of the impact of the distance on academic performance. Methodologically, data were collected through a web survey applied across a sample of undergraduate students at the University of Évora between March 5th- 20[th,] 2015[4]. By the end, 1075 questionnaires were validated for in-depth statistical analysis. This study was aimed at enhancing the sustained discussion over the topic, which is of utmost importance for students and their families, universities' student support services, and, ultimately, for authorities analyzing the territorial dispersion of higher education institutions in Portugal; the success of the study hinged on the challenge of catching the attention of the students and having them fill out the survey. Specifically, how would undergraduate students find the topic worthwhile among so many and different issues calling for their time and attention in the normality of their daily lives?

In the DISTANCE project, the strategy used to recruit students was entirely conducted online. Accordingly, an e-mail was sent to the students' mailing list, introducing the purpose of the study and inviting completion of a questionnaire. The e-mail was sent from one of the researchers' official e-mail, observing the following details:

- **E-Mail Sender:** An official e-mail account was used, easily recognized as it uses the official domain ending in @uevora.pt. This solution seemed proper because the survey clearly had institutional purposes related to an academic topic studied within the University of Évora.
- **E-Mail Recipient:** The institutional mailing list of the students was visibly used (mailto: <alunos[students]@uevora.pt>). Targeting only students with a specific mailing list was found useful because it deals with a topic close to their interests and fits the appropriate uses of such a mailing list. This is a well-known mailing list at the university. Similarly, there are other group mailing lists targeting specific categories within the university (e.g., teachers and collaborators), which are then used whenever the sender wishes to target collective messages.
- **Subject:** A first email was sent on March 3rd, 2015, with the subject line as follows:
Request to participate in a study | Undergraduate Students at UÉvora

Using this simultaneously short and incisive subject was a way of clearly presenting the purpose of the message, as long subject lines usually become incomplete in the preview mode of many devices such as laptops, smart phones, and tablets. Two further emails with polite reminders were sent later (on March 11ᵗʰ and 17ᵗʰ), calling for additional participation within the space of two weeks. The second and the third email slightly changed the subject line:

REMINDER: Request to participate in a study | Undergraduate Students at UÉvora
LAST CALL: Request to participate in a study | Undergraduate Students at UÉvora

Additionally, the first paragraph of the text body was also changed in both cases:

We contact you again to kindly request your participation in a short online questionnaire aiming to...

We contact you a third and final time to kindly request your participation in a short online questionnaire aiming to...

Changes in the subject line were introduced as a way of avoiding grouping messages in some specific email management platforms (e.g., Gmail). Using capital letters in introductory words or expressions in the subject line were also introduced, namely "REMINDER" and "LAST CALL." Additionally, right before the beginning of the body text, a short message between square brackets was included as a way of dispensing the reading from those who had already participated in the survey. This was particularly important because the research team did not intend to upset people by appearing to be sent just like irrelevant spam:

[This message is a last call for participation in the study "Influence of distance between the University and the Residence on Academic Performance." If you have already responded to the questionnaire, please accept our thanks and disregard this request. Thank you!]

- **Body Text:** A short body text message was sent to students asking for their participation in the survey. The text used a professional tone to formally invite students to participate in the study. The first email was sent on March, 3ʳᵈ at 11:20 pm. Students were introduced formally with *"dear students"* and a *"good night"* compliment. Afterwards, the purpose of the email was detailed as students were invited to participate in answering a small survey with the aim of collecting data from undergraduate students in the University of Évora in order to study the influence of distance between the University and the actual household residence on academic performance. A hyperlink to the survey was included afterwards, as well as information indicating that the survey will be quick and anonymous and the collected data will be used only for research purposes. Finally, the importance of participation was stressed by using a motivating phrase, and students were cordially invited to participate and share the link among their contacts network. A final thanks was then included:

Your participation is very important! Please participate and share the link on your contacts network, thus helping us to better understand a topic that interests both teachers and students.

Thank you, in advance, for your kind cooperation!

- **Signature:** Besides the thanks message, the email was signed with the explicit reference to the name of the research team members as follows:

With our best regards and thanks,
The Research Team
[name of the researchers involved]

Additionally, a small colored image containing a caption of the same image used in the header of the questionnaire was included in the signature. The image of a stylized landscape made of several buildings in an urban residential area was used to create a visually attractive element for the survey. Thus, when the students follow the hyperlink they will find the exact same image in the survey, intended to give them a sense of an aesthetic and professional atmosphere that they are welcome to engage with.

Moreover, the survey was designed in Google Forms from Google Drive. Since 2011, the official email service for students at the University of Évora is available from Google Apps for Education. The service has the interface, space, and quality of Gmail, but it keeps the institutional email address of the university. As Google platforms are well known and frequently used among services, this also contributed to create a very friendly participation environment for students.

To sum up, as a strategy for entering the normality of everyday life and to get the attention of students to participate in the survey, the research team of the DISTANCE project focused on the means of announcing the questionnaire in order to maximize response rates. Adopting a professional communication style and content improved the credibility of the study, yet these aspects did not take the topic out of the center of *their* daily life: It's something about *their* life, in *their* university, and to participate only requires a *quick answer* in a *well-known* and *friendly response environment*.

Entering the Idiosyncrasy of Multicultural Lives

For the purposes of exploring the challenge of entering into the idiosyncrasy of very different and multicultural lives, this section draws on a previous research developed in 2013 as an initiation project into scientific research, developed within the framework of the "Sociology of the Family" course [SOC2410] at the University of Évora during the academic year 2013-14. The project was titled "Personal Life at a Distance and University International Mobility" (VID@S),[5] and it was motivated by the assumption that Information and Communication Technologies (ICTs) occupy a central place in contemporary societies because their use is now widespread in the daily life of individuals and crosses various areas of social life. In economics, family, education, politics, and even religion or leisure, ICTs are not just a way of bringing individuals who are physically and temporally apart together virtually. ICTs are socially embedded; they have their own dynamics and construct new realities that need to be unveiled beyond the scope of common sense. From a sociological perspective, this project aimed to describe and understand the place of ICTs in the construction of the personal lives of students, teachers, and researchers who experience international university mobility. Specifically, this project attempted to identify and characterize the contexts of using ICTs, its contents and purposes, as well as its importance to, and meaning within, the construction of personal life at a distance. Ultimately, the study aimed to contribute to a deeper knowledge about a specific situation in the teaching-learning and researching process—the experience of university international mobility—which cannot be separated from the personal lives of individuals, with which it is greatly related, both in the academic and biographical sense.

This study aimed to understand the experiences of students, teachers, and researchers whose permanent residence was outside of Portugal, but who were at the time studying, teaching, or researching at the University of Évora. This comprised students of any course level and scientific area in Erasmus mobility, Erasmus Mundus mobility, Brazil and Angola mobility, or another; students with a partial or full course load in any level (bachelor, master's, or Ph.D.) at the University of Évora (e.g., double degree courses, students from Timor, Brazil, etc.); post-doc researchers; and teachers or visiting fellows at the University of Évora. Data were collected through an anonymous web survey using LimeSurvey®, an open-source survey application hosted at the University of Évora servers, between December 15th–31st 2013[6]. A total of 115 questionnaires with answers from a wide array of countries were validated for an in-depth statistical analysis; the represented countries included Brazil, Spain, Italy, East Timor, Angola, Germany, Bangladesh, Belgium, Bosnia and Herzegovina, Bulgaria, Cape Verde, Eritrea, Ethiopia, Finland, Philippines, France, Guinea-Bissau, Holland, England, India, Ireland, Mexico, Mozambique, Nepal, Poland, Czech Republic, Romania and Switzerland. Clearly, this study faced the challenge of catching the attention of many different possible respondents with a variety of background. Specifically, how would such individuals find the study relevant enough to take part; how could the survey connect through the idiosyncrasy of such multicultural lives?

As a solution, the strategy of recruiting respondents for this study was threefold. First, respondents were invited to participate in the study through an email message. Since possible respondents included students, post-doc researchers, and teachers or visiting fellows, this email message was sent to an already existing and official mailing list that would directly reach all these audiences. For this purpose, the research team used the general mailing list of the university intranet, <forue[academy]@uevora.pt>, <alunos[students]@uevora.pt>, and docentes[teachers]@uevora.pt>. The composition of this message followed the major principles presented earlier, namely regarding the email sender, email recipient, subject, body text, and signature.

Because academic mobility is experienced by individuals from many different nationalities and, consequently, different languages, the research team designed a bilingual survey in Portuguese/English and related materials.

A first email message asking for participation in the study was sent on December 16, 2013 with the following subject line:

Pedido de colaboração: Projecto Vid@s | Please circulate widely: Project Vid@s

The body text was also written in both languages. As the text started in Portuguese, the first line of the body text included square brackets referencing that the text in English will appear below, as follows:

[English below]

The body text message started with a reference of the project Vid@s[7] that served as the backdrop for the survey, including the address, via hyperlink, of the webpage where it was possible to find additional information, namely the framework, abstract, methodology, research team, findings, and affiliated institutions. The message then invited possible respondents to either participate or disseminate the web survey to their contacts whose permanent residence was outside of Portugal but who were at the time studying, teaching, or researching at the University of Évora.

Second, respondents were also recruited through written advertisements, which were posted throughout different university buildings, canteens and residence halls. These materials were written in both Portuguese and English and also embraced the same image used in the header of the questionnaire hosted on the LimeSurvey® platform to provide a visually attractive element. The text included the following message:

WEBSURVEY
url: https://inqueritos.uevora.pt/index.php/892925/lang-pt
ADDRESSED TO
Students, teachers and researchers whose permanent residence is outside of Portugal, presently studying, teaching or researching at the University of Évora
Available from: December, 15-31, 2013
Thank you!
Info: http://home.uevora.pt/~rosalina/vidas/

Third, the research team also took advantage of personal recruitment to raise awareness among potential respondents about completing the survey and to enhance the advantages of a purposive and snowball sample. Specifically, both in the doctoral school (The Institute for Advanced Studies and Research—IIFA), as well as in the residence hall António Gedeão, which is the hall that houses most of the students in mobility and is located on the outskirts of Évora's historical center, a face-to-face contact was established between the research team and students, teachers, and researchers. Because the exact URL location of the survey was hard to memorize, a printed flyer adapted from the poster was delivered by hand as a way of helping possible participants remember.

In answering the specific challenge of multiculturalism, recruitment as developed through the VID@S project was successful because it stressed the importance of each individual participant. Although the sample would always be restricted because the university is small, potential respondents were made to feel that each participant was *important* and participation *mattered*. Writing bilingually in both Portuguese and English, using written advertisements, and turning to personal face-to-face recruitment were strategies that clearly contributed to such a purpose.

Entering the Chaos of Busy Lives

For the purposes of exploring the topic related to the challenge of entering the chaos of busy lives, this section builds on previous research developed in 2015, consisting of a case study hoping to identify and understand the causes of dropout at the University of Évora, with a goal of defining and implementing appropriate preventive measures (DROPOUT)[8]. Specifically, this study was designed to identify, characterize, and analyze the causes of dropout among students who entered and left the University of Évora between September 1, 2011 and February 28, 2015; to identify and analyze the causes of dropout at the University of Évora in the last three years through the application, collection, and analysis of a survey among students; to deepen the understanding of the causes of dropout from the students' perspectives by conducting semi-structured interviews with students willing to talk about their experience; and, finally, to propose a set of preventive measures and respective times and modes of intervention that would show future effectiveness in identifying early dropout intentions considered "avoidable" and acting timely and effectively upon them.

In order to answer such topics, the research team analyzed available data from University services and designed an anonymous questionnaire aimed to be self-administered by students, which was hosted on the servers of the University of Évora through the platform LimeSurvey®[9]. In the end, from the total sent, there were 118 immediate returns (due to disabled accounts or mailboxes that exceeded maximum storage capacity) and an overall response rate of 42.2% (908) from the 2,150 that constituted the population.

Seeking to deepen the understanding of the causes of dropout, a semi-structured interview protocol was designed to apply to students whose enrollment at the University of Évora became idle over the preceding three years. Specifically, recruiting students for participation in the interview phase was conducted through a volunteer opportunity sample, which was constituted in three main phases over the months of September and October 2015. Firstly, an e-mail was sent to a number of students that explicitly pointed out in the questionnaire their availability for further participation with the research team in continuing such a study.

Students were primarily contacted through email. This email message followed the major principles presented earlier, namely regarding the email sender, e-mail recipient, subject, body text, and signature. The message was sent on September 28, 2015 through a separate email account with the domain of the University of Évora, created during the phase of the dissemination of the questionnaire, notably with the sender "University of Évora – Vice Rectory [studies]", corresponding to the email <vice-reitoria-estudos[vice-rectory-studies]@uevora.pt>. In this email, students were asked to complete a small online form in order to facilitate the scheduling of interviews[10].

For this specific purpose, a form was designed using Google Forms. After a small image header already used in the questionnaire in LimeSurvey®, introductory text was included to remind previous participants of the purposes of the contact:

This form is intended to facilitate the scheduling of interviews to be undertaken in the framework of the study "Causes of dropout at the University of Évora".

Please complete the form and wait for our email confirmation.

If you have any questions, please contact the research team via e-mail [vice-reitoria-estudos@uevora.pt].

Thank you in advance for your cooperation!

The following questions were available for filling (*required):

Name*: _____
E-mail*: _____
Preference regarding the form of the interview (Please tell us if you prefer to schedule a personal or a
    distance interview)*
    ◦   Face-to-face interview (to be held in Évora)
    ◦   Distance interview (via Skype platforms, Google Hangout, etc.)
Details for completing the interview

Face-to-face interview: Please suggest a place of your convenience to complete the interview (e.g., a public place, university, private address, etc.): _____

Distance interview: Please suggest a platform of your convenience to use (e.g. Skype, Google's Hangout, Other): _____

Please indicate up to three dates of your availability so that we can schedule the interview:

Date (1st Option)*: [Dropdown question within a selected time frame]

Suggested Time*: [Hrs. | Min | AM/PM]

Date (2nd Option): [Dropdown question within a selected time frame]

Suggested Time: [Hrs. | Min | AM/PM]

Date (3rd option): [Dropdown question within a selected time frame]

Suggested Time: [Hrs. | Min | AM/PM]

Phone (This contact will only be used in case of trouble in communication via email): _____

A member of the research team was responsible for constantly checking the Google spreadsheet in order to acknowledge and confirm (via email) the availability to conduct the interview on the first date suggested by the student. In cases of calendar overlapping, the researcher simply looked for the second or third suggestion, then confirmed the interview.

In the end, a total of 20 interviews resulted from both men and women representing different aspects of the intended student body; the interviews were successfully conducted and validated for an in-depth qualitative data analysis. As suggested by students, the interviews took place in settings of their preference. Some face-to-face interviews were conducted in Évora and some others at a distance, especially in cases when traveling to Évora was difficult or even impossible. Overall, a quarter of the interviews took place in person in places suggested by the interviewee (e.g., at the university, in a public place such as a coffee shop or snack-bar) and the remaining interviews were conducted through Skype, Google Hangout, or a free phone call.

Similarly to what happened with the survey, the research team believes that the success of this phase was due to multiple reasons. Firstly, using Google Forms seemed a very quick and easy way of agreeing on a time and venue to conduct the interview, thus avoiding several email exchanges that would annoy the potential interviewee. Secondly, there was a constant association between the study and the University of Évora, in particular the Vice-Rectory. The need to pass on to the participants the importance, seriousness, and relevance of the study was reflected in the options around the clarity and professionalism demonstrated at all times and communication materials, as well as in the form layout, which was also specifically prepared to convey this same message of institutional association with the university (e.g., including in the header a photograph of Renaissance tiles, which are very iconic of the university, and the university's official symbol at the end). Thirdly, it should be noted that the management of the email account was a subject of constant attention. Monitoring such an email account was important to convey not only the idea of a prompt and personalized answer, but also to be attentive to non-delivery and/or the return of emails. To a lesser extent, this email account was also a tool for communicating with potential respondents who asked specific questions or informed the research team about changes of dates and venues.

In dealing with the specific challenge of entering the busy lives of individuals with the aim of asking for time to participate in an interview, the strategy of a personalized contact in a seemingly cold and impersonal environment as online email proved to be a very successful solution in the DROPOUT project. Thus, allowing possible respondents to choose their own availabilities to participate in an interview and allowing them to choose the format of the interview (face-to-face, via Skype or Google Hangout), coupled with an attentive and almost synchronous strategy of monitoring the email account to negotiate further details, was used to overcome difficulties in scheduling a time-space of mutual accordance without imposing researcher preference upon interviewees. Broadly, this strategy is anchored in the purpose of making the approach more like traditional face-to-face interactions when individuals try to agree on a time and place to meet. Moreover, the email was also used to give explicit acknowledgment and encouragement when asking for questions or raising doubts, thus making people feel their responses were useful and interesting. This is particularly important because, through email, only visual elements and text might replace the nodding and different signs of interest the researcher would usually display in a face-to-face interaction.

ESTABLISHING AND EVALUATING CREDIBILITY WITHIN ONLINE RECRUITMENT STRATEGIES

Based on the several best practices explored previously, Table 1 summarizes key-criteria to be established by researchers when designing strategies aimed at the online recruitment of participants within a framework of scientific research. Because those strategies are often based upon sending an email message, Table 1 is structured according to respective main fields, namely sender, recipient, subject, body text, and signature.

Table 2 presents a checklist to be answered by Internet users in order to evaluate the credibility within recruitment emails used for scientific purposes. Again, the checklist comprises five overarching criteria for evaluation, which aggregate the basic information when analyzing an email message.

Both Tables 1 and 2 give beginning researchers and Internet users a simple, fast, and flexible way to understand the basic elements of online credibility, either for establishing and sustaining it, as when the purpose is to design recruitment strategies, or to evaluate it, when one is the subject of such strategies.

FUTURE RESEARCH DIRECTIONS

There is a tendency to look at Internet research as a quick and easy procedure, yet this often turns out not to be the case. Particularly, observing ethical procedures is always time-consuming, and this simply cannot be done in a hurry. Existing ethical research practices also apply to online data collection and analysis, even if they need some adaptation (Eynon & Schroeder, 2008; Kimmel, 1988). As such, future researchers need to attend to the ethical issues of Internet research because digital ethos is constantly evolving.

On one hand, the future asks for creative ways of gaining informed consent and protecting research participants' privacy. It is well known that potential respondents are not sensitive to long and detailed emails. Nonetheless, a certain amount of in-depth information has to be given in a very clear and understandable way. Moreover, participants need to give their consent to be part of the study. Such questions are always complex: The researcher has to reconcile efforts to avoid the chances of drop-out with the ethical obligations of providing pertinent information. Several strategies can be undertaken: increase the readability of consent forms using headings and highlighting and limit the amount of text and avoid

Table 1. Key-criteria in establishing credibility within recruitment emails for scientific purposes

Sender
• Use an official email account
• Alternatively, use a personal email clearly identified with your name and surname

Recipient
• Use individual recipients' emails
• Avoid using multiple recipients in visible mode. Instead, use BCC field to add recipients and put yourself in CC field

Subject
• Use a simultaneously short and incisive subject text line. Remember that long subject lines usually become incomplete in the preview mode of many devices such as laptops, smart phones, and tablets
• When sending reminders calling for additional participation, do it with at least a one week interval and no more than twice (e.g., one in the middle of the period estimated for data collection and a second before the end of the period but with enough time so that late participants can answer)
• Remember to change the subject line slightly to avoid grouping messages in some specific mail management platforms (e.g., Gmail). You can use introductory words or expressions (eventually capital letters) such as "REMINDER" for a second call and "LAST CALL" for the final call

Body Text
• Use a simultaneously professional and polite tone when inviting individuals to participate in the study
• Briefly present yourself; the study framework and aims; the type of participation expected; anonymity and confidentiality procedures; the final purpose; and ways of storing and using the collected data
• When writing reminders, please remember to include a short message, eventually between square brackets, as a way of filtering the reading for those who already answered/participated in the study
• Remember to use a bilingual message if you are targeting multiple linguistic participants
• Use hyperlinks to further information such as the university, project, or funding partners' webpage
• Use a hyperlink to the survey and be sure that it is functioning (the URL is constituted by transfer protocol, sub-domain, domain, directory of the domain, filename, and file type). Alternatively, write the complete URL and kindly ask participants to copy and paste it into a web browser
• When aiming the participation in a web survey, be sure to use a renowned platform whose domain can be easily recognized. If you think the participant does not know the platform, use some words to present it briefly or be sure to host the survey in a trustful web server
• Make reference to additional recruitment strategies (if any) such as written advertisements (e.g., posters and flyers to be distributed by hand or personnel recruitment through face-to-face contact in key contexts, using either the hyperlink or an OCR code image)
• Always check for typos, spelling, and grammar errors
• Include a final thanks message
• Include contacts for further questions or doubts and be sure that you will be available to answer them in a reasonable amount of time

Signature
• Sign with your name and the other research team members' names and contacts
• Add information about the institution where the study is being developed (University, Research Center, Company, etc.)
• Include some logo or image as a header or footer to make the connection with the email content, giving a sense of an aesthetic and professional atmosphere

Source: Own elaboration.

the use of technical terms and jargon. On the other hand, regarding harm and injury, the researcher will need to think creatively about ways of evaluating these negative dimensions in a truly effective way. In contrast to face-to-face experiences, when conducting a web survey, the researcher cannot rely on the immediacy of visual clues such as facial expressions, body language, or silences to determine the impact of questions or processes on participants. It is therefore important to listen to the feedback of respondents with regard to the ways web-based research is being conducted.

While the movement for open access (e.g., making publicly funded research freely available) seems to be pervasive and irreversible, it is not free from challenges from an ethical point of view because it allows for a quick and easy location (e.g., using standard search engines) and eventual recognition of

Table 2. Checklist to evaluate credibility within recruitment emails for scientific purposes

Sender
□ Does the email sender use an official email account?   □ Can you clearly identify the name and origin of the email?
Recipient
□ Is this a personalized email?   □ Was the email sender careful in hiding the email addresses of the other recipients using BCC?
Subject
□ Can you clearly understand the subject of the message?   □ Is the researcher always annoying you with reminders, even after you answer or participate?   □ Does the researcher demonstrate attention in changing or slightly adapting the subject line in reminders?
Body Text
□ Is the language clear, in a simultaneously professional and polite tone?   □ Does the researcher present him/herself, the study framework and aims; type of participation expected; anonymity and confidentiality procedures; final purpose; and ways of storing and using the collected data?   □ Does the researcher show any attention to those who have already answered/participated in the study?   □ Was there any effort given to translating the email content into different languages?   □ Are there any hyperlinks for further information such as the university, project or funding partners' webpage?   □ Do the hyperlinks presented appear to be functioning (including transfer protocol, sub-domain, domain, directory of the domain, filename and file type)? Alternatively, is it possible to copy and paste the URL into a web browser?   □ If there is an invitation to participate in a web survey, is the platform renowned or hosted by a trustworthy web server?   □ Does the email meet additional recruitment strategies (if any) such as written advertisements (e.g., posters and flyers previously distributed in hand or personal recruitment through face-to-face contact in key contexts, using either the hyperlink or an OCR code image)?   □ Are there any (or too many) typos, spelling, and grammar errors?   □ Is there a final thanks message?   □ Was contact information for further questions or doubts provided?
Signature
□ Is the email message signed with the name of the sender, perhaps later even other research team members' names?   □ Is there any further information about the institution where the study is being developed (University, Research Center, Company, etc.)?   □ Is there any logo or image used as a header or footer that somehow makes a connection with the email content, giving a sense of an aesthetic and professional atmosphere?

Source: Own elaboration.

the participants in data collection inquiries. This is especially interesting in the framework of active research that gives people access to the research at various stages; special attention to the guarantee of anonymity must be provided, especially with the incorporation of data from qualitative studies, which are often made visible using verbatim transcripts and direct quotations (Berg, 2009; Clesne, 1999; Maxwell, 2005). There are some strong reasons to be cautious about putting raw data in an accessible online format because some forms of data might allow research participants to recognize themselves or be recognized by others. In such cases, the researcher (or the research team) should think carefully about the advantages of making data freely accessible versus more restricted forms of distribution that might be more appropriate.

Finally, the Internet will continue to be part of everyday life. This means that it will probably be even more difficult to recruit participants in the future as requests keep increasing. Accordingly, researchers might simply think of alternative strategies such as paying respondents directly or using marketing research firms to find respondents in the target group. Online recruitment is sometimes difficult, but how ethical are these aforementioned strategies? If Internet researchers ultimately end up paying for responses, will they be seen as more or less credible than other academic researchers? The question is far from being answered, and, again, many of these strategies have already been used in existing paper or face-to-face research methods and are therefore not specifically brand new questions arising solely in the context of the Internet and big data. Moreover, as researchers are interested in using the Internet to collect data, they have to be aware that informatics tools change constantly, thus requiring the development of continuously new knowledges regarding the specific skills needed to create, use, and take advantage of multiple unique, and constantly evolving, online tools. As advocated elsewhere, current—and future—researchers have to be a geek (Costa, 2013). This is particularly important because the digital divide still exists. Because Internet access is not uniform, researchers must pay special attention to testing their instruments and making their research accessible for everyone, thus avoiding a double digital divide.

CONCLUSION

Credible online recruitment eliciting techniques for scientific purposes have gradually attracted social scientists' attention as the Internet became a mainstream technology widely available across society. As with any form of research, those using the Internet for research purposes are expected to be sensitive to the possible concerns of participants and develop appropriate responses to each situation.

The growing body of literature on Internet research provides helpful advice when considering design, collection, and ethical issues, yet it lacks awareness of the importance of writing to audiences when facing the need for recruitment. In such a fuzzy online environment with an absence of face-to-face presence, and where social scientists compete with numerous companies, advertisers, and marketers, each one trying to catch the attention, time, and action of the user—consumer—participant, how can social scientists harness digital ethos to successfully recruit participants? Following some basic "netiquette" rules or trusting the seeming appeal of a user-friendly interface is simply not enough.

Based on a number of illustrations from both quantitative and qualitative inquiries recently carried out by the author, this chapter adds new knowledge by presenting and discussing credible online recruitment eliciting techniques for scientific purposes adjusted to the digital age. While several best practices and much empirically tested advice were presented throughout this chapter regarding three main challenges (e.g., entering the normality of the everyday life, entering the idiosyncrasy of multicultural lives, and entering the chaos of busy lives), the chapter ends with a toolbox for researchers to establish—and users to evaluate—(dis)credibility within online recruitment strategies adjusted to different design studies that are rapidly growing in number and focus.

Traditional recruitment for scientific purposes, often referred to as "knockin' on doors," was based essentially in person-to-person communication, which, in turn, was anchored in external factors such as the credibility of the organizing or funding institution (usually a university or research center), and the researcher or research team reputation. Nowadays, successful data collection, particularly online, seems to rely, as ever, on internal factors of the communication process as mirrored in e-mail content, design choices, and related strategies. When "knockin' on digital doors," it is therefore important to properly design the instruments with this idea in mind, with particular attention being paid to establish the initial approach for potential respondents. This task is particularly demanding because the Internet, notably within email contexts, somehow reduces the available communicative resources of the personal presence of the author primarily to text and image. To counterbalance this, researchers have to create a richer environment by focusing on getting the most out of the only tools they have at their disposal, namely by attending to the professional and inclusive use of text and image in digital communication such as email.

As the future seems to be the time-space where trust (still) matters, researchers must raise consciousness and develop skills in building online trust relations when writing to potential respondents because this seriously impacts what they will unearth and share later with the social scientists' broader community. In the end, neither the scientists nor the participants can afford to be deceived.

ACKNOWLEDGMENT

The author wishes to express her gratitude to the editors of this volume and the three anonymous reviewers for their careful and attentive reading and fruitful comments and suggestions regarding the chapter. A draft version of this paper was discussed at the Universidad Complutense de Madrid in May 2016, during a Staff Mobility for Teaching under the ERASMUS+ Higher Education Mobility Agreement. The author gratefully acknowledges the constructive comments and suggestions therein pointed by Millán Arroyo Menéndez, Vicedecano de Investigación y Estudios de Doctorado, and all the students, who freely and enthusiastically participated in the related seminars held on the Facultad de Ciencias Políticas y Sociología (Campus de Somosaguas).

REFERENCES

Becker, H. S. (1986). *Writing for social scientists*. Chicago, IL: The University of Chicago Press.

Berg, B. L. (2009). *Qualitative research methods for the social sciences* (7th ed.). Boston, MA: Allyn & Bacon.

Bryman, A. (2008). *Social research methods* (3rd ed.). Oxford, U.K.: Oxford University Press.

Buckingham, D. (2008). *Youth, identity and digital media*. Cambridge, MA: MIT Press.

Clesne, C. (1999). *Becoming qualitative researchers: An introduction* (2nd ed.). New York, NY: Longman.

Costa, R. (2013). (Re)Pensar o Ofício do Investigador Qualitativo, Hoje: Metáforas, Ferramentas e Competências em CAQDAS. *Indagatio Didactica, 5*(2), 1118–1127. Available at: http://revistas.ua.pt/index.php/ID/article/view/2513/2379

Couper, M. P. (2005). Technology Trends in Survey Data Collection. *Social Science Computer Review*, (Winter): 23, 486–501. doi:10.1177/0894439305278972

Denscombe, M. (1998). *The good research guide for small-scale social research projects*. Buckingham, UK: Open University Press.

Denzin, N. K., & Lincoln, Y. (Eds.). (2000). *Handbook of qualitative research* (2nd ed.). Thousand Oaks, CA: Sage Publications.

Eynon, R., Fry, J., & Schroeder, R. (2008). The ethics of Internet research. In N. Fielding, R. M. Lee, & G. Blank, G. (Eds.), The SAGE handbook of online research methods (pp. 42-57). London, U.K.: SAGE Publications, Ltd. doi:10.4135/9780857020055.n2

Fielding, N., Lee, R. M., & Blank, G. (Eds.). (2008). *The SAGE handbook of online research methods*. London: SAGE Publications, Ltd. doi:10.4135/9780857020055

Flick, U. (2015). *Introducing research methodology: A beginners' guide to doing a research project* (2nd ed.). London, UK: Sage.

Folk, M., & Apostel, S. (2013). *Online credibility and digital ethos: Evaluating computer-mediated communication*. Hershey, PA: IGI Global. doi:10.4018/978-1-4666-2663-8

Gaiser, T. J., & Schreiner, A. E. (2009). *A guide to conducting online research*. London, UK: Sage. doi:10.4135/9780857029003

Gilbert, N. (2001). *Researching social life*. London, UK: Sage.

Hargittai, E. (2010). Digital na(t)ives? Variation in internet skills and uses among members of the 'net generation'. *Sociological Inquiry*, 80(1), 92–113. doi:10.1111/j.1475-682X.2009.00317.x

Hewson, C., Yule, P., Laurent, D., & Vogel, C. (2003). *Internet research methods: A practical guide for the social and behavioural sciences*. London, UK: Sage Publications. doi:10.4135/9781849209298

Hooley, T., Wellens, J., & Marriott, J. (2012). *What is online research? Using the Internet for social science research*. London, UK: Bloomsbury Academic.

Hughes, J. (Ed.). (2012). *SAGE Internet research methods*. London, UK: SAGE. doi:10.4135/9781446263327

Hyde, M. J. (Ed.). (2004). *The ethos of rhetoric*. Columbia, SC: University of South Carolina Press.

Janesick, V. (1998). *Stretching exercises for qualitative researchers*. Thousand Oaks, CA: Sage Publications.

Kimmel, A. J. (1988). *Ethics and values in applied social research*. Newbury Park, NJ: Sage Publications. doi:10.4135/9781412984096

Lee, L. (2008). The impact of young people's Internet use on class boundaries and life trajectories. *Sociology*, 42(1), 137–153. doi:10.1177/0038038507084829

Livingstone, S., & Helsper, E. (2007). Gradations in digital inclusion: Children, young people and the digital divide. *New Media & Society*, 9(4), 671–696. doi:10.1177/1461444807080335

Maxwell, J. (2005). *Qualitative research design: An interactive approach* (2nd ed.). Thousand Oaks, CA: Sage Publications.

Miles, M. B., & Huberman, A. M. (1994). *Qualitative data analysis: An expanded sourcebook* (2nd ed.). Thousand Oaks, CA: Sage Publications.

Neuman, W. L. (2011). *Social research methods: Qualitative and quantitative approaches*. Boston, MA: Pearson.

Patton, M. Q. (2002). *Qualitative evaluation and research methods* (3rd ed.). Thousand Oaks, CA: Sage Publications.

Punch, K. F. (2014). *Introduction to social research: Quantitative and qualitative approaches* (3rd ed.). London: Sage Publications.

Salmons, J. (2010). *Online interviews in real time*. London, UK: Sage.

Schostak, J. (2006). *Interviewing and representation in qualitative research*. Glasgow, UK: Open University Press.

KEY TERMS AND DEFINITIONS

Asynchronous: Communications that are subject to delays in transmission and/or between the sender and the recipient.

Client-Side Internet Survey: A survey that collects data using a survey that is executed on a respondent's machine.

Internet Inquiry: A form of inquiry that is based on Internet facilities to communicate, using either written, audio, or video capabilities.

Operating System: Abbreviated as OS, an operating system is a powerful, and usually large, program that controls and manages the hardware and other software on a machine computer.

Paper-Based Questionnaire: A survey that collects data and is presented to the respondent on a paper support, either face-to-face or using the postal service.

Self-Administrated Questionnaire: A questionnaire that is administrated by the respondent, who reads the questions and then points the answers.

Server-Side Internet Survey: A survey that collects data using a survey that is executed on the survey organization's web server.

Synchronous: Communications that appear directly on a recipients' computer.

ENDNOTES

[1]   The title of this paper is inspired in "Knocking' on Heaven's Door", the title from a song written and sung by Bob Dylan, for the soundtrack of the 1973 film *Pat Garrett and Billy the Kid*.

[2]   Surveymonkey®, Qualtrics and Google Forms are similar platforms. In academic settings, LimeSurvey® is also a very well-known and prestigious platform.

[3]   In addition to the author, the research team further comprised Carlos Vieira and Isabel Vieira (Universidade de Évora, Portugal).

[4]   The survey was available at url: https://docs.google.com/forms/d/1alt6XyqKEYWwePL0BvkfZ UnmaYJqSOn5yf5Oqx-5AsI/closedform

[5]   Besides the author, the research team further comprised Rafanelly Lopes (Universidade Federal Fluminense, Brazil), Alexandra Batista, Helena Patronilho and Liliana Piegas (Universidade de Évora, Portugal).

[6]   The survey was available at url: https://inqueritos.uevora.pt/index.php/892925/lang-pt

7   The webpage of the Project Vid@s: Personal Life at a distance and University International Mobility is still available at url: http://home.uevora.pt/~rosalina/vidas

8   Apart from the author, the research team further comprised Paulo Infante, Cristina Centeno, Aida Serra Lobo, Dália Cristóvão, Maria Beatriz Castor and Luís Pardal (Universidade de Évora, Portugal), and counted with the collaboration of Liliana Piegas (Universidade de Évora, Portugal).

9   The survey was available at url: https://inqueritos.uevora.pt/index.php/698335/lang-pt

10   The form was available at url: https://docs.google.com/forms/d/1ZWYMu1fUNiPxh3vk7Dv4_i5FL-OP5VMOsiD93VYbXN8/closedform

Chapter 4
Who Is Tracking You?
A Rhetorical Framework for Evaluating Surveillance and Privacy Practices

Estee Beck
The University of Texas at Arlington, USA

ABSTRACT

Exchanging information online often involves a degree of assessing the credibility and reliability of websites, which include the authors, sources, and content. This chapter argues for an additional assessment category: evaluating privacy and/or data use statements of websites because of the underlying ideologies, methods of tracking technologies used to collect data, and the need for comprehension of what website terms and conditions mean for the average person. This chapter provides a rhetorical framework as suggested guidelines to follow when evaluating privacy and/or data use statements of websites.

INTRODUCTION

As Adrienne Lafrance (2015) noted, the average lifespan of a webpage is only 100 days; however, as of late 2015, there are over 1 billion webpages in existence (Internet Live Stats, 2016). With the volume of webpages in existence, there is often a need to assess the credibility and reliability of websites in order to establish the validity of the information contained therein. To help with such an endeavor, the International Federation of Library Associations has provided research on methods for evaluating sources as part of a larger literacy and reading integration matrix (Farmer & Stricevic, 2011). Concurrently, the American Library Association has devoted space for an online lesson plan database providing professionals with curriculum materials—including lesson plans on evaluating websites (Lomanno, n.d., Ricker, n.d., Steinhauser, n.d.). Even the Reference and User Services Association, a Division of the American Library Association (2015), has a dedicated site for finding, evaluating, and using primary resources on the web. Much of the literature and professional reports result from the need to teach students how to evaluate websites in an age where anyone can launch a webpage with unreliable and untrustworthy information. Studies from the mid-2000s reveal many students do not critically evaluate website content

DOI: 10.4018/978-1-5225-1072-7.ch004

(Killi, Laurinen, & Marttunen, 2008; Kuiper, Volman, & Terwel, 2005; New Literacies Research Team & Internet Reading Research Group, 2006).

The research on evaluating the credibility of websites suggests evaluation metrics under categories such as author affiliation and authority, evidence of authenticity or bias; currency or recency; and website content. While these areas provide a strong foundation for evaluating website credibility, an often overlooked area is analyzing websites based on surveillance tracking technologies alongside website privacy policy statements. This is potentially problematic given the often complex ideologies governing policies and procedures of websites, not to mention the sophisticated methods for collecting, storing, and profiting from the data of its customers or users employed by many websites such as Google, Facebook, Amazon, Netflix, and Dictionary.com use (Beck, 2015). Tracking cookies—small alphanumeric files used to track browsing histories—are part of a refined approach to collecting intimate data on individuals. Many websites use tracking cookies; however, in many cases it is less clear how the websites use the data—whether it is for internal purposes or for profit. Existing research in this area indicates there is reason to apply caution before consenting to the terms and conditions of websites because businesses more often use data to identify, track, and intervene on private citizen's lives without real cause (Hoback, 2013; Degli Esposti, 2014).

In light of the complex mechanisms governing website terms and conditions, tracking technologies, and website policies, this chapter seeks the inclusion of a rhetorical framework—a set of guiding heuristics grounded in the rhetorical tradition—for evaluating website surveillance and privacy practices in order to explore how one might come to view information—and accurately assess—the credibility and reliability of websites from a privacy and security perspective. Since evaluating sources is not a new concept to critical thinking or the research process, my discussion herein focuses on surveillance culture generally, with a deepened emphasis upon evaluating website credibility through surveillance techniques and privacy policy statements. Digital surveillance and privacy play an integral role in networked communication. Making decisions about *which sites* get *what data* from website customers/users is part of developing a digital literacy skillset. This chapter provides background for the importance of this evaluation area, and then moves to contemporary scholarship and news media sources addressing surveillance and privacy issues online, ending with strategies for developing a rhetorical framework based upon localized and individual needs.

BACKGROUND

Although most websites have some type of data and/or privacy policy statement disclosing how the site collects, uses, and discloses user data, it can be difficult to understand the legal protections offered to people. In the United States, for example, there are no federal privacy laws mandating that companies issue data/or privacy policy statements—or any type of industry or legal consortium offering common guidelines for developing statements for website users to understand with ease. However, there are three U.S. federal acts giving provisions to website operators for areas of finances, health, and the protection of children[1] under the age of 13. Yet, these three laws are written for the protection of companies with websites in the United States against privacy lawsuits. On the other hand, the European Union adopted a directive in 1995, the Data Protection Directive (Directive 95/46/EC) that provides a data protection system for privacy within and across EU borders for individuals. Additionally, this directive has had a direct impact on American industry seeking to do business in the EU with ramifications felt in international law and international trade rules (George, Lynch, & Marsnik, 2001; Shaffer, 2002). With respect to EU guidelines, they are more comprehensive and offer greater privacy protection than US privacy laws.

Given the disparate nature of privacy protection laws by governing bodies, some researchers sought to examine how website users understood or trusted websites based on privacy policy statements. Earp et al., (2005) surveyed more than1,000 Internet users and analyzed more than 50 website privacy policy statements to examine Internet users' perceptions and expectations with website privacy. Their study revealed privacy policy statements often do not offer enough privacy and that many people do not trust or understand website privacy policy statements. Other studies have shown that privacy policies are difficult to understand (Milne & Culnan, 2004) and the complex sentence structures of many privacy policy statements require some sort of college education to parse out the meaning (Antón et al., 2004). Finally, Pollach (2009) argued that websites should redesign privacy policy statements for "content, language, and presentation format" (p. 103) to encourage users to engage with reading privacy policy statements and to establish website trust and further website credibility and reliability with privacy protections.

Even though Pollach (2009) defined a method for websites to revise their privacy policy statements with language and presentation design at the forefront, private industry has been slow to adopt such measures. The aforementioned research of Earp et al., along with Solove's taxonomy of information privacy practices (2007), allowed Xu et al., (2011) to further test the connections between user understanding and trust of website privacy policy statements through a survey of 823 users of four different types of websites: ecommerce, social networking, financial, and healthcare sites. Their research reveals a perceived privacy risk with the loss of personal information among users. However, it may be argued that there is a level of difficulty in communicating the findings of Pollach (2009) to a global, non-academic audience.

Some segments in the public and private sectors in the United States and the United Kingdom, however, have realized the need to have commonly agreed upon content, language, and design principles for website privacy policy statements to help address consumer/user concern over privacy. A range of professional merchants, providers, and organizations recognize a need for providing templates and guidelines for website operators. Such a range includes reputable organizations offering information to web marketing companies providing templates—with the caveat such guidance does not substitute for legal advice. For example, the U.S. Better Business Bureau (BBB) offers both a template and guideline[2] for BBB-accredited businesses to use for their websites (n.d.). Elsewhere, marketing company RedFusion Media offers a sample privacy policy statement, "as a starting guide, and no way gaurantee [sic] it." Further, a registered UK private limited company, Quality Nonsense, owns and operates a site for US customers titled, "PrivacyPolicies.com" and offers a custom policy for $19.99 for commercial use. While there is no commonly agreed upon privacy policy set of guidelines for the US, and some websites appear to offer a range of templates for website operators, the data and/or privacy policy statements do provide rich details about how a website uses, shares, and protects customer data. To that end, examining such statements provides an additional method for establishing website credibility, and more importantly, establishing relevance for the individual.

Although not largely visible, the cognitive relationship an individual forms when examining privacy policy statements and assessing website credibility is central to determining best practices for information design and delivery (Xu et al., 2011). Such work could also be extended into examining how website users assess website credibility and reliability, especially with privacy policy statements, in order to establish trust and evaluate risk. At this time, with many websites having disparate privacy policy and terms & use statements available, the burden to evaluate website reliability is transferred to the website customer/user.

POSSIBLE PRIVACY PROTECTION GUIDELINES

Companies and website operators have only adopted data and/or privacy policy statements with the commercialization of the Internet, as Papacharissi and Fernback reported in their 2005 analysis of website privacy statements. The U.S. Federal Trade Commission (FTC) began responding to American concerns of sharing personal information with web-based retailers in the late 1990s, by issuing a report to Congress titled, "Self-Regulation and Privacy Online" in 1999. The report authors acknowledged the commercialization of the World Wide Web and the industry adoption of collecting data about consumers to tailor products and services and offer targeted advertising. Additionally, the authors shared consumer anxiety with privacy and personal information online. Responding to consumer privacy protection concerns, the FTC outlined a series of industry self-regulation efforts to address fair information practices online, including the development of the Online Privacy Alliance (a coalition of industry groups that established member guidelines for the adoption of privacy policy notices) and online seal programs that offered compliance monitoring of licensees, who displayed a privacy seal on their website. As a result of these industry gestures toward self-regulation, the FTC recommended no legislative action for federal guidelines for consumer privacy protection.

The general tenor of the 1999 report adopts a wait-and-see approach to industry responses for self-regulation of privacy protection for consumers. Because of the relative infancy of the Internet and rapid growth in the technology and consumer sectors, the FTC acknowledged the nascent nature of the Internet's potential. Allowing for the industry to respond to consumer privacy concerns with agreed upon guidelines permitted myriad legal statements of scope and scale. At the time, not wanting to move on federal legislative action might have been a smart, if not cautionary, move on the FTC's behalf. Since the 1999 report, the increased reliance upon the Internet for information exchange and marketplace commerce has opened new methods for collecting consumer data—from sophisticated tracking technologies that allow for individual personalization of information (cf. Ghostry's "Tracker Basics") to data breaches of personal health, financial, educational records (cf. McCandless, et al., 2016).

However, the hands-off approach to industry self-regulation in the optimistic days of the Internet were curtailed in the final FTC report on privacy protection issued in 2012. In "Protecting Consumer Privacy in an Era of Rapid Change: Recommendations for Businesses and Policymakers," the FTC recommended congressional action for "baseline privacy protection" with additional calls for "data security legislation" (p. i). In the final report, the FTC provides a framework for industry best practices that collected, used, and shared consumer data and urged companies to adopt said practices at more rapid rate than historically acted upon. The five advanced areas of privacy protection include:

1. **Do Not Track Technologies:** Signaling consumer choice about tracking technologies online;
2. **Mobile Disclosure Guidelines for Small Screen Technologies:** i.e., finding ways to provide succinct and efficient means of delivering guidelines on small-screen devices;
3. **Data Broker Collection and Use of Consumer Data:** Especially with the invisible and apparent lack of consumer control over the information large data broker companies have on consumers;
4. Methods for addressing how large Internet service providers, including social media companies, media and telecommunications companies, and operating system providers track consumer online activities; and
5. Developing a Project to Promote Self-Regulation and Enforcement of privacy codes and conduct for consumer protection.

In order to offer broad-based consumer privacy protections, the FTC, in this final report, takes both a targeted and broad view of privacy protection. In soliciting public comments on privacy regulation and protection, the FTC found responses ranging from the benefits and constraints of privacy harm to negative economic impact of increased—and federal regulated—privacy laws. However, the larger context of the final report gestures toward the need for some type of federal baseline privacy protection. The FTC acknowledged it is in a position to assist and support efforts with do not track tools or system; privacy protections for mobile services; consumer access to information held by a data broker; a public workshop regarding large Internet Service Providers tracking consumer activity online; and, enforceable self-regulatory codes. Despite these nods towards increased protection and options for consumers in the United States, many industry leaders continue to respond employ tracking technologies and collect consumer data without providing consumers much access. Because of the perceived failure of the industry to provide adequate consumer protection, everyday people face real challenges when evaluating the credibility of website privacy and/or data use policy statements.

ISSUES, CONTROVERSIES, AND PROBLEMS

This section introduces a series of vignettes for consideration as possible solutions for website operators to incorporate in revised privacy policy statements. While much of the suggestions in this section far exceed the boundaries of the purpose of this chapter, i.e., providing a rhetorical framework for evaluating websites for surveillance and privacy practices, this contribution takes up some of the more challenging areas of information design on websites to acknowledge there are possible solutions to a widespread problem of misunderstanding privacy policy statements writ large.

Because of the lack of agreed upon principles for privacy and/or data use policy statements, consumers who use the Internet face challenges when deciding to use a website for information exchange, commerce, education, or entertainment, among other such uses. Acknowledged as another box to check when signing up for goods and services, many consumers/users simply do not read website terms and conditions—as demonstrated in the documentary *Terms and Conditions May Apply* (Hoback, 2013). A factor in blindly accepting website statements by checking a box arises with the currency of time. Often, the time needed to read through many terms and conditions appears substantial and not worth an effort. This is not because the average person does not possess the mental faculties to comprehend the statements. Rather, the terms and conditions are often lengthy legal documents, written in legalese—as Vie (2014) noted in her discussion of privacy policy statements and video gaming—and carry with them a low-context barrier to appreciating the domain knowledge of privacy law and its implications for consumers.

Privacy and/or data policy statements, after all, are written for the express purpose of protecting a company or website operator from legal damages. Certainly, consumer education about how website operators use customer data belongs as a secondary purpose of such statements; however, any industry self-regulation efforts to increase consumer education about terms and conditions have fallen flat. In a 2014 Pew Research Center report "What Internet Users Know about Technology and the Web" that surveyed a nationally representative sample of 1,066 Internet users through 17 questions on technology, only 44% of respondents understood[3], ". . . that when a company posts a privacy statement, it does not necessarily mean that they are actually keeping the information they collect on users confidential" (para. 7). Currently, there are no incentives to the average person—who is unconcerned about how website operators collect, use, and share their data—to learn about the key aspects of privacy and/or data use statements. If we understand the Internet as a platform for goods, services, and information exchange, and we truly consider how everyday people encounter privacy and/or data use policy statements, then we must discern how to integrate the critical thinking skills necessary to assess the credibility of a site—based in part on their terms of use—into our curricula.

Another challenge ripe for confusing and laborious effort is the myriad content and design structures of privacy and/or data use statements. Depending upon the complexities of goods, services, and information exchange offered on a website, the terms and conditions may be of considerable length and varied design structures. As an illustrative case for regulatory oversight by a public entity, the U.S. Food and Drug Administration's supervision of the nutritional facts label—which provides one label for consumers to know information quickly and effectively about the nutritional values of a labeled food item—provides an agreed upon template that manufactures of food items must comply with when producing and distributing food in the United States. The potential to use such a template—even a set of agreed upon content, language, and design guidelines—with website privacy policy statements represents a possible solution and a means of achieving accountability for fair information practices and standards. Such user-friendly guidelines and agreements may aid in helping customers/users understand and evaluate website reliability and credibility with ease. Although it may be argued that it took decades for the FDA to achieve the nutritional facts label, it is clear that successive public policy interventions cleared the way. U.S. President John F. Kennedy's Consumer Bill of Rights (1962)—the right to be safe, to be informed, to choose, and to be heard—represents a milestone that later helped launch the 1965 Fair Packaging and Labeling Act, which required honest and informative labels in consumer products. Not until much later, in 1990, did the United State pass the Nutritional Labeling and Education Act requiring packaged foods to have consistent labeling and health claims. These significant rights and acts signaled to the public a sense of regulatory oversight, trust, and reliability for manufactured food products. In many ways, this type of administration and regulation allows for greater confidence and consumer protection, a necessity for consumers in vulnerable positions, especially when they may be in situations where no outward hint of danger exists. The time seems ripe for the U.S. government to pay similar attention to the area of website privacy policy statements. The uniform standard, regulations, and procedures for labeling helped instill greater trust among people, and being able to establish that level of trust among people on websites is just as necessary.

Almost every website has some sort of privacy policy, data use, and/or terms and conditions statement governing how website users may operate the site. Most of the language focuses on protecting the financial and legal interests of the website operator; however, there are some exceptions. For example, the FTC (accessed January 6, 2016) website discloses the use of single-session cookies (data files expiring at the close of the page session that are used to aid in website navigation) and multi-session cookies (stored on the individual computer and used to record website visits), along with the vendor names associated with the development of each cookie used on their website, such as Google, Lockheed Martin, and ForSee Results. A website governed by EU laws also provides additional measures to inform users about cookie collection through the use of banners or alerts. These advancements are far different than other website operators, such as Facebook, who, in its 2,600-word data use statement (accessed December 13, 2015), provides users an overview about the collection of data with little transparency or detail on the vendors. Additionally, the two websites use different types of accessing aids (document navigation tools) of bright colors, informative headers and subheaders, and chunked information in single or multi-column formats. What is clear from this example is how the FTC and Facebook—only two websites used for the purposes of illustration of variance—privilege various content, technical, and design principles over others. The divergence in website operator ideologies about policy and disclo-sure, the privileging of certain information over others, and the technical design principles adds to the potential for misunderstanding the nuances of each website operator's terms and conditions. Thus, the statements reflect a networked spectrum of values that may prove difficult for the average website user to assess when evaluating website credibility, especially if time and low-context barriers exist in the process of assessment. Thus, there is validity in providing a solution to a real challenge, from a website operator perspective, of having uniform guidelines and agreed upon principles to guide website user's trust and risk assessment with relative efficiency and ease. There is a real need for further regulatory or legislative oversight in this area to engender trust among website users.

VIEWPOINTS, VISION, AND VISIBILITY

It is important to acknowledge the larger role surveillance plays in the context of this argument. We live in a surveillance state. Our online clicks and strokes, attitudes, connections, habits, histories, move-ments, and searches are monitored, shared, stored, and tracked. Our invisible digital identities (Beck, 2015)—developed by online companies, data brokers, and even health, financial, legal, educational, and consumer databases (e.g., loyalty cards)—paint a portrait of who we are and what we do. In order to understand the implications of website privacy policy statements, tracking technologies, and the role nation-states and large corporations have in creating and sustaining online surveillance, a broad overview of scholarly discussion is in order.

In an attempt to overview the cross-disciplinary field of surveillance studies, sociologist and pioneer of the field Lyon (2007) provided three broad themes of surveillance culture: viewpoints, vision, and visibility. Lyon described each theme as a consequence of goal-directed activity to monitor, control, and shape the masses. The primary goals of surveillance-driven democratic society, of course, work to establish order and safety; however, with the entry of capitalism and neo-liberal ideologies, shifts toward influencing and controlling individuals on a large scale occur—whether by the design of those in power or those in the populace who use technologies to disrupt the status-quo of the elites.

In Lyon's viewpoints context of surveillance studies, the foundation for a surveillance state forms as a focused and sustained purpose for overseeing, protecting, or supervising human behavior. Closed circuit televisions, for instance, remain a popular and ubiquitous form of recording people's actions. For instance, the monitoring of European citizens with the use of CCTV technology in public spaces is widespread (Norris, McCahill, & Wood, 2004), despite the public's concern and opposition to the installation and use of millions of cameras in public areas. The continued use of surveillance technologies also includes recording suspicious behavior on public sidewalks (Norris & Armstrong, 1999) and in online spaces, mining meta-data from websites and mobile app technologies (Degli Espoti, 2014). The conclusion to draw from viewpoints is not necessarily one of acknowledging the surveillance technological apparatus of classifying, sorting, and targeting individuals and mass groups; it is instead in addressing the ideological forces that assume such identification and segregation of people. In many ways, website privacy policy statements, which provide greater legal and financial protection for website operators, exist within a surveillance network whenever tracking technologies, especially multi-session cookies, are used. This idea is central for any critical thinking about privacy and/or data use policy evaluation when assessing the overall credibility of a website, i.e., what underlying viewpoints *or* ideologies drive the terms and conditions, and to what degree is a person comfortable with such views?

As the theme of vision suggests, the recording method for a system of control—or how surveillance operates in tandem with technologies—is just as important as the underlying vision, or impetus, for the policies and procedures for recording or watching people. Representative methods for surveillance culture, face-to-face surveillance, file or database surveillance, bureaucratic record keeping, CCTV monitoring, and computer interface surveillance are generally recognized by government and industry leaders as appropriate vehicles for enacting hierarchal power relations over those monitored or watched—especially without express knowledge of such surveillance activities.

One strikingly gross characterization of the nature of mass surveillance is the outrage some United States senators expressed when they learned the NSA eavesdropped on private conversations of members of Congress who were involved in negotiations with Israeli Prime Minister Benjamin Netanyahu and his team on the Iran Deal. Journalist Glenn Greenwald (2015) reported on the public outrage the GOP chairman of the House Intelligence Committee, Pete Hoekstra, tweeted when he learned of a *Wall Street Journal* report that the NSA spied on Congress: "WSJ report that NSA spied on Congress and Israel communications very disturbing. Actually outrageous. Maybe unprecedented abuse of power" (Hoekstra, 2015). As this tweet suggests, the work of NSA spying is a goal-directed activity pointing away from those in positions of power in the United States, especially those who support and defend the use of surveillance on others. With such an explosive condemnation of the surveillance capabilities and usage of the NSA, one might conclude that those who occupy positions of power do not support a super-system of surveillance that gazes upon the unsuspecting subject (Foucault, 1979) when such a system targets power brokers, i.e., U.S. elected officials, and more importantly, *public* holders of office. Taken under the theme of vision, the methods for surveillance and the authority to monitor employees and/or the public takes on an Orwellian feel—regardless of the authority granted by a public office, the overriding surveillance apparatus of the United States reigns as the de-facto system for observing and monitoring people's actions. Taken another way, albeit seen through a pro-surveillance stance, the abuse of power is not the NSA's reach, but instead the abuse of power senators display when expressing outrage over being spied on—they are anything but exempt from surveillance activities as public employees of the state.

There are three inferences to conclude from vision that directly connect to an individual's method for assessing the credibility of privacy and/or data use statements within websites. First, and perhaps the most obvious, is the technologies that enable surveillance—CCTVs, files, and online tracking technologies (among others). Second, and perhaps most connected to viewpoints, is the overall grand scheme, the larger mission or view of using surveillance technologies for a greater purpose. Finally, how the methods of surveillance and the larger scheme result in judgments and actions that affect people's lives for the good or bad. The most insidious of such decisions results in adversity, discrimination, and assumptions about what people want to experience in their lives. For everyday people who want goods, services, and information provided by websites and opt-in to a critical decision-making approach to assessing website credibility, developing a sophisticated framework for uprooting the political, social, and financial ideological motivations of website operators may prove a challenging skill to harness. However, building a rhetorical framework for evaluating surveillance and privacy practices online helps an individual take control and make decisions about how to participate in a surveillance society, which may lead to forms of activism and education in local and national networks.

It is important to note why a rhetorical framework matters in the context of vision. Social media spaces, search engine and web providers, large data brokers, and computer device manufacturers persist in the work of digital algorithmic surveillance. Digital algorithmic surveillance, a term originally introduced by sociologists Clive Norris, Jade Moran, and Gary Armstrong (1998), describes how surveillance technologies store, categorize, and sift through complex datasets with step-by-step procedures for specific results. Social media sites, for example, use hundreds of algorithms, and some categorize people based on how they navigate and use the sites. This form of algorithmic surveillance can also be seen through web cookies and beacons that provide information about people's web habits to companies and governments. Companies like Facebook, Amazon, Google, and Netflix use digital algorithmic surveillance to personalize information for its users as well. In his research on Facebook, Pariser (2011) presented research on how the social media company filtered information on Facebook accounts using data collected from site usage. This "filter bubble," as Pariser named it, works through algorithms ranking and calculating a person's clicks on the site. What's questionable, as Pariser argued, about this operation is how this type of social sorting changes people's cognitive frameworks. This means filtering can reinforce a person's value and belief systems, all the while limiting access to information he or she does not necessarily agree with politically, socially, or culturally. Even more problematic is how Facebook hides how personalization works:

While the Internet has the potential to decentralize knowledge and control, in practice it's concentrating control over what we see and what opportunities we're offered in the hands of few people than ever before...What's troubling about this shift toward personalization is that it's largely invisible to users and, as a result, out of our control. (Pariser, 2011, p. 218)

The essential political notion of social sorting, as seen in the example of the filter bubble, is a purpose-driven classification scheme to drive people into distinct classes for content delivery relevant for people in certain cultural, economic, educational, political, and social classes. Of course, this particular model is alarming for democracy and civic performance. If people see content aligned with their values, beliefs, and identity markers (including advertisements), then civic performance erodes. However, what is more questionable is the power Facebook has to control such a surveillance apparatus—all without the users' knowledge, input, or explicit understanding of the process for social sorting.

Such a perspective offers evidence to the third theme of surveillance studies—visibility, or how people respond to systems of surveillance. Questions of how writers and the media portrays surveillance systems—as a fear-mongering tactic, a cautionary tale, or an emblem of liberty and freedom arise. For instance, Orwell's *Nineteen Eighty-Four* illustrates the loss of personal dignity and freedom through the watchful eye of a totalitarian state, while television show Big Brother celebrates surveillance culture by monitoring a group of people inside a large house, cut off from the outside world over a period of months, for a network audience to view from the comfort of their own homes. For the contestants on the show, the temporary loss of liberty and freedom occurs as an agreed upon parameter; the promise of reward for being the final contestant is winning the cash prize, which allows for greater financial freedom than previously experienced. But, as Andrejevic (2004) noted of reality television shows like Big Brother, the contestants are not the real winners; instead, the real winners are the television producers, networks, and people who invested capital into the enterprise—all those who reap more rewards than the contestants. In many ways, the reaction of surveillance culture, as seen in literature and media, represents an internalization and desensitization to cultural and social control of power. The everyday citizen understands, participates (as spectator or surveilled), and chooses to analyze and/or consume the affective power and control of a surveillance apparatus. When such a citizenry decides to respond to surveillance culture, evidence of dissent, reaction, and hacking surface in movements to protect privacy and/or curtail corporate and/or government [ab]uses. The critical lesson of visibility is how various stakeholders, in positions of power in media, government, or corporations respond and react to the surveillance state—whether it's exploiting or monetizing surveillance for financial gain or otherwise.

RHETORICAL FRAMEWORK

Based upon the current state of privacy and/or data use statements and the problems industry and the US government face with self-regulation, assessing credibility presents challenges for individuals when evaluating terms and conditions. However, based upon the discussion herein of these issues, the researcher proposes a three-part rhetorical framework, formed, in part, upon Lyon's thematic categories for surveillance studies, in order to evaluate website credibility based on privacy and/or data use statements, including:

1. Ideological viewpoints, or assessing the views and beliefs assumed in terms and conditions;
2. Methodological vision, or evaluating the underlying purpose and collection method (i.e., technologies to determine individual alignment with websites); and,
3. Design of visibility and transparency, or assessing how the website operator designs statements for efficient, easy use and comprehension along with transparent data practices.

The researcher selected Lyon's categories to help address and uncover larger ideological patterns of thinking and policy implementation in order to address deeper human needs and rationales, as well as to offer a heuristic model for examining the reliability and credibility of website privacy policy statements. This framework takes into consideration Aristotle's (2007, trans.) persuasive appeals—ethos (ethics), logos (logic), and pathos (emotions)—with information design and user experience factors. By developing a routine practice for assessing the credibility of a website from terms and conditions, students will become stronger purveyors of critical thinking and potentially influential in conceptualizing new design practices and principles for delivering lengthy legal documents.

SOLUTIONS AND RECOMMENDATIONS

Admittedly, one of the main challenges most people will face when assessing the credibility of privacy and/or data use statements will be time. It is much easier—and woefully uninformed—to blindly accept the terms and conditions in order to receive the perceived benefits of the website. Despite this potential behavior and the issue of time, investing personal time in developing an individual framework encourages people to investigate the apparent and underlying ideologies and real legal effects of said statements. When assessing the credibility of website terms and conditions, the researcher is in agreement with Ke and Hoadley (2009) that a one-size-fits-all evaluation model may not meet the needs of everyone, nor—as Apostel and Folk (2008) noted—a checklist approach. However, the researcher also acknowledges that examples of practical applications of a suggested rhetorical framework may inspire people to work on their own guidelines—either through using the framework suggested herein or modifying the base concepts for their own value systems about surveillance and privacy online. To that end, the researcher offers the following practical rhetorical strategies for working within the framework:

Ideological Viewpoints

- Take some time to think and possibly record thoughts, feelings, and ideas about your beliefs and values about government and industry surveillance and privacy practices.
    - It may be for some there is a high degree of implicit trust[4] about how website operators collect and store data. For others, a more cautious or low degree of trust may be present—learning about how you'd feel about having data exposed online, including financial, health, legal, educational, and social records prior to signing up for goods, services, or information exchange websites or databases may help in making decisions about what data to disclose or what websites to give away data too.
- After identifying key areas of concern with surveillance and privacy practices, make it a habit to skim or, if possible, read privacy and/or data use statements.
    - Even if time is a factor, there are multiple websites online dedicated to providing highlights of terms of conditions, including Ghostry.com, which offers a web extension and Terms of Service; Didn't Read project (n.d.), which evaluates website statements on a scale and gives a top-level overview of what matters most in terms of privacy and data protection.
- Be prepared to opt-out of a website operator's terms and conditions by using obfuscation practices or no longer using a website—and live with the choice with periodical benefit/risk updates.
    - In Burton and Nissenbaum's (2015)*Obfuscation: A User's Guide for Privacy Protest*, the authors provide an entry for people to use obfuscation practices to opt-out or subvert unwanted surveillance. On the more extreme side, making a decision to no longer use a website, as the researcher did when she left Facebook [5](cf. Beck, 2014) after seven years of use, might be a viable decision based on the benefits and constraints of what the site offers (or does not).

Methodological Vision

- Attempt to identify the use of certain technologies to monitor, collect, store, and share data.
    - While the FTC cookie page provides the purpose and vendor for each single-session and multi-session cookie it uses, not all website operators will go to such lengths for transparency. You may have to rely upon installing Ghostry's web extension or visiting the Online Behavior Alliance's consumer opt-out page to view who's tracking you online in order to opt-out of those trackers.
- Determine how the methods of collection and sharing correspond to the website operator's vision or general views about goods, services, or information exchange.
    - This particular area may take up more time than other areas because this domain requires abilities to define, analyze, and synthesize information. Take Facebook's data use policy for instance. The lengthy document provides a broad overview that it collects and shares data along multiple indexes and points, but it is not entirely clear how such collection corresponds to Facebook's larger vision about its role in social media.
- When in doubt about conflicting information or uncertainty about methods of collection, write to the website operator.
    - Most privacy and/or data use statements have contact information for the operator. Take the time to send an email or write a letter to seek out clarification.

Design of Visibility and Transparency

- Assess how the website operator designs the privacy and/or data use statements for visibility and transparency for the average person to comprehend with efficiency and ease.
  - This area will be perhaps the quickest to complete because a preliminary scan of the design elements of the page—from descriptive headers to the use of accessible aids and hyper-links—will help determine the credibility and care the website operator has put forth in making terms and conditions transparent and comprehensive.
- Determine whether the values of the website operator are transparent enough so that the average person can make informed decisions about opt-in and opt-out practices.
  - Chances are if the website uses plain language invoking the second person in the active voice, along with an 8th grade readability level, then the website operator is making an effort for the average person to engage and understand the terms and conditions.

Assessing the credibility of a website based on its privacy and/or data use policy statements provides people with the means to take control over their information online. Those who take the time to consider how surveillance and privacy impact their day-to-day routine will undoubtedly uncover challenges when figuring out the best course of action when participating with websites. Additionally, the researcher would be remiss to not acknowledge that privacy is not the antidote to surveillance—as Stalder (2002) argued in an opinion piece. Individual privacy is personal; the concept varies wildly among people. As Stalder noted, the sustainable approach to addressing surveillance is holding those in power—or those who surveill—accountable for their actions. The real change for greater privacy protection online—whether that's through self-regulation, government oversight, or even individually assessing credibility—is taking up the matter with policy makers and industry leaders in an organized, vocalized, and sustained movement. However, as educators, we can take steps now to inform our students about website terms and conditions, thereby providing them with the critical skills needed to make healthy decisions about sharing information and data online.

FUTURE RESEARCH DIRECTIONS

Working with the rhetorical framework allows website users and students to negotiate the immediate and long-term trust and risk needs when consenting to use a website with privacy policy statements. As such, integration of such a framework requires longitudinal empirical research with diverse research participants to assess the validity of such a framework. Additionally, as Xu et al. (2011) supported, there is a real need to understand the cognitive frameworks when website users participate in understanding and evaluating website privacy policy statements. More research into the behaviors and knowledge website users present when examining disparate statements will help website operators design content, language, and information design standards (Pollach, 2009).

However, the larger scale implications of this chapter illuminate the need for website operators to engage in standardized privacy policy statements through regulatory oversight and agreed-upon guidelines. This could involve partnerships with government leaders from multiple nation-states across the globe, private industry leaders, legal scholars, and academic researchers, enabling such a team to define, pass, and distribute directives or oversight regulations. Large-scale research in this area may include industry white papers and empirical data from studies.

CONCLUSION

It is the researcher's hope that this chapter serves as a guide for educators, regardless of disciplinary alignment, to understand the problems and challenges with privacy and/or data use statements and to teach students how to develop a rhetorical framework that evaluates website terms and conditions based upon their individual ideologies. Additionally, the researcher hopes that this chapter provides ground for future research, including qualitative and quantitative studies on comprehending website terms and conditions, or even intervention studies addressing a common design for website operators to adopt. More prominently, the overall purpose of this chapter is to introduce inclusion of privacy and/or data use policies in overall evaluations of websites. For educators teaching introductory courses, this might mean simply highlighting and acknowledging website terms and conditions alongside author affiliation, source handling and citation, and any apparent bias within the content. Understanding the scope of opaque or invisible processes underneath the textual layer of a website is just as important as the visible layers that we all too often focus upon. The ability to make decisions about all the available pieces helps students become smart and discerning online citizens.

REFERENCES

Andrejevic, M. (2004). *Reality TV: The work of being watched*. Lanham, MD: Rowman and Littlefield.

Antón, A. I., Earp, J. B., He, Q., Stufflebeam, W., Bolchini, D., & Jensen, C. (2004). The lack of clarity in financial privacy policies and the need for standardization. *IEEE Security and Privacy*, 2(2), 36–45. doi:10.1109/MSECP.2004.1281243

Apostel, S., & Folk, M. (2008). Shifting trends in evaluating the credibility of CMC. In S. Kelsey & K. St. Amant (Eds.), *Handbook of research on computer mediated communication* (pp. 185–195). Hershey, PA: Idea Group Reference. doi:10.4018/978-1-59904-863-5.ch014

Aristotle, . (2007). *On rhetoric: A theory of civic discourse* (G. A. Kennedy, Trans.). Oxford, UK: Oxford UP.

BBB offers sample privacy policy for businesses. (n.d.). Retrieved December 16, 2015, from https://www.bbb.org/dallas/for-businesses/bbb-sample-privacy-policy1/

Beck, E. (2014). Breaking up with Facebook: Untethering from the ideological freight of online surveillance. *Hybrid Pedagogy*. Retrieved January 9, 2016, from http://www.hybridpedagogy.com/journal/breaking-facebook-untethering-ideological-freight-online-surveillance/

Beck, E. (2015). The invisible digital identity: Assemblages of digital networks. *Computers and Composition*, 35, 125–140. doi:10.1016/j.compcom.2015.01.005

boyd, d. (2013). *Where 'nothing to hide' fails as logic*. [web log]. Retrieved January 9, 2016, from http://www.zephoria.org/thoughts/archives/2013/06/10/nothing-to-hide.html

Burton, F., & Nissenbaum, H. F. (2015). *Obfuscation: A user's guide for privacy and protest*. Cambridge, MA: The MIT Press.

Children's Online Privacy Protection Rule ("COPPA"). (n.d.). Retrieved January 9, 2016, from https://www.ftc.gov/enforcement/rules/rulemaking-regulatory-reform-proceedings/childrens-online-privacy-protection-rule

Data use policy. (n.d.). Facebook. Retrieved January 2, 2016, from https://www.facebook.com/policy.php

Degli Esposti, S. (2014). When big data meets dataveillance: The hidden side of analytics. *Surveillance & Society*, *12*(2), 209–225.

Directive 95/46/EC of the European Parliament and of the Council of 24 October 1995 on the protection of individuals with regard to the processing of personal data and on the free movement of such data, 1995 O.J. L 281, 23/11/1995.

Earp, J. B., Antón, A. A., Aiman-Smith, L., & Stufflebeam, W. H. (2005). Examining Internet privacy policies within the context of user privacy values. *IEEE Transactions on Engineering Management*, *52*(2), 227–237. doi:10.1109/TEM.2005.844927

Facebook. (2015). Data policy. *Facebook*. Retrieved December 13, 2015, from https://www.facebook.com/about/privacy

Farmer, L., & Stricevic, I. (2011). Using research to promote literacy and reading in libraries: Guidelines for librarians. *IFLA Professional Report: 125*.

Federal Trade Commission. (2012, March). *Protecting consumer privacy in an era of rapid change: Recommendations for business and policymakers*. FTC Report.

Federal Trade Commission. (2016). *Internet cookies*. FTC. Retrieved January 16, 2016, from https://www.ftc.gov/site-information/privacy-policy/internet-cookies

Foucault, M. (1979). *Discipline and punish: The birth of the prison*. New York: Vintage Books.

George, B. C., Lynch, P., & Marsnik, S. J. (2001). U.S. multinational employers: Navigating through the "safe harbor" principles to comply with the EU data privacy directive. *American Business Law Journal*, *38*(4), 735–783. doi:10.1111/j.1744-1714.2001.tb00906.x

Ghostry. (2016). Tracker basics: What you need to know about trackers. *Ghostry*. Retrieved June 24, 2016, from https://www.ghostery.com/intelligence/tracker-basics/

Gramm-Leach-Bliley Act. (n.d.). Retrieved January 9, 2016, from https://www.ftc.gov/tips-advice/business-center/privacy-and-security/gramm-leach-bliley-act

Greenwald, G. (2013, June 6). NSA collecting phone records of millions of Verizon customers daily. *The Guardian*. Retrieved July 3, 2013, from http://www.theguardian.com/world/2013/jun/06/nsa-phone-records-verizon-court-order

Greenwald, G. (2015, December 30). *NSA cheerleaders discover value of privacy only when their own is violated*. Retrieved January 2, 2016, from https://theintercept.com/2015/12/30/spying-on-congress-and-israel-nsa-cheerleaders-discover-value-of-privacy-only-when-their-own-is-violated/

Hoback, C. (Director). (2013). *Terms and conditions may apply* [Motion picture].

Hoekstra, P. [peetehoekstra]. (2015, December 30). *WSJ report that NSA spied on Congress and Israel communications very disturbing. Actually outrageous. Maybe unprecedented abuse of power.* [Tweet]. Retrieved from https://twitter.com/petehoekstra/status/682007598476873728

Internet Live Stats. (2016). Retrieved March 2, 2016 from http://www.internetlivestats.com/watch/websites/

Ke, F., & Hoadley, C. (2009). Evaluating online learning communities. *Educational Technology Research and Development, 57*(4), 487–511. doi:10.1007/s11423-009-9120-2

Kennedy, J. F. (1962). *93-Special message to the Congress on protecting the consumer interest.* Retrieved April 7, 2016, from http://www.presidency.ucsb.edu/ws/?pid=9108

Killi, C., Laurinen, L., & Marttunen, M. (2008). Students evaluating Internet sources: From versatile evaluators to uncritical readers. *Journal of Educational Computing Research, 39*(1), 75–95. doi:10.2190/EC.39.1.e

Kuiper, E., Volman, M., & Terwel, J. (2005). The Web as an information resource in K–12 education: Strategies for supporting students in searching and processing information. *Review of Educational Research, 75*(3), 285–328. doi:10.3102/00346543075003285

Lafrance, A. (2015). How many websites are there? *The Atlantic.* Retrieved March 2, 2016, from http://www.theatlantic.com/technology/archive/2015/09/how-many-websites-are-there/408151/

Lomanno, K. (n.d.). Savvy suffers: Website evaluation and media literacy. *AASL Learning4Life Lesson Plan Database.* Retrieved March 24, 2016, from http://www.ala.org/aasl/sites/ala.org.aasl/files/content/conferencesandevents/ecollab/lpd/SavvySurgersWebsiteEvaluationandMediaLiteracy.pdf

Lyon, D. (2007). *Surveillance studies: An overview.* Cambridge, UK: Polity Press.

McCandless, D., Evans, T., Quick, M., Hollowood, E., Miles, C., & Hampson, D. (2016). World's biggest data breaches. *Information is Beautiful.* Retrieved June 24, 2016, from http://www.informationisbeautiful.net/visualizations/worlds-biggest-data-breaches-hacks/

Milne, G. R., & Culnan, M. J. (2004). Strategies for reducing online privacy risks: Why consumers read (or don't read) online privacy notices. *Journal of Interactive Marketing, 18*(3), 15–29. doi:10.1002/dir.20009

New Literacies Research Team & Internet Reading Research Group. (2006). *Results summary report from the Survey of Internet Usage and Online Reading for School District 10–C (Research Rep. No. 1).* Storrs, CT: University of Connecticut, New Literacies Research Lab.

Norris, C., & Armstrong, G. (1999). *The maximum surveillance society: The rise of CCTV.* Oxford, UK: Berg.

Norris, C., McCahill, M., & Wood, D. (2004). Editorial. The growth of CCTV: A global perspective on the international diffusion of video surveillance in publicly accessible space. *Surveillance & Society, 2*(2/3), 110–135.

Norris, C., Moran, J., & Armstrong, G. (1998). Algorithmic surveillance: The future of automated visual surveillance. In C. Norris, J. Moran, & G. Armstrong (Eds.), *Surveillance, closed circuit television, and social control.* Aldershot, UK: Ashgate.

Orwell, G. (1950). *1984: A novel*. New York: Signet Classic.

Papacharissi, Z., & Fernback, J. (2005). Online privacy and consumer protection: An analysis of portal privacy statements. *Journal of Broadcasting & Electronic Media, 49*(3), 259–281. doi:10.1207/s15506878jobem4903_1

Pariser, E. (2011). *The filter bubble: What the Internet is hiding from you*. New York: Penguin Press.

Pollach, I. (2007). What's wrong with online privacy policies? *Communications of the ACM, 50*(9), 103–108. doi:10.1145/1284621.1284627

Protecting consumer privacy in an era of rapid change: Recommendations for businesses and policymakers. (2012, March 1). Retrieved January 2, 2016, from https://www.ftc.gov/sites/default/files/documents/reports/federal-trade-commission-report-protecting-consumer-privacy-era-rapid-change recommendations/120326privacyreport.pdf

Reference and User Services Association. (2016). *American Library Association*. Retrieved from http://www.ala.org/rusa/

Ricker, J. (n.d.). *Evaluating websites. AASL Learning4Life Lesson Plan Database*. Retrieved March 24, 2016, from http://www.ala.org/aasl/sites/ala.org.aasl/files/content/conferencesandevents/ecollab/lpd/EvaluatingWebsites.pdf

Self-regulation and privacy online: A report to Congress. (1999, July 1). FTC. Retrieved January 2, 2016, from https://www.ftc.gov/system/files/documents/reports/self-regulation-privacy-onlinea-federal-trade-commission-report-congress/1999self-regulationreport.pdf

Shaffer, G. (2002). The power of EU collective action: The impact of EU data privacy regulation on US business practice. *European Law Journal, 5*(4), 419–437. doi:10.1111/1468-0386.00089

Solove, D. (2007). I've got nothing to hide' and other misunderstandings of privacy. *The San Diego Law Review, 44*. Available http://papers.ssrn.com/sol3/papers.cfm?abstract_id=998565

Stalder, F. (2002). Opinion. Privacy is not the antidote to surveillance. *Surveillance & Society, 1*(1).

Steinhauser, C. (n.d.). *Web evaluation. AASL Learning4Life Lesson Plan Database*. Retrieved March 24, 2016, from http://www.ala.org/aasl/sites/ala.org.aasl/files/content/conferencesandevents/ecollab/lpd/WebEvaluation.pdf

Terms of Service. Didn't Read. (n.d.). Retrieved December 7, 2015, from https://tosdr.org/index.html#services

Vie, S. (2014). 'You are how you play': Privacy policies and data mining in social networking games. In J. deWinter & R. Moeller (Eds.), *Computer Games and Technical Communication: Critical Methods and Applications at the Intersection*. Ashgate.

What Internet users know about technology and the web. (2014, November 25). Retrieved January 2, 2016, from http://www.pewinternet.org/2014/11/25/web-iq/

Xu, H., Dinev, T., Smith, J., & Hart, P. (2011). Information privacy concerns: Linking individual perceptions with institutional privacy assurances. *Journal of the Association for Information Systems, 12*(12), 798–824.

KEY TERMS AND DEFINITIONS

Digital Literacy: An area of study focused on developing comprehension of symbolic communication in online, networked spaces.

Ethos: One of three of Aristotle's persuasive appeals (along with logos and pathos) used as a means to appeal to a speaker's character or credibility.

Logos: One of three of Aristotle's persuasive appeals (along with ethos and pathos) used as a means to appeal to rational thought and order.

Pathos: One of three of Aristotle's persuasive appeals (along with ethos and logos) used as a means to appeal to emotion.

Privacy Policies: A statement or legal document used to define and disclose how a website, business or party collects, distributes, manages, and stores a customer's personal data.

Surveillance: Physical observation or automated methods used to collect, distribute, and store personal details to influence and supervise individuals and populations.

Standards: A set of guidelines for interoperability of content across time, space, and place allowing for fair access to content online.

Terms and Conditions: A statement or legal document used by websites to define and disclose how a website, business or party specifies how the website and content may be used, provides a disclaimer of liability, and discloses any statutory rules governing the website.

ENDNOTES

[1] The Gramm-Leach-Bliley Act (n.d.) requires financial institutions or companies that offer an array of financial advice to disclose how the institution or company shares and protects sensitive customer data. The Health Insurance Portability and Accountability Act (HIPPA) requires health care services to disclose privacy practices of the provider to patients—even in instances of related online health data. Finally, the Children's Online Privacy Protection Act (n.d.) imposes stricter requirements on websites that collect data from children under 13 years of age.

[2] In order to meet the BBB accreditation standards, privacy policies must address six areas: policy, or how information is collected; choice, customer options about how such data is used; access, ways a customer can change or correct information; security, or how the site will protect customer data; redress, or what options a customer has if a privacy policy is not met; and, how the website will communicate updates to the policy.

[3] The respondents were only able to answer true or false to the question.

[4] Hopefully, the implicit trust does not stem from the argument or belief of "I've Got Nothing to Hide." Some students—or perhaps even readers of this chapter—may believe in said position. For scholarly support on misunderstandings about the argument and what privacy means, reference danah boyd (2013) and Daniel Solove (2007).

[5] The researcher realizes in suggesting to opt-out of using a website, or taken another way—leaving for good, presents diverse opinions on the subject. For example, since the researcher published on her decision to leave Facebook, she has encountered a range of opinions on the topic—all from well-meaning loved ones, friends, and colleagues. Some people agree with the decision and know Facebook uses multiple algorithms and tracking technologies to gather and use data on them,

but they perceive the benefit of social connection through the site is of more benefit than harm. Others have suggested they could never leave the site because to be an educator and/or activist of surveillance and privacy issues means to work within "the system" to make change happen. The researcher provides these anecdotes to illustrate that each person has a different need, belief, and comfort level about data collection and privacy provisions.

Section 2
Evaluating Digital Ethos and Online Credibility in Medical Contexts

Because the number of people who desire access to heath information continues to grow (and the amount of health information available to those people continues to grow as well), this section offers advice for assessing the credibility of online health information. Considering that many people around the world lack access to adequate health care but can easily access online health information, this section offers a range of advice that is very important for a wide audience to consider.

Chapter 5
Ethos in E-Health:
From Informational to Interactive Websites

Abigail Bakke
Minnesota State University, USA

ABSTRACT

The proliferation of medical information online, without physicians or peer reviewers as gatekeepers, has made e-health an important focus for credibility research. Web 2.0, enabling lay users to contribute content, has complicated patients' challenge of deciding who to trust. To help inspire trust, an e-health website must convey a credible ethos in its homepage and other pages that constitute a user's first impression of a site. This chapter compares the visual and textual ethos strategies of three major e-health sites that represent a continuum from informational to interactive: a government site, a commercial site, and a patient social networking site. The findings reveal a variety of features, such as scientific imagery, privacy seals, and video of patient stories, that can ultimately contribute to an ethos based in expertise and/or in community. This study has implications for the design and evaluation of trustworthy e-health communication.

INTRODUCTION

Medical information has been accessible on the Internet for years, and looking up conditions and symptoms has become a common patient practice. Today, many types of e-health sites are available, from traditional information-based sites to more social, interaction-based sites.

As the web has grown as a resource for today's patients, so have concerns about the credibility of that information. As early as 1995, medical professionals were formally meeting to address concerns with the credibility of health information on the web (Adams & Berg, 2004). Current issues like the anti-vaccination movement or global health crises like Ebola have highlighted the need for credible, trustworthy online information today. Web 2.0, or the participatory web, has raised special complications.

Web 2.0 in itself is nothing new; what is newer and significant is that the values that characterize Web 2.0—openness, transparency, sharing (Eysenbach, 2008)—are extending into medicine and other areas that have been characterized by hierarchy and limited access. Web 2.0 has granted today's patients

DOI: 10.4018/978-1-5225-1072-7.ch005

unprecedented levels of access to, and interactivity with, medical information and other patients. In this new context of the patient-participatory web (my term for online spaces where patients can contribute and comment on health information rather than just consume it), it is not uncommon for patients to discuss health questions in a social media site in lieu of a call to the doctor. Along with much helpful medical information online, patients may encounter unproven information, well-intentioned misinformation, and outright scams. Without the gatekeeping mechanisms of peer review or physician guidance, patients are left with the difficult decision of what to trust.

By extension, e-health organizations, whether established or novel, are left with the challenge of promoting patients' trust in their sites. One of the main rhetorical means by which e-health organizations promote trust is constructing a credible ethos. However, there are limitations to traditional ways of establishing credibility online, particularly given the shift from passive information consumption to more active participation.

Given this shift, what is needed is a greater understanding of the rhetorical strategies diverse e-health websites use to establish ethos. Therefore, this chapter compares popular e-health sites to paint a broader picture of how these sites attempt to inspire trust.

This chapter first sets the background, addressing trends in e-health as well as the rhetorical concepts that help illuminate how websites secure users' trust. Then, the chapter moves to an in-depth rhetorical analysis of the homepages and other promotional pages of three major e-health sites that represent a continuum from informational to interactive: the government site for the National Institutes of Health (NIH.gov), a commercial site (WebMD.com or "WebMD"), and a medical social networking site driven by patient input and crowdsourced data (PatientsLikeMe.com, or "PLM").

Overall, the findings of this analysis point to a broad range of strategies for securing users' trust in e-health sites. Expected ethos markers for health and medical information, such as expertise and scientific authority, are present across all the sites. However, the more interactive sites also encompass personal and social features. These ethos strategies are innovative and underexplored within the context of medical information. Therefore, as will be explained in the conclusion, these findings are significant for scholars, instructors, and designers of e-health communication.

BACKGROUND

E-Health

In order to understand the ethos strategies of today's e-health websites, it is important to place them in the larger context of e-health. The term "e-health" has been used since the early 2000s to characterize the broad overlap between the Internet and medicine. Eysenbach (2001) defined it as a field "referring to health services and information delivered or enhanced through the Internet and related technologies" (para. 3). Of U.S. Internet users, 72% have gone online to research health topics, and 35% could be considered "online diagnosers"—meaning they have gone online specifically to decide whether to seek medical attention to or learn to treat a condition themselves (Fox & Duggan, 2013).

E-health resources have been expanding on the web in terms of types and levels of interactivity, which suggests a need for a nuanced, rather than monolithic, approach to e-health sources (Arduser, 2015; Neubaum & Krämer, 2015; Sillence & Briggs, 2015). Standard informational e-health sites abound, including WebMD, NIH.gov, and MayoClinic.org. More patient-participatory sites include personal blogs, patient social networks, and support communities (such as DailyStrength.org), which have been praised for their ability to connect patients with others, especially those with rare diseases (Meyer, 2012); in addition, health information sharing sites (such as PatientsLikeMe.com, 23andMe. com, and CrowdMed.com) collect and crowdsource patient health data. Such sites have been projected to contribute to medical advances (Swan, 2009). In general, the patient-participatory web both reflects and promotes the move towards greater patient involvement in their healthcare, with a flattening of the traditional hierarchy between patient and physician.

The patient-participatory web is, however, a double-edged sword. As Rheingold (2012) put it, "along with the latest word on cutting-edge drug trials are unsubstantiated claims, rumors, and outright quackery" (para. 4). Indeed, credibility in e-health has been an extensive and ongoing conversation in fields ranging from medicine to health informatics to information science to technical communication. The focus of the work has often been on evaluating the objective accuracy of e-health information (e.g., Kunst, Groot, Latthe, Latthe, & Khan, 2002) or users' processes for evaluating its credibility (e.g., Moturu, Liu, & Johnson, 2008). Such work has been, in part, driven by concerns about users trusting inaccurate information and experiencing negative effects (whether physical harm or "cyberchondria"), and reflects broader concerns with the Internet's lack of traditional gatekeeping and quality controls. When it comes to the question of how people navigate this information online and the rhetorical features that guide them, the theoretical concepts of ethos and trust can provide some answers.

Ethos and Trust

The concept of ethos from the rhetorical tradition is well suited to understanding the complexity of e-health, especially when combined with broader, interdisciplinary bodies of work on online trust. According to Folk and Apostel (2012), "Many people tend to associate ethos with credibility based on establishing a trustworthy personal character, thus often using ethos as a shorthand for credibility" (p. xviii). The "plasticity" of the concept makes it difficult to land on a single definition; nonetheless, ethos "provide[s] a powerful, flexible tool to consider nuances of credibility in digital contexts" (p. xviii).

In *On Rhetoric,* Aristotle (2007) used the term *ethos* to refer to the character of the speaker as a mode of persuasion. Aristotle was the first to place ethos within a systematic framework of persuasion, alongside of *logos* (or reasoning in the speech) and *pathos* (or the emotional state of the audience). In the Aristotelian conception, persuasion through ethos takes places "whenever the speech is spoken in such a way as to make the speaker worthy of credence; for we believe fair-minded people to a greater extent and more quickly [than we do others]" (p. 38). He saw that *pisteis*, or belief (or trust), results from "speech that reveals character" (p. 74). To Aristotle, ethos is strictly artistic (or invented), meaning that situated aspects such as the speaker's prior reputation would not fall within the definition of the proof through ethos. Mackiewicz (2010), in her adaptation of the invented/situated ethos pair for online interactive environments, notes that online authors can construct and draw attention to their situated ethos. Thus, while prior reputation and other situated elements of credibility do contribute to persuasiveness, what is said within the text itself—the ethos—has the power to reflect and influence that reputation.

Miller (2003) summarized Aristotle's three components of ethos: "We trust those in whom we sense goodwill (*eunoia*), those with moral qualities (*arete*), and those whose knowledge can be applied to our practical problems (*phronesis*)" (p. 202). She observed that, at least in the context of risk communication, ethos and expertise have often been conflated, thereby edging out goodwill and virtue, the more relational aspects of ethos: "The impersonality of an ethos of expertise runs the risk of being persuasive to no one" (p. 202). This quotation serves as an important reminder of the value of the sometimes-overlooked relational aspects of ethos when considering the trustworthiness of online medical information.

Closely related to the matter of reputation is the question of whether a rhetor's ethos results from actual character or whether it is merely the projection of good character. Reflecting an ongoing debate about ethos, others in the classical period interpreted the persuasive role of character in ethos more expansively than Aristotle. To Aristotle (2007), ethos was about *seeming* trustworthy (p. 38). Quintilian (2015), though, linked it more clearly to genuine character, defining a rhetor as "a good man speaking well" (p. xxxi). Of course, inherent character and trustworthiness are not measurable with the tools of rhetorical analysis. Nonetheless, information accuracy and authors' sincerity is an ongoing concern in discussions of e-health, particularly given some patients' special vulnerability to scams and claims of "quick cures," and rhetorical analysis can provide one angle on this broader, complex problem.

Modern rhetoricians have extended ethos in further directions; for instance, tracing the word back to its etymological roots as "a habitual gathering place" (Halloran, 1982, p. 60) draws out the communal dimensions of ethos. Scholars of Internet communication (Gurak, 1997; Warnick, 2007) have found this concept of ethos, which emphasizes social values and community, to be particularly relevant to online contexts. Ethos is an especially valuable tool for understanding persuasion in digital environments, because users can control the presentation of their identity in distinct ways. Website designers, corporate public relations departments, and participants in online communities are able to make textual and visual choices that persuade others towards trusting them.

Within the field of rhetoric and technical communication, researchers have drawn on ethos for strategies for evaluating, designing, and revising websites. For instance, Hunt (1996) distinguishes between web designers' choice of conveying a traditional, professional ethos, or a communal ethos that emphasizes common values between the website creators and their audiences. Brock (2012) analyzed the official ethos conveyed by proprietary software websites compared to the more participatory ethos of open source software websites. Coney and Steehouder (2000) and Swenson, Constantinides, and Gurak (2002) discussed the importance of a trustworthy online presence and of understanding the audience's values and needs. Spoel (2008), in her analysis of Canadian midwifery websites, equates ethos with an organization's "identity and value" (p. 267) and pays particular attention to the relationship the midwifery organizations constructed with their audiences.

As these examples from technical communication suggest, ethos on websites is often conveyed through shared values and relationship with the audience. In summary, while classical to modern rhetoricians have debated the particulars of ethos, a commonly accepted facet of ethos is that it has to do with the character of the speaker; in other words, it is linked to identity, whether of an individual, organization, or community. Likewise, technical communication scholars have defined ethos, in terms of web design, as an organization's persona or presence. For the purposes of this chapter, the word ethos is used to refer to the rhetor's projection of their character and credibility. Focusing on the projection of character is not meant to discount the true character or trustworthiness of the speaker. Still, a website's ethos is often the only factor, or at least an influential factor, that patients use when choosing whether to trust. The plasticity of ethos also makes it able to account for both familiar and novel means of establishing trust online.

Like the word *ethos*, *trust* does not lend itself easily to universal definitions. Basic definitions of trust center on the notion of belief; for instance, Fogg and Tseng (1999) defined trust as "a positive belief about the perceived reliability of, dependability of, and confidence in a person, object, or process" (p. 81). More than just belief, though, trust involves an orientation to action: it requires a "leap of faith" or "bet on the future," as some have described it (e.g., Bargh & McKenna, 2004; Sztompka, 1999).

The relationship between ethos and trust is relatively straightforward in that ethos is a rhetorical means of gaining trust. Because analyses of ethos, coming out of the field of rhetoric, may not account for the full range of ways that trust operates online, it is useful to look beyond that body of scholarship in order to supplement ethos analysis.

In fields like human-computer interaction and psychology, there has been an abundance of research addressing the question: What elements of websites contribute to trust? Much of this work was driven by e-commerce in the early 2000s and the need for trust in online business transactions. At that time, the topic of trust in websites was of particular interest because online retailers were adapting to an environment in which there were no in-person salespeople or brick-and-mortar buildings to represent the company as in traditional commerce; instead, the website had to do the work of conveying the company's values and credibility in order to persuade users to take the "leap of faith" of making a purchase, creating an account, joining a mailing list, etc.

Research suggests that trust assessment is an iterative process rather than a one-time judgment: Web users first look to the surface appearance of the website. If the website appears credible at first glance, the user moves on to a closer look at the information contained within the site (Wathen & Burkell, 2002). According to several synthesis studies of online trust (Beldad et al., 2010; Fogg, 2002; Wang & Emurian, 2005; Wathen & Burkell, 2002), two trust-inducing features are visual appearance (e.g., images, color, page design) and usability (e.g., navigation, speed). Other credibility features of websites include third-party guarantees such as seals of approval, privacy disclosures, brand or company reputation, and social presence cues (or a sense of connection to a real human or real offline organization) (Wang & Emurian, 2005).

While this literature from e-commerce is still relevant, today the Internet offers much more than just shopping and information consumption. As the popularity of social networking and Wikipedia attests, participation is now a defining feature of the Internet. Along with this growth of collaborative and social websites, studies in communication and rhetoric have identified more social contributors to trust. Recent empirical studies point to a growing dependence on peers compared to traditional authorities when assessing online information (Metzger, Flanagin, & Medders, 2010). Similarly, Warnick (2007) found that the site Indymedia, which allows for anonymously authored news stories, established an ethos of free speech and openness in contrast to mainstream media sites' ethos of quality control and identifiable authorship.

More recently, social psychologists Neubaum and Krämer (2015) compared users' reactions to personal blogs and institutional websites providing HIV information. They found that institutional websites were found to be credible, and personal blogs led to greater attention and recall. Similarly, a comparative rhetorical analysis of vaccine-related websites showed that pro-vaccine sites demonstrated a unidirectional, non-interactive model that played up the expertise of their sources, while vaccine-skeptical sites employed a wider variety of features and sources with a particular focus on creating communities (Grant et al., 2015). At the same time, issues of usability, organization, and structural features still matter even in the most participatory of spaces—online patient communities (Hajli et al., 2015).

In sum, what is trustworthy online depends not only on institutional, expert credentials, or on usability and design, but also on context and on a website's shared values with their audience. By incorporating interdisciplinary literature into the rhetorical toolkit, ethos analysis can show how a broad range of elements—visual design, organization, and even discourse on the site that positions the audience in particular ways—helps secure users' trust. This broader, more dynamic view of web credibility is particularly helpful for understanding why sites like Wikipedia or Twitter can be seen as trustworthy to users, despite their lack of verifiable authorship or information review processes.

The preceding literature review has shown that trust in online medical information is complicated due to the potential for misinformation. Even standard, information-based e-health sites raise questions about trust because of the novelty of patient access to medical information without the physician as gatekeeper. Particular features of websites can help form a trustworthy ethos, bringing users back to the site and encouraging them to explore it more deeply. The following analysis addresses how three different e-health organizations construct their ethos in order to secure users' trust. The process of selecting websites, narrowing to pages within the websites, and rhetorically analyzing the webpages will be described first.

METHODS

The selection of sites for analysis represents a continuum from informational to interactive, allowing me to observe the range of ethos strategies used by traditional, top-down e-health sites versus patient-based, bottom-up ones. Specifically, NIH.gov, WebMD, and PLM are analyzed. WebMD and NIH.gov are the two most popular e-health sites (Top 15 Most Popular Health Websites, 2014). While PLM receives much less traffic than the other two, some consider it the largest and best-known medical social networking site (Swan, 2009). It has seen major growth since its start in 2004: According to its homepage, as of 2014, it had over 250,000 members representing over 2,000 conditions (PatientsLikeMe, 2014b).

Trust begins to be established before users even access the information within a website; the process of establishing trust (or not) begins at the moment of users' first impressions of the site and the organization's identity and values. As mentioned previously, surface appearance is a key factor in trust assessment. This is not to say that patients always access specific e-health sites directly. In fact, users typically access medical information pages through a search engine rather than by starting at a single e-health website (Fox & Duggan, 2013). However, many people still do approach it in this linear fashion, or even if they land on the information page first, may go back to investigate the website at a general level. Therefore, home pages and other easy-to-access pages like "about" pages, employee profiles, and privacy policies are all logical places for analyzing ethos. This chapter looks at comparable pages across the three websites. All pages are fully public and, for consistency, were captured and analyzed during a common timeframe (fall 2014).

Rhetorical analysis is an appropriate method for revealing how the websites persuasively establish trust using ethos. Though each site's ethos may not be persuasive for all audiences (and indeed, rhetorical analysis is not intended to measure the success of a site's rhetoric), each site is quite popular, suggesting that there are broad audiences that do find them at least somewhat persuasive. The success of these sites is likely due in part to the careful work each organization has done to signal their credibility. Rhetorical analysis, while it cannot tell us about the effect or success of rhetorical features, can describe those features in depth and estimate their success based on prior research. Similarly, rhetorical analysis, when focusing on a rhetor's projection of their character, cannot fully account for audience-specific features that contribute to trust. As other disciplines' research has shown, these features intrinsic to the trustor consist of their prior knowledge of a disease, their propensity to trust, their familiarity with an organization's reputation, or experience with technology generally (e.g., Beldad, et al., 2010; Neubaum & Krämer, 2015). Nevertheless, the way that sites construct and position audiences through design and discursive features suggests something about the audiences being targeted.

The flexibility of rhetorical analysis also makes it an especially suitable method for study of websites: It accounts for the rhetorical role of non-textual features on the site, such as visuals, video, and even navigational features. Warnick (2005) argued that digital texts, with their personalization, interactivity, and complex authorship, require broader critical approaches than typical "print-centric" criticism. Moreover, comparative rhetorical analysis enables authors to make better claims about the range of variation of rhetorical features. For instance, both Brock (2012) and Spoel (2008) compared websites in terms of how each presented its ethos.

Previous work on trust and e-commerce, reviewed above, helped me identify features that have been found to contribute to trust in websites, such as third-party guarantees and social presence cues. At the same time, I attended to the ways each site establishes its identity and values in relation to the audience, reflected in things like mission statements and visual focal points. These discursive means of positioning the audience as more or less engaged also contribute to the persuasiveness of the site.

ANALYSIS: ETHOS IN E-HEALTH SITES

NIH.gov and WebMD already have credible reputations due in part to their history and significant funding sources that have enabled them to invest into their public presentation. NIH.gov may appeal more to users who already privilege expert, science-based information as more trustworthy. As will be shown in the analysis, WebMD also emphasizes its professionally reviewed information, but in addition to an emphasis on accessibility and personalization. PLM is lesser known and therefore may need to do more work to construct a credible ethos, but it is still a commercial website with the resources to invest into rhetorically shaping the content and design of its site. Its audience may consist of users who are more technologically skilled to be able to contribute. Its audience may also be more specialized to those with chronic illness (as the communities are devoted to such conditions). While the target audiences of each site are not exactly the same, e-health users rarely visit one e-health site in isolation. Because it is typical for users to consult information from a variety of sources (Fox & Duggan, 2013), there is likely some overlap of audience among the three sites.

As illustrated in the remainder of this chapter, all three e-health organizations project a strong ethos. However, each does so in a different way. NIH.gov relies primarily upon expertise to project an ethos of governmental and scientific authority. WebMD likewise relies upon expertise, in addition to patient-centered features, to project a professional yet personal ethos. PLM uses some reference to expertise, but mainly uses personal and communal features to project a participatory ethos.

Ethos on NIH.gov

The NIH (National Institutes of Health) is the U.S. medical research agency and the largest source of medical research funding in the world. Its website, NIH.gov, serves as a source of information about the institutes' history, mission, and research agenda. The site also serves as a portal to governmental medical literature. Founded in the 1800s, the NIH has the longest history of the three organizations.

On the continuum of informational to interactive, NIH.gov represents an informational site, because it is a primarily unidirectional website where users go for the main purpose of *consuming* medical information as published by the organization, not *contributing* to knowledge or interacting with the organization or others.

The NIH.gov website makes its governmental identity clear. The name and logo of the U.S. Department of Health & Human Services can be found in the upper left corner of the NIH homepage (NIH, 2014d). The website's information is organized according to the menu across the top, which consists of five drop-down categories including Health Information, Grants & Funding, and Research & Training. These categories quickly tell a story about the purpose of the organization and what it can provide for users, which is primarily information about its institutes and research.

The webpage has both textual and visual elements, with the focal point of the page a revolving slideshow of featured articles. To the right of them are three recent "in the news" articles, showing that the organization stays up-to-date. The focus on Ebola is also understandable because of the timing (fall 2014). During the Ebola outbreak in West Africa, with some isolated cases in the United States, many were looking to the government for information about how it would handle the situation. The subtitle "Get the facts about Ebola" suggests that the NIH sees itself as an official source of facts at a time when it was easy to be misinformed by rumor and speculation.

Scrolling down the homepage, an information tab, "NIH at a Glance," is placed above an aerial photograph of the NIH campus in Bethesda, Maryland. The photograph along with a Visitor Information link serve as a social presence cue, making it clear that this is a real, physical location. To the right is a photo of the NIH director, Francis Collins. As with the photograph of the campus, this image of an individual emphasizes the NIH's "realness" as an organization. He is referred to as Dr. Francis S. Collins, drawing attention to his expertise as a doctor. Next to his picture, icons indicate other ways to stay updated (Twitter, his blog, etc.), which serve to present him as somewhat accessible and open. At the same time, the NIH's and Collins's social media pages create opportunities for user interaction, in that users can comment on tweets and blog posts. That these opportunities for participation are relegated to external websites suggests that participation is still not a central purpose for NIH.gov. The NIH also describes Collins as "a physician-geneticist noted for his landmark discoveries of disease genes and his leadership of the international Human Genome Project," and his various awards and memberships are listed (NIH, 2014b). This is unsurprising information to include in the NIH director biography – his discoveries and credentials align with the NIH's research mission.

The homepage includes images associated with each posted article, such as a stock photograph of a person or a medical image such as a brain scan. Additional scientific imagery such as the Ebola virus, microscopes, or photographs of scientists at work all signal scientific expertise to build the organization's ethos of scientific authority. Meanwhile, word choices on the homepage suggest how users are to engage with the site. For instance, verbs suggest that users' actions include learning and finding: "Learn about a new Presidential focus aimed at revolutionizing our understanding of the human brain," "Find information," etc. These headings are in line with the site's purpose as informational—there is no place for users to log in to engage with the site in a more interactive way or to post content of their own.

The scientific theme is carried through in the text of the About page (NIH, 2014a), which relies heavily on statistics and facts to build the NIH's trustworthy ethos. For instance, it reads, "Life expectancy in the United States has jumped…" and "More than 80% of the NIH's budget goes to more than 300,000 research personnel…" The page includes a section on history, and notes that 145 Nobel Prize winners have received support from the NIH. The About page also explains that "Successful biomedical research depends on the talent and dedication of the scientific workforce." In all, the central message conveyed is that the NIH exists for the benefit of the public and that the NIH has played a historical role in supporting health and medical advances.

NIH.gov includes an easy-to-find privacy notice (NIH, 2014e). Privacy protection may not be as important of a concern for informational sites as it is for sites where users post personal information, and as with most privacy policies, it is not particularly reader-centered. Nonetheless, the policy is relatively thorough and transparent, addressing topics such as cookie use. Moreover, the presence of the policy in and of itself can contribute to trust on a website (Beldad et al., 2010).

Despite NIH.gov's strengths in conveying a consistent scientific ethos, the website does not seem designed with the everyday user in mind. The site's organization is not especially intuitive, and it is not clear exactly who the site is for: At various points the articles refer to providing information for "health professionals," "the public," "employees," "parents," and "caregivers." In other words, patients or users are not central. Instead, there is an emphasis on the NIH serving as a source of official guidelines and facts. This official, authoritative ethos is shown in the NIH's definition of itself: "*The* nation's medical research agency" (emphasis added). Patients are here positioned more as passive recipients than as active agents in healthcare.

Another indicator of the organization's official ethos appears in the FAQs section (NIH, 2014c), which addresses questions not just about the NIH but about more general health issues such as, "Can NIH offer any advice when searching for health information on the Internet?" or "Where can I find information about alternative medicine?" This suggests that the NIH is seen as a trusted organization that can serve as a source for common health questions, as well as advise patients on how to navigate other potentially less credible health information sources.

The NIH has built up a trustworthy ethos by highlighting its link to a real physical location with a history, the expertise of its director and employees, and its quantifiable scientific and health impact. Scientific imagery, a largely non-interactive design, and official rather than user-centered language contribute to the NIH's ethos of scientific rigor and official government authority, and highlight its central purpose as providing information. Such features are important in showing how the NIH stands out in an age where misinformation can flourish online. While NIH.gov offers little room for user participation, WebMD, which is a commercial site and has moved in a more interactive direction than NIH.gov, offers some interesting contrasts.

Ethos on WebMD.com

WebMD emerged during the e-health boom of the early 2000s and is best known as a medical information site, publishing news and reference articles on a wide range of health topics. Besides just reading information, patients can interact with information and peers using the site's individualized tools and support communities (discussion forums). As such, WebMD reflects a hybrid site where informational and interactive features are blended.

WebMD's very name shows that its ethos is grounded in medical expertise. However, it is clear that WebMD is a commercial website, with its .com domain name and banner ads along the top and sides of the homepage (WebMD, 2014b). Sign-in and social media links can be found at the top right. Like NIH.gov, the site's major categories are listed across the top as drop-down menus, including Health A-Z and News & Experts. While the NIH's categories refer more to organization-specific information, WebMD's categories are user-focused, leading users directly to relevant health topics.

The homepage is designed somewhat like a news site, with a main article and video as the focal point of the page. Another notable section is labeled "Conversations," which displays a selection of WebMD's recent social media posts. WebMD redesigned its site from summer 2014 to fall 2014, and one of the major changes was to emphasize social media. This emphasis shows a move towards a social media presence being an important element of an organization's ethos: Having over a million Twitter followers serves as a modern-day form of an age-old contributor to trust, social validation. At the same time, the Conversations section showcases WebMD's affiliations with celebrities and other trusted organizations and news outlets and shows WebMD to be up-to-the-minute with content.

Below the Conversations section are diverse, multimodal articles and interactive tools. Article topics include celebrities, recipes, and facts about disease, making it clear the audience is broad. This breadth of content, placing celebrity diet tricks next to medical articles, may make the site appear less serious and focused, detracting from its credibility. Similarly, commercialism and overall "clutter" can detract from credibility on websites (Fogg, 2002). The fall 2014 redesign also involved streamlining the page and providing more white space. This more minimalistic design suggests that the organization is aware of the importance of maintaining a current and credible page design.

Further supporting the site's trustworthy ethos, the bottom of the homepage includes third-party guarantees or trust seals (TRUSTe, HON, etc.) to supports the site's privacy practices and information quality. As with NIH.gov, WebMD has a relatively accessible privacy policy (WebMD, 2014c) that aligns with the claims in the privacy seal.

Another conspicuous feature on the homepage is the Symptom Checker, one of WebMD's most popular interactive tools. Such tools enable interaction primarily between the user and the website (i.e., users can input personal symptoms and receive a list of possible diagnoses). The results page for the Symptom Checker does include a link to relevant patient communities on WebMD to support interaction with peers as well. However, the community feature is not well advertised and is not accessible from the homepage, at least without being logged in. The presence of both member-created and WebMD-moderated communities suggests that the credibility and value of the community still comes, at least in part, from medical expertise.

It is on the WebMD About page (WebMD, 2014a) where the company starts to be more intentional about shaping its ethos as a credible source of health information, not just as a useful, broad, or entertaining source. The About page uses headings such as "Our award winning content," and uses corresponding visuals such as a stethoscope, employees in suits, and a trophy, all of which form a picture of WebMD as a quality-focused and transparent medical organization.

Besides linking to awards, the About page also links to employee biographies (WebMD, 2014d), which feature the main medical editors and senior editorial staff (noted as MDs). The page description states that WebMD works with over 100 doctors and health experts to ensure "up to date, accurate" content. The biographies are written in third person, and describe the employees' academic and medical backgrounds, as well as relevant volunteering and media experience. This combination of credentials and personal details serves WebMD's dual goals of being both trusted and entertaining.

These biographies are significant on WebMD because many of the WebMD medical articles hyperlink to them. It seems that WebMD, by so explicitly emphasizing the quality, accuracy, and credibility of its information, is setting itself apart from unverified and low-quality health information on the Internet. These overt links to expert authorship help to support WebMD's claims of information quality, and, ultimately, its expert ethos.

In summary, WebMD's main role is to serve as a health news and information site, and credibility is enhanced through multiple references to its expert medical doctors and quality review process, and through third-party seals repeated throughout the website. Meanwhile, in the design of the site, WebMD strives to make content relevant and accessible for a lay reader; the user-centeredness is reflected in the breadth of topics and the options for customizing information beyond just searching and browsing. The expert-authored information is the hallmark of the site, but WebMD opens up some options for more user participation by having a sign-in option and WebMD communities. So, while WebMD's ethos is ultimately a professional, expert one, as suggested by the "MD" in its title, it also has moved in a more user-centered, interactive direction. Patients are recipients of expert medical information, but they can also personalize and discuss that information as participants in their own care.

Ethos on PatientsLikeMe.com

PLM is the newest of the three e-health sites and is the least conventional because it relies on the input of patient data to generate information about conditions and treatments. Users fill in a detailed profile in which they track their medical information (like a publicly posted electronic health record). Users can then search profiles to find "patients like them." PLM aggregates the data from individual user profiles into reports for each condition, uses that data for in-house research, and sells de-identified data to pharmaceuticals for research. Another major service of the site is forums, providing patient-to-patient communication like WebMD's communities. By making users the main participants and, in a sense, the authors of information, such sites aim to turn the traditional unidirectional model for medical information on its head. In that sense, this is an important, novel type of site to examine for ethos appeals.

PLM's design features make the site visually engaging and navigable, while also placing the website clearly in the category of a social network site. Like many social networking site homepages, PLM's homepage (PatientsLikeMe, 2014b) serves as a front page meant to acquaint users with the purpose and benefits of the site, and to emphasize the importance of becoming a member in order to experience those benefits. The most prominent visual feature is a video and slogan, "Live better, together!" Below the slogan, it reads, "Making healthcare better for everyone through sharing, support, and research." This is superimposed on a faded blue and green background image of eight adults holding hands. The green "Join now" button below the slogan is also a central feature of the page. To prioritize an informative video about the website makes sense, given that PLM is a novel e-health site – it has more persuasive work to do before users will buy into the company's mission.

At first glance, PLM's homepage is very clean and uncluttered. There are no advertisements. Even the color scheme contributes to a trustworthy ethos: Some research has found that users find cool, pastel color schemes to be more credible in websites (Wang & Emurian, 2005). At the top of the homepage are the company name, a search bar (inviting searches for conditions, symptoms, and treatments) and sign-in fields. Users' possible actions with the site include signing in, searching, and watching the video.

Scrolling down on the homepage reveals a brief history of PLM, including a photo of the co-founders with their brother, an ALS patient. Displaying numbers of members, published studies, and data points about disease all suggest how PLM is aligning itself with the credibility of statistics and peer-reviewed, published studies.

Once users click into the About page (PatientsLikeMe, 2014a), they encounter a familiar page design, helping to establish the company's brand. A lower-case logo provides an informal feel. Along with design features, PLM signals credibility by "borrowing" from the credibility of recognized organizations. For instance, a news item on the homepage advertises a partnership with the cancer treatment center at a regional hospital. Employee profiles (PatientsLikeMe, 2014d) also refer to PLM's partnerships with nonprofits. These various references build on the credibility of the mainstream medical system while also aligning with the innovative, independent spirit of grassroots research groups.

PLM also leverages its affiliations with popular media publications and organizations to enhance ethos across its website. References to profiles of the company published in *The New Yorker* and *60 Minutes* all help to develop the company's ethos as sincere, in that the family's own medical struggles served as motivation for starting the company, in contrast to commercial motives.

In addition, the inclusion of a prominent social media block on the About page, labeled "Stay connected," shows that PLM has a broad social media presence. PLM's social media block provides a variety of spaces to feature patient voices: While some are filtered through PLM, such as the testimonials page and YouTube page of professionally made video interviews with users, PLM also shows itself to be open to communicating with its users via informal avenues like Twitter or YouTube comments. PLM's social media presence shows that PLM is a web-savvy company that is followed by thousands across several well-known sites.

PLM's mode of choice for conveying information is videos of interviews with patients, quotations, and narratives. PLM conveys a message of concern for its users as individuals, while helping those individuals to see themselves as part of a larger community with a larger purpose. For example, the "Member stories" video, the focal point of the homepage, draws attention to real users of the site. Patients, representing a variety of chronic conditions, describe feeling fear and lack of community. By showing real patients who have benefited from the site, potential users can imagine themselves in the position of these patients. PLM also makes explicit their appreciation for patients by stating on their About page, under "Our promise," that they are "committed to putting patients first." While this might seem like an empty claim by itself, the use of images, video, and personal narrative highlights specific past and present users.

PLM effectively balances the emphasis on individual empowerment with a sense of community. Many of the references to people portray them in community or relationship, displaying the participatory nature of the site. As an example, the company name, slogan, and background image of people holding hands on the homepage all support the message of community. The "Member stories" video illustrates the relationship between the individual and the community very well: It opens with puzzle pieces, which each have pictures of individual users, falling into place to form a larger whole. While the video starts with individuals talking about their own experiences and about feeling alone, as the video progresses, they talk about how they transformed their individual challenges into opportunities to help others. One user talks about "the chance to help someone who has psoriasis like me to live a little bit of a better life." The patients in the video also talk about an even broader community, joining in the overarching goal of finding treatments and cures. As one patient says in the video, "we can do much better fighting the disease as a group than we can as individuals."

This theme of the greater good and a common vision comes through even in the privacy policy (PatientsLikeMe, 2014e), which, interestingly, opens with a statement about its openness and how a "shared belief" in openness contributes to "collective knowledge" on disease and health. Because users take on greater risk when they share health information online versus just read it, it makes sense that PLM would take a different rhetorical approach to privacy than more informational e-health sites. Indeed, the more personal language in the privacy policy, along with instantly referring users to the site's "Openness philosophy" (PatientsLikeMe, 2014c) work to create a social paradigm around privacy (or lack thereof). One of PLM's few mentions of medical professionals also occurs in the Openness philosophy, stating that patients' data belongs to patients to share with doctors to "improve dialogue." The message is that patients are empowered by owning the data that they track and generate, which reverses the classic information hierarchy in which medical institutions are the primary holders of patient data.

PLM as a company constructs its patients as important both for their individual stories and as contributors to a larger mission; the company also strategically constructs itself in relation to those patients to convey their sincerity and caring. For instance, the co-founders are featured across the website, showing PLM to be not an impersonal company, but a company with real people and a history behind it. One of their profiles is written in first person and includes a few mistakes. On WebMD or NIH.gov, errors like this would surely detract from credibility, but in the greater context of PLM's personal ethos, such errors instead make him appear relatable. Additionally, instead of medical degrees and credentials in their profiles, as was found on the doctor profiles on the other sites, the brothers tell their personal story. Moreover, users are positioned as innovators, along on a shared journey with the creators. One video states, "Our patients have really put a lot of trust in the community and us as a company to work with them on that journey." Whereas the mainstream medical system is characterized by problem-solving and efficiency, PLM establishes an overall ethos that is characterized by personal connection and community.

Comparison

All three organizations—NIH.gov, WebMD, and PLM—have textual, visual, and even interactive features on their websites that form a successful ethos (at least in some ways and for some audiences). In fact, the websites are similar in many ways: They are all highly visual, hypertextual, generally well-designed, and well-maintained. All of the websites are reasonably easy to navigate and meet basic, common criteria for website credibility; for instance, each has an easily accessible privacy policy and shows that their website is up-to-date.

All of the websites emphasize, to some extent, the credibility inherent in peer-reviewed or expert-reviewed content, and all of them use the strategy of highlighting affiliations with well-recognized organizations. Each of the e-health websites has a strong social media presence that is quickly noticeable from their respective homepages. Advertising a social media presence may be a newer factor in forming a website ethos, and it is a sign that the web, in general, is actively growing towards the social.

There are, however, important ways in which each website's ethos differs. Both NIH.gov and WebMD accentuate expertise, but of different types: NIH.gov does so through its history and scientific and governmental authority, while WebMD accentuates the expertise of its physicians and reviewers. While the commercialism of the WebMD homepage detracts from its credibility, the website succeeds in ways that NIH.gov does not: WebMD keeps users central by offering ways to personalize the experience such as the Symptom Checker. Multiple access points to health information reinforce that the intended audience is the lay information searcher.

The visuals further underscore contrasts: NIH.gov and WebMD feature occasional images of company employees or stock photos of people, but PLM incorporates far more (and real) representations of patients, contributing to the site's personal ethos. In addition, when clinical advancement is discussed, the NIH focuses on its value to patients, while PLM addresses patients not just as the beneficiaries of advances, but also as the agents.

PLM builds on the more expected credibility features for medical information, such as references to research studies and medical institutions, but also emphasizes the sincerity of the site creators and the experience of individual patients. Therefore, while PLM does not rely as heavily upon researcher or physician expertise, a longstanding contributor to the ethos of medical information, the organization does emphasize an unconventionally valued expertise—that of the patient, as evidenced by the predominance of patient testimonials and personal narrative. The employee profiles on NIH.gov and WebMD both emphasize credentials, polish, and accuracy, with the WebMD profiles showing a more personal side. PLM's profiles take the personal aspect a step further with informal language and visuals to present the company's co-founders as people to identify with.

On NIH.gov and WebMD, the main features on the homepage are the articles, implicitly communicating the websites' purpose as repositories of information. However, WebMD, in including communities, topics of broad interest, and interactive tools, serves as a hybrid site that encourages greater user engagement. Unlike NIH.gov and WebMD, PLM has no main menu to organize the site. Even the privacy discourse in each site highlights either more expertise-based or more community-based values. On the whole, PLM encourages user engagement, but not just as an added feature: Connection is the core of the site.

This analysis shows a range of e-health sites and the corresponding range of features used to construct a successful ethos. Unidirectional information sites like NIH.gov may represent the standard model for health information, positioning patients as consumers and projecting an official governmental, scientific ethos. As such, it may appeal to audiences who are more familiar or are more comfortable with the traditional doctor-patient hierarchy. WebMD, with its ethos of professional expertise balanced with user-friendliness, and PLM, with its personal, communal ethos, both display how some websites are starting to shift that structure. In the most interactive site, PLM, patients are constructed as active participants in a fight together, not only against disease, but against the established, slow, closed system of clinical research, and against a medical system that views patients as numbers rather than as people. This analysis shows how design elements, including opportunities to interact with the sites, along with discursive means of positioning the organization and the audience, can be included among the features that form a site's ethos.

FUTURE RESEARCH DIRECTIONS

While the preceding analysis highlights the broad range of strategies e-health sites can use to form a trustworthy ethos, a key dilemma remains: By opening up e-health to patient contributions in order to cultivate a communal ethos, an e-health organization may also open the doors to misinformation, scams, and trolls. Future research directions should examine both sides of the double-edged sword posed by the patient-participatory web.

For instance, future research might further explore how communal and personal features operate to induce trust in contexts beyond an e-health organization's homepage. As one example, studies could focus on the ethos strategies used in websites' actual medical content, to see how a range of e-health sites communicate the credibility of their information at a deeper level. In addition, future research on how informational and interactive e-health sites cultivate ethos not only within their websites, but also within their social media presence as a whole, could illuminate the ways that sites are moving towards greater interactivity.

In addition, rhetorical analysis can only account for how rhetoric operates in the text—it does not provide direct access to authors' motives or character, or audiences' perceptions. Future research could incorporate methods such as interviews, usability tests, or surveys to provide better insights into the effect of the persuasive strategies revealed by rhetorical analysis. Additional methods could also better explore solutions to the problem of misinformation on the web.

Finally, one theoretical implication of this research is the value of incorporating scholarly work on trust, from fields like human-computer interaction or psychology, into rhetorical understandings of e-health. Bringing this scholarship together provides a more robust understanding of how trust is established persuasively online. Future research should further address rhetorical perspectives on trust.

CONCLUSION

This chapter has focused on how e-health organizations construct ethos in their homepages and other promotional webpages as a means of inspiring trust. Comparing informational to interactive sites shows a range of successful strategies, some of which align with—and others which diverge from—traditional criteria for credible medical information. NIH.gov and WebMD's ethos of expertise is in line with how medical information has long been transmitted according to a standard doctor-patient hierarchy, with experts sharing information unidirectionally with patients. On the other hand, PLM and, to a lesser degree, WebMD demonstrate how some sites are positioning patients as active participants. These newer e-health sites display the role of the patient voice in forming an organizational ethos. As the patient-participatory web grows, the construction of the audience—as recipients of expert information, as active participants in healthcare, or anywhere in between—may become a more salient factor in e-health organizations' ethos.

These findings have implications for the design and evaluation of trustworthy e-health communication. For health writers, web designers, and the rhetoric and writing instructors preparing students for these jobs, knowledge of the features that promote trust is essential. Legitimate health organizations need to know how to make their websites stand out amid false, misguided, or incomplete medical information. Of course, many patients deliberately seek out official, expert, information-based sites already, because these patients trust that kind of information. Often, users find both expertise and social elements to be persuasive in e-health (Hu and Sundar, 2010). Therefore, there is no evidence that such sites will or should go away.

However, according to this study's findings, e-health sites of all types seem to be growing towards the social, even if only in constrained ways (e.g., NIH.gov links to social media). Patient-participatory sites like PLM and, to a lesser extent, WebMD enable sharing and information exchange in even more complex ways that patients seem to value. Therefore, the persuasiveness of patient experience might be leveraged in addition to more traditional credibility strategies that emphasize physician expertise. Returning to Miller's (2003) argument, an ethos consisting strictly of expertise limits trust.

To grasp the import of this argument, picture a governmental website attempting to get the word out about vaccines. Recalling studies addressed earlier such as Neubaum and Krämer (2015) and Grant et al. (2015), in which lay and institutional health websites were compared, we know that patients can find person-centered health websites to be trustworthy (along with, or at times in contrast to, professional sites). Studies that assess e-health websites only on the basis of their quality and accuracy do not reveal much about *why* patients trust the information, good or bad; rhetorical perspectives can help to do that. This is not to say that accuracy of information and the underlying character of an e-health organization are not important. However, because neither patients nor rhetorical scholars can fully measure medical accuracy, exploring the factors that do lead to trusting the delivery of that information is essential.

As numerous trust researchers have found (e.g., Fogg & Tseng, 1999; Sillence & Briggs, 2015), users may reject or trust websites quickly based on first impressions of design and content. A site's ethos, or projection of its character and trustworthiness, is a user's first step in choosing to trust an organization more deeply; as such, it is important to understand ethos elements that stand out. Physicians and officials concerned with misinformation online have often been interested in driving users away from potentially harmful websites. Instead, to promote good quality information, web designers for e-health might take cues from what actually seems to work in terms of trust.

At a practical level, class activities for first-year writing, technical and professional writing, or medical writing can help students develop a sense of the rhetorical complexity of ethos in e-health. As health and medical writing grows as a subfield within technical and professional communication, greater attention to health writing in digital formats such as websites is crucial. Students can evaluate ethos, looking at a continuum of websites as analyzed in this chapter. For students training for such careers, rhetorically analyzing different types of e-health websites could reveal variation in tone, visuals, interactivity, audience positioning, purpose, and context.

As mentioned above, the carefully formed ethos of an e-health site does not always align with the actual quality of health information within the site. Instructors can cultivate a critical stance towards e-health sites in students, possibly by assigning an analysis of sites with varying degrees of reliability, such as MayoClinic.org and RYTHospital.com. The latter is persuasively designed to look legitimate, but it is a known hoax. A goal of this activity would be for students to see how the false site strategically replicates some elements of a credible site—a fake physical address, a photo of the president, a contact form, and references to medical doctors—for the purpose of deception. Instructors might talk about how those first impressions can serve as a valuable heuristic for credibility assessment, but that they are not foolproof. Critical activities like this can be a jumping off point for deeper discussions of the ethical dimensions of writing and designing technical content. Indeed, students as well as scholars must continue to explore new ethical, rhetorical, and communal dimensions brought about by exciting shifts in the e-health landscape.

REFERENCES

Adams, S., & Berg, M. (2004). The nature of the Net: Constructing reliability of health information on the Web. *Information Technology & People, 17*(2), 150–170. doi:10.1108/09593840410542484

Apostel, S., & Folk, M. (Eds.). (2012). *Online Credibility and Digital Ethos: Evaluating Computer-Mediated Communication*. Hershey, PA: IGI Global.

Arduser, L. (2011). Warp and weft: Weaving the discussion threads of an online community. *Journal of Technical Writing and Communication, 41*(1), 5–31. doi:10.2190/TW.41.1.b

Aristotle, . (2007). *On rhetoric: A theory of civic discourse* (G. Kennedy, Trans.). Oxford, UK: Oxford University Press.

Bargh, J. A., & McKenna, K. Y. A. (2004). The Internet and social life. *Annual Review of Psychology, 55*(1), 573–590. doi:10.1146/annurev.psych.55.090902.141922 PMID:14744227

Beldad, A., de Jong, M., & Steehouder, M. (2010). How shall I trust the faceless and the intangible? A literature review on the antecedents of online trust. *Computers in Human Behavior, 26*(5), 857–869. doi:10.1016/j.chb.2010.03.013

Brock, K. (2012). Establishing ethos on proprietary and open source software websites. In M. Folk & S. Apostel (Eds.), *Online Credibility and Digital Ethos* (pp. 56–77). Hershey, PA: IGI Global.

Coney, M. B., & Steehouder, M. (2000). Role playing on the Web: Guidelines for designing and evaluating personas online. *Technical Communication (Washington)*, *47*(3), 327–340.

Eysenbach, G. (2001). What is e-health? *Journal of Medical Internet Research*, *3*(2), e20. doi:10.2196/jmir.3.2.e20 PMID:11720962

Eysenbach, G. (2008). Medicine 2.0: Social networking, collaboration, participation, apomediation, and openness. *Journal of Medical Internet Research*, *10*(3), e22. doi:10.2196/jmir.1030 PMID:18725354

Fogg, B. J. (2002). *Stanford guidelines for web credibility*. Retrieved from http://credibility.stanford.edu/guidelines/#chi00

Fogg, B. J., & Tseng, H. (1999). The elements of computer credibility. In Proceedings of the SIGCHI conference on Human Factors in Computing Systems (pp. 80–87). ACM. Retrieved from http://dl.acm.org/citation.cfm?id=303001

Fox, S., & Duggan, M. (2013). *Health Online 2013*. Washington, DC: Pew Internet and American Life Project. Retrieved from http://www.pewinternet.org/2013/01/15/health-online-2013/

Grant, L., Hausman, B. L., Cashion, M., Lucchesi, N., Patel, K., & Roberts, J. (2015). Vaccination persuasion online: A qualitative study of two provaccine and two vaccine-skeptical websites. *Journal of Medical Internet Research*, *17*(5), e133. doi:10.2196/jmir.4153 PMID:26024907

Gurak, L. J. (1997). *Persuasion and privacy in cyberspace: The online protests over Lotus Marketplace and the Clipper Chip*. New Haven, CT: Yale University Press.

Hajli, M. N., Sims, J., Featherman, M., & Love, P. E. D. (2015). Credibility of information in online communities. *Journal of Strategic Marketing*, *23*(3), 238–253. doi:10.1080/0965254X.2014.920904

Halloran, S. M. (1982). Aristotle's concept of ethos, or if not his somebody else's. *Rhetoric Review*, *1*(1), 58–63. doi:10.1080/07350198209359037

Hu, Y., & Sundar, S. S. (2010). Effects of online health sources on credibility and behavioral intentions. *Communication Research*, *37*(1), 105–132. doi:10.1177/0093650209351512

Hunt, K. (1996). Establishing a presence on the World Wide Web: A rhetorical approach. *Technical Communication (Washington)*, *43*(4), 376–387.

Kunst, H., Groot, D., Latthe, P. M., Latthe, M., & Khan, K. S. (2002). Accuracy of information on apparently credible websites: Survey of five common health topics. *BMJ: British Medical Journal*, *324*(7337), 581–582. doi:10.1136/bmj.324.7337.581 PMID:11884323

Mackiewicz, J. (2010). The co-construction of credibility in online product reviews. *Technical Communication Quarterly*, *19*(4), 403–426. doi:10.1080/10572252.2010.502091

Metzger, M. J., Flanagin, A. J., & Medders, R. B. (2010). Social and heuristic approaches to credibility evaluation online. *Journal of Communication*, *60*(3), 413–439. doi:10.1111/j.1460-2466.2010.01488.x

Meyer, E. (2012, June 12). Online networking a godsend for those with rare diseases. *Chicago Tribune*. Retrieved from http://articles.chicagotribune.com/2012-06-12/news/ct-met-medical-social-networking-20120612_1_rare-diseases-social-media-social-networks

Miller, C. R. (2003). The presumptions of expertise: The role of ethos in risk analysis. *Configurations*, *11*(2), 163–202. doi:10.1353/con.2004.0022

Moturu, S. T., Liu, H., & Johnson, W. G. (2008). *Trust evaluation in health information on the World Wide Web*. Vancouver, BC: Engineering in Medicine and Biology Society. doi:10.1109/IEMBS.2008.4649459

Neubaum, G., & Krämer, N. C. (2015). Let's blog about health! Exploring the persuasiveness of a personal HIV blog compared to an institutional HIV website. *Health Communication*, *30*(9), 872–883. doi:10.1080/10410236.2013.856742 PMID:24885514

NIH. (2014a). *About NIH*. Retrieved from http://nih.gov/about/

NIH. (2014b). *Biographical Sketch of Francis S. Collins, M.D., Ph.D*. Retrieved from http://nih.gov/about/director/directorbio.htm

NIH. (2014c). *Frequently Asked Questions*. Retrieved from http://nih.gov/about/FAQ.htm

NIH. (2014d). *Homepage*. Retrieved from http://nih.gov/

NIH. (2014e). *NIH Web Privacy Notice*. Retrieved from http://nih.gov/about/privacy.htm

PatientsLikeMe. (2014a). *About Us*. Retrieved from http://www.patientslikeme.com/about

PatientsLikeMe. (2014b). *Homepage*. Retrieved from www.patientslikeme.com

PatientsLikeMe. (2014c). *Openness Philosophy*. Retrieved from http://www.patientslikeme.com/about/openness

PatientsLikeMe. (2014d). *Our Team*. Retrieved from http://www.patientslikeme.com/about/team

PatientsLikeMe. (2014e). *Privacy Policy*. Retrieved from http://www.patientslikeme.com/about/privacy

Quintilian, . (2015). *Quintilian on the teaching of speaking and writing: Translations from books one, two, and ten of the Institutio Oratoria* (2nd ed.). (J. J. Murphy, Trans.). Carbondale, IL: SIU Press.

Rheingold, H. (2012, May 9). How to use the Internet wisely, for your health and your country's. *The Atlantic*. Retrieved from http://www.theatlantic.com/technology/archive/2012/05/how-to-use-the-internet-wisely-for-your-health-and-your-countrys/256898/

Sillence, E., & Briggs, P. (2015). Trust and engagement in online health: A timeline approach. In S. S. Sundar (Ed.), *The Handbook of the Psychology of Communication Technology* (pp. 469–487). Chichester, UK: Wiley Blackwell. doi:10.1002/9781118426456.ch21

Spoel, P. (2008). Communicating values, valuing community through health-care websites: Midwifery's online ethos and public communication in Ontario. *Technical Communication Quarterly*, *17*(3), 264–288. doi:10.1080/10572250802100360

Swan, M. (2009). Emerging patient-driven health care models: An examination of health social networks, consumer personalized medicine and quantified self-tracking. *International Journal of Environmental Research and Public Health*, *6*(2), 492–525. doi:10.3390/ijerph6020492 PMID:19440396

Swenson, J., Constantinides, H., & Gurak, L. J. (2002). Audience-driven Web design: An application to medical Web sites. *Technical Communication (Washington)*, *49*(3).

Sztompka, P. (1999). *Trust: A sociological theory*. Cambridge, UK: Cambridge University Press.

Top 15 Most Popular Health Websites. (2014, September). Retrieved from http://www.ebizmba.com/articles/health-websites

Wang, Y. D., & Emurian, H. H. (2005). An overview of online trust: Concepts, elements, and implications. *Computers in Human Behavior*, *21*(1), 105–125. doi:10.1016/j.chb.2003.11.008

Warnick, B. (2005). Looking to the future: Electronic texts and the deepening interface. *Technical Communication Quarterly*, *14*(3), 327–333. doi:10.1207/s15427625tcq1403_11

Warnick, B. (2007). *Rhetoric online: Persuasion and politics on the World Wide Web* (Vol. 12). New York, NY: Peter Lang.

Wathen, C. N., & Burkell, J. (2002). Believe it or not: Factors influencing credibility on the Web. *Journal of the American Society for Information Science and Technology*, *53*(2), 134–144. doi:10.1002/asi.10016

WebMD. (2014a). *About WebMD*. Retrieved from http://www.webmd.com/about-webmd-policies/default.htm?ss=ftr

WebMD. (2014b). *Homepage*. Retrieved from http://www.webmd.com/

WebMD (2014c). *Privacy Policy*. Retrieved from http://www.webmd.com/about-webmd-policies/about-privacy-policy?ss=ftr

WebMD (2014d). *Who We Are*. Retrieved from http://www.webmd.com/about-webmd-policies/about-who-we-are

KEY TERMS AND DEFINITIONS

E-Health: Online health and medical information or services.

Ethos: A rhetor's projection of their character and credibility for the purpose of gaining trust.

Health Information Sharing Website: A website where patients share medical data for crowdsourcing cures and treatments.

Informational Website: A website whose primary purpose is to convey information unidirectionally.

Interactive Website: A website whose primary purpose is to facilitate user engagement and contribution.

Patient-Participatory Web: The participatory web for patients; online spaces where patients can interact and contribute e-health information.

Social Presence Cues: Features of a website that signal a connection to a real person or location.

Third-Party Seals: Seals included on websites that indicate a third party's evaluation or validation of the site in areas such as privacy protection and information quality.

Trust: The goal of ethos; a confident belief in another's reliability or credibility to the extent that one would act on that belief.

Chapter 6
Adopting a Parasocial Connection to Overcome Professional Kakoethos in Online Health Information

Andrew W. Cole
Waukesha County Technical College, USA

Thomas A. Salek
University of Wisconsin-Stevens Point, USA

ABSTRACT

This chapter approaches online ethos rhetorically to argue that professional medical sources (e.g., practitioners, organizations) must overcome a rhetorically constituted kakoethos in order to influence online health information seekers. Professional medical source kakoethos is established through a lack of identified, authentic personal experience with specific medical conditions, and health information message content that focuses exclusively on the science behind the condition. Conversely, lay health information sources fashion ethos through identifying personal experience with specific medical conditions, and employing emotionally supportive messages. The result is an online health rhetoric appearing credible and authentic. Rhetorically crafting a parasocial connection to online health information seekers may offer a means for professional medical sources to overcome the kakoethos established through lack of personal experience.

INTRODUCTION

The Internet has changed how individuals interact with health information. Online health information seekers can easily find themselves overwhelmed with health messages from a vast number of potential sources. For better or for worse, the massive amount—and instantaneous availability—of health information available online can provide individuals with a swift avenue to self-diagnose. Findings from the Pew Research Center (Fox & Duggan, 2013) suggested that approximately three-fourths of Internet users

DOI: 10.4018/978-1-5225-1072-7.ch006

search for health information online. Over half of those users reported searching for health information to assist in determining a medical diagnosis, either for themselves or for a close other, such as a friend or family member.

Whether accessing symptom checkers to make a self-diagnosis, considering the health advice embedded within friends' posts on social media, or reading emotionally supportive posts on online support discussion boards, individuals are bombarded by health messages online. The wide array of online health information sources problematizes traditional notions of expertise and credibility when it comes to health information and advice messages. In order to increase influence on online health information seekers, professional medical sources (e.g., practitioners, organizations) must overcome the *kakoethos* or *"anti-ethos"* (Johnson, 2010) constructed in professional medical online health information. *Kakoethos* can be fashioned through a lack of authentic, personal experience with the particular medical condition, as well as a rhetoric that focuses exclusively on the science behind a medical condition without including any elements of emotional support. Creating a parasocial connection between professional medical sources and online health information seekers may offer a means to overcome the *kakoethos* constructed in much online health information provided by professional medical sources.

This chapter differentiates how *ethos* and *kakoethos* are crafted and maintained in the rhetoric of online health information. Analyses of lay and professional medical online health information concerning Multiple Sclerosis (MS) are presented to provide further insight into how *ethos* and *kakoethos* are rhetorically constituted in online health information. As a multitude of information on the condition from both lay and professional sources is available online, MS serves as an appropriate topic in which to rhetorically examine online health information. Using previous rhetorical and social science research, as well as the MS examples analyzed within, the chapter contends that a rhetorically grounded parasocial connection may offer professional medical sources a way to counteract the *kakoethos* constructed in their rhetoric. Through examples of medical health professional websites, as well as lay health information sources, this chapter offers case studies about how *kakoethos* can be overcome through personalized rhetoric. Similarly, this chapter diagnoses that an ill of many professional online health information sites is rhetoric that lacks personal experience with specific conditions. Offering this kind of personalized rhetoric alongside professional medical advice can help practitioners build a sense of shared identity, which can enhance their general *ethos* or credibility.

BACKGROUND

A conception of *ethos* as credibility is challenged by the (seemingly) anonymous online environment. Frobish (2013) suggested that classic notions of *ethos* may no longer apply to the online environment because *digital ethos* suggests that the notion of credibility may be "freed," or more fluid, in the online environment. However, this chapter contends that Aristotle's (2007) artistic and inartistic proofs can still aid in conceptualizing and understanding *ethos* in online health information messages. Artistic proofs concern the dimensions discursively constructed in a text. Conversely, inartistic proofs address elements extrinsic to the text itself. In order to understand credibility in the online environment, the intrinsic (i.e., that which is available to an audience discursively within a text) must be distinguished from the extrinsic (i.e., that which is the subject position of the text's author). More specifically, as such expertise solely represents inartistic proof, a traditional medical credibility arising from expert power (see French & Raven, 1959), when divorced from the professional setting of a physical medical space (i.e., a doctor's office), may not necessarily have the same influence to persuade online health information seekers.

In a hyper-mediated public sphere, online health information seekers find themselves bombarded with cascading levels of health information from a staggering amount of potential sources. Gilewicz and Allard-Huver (2013) suggested that construction of *ethos* in online spaces depends on a balance between the anonymity present in the online environment and the traditionally "transparent" nature of public discourse. Alongside authoritative medical websites such as the Mayo Clinic or WebMD.com, a variety of other potential lay health information sources exist. Therefore, in the context of online health information, the notion of an *online* ethos moves beyond visual anonymity and into the midst of a rhetorical dilemma, where the quality of content within a health information message alone does not determine its credibility or influence. As seen in the large variety of lay health sources providing health information online through avenues such as blogs, discussion forums, and YouTube videos, providing scientifically accurate medical information alone is not enough to encourage health information seekers to "buy in" and modify health behaviors or make health decisions.

In terms of artistic proofs, different online health information messages each constitute different texts, with some sense of *ethos* built discursively in the content. This chapter argues that the artistic (intrinsic) elements of online health information provided from professional medical sources often construct a *kakoethos,* or a type of "anti-ethos" (Johnson, 2010), which serves to diminish the health information's potential influence. Building from a framework established by Quackenbush (2011), Salek (2014) explained that *kakoethos* could limit a rhetor's potential persuasiveness to audiences. However, Salek advised that a rhetor could rhetorically address and overcome *kakoethos* by speaking "both as and of…a discrediting trait" (p. 178) or using discourse that appears to be based in personal experience and subject matter expertise. For online health professionals, ignoring the *kakoethos* rhetorically constructed in messages, or otherwise dismissing its importance while continuing to focus exclusively on providing scientifically accurate information, may limit the persuasive potential of the online health information provided. To advance this chapter's argument, the next section is grounded in findings from previous research on health information, social support, and source credibility to illustrate how online health information seekers often privilege the emotionally supportive elements present in much online lay health information.

MAIN FOCUS OF THE CHAPTER

Before relating *ethos* and *kakoethos* to specific instances of online professional medical and lay health information rhetoric, a framework for understanding health information seekers' relationships with online health information is needed. The way that online users interact with online health information can be understood through Williams's (2003) notion of "flow." Although Williams applied flow to television, this chapter applies flow to the online environment, where the boundaries between different technologies (i.e., computers, smartphones, tablets) continue to blur. Williams contended that a personal medium, such as television, facilitates a process whereby viewers allow the images to flow by them. The process amalgamates information provided by different sources, with viewers incorporating information gained from various sources together. More specifically, according to Williams, television viewers blend the content of a specific show with information from advertisements embedded within the show. In essence, the messages' content from both contexts, though unrelated in substance, "flows" together.

Just as television viewers may not necessarily remember a specific show, but instead the sequence in which it appeared (i.e. the show, commercials, placement to the next show), online health information seekers may easily and quickly move from hyperlink to hyperlink, and source to source, without later remembering specifically where they got specific information, and the specific sources from which they received information. Health information seekers' interactions with online health information often involve "Googling" and following hyperlinks from one article to the next with varying degrees of information content, quality, and trust in any given source (Buis & Carpenter, 2009; Hu & Haake, 2010; Kwon, Kye, Park, Oh, & Park, 2015). However, as online health information seekers move from one site to another, they do not necessarily process the health information they receive in its authentic context. As health information seekers navigate between online health sources, they may completely lose track as to what information they received from professional medical sources (e.g., Mayo Clinic), and what information they received from lay sources, (e.g., personal YouTube videos). Considering Williams's (2003) notion of flow, such information is digested through the sequence of clicks.

As online health information seekers process the information they encounter, they make judgments about the information value. All discourses are subject to evaluative judgments based not only on power, but also are granted power through reinforcement based on quantity, not necessarily overall quality. Burke (1969) noted that persuasion can happen in part due to the number of times that one is exposed to a discourse. In other words, a health message's referential power (see French & Raven, 1959) to an online health information seeker grants power to its persuasive appeal. Accumulating seemingly personalized messages helps serve as "visual labor" to help increase the persuasiveness of a message (Tatarchevskiy, 2011). The more a particular discourse is seen by a health information seeker, as well as how personally and emotionally connected the individual is to the message, the more likely it is to impact the message's persuasive potential. Burke labeled the process through which humans process and grant power to discourses as "identification." For Burke, identification occurs when human agents coalesce around a rhetorical act, using its intrinsic content and a human's extrinsic situation as motivation for future acts. Professional medical sources, therefore, are tasked with providing not only medically accurate health information, but information that stands out among the vast amount of online health information messages online.

The online environment allows cascading forms of communication to spread rapidly across social networks. Contrary to the face-to-face (FtF) communication exchanges in traditional physician-patient office settings, much online health information does not necessarily represent professional medical opinions. The relationship between health information and a health information seeker's use of such information therefore may lay in the power of health discourses and the degree to which an individual identifies with the discourse. In an analysis of Facebook posts concerning the Egyptian revolution, Gamie (2013) argued that a "communal" *ethos* can be built through shared identity. A communal identity based in experience with a particular heath condition and fashioned through emotionally supportive lay health information messages can help explain how online health information seekers coalesce around information that could even run counter to the health information and advice available from professional medical sources.

Social Support

Social support describes messages offering information with a personal connection by a sender and an emotional connection with that information by a receiver. Individuals typically provide social support in response to perceptions that another individual is troubled (Goldsmith, 2004). Communication researchers generally divide social support into three distinct categories: emotional support, informational support, and tangible support (Burleson, 2003; Goldsmith, 2004; Thoits, 2011). Emotional support includes messages of care and empathy (e.g., listening). Informational support includes messages containing information (e.g., giving advice). Tangible support concerns the ability to materially assist another (e.g., providing financial assistance). Empirical research suggests that these three support categorizations carry over to the online environment in addition to FtF (Blight, Jagiello, & Ruppel, 2015). A rhetorical understanding of social support provides insight into cultivating identification, and ultimately, a parasocial connection. Goldsmith (2004) explained that a rhetorical approach to social support examines how situations "can shape and constrain what is likely to be effective but also recognizes the ways in which language shapes and constrains how we see a situation and what we see as relevant within a situation" (p. 50). The rhetorical challenge for professional medical sources is providing health information that balances accurate medical information with support for a health information seeker's emotional needs.

Though communicating social support is commonly associated with close others such as friends and family (see Goldsmith, 2004), medical professionals are also often tasked with providing support to patients and families as part of their duties. Professional caregivers, in particular, often find themselves providing support to patients and their families. In one study, Stone (2013) interviewed nursing staff working with individuals and families experiencing Alzheimer's disease. In Stone's qualitative analysis, professional caregivers felt challenged by attempting to balance the need to provide accurate health information alongside the need to support patients and their families emotionally. Stone's participants often reported struggling with providing information to patients' families in a way that was accurate but did not discourage family members from maintaining hope about the condition of their loved ones. The interpersonal challenge faced by the medical professionals in Stone's research challenges professional medical sources providing health information online as well. Of particular importance in the online environment is establishing credibility.

Source Credibility

The overwhelming number of health information sources online leads to a situation where the veracity and quality of information is not always clear. Though Williams's (2003) notion of "flow" suggests that health information seekers may not always remember the exact source from which they receive information, how they process the credibility of the information they receive might influence the information they use in health decision-making. Further complicating matters, individual identity in the online environment is not based in absolute certainty. Jordan (2005) argued that online identity is a rhetorical exercise between author, text, and audience. In other words, a text's authenticity and credibility, *and* a rhetor's identity and credibility, is constructed through the interaction of online user and text. Recognizing the information source as credible constitutes a rhetorical exercise between both the artistic qualities intrinsic to the text and the inartistic, or extrinsic, elements of the source.

Though the interaction between an online health information seeker and an online text's content is a rhetorical exercise, the online health information in itself is also a rhetorical exercise. Although online health information available on websites such as WebMD or the Mayo Clinic's website may provide evidence-based medical information with citations to outside scholarly sources, information also becomes credible, and potentially persuasive, through a process that privileges one idea over another. For example, in analyzing a Twitter "controversy," Salek (2015) described the creation of a para-context. A para-context, according to Salek, describes the mere existence of an online discourse disconnected to widely acknowledged and accepted facts. Thus, Salek argued that online information often exists in a para-context where the accumulation of information, the reposting of this information, and phatic gestures such as "likes" on Facebook or "retweets" on Twitter generate an appearance of information credibility, and even wide-scale acceptance, that may run counter to offline reality. The para-context may well contain facts, but the credibility of the information lies in the accumulation of information, including phatic responses, rather than the factual accuracy of the information. In this regard, perceptions of the information in a para-context are rooted more in the presence of information and the social weight given to the information through phatic responses, rather than the quality and accuracy of its overall content.

The understanding of online para-contexts outlined above provides insight into how online health information seekers may process source credibility in the online environment. Grant and colleagues (2015) conducted a study comparing websites that supported vaccination use ("provaccine websites") and websites that advocated against the use of vaccines (anti-vaccination, or "vaccine-skeptic websites"). The researchers found that the websites supporting vaccines, primarily government or professional medical organization websites, focused exclusively on providing scientific and evidence-based information on vaccines. These provaccine websites also offered very little hyperlinking to outside sources and offered no opportunity for online health information seekers to comment on, or otherwise engage in, the content provided on the site. The researchers suggested that such a uni-directional format for health communication messages can result in "an image of unsympathetic authoritarians who only care about well-being at the level of the public instead of at the level of the individual" (p. 16). Conversely, the researchers found that the "vaccine-skeptical" websites relied heavily on the information provided by communities of online users who shared personal experiences with vaccines. Rather than directly counter the types of medical claims that professional medical sources on the topic might use, the "vaccine-skeptical" sites instead focused on countering the credibility of science-based messages and professional medical sources, more generally, and they privileged individualized personal experiences with vaccines. The contrasting rhetorical approaches present in Grant et al.'s research demonstrate well how lay health sources and professional medicals cast *ethos* differently in the online environment.

Lay Health Source *Ethos*

As evidenced by Grant et al.'s (2015) study, an online para-context can be observed in how lay health information sources face fewer rhetorical obstacles than professional medical sources when communicating about health and providing social support. Because lay health sources do not necessarily represent scientifically accurate medical opinions, usually relying on personal experiences instead, they have much more flexibility than professional medical sources to address the audience's emotional needs. It is therefore not surprising that previous empirical research supports lay health sources as influential in health information-seeking and decision-making (Chiu & Hsieh, 2012; Frohlich & Zmyslinski-Seelig, 2012). Like professional medical sources, lay health sources provide informational support. However, unlike professional medical sources, lay sources are not constrained by the need to balance an accurate presentation of medical information with the emotional needs of the audience. Frohlich and Zmyslinski-Seelig (2012) conducted a study examining YouTube comments on videos about inflammatory bowel disease and ostomies. The researchers found that YouTube user comments posted in response to lay videos on the topic contained as much as five times the amount of emotional support than could be found in comments on professional videos on the same topic. Such findings suggest that contrary to the primarily scientific information-based messages of professional medical sources, lay health sources can fashion primarily emotionally supportive messages that still contain kernels of health information.

One reason lay health information may influence online health information seekers lies in the sense of credibility established only though the authenticity derived from personal experience with a specific medical condition. Online lay health information sources providing information forged from personal experience rhetorically establish *ethos* when providing personal anecdotes and giving health advice based on previous personal experiences. Such examples help to rhetorically construct what Dubrofsky and Wood (2014) explained as the "call to authenticity," which establishes a more "natural-seeming" inter-personal tone (p. 282). For Dubrofsky and Wood, an authentic or personalized discourse is constructed rhetorically through artistic proofs, and this "call-to-authenticity" can be leveraged to build credibility. Further, Banet-Weiser (2012) stressed that authenticity can be a deliberate rhetorical strategy available to those wishing to create a non-commercialized discourse.

Previous research in online support groups supports the notion that, though support messages from lay sources often provide emotional support as a primary goal, they provide informational support as well. Donovan, LeFebvre, Tardif, Brown, and Love (2014) analyzed discussion posts in an online support group for young cancer survivors. The researchers found many individuals expressing high levels of uncertainty in their posts. They further found that individuals who expressed higher levels of uncertainty were more apt to receive messages containing informational support, such as directive advice, in response from members of the online community. More than three-fourths of the responses, even those containing emotionally supportive elements, contained some form of informational support. Supporting the potential persuasive power of the "call to authenticity" (Dubrofsky & Wood, 2014), individuals who posted messages of informational support often featured information rooted in their own personal experiences.

For this chapter, a search was conducted for an online MS support group to examine messages posted on the site. One website ("Multiple Sclerosis (MS) Support Group", 2012) served as an example of a website offering health information and support not directly originating from a professional medical source. The forum's purpose as an information source appeared specifically in the text, which described itself as providing users with "free, anonymous support from *people just like you*" (emphasis added). The website offered a basic overview of MS symptoms and treatments, as well as a series of message boards allowing individuals to interact with each other. The community message boards, which were still active at the time of this writing, provided individuals the opportunity to post questions and provide answers on topics ranging from which medicines can be successfully used to treat MS symptoms, and what lifestyle changes individuals made following MS diagnoses.

Many discussion board questions observed for this analysis asked the community whether others were currently experiencing, or had ever experienced, the symptoms that the poster was currently experiencing. Other users would then post affirming responses attesting to the normalcy of the symptoms. In response to such posts seeking reassurance as to whether particular symptoms were "normal," other users would post confirming statements such as, "That is one of my most common symptoms." On one level, these confirming messages addressed the normalcy of symptoms to rhetorically counteract messages received as part of a medical diagnosis that can make individuals feel as though they are no longer "normal" (Hayden, 1993; Parsloe, 2015). Responses such as those posted in the support group message board acted to rhetorically normalize the experience associated with the symptom within the context of the group and foster a shared identity through reconstructing the individual as "normal" in relation to the group.

Text-based online message boards offer one avenue in which to receive lay health information, but online videos, prevalent on websites such as YouTube, represent another common source of online lay health information. YouTube videos, in particular, offer potential for reciprocal social support avenues because the videos themselves can offer supportive messages toward an audience, and audience members can post supporting comments toward the person (or persons) featured in the video. YouTube videos providing health information are very common. For this chapter, a YouTube search for "multiple sclerosis" returned over 120,000 videos. Some videos consisted of professional educational videos made by hospitals and health organizations, while other videos featured laypeople speaking about personal experiences directly into a webcam or camera. The first page of search results offered a video, occurring as part of a series of weekly videos (Schuplin, 2014a; Schuplin, 2014b; Schuplin, 2014c), by an individual describing the progression of MS symptoms that seemed to represent the types of lay health discourses described above [e.g., Dubrofsky and Wood's (2014) "call to authenticity"].

As part of the weekly video series, the speaker outlined several key symptoms of MS, detailed the impacts of MS on her life, and described specific experiences with medical professionals she encountered since first experiencing symptoms. In the description section of each of the videos, the following disclaimer was posted: "*NOTE* I am NOT a doctor! I am sharing my experiences with you because having MS can be incredibly overwhelming." Although using personal experience with MS as the basis for the information in the videos, she directly informed the audience that the videos are meant to be informational, but primarily as a means of social support. Each of the videos has a common interpersonal quality that begins with candid speech to the camera enthusiastically greeting viewers of the video. The videos provided information about MS, specifically on how the condition progresses, but did so completely through the use of personal examples and anecdotes.

To connect with online health information seekers interpersonally, the speaker frequently referenced her desire to help others feel empowered about their condition. She further announced her goal as assisting others with MS in getting out of "limbo," so that they could better understand what is happening with their bodies and thereby share experiences via an online support system. In addition to talking about her personal experience with symptoms of MS, the speaker connected with the audience interpersonally through self-disclosure of information about her personal life, including how she ultimately realized the cause of her symptoms by conducting web searches. Although visits with physicians and information gleaned from professional medical sources are mentioned throughout the video series, the speaker's credibility in the videos appeared to be based primarily on her personal experiences and the interpersonal rapport she established with the audience through a conversational tone and the frank communication of personal experiences.

The speaker further warned those watching the video about the possibility that physicians and family members may not understand the reality of how somebody experiences MS symptoms. Such comments exemplify how *ethos* can be established through personal experience. The personal narrative in the videos provided health information seekers an informal, yet informative, explanation of the symptoms and effects of MS, as well as how to positively understand and re-frame interactions with others. As a whole, the videos' primary focus appeared to be on understanding symptoms, rather than scientific explanations of what MS does to the body. The speaker's *ethos* is constructed not only through personal experiences with the physical pain associated with MS, but also through identification with audience members rooted in the emotional struggle that individuals diagnosed with the condition must come to terms with.

Professional Health Source *Kakoethos*

The rhetoric of professional medical sources appears to construct credibility differently than in the lay social support message boards or YouTube videos discussed above. In contrast to the anecdotal, personal experience-oriented, and socially supportive approach adopted by the lay online health information sources described above, the messages provided by professional medical sources are often devoid of emotionally supportive elements. This rhetoric, though highly credible and communicating authoritative, scientifically accurate health information, may not influence online medical information seekers' health behaviors. In a study targeting online health information-seeking behaviors in the context of HIV, Neubaum and Krämer (2015) examined a "person-centered" lay blog on HIV and a "non-person-centered" institutionally affiliated HIV blog. They found that participants largely considered the institutionally affiliated blog more credible, and yet still reported higher levels of self-efficacy in relation to the diagnosis after reading the lay blog. The personalized messages from lay sources may make understanding conditions, and ultimately the process of health decision-making, more accessible than the generally information-based rhetoric of professional medical sources.

The rhetorical challenge for medical professionals in online and FtF settings thus becomes providing medically accurate health information while maintaining an apt online "bedside manner" in a rhetorical sense. One example, WebMD's (2015)*Multiple Sclerosis Health Center*, stated the following:

People with multiple sclerosis (MS) tend to have their first symptoms between the ages of 20 and 40. Usually the symptoms get better, but then come back. Some may come and go, while others linger. Keep track of your symptoms to help your doctor know whether MS or another condition is to blame. (n.p.)

In the above example, the audience is rhetorically constructed as symptomatic of MS through phrases such as "your symptoms" and "your doctor." Such rhetoric contrasts previous research on health information-seeking behaviors that suggested online health information seekers are often motivated more by fears of potential illness than from current health status (Baumgartner & Hartmann, 2011). However, the above example rhetorically constructs the uncertainty as to whether MS or another condition was present in the audience, not whether or not a medical condition was present at all. If an individual was considering whether or not to seek medical advice, a disconnected and potentially fear-inducing rhetoric could lead to potentially negative responses such as defensively avoiding future messages on the topic (Witte & Allen, 2000). Despite an accompanying disclaimer that the site did not diagnose illnesses, the audience was rhetorically constructed by the text as having the condition. If such a diagnosis were delivered interpersonally, some level of social support would likely have been provided by a professional caregiver. However, despite the rhetorical construction of diagnosis by the online text, no immediate elements of emotional support accompanied the informational discourse.

A similar rhetorical approach was found in an example appearing on the Mayo Clinic's website. A webpage attributed to Mayo Clinic Staff (2015) offered approaches to addressing symptoms of MS, including general health management techniques. However, the page also informed visitors of the importance of "Coping and support." The "Coping and support" section of the webpage explained that "Living with any chronic illness can be difficult," and further suggests that the audience "Maintain normal activities as best you can; Stay connected to friends and family; Continue to pursue hobbies that you enjoy and are able to do; Contact a support group, for yourself or for family members; Discuss your feelings and concerns about living with MS with your doctor or a counselor." The discourse of the web page first rhetorically dissociated the personal nature of living with the specific condition of MS (e.g., "living with any chronic illness can be difficult"), but then personalized the suggestions for coping with the condition. Such rhetoric appears in contrast to the rhetoric of lay support message board posts, which largely served to reconstruct users as "normal" in relation to the shared group identity. Instead, the suggested items under "Coping and support" ranged from "othering" the audience with appeals to outside perceptions of normalcy (e.g., "Maintain normal activities as best you can"), to rhetorically re-casting focus to others impacted by the individual's condition (e.g., "Contact a support group, for yourself or for family members.").

As detailed in Grant et al.'s (2015) comparison between vaccination websites, professional medical online health information often appears as rhetor-centered, rather than audience-centered. In a video found on the Mayo Clinic website (Keegan, 2015), the speaker explained the science behind progressive MS and the escalating symptoms that those with MS can expect to experience. In contrast to the lay YouTube video series described above, however, the Mayo Clinic website video featured no greeting, closing, or other means of interpersonal connection to the audience. In terms of information quality and ease of use, the video likely offered website visitors a valuable guide to understanding MS. However, the authority figure (i.e., medical doctor) explained the causes and symptoms of MS through a technical and solely informative rhetoric devoid of interpersonal connection and emotionally supportive elements. Though the speaker may be highly credible and the health information very scientifically accurate, the technical, disconnected rhetoric provided may impact health information seekers' likelihood to be influenced by the messages. Therefore, despite a basis in accurate medical knowledge, the rhetoric itself casts a *kakoethos,* in terms of inartistic and artistic proofs, toward the targeted audience due to its dissociation from the personal experience of the condition and the formal, informative tone.

SOLUTIONS AND RECOMMENDATIONS

The rhetorical approach outlined throughout this chapter suggests that the *kakoethos* constituted in the rhetoric of professional medical sources can be addressed through identifying a lack of personal experience, then building a parasocial connection to online health information seekers. Instead of viewing each body as a unique, personal construct, professional medical rhetoric that focuses only on the science of the medical condition and breaks the body down into mechanical component parts that fail, re-affirms audience members as not "normal" in the very way that the rhetoric of lay health information appears to counteract. Professional medical rhetoric such as the examples detailed above further remove the individual from the discussion on the condition being experienced. Without the opportunity to engage an online community and have personal experiences and symptoms affirmed by similar others, such rhetoric can construct the audience as voyeurs who are only able to sit outside the discourse and watch experts discuss the conditions they experience with almost no ability to enter into the conversation (Cole & Salek, 2014). As a result of this kind of rhetorical positioning, audience members are distanced from the professional medical rhetoric and may feel less like informed patients or consumers, and more like the targets of a discourse about a debilitating medical condition.

Though the *kakoethos* constructed by professional medical rhetoric described above may negatively impact professional medical sources' influence on health information seekers, Salek (2014) argued that *kakoethos* can be overcome. In order to improve the chances of influencing online health information seekers' health behaviors and decision-making, professional medical sources can rhetorically address, and overcome, *kakoethos* by identifying professional experience treating specific conditions, acknowledging a lack of direct personal experience with the specific condition, and inviting the audience into the discourse. To that end, the messages sent by professional medical sources should move beyond scientific accuracy alone to recognize the individual humanity of the audience as well. For example, the rhetoric of professional medical sources could employ emotionally supportive elements similar to those in lay health information messages. Once the *kakoethos* crafted through the lack of personal experience with the condition is addressed, professional medical sources can work toward building *ethos* through forging a rhetorically constructed interpersonal connection and inviting online health information seeker feedback and participation.

It may be impossible to temper the flow of health information in the clickable online environment, but professional medical sources can take steps to ground the legitimacy and suasory potential of their rhetoric by leveraging authoritative, scientifically accurate information with personal experience, humanizing elements of interpersonal social support, and providing online health information seekers the opportunity to provide feedback. Identification, persuasion, and trust likely work together through rhetoric based in an individual's personal connection to the message content, particularly when something as personally relevant as individual health is involved. French and Raven (1959) noted the persuasive appeal of referent power, or the ability for individuals to be influenced through identification with another person. As previously suggested, identification with discourse is based in a nexus of intrinsic and extrinsic factors. Despite the numerous reasons for trusting the expert opinion of a physician or other professional medical source, individuals evaluate the veracity and usefulness of health information due to a personal connection to the discourse, as well as the presence of this type of discourse across multiple health sources. Creating a parasocial connection to audience members through online health rhetoric, therefore, could become a key part of professional medical online health information.

Previous research suggests that a parasocial connection could be built between a professional medical source with scientifically accurate information and online health information seekers. A parasocial connection can be described as a mediated relationship, forged by mass communication, that incorporates psychologically beneficial elements present in FtF interpersonal relationships (Rubin & Rubin, 1985; Rubin & McHugh, 1987). Horton and Wohl (1956) first identified a theory of parasocial relationships with mass media characters, and they noted that parasocial connections between audience members and the characters served similar purposes—and offered similar benefits—to FtF interpersonal communication.

Parasocial connections can even influence audience members' beliefs. Schiappa, Gregg and Hewes (2005) charted a correlation between parasocial communication and changes in individuals' attitudes and beliefs. Examining parasocial communication and audiences' relationships with television programs and celebrities, Schiappa et al., noted that humans develop interpersonal feelings and connections to fictional characters and celebrities. Returning to French and Raven's (1959) conception of referent power, such parasocial connections could potentially influence audience members without the source ever becoming aware.

The online environment further potentially fosters parasocial connections because the "characters," though not interpersonally acquainted with the audience, are not fictional. Specifically, in the online environment, Marshall (2010) examined the parasocial connection constructed between celebrities and fans through celebrities' social media use. Marshall argued that celebrities capitalize on social media's interpersonal nature to increase social capital and forge a stronger presence in the public sphere. Marshall contended that a "parasocial interpersonal" pathway that offers audience members an appearance of celebrity authenticity has become a vital aspect of contemporary celebrity culture. He explained that, "The parasocial self is a pragmatic understanding that it is impossible to communicate individually with thousands and millions; and yet in this shifted on-line culture some effort has to be made" (p. 43). A similar understanding of parasocial relationships can therefore contribute toward developing *ethos* in professional medical online health information.

As demonstrated in the above analysis, scientifically accurate medical information that relies solely on the science to convey a message tends to lack emotionally supportive elements. Such rhetoric lacks the shared identity enacted by online lay health information and reinforces notions the individual with the condition seeking such information is not "normal." A rhetorically constructed interpersonal connection offers a potential avenue to break through the *kakoethos* fashioned in the traditionally disconnected, science-focused professional medical rhetoric. Parasocial connections offer a potential means to overcome *kakoethos*. In order to discursively construct *ethos* with online health information seekers, professional medical sources would do well to personalize and humanize the health information they provide in a way similar to the parasocial connections fashioned by celebrities online.

FUTURE RESEARCH DIRECTIONS

Due to the flow of information on the Internet, online health information seekers encounter varying types of information. The difficulty for professional medical sources online is finding a way to attenuate the *kakoethos* associated with their rhetoric so that the scientifically accurate medical information they provide will stand out among the din of health messages online and be retained by online health information seekers. As documented in previous research (Hayden, 1993; Parsloe, 2015) and the current analysis, many individuals experiencing illness feel stigmatized and "not normal" due to medical symptoms and diagnoses. In the case of professional medical sources, *kakoethos* is constructed through a lack of personal experience with specific conditions and symptoms and is further supported through discourse that normalizes the lack of a particular medical condition. It therefore may be unsurprising that many online health information seekers prefer lay health information that casts the individual as part of a shared identity organized around normalizing experiences associated with the condition.

With increasing demands for healthcare and growing physician and nurse shortages (American Association of Colleges of Nursing, 2014; Association of American Medical Colleges, 2015), one-on-one interpersonal relationships between medical professionals and all potential patients is becoming a less attainable goal. Therefore, future research should examine how individuals' health behaviors are impacted by access to lay health information online, especially considering they will likely have much more exposure to online health information before ever speaking to a doctor or nurse directly. Although this study uses a rhetorical approach to understanding the nature of *ethos* in online health information, future research could examine this phenomenon from qualitative and quantitative perspectives as well. Rhetorical analysis provides a productive academic path to diagnose discursive problems that exist in public culture by examining the ways that issues are framed in public culture (Brummett, 1984). Moreover, rhetorical analysis may not provide specific solutions, but it does offer experts and lawmakers insight into current ills and how to productively solve pressing public problems (Ehninger et al., 1971). Although this chapter uses rhetorical analysis as a means to examine online health information, much of this chapter used social scientific findings as a foundation for inquiry. Future research can build on this chapter's diagnosis of a rhetorical problem and recommendations, further illustrating how they can be measured through the scientific method.

CONCLUSION

Illness is a personal experience. With so many different potential channels and sources through which to receive health messages, previous research suggests that many individuals prefer health messages from lay persons who have personally experienced a specific health issue over messages from medical professionals (Chiu & Hsieh, 2012; Frohlich & Zmyslinski-Seelig, 2012). In the online environment where information "flows" (Williams, 2003) together and individuals receive health information and social support from multiple kinds of resources, professional medical rhetorics of health should not rely strictly on inartistic proofs. The cold, "matter of fact," exclusively scientifically accurate rhetoric of professional medical web pages is offset by the rhetoric of online lay health information that balances artistic and inartistic proofs while employing authenticity and personal experience to create inviting spaces where online health information seekers can feel as though they have entered a community with a shared identity. Because personal experience forms the basis of much lay health information online, professional medical sources may find success in overcoming the *kakoethos* established through the lack of direct and identifiable personal experience with a particular medical condition only by addressing that lack of direct personal experience with the condition, reframing the discourse on direct experiences in treating the condition, and allowing online health information seekers opportunity to participate in the discussion.

Given the sense of shared identity extant in much lay health information online, online health information seekers may evaluate source credibility more on personal experience and the anecdotal successes and failures of somebody else with the condition, rather than through authoritative, scientific, and evidence-based medical information. Given this tendency, health communication scholars, rhetoricians, physicians, and even health information seekers themselves, must critically examine online health rhetorics. This chapter described how viewing online health information rhetorically can assist in identifying how health discourses gain credibility online. In order for professional medical sources to establish credibility online and effectively influence the health behaviors and decision-making of an increasing number of online health information seekers, they must overcome the *kakoethos* inherent within their institutionalized rhetoric. The prescription for this problem may come from previous research into parasocial connections established by celebrities. Adapting a more humanized, emotionally supportive tone to messages of informational support, interweaving human elements such as personal narratives into institutionalized rhetoric, and allowing feedback from online health information seekers would assist professional medical sources in constructing *ethos* online. Such a rhetorical adjustment may ultimately aid in more effectively influencing information seekers' health behaviors and decision-making as social constraints continue to make FtF access to professional healthcare more challenging.

REFERENCES

American Association of Colleges of Nursing. (2014, April 24). *Nursing shortage fact sheet*. Retrieved from http://www.aacn.nche.edu/media-relations/NrsgShortageFS.pdf

Aristotle, . (2007). *On rhetoric* (G. A. Kennedy, Trans.). New York: Oxford University Press.

Association of American Medical Colleges. (2015). *Physician supply and demand through 2025: Key findings*. Retrieved from https://www.aamc.org/download/426260/data/physiciansupplyanddemandthrough-2025keyfindings.pdf

Banet-Weiser, S. (2012). *Authentic: The politics of ambivalence in a brand culture*. New York: New York University Press.

Baumgartner, S. E., & Hartmann, T. (2011). The role of health anxiety in online health information search. *Cyberpsychology, Behavior, and Social Networking*, *14*(10), 613–617. doi:10.1089/cyber.2010.0425 PMID:21548797

Blight, M. G., Jagiello, K., & Ruppel, E. K. (2015). "Same stuff different day:" A mixed-method study of support seeking on Facebook. *Computers in Human Behavior*, *53*, 366–373. doi:10.1016/j.chb.2015.07.029

Brummett, B. (1984). Rhetorical theory as heuristic and moral: A pedagogical justification. *Communication Education*, *33*(2), 97–107. doi:10.1080/03634528409384726

Buis, L. R., & Carpenter, S. (2009). Health and medical blog content and its relationships with blogger credentials and blog host. *Health Communication*, *24*(8), 703–710. doi:10.1080/10410230903264014 PMID:20183379

Burke, K. (1969). *A rhetoric of motives*. Berkeley, CA: University of California Press.

Burleson, B. R. (2003). Emotional support skills. In J. O. Greene & B. R. Burleson (Eds.), Handbook of communication and social interaction skills (pp. 551-594). Mahwah, NJ: Lawrence Erlbaum Associates Publishers.

Chiu, Y.-C., & Hsieh, Y.-L. (2012). Communication online with fellow cancer patients: Writing to be remembered, gain strength, and find survivors. *Journal of Health Psychology*, *18*(12), 1572–1581. doi:10.1177/1359105312465915 PMID:23221492

Cole, A. W., & Salek, T. A. (2014). Rhetorical voyeurism: Negotiation of literal and rhetorical audience in response to Kinsey's *Sexual Behavior in the Human Female*. *Journal of Communications and Media Studies*, *2*(1), 22–36.

Donovan, E. E., LeFebvre, L., Tardif, S., Brown, L. E., & Love, B. (2014). Patterns of social support communicated in response to expressions of uncertainty in an online community of young adults with cancer. *Journal of Applied Communication Research*, *42*(4), 432–455. doi:10.1080/00909882.2014.929725

Dubrofsky, R. E., & Wood, M. W. (2014). Posting racism and sexism: Authenticity, agency and self-reflexivity in social media. *Critical Studies in Media Communication*, *11*, 282–287. doi:10.1080/14791420.2014.926247

Eningher, E., Benson, T. W., Ettlich, E. E., Fisher, W. R., Kerr, H. P., Larson, R. I., . . . Niles, L. A. (1971). Report of the committee on the scope of rhetoric and the place of rhetorical studies in higher education. In L. F. Bitzer & E. Black (Eds.), The prospect of rhetoric: A report of the national development project (pp. 208-219). Englewood Cliffs, NJ: Prentice-Hall, Inc.

Fox, S., & Duggan, M. (2013, January 15). Health online 2013: Information triage. *Pew Research Center: Internet, Science & Tech*. Retrieved from http://www.pewinternet.org/2013/01/15/information-triage/

French, R. P., & Raven, B. (1959). The bases of social power. In D. Cartwright (Ed.), *Studies in social power* (pp. 150–167). Ann Arbor, MI: Institutive for Social Research, University of Michigan.

Frobish, T. S. (2013). On pixels, perceptions, and personae: Toward a model of online ethos. In M. Folk & S. Apostel (Eds.), *Online credibility and digital ethos: Evaluating computer-mediated communication* (pp. 1–23). Hershey, PA: IGI Global. doi:10.4018/978-1-4666-2663-8.ch001

Frohlich, D. O., & Zmyslinski-Seelig, A. (2012). The presence of social support messages on YouTube videos about inflammatory bowel disease and ostomies. *Health Communication, 27*(5), 421–428. doi: 10.1080/10410236.2011.606524 PMID:21962112

Gamie, S. (2013). The cyber-propelled Egyptian revolution and the de/construction of ethos. In M. Folk & S. Apostel (Eds.), *Online credibility and digital ethos: Evaluating computer-mediated communication* (pp. 316–331). Hershey, PA: IGI Global. doi:10.4018/978-1-4666-2663-8.ch018

Gilewicz, N., & Allard-Huver, F. (2013). Digital *parrhesia* as a counterweight to astroturfing. In M. Folk & S. Apostel (Eds.), *Online credibility and digital ethos: Evaluating computer-mediated communication* (pp. 215–228). Hershey, PA: IGI Global. doi:10.4018/978-1-4666-2663-8.ch012

Goldsmith, D. J. (2004). *Communicating social support.* New York: Cambridge University Press. doi:10.1017/CBO9780511606984

Grant, L., Hausman, B. L., Cashion, M., Lucchesi, N., Patel, K., & Roberts, J. (2015). Vaccination persuasion online: A qualitative study of two provaccine and two-vaccine-skeptical websites. *Journal of Medical Internet Research, 17*(5), e133. doi:10.2196/jmir.4153 PMID:26024907

Hayden, S. (1993). Chronically ill and "feeling fine": A study of communication and chronic illness. *Journal of Applied Communication Research, 21*(3), 263–278. doi:10.1080/00909889309365371

Horton, D., & Wohl, R. R. (1956). Mass communication and para-social interaction. *Psychiatry, 19,* 215–229. PMID:13359569

Hu, Y., & Haake, J. (2010). Search your way to an accurate diagnosis: Predictors of Internet-based diagnosis accuracy. *Atlantic Journal of Communication, 18*(2), 79–88. doi:10.1080/15456870903554916

Johnson, J. (2010). The skeleton on the couch: The Eagleton Affair, rhetorical disability, and the stigma of mental illness. *Rhetoric Society Quarterly, 40*(5), 459–478. doi:10.1080/02773945.2010.517234

Jordan, J. W. (2005). A virtual death and a real dilemma: Identity, trust, and community in cyberspace. *The Southern Communication Journal, 70*(3), 200–218. doi:10.1080/10417940509373327

Keegan, B. M. (2015). *Progressive multiple sclerosis.* Mayo Foundation for Medical Education and Research. Retrieved from http://www.mayoclinic.org/multiple-sclerosis-diagnosis/vid-20135054

Kwon, J. H., Kye, S.-Y., Park, E. Y., Oh, K. H., & Park, K. (2015). What predicts the trust of online health information? *Epidemiology and Health, 37,* e2015030. doi:10.4178/epih/e2015030 PMID:26212505

Marshall, P. D. (2010). The promotion and presentation of the self: Celebrity as marker and presentational media. *Celebrity Studies, 1*(1), 35–48. doi:10.1080/19392390903519057

Mayo Clinic Staff. (2015, October 1). *Self-management.* Retrieved from http://www.mayoclinic.org/diseases-conditions/multiple-sclerosis/manage/ptc-20131886

Multiple Sclerosis (MS) Support Group. (2012). *Daily Strength.* Retrieved from http://www.dailystrength.org/c/Multiple-Sclerosis-MS/support-group

Neubaum, G., & Krämer, N. C. (2015). Let's blog about health! Exploring the persuasiveness of a personal HIV blog compared to an institutional HIV website. *Health Communication, 30*(9), 872–883. doi:10.1080/10410236.2013.856742 PMID:24885514

Parsloe, S. M. (2015). Discourses of disability, narratives of community: Reclaiming an autistic identity online. *Journal of Applied Communication Research, 43*(3), 336–356. doi:10.1080/00909882.2015.1052829

Quackenbush, N. (2011). Speaking of—and as—stigma: Performativity and Parkinson's in the rhetoric of Michael J. Fox. *Disability Studies Quarterly, 31*(3). doi:10.18061/dsq.v31i3.1670

Rubin, A. M., & Rubin, R. B. (1985). Interface of personal and mediated communication: A research agenda. *Critical Studies in Mass Communication, 2*(1), 36–53. doi:10.1080/15295038509360060

Rubin, R. B., & McHugh, M. P. (1987). Development of parasocial interaction relationships. *Journal of Broadcasting & Electronic Media, 31*(3), 279–292. doi:10.1080/08838158709386664

Salek, T. A. (2014). Faith turns political on the 2012 campaign trail: Mitt Romney, Franklin Graham, and the stigma of nontraditional religions in American politics. *Communication Studies, 65*(2), 174–188. doi:10.1080/10510974.2013.851097

Salek, T. A. (2015). Controversy trending: The rhetorical form of Mia and Ronan Farrow's online firestorm against #WoodyAllen. *Communication, Culture & Critique.* doi:10.1111/cccr.12123

Schiappa, E., Gregg, P. B., & Hewes, D. E. (2005). The parasocial contact hypothesis. *Communication Monographs, 72*(1), 92–115. doi:10.1080/0363775052000342544

Schuplin, M. [Mallery Schuplin]. (2014a, April 21). *Multiple Sclerosis Monday—Being JCV Positive Tysabri* [Video file]. Retrieved from https://youtu.be/QMvplQmlDU4

Schuplin, M. [Mallery Schuplin]. (2014b, April 28). *Multiple sclerosis Monday – the early symptoms* [Video file]. Retrieved from https://youtu.be/4DGoxl0lDAs

Schuplin, M. [Mallery Schuplin]. (2014c, May 5). *Multiple sclerosis Monday – the scariest day of my life* [Video file]. Retrieved from https://youtu.be/aykvwXMgZ_I

Stone, A. M. (2013). Dilemmas of communicating about Alzheimer's disease: Professional caregivers, social support, and illness uncertainty. *Journal of Applied Communication Research, 41*(1), 1–17. doi:10.1080/00909882.2012.738426

Tatarchevskiy, T. (2011). The "popular" culture of Internet activism. *New Media & Society, 13*(2), 297–313. doi:10.1177/1461444810372785

Thoits, P. A. (2011). Mechanisms linking social ties and support to physical and mental health. *Journal of Health and Social Behavior, 52*(2), 145–161. doi:10.1177/0022146510395592 PMID:21673143

Web M. D. LLC. (2015). *Multiple sclerosis health center.* Retrieved from http://www.webmd.com/multiple-sclerosis

Williams, R. (2003). *Television.* London: Routledge.

Witte, K., & Allen, M. (2000). A meta-analysis of fear appeals: Implications for effective public health campaigns. *Health Education & Behavior, 27*(5), 591–615. doi:10.1177/109019810002700506 PMID:11009129

KEY TERMS AND DEFINITIONS

Emotional Support: Messages of social support that focus primarily on providing the receiver a sense of understanding and connection.

Health Information Seeker: An individual who searches for health information, for oneself or for another, on specific medical conditions and/or symptoms.

Informational Support: Messages of social support that focus primarily on providing the receiver with information on a topic. Informational support is often directive, as with advice.

Kakoethos: A form of "anti-ethos" where a lack of credibility, and/or influence, is rhetorically constructed.

Lay Health Source: An individual that provides others with health information despite not necessarily being formally educated on the topic, nor being a medical and/or health professional.

Parasocial Relationship: A type of mediated relationship between individuals who are not acquainted, where one individual may even be fictional. Parasocial relationships can offer many psychological benefits of interpersonal relationships.

Professional Medical Source: An individual and/or organization that provides others with health information based in formal medical training and education, health expertise, and related work experience.

Rhetor: The author of a text. Texts can be communicated personally, as in the context of public speaking, or through mediated means, as in the context of online communications.

Chapter 7
The Social Determinants in the Process of Credibility Assessment and the Influence of Topic Areas

Lluïsa Llamero
Blanquerna-Ramon Llull University, Spain

ABSTRACT

This chapter reflects on the process of truth representation in different topics of human knowledge to reach an understanding of differences in online credibility assessment. The author argues that new cultural trends for legitimizing second-hand information –as wisdom of crowds, self-sufficiency or gate-watching– may cause friction with symbolic cultural factors and social structures settled by historical processes. This makes the evaluation of credibility an issue under negotiation. Analysis of qualitative data into the areas of health, economy and tourism allow to propose a processual theoretical model of credibility assessment.

INTRODUCTION

Being informed outside the range of direct experience is a necessity for almost everybody in the globalized world. Many activities of daily life are conducted based on information available online, and, for many people, the World Wide Web has become the window to discover the planet. This window has introduced important novelties to the nature of information that impact people's information behavior and knowledge acquisition. Evaluating information provided by others has always been problemàtic because the data recipient may be intentionally or accidentally misled. Thus, second-hand information needs to be legitimized in order to overcome the initial distrust about what others say (Wilson, 1983). The notion of credibility contributes to that exercise of legitimation because it is closely connected to representations of truth in society.

DOI: 10.4018/978-1-5225-1072-7.ch007

Traditional rhetoric established that the ethos, or character of the speaker, was the determining factor in giving credit to a speech and, consequently, in reaching persuasion (Aristotle, trans. 1968). The rhetor had to convey intelligence, knowledge and moral virtuosity to gain a positive ethos. However, Aristotle and other rhetoricians of the Greek Classical Age developed their theories in a communication system where oral speech was the prevailing channel of communication; therefore, the rhetor and the audience were physically and directly connected, which is often not the case with computer-mediated communication. Contemporary rhetoricians emphasize that web technologies have blurred the connection between the rhetor and the audience, but they nevertheless still argue that those who want to act as rhetors online can establish their ethos by appealing to community identification and goodwill; moral character and virtue; intelligence and knowledge; and verbal and design competence (Frobish, 2013). Both verbal and design competence have risen in level of importance because of the ubiquity of computer-mediated communication and their ability to translate traditional ethos to the digital environment.

Despite rhetors being able to develop communicative strategies for persuading the audience of their positive ethos, each member of the audience ultimately takes responsibility for judging messages and deciding whether a rhetor deserves credibility or not. This has motivated scholars to investigate how individuals grant credibility to the plethora of information sources available on the Internet. Overall, research has applied and adapted theoretical developments from interpersonal communication to the digital environment (Choi & Stvilia, 2015). Credibility is treated as an epistemic tool to recognize the truth of information provided by others. On the other hand, it has been indicated that social structures and normative values have a strong influence on truth representation and also impact credibility judgments (Burbules, 2001; Wilson, 1983). Regarding this facet, it is relevant to point out that virtual communities have introduced new normative values about knowledge production, circulation, and legitimation (Bruns, 2005; Surowiecki, 2004). Those values would determine the moral virtuosity of digital ethos beyond the technical updates of rhetorical techniques. However, it lacks enough empirical and theoretical research to address how those new values interplay with the morality of traditional ethos. Do the values of digital ethos challenge the established cultural assumptions and social power relations on knowledge production and truth representation? Or are those values integrated with the collective cultural assumptions of our contemporary times? In order to reflect on these intriguing questions, this chapter explores how the ontology and axiology of different fields of knowledge construct a common representation of truth and, consequently, how that constructed common truth influences online credibility evaluation. The author will present an analysis of empirical data, operationalized through three different topic areas—health, economy, and tourism—that range from closed knowledge and semi-open knowledge to open knowledge, inspired by Patrick Wilson's (1983) distinction between knowledge and opinion. Findings support the emergence of a processual model, which will be discussed in relation to how the interplay between traditional and digital ethos influences credibility evaluation.

BACKGROUND

Conditions for Online Credibility Assessment

The role of social structures in judging information was clear before the Internet's advent. We depended on a range of intermediaries to gather information and ideas to interpret its truthfulness. Communication and sociology explained it by the theory of gatekeeping, which depicted how a few people managed information dissemination in a top-bottom relationship. The ethos of gatekeepers was legitimated under clear codes of conduct and systematic procedures for reporting information. Different professions contributed to settle the truth in their domain (Wilson, 1983), whereas the media were the main institution that provided the general picture to the big audience. Their procedures in processing raw data and transforming it into stories understandable by a lay public were the landmark of the journalism profession. Media translated the knowledge produced by specialists, intel·lectuals, and politicians, among others. In this paradigm, the author's identity (both individuals and institutions) and reputation were markers that guaranteed the quality of information for receivers. These markers often lack on the Internet (Metzger, 2007) or can be easily manipulated (Burbules, 2001), thereby causing difficulties for traditional credibility evaluation.

In this unsteady communication landscape, research on online credibility has devoted much effort to investigating how audiences cope with the difficulties of assessing the reliability of sources, messages, and media. The focus has been put on how individuals process information and what markers of Internet artifacts convey credibility (see Fogg, 2003; Choi & Stivila, 2015; Jeon & Rieh, 2014; Metzger, Hartsell, & Flanagin, 2015) Overall, research assumes that by focusing on the subject of credibility, theoretical development would be able to explain credibility assessment regardless of the objects under investigation (Choi & Stivila, 2015). The impact of context—social structures and cultural assumptions—has been taken into account both considering the particular goals of the information task and the cultural background and social situation of the receivers (Metzger, 2007). For example, Fogg (2003) argued that the user's assumptions derived from their culture, past experiences, topic competence, and situational norms influence interpretation. In support of this statement, Hilligoss and Rieh (2008) found that context constrains the selection of resources and bound judgments. Therefore, "credibility is not viewed as an absolute but rather may be seen as relative given its relationship to certain contexts of information seeking and use" (Hilligoss & Rieh, 2008, p. 1480). In other words, the judgments are accommodated to the situation the user wants to employ the information for. However, the measurements of individuals' perceptions overshadow the study of how contextual factors impact on individuals.

The Theory of Cognitive Authority (Wilson, 1983) can help us add social perspective to the analysis of credibility. It stated that consumption of second-hand information is a moral imperative as "to be well informed is a virtue among all classes, but what constitutes being well informed varies with social location" (Wilson, 1983, p.149). The notion of being well informed is obviously related to credibility and connected to the acceptance of truth claimed by others. This theory suggests that people rely on specific sources (individuals or institutions) to legitimate second-hand information, granting them the status of cognitive authority. Wilson defined cognitive authority as a kind of influence on one's thought. The epistemic exercise employed by a person to recognize cognitive authority follows the assumption that "there are people who know what they are talking about" (Wilson, 1983, p.15). To be considered a cognitive authority, a source has to be perceived as competent and trustworthy, attributes in line with theories addressed to explore credibility and traditional ethos. Therefore, despite using a different terminology, the Theory of Cognitive Authority has been employed in various studies that addressed online information assessment: Savolainen (2007) found evidence that cognitive authority recognition depends on the topic of interest and the ideology of users; Huvila (2013) concluded that search activity on major search engines has become a cognitive authority in itself.

The Social Construction of Truth: Professions' Prerogatives and Challenges

Philosophy, anthropology, and sociology have deeply studied social processes of truth construction. In the view of social epistemology—the sub-discipline of philosophy that analyzes the social dimensions of production, distribution, and utilization of intellectual products (Wilson, 1983)—scholars state that in open democratic societies, a plethora of content providers compete for end-users' approval. In that competition, cultural symbolic representations conform to the rules of what must be considered true. The veracity of information is judged through common sense when it applies to an orienting function (Savolainen, 1995) or through the acceptance of expert knowledge when it applies to carry out specific tasks (Wilson, 1983). Common sense is defined as a cultural system that interprets daily experience by presenting reality without sophistication (Geertz, 1999). It assumes that every individual has an elementary mental outfit to judge reality. Just like any other interpretative system (e.g., myth, picture, science) it is historically constructed; it can also be developed, formalized, questioned, and even taught, and it can dramatically differ from one culture to another. Although common sense has a strong impact on judgements in everyday life, the historical evolution of science and the rise of professions have established the idea that expert knowledge is more rational and closer to the truth. This was driven by an ideology of professions, which—as in the case of medicine—gained administrative prerogatives (Freidson, 1978).

In order to discern whether people are prone to use common sense or to trust professionals, we can rely on Wilson's (1983) distinction between knowledge and opinion, or "closed and open questions" (p. 16). Knowledge is defined as the set of closed questions that conform to the stock of beliefs settled beyond a doubt in a historical moment, whereas opinion is a set of unsolved questions, always open and under debate. He acknowledged that the distinction is rough and practical but argued that the distinction worked for the ordinary purposes of ordinary life. Members of professions are responsible for monitoring the development of knowledge in the profession's body of technique and information. Thus, they are constantly confronted with the task of judging information in a systematic and reliable fashion. They are not exempt to criticism—by other professions, for exemple—but one of the central arguments of the ideology of professions is that outside critics are unable to judge their body of knowledge (Freidson, 1978; Wilson, 1983). In the competitive environment of modern societies, people will judge second-hand information according to an initial stock of beliefs that is characteristic of the social place that every individual has in the world. Cultural capital enables people to assess information based on a common-sense analysis of the inherent plausibility of messages, but in areas of closed knowledge, laypersons are unable to carry out that test. Thus, they are compelled to trust experts.

Digital Ethos: Aggregation, Self-Sufficiency, and Transparency

As aforementioned, virtual communities have developed new values that entail new forms of knowledge production and legitimation. To understand how this trend is being articulated with deep-rooted social validation of knowledge, it is necessary to reflect on the basis that forms the virtuosity of digital ethos.

Regarding knowledge production, virtual communities have advocated for a sense of superiority on collectivities since the very beginning of the Internet's advent. James Surowiecki's (2004) highly influential *The Wisdom of the Crowds* (2004) popularized the idea that the aggregation of information in groups can generate a more accurate overall answer than one generated by an expert. His thesis depicts the Internet as the perfect place where this idea can thrive because the ethos of the Net is hostile to the idea that power and authority should belong to a select group of people. Expertise and reputation, thus, would have moved from professional gatekeepers to the crowds. Recent empirical research proved that the success of Wikipedia relies on this argument and has reached a common legitimation, being gradually accepted by even the social stratum of teachers (Lim, 2013).

Bruns (2005) developed the thesis of collective wisdom and coined the terms "producer" and "gatewatching." Producers are the result of the convergence between the producers and the receivers (users) of content in 2.0 environments. In other words, they are people who create texts and use texts. The old separation between producers and users has been substituted by a bidirectional dynamic. This trend especially impacts the gatekeeper role of legacy journalism, but may be extended to other areas. Producers access not only news stories written by journalists, but also content written by primary sources. They can compare and debate the reasons for gatekeeping, resulting in a collective watch or a gatewatching—in Bruns's terms—of motivations (be they commercial or political, long-established journalistic rutines, etc.). Therefore, the construction of truth is an outcome of a new set of power relations (presumably horizontal relations) on a community and not the acceptance of the proposals of a superior hierarchical group. In addition, Lankes (2008) contended that assessment into 2.0 platforms is based on reliability and points to less dependence on authority. Users would determine credibility by synthesizing multiple sources (including primary sources and raw data) and analyze whether what each source says is consistent. The traditional expertise of professionals would be, thus, somehow replaced by a perceived self-sufficiency because data is accessible to everyone.

Other scholars do not depict a decline on the role of authorities but propose the reshaping of its role. Eysenbach (2008) coined the neologism "apomediation" for depicting a new way for users to identify credible information. Apomediation is a special form of disintermediation that substitutes dependence on traditional intermediaries (gatekeepers) for guidance from apomediaries. By using the latin prefix apo-, which means separate, Eysenbach signaled that apomediaries are detached from the process of data gathering, selection, and presentation in a particular narrative. They cannot alter or select the information that is being brokered. The task of apomediaries (personal sources or systems) is saying whether a document can be of certain quality. Eysenbach noted that whether consumers prefer apomediation, intermediation is highly situation-specific, depending on variables of self-perceived autonomy, self-efficacy, and knowledge on a topic.

The advent of Web 2.0 put the focus on considering digital environment a venue that somehow mirrors interpersonal communication. Trust in interpersonal communication is built on individual perception of honesty and consistent behavior. However, the Internet challenges this way of building trust. Jessen and Jørgessen (2011) proposed the Theory of Aggregated Trustworthiness to argue that multiple streams of social opinions from other users (comments, votes, ratings, etc.) play an important role in forming the perceived trustworthiness of content. This dynamic is unique to the Web and is made possible by factors not attainable in any off-line setting. According to the Theory of Aggregated Trustworthiness, credibility judgments may be formed by pondering social feedback and collective judgment: "Aggregating a wealth of trustworthiness cues provide the most robust form of evaluation, when author credentials are hard or impossible to come by" (Jessen & Jørgessen, 2011, para. 14).

THE STUDY: ENCOUNTERS OF TRADITIONAL ETHOS AND DIGITAL ETHOS IN THREE AREAS OF KNOWLEDGE

We have seen how the literature acknowledges the role of social determinants (power relations, ideology of professions, socially shared assumptions on truth) in shaping credibility judgments and how those judgments have a fundamental epistemic dimension (expertise) and a normative dimension (trustworthiness). We have also seen how virtual cultures are challenging taken-for-granted assumptions about knowledge production and trust dynamics. But research has insufficiently addressed the effects of this cultural tension. For that reason, it would be valuable to investigate the articulation of these two trends in daily life settings. This study pursues this goal by reflecting theoretically on the degree of social prominence of three professions—medicine, economy, and tourism—and analyzing qualitative data from a sample of professionals, laypersons, and producers.

As credibility is a process of meaning attribution, a qualitative approach was adopted because it offers the advantages of examining a process in great detail and its rationalities (Wimmer, Dader, & Dominik, 1996). To operationalize the goals of the research, the author constructed a scale of areas of knowledge inspired by Wilson's distinction between open and closed questions. The ranges of the scale are: closed knowledge, semi-open knowledge, and open knowledge.

Health information is situated into an area of closed knowledge. Although health is a complex concept, the historical process of medicalization marks the biomedical paradigm as the hegemonic paradigm for health management (Rosen, 1985). This paradigm establishes that health information must be based on objective empirical evidence and holds a positivist view of science. Literature on medicine recognizes contention in some areas, especially in the field of mental health (Castel, 1983). The World Health Organization (2001) itself established that cultural features shape what is considered a mental health disorder. Thus, the power of objectivity may become disputed. However, if a medical issue is solved under knowledge that fits the biomedical paradigm, we can arguably consider the question settled beyond a doubt, which is what Wilson described a closed question.

Economy fits into an area of semi-open knowledge because it is located at a midpoint between a stable truth and a disputed opinion. In economy, empirical data is used, mostly in the form of quantitative indicators. They can be considered objective, although they are more dependent on human construction than evidence used in natural sciences. Besides, unlike natural sciences, the acceptance of outcomes from data is not universal. For instance, many theories whose validity is asserted following cultural traditions, moral values, and ideologies around how wealth is produced and distributed among the population are under debate (Harris, 1990; Cameron, Neal, & Coll, 2005). Consequently, truth is subject to processes of agreement and disagreement among different social groups. The Internet has aroused disruptive discourses on the prevailing schools of thought of Neoliberalism and Keynesianism, although they remain marginal. Wikinomics (Tapscott & Williams, 2008) is one of these discourses.

Finally, tourism is situated in an area of open knowledge. Despite the importance of objective data (e.g., schedules and companies that provide hospitality services or transportation), the personal tastes of tourists are the main factor that molds credibility judgements. Literature on tourism recognizes the influence of social structures into the behavior of tourists, but it treats information assessment as a question of individual preference (Ayeh, Au, & Law, 2013; Guex, 2010). Thus, all questions in the field are subjected to a great deal of debate.

METHODOLOGY

Participants

As the aim of the study was investigating how traditional social construction of truth coexists with new forms of knowledge legitimation, the sample was designed following purposive criteria. Data from 53 participants was gathered in Spain between 2011 and 2014 by employing semi-structured interviews, observations, and focus groups. Potential participants were selected according to the following factors: profession, interest on the topic, ideology, and virtual community engagement. Pilot tests were conducted through a focus group session (N=7) and interviews with professionals, lay users, and bloggers (N=6). This procedure was used in order to refine a previous discussion guide elaborated from the literature revision, which found new themes involved in credibility judgments such as the necessity to learn about a topic. The final discussion guide asked participants about their motivations and general information-seeking behavior (e.g., types of websites accessed online and usual sources of online and offline information), overall understanding of credibility as a notion (i.e., values for believing and using information), specific strategies for evaluating information (e.g., learning about a topic, identifying sources, using raw data, comparing sites) and conditions where credibility is more and less important. It should be noted, however, that the questions were just a guide to foster conversation and to encourage reflection. On the other hand, after having analyzed all data, test-data provided useful insights and, consequently, was included in the sample of this study (N=53).

The sample includes a variety of profiles, distinguishing among professional practitioners specialized on each topic (N= 24), lay users (N=22) and producers bloggers (N= 7) writing about the respective topics in their personal website. Recruitment was done through professional associations, civic organizations, pages of social media, and snowball sampling. The health sub-sample case study consists of physicians (N=5), patients and caregivers (N=5), one physician blogger, and one patient blogger. The economy sub-sample case study consists of a variety of economy professionals (scholars, financial advisors, unionists, consultants) (N= 6), lay users (N= 7) and producers bloggers (N= 2). The tourism sub-sample case study consists of a variety of tourist professionals (consultants, travel agents, marketing specialists, and academic researchers) (N=5), lay users (N=5), and producers bloggers (N=3). Finally, participants were selected to fit the most common demographics of the Internet users that Spanish statistics describe. According to the Spanish Statistical Office (Instituto Nacional de Estadística, 2012) people who used the Internet were mostly individuals between 16 and 44 years old, with a high school level of education or a university degree, roughly equal in terms of gender, and lived in urban areas of more than 50,000 residents.

Data Collection

This study adopted two main methods for data gathering: semi-structured interviews and participant observation. The use of semi-structured interviews was considered suitable as a means to obtain representative narratives of meaning attribution (Wimmer, Dadder, & Dominik, 1996) since they have proven "useful for systematically studying the intricate connection between the social and the individual through particular cases" (Meyer, 2008, p.76). Interviews took place in the natural settings (workplace or home) of respondents and lasted 90 minutes on average.

The inclusion of observation was stimulated by Metzger's (2007) call for employing the most naturalistic methods available in order to overcome the potential discrepancy between self-reported procedures of credibility assessment and actual behaviors. Social pressures may impel people to state that they should critically analyze online information, yet factors such as time constraints often prevent people from doing so. In this study, observation was conducted through the think aloud protocol. This technique stems from usability research, but it has also been implemented in computer-mediated communication studies (Guan, Lee, Cuddihy, & Ramey, 2006; Kendall, 2004). The exercise suggested informants browse the Web freely to illustrate their reasoning and allowed them to propose a revision of specific websites. Respondents were invited to verbalize the thoughts that arise from the consumption of online information. They were not trained respondents in thinking aloud; the gaps that tend to occur with novices were overcome by asking them what they were thinking when they remained silent. The exercises happened at the end of interviews. Recordings of the interviews and the think aloud exercise were transcribed and analyzed using the grounded theory approach.

RESULTS

A Three-Stage Model of Credibility Assessment Based on the Social Construction of Truth

A processual model of credibility assessment was inferred from data analysis, since credibility judgements have been proven to not be static but to evolve. The framework provides three sequential stages that users follow to evaluate credibility. In the first stage, users make an initial identification of the truth socially established in a topic area. Out of this evaluation they associate the truth as the outcome of social rules that apply in areas of closed knowledge, semi-open knowledge, and open knowledge, and they become familiar with the ethos of each domain. Within the closed area of knowledge, traditional ethos prevails and is established through the rules promulgated by professions and scientific criteria. Individuals are very conditioned by social hierarchies to assess the truthfulness of a particular piece of information. In fields of semi-open knowledge, both traditional ethos and digital ethos play a role, and the individual is less obliged to accept a statement of truth that social strata impose. In fields of open knowledge, truth is considered a relative notion and the values of digital ethos play a more influential role, especially aggregated trustworthiness and self-sufficiency.

Although users identify how different knowledge areas entail different rules for assessing information, they do not feel confident making a reasoned judgement by themselves in their first contact with a piece of information. Hence, they move to a second stage where they follow a learning process about the field in question because, without first having acquired a reasonable level of knowledge, the judgement of the appropriateness of any claimed truth is not critically performed. In the case of professionals, we must think that this stage is part of their formal training and working experience.

Finally, on a third stage, users feel empowered to make reasoned judgments about specific information sources and content. Their initial cultural capital surrounding a topic has been deployed to assess credibility. Those judgments can be a reproduction, a negotiation, or a critique of the social construction of credibility in relation to a socially shared idea of truth.

Figure 1. A three-stage model of credibility assessment based on the social construction of truth

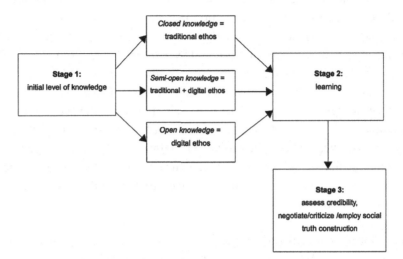

The values of the digital ethos did not mark a difference in relation to the a priori most engaged profiles: the producer bloggers. Hence, the author argues that the adoption of virtues of the digital ethos is transversal and moderated by the general assumptions of truth construction. A summary of the three stages of credibility evaluation is presented on figure 1. A deep understanding of the framework will be comprehended through the arguments of participants.

Health Case Study: Closure of Knowledge Slows Down Digital Ethos Adoption

Participants in this study identified truth construction with the procedures and codes of conduct of the medical professions. The expansion of electronic-health information is dramatically changing traditional ways of information consumption, but it is unclear whether digital values play a role in credibility evaluation. Deep-rooted cultural values and social structures are strongly influential. To understand credibility assessment in this study, we should refer to medicalization in Spain. Their specific characteristics are: a tax-funded universal healthcare system, the mutual legitimation between state and doctors, the government's attempt to persuade the population that healthy lifestyles are moral virtues (Bernabeu, 2007), and the perception of doctors as strong authority figures among the population (Allué, 2013).

The biomedical paradigm is very pervasive in the processes of credibility evaluation. Professionals stated that credible information should conform to a particular conceptualization of truth derived from scientific criteria. In the words of doctor P20[1], "Credibility would be associated to a truthfulness capable of being proven through what we call evidence-based medicine." On their part, patients showed a special awareness of the importance of being rigorous in assessing credibility. Specifically, they stated, "In health you must accurately pay attention to the source of information; it is not so important when you search for a cooking recipe" (P17, lay user) or "When you look for ideas to buy shoes" (P19, lay user). Thus, we can see how users associate health information with a different area of knowledge in a first stage of information processing. Patients accept medical professions as credible sources because they hold expert knowledge, which is supposed to be the best type of knowledge in the area of health.

Despite the fact that the biomedical paradigm was fully accepted by all the interviewed patients, access to this kind of information can cause friction between patients and the physician's social prerogatives. One example was provided by patient 18, who trusted a website devoted to the risks of taking drugs during breastfeeding. The website was authored by a group of pediatricians and provides not only a rating of the risks but also biomedical literature that sustains that rating. She explained that when she got mastitis she consulted the web and found that she could take Ciprofloxacin, an antibiotic with a very low risk level for the age and weight of the baby she breastfed. However, when she requested the prescription, her family doctor "refused, despite the fact that I [referenced] the website; she argued that Ciprofloxacin was contraindicated according to vade mecum" (P18 lay user blogger) and continued to add, "but vade mecums are not always accurate because they're written by lawyers of the pharmaceutical industry and are very conservative and not rigorous with current scientific knowledge." A family doctor reported another example of friction:

Once, a well-documented patient asked me for a brand drug arguing that it was the only drug with evidence for treating his disease. Of course I wasn't able to refute him and I was compelled to inform him that the healthcare system did not subsidize that drug and that the protocol established the prescription of a generic. (P12 professional)

These two quotations show how, despite the fact that laypersons are capable of dealing with health information in equal terms as experts, social structures—in this case laws and economy factors—prevent the adoption of an egalitarian relationship; doctors retain the administrative authority that society has granted them.

Apart from doctors, patients also consider an expert as "someone who has lived through a disease and reports a personal experience" (P17, lay user). Reporting a personal experience in venues of user-generated content (UGC) is a way of truth construction that complements the truth settled by physicians. However, it has a different status and is only used to cope with emotional issues related to suffering a disease (lay users P17, 19, 13).

A great amount of scientific information is available online both for physicians and laypersons, but the closure of knowledge in health does not allow for collaborative knowledge production and reliance on the wisdom of the crowds. Doctors argued that their extensive academic training and clinical experience equip them to properly understand health information since "there's objective data, but objective data is based on big populations. Not everybody can extrapolate a conclusion out of data for a particular situation. Doctors have the ability to interpret data. We're paid for that job" (P21, professional). Therefore, doctors situate themselves as cognitive authorities for establishing the truth, stressing that they have a preeminent position on society, as we can infer from the statement "we're paid for that job."

Accounts of patients showed a variety of attitudes in assessing e-health information. Overall, many patients did not consider themselves prepared enough to understand medical literature, but they valued the possibilities for learning that Internet offers. The availability of biomedical information online makes laypersons access that information because they are motivated by a psychological need for learning what will happen to them in the course of their malady. Some patients speak with their physicians about what they have read on the Internet but they do this with "reluctance," as doctors usually notice (P20, P21, P14). The traditionally superior status of doctors may explain this attitude, along with negative comments made by some doctors, who often use such pejorative expressions as, "Yes, you read something on Google again, my doctor tell me sometimes" (P17, lay user). However this attitude is changing, and the doctors interviewed recognized that if "we're receptive, patients immediately ask us for help to interpret scientific information" (P20, professional). Physicians, thus, become apomediaries by guiding patients to understand the obscure jargon of medical literature and giving them reasoned opinions about the reliability of content. They also recommended web resources to patients in order to get further information about their conditions. In this way, patients can follow an apomediated learning process and become more health literate. Consequently, credibility judgments change over time: initially, they are based on expertise recognition and interpersonal trust of their physicians, whereas in the end they are based on self-sufficiency that judges if messages are plausible and have a logical basis.

Although motivation to be rigorous is high for all profiles, we can explain the process of credibility assessment relying on heuristics[2]. Informants acknowledged that they have taken-for-granted habits. Thus, most of the time they assess credibility by intuition. However, they qualify intuition "not as a spontaneous impulse but as an experience not rationalized" (P20, professional). In the daily consumption of information, the social construction of truth shows a correlation to a series of heuristics (see Table 1). The medical profession constrains the selection of resources and bound judgements, both in the case of physicians and in the case of patients. Heuristics can be grouped in expertise, trustworthiness, and plausibility dimensions. In the expertise dimension, all informants accept markers of the biomedical paradigm as signals of truth and reject proposals of so-called alternative medicines. Universities, scientific societies, and databases of medical journals are considered the more credible sources. A heuristic exclusively employed by patients is the recognition of other patients as experts. The trustworthiness dimension generates heuristics that see in the ethical codes of medical professions a way for assessing the moral behavior of sources. The authority of doctors make their apomediation a valid heuristic for patients. They also take for granted that other patients writing in UGC venues have goodwill in relating their experiences and consequently trust them. Finally, on the plausibility dimension, we find the inclusion of evidence and consistency with previous knowledge as heuristics common to doctors and patients.

Observation showed that doctors do not always rely on the heuristics derived from professional procedures, as they claimed. Two doctors performed similar practices to laypersons during the exercise proposed by the researcher. They used Google to search for keywords to get a quick answer to a doubt. In one case, doctor P12 looked up the drug "diazepam" and came across to a website (www.prospectos.net) not run by an official healthcare provider. In another case, physician P14 searched for "spirometry" to check if a value measured on the consultancy was a medical issue or not, and he came across a non-official website as well. This is in conflict with their claim of consulting scientist sources expressed during the interviews. Both argued that the reliability of the source was not of major importance because data are objective, with no room for discussion, and that in the consultancy, they were constrained by time pressure.

Economy Case Study: Situational Coexistence between Traditional Ethos and Digital Ethos

The higher degree of openness in economic knowledge results in a higher reliance on some of the values of digital ethos, but these digital ethos elements coexist with traditional ethos due to the influence of professionalism. All informants interviewed in this case study saw the truth as more flexible than informants interviewed for the health case study. However, significant differences in mindsets depending on social situations can be observed. The most important social determinant that molds credibility assessment is a profession related to the economic sector.

Table 1. Inventory of heuristics in three areas of knowledge (closed, semi-open and open) differentiated by the social determinant of profession

Attribute Dimension	Professionals	Laypersons
Closed Knowledge (Health)		
Expertise	• Biomedical paradigm. • Reputed sources (universities, journals, medical databases...).	• Biomedical paradigm. • Reputed sources (universities, journals, medical databases...). • Patients.
Trustworthiness	• Medical Ethical code.	• Medical Ethical code. • Apomediation by doctors. • Goodwill of patients in UGC.
Plausibility	• Methodology. • Inclusion of evidence. • Consistency with knowledge background.	• Inclusion of evidence. • Consistency with acquired health literacy.
Semi-Open Knowledge (Economy)		
Expertise	• Traditional reputation. • Endorsement from colleagues. • Officiality (institutional post holders, statistic data).	• Informal (anyone can become an expert). • Comprehensiveness of content.
Trustworthiness	• Primary sources. • International quality press.	• Source reputation background (includes digital nickname identity). • Endorsement by opinion leaders. • Journalism values (fact dissemination, neutrality, agenda setting). • Homophily in opinions.
Plausibility	• Comparison. • Time makes rumors become news.	• Commonsense evaluation. • Digital social validation.
Open Knowledge (Tourism)		
Expertise	• Informal (anyone can become an expert). • Access primary sources. • Currency.	• Informal (anyone can become an expert). • Currency.
Trustworthiness	• UGC integrity. • Experts' integrity. • Homophily. • Digital reputation and popularity.	• UGC integrity. • Homophily. • Trust built through time.
Plausibility	• Objectivity of pictures. • Crowd consensus. • Not marketing language. • Quality of information. • Comparison for quality and price of tourist services.	• Crowd consensus. • Dialog dynamic (accuracy question/answer). • Objectivity of pictures. • Not marketing language

* Heuristics of producers bloggers are included into professionals and laypersons, as they adopt digital ethos in a similar way.

The economic professionals stated that they have to use a lot of second-hand information for developing their work and showed awareness of the risks of relying on second-hand sources. The references to the risks prove that the result of an initial examination of knowledge leads to identify it as a semi-open field. In order to overcome the risks, economic professionals assess information following the rules of their profession. Sources must have a reputation in the industry to be perceived as credible. Therefore, professionals do not use the Web to come across any source, instead, "We use the Internet as a consultation tool to go to very specific sites: financial entities, specialized news agencies—for example, Bloomberg or Reuters—or Stock Exchange official websites" (P10, professional). One informant used a metaphor to illustrate his browsing habits:

For me the Net is like a library. It's obvious that when you go to a library you don't pick up any book; you search for those books of your interest, which have references about their quality. I can use Wikipedia, but I don't grant Wikipedia a lot of credibility. Maybe it's a restricted way of using the Internet, but it's the right way to do a good job. P4 (professional)

The trustworthiness dimension is important in economy since many sources can have vested interests, whether commercial or political. The most important factor to build a trust relationship is that the source demonstrates a record of professionalism and honest behavior over time:

You contrast reputation as time goes on. Financial websites were the first to appear. Thus, time has proven what websites are aggressive and disseminate rumors that end up being false, and what websites disseminate real news, with fact-checked data. The second ones give you more security. P2 (professional)

Users in this study manifested an open attitude to trust amateur digital sources according to the semi-open nature of economy that allows room for granting credibility to non-traditional and professional experts. The prevalent argument is:

I think that every source has to gain its credibility. If you like economy and you run a blog, it doesn't matter if you are a taxi driver, what matters is that you analyze data properly and express an opinion, because data in economy is a matter of opinion. (P46, lay user)

Trust is built through what they call "digital identity," which can be either a real name or a nickname, provided that the source shows consistency in their posts (P32, 33, 6, 7, 9). Although it can be assumed that the political orientation of users may influence the acceptance of non-traditional sources, in this study political orientation has not been revealed as an influential factor and all profiles of informants—leftists, liberals and conservatives—are open to the idea that anyone can write authoritatively on the economy. The job is the factor that acts as a social determinant. In this way, professionals interviewed stated that although they trust some non-traditionally reputed sources, they cannot use them at work because it would jeopardize their own reputation in front of their clients (P1, 2, 8, 10, 38, 42, 41). Nevertheless, professionals complained because now they, "have to supply detailed explanations to some clients, who browse the Internet and find solutions not suitable for their financial situation" (P38 professional).

As it can be appreciated by the last quotation, a common idea is that knowledge about the economy is not restricted to a group of professionals; anyone can learn. The abundance of documents, opinions, and interactions makes laypersons think that the Internet enables self-learning. Thus, if we take into account the Internet as a whole, the medium holds an advantage of credibility in comparison with former ways of accessing information such as interpersonal relationships and mass media. However, layusers were skeptical of all economic information, regardless of the source. Consequently, they accounted for a complex assessment process of credibility evaluation that banks not only on expertise and trustworthiness cues but, more significantly, on plausibility. Informant P3 offered a paradigmatic example as he reported to start from the assumption that "50% of news stories are rumors and not fact-checked data." Paying attention to potential bias is an example of a strategy developed to cope with this skepticism:

I always try to guess the intention of the source. For example, if a car company delivers a press release informing about some problem with the cars it sells because quality controls detected some failure, it'll be credible to me. On the contrary, if the press release says that their car is the best in the market and has been awarded, it won't be credible. The same source, but depending on the intention of the message, I assess it differently. P6 (lay user)

Journalism plays a role in this area of knowledge in contrast to the health area, where laypersons identified their doctors and scientific literature as providers of the most credible second-hand information. All economic informants relied on media outlets because, as P6 (lay user) stated, "They set the agenda." However, journalism is perceived as an institution not to be trusted but to be watched. Trust in legacy media is migrating to economic blogs due to the preference for dialogue, which encourages gatewatching and leads to collective wisdom, a benchmark value of the digital ethos. The observation exercise showed how bloggers devoted a great importance to dialogue:

Blogs are a bidirectional channel. As you can see in this post, I wrote an opinion and my readers can refute me or expand the arguments. Many times they endorse a piece of news. They post a link. This is useful to improve the initial content or to demonstrate that I'm wrong. (…) If your community is big enough, people may appear with better knowledge than yours and direct you to primary data. P32 (blogger)

Experience in consuming economic information, both on the Internet and offline, have leads to the development of a series of heuristics to assess credibility. Professionals employ traditionally reputed sources endorsed by colleagues and officials (e.g., institutional post-holders such as economic ministers and CEOs and statistical data) to establish rules used in evaluating the expertise of information. Laypersons are more open to accepting both people with academic credentials and/or professional backgrounds—as well as amateur sources—as experts. Comprehensiveness of content is a signal of expertise for them, too.

Despite a certain degree of skepticism, laypersons grant a generic trust to online economic information, which can increase or decrease according to the perception of vested interests and biases within sources; this constitutes a process of learning about the field (second stage of credibility assessment). Thus, they rely on the background reputation of the source, identified by a real name or their nickname. Endorsement by opinion leaders is a second heuristic. Although they are cautious to trust media, laypersons appreciate the traditional journalism values of fact dissemination, neutrality, and agenda selection. To trust opinion content, they use the homophily rule, which is defined in terms of sharing a political ideology. On their side, professionals trust primary sources to learn about factual data and the international quality press (they mentioned *Financial Times* and *Wall Street Journal* as examples).

Assessing credibility through heuristics of plausibility follows two strategies for economic professionals: comparing information on several websites (stage three of the framework) and letting time pass to see if rumors become news. Thus, a piece of news not confirmed by primary sources is not considered relevant to make a judgment about potential truth. On the other hand, laypersons and bloggers use common sense as a heuristic rule to evaluate the consistency of content. They attribute a value of truth to pieces of news with documentary support, such as pictures or primary data. The other strategy employed by these informants infers that a story will be real if it appears on many websites. Thereby, aggregation of data contributes to a higher perception of the chances to grasp the truth, "because you can read the same thing on twenty different sites and form your own opinion" (P6, lay user).

Tourism Case Study: Digital Ethos Adoption

Web 2.0 has dramatically changed tourists' habits and behaviors of planning, consuming travel products, and sharing their travel experiences. The openness of tourism boosted new habits of information management to such a degree that tourism scholars talk about a change of paradigm in the industry (Buhalis & Law, 2008). Because of new e-business and information sources, traditional intermediaries such as travel agencies or specialized magazines are in serious decline. In this field, the importance of the end-users' ability to judge information is essential due to the intangible nature of tourism products, which offer very limited physical cues for evaluation before purchase (Ayeh, Au & Law, 2013).

According to data in this study, the impact of social determinants is weak. Participants defined truth as a personal opinion because "every traveller has their way of traveling" (P22, lay user). Thus, in a first stage, they classified tourism as a field of open knowledge. This assumption dismisses the role of social determinants in assessing credibility. Consequently, different travelers' profiles share similar patterns of assessment, and to be a member of a profession related to tourism does not entail specific rules for truth recognition.

As truth is a question of personal preference, tourists look for markers to identify whether the content would match their tastes. Although markers are numerous, the first one users take into account is the source. Generally, tourists are aware of the presence of commercial bias in traditional sources, especially from tourist suppliers and official marketing sites. This pre-established idea favors UGC venues because travelers posting in such venues are supposed to be disinterested sources of information. Therefore, information disseminated by peer travelers possesses an advantage of trustworthiness and the assessment of credibility is simplified, as shown in the following quote:

When I look for information in an official website I already know that they are going to say the wonders of the place and not the negative things. If the place has awful public transportation, the official website won't say it. I just know that. When I browse review websites I really look for credibility. I just look for this objectivity, that whoever writes a post will tell me what they really think. P26 (professional)

The amount of data in UGC platforms is overwhelming, but classifying reviews by topic and search engines help tourists. They look for homophily (in this case defined as shared interests and shared mindset) because travelers rely on the strategy of looking for the places and types of travel experiences that they prefer. Two examples illustrate this practice:

If I'm interested in culture or in hiking I'll go directly to look at these options. [This way I don't read all reviews], I do a previous selection. P29 (lay user)

I trust, depending on who recommends something. If they match my way of life or have the same hobbies than me, I'll give them more value. P27 (professional)

This practice does not invalidate the acceptance of the veracity of other possible views on a hypothetical plane, but, in general, users ignore much content due to lack of interest.

Comparing opinions to find crowd consensus is another value of the digital ethos widely used as a basic verification form by tourists and tourism professionals. One participant talked about the issue of accepting one opinion above others by saying, "If I see that everybody agrees with the opinion that a destination is worth seeing, I trust that general idea" (P27, professional).

First-hand accounts of travelers seem to be a way of acquiring the most accurate information about unknown destinations and tourist services. Thus, a background of travel experience and the appeal of stories are the markers that provide the status of expertise. This is in contrast with other areas of knowledge, as P30 (professional) acknowledged, "In economics if a guy comes from Harvard [University] you may think he's a guru, but in traveling you should consider the way of thinking more, the way of presenting the places."

Tourists also take into account the genre of information to adopt a strategy for evaluating its credibility. This way, whereas users trust first-hand reports not biased by commercial interests when they talk in general, when they look for accurate information, they rely on experts, not casual UGC providers. For example, to get information about the quality of the cultural agenda in a city, they consider the information more reliable if it comes "from an expert who knows the atmosphere very well; it would be more interesting than the opinion of a lot of people" (P26 professional). Experts are also a guarantee of trust in a medium where "everybody copies and pastes" (P37 blogger) because they would provide quality information in order to preserve their reputations. Plausibility is employed to give a general evaluation. For example, users consider that a description about a place should be consistent with their general knowledge and common sense.

On the other hand, observation revealed a strategy to buy tourist products that is the result of self-training on how commercial practices work. P31, one of the professionals interviewed, performed an example of how she would plan a trip for Bilbao, a northern city of Spain. First, she said that because she has never been at the destination, she would make a query on Google with the keywords "flights to Bilbao" to look for an airline. After that, she pointed out that Google has commercial interests, so she usually chooses among the results taking into account her previous travel background. Therefore, she would choose reputable companies and then "I like to go directly to the company [website]" because she thinks she would save time. She also uses search engines because, "They give you a comparison of prices from many airlines." This informant, as several others, emphasized that specialized search engines and comparison-booking sites tend to include UGC, which she consulted to verify information with respect to the quality of an accommodation. This observation showed how users interpret raw data to buy a product applying the concept of reliability identified by Lankes (2008), but at the same time, it revealed how searching at e-WOM venues acts as a cognitive authority in line with Huvila (2013).

This mindset of strategies and values ascribed to tourism information correlates with a set of heuristics (see Table 1), with few differences among professionals and laypersons. As aforementioned, both profiles rely on the recognition of informal digital expertise. They also rely on the currency of information and professionals mentioned in the selection of primary sources (commercial, official sites of promotion, official statistics websites) as a rule. Heuristics of the trustworthiness dimension assume that UGC lacks commercial bias. Homophily to select suitable information is another popular heuristic. Laypersons mentioned that trust is built on the basis of consistency over time, whereas professionals reported that they rely on reputation and popularity. In this area of knowledge, plausibility heuristics are the following: crowd consensus, the accuracy of question/answer dynamics, the employment of a non-marketing language (defined by informants as a language that does not enhance the beauty and virtues of destinations or tourist services), the quality of information, the objectivity of pictures, and the comparison of quality and price of tourist services.

CONCLUSION

Previous studies on credibility used factor analysis approaches to measure indicators that result in a multiplicity of constructs of credibility and complicate our understanding of online information consumption (Choi & Stivila, 2015). On the other hand, qualitative studies found that users' conceptualization of credibility were bounded by context and ideology (Hilligoss & Rieh, 2008; Savolainen, 2007). Despite the importance attributed to contextual factors, scholars are still devoted to investigating how audiences cope with the intrinsic features of online content, be they related to the source, the quality of messages, or the dynamics of participation. The role of power structures and cultural mindsets associated with types of information is still largely ignored and missunderstood. The social epistemology approach of credibility assessment applied in this study contributes to connect the rise of new values of information legitimation aroused by virtual communities—the collective digital ethos—with social determinants.

At least two interesting findings were noted when truth, knowledge, and social context are undertaken to explain credibility judgments. First, digital ethos tends toward eliminating hierarchies in knowledge production, but traditional structures struggle in retaining the hegemony of their ethos. The smaller the area of knowledge, the bigger the resistance to adopt new procedures and values (e.g., reliance on crowd consensus) becomes. Second, laypersons do not question the ethos of professions ascribed to areas of closed knowledge, but they feel capable of pursuing a learning process and discussing, at the very least, similar terms with traditional authorities. In presenting the interplay among social structures, epistemic styles of thinking, normative values, and the pressures of digital ethos, this chapter identifies new direction for future research in credibility.

On the other hand, this approach has implications for digital literacy programs. By taking into account the social dynamics of truth construction, literacy programs can develop approaches that promote critical thinking connected with the ontology of knowledge areas. Understanding how knowledge production works would enable people to consider the pros and cons of traditional procedures of truth construction and the limits that social actors impose on adopting new thinking styles. At the same time, critical thinking would balance the advantages and disadvantages of the procedures of truth construction adopted by the champions of digital ethos. Critical thinkers would take advantage of the Internet as a repository of information and would be empowered in their relationship with specialists because they would be able to deal with data and arguments on similar terms. This involves a learning effort that can be quite substantial and ongoing. Finally, such critical thinking and involvement with different methods of source evaluation in relatively unfamiliar topics can foster important discussion on normative factors needed to improve equity in social relations.

Understanding credibility as a process embedded in social epistemology enables us to thoroughly depict the role of social determinants. The model herein demonstrates the importance of understanding the differences in placing information in areas of knowledge for employing different evaluation procedures. Thus, we have seen how the closure of knowledge conditions the degree of objectivity in evaluating credibility and the power relations played by social strata. Although the study approached three different areas of knowledge, it has limitations since other fields in each area might entail new parameters and/or restrictions for legitimating (online) information. However, it seems a broadly shared assumption that the comprehensiveness of the Internet as a repository of human knowledge enables people to learn and reach self-sufficiency (Lankes, 2008).

Tackling the role that social structures play also allows us to reflect on the establishment of normative values and its acceptance by individuals. In this way, we can diagnose how credibility may be split between the perception of the accepted credibility in a particular social sphere and the particular credibility definition deployed by each individual.

Finally, this research has implications for methodology when investigating credibility evaluation. Discursive explanations have proven valuable in discerning the rationalities of individuals. However, observation of their actual behavior has detected some inconsistencies that help us to better understand processes of evaluation and to better elicit change in consumption habits and meaning interpretation. Despite not being entirely a naturalistic approach, think aloud protocol has proven useful in unveiling implicit judgements.

REFERENCES

Allué, M. (2013). *El Paciente inquieto: los servicios de atención médica y la ciudadanía*. Barcelona: Edicions Bellaterra.

Aristotle. (1998). Retórica. Madrid: Alianza.

Ayeh, J. K., Au, N., & Law, R. (2013). "Do We Believe in TripAdvisor?" Examining Credibility Perceptions and Online Travelers' Attitude toward Using User-Generated Content. *Journal of Travel Research*, *52*(4), 437–452. doi:10.1177/0047287512475217

Bernabeu, J. (2007). Medicina e ideología: reflexiones desde la historiografía médica española. In R. Campos, L. Montiel, & R. Huertas (Eds.), *Medicina, ideología e historia en España (siglos XVI-XXI)* (pp. 17–50). Madrid: Consejo Superior de Investigaciones Científicas.

Bruns, A. (2005). *Gatewatching: Collaborative online news production* (Vol. 26). Peter Lang.

Burbules, N. (2001). Paradoxes of the Web: The ethical dimensions of credibility. *Library Trends*, *49*(3), 441–453.

Cameron, R. E., Neal, L., & Coll, M. Á. (2005). *Historia económica mundial: desde el Paleolítico hasta el presente*. Madrid: Alianza.

Castel, R. (1983). *La Gestión de los riesgos: de la anti-psiquiatría al post-análisis*. Barcelona: Anagrama.

Choi, W., & Stvilia, B. (2015). Web credibility assessment: Conceptualization, operationalization, variability and models. *Journal of the Association for Information Science and Technology*, *66*(12), 2399–2414. doi:10.1002/asi.23543

Eysenbach, G. (2008). Medicine 2.0: Social networking, collaboration, participation, apomediation, and openness. *Journal of Medical Internet Research*, *10*(3), e22. doi:10.2196/jmir.1030 PMID:18725354

Fogg, B. J. (2003). *Persuasive technology: using computers to change what we think and do*. Amsterdam: Morgan Kaufmann Publishers.

Freidson, E. (1978). *La Profesión médica: un estudio de sociologia del conocimiento aplicado*. Barcelona: Península.

Frobish, T. S. (2013). On pixels, perceptions, and personae: Toward a model of online ethos. In M. Folk & S. Apostel (Eds.), *Digital ethos: Evaluating computer-mediated communication* (pp. 1–23). Hershey, PA: IGI Global. doi:10.4018/978-1-4666-2663-8.ch001

Geertz, C. (1999). El sentido común como sistema cultural. In *Conocimiento Local. Ensayos sobre la interpretación de las culturas* (pp. 93–116). Barcelona: Paidós Ibérica.

Guan, Z., Lee, S., Cuddihy, E., & Ramey, J. (2006). The validity of the stimulated retrospective think-aloud method as measured by eye tracking. In *Proceedings of the SIGCHI conference on Human Factors in computing systems - CHI '06* (pp. 1253-1262). Montreal, Quebec, Canada: ACM Press. doi:10.1145/1124772.1124961

Guex, V. (2010). A Sociological View of the Cybertourists. In Information and Communication Technologies in Tourism 2010 (pp. 417-428). Springer. doi:10.1007/978-3-211-99407-8_35

Harris, M. (1990). *Antropología cultural*. Madrid: Alianza.

Hilligoss, B., & Rieh, S. Y. (2008). Developing a unifying framework of credibility assessment: Construct, heuristics, and interaction in context. *Information Processing & Management, 44*(4), 1467–1484. doi:10.1016/j.ipm.2007.10.001

Huvila, I. (2013). In Web search we trust? Articulation of the cognitive authorities of Web searching. Information Research, 18(1).

Instituto Nacional de Estadística. (2012). *Survey about Household Equipement and Use of Technology 2012*. Retrieved December 13, 2013, from http://www.ine.es/jaxi/menu.do?type=pcaxis&path=%2Ft25/p450&file=inebase&L=0

Jeon, G. Y., & Rieh, S. Y. (2014). Answers from the Crowd: How Credible are Strangers in Social Q&A? iConference 2014 Proceedings (pp. 663-668). iSchools.

Jessen, J., & Jørgensen, A. (2011). Aggregated trustworthiness: Redefining online credibility through social validation. *First Monday, 17*(1). Retrieved from http://firstmonday.org/htbin/cgiwrap/bin/ojs/index.php/fm/article/viewArticle/3731

Kendall, L. (2004). Studying the day-to-day meaning of email through a hybrid think-aloud protocol/In depth interview research method. In *2nd Symposium New Research for New Media*.

Lankes, R. D. (2008). Credibility on the internet: Shifting from authority to reliability. *The Journal of Documentation, 64*(5), 667–686. doi:10.1108/00220410810899709

Lim, S. (2013). Does formal authority still matter in the age of wisdom of crowds? Perceived credibility, peer and professor endorsement in relation to college students' wikipedia use for academic purposes. *Proceedings of the American Society for Information Science and Technology, 50*(1), 1–4. doi:10.1002/meet.14505001118

Metzger, M. (2007). Making sense of credibility on the Web: Models for evaluating online information and recommendations for future research. *Journal of the American Society for Information Science and Technology, 58*(13), 2078–2091. doi:10.1002/asi.20672

Metzger, M. J., Hartsell, E. H., & Flanagin, A. J. (2015). Cognitive Dissonance or Credibility? A Comparison of Two Theoretical Explanations for Selective Exposure to Partisan News. *Communication Research*, 1–26.

Meyer, A. (2008). Investigating Cultural Consumers. In M. Pickering (Ed.), Research Methods for Cultural Studies (pp. 68-87). Edimburgh, UK: Edinburgh University Press.

Rosen, G. (1985). *De la policía médica a la medicina social: Ensayos sobre la historia de la atención a la salud*. México: Siglo XXI.

Savolainen, R. (1995). Everyday Life Information Seeking : Approaching Information Seeking in the Context of «Way of Life». *Library & Information Science Research, 0*(17), 259–294. doi:10.1016/0740-8188(95)90048-9

Savolainen, R. (2007). Media credibility and cognitive authority. The case of seeking orienting information. *Information Research, 12*(3).

Surowiecki, J. (2004). *The wisdom of crowds*. New York: Anchor Books.

Tapscott, D., & Williams, A. D. (2008). *Wikinomics: How mass collaboration changes everything*. Penguin.

Wilson, P. (1983). *Second-hand knowledge: An inquiry into cognitive authority*. Greenwood Press Westport.

Wimmer, R. D., Dader, J. L., & Dominick, J. R. (1996). *La Investigación científica de los medios de comunicación: una introducción a sus métodos*. Barcelona: Bosch.

World Health Organization. (2001). *The World Health Report 2001. Mental health: new understanding, new hope*. Retrieved from http://jama.jamanetwork.com/article.aspx?articleid=194394

KEY TERMS AND DEFINITIONS

Apomediation: Neologism coined by Gunter Eysenbach in 2008 for depicting a special form of disintermediation that has emerged on the Internet. By apomediation Internet users substitute the dependence on traditional intermediaries of information (gatekeepers) for guidance from apomediaries, who help them to identify credible information by saying if a document is of certain quality, but without altering the raw data or providing a particular narrative.

Closed, Semi-Open and Open Knowledge: A scale for knowledge classification based on the disctinction between closed and open questions. A closed knowledge area is one where a set of statements is established beyond doubt in a historical moment (e.g. medicine in this study), a semi-open knowledge area includes both undoubted statatements and issues on debate and contention (e.g. Economy in this studiy), and, finally, an open knowledge area is a domain totally conformed by opinions on debate and subjectivity (e.g. tourism in this study).

Cognitive Authority: A theory by Patrick Wilson (1983) that establishes that people grant especial status to other sources of information and knowledge to legitimate second-hand information. Cognitive authorities have an influence on people's thoughts because they are perceived to be competent and knowledgable in a sphere of knowledge and also morally virtuous persons (or institutions).

Common Sense: A cultural system of interpretation historically constructed that presents the reality in a simple manner. It assumes that every individual has an elementary mental outfit to judge the reality.

Gatewatching: The outcome of the debate carried on by producers (see below) in Internet venues, who compare and discuss about the motivations of information providers for gatekeeping data, be they commercial or political, long-established journalistic/editorial routines... As a result, the construction of truth is performed through a new set of power relations (presumably horizontal relations) on a community and not the acceptance of the proposals of a superior hierarchical group.

Producer: A profile of Internet consumer who is engaged in producing texts and using texts at the same time. This type of consumer challenges the old separation between active producers and passive audiences. Producers can be bloggers, micro-bloggers, commentators or members of virtual communities.

Professionalism: The ideology that considers expert knowledge as more rational knowledge than general knowledge or common sense. It is usually supported by administrative prerogatives, e.g. medicine, law.

Second-Hand Information Legitimation: Individual practice, influenced by social determinants, by which information provided by others (initially distrusted) is considered valid information and suitable to use. This exercise relies on notions of credibility and representations of truth.

Self-Suffiency: An information assessment based on reliability, popular into 2.0 platforms where users are able to synthesizing data from multiple sources and analyzing its consistency.

Wisdom of Crowds: A theory by James Surowiecky (2004) that attributes superiority to the knowledge produced by the aggregation of individual decisions in groups. The theory questions the traditional idea of quality knowledge produced by training and specialized experts. Virtual communities have adopted this idea as a value for knowledge production and legitimation.

ENDNOTES

[1]   Throughout, quotations from the data are indicated by a reference to the participant (P), complemented by the basic profile definition of professional, lay user, and blogger.

[2]   Cognitive heuristic rules are information processing strategies that ignore certain information to make decisions quickly and with less effort than complex methods as systematic analysis. They act as rules of thumb or mental shortcuts for recognizing credibility attributes.

Chapter 8
Credible to Whom?
The Curse of the Echo Chamber

Nathan Rodriguez
University of Wisconsin – Stevens Point, USA

ABSTRACT

This chapter adopts a case study approach to examine the echo chamber effect online. Individuals cobble together personalized newsfeeds by active choice and those choices are often accompanied by subtle manipulations in social media and online search engine algorithms that may shape and constrain the parameters of information on a given topic. In this chapter, the author studied vaccine-hesitant discourse in an online forum over a five-year period. Those conversations exhibited characteristics of what would be considered an echo chamber, as defined by Jamieson and Cappella (2008). The implications of this case study suggest that the echo chamber within the realm of vaccination can lead individuals toward content and information of dubious veracity, with significant implications for public health.

INTRODUCTION

Search engines, mobile apps, and social media have radically reconstituted the process of acquiring information. Traditional intermediaries with specialized knowledge now vie for attention in the digital realm. Motivated participants in online spaces may actively contest notions of what constitutes expertise, and what authors, sources and narratives enjoy the digital ethos that can persuade others.

In many instances, this commingling of experts and laity is innocuous and user-friendly. Personalized online experiences may help individuals decide which movie to stream on Netflix, which restaurant to patronize, or which tourist destination might be worth a visit. At the same time, a significant middle ground exists where a lack of exposure to alternative points of view has a variety of consequences on a personal and societal level.

Communication has been transformed from a supply- to a demand-economy due to declining advertising revenues and the evolving habits of readers and viewers (Brants, 2013; Van Cuilenburg et al., 1999). This means that consumers who formerly had a narrow range of media options now have a panoply of voices vying for their attention: alternative media outlets, bloggers and vloggers, close friends and distant

DOI: 10.4018/978-1-5225-1072-7.ch008

relatives, and professional journalists at legacy media institutions. In this restructured setting, individuals assemble a daily information flow that may or may not contain viewpoints that contradict their own, resulting in a positive feedback loop, or echo chamber (Jamieson & Cappella, 2008). The consumers of news have now become the gatekeepers.

Viewers and readers not only have access to a broader range of media sources, but also the ability to connect with one another to discuss those representations. One of the most fundamental changes in the digital era is not that individuals have an enhanced ability to seek out information, but that information is pushed back to the individual at an increased rate through social media networks. The notion that people receive more information from friends and family than mass media has circulated for several decades, with studies confirming three-quarters of people follow the news primarily for social purposes (Katz & Lazarsfield 1955; Kovach & Rosenstiel, 2010, p. 150). Social recommendations therefore have a significant influence on whether individuals choose to click on stories, the assumptions they make regarding credibility, and whether they decide to share the story (Cole & Greer, 2013, p. 676; Xu, 2013, pp. 769-771).

Individuals no longer access information through one or a few mass media sources, but "literally assemble information associatively by interacting with it online" (Peters & Broersma, 2013, pp. 4-5). Social networking platforms have become a critical part of information flow, even more so for younger individuals, and these trends are likely to persist because media consumption patterns developed in early adulthood tend to endure (Davies & Enyon, 2013; Rankin, 2013, pp. 105-106; p. 154). If the acquisition and recirculation of news and information is fundamentally a social process, an individual's desire to seek out information inside or outside this personalized echo chamber may be determined by social ties.

Finally, readers and viewers continue to drift at greater rates into niche-based interpretive communities, and the (re)construction of events becomes a more active and involved process as official discourses blend with vernacular narratives. Certain interpretive communities perceptually lie beyond the bounds of more mainstream or acceptable political discourse, and such groups deserve greater academic attention to better describe the nature of online conversations that bind these individuals together, often in opposition to representations by mainstream media outlets.

This chapter begins with an overview of how the circulation and recirculation of news and information has changed during the past few decades in order to argue how the architecture of new media systems makes a personalized echo chamber a more likely outcome than in the past. Conspiracy theories in particular complicate discussions of credibility, and a case study approach toward vaccine-hesitant discourse is used to demonstrate the relative perils of ascertaining the credibility of information found online. The concluding discussion evaluates the implications of this continually evolving media environment.

BACKGROUND

Legacy Media Meets Social Media

In the halcyon days of network television in the mid- and late-20th century, legacy media institutions helped form an agreed-upon "grand narrative" (Lyotard, 1979) that could at least offer a recognizable point of reference for current events. By selecting what was considered fit for discussion, that grand narrative also dictated the "bounds that are set on thinkable thought" (Chomsky, 1989, p. 147). The digital era removes intermediaries from the process of accessing and recirculating information, and it allows individuals to access, comment upon, and share information from a dizzying array of sources that offer the allure of click-worthy content.

Technological advances have changed the way information moves, and the process of acquiring information has become more personalized. Digital devices changed the way people communicate and also changed the way people receive and share information, including news. The ways individuals produce, access, circulate, and share information has changed in the last few decades as internet access and smartphones allow people to adopt mass communication techniques, offer commentary on news stories, and access narratives that suit personal preferences. The 20th century top-down structure of media flow, with its binary of producer and consumer, is supplemented—and in some ways supplanted—by outside voices: bloggers, content aggregation sites, and alternative media sources.

Journalism, particularly in the broadcast era, constructed and recalled shared memories that helped unify viewers/readers into communities based on common ground (Kitch, 2002). In that way, journalists may be said to lead interpretive communities. Of course, this process marginalized other groups with alternative version of the same events (Zelizer, 1995). The digital era complicates the process a bit more, as the "people formerly known as the audience" have the ability to directly affirm, contest, or subvert such messages through social media (Rosen, 2006). The process of constructing the past has always involved a commingling between official and individual narratives, but individuals now have the ability to disseminate their thoughts on the same platform. Now the baggage of the masses often accompanies what were once the stand-alone official accounts by officials, experts, and gatekeepers of incidents and events in a community.

When the Mainstream Is Marginalized and the Marginalized Is Mainstream

Public opinion polls in recent years clearly indicate most Americans do not trust mainstream media sources. A 2012 Gallup poll showed 60 percent of Americans had "little or no trust" in mass media (Morales, 2012). Pew reported double-digit declines in "believability" ratings for thirteen of the largest news organizations in print, cable and radio from 2002 to 2012 ("Further Decline...," 2012). A 2013 Gallup poll indicated only one in five Americans agreed that print and television journalists have "high or very high" honesty and ethical standards (Swift, 2013). Warner (2010) showed that highly partisan content (e.g., Sean Hannity and *The Nation*) is perceived as "equally trustworthy" and "equally objective" when compared side-by-side with a mainstream media source—in this case, *The New York Times* (p. 442).

Individuals may seek out, receive, and (re)circulate information from a wider array of sources than ever before. A variety of outcomes may occur when someone is dissatisfied with, or distrustful of, mainstream media sources. In the digital era, this frequently results in individuals seeking out alternative sources of news and information online that align more closely with their interests (Hanitzsch, 2013, pp. 206-208; Hwang et al., 2006; Tsfati & Cappella, 2003). Alternate sources of information, by virtue of a willingness to interrogate specific issues of interest to a particular niche, thus begin to occupy a position of greater prominence (Aaronovitch, 2010, p. 158). The sheer number of sources can complicate the assessment of credibility (Franklin & Carlson, 2011; Kovach & Rosenstiel, 2010). When mainstream media sources are generally held in low esteem, it becomes less surprising that an increasing number of readers and viewers drift to sources of sometimes-dubious veracity.

This means that claims that were once isolated and seen as beyond the bounds of mainstream discourse are able to spread more rapidly online. The Internet allows strangers to connect across physical distances, and information that was "once scattered, forgettable and localized is becoming permanent and searchable" (Solove, 2007, p. 4). In the past, those who held marginalized beliefs about disparate issues often lacked the ability to articulate those views before a significant number of people. For years, advocates of conspiracy theories had a relatively limited toolkit to express their viewpoints, including pamphlets, late-night radio programs, VHS tapes, or an occasional convention—all of which offered sporadic engagement rather than constant immersion. As a result, outsider views were often relegated to the margins of public discourse, the product of isolated individuals. The dissemination of that same information online becomes cumulative, searchable and transmittable with a few keystrokes. In recent years, individuals who espouse conspiracy theories have connected with a receptive audience online (Aaronovitch, 2010, p. 232; Byford, 2011; Wood, 2013, p. 31). This suggests that conspiracy theories can spread more easily and further cloud—or cast doubt upon—depictions of events by mainstream media outlets.

What remains murky is the extent to which alternative sources of information might dominate an individual's media diet. Some work suggests individuals filter information they receive from those with differing viewpoints in their social media feed (Rainie & Smith, 2012), while other studies suggest that in spite of using the internet to seek out shared opinions, individuals tend to not intentionally avoid information that might result in dissonance (Holbert, Hmielowski & Weeks, 2012; Garrett, 2009 in Gvirsman, 2014, pp. 78-79; Tewksbury, 2006). Immersion in such informational environments provides participants with the illusory notion that true public opinion closely matches one's own opinion (Wojcieszak, 2010). Whether it is through face-to-face interactions with acquaintances or virtual interactions with like-minded others online, individuals now have the ability to connect with others who have similar viewpoints—regardless of how far beyond the realm of mainstream discourse those viewpoints might be.

By their very nature, conspiracy theories lie beyond the realm of traditionally mainstream discourse, to varying degrees. As with most narratives, conspiracy theories differ greatly in terms of content and implications for a broader worldview. What links these narratives is a contrast from an "official" version of events that posits a more nefarious scheme occurred with more than one agent acting insidiously during its execution and/or subsequent cover-up. Mere exposure to conspiracy theories has been shown to increase belief in such theories (Jolley, 2013, p. 35; Lantian, 2013, p. 19). This means that alternative sources of information can become viewed as more accurate or even credible on a particular topic that exists beyond the purview of most mainstream discussions. As individuals delve more deeply into alternative texts, they may begin to (rightly) associate mainstream media outlets with the official, or in their view, flawed version of events. The result is that conspiracy theories, by circulating with greater ease, can cloud—or at least cast doubt upon—depictions of events by mainstream media outlets.

A Self-Selected Echo Chamber

While a number of circumstances coalesce to influence media choices made by individuals, it is worth reviewing two phenomena that tend to explain how someone may actively move toward what might be considered an echo chamber. Hostile media theory emerged in the 1980s to describe the idea that partisans can view the same neutral story as biased in favor of the opposition (Vallone, Ross & Lepper, 1985). Media dissociation, proposed by Hwang et al., (2006), is a variation of hostile media theory and describes a situation where individuals perceive their worldview at odds with that articulated by mainstream media outlets. It differs from hostile media theory in that it focuses on an individual's perceived relation to the content of mainstream media, and does not rely upon a "neutral" story viewed by those with partisan political beliefs. Research suggests the more individuals feel their views differ from those portrayed in mainstream media outlets, the more motivated they become to rely upon the Internet for information and social connections (Hwang et al., 2006, p. 462, 476).

The information age can be viewed as the affirmation age when individuals actively select content that aligns with their existing viewpoint. People tend to seek out and read what they prefer to believe (Garrett, 2009; Hart et al., 2009; Iyengar & Hahn, 2009; Warner, 2010). This may result in an effect known as the echo chamber, which depicts the ways "messages are amplified and reverberate...[within] a bounded, enclosed media space that has the potential to both magnify the messages delivered within it and insulate them from rebuttal...[It] creates a common frame of reference and positive feedback loops for those who listen to, read, and watch these media outlets" (Jamieson & Cappella, 2008, p. 76). As daily patterns of acquiring information become calcified over time, beliefs about source credibility begin to take root, and information that does not provide the satisfaction of affirmation may be sacrificed to maintain consonance in the echo chamber.

Studies have examined the echo chamber metaphor within the online context in a variety of ways, with uneven standards for what might constitute an echo chamber. Adamic and Glance (2005) performed a citation analysis of political blogs, examining whether external citations were left- or right-leaning. Some researchers have conducted pre- and post-tests for individuals exposed to a cluster of informational sources that represented an echo chamber (Warner, 2010). Others have examined reader comments on blogs, arguing that an echo chamber should be defined as a blog "on which more than 64% of the opinionated commenters agree with the blogger" (Gilbert, Bergstrom & Karahalios, 2009). Some have suggested that conspiracy sites retain the hallmarks of an echo chamber (Sunstein & Vermeule, 2009, p. 210), but there have not been any studies to determine whether conspiracy-themed websites functionally serve as echo chambers (Wood, 2013, p. 33).

Helpfully, a few key observations first mentioned by Jamieson and Cappella include perhaps the most comprehensive description of the characteristics of an echo chamber. Three broad themes emerge in their work: consistent redundant framing, metacommunication about frames from the mainstream, and elements of an in-group mentality.

Consistent redundant framing is said to offer the audience a way to navigate content and resolve competing frames (Jamieson & Cappella, 2008, p. 142). This results in a consistent way of viewing events, focusing on certain aspects while excluding others. The presence of semantic priming—or specific word choices—can "increase the salience of those words and their associated concepts, topics, or issues" (p. 143). This generates a common vocabulary for participants and enhances the appeal of certain modes of thought.

Metacommunication about mainstream media frames concerns the relative valence (positive or negative) individuals have with respect to mainstream sources (Jamieson and Cappella, 2008, pp. 151-152). In this way, the group not only frames current events, but "reframes the content and identity" of competing media options (p. 152).

Several factors converge to comprise an "in-group mentality." Jamieson and Cappella argue such groups exhibit a distinctive common vocabulary, tend to exaggerate differences with out-groups, and tend to perceive the out-group as more homogenous (pp. 177-180). The process of creating a common enemy is key to establishing a group identity (p. 180), and the use of ridicule or polarizing labels both distances the group from such entities and demonstrates a "common understanding of the enemy" (p. 184).

These findings certainly build upon basic tenets of social identity theory proposed by Tajfel et al (1971) that suggested as individuals self-categorize into groups, competition is a norm of human behavior, and that once certain categories or issues become more salient, depersonalization can occur because as a "category becomes salient, people come to see themselves and other category members less as individuals and more as interchangeable exemplars of the group prototype" (Hornsey, 2008, p. 208).

The case study selected for this chapter reveals some of the ways in which these characteristics are operationalized in discussions of vaccination. The patterns of behavior discussed thus far have focused upon some of the more deliberate choices individuals may make that help shape the content of their daily newsfeed. But in conjunction with these choices, the architecture of the Internet marshals information, sources, and suggestions in a manner that narrows, rather than broadens, perceived options—and it does so seamlessly, in a way that remains opaque to the user.

The Filter Bubble and the Invisible Architecture of the Internet

The marketplace of ideas metaphor posits that "truth" emerges through the comparison of competing viewpoints, but this fails to account for the realities of the digital era. If one were to research a conspiracy theory by using Google and YouTube, a search for "truth" may yield more questions than clarity. A "filter bubble" adjusts web search results based on a user's historic preferences (Pariser, 2011) and videos played on YouTube feature suggested clips regarding a similar premise (Ito et al., 2009, p. 46). So, even if someone were to investigate the veracity of a particular conspiracy theory claim, the results on search engines and YouTube become re-oriented by algorithms that generally lead an individual deeper into the conspiracy texts. The Internet may allow an individual to adopt the tools of mass communication, but its architecture generates a stream of information that often reaffirms certain views.

Some of the more outlandish conspiracy theories may appear to have more proponents than skeptics if the narrative resides far beyond the bounds of mainstream discussions. When one executes a web search for "FEMA death camps," "reptilian agenda," or any one of the more far-fetched conspiracy theories, advocates often outnumber skeptics by virtue of occupying terrain that others have not bothered to explore. For example, at the time of this writing, a Google search (on a cleared incognito browser) for "FEMA death camps" generates just two links on the first page that dismiss the theory, alongside eight links in favor of the argument. The first link is a YouTube video, "FEMA DEATH CAMPS EXPOSED (CIA IS AWARE)," the second is "Images for FEMA death camps" with four thumbnails of Google Image results. The two sources on the first page to debunk the theory, RationalWiki.org and PopularMechanics.com, compete "below the fold" with results including: "List of All FEMA Concentration Camps in America," "*CBS News* Admits FEMA Camps Are Real," and a *Yahoo! Answers* link with a "Best Answer, Chosen by Voters" that affirms the theory. Similarly, a Google search for "reptilian shape-shifters" yields zero links on the first page that debunk the theory. These web search results belie the actual acceptance rate of such theories, as national polls data show just 4 percent of Americans profess a belief in reptilian shape-shifters (Public Policy Polling, 2013). Those who articulate conspiracy theories in the digital era therefore often produce the dominant texts on search engine result pages by virtue of the more marginalized issues existing beyond traditional journalism beats and popular public discourse. The result for readers can be a confusing mélange of detailed conspiracy theory texts that often overwhelm the sparse, surface-level treatment accorded to the discourse by mainstream publications. At that point, it becomes more difficult to discern the credible expert on that issue.

The era of digital balkanization means individuals may unwittingly create a web of facticity that may offer an illusion of confirmation. Individuals tend to circulate within their preferred pockets of the newsphere (Tracy, 2012), often without wider knowledge of potentially valid perspectives on a particular subject. Often, those pockets of the newsphere form a self-reinforcing web of similar claims that complicate questions of credibility because certain reporters and outlets may garner credibility by virtue of referencing others who have credibility within those circles.

Participants in online conspiracy theory forums, as with many other online forums, frequently reference sources and experts they deem credible. Once a quorum of "credible sources" is achieved, an individual tends to form an opinion regarding an issue. The formation of that opinion is built upon arguably reasonable inferences from a casual reader or viewer, due to the veneer of credibility some sources attain by making use of the architecture of the Internet.

Conspiracy theorist Alex Jones has emerged as a leader within a burgeoning conspiracy theory movement, boasting a larger digital presence than Rush Limbaugh and Glenn Beck combined (Zaitchik, 2011). Jones's conspiracy theorizing proves to be an popular entry point for discussions of conspiracy theories, as his websites, Infowars and PrisonPlanet, generate around 28 million unique hits each month (Seitz-Wald, 2013). Those online discussions can cause someone predisposed to a particular belief to articulate that belief with greater conviction in the presence of other like-minded individuals (Sunstein, 2009). As will be shown in the following case study, however, even heterogeneous online forums where claims are subject to intense debate and individuals are exposed to different points of view may prove to be little more than a convenient meeting place for participants to articulate rather than challenge their own viewpoints.

CASE STUDY: VACCINE-HESITANT DISCOURSE

Amplifying Adverse Reactions: The Online "Debate" Regarding Vaccination

The medical debate regarding vaccines bears some resemblance to the scientific discussion concerning global warming, in that most experts consider it a question that has been asked, answered, and settled. With respect to vaccinations, an overwhelming amount of data demonstrates the procedure itself is a safe and effective way to combat disease. Vaccines may have varying rates of efficacy, but there is no credible evidence to suggest they are linked to a rise in Autism Spectrum Disorder diagnoses. But concerns about vaccines have persisted, and as more people have abandoned the recommended inoculation schedule in recent years, vaccine-preventable infectious diseases have returned to the United States.

The argument in favor of vaccines is reasonably straightforward: inoculating the public prevents the spread of curable disease, in a safe and cost-effective manner. Vaccines, and those who develop them, have been indispensable in eradicating smallpox, as well as preventing the spread of pertussis, measles, and polio (Dube et. al., 2013, p. 1763; Poland & Jacobson, 2012). Hailed as the "most important public health achievement of the last century," vaccines have been credited with saving 2.5 million lives globally each year (Bean, 2011, p. 1874; Chan, 2014). Numerous studies indicate adverse reactions to vaccines are generally rare (Peltola & Heinonen, 1986; Zhou et al, 2003, p. 1). The Centers for Disease Control and Prevention (CDC) found that severe reactions "occur so rarely that the risk is difficult to calculate"

(Frequently Asked Questions, 2011). Given their preventative success rate, vaccines are also seen as cost-effective by reducing future medical expenses and limiting productivity losses (Lieu et. al., 1994; Sanders & Taira, 2003). Belief in the efficacy of vaccines is not limited to western medical science, as dozens of nation-states require travelers to provide documentation of immunization ("International Travel," 2014). In short, decades of research by members of the medical community approach near-consensus in the argument that vaccines safely prevent the spread of infectious disease.

Public polling data indicate widespread confusion regarding the basic claim that vaccines cause autism. A Harris poll found that one in three parents link vaccines and autism (Survey, 2014). Another study indicated just 44 percent of Americans disagreed with the statement "Doctors and the government still want to vaccinate children even though they know these vaccines cause autism and other psychological disorders (Oliver & Wood, 2014). The implications of these findings are indicative first of significant public concern regarding the safety and effectiveness of vaccination, and second, of significant public concern regarding the general trustworthiness of doctors and the government. It would not be unreasonable to suggest the convenience of search engines has, for some individuals in certain cases, diminished the influence of traditional experts who have acted as information intermediaries—even medical professionals.

Online search engines have fundamentally changed the way individuals become informed about issues. Three in four Americans who use the Internet have sought out health information online during the past year (Fox & Duggan, 2013). If and when people try to investigate the inaccurate claim that vaccines cause autism or are unsafe, they may consult a health care professional at some point during the process, but people frequently turn to an online search to resolve such matters (Ruiz & Bell, 2014, p. 5777). In executing an online search, it can be difficult for a layperson to separate fact from speculation, conjecture or outright fiction without additional research, which often leads further into anti-vaccination literature. This is because search engine results for "vaccines" will often produce texts from the *Centers for Disease Control and Prevention* alongside information from the National Vaccine Information Center. The latter organization, bearing a moniker that may appear objective to a member of the laity, is indeed a curator of anti-vaccination literature.

Although the results might be a bit dated (as Lycos, Metacrawler, and AOL were used alongside Google, Yahoo, and MSN), one study found that 93 percent of parents found anti-vaccination sites in their first 10 search results, and, of greater importance, that simpler search terms tended to yield more anti-vaccination websites (Downs, de Bruin & Fischhoff, 2008, p. 1604). This contrasted with more sophisticated searches that were more likely to generate official public health sites on the first page of results, which is troubling because it indicates that people who may be less knowledgeable regarding vaccines are more likely to encounter information of dubious veracity. The authors also reported that many parents said they would rather search online than ask their physician for additional information regarding vaccinations.

So the basic way that many people tend to verify claims—an online search--can lead to greater confusion regarding vaccination. This not only impacts a layperson who executes a purposive live search, but also those who encounter such claims by chance through social networks. One problem is that even brief exposure to anti-vaccination websites has been shown to increase a person's perception of risk and reduce the likelihood that parents will vaccinate their children several months later (Betsch & Renkewitz, 2009).

There is near-consensus in the persuasion literature that online forums are more effective at persuasion relative to traditional media (Daugherty, Gangadharbatla & Bright, 2010). Finally, Kareklas, Muehling and Weber (2015) demonstrated that public service announcements regarding vaccination did not influence individual opinions regarding vaccination, but that online comments regarding those PSAs did influence opinions. This is a particularly significant finding that demonstrates the power of collaborative filtering, and the primacy individuals tend to place on the opinion of other—often anonymous—members of the public compared to the value given to expert opinions on the matter.

With respect to vaccine-hesitant views, then, the process of self-education through online searches seems to make it more likely that vaccine-hesitant views become calcified. Individuals who begin with curiosity may instead become swept up by evolving search algorithms and filter bubbles that generate anti-vaccine texts.

Vaccine-Hesitant Discourse Online

The author studied online discussions over a five-year period regarding vaccination on the conspiracy theory based website, *AboveTopSecret* (ATS). The user-generated nature of the content on discussion boards allows for topics of interest to emerge organically in comparison to the genre of top-down, text-producing sites, and can therefore yield a better glimpse at which vaccine-related claims hold suasive force for a cross-section of vaccine-hesitant individuals.

In the process of examining suitable user-generated message boards, emphasis was placed upon finding message boards that facilitated the circulation of conspiracy theories. Concern regarding vaccine safety may not necessarily be conspiratorial in nature, but such sites, it would seem, might be more conducive to attracting ample debate. Furthermore, public opinion polls mentioned previously classify the belief as a conspiracy theory: Observers have noticed "conspiracy theories lie at the heart of the anti-vaccine movement" (Offit, 2011, p. 203).

It has been said "the soul of interaction" in online groups is "strong, often vehement disagreement" that is "sometimes...emotional" and "sometimes...highly rational" (Kelly, Fisher, & Smith, 2005, p. 91). And while caustic interactions were present to some degree, the site structure, active moderation, and nature of conversations on ATS promoted more reasoned dialogue. In other words, the conversations on ATS seemed to offer greater substance and depth than were found in the other forums. For these reasons, ATS was selected as the site of study for the project.

To briefly situate the discussion site within a broader context, ATS advertises itself as the "largest and most popular discussion board community dedicated to the intelligent exchange of ideas and debate on a wide range of 'alternate topics'" ("About," 2014). ATS has been characterized by participants on other conspiracy theory sites as "the biggest conspiracy forum" (Dubay, 2010). The site's 300,000+ registered users have created more than one million topic threads, with an average of 18 responses per thread. A snapshot of the aggregate statistics of the site demonstrates just a few thousand participants produce the vast majority of the content.

As its name might suggest, ATS is, for the most part, friendly toward conspiracy theorizing. This ought not be conflated with being accepting or uncritical toward such ideas—there are plenty of threads with more skeptics than proponents. Rather, the site is maybe best seen as a gathering place to discuss (and discard) ideas that may fall within, along, and beyond the boundaries of typical mainstream discourse. In a number of cases, the person initiating a thread may not have a particularly strong opinion on the matter, and is merely brought something to the attention of other board members to discuss.

METHODS

This methodology used in the case study is rooted in grounded theory that seeks to probe vaccine-hesitant discourse with the intention of developing a better answer to the basic question, "What's happening here?" (Glaser, 1978). Because the discourse occurs online, the raw data is the content posted by participants, and the analysis necessarily borrows techniques from ethnography and content analysis (Steinmetz, 2012, pp. 27, 30).

My approach to the topic resembles what Altheide and Schneider (2013) call *tracking discourse*, or "following certain issues, words, themes and frames over a period of time and analyzing the discourse interactively and inductively" (pp. 117-118). An inductive approach to online discussions is often recommended given that such conversations are often lively and granular in nature, with participants often debating multiple individuals or claims within a single post (Gasson & Waters, 2013, p. 106).

Baym (2009) observed that generalizability in qualitative work is "neither relevant nor possible" given the fluid nature of reality, so the goal should be to generate analyses with thick descriptions that could then be compared to other contexts (pp. 175, 186). The hope is to achieve what has been called "limited triangulation" where certain patterns are identified and might be of utility to researchers in a similar area of interest (Lincoln & Guba, 2000).

In all, 62 threads from 2010-2014 were selected for close reading, which resulted in review of roughly 6,580 user comments. During this time period, it is clear there was a rotating cast of participants on both sides of the debate. Within the sample, 57 authors created the 62 threads, and no participant started more than two threads. While it might be expected that the majority of threads in the forum might exhibit clear anti-vaccination phrasing, a quick glance at the valence of thread titles revealed roughly half of all thread titles seemed to favor an anti-vaccination narrative, while the remaining half were either open-ended or clearly pro-vaccination in nature.

Finally, to determine which aspects of communication might be considered distinctive, it is suggested one look to intensity and frequency of various features (Foss, 2009, p. 389). In an online context, this means examining what occurs within and across threads, and how participants engage both the topic and one another (Gasson & Waters, 2013, p. 102). Approximately one-third of the way through the coding process, recurring patterns of claims and behavior emerged. After refining those initial observations, a saturation point was reached and key themes in the debates regarding vaccines were identified. Credibility-related themes are unpacked in the following section to better understand the nature of vaccine-hesitant discourse online, and the process of meaning-making that occurs in such spaces.

"Links on Both Sides": *Natural News* and the Veneer of Plausibility

An observation from the ATS study is that participants on opposite ends of the vaccine-hesitancy spectrum frequently, though not always, have divergent views as to what constitutes a credible source of information (Rodriguez, 2015). Empirical evidence regarding the effectiveness of vaccination and peer-reviewed scientific studies were often cited by those in favor of inoculation, while those who were opposed to, or hesitant regarding, vaccination circulated their own historical anecdotes as reasons to question statements by authoritative sources. Disagreements regarding what constituted expertise or evidence were therefore common.

Many anti-vaccine arguments may appear compelling at first glance because there is a veneer of plausibility to many claims made by individuals in the vaccine-hesitant camp. The most common argument leveled against the CDC's recommended inoculation schedule was a variation of "Too many, too soon," in other words, too many vaccines are administered to children too early in the child's development, resulting in adverse reactions. Evidence in favor of vaccine-hesitancy is frequently speculative and scattered, but cumulatively can lend the illusion of an active controversy. This can cause some individuals to seek out and connect with others who share the interest, as one participant on ATS observed: "We are in this together and need to string together evidence as it emerges" (CorruptionExposed, 2013). It should be noted that ATS is a heterogeneous forum in which participants engage in lively and substantive debate. This distinction is meaningful because a number of online platforms, particularly Facebook groups, exist more as insular support groups with some administrators banning users who articulate a different viewpoint.

There was substantial disagreement as to what constituted evidence and who may be considered an expert. One of the most-circulated sites used by those in favor of the inoculation schedule is Science-BasedMedicine.org, which is run by physicians and attempts to methodically examine many claims made by the more vociferous anti-vaccine sites. Vaccine skeptics have referred to it as a "well known Big Pharma propaganda site, one of the worst places you could go to find out more about this, even CNN is better than that..." (HiddenCode, 2014). A number of participants who were vaccine-hesitant expressed cynicism regarding both the mainstream scientific community and legacy media institutions. In turn, when pressed for evidence that supports their beliefs regarding vaccination, many of those participants would proffer a link from a site of dubious veracity, e.g., Mercola.com or *Natural News*.

In recent years, a prominent hub for circulating information on alternative treatments is the website *Natural News*. Created by self-described "activist-turned-scientist" Mike Adams, the website enjoys between six million and seven million visits each month ("About Natural News," 2014; "Health Ranger," 2013; "NaturalNews.com," 2015). Not just some but many of the stories on *Natural News* demonstrate little regard for reality. In the recent past, the site opined that President Obama has "been plotting what can only be called a total government takeover of America," that eating whole lemons prevents cancer, and that homeopathic remedies can cure Ebola (Engel, 2014; Johnson, 2014; Palmer, 2014). Perhaps even more disturbing, the site has "achieved astonishing traction on social media, garnering Facebook shares in the high-five and low-six figures" (Palmer, 2014). The website is therefore not just a prominent alternative health site, but an exemplar of the ways in which information can circulate unchecked within the digital realm.

In the ATS discussions, *Natural News* emerged as perhaps the most prominent website that circulated anti-vaccine claims and was used by participants in dozens of interactions. It was striking to discover that the website was quickly critiqued nearly every time it was used, but, more remarkably, there were zero recorded instances of any participant attempting to defend the credibility of the site. Rather, it was common for the person advancing a claim with a *Natural News* link to impugn the credibility of any data, studies, government agencies, or scientists redeployed by those on the other side of the debate. On other occasions, the person stopped advancing the argument altogether, or continued with a variation of the argument's basic premise without mentioning *Natural News*, or argued the site merely hosted the link. But no participants proved willing to defend *Natural News*, and those in favor of the inoculation schedule crafted a variety of rejoinders that ranged from sarcasm to exasperation.

Other participants simply refuse to engage in discussion: "I'm not going to accept stories on sites like natural news, no one should" (SpearMint, 2013). On other occasions, participants indicted *Natural News*, but were careful to add specific problems with the claims presented as well: "You really shouldn't use natural news as a source. It's terrible. Again, I'm not using that as a reason why what the things you posted are wrong. It's just being said in addition to reasons why they are manipulating facts, or leaving things out" (Ghost375, 2013). The reputation of the site among participants on ATS was so dreadful that it was used as an exemplar of low-quality information even when it had not been used by anyone else in the thread: "Please source your statistics or admit to making up these numbers. Not even *Natural News* blows the numbers out of proportion so extremely" (opopanax, 2013).

Again, the most common response by individuals who posted *Natural News* links was to question the motives of other sources, rather than defend the site itself. A typical back-and-forth regarding the site featured one person indicating *Natural News* "literally MANUFACTURES stories. LITERALLY. They are a known hoax site" (raymundoko, 2014; emphasis in original). That person then included a link to Snopes.com, a site often used to dispel rumors and theories. In response, the person who provided the *Natural News* link did not defend the site but rather argued that Snopes.com could not be trusted because it had received funding from George Soros. And so it goes.

That example was one of several instances where seemingly neutral arbiters of truth were recast as part of the problem, in a way that at times appeared to be infinitely regressive. It is thus court cases, research-in-progress, misleading charts, questionable journal articles, informational sources of dubious veracity such as Mercola.com and the oft-maligned *Natural News*, and *YouTube* clips that proved to be the foundation for the vast majority of claims made by vaccine-hesitant individuals in the discussions studied (Rodriguez, 2015). Quality notwithstanding, the mere presence of headlines and URLs allowed the more ardent of those who oppose vaccines to make the argument that there are "links on both sides." This particular trope attempted to neutralize (or equalize) scientific investigation of the matter by implying an open debate is underway. As this section has shown, standards for what constituted proper evidence varied widely. When the proper framework for debate cannot be agreed upon, the discovery of common ground becomes more difficult.

A Different Present, a Different Past, an Uncertain Future

As mentioned above, empirical evidence regarding the efficacy of vaccines was often dismissed or contested by a number of vaccine-hesitant individuals. Perhaps more importantly, divergent interpretations regarding present-day issues extended to the past, as once-objective successes of inoculation became subject to revisionist history. For proponents of the inoculation schedule, such claims may be puzzling at first, given what would seem to be an impressive track record of efficacy in eradicating measles, polio, and other diseases.

The basic claim made in such debates is two-fold: first, evidence was cited to demonstrate a particular disease had already begun to wane before the introduction of a vaccine; second, claims were frequently made that improvements in sanitation were responsible for the eradication of most diseases. The primacy of historical analogues and anecdotes for many vaccine-hesitant individuals appears to be a relatively new observation regarding such discourse. To be sure, a number of researchers have examined the historical roots of vaccine-hesitant discourse, but at the time of this analysis, there seems to be little appreciation of how vaccine-hesitant individuals might redeploy historical examples to justify their beliefs.

The past is constantly (re)constructed in narratives by different groups in different ways for different reasons, and that process of meaning-making determines the condition of the present and influences the parameters and potentialities of the future. Halbwachs (1950) recognized the fundamentally social nature of remembering, and subsequent scholarship has emphasized the significance of remembrance for strengthening ties within communities (Radley, 1990; Brockmeier, 2002). Therefore, the ways in which individuals characterize the past informs us not only of their perception of an event, but their own lived experience, and the groups with which they identify. Those viewpoints now circulate on a much wider scale than at any point in human history, for better and for worse.

CONCLUSION

This case study examined vaccine-hesitant discourse in a heterogeneous online forum, and found that the arguments proffered by those opposed to vaccination exemplified characteristics typically seen in an echo chamber. Jamieson and Cappella's (2008) observations of semantic priming, metacommunication regarding mainstream media frames, and the development of an in-group mentality were all present in discussions on ATS. Those three traits are often blended in conversations, but semantic priming was observed in frequent mentions of "Big Pharma," which was intended to cast aspersions on the credibility of particular studies. Metacommunication about mainstream frames was shown in the contestation of empirical evidence of the effectiveness of vaccines, as well as comments that maligned "MSM" generally while lauding the work of "independent" researchers and outlets including Mercola.com and Natural-News.com. An in-group mentality was observed by some of the more ardent voices against vaccination, who would occasionally refer to their opponents as "pro-vaxers" or "vax-deniers," while also providing social support for those who claim to have been personally impacted by adverse reactions to vaccines.

The case study also revealed how these echo chamber characteristics became operationalized, as participants exhibited divergent views on digital ethos, and what constituted credible information. Peer-reviewed scientific evidence in favor of vaccination was met by accusations of "Big Pharma" ties and alternate history narratives that attempted to diminish the authoritative and suasive force of mainstream science. Cynicism regarding mainstream media outlets was often accompanied by links to alternative health news websites, notably Natural News—though when pressed to defend that particular source, there were zero recorded instances of participants attempting to defend the credibility of the site. Future efforts could examine user perceptions of the credibility of popular alternative health websites in an effort to better understand how and why such messages seem to resonate, regardless of the digital ethos of the messenger.

The digital era allows individuals to connect with others in asynchronous communication, meaning that articulations and utterances that were once scattered, contemporaneous, and possibly forgettable are now frequently captured, catalogued, and (re)circulated. Issues that were once considered to lie beyond the bounds of mainstream discourse may be summoned with a few well-placed keystrokes. In some cases, this may be beneficial because information in theory becomes democratized. As this case study has shown, however, the conscious decisions that individuals make with respect to their choices of news and information, as well as the architecture of the Internet itself, has made it more likely that exotic and occasionally dangerous belief systems are reinforced rather than challenged.

A broad and speculative appraisal at the time of this writing is that those who might benefit most from exposure to different viewpoints are those who are less likely to seek them out and are generally less aware of how their own worldview is subtly reinforced through their online activities. The individual consideration of credibility is, itself, a calculation as personalized as the algorithms that determine our daily newsfeed. One person's *Newsweek* may be another person's *Natural News*, so in any discussion of credibility, it is fair to ask, "Credible to whom?"

REFERENCES

Aaronovitch, D. (2010). *Voodoo histories: The role of the conspiracy theory in shaping modern history.* New York, NY: Riverhead Books.

About AboveTopSecret.com. (2014). *AboveTopSecret.* Retrieved from http://www.abovetopsecret.com/about_abovetopsecret.php

About Natural News. (n.d.). *Natural News.* Retrieved from http://www.naturalnews.com/About.html

Adamic, L. A., & Glance, N. (2005, August). The political blogosphere and the 2004 US election: Divided they blog. In *Proceedings of the 3rd international workshop on Link discovery* (pp. 36-43). ACM. doi:10.1145/1134271.1134277

Adams, M. (2012). *Obama seizes control over all food, farms, livestock, farm equipment, fertilizer and farm production across America.* Natural News. Retrieved from http://www.naturalnews.com/035301_Obama_executive_orders_food_supply.html

Altheide, D. L., & Schneider, C. J. (2013). *Qualitative media analysis* (2nd ed.). Los Angeles, CA: Sage.

Baym, N. K. (2009). What constitutes quality in qualitative internet research? In A. N. Markham & N. K. Baym (Eds.), *Internet inquiry: Conversations about method* (pp. 173–189). Los Angeles, CA: Sage Publications. doi:10.4135/9781483329086.n16

Bean, S. J. (2011). Emerging and continuing trends in vaccine opposition website content. *Vaccine, 29*(10), 1874–1880. doi:10.1016/j.vaccine.2011.01.003 PMID:21238571

Betsch, C., & Renkewitz, F. (2009). Langfristige Auswirkungen einer Informationssuche auf impfkritischen Internetseiten. *Prävention, 32,* 125–128.

Brants, K. (2013). Trust, cynicism, and responsiveness: the uneasy situation of journalism in democracy. In C. Peters & M. Broersma (Eds.), *Rethinking journalism: Trust and participation in a transformed news landscape* (pp. 15–27). New York, NY: Routledge.

Brockmeier, J. (2002). Remembering and forgetting: Narrative as cultural memory. *Culture and Psychology, 8*(1), 15–43. doi:10.1177/1354067X0281002

Byford, J. (2011). *Conspiracy theories: A critical introduction.* New York, NY: Palgrave-MacMillan. doi:10.1057/9780230349216

Chan, M. (2014, March 5). *WHO Director-General addresses vaccine and immunization research forum (transcript)*. World Health Organization. Retrieved from http://www.who.int/dg/speeches/2014/research-uhc/en/

Chomsky, N. (1989). *Necessary illusions: thought control in democratic societies*. Cambridge: South End Press.

Cole, J. T., & Greer, J. D. (2013). Audience response to brand journalism: The effect of frame, source, and involvement. *Journalism & Mass Communication Quarterly*, *90*(4), 673–690. doi:10.1177/1077699013503160

CorruptionExposed. (2013, January 16). *Re: Vaccine Court Awards Millions to Two Children with Autism* [Online forum comment]. Retrieved from http://www.abovetopsecret.com/forum/thread918559

Daugherty, T., Gangadharbatla, H., & Bright, L. (2010). Presence and persuasion. In C. Campanella Bracken & P. Skalski (Eds.), *Presence and popular media: Understanding media users' everyday experiences*. Mahwah, NJ: Lawrence Erlbaum.

Davies, C., & Eynon, R. (2013). *Teenagers and technology*. London: Routledge.

Downs, J. S., Bruine de Bruin, W., & Fischoff, B. (2008). Parents' vaccination comprehension and decisions. *Vaccine*, *26*(12), 1595–1607. doi:10.1016/j.vaccine.2008.01.011 PMID:18295940

Dubay, E. (2010, September 22). *Re: Above Above Top Secret.com* [Online forum comment]. Retrieved from http://www.atlanteanconspiracy.com/2008/06/above-above-top-secret-com.html

Dube, E., Laberge, C., Guay, M., Bramadat, P., Roy, R., & Bettinger, J. (2013). Vaccine hesitancy: An overview. *Human Vaccines & Immunotherapeutics*, *9*(8), 1763–1773. doi:10.4161/hv.24657 PMID:23584253

Foss, S. K. (2009). *Rhetorical criticism: Exploration and practice* (4th ed.). Long Grove, IL: Waveland Press.

Fox, S., & Duggan, M. (2013). *Health online 2013*. Pew Internet. Retrieved from http://www.pewinternet.org/files/old-media/Files/Reports/PIP_HealthOnline.pdf

Franklin, B., & Carlson, M. (2011). *Journalists, sources, and credibility: New perspectives*. London: Routledge.

Frequently asked questions about vaccine safety. (2011, February 8). *CDC*. Retrieved from http://www.cdc.gov/vaccinesafety/Vaccines/Common_questions.html

Further decline in credibility ratings for most news organizations. (2012, August 16). *People-Press*. Retrieved from http://www.people-press.org/2012/08/16/further-decline-in-credibility-ratings-for-most-news-organizations/

Garrett, R. K. (2009). Politically motivated reinforcement seeking: Reframing the selective exposure debate. *Journal of Communication*, *59*(4), 676–699. doi:10.1111/j.1460-2466.2009.01452.x

Gasson, S., & Waters, J. (2013). Using a grounded theory approach to study online collaboration behaviors. *European Journal of Information Systems*, *22*(1), 95–118. doi:10.1057/ejis.2011.24

Ghost375. (2013, February 2). *Re: Why Vaccines are Great.* [Online forum comment]. Retrieved from http://www.abovetopsecret.com/forum/thread923268

Gilbert, E., Bergstrom, T., & Karahalios, K. (2009, January). Blogs are echo chambers: Blogs are echo chambers. In *System Sciences, 2009. HICSS'09.42nd Hawaii International Conference.*

Glaser, B. G. (1978). *Theoretical sensitivity: Advances in the methodology of grounded theory.* Mill Valley, CA: Sociology Press.

Gvirsman, S. D. (2014). It's not that we don't know, it's that we don't care: Explaining why selective exposure polarizes attitudes. *Mass Communication & Society, 17*(1), 74–97. doi:10.1080/15205436.2 013.816738

Halbwachs, M. (1950). *On Collective Memory.* New York: Harper.

Hanitzsch, T. (2013). Journalism, participative media and trust in a comparative context. In C. Peters & M. Broersma (Eds.), *Rethinking journalism: Trust and participation in a transformed news landscape* (pp. 200–209). New York, NY: Routledge.

Hart, W., Albarracín, D., Eagly, A. H., Brechan, I., Lindberg, M. J., & Merrill, L. (2009). Feeling validated versus being correct: A meta-analysis of selective exposure to information. *Psychological Bulletin, 135*(4), 555–588. doi:10.1037/a0015701 PMID:19586162

HiddenCode. (2014, August 28). *Re: BREAKING: CDC Whistleblower Confesses to MMR Vaccine Research Fraud.* [Online forum comment]. Retrieved from: http://www.abovetopsecret.com/forum/thread1029670

Holbert, R., Hmielowski, J. D., & Weeks, B. E. (2012). Clarifying relationships between ideology and ideologically oriented cable TV news use: A case of suppression. *Communication Research, 39*(2), 194–216. doi:10.1177/0093650211405650

Hornsey, M. J. (2008). Social identity theory and self-categorization theory: A historical review. *Social and Personality Psychology Compass, 2*(1), 204–222. doi:10.1111/j.1751-9004.2007.00066.x

Hwang, H., Schmierbach, M., Paek, H. J., Gil de Zuniga, H., & Shah, D. (2006). Media sissociation, internet use, and antiwar political participation: A case study of political dissent and action against the war in Iraq. *Mass Communication & Society, 9*(4), 461–483. doi:10.1207/s15327825mcs0904_5

International travel and health. (2014). World Health Organization. Retrieved from http://www.who. int/ith/en/

Ito, M. (2009). *Hanging out, messing around and geeking out: Kids living and learning with new media.* Cambridge, MA: MIT Press.

Iyengar, S., & Kyu, S. H. (2009). Red media, blue media: Evidence of ideological selectivity in media use. *Journal of Communication, 59*(1), 19–39. doi:10.1111/j.1460-2466.2008.01402.x

Jamieson, K. H., & Cappella, J. N. (2008). *Echo chamber: Rush Limbaugh and the conservative media establishment.* New York, NY: Oxford University Press.

Jolley, D. (2013). The detrimental nature of conspiracy theories. *PsyPAG Quarterly, 88*, 35–39.

Kareklas, I., Muehling, D., & Weber, T. J. (2015). Reexamining health messages in the digital age: A fresh look at source credibility effects. *Journal of Advertising*, *44*(2), 88–104. doi:10.1080/00913367. 2015.1018461

Katz, E., & Lazarsfeld, F. P. (1955). *Personal Influence*. New York, NY: Free Press.

Kelly, J., Fisher, D., & Smith, M. (2005). *Debate, Division, and Diversity: Political Discourse Networks in USENET Newsgroups*. Stanford Online Deliberation Conference DIAC'05.

Kitch, C. (2002). "A death in the American family": Myth, memory, and national values in the media mourning of John F. Kennedy Jr. *Journalism & Mass Communication Quarterly*, *79*(2), 294–309. doi:10.1177/107769900207900203

Kovach, B., & Rosenstiel, T. (2010). *Blur: How to know what's true in the age of information overload*. New York, NY: Bloomsbury.

Lantian, A. (2013). A review of different approaches to study belief in conspiracy theories. *PsyPAG Quarterly*, *88*, 19–21.

Lieu, T. A. et al.. (1994). Cost-effectiveness of a routine varicella vaccination program for U.S. children. *Journal of the American Medical Association*, *271*(5), 375–381. doi:10.1001/jama.1994.03510290057037 PMID:8283587

Lincoln, Y. S., & Guba, E. G. (2000). Paradigmatic controversies contradictions and emerging confluences. In N. K. Denzin & Y. S. Lincoln (Eds.), *The handbook of qualitative research* (pp. 163–188). Beverly Hills, CA: Sage Publications.

Lyotard, J. F. (1979). *The postmodern condition: A report on knowledge*. Paris: Minuit.

Morales, L. (2012, September 21). U.S. distrust in media hits new high. *Gallup*. Retrieved from http://www.gallup.com/poll/157589/distrust-media-hits-new-high.aspx

Offit, P. A. (2010). *Deadly choices: How the anti-vaccine movement threatens us all*. Basic Books.

Oftedal, K. (2014). Treating Ebola with homeopathy. *Natural News*. Retrieved from http://blogs.naturalnews.com/treating-ebola-homeopathy/

Oliver, J. E., & Wood, T. J. (2014). Conspiracy theories and the paranoid style(s) of mass opinion. *American Journal of Political Science*, *58*(4), 952–966. doi:10.1111/ajps.12084

opopanax. (2013, December 19). *Re: Are all vaccines dangerous? Even Tetanus shots?* [Online forum comment]. Retrieved from http://www.abovetopsecret.com/forum/thread988907

Palmer, B. (2014). Himalayan bath salts will not save your life. Slate. Retrieved from http://www.slate.com/articles/health_and_science/medical_examiner/2014/02/natural_news_is_a_facebook_hit_never_click_on_itsr_stories_about_cancer.html

Pariser, E. (2011). *The filter bubble: What the Internet is hiding from you*. New York, NY: Penguin Press.

Peltola, H., & Heinonen, O. P. (1986). Frequency of true adverse reactions to Measles-Mumps-Rubella vaccine: A double-blind placebo-controlled trial in twins. *Lancet, 327*(8487), 939–942. doi:10.1016/S0140-6736(86)91044-5 PMID:2871241

Peters, C., & Broersma, M. (2013). *Rethinking Journalism: Trust and Participation in a Transformed News Landscape*. New York, NY: Routledge.

Poland, G. A., & Jacobson, R. M. (2011). The age-old struggle against the antivaccinationists. *The New England Journal of Medicine, 13*(2), 97–99. doi:10.1056/NEJMp1010594 PMID:21226573

Public Policy Polling. (2013, April 2). Conspiracy theory poll results.

Radley, A. (1990). Artefacts, memory and a sense of the past. In D. Middleton & D. Edwards (Eds.), *Collective remembering* (pp. 46–59). London: Sage.

Rainie, L., & Smith, A. (2012, March 12). *Social networking sites and politics.* Pew Internet & American Life Project. Retrieved from http://www.pewinternet.org/Reports/2012/Social-networking-and-politics.aspx

Rankin, D. (2013). *U.S. politics and Generation Y: Engaging the Millenials.* Boulder, CO: Lynne Rienner.

raymundoko. (2014, August 26). *Re: Vaccine Fraud: U.S. Mainstream Media Censors Whistleblower's Explosive Story.* [Online forum comment]. Retrieved from http://www.abovetopsecret.com/forum/thread1029262

Rodriguez, N. J. (2015). *Toward a better understanding of vaccine-hesitant discourse.* (Unpublished doctoral dissertation). University of Kansas, Lawrence, KS.

Rosen, J. (2006, June 27). *The people formerly known as the audience.* Retrieved from: http://archive.pressthink.org/2006/06/27/ppl_frmr.html

Ruiz, J. B., & Bell, R. A. (2014). Understanding vaccination resistance: Vaccine search term selection bias and the valence of retrieved information. *Vaccine, 32*(44), 5776–5780. doi:10.1016/j.vaccine.2014.08.042 PMID:25176640

Sanders, G. D., & Taira, A. V. (2003). Cost effectiveness of a potential vaccine for *human papillomavirus. Emerging Infectious Diseases, 9*(1), 37–48. doi:10.3201/eid0901.020168 PMID:12533280

Seitz-Wald, A. (2013, May 2). Alex Jones: Conspiracy Inc. *Salon.* Retrieved from http://www.salon.com/2013/05/02/alex_jones_conspiracy_inc/

Solove, D. J. (2007). *The future of reputation: Gossip, rumor, and privacy on the Internet.* Binghamton, NY: Vail-Ballou Press.

SpearMint. (2013, February 2). *Re: Why Vaccines are Great.* [Online forum comment]. Retrieved from http://www.abovetopsecret.com/forum/thread923268

Steinmetz, K. F. (2012). Message received: Virtual ethnography in online message boards. *International Journal of Qualitative Methods, 11*(1), 26–39.

Sunstein, C. R. (2009). *Going to extremes: How like minds unite and divide.* New York: Oxford University Press.

Sunstein, C. R., & Vermeule, A. (2009). Conspiracy theories: Causes and cures. *Journal of Political Philosophy, 17*(2), 202–227. doi:10.1111/j.1467-9760.2008.00325.x

Survey: One third of American parents mistakenly link vaccines to autism. (2014). National Consumers League. Retrieved from http://www.nclnet.org/survey_one_third_of_american_parents_mistakenly_link_vaccines_to_autism

Swift, A. (2013). Honesty and ethics rating of clergy slides to new low: Nurses again top list; lobbyists are worst. *Gallup.* Retrieved from: http://www.gallup.com/poll/166298/honesty-ethics-rating-clergy-slides-new-low.aspx

Tajfel, H., Billig, M., Bundy, R. P., & Flament, C. (1971). Social categorization and intergroup behaviour. *European Journal of Social Psychology, 1*(2), 149–178. doi:10.1002/ejsp.2420010202

Tewksbury, D. (2006). Exposure to the newer media in a Presidential primary campaign. *Political Communication, 23*(3), 313–332. doi:10.1080/10584600600808877

Tracy, C. (2012). *The newsphere: Understanding the news and information environment.* New York: Peter Lang.

Tsfati, Y., & Cappella, J. N. (2003). Do people watch what they do not trust? Exploring the association between news media skepticism and exposure. *Communication Research, 30*(5), 1–26. doi:10.1177/0093650203253371

Vallone, R. P., Ross, L., & Lepper, M. R. (1985). The hostile media phenomenon: Biased perception and perceptions of media bias in coverage of the "Beirut Massacre.". *Journal of Personality and Social Psychology, 49*(3), 577–585. doi:10.1037/0022-3514.49.3.577 PMID:4045697

Van Cuilenburg, J. (1999). On competition, access and diversity in media, old and new. *New Media & Society, 1*(2), 183–207. doi:10.1177/14614449922225555

Warner, B. R. (2010). Segmenting the electorate: The effects of exposure to political extremism online. *Communication Studies, 61*(4), 430–444. doi:10.1080/10510974.2010.497069

Wojcieszak, M. (2010). "Don't talk to me": Effects of ideologically homogeneous online groups and politically dissimilar offline ties on extremism. *New Media & Society, 12*(4), 637–655. doi:10.1177/1461444809342775

Wood, M. (2013). Has the Internet been good for conspiracy theorizing? *PsyPAG Quarterly: Special Issue: The Psychology of Conspiracy Theories, 88*, 31–34.

Wright, C. (2014). Lemon: The quintessential cancer destroyer and all-around health tonic. *Natural News.* Retrieved from http://www.naturalnews.com/043671_lemon_rind_cancer_cures.html

Xu, Q. (2013). Social recommendation, source credibility, and recency: Effects of news cues in a social bookmarking website. *Journalism & Mass Communication Quarterly, 90*(4), 757–775. doi:10.1177/1077699013503158

Zaitchik, A. (2011, March 2). Meet Alex Jones. *Rolling Stone*. Retrieved from http://www.rollingstone.com/politics/news/talk-radios-alex-jones-the-most-paranoid-man-in-america-20110302

Zelizer, B. (1992). *Covering the body: The Kennedy assassination, the media, and the shaping of collective memory*. Chicago: University of Chicago.

Zhou, W. (2003). Surveillance for safety after immunization: Vaccine Adverse Event Reporting System (VAERS) --- United States, 1991-2001. *MMWR. Surveillance Summaries*, *52*(1), 1–24. PMID:12825543

KEY TERMS AND DEFINITIONS

Conspiracy Theory: A narrative that contrasts the "official" version of events and posits a more nefarious scheme occurred with more than one agent acting insidiously during its execution and/or subsequent cover-up.

Echo Chamber: An environment in which an individual's beliefs remain generally uncontested and in which existing worldviews are reaffirmed.

Feedback Loop: A feedback loop occurs when incoming information regarding events reaffirms existing beliefs, and helps create conditions in which an echo chamber may characterize a person's exposure to information.

Filter Bubble: A filter bubble is a characteristic of the architecture of the Internet, and functions to limit, rather than broaden the perceived viewpoints or choices an individual may have.

Grand Narrative: A grand narrative refers to an accumulation of stories by mainstream media outlets that help shape a sense of common ground with respect to what constitutes mainstream concerns and discourse.

Hostile Media Theory: Holds that partisans on either side of an issue will view an objective news article as biased against their beliefs.

Media Dissociation: A variation of hostile media theory, media dissociation describes a broader sense of an individual perceiving their worldview as being at odds with narratives found in mainstream media.

Vaccine-Hesitant Discourse: A broader term that incorporates both individuals who might identify as "anti-vaccine," as well as individuals who have less defined beliefs on the topic. This suggests that beliefs regarding vaccines should be discussed as falling along a spectrum of confidence and hesitancy, rather than being identified as either "pro-" or "anti-vaccine."

Section 3
Addressing Anonymity in Digital Realms

Much advice on evaluating online information hinges on determining the author of a source, then making judgments about the credibility of that author's credentials. However, a vast amount of the digital information we encounter has no discernible author, much less an author whose background and credentials are readily available for evaluation. This section examines the benefits and drawbacks of anonymity with regard to establishing digital credibility, and it offers strategies for assessing information on sites where anonymity reigns.

Chapter 9
Ethos Construction, Identification, and Authenticity in the Discourses of AWSA:
The Arab Women's Solidarity Association International

Samaa Gamie
Lincoln University, USA

ABSTRACT

The chapter explores the complex emergent feminist ethos in two virtual spaces created by the San Francisco chapter of AWSA—the Arab Women's Solidarity Association International, an Arab women's activist group. First, the chapter discusses ethos and identity construction in cyberspace. Second, the chapter analyzes AWSA's cyber discourses to uncover the characteristics of its feminist ethos and the opportunities allowed or lost for authenticity and the role of anonymity in constructing its feminist ethos. Third, the chapter questions whether anonymity allows for the critical examination of the discourses and ideologies of the powerful in addition to the creation of a sustainable counter-hegemonic discourse or whether it heightens the threat of homogeneity and streamlining in cyberspace. The chapter, in its conclusion, calls for a critical investigation of the potential of the digital domain to challenge the concentration of power in virtual spaces and uncover frameworks through which revolutionary discourses can be sustained and disseminated.

INTRODUCTION

In both virtual or real communities and the rhetorical situations that transpire within and outside these discursive spaces, the construction of ethos emerges as a central component. Whether we view ethos as one's credibility displayed by one's good or moral character (Plato, 2001; Aristotle, 2001), an element of style (Quintilian, 2001), a "dwelling place" in which we should consider the situation and context within which rhetoric is applied (Hyde, 2004), a group quality (Gurak, 1999), or a network of communal discursive

DOI: 10.4018/978-1-5225-1072-7.ch009

practices that is ideally "multi-voiced and authentic," negotiated with social institutions (Brooke, 1991), or situated in "one's locatedness in various social and cultural 'spaces'" (Reynolds, 1993, p. 326), ethos in online discourses becomes key to the realization of identification with one's digital audience.

In online spaces, identity is formed and constituted through language interaction, making identity an "emergent product rather than the pre-existing source of linguistic and other semiotic practices" (Bucholtz & Hall as cited in Grabill & Pigg, 2012, p. 102). In digital interactions, the term identity-in-use emerges to elucidate how identity is formulated not only by broad categories like race, class, and gender, but also by discursive negotiations and interactions whereever digital identity is distributed and enmeshed in complex dialogical activity for the purpose of building social relationships, as Carolyn Miller (2001) suggested. In this light, online communication becomes "a complex negotiation between various versions of our online and our real selves, between our many representations of our selves and our listeners and readers, and, not least, between our many selves and the computer structure and operations through which we represent these selves to others" (Zappen, 2005, p. 323)—creating a complex discourse on identity that accounts for the multiplicity of selves constructed through online discursive interactions in "relation to embodiment and materiality" (Grabill & Pigg, 2012, p. 103). The complex discourse on identity elucidates the challenges associated with ethos construction and deployment in cyber spaces, making the term ethos-in-use equally relevant because the emergent digital ethos is formulated by online discursive negotiations and interactions and is, thus, non-static and ever-changing across time, across texts, and across spaces. In the discourses of the marginalized, ethos construction becomes, in itself, an act of struggle through language—a "struggle in language to recover…, to reconcile, to reunite, to renew" (hooks, 1989, pp. 146-147). Though ethos in these discourses is created in the margins, that locale "offers to one the possibility of radical perspective from which to see and create, to imagine alternatives, new worlds" (hooks, 1989, p. 207) and allows for the potentiality of transformation and the creation of radical inclusive spaces from which to recover those in the margins, create solidarity, and erase the categories of colonized and colonizer (hooks, 1989, p. 209).

The rich discourses on ethos stem from the central role feminism plays/ed in challenging and redefining the traditional conception of ethos, conventionally seen as emphasizing the conventional and the public rather than the private and the idiosyncratic. Undeniably, the traditional male-female divide in Muslim and Arab communities has found its replication in the real and virtual spaces Arab and Muslim women traverse, as Arab women activists' efforts have often been discredited for defying the male-constructed normative code of women's ethos of silence and invisibility. In the context of Arab culture, Arab women's voices become acts of dissidence and encroachments upon masculine spaces because these women defy the rigid separation between the public sphere of visibility of masculinity and the private sphere of silence and domesticity of femininity (Guéye, 2010, p. 162)—challenging a dichotomy that perpetuates the primacy of men in Arab societies. However, for these women, ethos is constructed from the margins of society (Rich, 1986; hooks, 1989; Haraway, 1988) and in the social space between "personal and public life" (Ronald, 1990, p. 37) and between writer and reader and speaker and listener (LeFevre, 1987, p. 45-46), and between the self and its locality within and outside the boundaries of social institutions and hierarchies. In their deconstruction and redefinition of the traditionalist constructions of women's ethos in their virtual and real communities, Arab women activists "displace the structures" from which they emerged and try to "create empty spaces, and new places, from which others may speak" (Schmertz, 1999, p.89). However, the success with which these women activists are able to traverse the conditions of their disempowerment in their communities and extend that liberation to other women in their societies is one that needs further examination to explore the potential of cyberspace to realize the empowerment and liberation of the dispossessed and the marginalized.

Hence, the paper's focus is to explore the complex emergent feminist ethos in two virtual spaces created by the San Francisco chapter of the Arab Women's Solidarity Association International (AWSA), an Arab women's activist group. The group's first virtual space was founded in 1999 to disseminate the organization's activist causes and messages. With its impassioned rhetoric and vehement rejection of Arab women's marginalization, the first virtual site showcased a feminist ethos that carried a forceful activist and political message that resisted women's material silencing by forcefully advocating against racism, sexism, Zionism, Arab women's political disenfranchisement, and violence against women. The second virtual space was launched in 2006, replacing the first site, and the feminist ethos in the second site appears more dispassionate, disengaged, and factual in its presentation of key Middle East issues about women's material being and human rights. In both virtual spaces, the dual role anonymity plays in ethos construction allows it to be an empowering tool that increases the outreach of AWSA's messages while bringing into question the sustainability of such activist discourses as the threat of homogenization and streamlining is ever lingering.

BACKGROUND

In deconstructing and rhetorically analyzing the discourses of the marginalized, feminist standpoint theory becomes central in critiquing hegemony (Hekman,1997, p. 355) and locating the authority of experience in the disenfranchised, making the epistemology of the marginalized marked by "a duality of levels of reality" and awarding them a deeper knowledge, a profound understanding of, and an ability to critique, the perspective of the powerful (Hartsock, 1983, p. 285). The rhetoric of the marginalized is, thus, based on "oppositional knowledges" and "multiple consciousness" that engage in "conscious" resistance of the hegemonic messages, shaping an anti-hegemonic and innovative discourse that opposes and challenges the limitations on the perspectives of the marginalized (McClish & Bacon,2002, p. 33). The heightened perspectives of the marginalized and their feminist discourses are not only a "reflection of one's viewpoint but a rhetorical product consciously created and mediated by the available means of persuasion" (McClish & Bacon, 2002, p. 31) and are founded in their unique gendered and racialized experiences, creating an "outsider-within" perspective—a "peculiar marginality" (Collins, 1990) that uses the lens of the social condition to look back at the self (Harding, 1998). Though some of the criticism against feminist standpoint theory focuses on its tendency to essentialize categories such as women and promote a "collective common" experience while erasing differences (Wood, 1997; Smith, 1998; Bell et al., 2000), Spivak (1990) countered that repudiation of essentialism and called for the deployment of strategic essentialism, situating it "at the moment, [to] become vigilant about our own practice and use it as much as we can rather than make the totally unproductive gesture of repudiating it" (p. 11). Such essentialismis to be strategically deployed and abandoned for the sake of getting to "pick up the universal that will give you the power to fight against the other side" (Spivak, 1990, p. 12) while naming one's subject position. In addition, Wood (1997) and Collins (1990) asserted that emphasizing a group does not jeopardize awareness of diversity and difference within a group because group identities are formed by the tension between multiplicity and commonality within the group (as cited in McClish & Bacon, 2002, p. 29). In using standpoint theory for rhetorical studies of feminist and racialized digital discourses, one must acknowledge how the construction of ethos in these discourses becomes inseparable from one's own experiences and standpoint; in fact, the construction of ethos is discursively negotiated in the intersection of social phenomena such as race, class, and gender—all of which are mutually constructed—as we acknowledge the fundamental tension between identification and difference because the goal of such discourses becomes to achieve "a sense of connectedness without suppressing differences or sacrificing the essentials of identity" (as cited in McClish & Bacon, 2002, pp. 32-33).

In addition to using Feminist Standpoint theory in the analysis of the two virtual spaces of the Arab Women's Solidarity Association International, the two central terms utilized to characterize the feminist ethos and standpoint emergent in these virtual discourses are subdued and tyrannical feminist ethos. A subdued feminist ethos is one that operates within the parameters of Western feminist thought and seeks consensus building and bridging cultural barriers and difference with non-Arab feminists. It has an apolitical standpoint and seeks the creation of social and economic justice in Arab communities, while avoiding exploring the explosive political justice issues in these societies. Within the framework of subdued feminism, an articulation, or rejection, of the social, cultural, economic, and political networks of oppression and victimization of Arab women and Arab people is absent or minimally vocalized in the interest of a moderate rhetoric of activism and inclusion that is highly objective, minimally-racialized, and factual. On the other hand, a tyrannical feminist ethos is one that operates within the parameters of an Arab feminism hostile to Western forms of feminism. It seeks some form of consensus building with non-Arab feminists in the interest of affirming the failure of the Western feminist trend in the genuine inclusion of Arab and non-White feminisms and affirms the singular authenticity of the Arab feminist experience. A tyrannical feminist ethos has a standpoint that vehemently articulates a rejection of the social, cultural, economic, and political networks of the oppression of Arab women and Arab people, while simultaneously condemning Arab and Western governments, not excluding patriarchy and Western feminists, for their collusion in that victimization, producing a highly explosive and racialized rhetoric.

In cyberspaces, cyber users are divided not only by the corporeal limits of their bodies as in face-to-face communication, but also by the limits of real time and space in a vast virtual universe. In these virtual spaces, the achievement of identification with one's audience becomes crucial for the survival of virtual spaces that champion the social and economic liberation of the marginalized through creating shared embodied experiences with the global audiences as peers in a global movement against political, social, and economic marginalization. Identification is achieved by creating an emergent peer ethos bound by a sense of community and shared identity in both material and virtual social spaces. In essence, through identification or a series of identifications, cooperation, virtuo-social cohesion, and community-building, a cyber identity or ethos is constructed and negotiated through which mutual embodied experiences of identification can be achieved. These emergent group identities or ethos, as Collins proposed, are based on the tension between commonality and multiplicity, allowing for solidarity and identification within a diverse group. That emergent ethos is not static but rather "shifts and changes over time, across texts, and around competing spaces" (Reynolds,1993, p. 326), becoming "a social act and as a product of [this] community's character" (p. 327). In fact, in *A Rhetoric of Motives*, Kenneth Burke writes that speakers can only persuade their audiences if they can "talk [their] language by speech, gesture, tonality, order, image, attitude, idea, identifying [their] ways with his" (1962, p. 55), thus creating an opportunity for identification between the speaker and the audience (Bridgeman, 2014, p.199). In creating identification with the audience, speakers create an interest in the audience to act with the speaker to achieve a common purpose, thus becoming one with a person other than oneself (Odom, 2014, p. 243). From that act of identification, a sense of community arises from "an understandable dream expressing a desire for selves that are transparent to one another, (with) relationships of mutual identification, social closeness and comfort" (Young, 1990, p.300), from "a feeling of connectedness that confers a space of belonging" (Foster,197, p. 29), and from a desire for unity and cohesion. Such identification is shaped by the verbally stated views of the audience, as well as by non-verbal factors; one such factor, is, which Katherine Bridgeman (2014) suggested, the "embodiment of both the speaker and the audience" (p. 199). When speakers identify their beliefs, values, or ways with those of the audience, they facilitate "a mutually embodied experience of rhetorical exchange" (Bridgeman, 2014, p. 199), making embodiment a central component for identification and a means of achieving persuasion. Thus, the paper will explore the opportunities allotted or lost by AWSA International's two virtual spaces to create identification with its virtual Arab and global audience through mutually embodied experiences of rhetorical exchange.

In this paper, and as part of the analysis of the emergent feminist ethos in these digital spaces, a question will be proposed that Lisa Nakamura (2002) also asked: Can the Internet propagate genuinely new and nonracist (and nonsexist and nonclassist but intersubjective) ways of being and identity construction that move beyond the reduction of the other; or is it merely a reflection and a tool of reenactment and reproduction of the dominant culture and discourses at large? Also, in the examination of the rhetorical spaces occupied by Arab women, do questions of cultural and racial authenticity in cyberspace become relevant or central to our conversation about racialized ethos construction in digital spaces? A third question posed by this research is: Can minority or dominated subjects create coherent digital identities that assimilate this digital medium to their own cultural and political needs or "are [they] inevitably compromised by its presence" as they tack together their identity from stereotypical cultural narratives in media sources and in dominant discourses, thus reenacting the narratives they seek to resist (Nakamura, 2008, p.87)? Just like Deleuze and Guattari posited the question "Why do [wo/men] fight for their servitude as stubbornly as though it were their salvation?" (as cited in Al-Nakib, 2013,p. 465),this chapter explores whether Arab women activists remain circumscribed by the structures that oppress them or whether they effectually challenge them? The chapter also ponders the question whether anonymity allows for the critical examination of the discourses and ideologies of the powerful and their role in perpetuating the domination over the marginalized, and whether anonymity allows for the creation of a sustainable counterhegemonic discourse or a new framework for defying hegemony and patriarchy.

CRITICAL VIEW OF RACE IN CYBERSPACE

In discussing the potential of cyberspace for empowering its racialized cyber users to create empowered and empowering digital identities (Gruber, 2001; Hawisher & Sullivan, 1999) in their virtual—and, eventually, material—communities comes the importance of investigating the metaphors describing that virtual space. Viewing the World Wide Web as a new frontier is one metaphor that promises enormous potential from excavating that site. However, such metaphor romanticizes colonial history (Ulmer, 1994; Ow, 2000) and constitutes that online space as one warranting colonial exploration in order to civilize it, casting doubt on its liberatory potential and warning of its potential abuses, especially when it comes to minority cyber discourses and identities. Another metaphor presents the WWW as the "information superhighway," a metaphor paralleling the federal highway system, which, according to Jeffery A. Ow (2000), not only connects communities, but also "disrupt[s] and disperse[s] communities through and over which they are built, namely communities of color" (p. 61), further problematizing the power and potential misuses of that virtual space and casting doubt on its potential as a space for the marginalized cyber users to create and affirm an empowered digital ethos that traverses the alienating virtual and material conditions of its Othering. Other discussions of cyberspace have invoked the metaphor of community, which according to Myers (1986), can result in the reproduction and maintenance of the existing, oppressive homogenizing power structures. In fact, Kurt Spellmeyer (1994) likened the community metaphor to "the 'shared conventions' of a prison" and calls for moving beyond the confining and delimiting metaphor of community to "'an image of social life...large enough, and loose enough, to make room for words and things and minds together'" (as cited in Walters, 1995, p. 823). The threat of homogenization inherent in the lingering use of the metaphor of community to describe cyberspace can be heeded by moving beyond that metaphor and investigating the interpretive communities and the historical processes and power structures that shape the production of knowledge in such digital pockets. Thus, it becomes crucial to investigate the immense power of cyberspace, viewing it as an instrument of power that could either facilitate or hinder the potential of that space to be a tool of empowerment, especially in the construction and facilitation of empowered, and empowering, racialized digital identities.

Regretfully, the taboo associated with discussions of race in offline and online communities has led to little scholarly work on how these new technologies shape or transform existing notions of race. This has led to assertions like those of Kali Tal (1996) that "it is finally possible to completely and utterly disappear people of color" in cyberspace as the avoidance of questions about race has led to, what Tal called the "whitinizing" of that new media, and like those of Ziauddin Sardar(1996),who viewed the Internet as the "darker side of the West" (p. 35) and as a new example of imperializing practices perpetuated by the West in its ongoing domination of other cultures and peoples. In *Race in Cyberspace*, Jennifer Gonzalez (2000) challenged the naïve yet pervasive notion that subjects that go online leave behind the social categories that define them in the "real world," including race and gender, and asserted that human subjects inevitably enact and perform their new identities through the sign systems they already inhabit. Lisa Nakamura(2002) further asserted that even though it is true that in virtual spaces the physical bodies of users are hidden from others, race has a way of asserting itself in the kinds of identities racialized bodies construct both through language and images (Stone, 1992; Balsamo, 1999; Takayoshi, 1999). In fact, as Daniel Punday (2000) explained: "quite contrary to the early belief that cyberspace offers a way to escape gender, race, and class as conditions of social interaction...recent critics suggest that online discourse is woven of stereotypical cultural narratives that reinstall precisely these conditions" (p. 199). These assertions cast doubt on the claims of a radical post-racial democracy associated with the early views of cyberspace as critics "have lost confidence in the socially transformative possibilities of online discourse" (Punday, 2000, p. 204) and as minorities and the disenfranchised often resort to the creation of stereotypical cultural representations that reinstate the disempowering conditions of their Othering. However, in feminist discourses, the realization and articulation of one's othering becomes not a means of one's victimization, but the means of one's empowerment, as one articulates and names the locale from which one speaks, thereby creating Donna Haraway's (1988) "situated knowledge" that acknowledges the possibilities, the partial perspective, and the limitations inherent in that act of naming (Schmertz,1999, p. 88).

ARAB FEMINISM AND CYBERFEMINISM

However, in computer-mediated communication, the premise upon which technological empowerment is based is the reduction, absence, or elimination of the technology user's entire corporeal body from the discourse environment (De Pew, 2003), this investment in erasing the marked subject is one that the online rhetorics of hyphenated women's groups have defied by rhetorically and visually affirming their gendered and racialized digital subjectivities (Gruber, 2001; Knadler, 2001). This is no less evident in the cyber feminist discourses of Arab women activists. Accordingly, the emergence of cyberfeminism, as a new form of feminism, in online spaces has, according to Plant (1996), "allowed women to escape the patriarchal control of centralized organizations and has offered them a safe haven where postmodern fragmented subjectivities can exist" (as cited in Stephan, 2013, p. 83). Other scholars, such as Christina Vogt and Peiying Chen (2001), have argued that the suitability of cyberspace for women's activism comes from the absence of "institutional and cultural norms [...] similar to the nontraditional spaces" women's movements have created (p. 371). The discourses of Arab cyberfeminism, whose limits and potential for activism are largely understudied, create a contested space to examine current postmodern identity fragmentation in the era of digital reproduction and challenge patriarchal gender roles while "questioning the sociocultural, economic, political and legal institutions constraining" women (Skalli, 2006, pp. 36-77).

Among the many challenges limiting Arab women's cyberactivism, according to Rita Stephan (2013), are the concentration of women's activism among the privileged (i.e., upper and upper-middle class women); limited Arab women's access to cyberspace due to high female illiteracy; unfamiliarity with foreign languages; limited and government-restricted Internet access; the patriarchal cultural discourse that views danger in giving women free access to the Internet; and the marginalization and alienation of Arab feminists in the diaspora by Arab men and Western feminists. According to Naber (2011), the disenfranchisement of Arab-American feminists by American feminists is evident because most of the political and feminist spaces are not available for them and appear to be "dominated by Orientalist perspectives about Arab women" (p. 88). Furthermore, Arab women are additionally "fragmented internally" on how much of the "negative" aspects of Arab culture they can expose within American media and academia (Stephan, 2013, p. 87); such exposure, which are deemed acts of betrayal of Arab heritage and as collusion with the Western colonialist agenda, furthers the alienation of these Arab women from their Arab communities because these feminists become "victims of the complex Arab perception of colonialism" (Ghoussoub as cited in Fayad, 1995, p.152; this results in the discrediting and disavowal of their activist agendas in the interest of preserving cultural purity, as Woman is constricted by the cultural narrative rather than becoming "an agent of [her] own history" (p. 152). Despite the challenges facing Arab women feminists, Arab and Middle Eastern women activists are increasingly resorting to cyberspace to advance their activism and "design their own forms of feminism," in order to construct their identities as members of real and virtual organizations, and "to resist and reform [the] masculine, patriarchal-feudal-religious disposition'" in their communities (Mojab & Gorman as cited in Stephan, 2013, p.88). AWSA is a case in point.

AWSA BACKGROUND

According to their online profile, the Arab Women's Solidarity Association International was started in Egypt in 1982 by a group of 120 women led by Dr. Nawal El Saadawi, an Egyptian feminist, doctor, and writer. By 1985, it had 3,000 members and was granted consultative status with the Economic and Social Council of the United Nations as an Arab NGO. Between 1982 and 1991, AWSA International organized several international conferences, developed projects for economically underprivileged women, and published books and literary magazines. After the vocal opposition of AWSA International to the Gulf War, the Egyptian government banned it, resulting in AWSA International moving its headquarters to Algeria. It later returned to Egypt in 1996, where it continues to operate. AWSA chapters in the US were founded in Seattle in 1994, which remained active till 1996, and in San Francisco in 1995,which proved to be its most progressive and radical chapter. The SF chapter was started by a group of vocal, radical feminists, mostly students at that time. According to Rita Stephens, one of the steering committee members of AWSA International, the birth of transnational feminism in the 1980s affected AWSA and caused Arab-American women to start organizing in light of the Israeli invasion of Beirut in the 1980s, adding that Cyber AWSA was meant to be a site targeting war, Zionism, and pro Arab-feminism (personal communication, August 2, 2010).However, shortly after the founding of Cyber AWSA and the e-mail listserv, conflicts arose over how much conservatism could be allowed on the listserv, which eventually led to several founding members quitting the listserv and forming their own organizations; only a few of the founding members remained (R. Stephan, personal communication, August 2, 2010).

Though AWSA International San Francisco's chapter was eventually dissolved and its last activity was recorded in June 2002, the AWSA's listserv remains active as a forum for the exchange of experience and knowledge among members. Hence, Cyber AWSA has continued as a venue for Arab feminists to assert their relevance in the feminist activist movement (Stephan, 2013).

THE OLD AWSA

AWSA's first website was founded by its North American San Francisco chapter in 1999to disseminate the organization's activist causes and messages. On the homepage ofAWSA International's first virtual space, the Arab Women's Solidarity Association's mission statement identified it as a progressive women's association founded in Egypt in 1982 by Nawal El Saadawi—an iconic Egyptian feminist, women's rights advocate, and writer, as well as a group of women who believed that the struggle to liberate Arab people from all forms of domination cannot be separated from women's liberation. From the start, the compelling feminist ethos is underscored by the reference to El Saadawi and Arab women activists and the struggle to achieve women's liberation by challenging the economic, cultural, and media structures that oppress and dominate not only women but also all Arab people. Such emergent feminist ethos and articulated standpoint stipulate the realization of freedom for women on freeing their societies and show the extent of the formidable task facing women who call for women's liberation in Arab societies. Despite the reference to El Saadawi as the founding member of the original AWSA, no other members are identified, making anonymity a central element of the emergent ethos and its most appealing factor because the movement is not defined by the naming of one or any of its members but by its goal of liberating and empowering Arab women and people. Anonymity in AWSA International SF became the means that unfettered it from the shackles of patriarchy because names "put people into slots, impose limits upon their creative possibilities, and stand for collective-based enunciations of conformism, linearity, and regimentation" (Guèye, 2010, p. 164); in short, anonymity provided the framework for the fluid construction of the group's feminist ethos.

In its mission statement, which occupies most of the homepage, readers are informed of the goal of AWSA International San Francisco's chapter, which was established in 1995, to"promot[e] Arab women's active participation in social, economic and political life," to substitute for the inability to create a material space for AWSA International chapters throughout North America, and to connect Arab women in North America with other Arab women and their international allies through the website and the Yahoo email list-serve. However, the means by which such cooperation can serve the activist mission of the organization and by which the organization promotes Arab women's active participation are not clearly

Figure 1. Cyber AWSA homepage

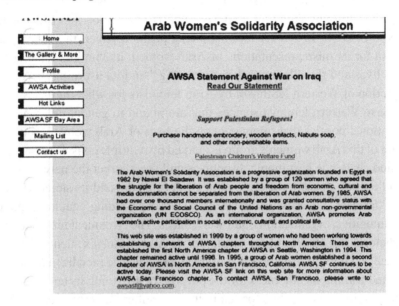

identified. The emergent ethos, from the onset, utilized a subdued feminist ethos with its cooperative rhetoric in the reference to "international" allies while articulating the conditions for ending women's marginalization. What lacks is the framework through which such activist goals can be materialized in women's real communities and pertinent information about the social, economic, and political conditions of Arab women that hinder their liberation.

The activist stances and engagements of the activist group in its San Francisco chapter are high-lighted further in the "Profile" section. These events include benefits for women victims of war, "a protest against the racist portrayal of Arab women in Israeli arts, a workshop on racist media images of Arab women and men, and empowerment-based events for Arab women and their communities," and an annual Arab film festival. All these references frame Cyber AWSA International as an Arab women's organization that is vocal in its views against war and the victimization of women and also against what it sees are unfair, racist portrayals of Arab men and women in art and media. They also present Cyber

Figure 2. Cyber AWSA profile

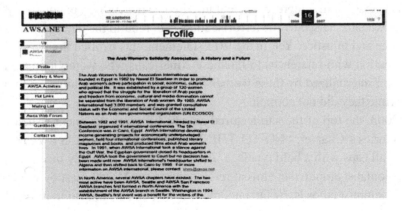

AWSA International as an organization that is taking steps to empower and educate its members and site visitors through its "training guide for activists" and its posted position paper that was presented in the Feminist Expo in 2000. In AWSA International's position paper, the vehement condemnation of Western feminism for its misrepresentations of Arab women, its "limited understanding of the big picture of women's lives and the dilemmas they are facing," and its usurping of Arab women's voice underscore the rejection of Western feminism by Arab feminists for what they view as a reductionism of Arab women due to Western feminist stances that are bound to gender and yet divorced from the national and international politics that impinge upon the lives of Arab women. The emergent feminist ethos and standpoint of this Arab women's group is marked by multiple consciousness, giving it a unique ability to critique and challenge hegemonic discourses and deconstruct the networks of Arab women's marginalization and erasure through the critique of western media and its stereotypical representation of Arab women as "faceless, voiceless and nameless," while providing equal critique of patriarchy in Arab societies, communities, organizations, and workplaces. The tyrannical feminist ethos that emerges from the activist rhetoric and stances of the group defies Arab women's silencing and invisibility and deconstructs the local and foreign structures that oppress women. The racialized feminist ethos blatantly invests in marking and naming its otherness for the purpose of affirming its authentic voice and its sole right to speak for the Arab woman, calling for "claiming our cultural identities, and defining and defending our rights," and stating "we are carving out our space, and pulling our seat up to the table, on our own terms, and with our own designs." Thus, this feminist ethos uses "strategic essentialism" to name its Arabness and womanhood and to present its feminist standpoint through its "engaged vision" that arises from these women's heightened understanding of the condition of Arab women in their societies and in the diaspora. The role anonymity plays in the construction of its tyrannical feminist ethos and the highly racialized rhetoric that utilizes the discourse of racial and cultural authenticity help in the construction of a coherent and defiant racialized digital identity that vehemently articulates a rejection of the social, cultural, economic, and political networks of the oppression of Arab women but also assimilates this digital media to its own activist and political needs.

The three additional links on the homepage provide access to AWSA International's response against the war on Iraq (located at the top of the homepage); the 9/11 terrorist attacks (located at the bottom of the homepage); and the Arab-American Anti-Discrimination Committee's (ADC) actions (also located at the bottom of the homepage). An impassioned and unyielding rhetoric highlights the feminist ethos of this Arab women's group: In these three political statements, they condemn not only the "horrible terrorist attacks" but also the threat to Arab-American communities, the erasure of Arab women's voices by the ADC, and the United States Middle East policy and the impending Iraq war. The use of cooperative rhetoric in the third person plural represents the unified voice of AWSA's members, who are driven by urgency to heal the wounds caused by the terrorist attacks, to rebuild the nation by "standing together," and to defy prejudice and injustice. Yet, in the 9/11 statement, this explicit urgency is bound by an explicit fear of persecution with references to Japanese Americans who were victimized, foregrounding the sense of injustice internalized by these women who feel their communities and families are being demonized for a crime they did not commit.

On April 10, 2003, the top of the site featured an anti-Iraq war statement issued by AWSA International North America's Chapter; "NO TO THE RACIST, COLONIALIST WAR ON IRAQ" was written in red font, all caps with a bold typeface. AWSA's rhetoric is highly incendiary and racialized, calling the US a colonialist empire that aims at re-colonizing the Middle East by waging a racist war in Iraq. The emergent feminist ethos is, by far, uncompromising and tyrannical in its condemnation of the

Figure 3. Cyber AWSA 9/11 press release

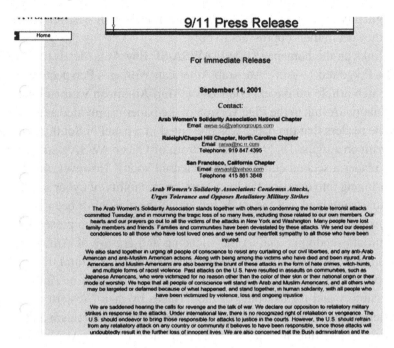

United States role in the UN-led sanctions in Iraq, U.S. support of Israel, and the "US-supported war" against the "ethnic cleansing of indigenous Palestinians from their homeland." The politicization of the group's mission marks a departure from the toned-down activist rhetoric of its mission statement, but it also aligns itself with a feminist identity that simultaneously affirms and resists the conditions of its Othering by articulating its subject position while deconstructing and rejecting the political networks of the oppression of Arab women and Arab people. The emergent feminist standpoint views the liberation of Arab women as contingent upon the liberation of their communities from all forms of domination and

Figure 4. Cyber AWSA Iraq War statement

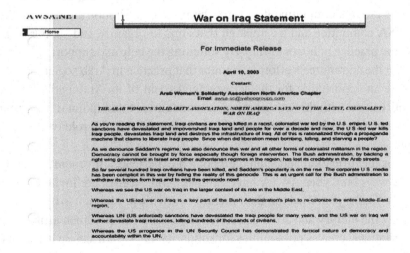

victimization, creating the dual persuasion standpoint theorists suggest, as AWSA's gendered and racialized "peculiar" marginality creates an epistemology that contrasts with—and critiques the epistemology of—what and who they deem their oppressors to be.

One of the side links on the homepage titled "AWSA SF Bay Area" leads to AWSA's statement on its paper, titled "The Forgotten '—ism': An Arab American Women's Perspective on Zionism, Racism and Sexism," a research article on the experiences of Arab American women with different forms of racism and discrimination. A link to the PDF version of the paper is provided at the top of the page. The statement informs the readers that the paper was presented in a panel in South Africa at the UN World Conference on Racism on August 18, 2001. The bottom of Cyber AWSA's statement introducing the paper promises the reader a second edition "to be released soon." However, no further edition of the paper is provided, bringing into question the long-term sustainability of cyber activism because activist sites are often left un-maintained and the goals for which the sites have been erected seem to be lost with time (Shapiro, 1995). AWSA's paper at the UN World Conference presents a feminist political, social, and humanitarian standpoint against the silencing and erasure of Arab-American women and of "the demonization of Arab women within Western academic and cultural traditions" (Naber, et. al., 2011, p. 7). The paper brings voice to the silenced and erased struggles of Arab women in the US as they resist their invisibility and the usurping of their voices by their Western counterparts, reject the Western-imposed stereotypes on them, and defy the different forms of racism and discrimination they encounter. In discursively resisting the injustices and prejudices faced by Arab women in their US communities and in challenging the oppressive dominant cultural and social structures that marginalize and intensify their subject-object binary, Cyber AWSA resorts to a rhetoric of authenticity that articulates, while strategically essentializing, the racialized experiences of these women. This produces a feminist ethos that utilizes an essentializing anonymity as it articulates its positioning from the margins of society and in the space within and between the realization of the self and its Otherness, while effectually critiquing and challenging privilege and hegemony.

Cyber AWSA's feminist ethos is underscored by a vocalization of one of the key issues affecting women's material being in Arab societies, which is honor killings—a traditional practice that victimizes Arab and Muslim women, especially in the Middle East and North Africa. In addition to providing multiple resources that feature articles and links on the issue of honor killing, the AWSA International statement on honor killing (found under the AWSA Activities link) vocalizes the concern of this Arab women's group by "the rising numbers of 'honor killings' of women and adolescent girls around the world." The activist group's commitment to fight the practice of honor killing is underscored by the creation of an AWSA committee and a campaign that aims to organize and support regional and local groups in fighting the practice of honor killing. By soliciting the help and support of AWSA International members to assist in the committee's effort to counter that practice in Arab societies, the virtual activist site is able to create an opportunity for the active engagement of its Arab audience and international allies, enable identification with the activist missions and feminist standpoint of the group in ending the victimization of women in their societies, and aid in deconstructing the role of patriarchy and culture in its perpetuation.

Opportunities for identification and shared embodied experiences for members and visitors are facilitated in various ways on Cyber AWSA International. Arab women are invited to contribute to that online community's "Gallery" and submit their literary or artistic production to be showcased on the site, and they also display the literary and artistic production of some Arab women artists and writers. Thus, Cyber AWSA International creates possibilities for solidarity and identification between Cyber AWSA's members and visitors—who include not only Arab women around the world but also international allies who subscribe to the activist group's mission and values—because the site's visitors and members can experience the singular and authentic experiences of these Arab women writers and artists through their works. Other opportunities for identification with the organization's mission are encouraged through the section titled "Contact Us," which includes an invitation to join the AWSA team, contact AWSA's United Nations Economic and Social Council (ECOSOC) representatives, or contact Cyber AWSA with questions. In the Profile, the Mailing and Chat, and AWSA International Web Forum sections, an invitation is extended to the site's visitors and group members to join the discussion and mailing listserv, which "serves as a network for Arab women…from all/diverse backgrounds and orientations" to connect with "their allies internationally."Arab women seeking AWSA International's listserv membership are asked to provide their name, where they live, what they do for a living, where they work, how they heard about Cyber AWSA International, and what they hope to gain from the membership; after AWSA San Francisco's steering committee reviews the information, the committee votes on whether the person should join the group. According to Stephan, AWSA's listserv has become increasingly exclusive as it "protects women" members and works on making it "a safe haven for other feminist activities"; thus, a full-fledged American or European woman cannot join the listserv until she proves she is interested and is "active in our [Arab and Arab women's]issues" (R. Stephan, personal communication, August 2, 2010). In addition, men are not readily allowed to join the listserv, unless they are referred and sponsored by an AWSA International woman member (R. Stephan, personal communication, August 2, 2010). According to Stephan, this restrictive selection process is in place to ensure the safety of AWSA members residing in countries such as Saudi Arabia and Iran, where there are immense restrictions on individual freedoms and where the safety and well-being of these women can be compromised if their identities are exposed. Here, anonymity becomes a means of empowering women by subverting the restrictions imposed upon Arab women in their physical spaces and in defying the oppressiveness of patriarchal supremacy in their societies.

Upon being accepted into Cyber AWSA's Yahoo group, which was started in August 2001, several guidelines are required for continuing one's membership, including the use of respectful dialogue and the lack of offensive language, personal attacks, or sexist or racist speech, etc.

Figure 5. Cyber AWSA mailing and chat page

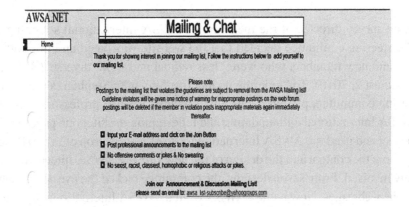

Hence, in joining the listserv, which had an average of 100 posts a month in 2005, the member achieves the highest level of interactivity with other members of Cyber AWSA, providing an opportunity for identification and shared embodied experiences as women post news about upcoming conferences, internships and scholarships for women, women's rights rallies and events, and news about human and women's rights issues in various Arab countries. Each post started a conversation thread that could extend daysor even weeks,as women shared their perspectives on news, ideas, reactions, and analyses of events, dissected the structures that oppress women in their societies, and reflected on the means of women's liberation, all of which, they acknowledged, is a formidable task. The conversations on the Yahoo listserv contained little bashing and molded the voices of Arab women and their international allies and friends, who were able to identify with the causes of the group to support Arab women's liberation from the cultural, social, patriarchal, and political networks that perpetuate their victimization. The threaded discussions on the Yahoo listserv allowed for mutually embodied experiences of activism and social and cultural protest by bringing the experience, voice, and interests of one activist into the mutually embodied experience of another and by allowing for a dialogic exchange that extended beyond "their computer screens, their living rooms, or their town centers and reach[ed] a global audience" (Bridgman, 2014, p. 203), whether Arab or non-Arab.[1]

Throughout the Cyber AWSA site, there are no visuals or pictures with the exception of the pages showcasing some Arab women's artistic production and graphic designs. Apart from the use of black font and muted background colors (white and grey with occasional purple lines and blue text), there are a few instances in which red font, bold-typeface, and all caps letters are used to visually re-enforce the group's heated rhetoric on central issues that affect the survival and physical being of Arab women and Arab people. The de-emphasis on the visual orientation of this online community illustrates Cyber AWSA International's emphasis on the text and words as the central medium through which the group's activist mission is conveyed and through which its feminist ethos is constructed. Furthermore, the deliberate absence of any graphics showcasing Arab women, whether in traditional Arab, Muslim or Western garb, indicates the community's interest in appealing to women of all faiths and ethnicities, in avoiding essentializing Arab women or AWSA's members, and in enforcing anonymity as a central element of its emergent ethos.

THE NEW AWSA

After a 2004 online survey directed at the members of AWSA International soliciting their views on Cyber AWSA, the steering committee decided that the website was dated and did not reflect the new identity of AWSA and new members who were "less radical and more diverse"(R. Stephan, personal communication, August 2, 2010). To "redefine its identity," in 2005, Stephan, a member of the AWSA International steering committee, put out a call for Computer Science professors at St. Edwards' University to help AWSA International with updating and redesigning the site; one professor volunteered to assist with the project and used the AWSA International site as a class project in an HCI class. In all the decision-making about the content and the design of the new site, the AWSA International steering committee was actively involved. From seven designs, the committee picked the eye design which dominates the top banner on the web pages. Now named AWSA United, AWSA International has transitioned from being an organization to being only a list group. In addition, the committee decided to remove all past postings and "all references from the past," making the AWSA cyber community primarily informative

Figure 6. AWSA United homepage

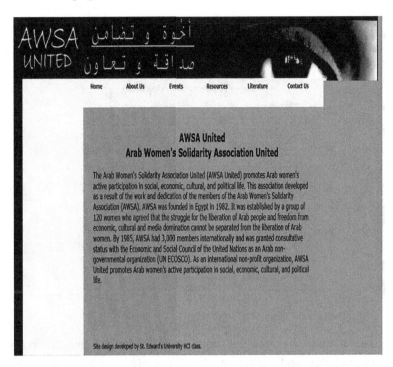

and mostly focused on directing the people to join and use the listserv to disseminate information, to promote activism, and to sign petitions, etc. (R. Stephan, personal communication, August 2, 2010). Thus, the second virtual space, AWSA United, was launched in 2006 to replace the first Cyber AWSA.

Though the new site has a cleaner design, it is missing many of the components and activist messages in the previous site. What is most striking is the absence of AWSA's position paper in the Feminist Expo; its position statements in response to 9/11, ADC practices, and to the potential war in Iraq; AWSA's campaign against honor killings; and AWSA's position paper "'The Forgotten -ism' on Zionism, sexism, and racism." The new site appears to have substituted its previous impassioned rhetoric in its critique of patriarchy, Western feminism, cultural imperialism, sexism, and racism for a subdued rhetoric that is factual and dispassionate. This is evident in the absence of any of the position statements that expound AWSA International's activist mission to realize Arab women's liberation and that of their societies from all forms of domination and to facilitate the construction of coherent racialized feminist identities that forcefully articulate the disjunctive relationship between the self and otherness. The emergent subdued feminist ethos is, thus, apolitical and seeks the liberation and freedom of Arab women and people, while avoiding exploring the explosive political, social, and economic justice issues in these societies. The new AWSA United site only provides links to Internet sources on honor killings and cultural and women's issues without providing a venue for this Arab women's group to voice its key activist positions and views to the site's other visitors and guests. The absence of AWSA International's central position statements on Arab women's rights, critiques of Western representations of Arab women and people, and commentaries on key political events in the joint Arab-American history marks a discursive departure from a large part of the history of that women's group and illustrates a divergence from the heightened political and ultra-feminist orientation evident in the discourses of its former virtual space. Hence, in

Figure 7. AWSA United profile

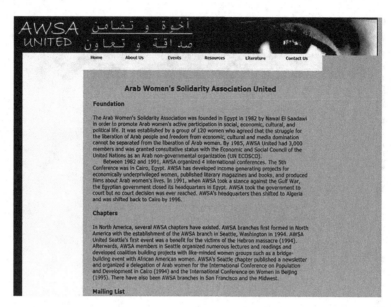

order to promote a more diverse cyberspace, a subdued feminist ethos and standpoint were substituted for the tyrannical feminist ethos and standpoint that dominated the previous Cyber AWSA. Its new ethos allows AWSA United new "less radical" and more "diverse" members to realize opportunities for identification with the organization's mission and emergent feminist ethos.

In AWSA United's new virtual space, the Home and About Us sections offer information about the organization and its founding—information similar to, though abridged, from that on the old Cyber AWSA homepage and Profile sections.

The use of cooperative rhetoric is evident in the references to AWSA United listserv as "a network for Arab women and their allies internationally," an "international network" inviting Arab women "from all backgrounds and orientations to come together and participate in AWSA United." Furthermore, the references to developing "coalition building projects" with "like-minded women groups," who "come together and participate" in the struggle to liberate Arab women highlight the subdued, less radical feminist standpoint and ethos that seek to build consensus and cooperation by bridging the cultural differences between Arab and non-Arab feminists. This subdued activist discourse is enforced rhetorically by the multiple references to "Arab women," "active participation," "liberation," and "allies" that reinforce the group members' identity as gendered and racialized subjects who are occupying this discursive virtual space and enhance the sense of civic engagement and identification between AWSA United members as partners aiming at promoting change in the material conditions of Arab women's existence. The emergent feminist ethos utilizes anonymity because the organization is not defined by any of its founding members but by the totality of members who share the same activist values and beliefs. Within the framework of a subdued feminist ethos, an articulation or rejection of the social, cultural, economic, and political networks of oppression and victimization of Arab women and Arab people is absent (or minimally vocalized) in the interest of a moderate rhetoric of activism and inclusion that is highly dispassionate, objective, and minimally racialized. The feminist standpoint portrayed in the new cyberspace for AWSA United does not, however, allow for the critical examination of the discourses and ideologies of the powerful and their role in perpetuating the domination over the marginalized, thus failing to create a counter hegemonic discourse or a new framework for defying these forms of domination.

The Horizontal toolbar offers a number of links, including Events, Resources, Literature, and Contact Us sections. The Events section is empty and does not include any past or recent events. The "Resources" section, on the other hand, includes the heading "Honor Killings." Yet, the page does not provide AWSA International's previous statement on honor killings or its campaign against this practice in women's materials spaces; the page merely provides links to external sites and resources about the history and practice of honor killing. Many of these links are similar to the ones on the old Cyber AWSA site and provide factual information to the AWSA United members about key social, cultural, political, and humanitarian issues affecting Arab women and their communities, effactually disseminating information to the activist members of the group about promoting women's activism in their digital and real spaces. Yet, the means by which this activism can be promoted or executed is not immediately evident on the site.

Though opportunities for identification and shared collective identity and consciousness between AWSA United members and visitors are made possible by the link on the Literature page for showcasing "the different types of literature submitted to the site" by AWSA United's members and friends, these opportunities fail to be realized because the page is empty and no literary production is posted. Similar to the previous Cyber AWSA, the new AWSA features a Contact Us section that provides information about joining AWSA United's mailing list and message board and provides an email contact for the organization, encouraging the members and visitors to join in the discussion and actively engage in the conversations of that online community. The page also includes a set of rules for posting messages on the Message Board, explaining that all membership requests must be approved by the moderator first before the member is allowed access to join the group, similar to the former Cyber AWSA.

Figure 8. AWSA United contact us page

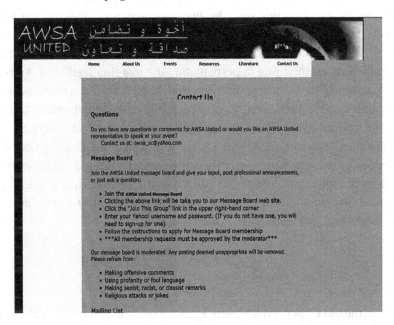

Thus, in joining the listserv, the maximum opportunities for identification with the group's activist mission and for shared embodied experiences among the listserv's members, Arab and non-Arab, are allowed, thereby providing AWSA United members with the highest level of interactivity with other members. In the Listserv, women share information about CFPs on upcoming conferences and publications of interest to Arab women activists and feminists, internships and jobs for women, women's and human rights' rallies and petitions, and news relating to human and women's rights issues in Arab countries and in the diaspora. The average number of posts on the YAHOO listserv dropped from 100 (evident with the previous Cyber AWSA around 2005) to a range of one to three post(s) a month in 2012-2013. The responses to posts have dropped from an average of ten responses in 2005 to a present average of one response recorded in May 2013, if any response is given at all. The current posts on the listserv no longer extend for weeks or even days—as with the previous Cyber AWSA. Most of the posts are left uncommented on and many of the conversations between AWSA United members are truncated and fail to allow for mutually embodied experiences of activism and social and cultural protest by minimally bringing the experience, voice, and interests of one activist into the mutually embodied experience of another, and by minimally allowing for a dialogic exchange that extends beyond the limitations of these women's physical and virtual spaces.

With minimal visual presence, the pages have a mocha background color with black utilized in the upper vertical and horizontal banners; the site features in its top banner a cropped image of a woman's face partially showing her dark brown eye, long dark lashes, her olive skin, and a cropped part of a black veil covering her eyebrow—representing the traditional Islamic head cover for Muslim women—making this image the only visual representation of Arab women on the site. The minimal use of Arabic in the top banner (next to the title AWSA United where four Arabic words: Sisterhood and Solidarity; Friendship and Cooperation are written) and the visual representation of an Arab woman align with the subdued feminist ethos of this Arab women's group and come across as an attempt to establish racial and cultural authenticity and to prove that this is an authentic space for the expression for Arab women. However, rather than providing an audible authentic voice for that emergent ethos, the new virtual AWSA inadvertently visually and discursively essentializes the idea of an Arab woman. Thus, the feminist standpoint projected by the new AWSA United site does not allow for a substantial critique of the discourses and ideologies of the privileged and their role in perpetuating the marginalization of Arab women or allow for the full corrective power of the discourse of the marginalized to displace the structures that mask and propagate these inequities and to create empty and new spaces from which other Arab women can find liberation. Despite the role anonymity plays as a central component of the emergent ethos and its part in increasing the appeal and outreach of AWSA's activist message, the phasing out of the new AWSA presence—as evidenced by the site being currently offline and the limited traffic on its listserv—sheds light on the limitations of utilizing anonymity in ethos construction because doing so poses challenges to the sustainability of such activist discourses and threatens the ability to continue ongoing critical examination of the discourses and ideologies of the powerful.

SUMMATION

The emergent ethos in the old Cyber AWSA's site is characterized by a tyrannical feminist orientation that espouses an anti-Western stance, yet reconciles it, at times, with a subdued call for cooperation with people of conscience of all backgrounds and races. The impassioned and often incendiary rhetoric employed in articulating the central feminist standpoints of the group creates a powerful feminist discourse and ethos that do not circumscribe to the normative representations of Arab women in Western or Arab contexts. It is a defiant ethos whose feminist discourses emerge as "a self-reflexive mode of analysis, aimed at articulating the critique of power in discourse with the affirmation of alternative forms of subjectivity" for self and otherness (Braidotti, 1994, p. 120). The strategic deployment of the discourse of cultural authenticity and essentialism gives credence and authority to the experiences and discourses of the Arab women's group, though, at times, it falls into the trap of reductionism and reverse racism, replicating upon the privileged otherness and the totalizing conditions the group seeks to resist. The opportunities inherent in the site for identification and shared, embodied experiences among the group's members, both Arab and non-Arab, allow for the construction of an empowered feminist identity that resists and deconstructs the cultural narratives of conformity in her society, hence constructing an alternative feminist vision for her and other women's liberated discourses and identities that is hindered at times due to the reliance on English as the sole language for communication on the site.

The different elements of the first AWSA International virtual space seem far from a reflection of the dominant Western discourses and representations of Arab women; instead, they showcase how this women's group assimilates this new digital medium to its own cultural and political needs, forcefully voicing its views and showcasing a heightened sense of civic engagement and awareness of the current political conditions and their effects on Arab women's virtual and material being. Thus, this virtual space does not reinstate stereotypical narratives of Arab women and/or their stories because the online community constructs a coherent, defiant, and activist feminist digital identity that assimilates this digital media to voice and affirm its views. With its fierce rhetoric and forceful political messages, Cyber AWSA's first virtual space carries a determination to resist Arab women's material silencing by resorting to virtual affirmation and engagement in that digital space, highlighting the WWW's ability to create a rhetorical and virtual space for the subaltern to reclaim and affirm her voice, her political views, and her civic activism. Through the use of English as the main language of communication on the site, thus giving access to the privileged English-speaking members and visitors, questions of the cultural and racial authenticity of that cyber space arise. However, the use of English as the only language of communication should not be seen as the usurping of the voices of the Arab subaltern by Western voices, for as one hopes in this virtual space, the Arab subaltern, whether as an English or Arabic-speaking one, can defy her material and virtual silencing through her English and/or Arabic voice and defy the colonial view of what constitutes a native informant as she constructs her hybrid virtual identity. Cyber AWSA's utilization of anonymity in its ethos construction elucidates and reveals how a feminist standpoint and ethos can be inextricably linked to transcend simplistic notions of native experience, voice, or language to encompass the Arab women's group's agency to write the story their own way.

With the new AWSA United site, a new identity is projected of the Arab women's group that is not of a radical feminist, progressive, political, women's rights organization so much as a subdued and moderate feminist, apolitical, women's rights organization that is invested in consensus building and cooperating with other women who share their values and beliefs in Arab women's liberation. Through the AWSA United listserv for Arab women, Arab women's groups, and activists can connect, share their stories, find support, seek sisterhood, speak against human rights' violations, and promote activism in their cyber and real spaces by signing petitions online or attending regional and local conferences. This new identity reflects a change in the cyber group's needs and demographics as the members became less radical and more diverse and also reflects a redefinition of the forms of activism that the community engages in. In the new cyber AWSA United, activism is seen as less political and more focused on the issues that matter to its members—which include advocating women's empowerment by providing a space for debate, networking, information-sharing, and member organizing, all of which they broach in their discussion and announcements on the Listserv—than on the founding members' political or social agendas. However, that new AWSA United virtual space seems to have lost its more forceful, feminist voice and standpoint and therefore possibly its appeal to some of its women activists. The inaction on the new AWSA United listserv and the phasing out of that activist domain, which is currently accessible only through the Wayback Machine (Arab Women's Solidarity, 2006; Arab Women's Solidarity, 2012), marks a loss for many women who were active AWSA members and who may have found their voices through this women's group. The innovation of other alternative social media and cyber networks have also meant a loss of some of the appeal of the listserv because some members migrated and resorted to these new networking media (R. Stephan, personal communication, August 2, 2010).

Despite the utilization of anonymity in its emergent ethos to increase the outreach of its messages, the new AWSA United site inadvertently reinstates stereotypical representations of women in its discourses and visuals by failing to challenge the Western discursive and cultural representations of Arab women and the structures that oppress Arab women in their societies, ultimately reinstating the conditions of their Othering and silencing. But is this qualification completely accurate? Nevertheless, the new AWSA United site has allowed the moderate Arab feminist to assimilate this digital medium to her own changing cultural and activist needs and to facilitate the construction of what she views as an empowered, and empowering, civically-engaged, feminist ethos and standpoint that seeks intersubjectivity with otherness and moves beyond the reduction of the privileged Other. However, in that act of renaming one's subject position, the feminist voice and ethos emergent from this digital space is generic, forgettable, and uncharismatic, unlike the forceful, impassioned, and charismatic feminist voice and ethos projected by the former Cyber AWSA. By projecting a bland, objective, dispassionate, and "rational" (Stephan,2013, p. 99), persona invested in consensus-building and cooperation with other Arab and non-Arab activists, the emergent ethos becomes a compilation of stereotypical representations of an Arab woman with a muted voice and a generic visual presence that is forgettable and meek. The use of English as the main language of communication illustrates the control the privileged have over language—where lack of access for non-English speaking Arab women cannot be overlooked—and where "being permitted to exist is not the same as equal representation or equal access" (Nakamura, 2008, p. 206), which illuminates the paradoxical relationship the marginalized have with their own discourse that adopts the language of the privileged. Though both AWSA sites use English as the language of communication, deploy anonymity to varying degrees, and instate the discourse of racial and cultural authenticity to tell their own story their own way and to legitimate the discourses of this Arab women's activist group, the new AWSA United resorts to the visual representation of the "authentic" Arab woman and merely suffices with repeated references to "Arab" and "Arab women." Thus, the new AWSA United fails to instate a discourse that voices the experiences and grievances of that Arabness or of these Arab women—losing the opportunities allotted by the strategic deployment of a feminist standpoint that articulates a rhetoric of authenticity to reinstate authority in the discourses of the racially unprivileged otherness.

FUTURE RESEARCH DIRECTIONS

Undoubtedly, the in-between space these women activists occupy between identification and dis-identification within the web of cultural performances that define womanhood allows for the production of a counter-hegemonic discourse that can become an instrument of cultural awareness and political change. Thus, the need arises to examine if and how the digital medium can promote and sustain the discourses of activism and revolutionary work, as well as the need to examine the means of subverting the limitations of the virtual and physical domain and uncover opportunities and frameworks through which revolutionary and activist discourses can survive the short memories and attention spans of digital users who often migrate to emerging forms of digital media. This requires further examination of how the construction of ethos in these discourses becomes inseparable from one's experiences and one's standpoint and is discursively negotiated in the intersection of race, class, gender, intentionality, and language, as well as how these discourses can confer a sense of connectedness without suppressing differences or sacrificing the essentials of identity to produce alternative liberatory discourses. Such discourses can provide the framework through which the marginalized can free themselves from oppressive confining structures that limit their intentionalities and access and dismiss their capacities as transcendent subjects.

CONCLUSION

The folding of AWSA International's San Francisco chapter in 2002, the disappearance of Cyber AWSA from the web, and the dwindling presence of AWSA United in its listserv raise questions about the sustainability of online activist spaces. On one hand, the utilization of anonymity in AWSA's ethos construction, whereby the organization is defined by the totality of members who share the same values and mission, increases the appeal of its message to both Arab and non-Arab members. On another hand, the ease with which online users can move from one on-line community to another and the lack of a charismatic figure that carries forth the organization's activist message raise skepticism about the potential of anonymity in online interaction to create sustainable online spaces of belonging and being that can result in sustainable tangible change in real communities (Lockard, 1996; Healy, 1996) and that can defy the threat of homogenization and streamlining.

As online users lose interest, new social sites and virtual media are invented, sites are left unmaintained, and the goals for which the sites have been erected are lost with time, it becomes difficult to maintain a sense of unity and belonging in these virtual spaces. The realization of identification and creating opportunities for shared embodied experiences and "connectivity" with others in internetworked spaces in which "a person's boundaries are relatively fluid so that a person feels a part of significant others" (Joseph,1993, p. 425) becomes difficult to maintain because cyber users face "internal conflicts, external pressure, and technological shifts to other means of media" (Stephan, 2013, p. 97), erecting obstacles against building strong and lasting online pockets of activism. Though the role of anonymity in ethos construction allows for the critical examination of the discourses and ideologies of the powerful and their role in perpetuating the domination over the marginalized, as is evident in the first AWSA site, anonymity fails to create a sustainable counterhegemonic discourse or a new framework for defying these forms of domination.

For many, the Internet is a powerful medium with a tremendous potential to challenge patriarchy, oppression, and the concentration of power in real and virtual spaces. However, that narrative is one that oversimplifies the problematics of access for minorities and the socially, culturally, and economically disadvantaged, and disregards the marginalized in third world communities whose stories are left untold, which should make people questions the relevance of cyber space as a means of disseminating activist discourses and messages to dismantle the dynamics of silencing and erasing the marginalized or racialized other. That narrative also oversimplifies the dangers and possible opportunities inherent in the instatement of the discourses of racial authenticity and purity in cyberspace, which can inadvertently perpetuate the silencing of those deemed non-native enough, thereby alienating them from their discourses and societies if they break the silence code, while also allotting the right to speak exclusively to others deemed more native and more culturally and racially pure/authentic. However, the opportunities allotted in the discourses of racial authenticity in cyberspace lie in the awarding of authority to untraditional voices and the reinstating of authority in conventionally nonauthoritative spaces, discourses, and experiences of the racialized other. In addition, with the absence of millions from the cyber narrative, can one truly investigate the potential of cyberspace to propagate genuinely new and nonracist (and nonsexist and non-classist but intersubjective) ways of being and ethos construction that can move beyond one's othering or the reduction of otherness? Probably not. However, what we can do is open the door for extensive discussions of race and the study of what Nakamura (2002) called "cybertypes," or the images and representations of racial identity in this digital medium, and the implications of such representations in furthering or challenging the marginalization of Otherness. Only then can we initiate a genuine polyphonic discussion of the narrative of cyberspace, and only then can we assess whether and how cyberspace has facilitated or obstructed the creation of empowered digital racio-identities and/or the construction of an empowered and empowering ethos that challenges privilege and the digital and material silencing and erasure of the marginalized. In the cyber discourses of marginalized rhetors, we need to investigate what Judith Butler (1990) pointed out—the weaknesses and contradictions in the discursive resistance of the oppressed as they employ "the strategy of the oppressor instead of offering a different set of terms" (p. 13) and which ends up replicating the totalizing conditions of their disempowerment and extending their subjugation—and find means for the proliferation of resistant and subversive strategies that dislodge the discursive and ideological power of the oppressor. This act of displacement requires a more substantial role for feminist standpoint theory in investigating the discourses of the marginalized and illuminating the ideological challenges and strategic omissions in their discourses as they attempt to critique, dismantle, and displace the oppressive epistemology of the powerful and create a new set of terms for creating liberatory discourses and ideologies.

RERERENCES

Al-Nakib, M. (2013, Winter). Disjunctive synthesis: Deleuze and Arab feminism. *Signs (Chicago, Ill.)*, *38*(2), 459–482. doi:10.1086/667220

Arab women's solidarity association. (2006, May 9). *Wayback Machine*. Retrieved from https://web.archive.org/web/20060216031423/http://www.awsa.net/

Arab women's solidarity association. (2012, September 5). *Wayback Machine*. Retrieved from https://web.archive.org/web/20110105211814/http://awsa.net/

Aristotle. (2001). Rhetoric. In P. Bizzell & B. Herzberg (Eds.), The rhetorical tradition: readings from classical times to the present (2nd ed.; pp. 179-240). Boston, MA: Bedford/St Martins.

Balsamo, A. (1999). *Technologies of the gendered body: Reading cyborg women*. Durham, NC: Duke University Press.

Bell, K. E., Orbe, M. P., Drummond, D. K., & Camara, S. K. (2000). Accepting the challenge of centralizing without essentializing: Black feminist thought and African American women's communicative experiences. *Women's. Studies in Communications, 23*, 41–62.

Braidotti, R. (1994). *Discontinuous becomings: Deleuze on the becoming-woman of philosophy. In Nomadic Subjects: Embodiment and Sexual Difference in Contemporary Feminist Theory* (pp. 111–123). New York, NY: Columbia University Press.

Bridgman, K. (2014). (Re)framing the interests of English speakers: "We are all Khaled Said. In M. Ballif (Ed.), *Re/Framing Identifications* (pp. 198–204). Chicago, IL: Waveland Press.

Brooke, R. E. (1991). *Writing and sense of self: Identity negotiation in writing workshops*. Urbana, IL: NCTE.

Burke, K. (1962). *A rhetoric of motives*. Cleveland, OH: Meridian.

Butler, J. (1990). *Gender trouble: feminism and the subversion of identity*. New York, NY: Routledge.

Collins, P. H. (1990). *Black feminist thought: Knowledge, consciousness, and the politics of empowerment*. New York, NY: Routledge.

De Pew, K. E. (2003). *The rhetorical process of digital subjectivities: Case studies of International TAs negotiating identity with digital media*. (Unpublished doctoral dissertation). Purdue University, West Lafayette, IN.

Fayad, M. (1995, Summer). Reinscribing identity: Nation and community in Arab women's writing. *College Literature, 22*(1), 147–160.

Foster, D. (1997). Community and identity in the electronic village. In D. Porter (Ed.), *Internet Culture* (pp. 23–37). New York, NY: Routledge.

Gonzalez, J. (2000). The appended subject: Race and identity as digital assemblage. In B. E. Kolko, L. Nakamura, & G. B. Rodman (Eds.), *Race in Cyberspace* (pp. 28–50). New York, NY: Routledge.

Grabill, J. T., & Pigg, S. (2012). Messy rhetoric: Identity performance as rhetorical agency in online public forums. *Rhetoric Society Quarterly, 42*(2), 99–119. doi:10.1080/02773945.2012.660369

Gruber, S. (2001). The rhetorics of three women activist groups on the web: Building and transforming communities. In G. Rosendale & S. Gruber (Eds.), *Alternative rhetorics: Challenges to the rhetorical tradition* (pp. 77–92). Albany, NY: State Univerity of New York Press.

Guèye, K. (2010, Summer). "Tyrannical femininity" in Nawal El Saadawi's *memoirs of a woman doctor. Research in African Literatures, 41*(2), 160–172. doi:10.2979/RAL.2010.41.2.160

Gurak, L. (1999). The promise and peril of social action in cyberspace: Ethos, delivery, and the protests over marketplace and the clipper chip. In P. Kollock & M. Smith (Eds.), *Communities in cyberspace* (pp. 243–263). London: Routledge.

Haraway, D. (1988). Situated knowledges: The science question in feminism and the privilege of partial perspective. *Feminist Studies*, *14*(3), 575–599. doi:10.2307/3178066

Harding, S. (1998). *Whose science? Whose knowledge? Thinking from women's lives*. Ithaca, NY: Cornell University Press.

Hartsock, N. C. M. (1983). The feminist standpoint: Developing the ground for a specifically feminist historical materialism. In S. Harding & M. B. Hintikka (Eds.), *Discovering reality: feminist perspectives on epistemology, metaphysics, methodology, and philosophy of science* (pp. 283–310). Dordrecht, The Netherlands: D. Reidel.

Hawisher, G. E., & Sullivan, P. (1999). Fleeting images: Women visually writing the web. In G. Hawisher & C. Selfe (Eds.), *Passions, pedagogies and 21st century technologies* (pp. 268–291). Logan, UT: Utah State University Press.

Healy, D. (1996). Cyberspace and Place: The Internet as middle landscape on the electronic frontier. In D. Porter (Ed.), *Internet culture* (pp. 55–68). New York, NY: Routledge.

Hekman, S. (1997). Truth and method: Feminist standpoint theory revisited. *Signs (Chicago, Ill.)*, *22*(2), 341–365. doi:10.1086/495159

hooks, b. (1989). *Yearning: Race, gender, and cultural politics*. London: Turnaround.

Hyde, M. J. (Ed.). (2004). *The ethos of rhetoric*. Columbia, SC: University of South Carolina Press.

Joseph, S. (1993). Gender and relationality among Arab families in Lebanon. *Feminist Studies*, *19*(3), 465–486. doi:10.2307/3178097

Knadler, S. (2001). E-Racing difference in e-Space: Black female subjectivity and the web- based portfolio. *Computers and Composition*, *18*(3), 235–255. doi:10.1016/S8755-4615(01)00054-8

LeFevre, K. B. (1987). *Invention as a social act*. Carbondale, IL: Southern Illinois UP.

Lockard, J. (1996). Progressive politics, electronic individualism and the myth of virtual community. In D. Porter (Ed.), *Internet culture* (pp. 219–231). New York, NY: Routledge.

McClish, G., & Bacon, J. (2002). "Telling the story her own way": The role of feminist standpoint theory in rhetorical studies. *Rhetoric Society Quarterly*, *32*(2), 27–55. doi:10.1080/02773940209391227

Miller, C. M. (2001). Writing in a culture of simulation: ethos online. In P. Coppock (Ed.), The Semiotics of writing: Transdisciplinary perspectives on the technology of writing (pp. 253-272). Turnhout, Belguim: Brepols Publishers.

Myers, G. (1986, February). Reality, consensus, and reform in the rhetoric of composition teaching. *College English*, *48*(2), 154–174. doi:10.2307/377298

Naber, N. (2011). Decolonizing culture: Beyond orientalist and anti-orientalist feminisms. In Ed. R. Abdulhadi, E. Alsultany, & N. Naber (Eds.), Arab and Arab American feminisms: Gender, violence and belongings (pp. 10-28). Syracuse, NY: Syracuse University Press.

Naber, N., Desouky, E., & Baroudi, L. (2001). The forgotten '—ism': An Arab American women's perspective on zionism, racism and sexism. *The UN World Conference on Racism*. Retrieved from https://web.archive.org/web/20050306042931/http://www.awsa.net/Positionpaper.htm

Nakamura, L. (2002). *Cyber types: race, ethnicity, and identity on the Internet*. New York, NY: Routledge.

Nakamura, L. (2008). *Digitizing race: Visual cultures of the Internet*. Minneapolis, MN: University of Minnesota Press.

Odom, J. (2014). Identification, consubstantiality, interval, and temporality: Luce Irigaray and the possibilities for rhetoric. In M. Ballif (Ed.), *Re/Framing identifications* (pp. 230–248). Chicago, IL: Waveland Press.

Ow, J. A. (2000). The revenge of the yellowfaced cyborg terminator. In B. E. Kolko, L. Nakamura, & G. B. Rodman (Eds.), *Race in cyberspace* (pp. 51–70). New York, NY: Routledge.

Plato. (2001). Gorgias. In P. Bizzell & B. Herzberg (Eds.), The rhetorical tradition: Readings from classical times to the present (2nd ed.; pp. 87-138). Boston, MA: Bedford/St. Martins.

Punday, D. (2000). The narrative construction of cyberspace: Reading *Neuromancer*, reading cyberspace debates. *College English*, *63*(2), 194–213. doi:10.2307/379040

Quintilian. (2001). Institutes of oratory. In P. Bizzell & B. Herzberg (Eds.), The rhetorical tradition: Readings from classical times to the present (2nd ed.; pp. 364-428). Boston, MA: Bedford/St. Martins.

Reynolds, N. (1993). Ethos as location: New sites for understanding discursive authority. *Rhetoric Review*, *11*(2), 325–338. doi:10.1080/07350199309389009

Rich, A. (1986). *Notes toward a politics of location. In Blood, read, and poetry: selected prose 1979-1985* (pp. 210–231). New York, NY: Norton.

Ronald, K. (1990). A reexamination of personal and public discourse in classical rhetoric. *Rhetoric Review*, *9*(1), 36–48. doi:10.1080/07350199009388911

Sardar, Z. (1996). alt. civilizations.faq cyberspace as the darker side of the west. In J. R. Ravetz & Sardar, Z. (Eds.), Cyberfutures: culture and politics on the information superhighway (pp. 14-41). New York, NY: Routledge.

Schmertz, J. (1999). Constructing essences: Ethos and the postmodern subject of feminism. *Rhetoric Review*, *18*(1), 82–91. doi:10.1080/07350199909359257

Shapiro, A. L. (1995, July3). Street corners in cyberspace. *Nation (New York, N.Y.)*, *261*(1), 10–14.

Skalli, L. (2006). Communicating gender in the public sphere: Women and information Technologiesin MENA. *Journal of Middle East Women's Studies*, *2*(2), 35–59.

Smith, V. (1998). *Not just race, not just gender: Black feminist readings*. New York, NY: Routledge.

Spivak, G. (1990). *The postcolonial critic: Interviews, strategies, dialogues* (S. Harasym, Ed.). New York, NY: Routledge.

Stephan, R. (2013). Creating solidarity in cyberspace: The case of Arab Women's Solidarity Association United. *Journal of Middle East Women's Studies, 9*(1), 81–109. doi:10.2979/jmiddeastwomstud.9.1.81

Stone, A. R. (1992). Will the real body please stand up? Boundary stories about virtual cultures. In M. Benedikt (Ed.), *Cyberspace: First steps* (pp. 81–118). Cambridge, MA: MIT Press.

Takayoshi, P. (1999). No boys allowed: The World Wide Web as a clubhouse for girls. *Computers and Composition, 16*(1), 89–106. doi:10.1016/S8755-4615(99)80007-3

Tal, K. (1996). *The unbearable whiteness of being: African American critical theory and cyberculture.* Retrieved from http://gse.buffalo.edu/fas/bromley/classes/socprac/readings/Kali-Tal-unbearable.htm

Ulmer, G. (1994). *Heuristics: The logic of invention.* Baltimore, MD: Johns Hopkins University Press.

Vogt, C., & Chen, P. (2001, September). Feminisms and the Internet. *Peace Review, 13*(3), 371–374. doi:10.1080/13668800120079072

Walters, F. D. (1995, November). Writing teachers writing and the politics of dissent. *College English, 57*(7), 822–839. doi:10.2307/378405

Wood, J. (1997). *Communication theories in action: An introduction.* Belmont, NY: Wadsworth.

Young, I. M. (1990). The ideal community and the politics of difference. In L. Nicholson (Ed.), *Feminism/Postmodernism* (pp. 300–323). New York, NY: Routledge.

Zappen, J. P. (2005). Digital rhetoric: Toward an integrated theory. *Technical Communication Quarterly, 14*(3), 319–325. doi:10.1207/s15427625tcq1403_10

KEY TERMS AND DEFINITIONS

Anonymity: It is the framing of theorizations on postcolonial/post-print constructions of authorship where the lack of a defined or named author becomes an expedient and credible form of authorship that legitimizes identity, authority, and experience inanonymous digital discourses.

Communal: It refers to a network of discursive practices and conventions for knowledge production and dissemination to which a certain community has consented.

Cyberfeminism: It is the deployment of cyberspace as a platform for advocating women's activism against the social, cultural, economic, and legal frameworks constraining them.

Essentialism: It is traditionally viewed as promoting collective common experiences while erasing differences, which can be strategically deployed to instate authority in the experiences of the marginalized.

Ethos: It can refer toone's good or moral character, an element of style, a "dwelling place," a group quality, or a network of communal discursive practices that is ideally polyphonic and authentic. One's digital ethos is formulated by online discursive negotiations and interactions and is ever changing across time, texts, and spaces.

Feminist Standpoint: It is a feminist theory that locates authority in the experiences and epistemology of the disenfranchised because their unique situatedness awards them a deeper knowledge, a profound understanding of, and an ability to critique and consciously resist, the perspective and discourses of the powerful.

Identification: It means to identify with one's audience's needs and norms in a more empathetic and dialogic approach, ultimately achieving persuasion. By identifying the rhetor's ways with the audience's, one creates an opportunity for identification between the speaker and the audience and for creating a sense of community.

Subdued Feminist Ethos: It is an ethos that operates within the parameters of Western feminist thought and seeks consensus building and bridging cultural barriers and differences with non-Arab feminists. It has an apolitical standpoint and seeks the creation of social and economic justice in Arab communities, while avoiding exploring the explosive political justice issues in these societies.

Tyrannical Feminist Ethos: It is an ethos that operates within the parameters of an Arab feminism hostile to Western forms of feminism. It seeks some form of consensus building with non-Arab feminists in the interest of affirming the failure of the Western feminist trend in the genuine inclusion of Arab and non-White feminisms and also affirming the singular authenticity of the Arab feminist experience.

ENDNOTE

[1] My encounter with the listserv came about while doing research on AWSA for a graduate course in my doctoral program back in 2005. After sending an email to the AWSA steering committee with my biographical information, I was admitted into the listserv and am still a member today. However, my membership on the AWSA listserv has been marked by short periods of activity followed by long periods of inactivity. Part of the reason I often abandon the listserv is my skepticism at my/Cyber AWSA's ability to realize tangible change in the lives of millions of Arab women who have often occupy a marginal space in their patriarchal communities, or in the lives of Arab people generally who suffer under the grip of dictators and despotic regimes that usurp the voices of both men and women.

Chapter 10
Credibility and Crisis in Pseudonymous Communities

Sarah Lefkowith
University of Oxford, UK

ABSTRACT

Information credibility is difficult to ascertain online, especially when identity is obscured. Yet increasingly, individuals ascertain credibility of emerging information in such contexts, including in the midst of crises. The authors, using data from reddit, examine the influence of potentially credibility cues in a pseudonymous context, investigating not both general effects and whether cues affecting credibility perceptions maintain their effects during crises. Findings include a positive relationship between commenter reputation and perceived credibility in non-crises; a positive relationship between perceived credibility and the use of persuasive appeals relating to one's character or experiences during crisis; and a positive relationship between perceived credibility and the use of a link during crisis. The authors explore how reddit's structure impacts credibility perception, describe how persuasion is operationalized, and elaborate a typology of highly credible comments. Through this study, the authors contribute to both credibility research and crisis informatics.

INTRODUCTION

In times of uncertainty, individuals and organizations must be able to determine who—or what—to believe. Yet in the digital age, ascertaining credibility is growing increasingly complex. A combination of forces, from source proliferation to evolving content production and consumption roles, challenge traditional strategies of assessing credibility and verifying information (Flanagin & Metzger, 2000; Metzger, Flanagin, & Medders, 2010; Sundar, 2008). This is particularly pronounced in contexts where markers of "author" and "source" are obscured, as occurs in much social media. In spite of these challenges, everyday users, media organizations, and governmental institutions must turn to the Internet for information on emerging events, utilizing "officially vetted" information alongside information that surfaces in social networks to guide decision making and response (Singer, 2014; Glenski, Johnston, & Weninger 2015).

DOI: 10.4018/978-1-5225-1072-7.ch010

The results of such efforts are often positive, enabling rapid dissemination of accurate information and service coordination. In crisis events such as natural disasters or public shootings, social media platforms are increasingly valuable because they allow for speedy aggregation of emerging, highly critical information that is otherwise difficult to obtain (Huey, Nhan, & Broll, 2012; Sutton, Palen, & Shklovski, 2008). However, these platforms are still home to rumor-mongering and potential misinformation, occasionally sparking bona fide crises of their own. Famously, reddit was the site of the misidentification of the Boston Marathon bombing suspects in 2013, resulting in the public accusation of multiple innocent individuals including one deceased missing person (D'Orazio, 2013; Kang, 2013). Though this event has led to increased scrutiny, issues of misinformation through social media persist, as has been witnessed in the wake of the November 2015 attacks in Paris (Rogers, 2015). Clearly, mis-assessing credibility can have profound effects.

Since credibility judgments occur across multiple platforms, many of which evolve rapidly, the institution of a comprehensive and imminent automatic intervention to determine content veracity seems unlikely. Addressing information verification and contemporary credibility assessment, however, is clearly necessary (Flanagin & Metzger, 2000; Singer, 2014). Consequently, we ought to unravel exactly what about this information inspires perceptions of credibility. What factors, exactly, lead us to believe information we find online?

This chapter investigates whether certain information characteristics are associated with perceived credibility in pseudonymous contexts and whether these associations change during a crisis. The author begins with a discussion of credibility and crisis informatics research, identifying factors popularly attributed to influencing credibility perceptions and exploring contemporary challenges. Using reddit as a primary data source, the authors then analyze information generated in response to both crises and non-crises using qualitative and quantitative methods. Our results indicate that, while some factors appear to be associated with perceived credibility in both crisis and non-crisis conditions, important variations exist with substantial consequences for crisis responders, journalists, everyday citizens, and future research.

BACKGROUND

Credibility Defined

Definitions of credibility vary; words like believability, accuracy, trustworthiness, reliability, and attractiveness all appear in past research (Melican & Dixon, 2008; Metzger, Flanagin, Eyal, Lemus, & McCann, 2003). For clarity, the authors adopt a definition derived from the Oxford English Dictionary, simply "the capacity to elicit belief" (Blank, 2006).

Credibility is a multidimensional construct applied to sources, messages, and media. "Source" refers to the origin of information, e.g., an individual or organization (Wathen & Burkell, 2002). "Messages" are the content of information, and "media" refers to the technologies and platforms through which a message is transmitted (Wathen & Burkell, 2002; Johnson & Kaye, 2004). Key components of source credibility are trustworthiness and expertise; put simply, sources that seem trustworthy and expert are perceived as credible (Fogg, Cuellar, & Danielson, 2002). Message credibility results from the interaction between source characteristics (e.g., experience, trustworthiness), message characteristics (e.g., articulation, internal logic), and receiver characteristics (e.g., cultural background, existing beliefs) (Wathen & Burkell, 2002; Melican & Dixon, 2008).

The process of establishing credibility is inherently relational, requiring both a source and an audience whose perceptions are at stake (Fogg, Cuellar, & Danielson, 2002; Blank, 2007). Perceptions can be manipulated; characteristics such as reputation, timing, and articulation can be strategically engineered even by those with minimal technical sophistication (Morris, Counts, Roseway, Hoff, & Schwarz, 2012). Further, perceptions do not necessarily reflect the actual character of information; in other words, perceived credibility is not equivalent to accuracy or proximity to truth (Fallis, 2008; Morris, Counts, Roseway, Hoff, & Schwarz, 2012; Westerman, Spence, & Heide, 2014).

Contemporary Challenges to Credibility Assessment

Before widespread Internet use, the comparative scarcity of media sources rendered credibility assessment primarily a matter of assessing source reputation (Metzger, Flanagin, & Medders, 2010; Sundar, 2008). Verification mechanisms were established and widely understood; consumers relied on editorial processes of media institutions, genre divides between information sources (e.g., entertainment versus reference), and the advice of trusted others (Flanagin & Metzger, 2000). The Internet, specifically Web 2.0 and social computing, rendered these strategies both less effective and potentially more necessary (Flanagin & Metzger, 2000; cf. Fogg, Cuellar, & Danielson, 2002; Sundar, 2008; Warnick, 2004). Traditional gatekeeping, editorial, and quality-control mechanisms can be eschewed, and the origin of information can be unclear (Fogg, Cuellar, & Danielson, 2002; Melican & Dixon, 2008; Sundar, 2008). These developments, among others, make it "next to impossible for an average Internet user to have a well-defined sense of the credibility of various sources and message categories on the Web." (Sundar, 2008, p. 74.)

Digital media uncouples credibility and authority at unprecedented levels, rendering source ambiguity a rule rather than exception (Fogg, Cuellar, & Danielson, 2002; Metzger, Flanagin, & Medders, 2010). This is particularly true of anonymous and pseudonymous platforms, which by design obscure users' identities. In such environments "users know little about the expertise, qualifications, and potential biases that may be infused into the information they obtain therein" (Metzger, Flanagin, & Medders, 2010, p. 415), even though some argue that this pseudonymity may in fact have beneficial effects in that it can enable sensitive or political discourse (Gamie, 2012). Regardless, such sites are a common information resource, raising questions about how the tension between lack of source identity and information verification is effectively navigated.

Crises may pose further challenges. The impact of crisis on credibility perceptions is under-researched (Westerman, Spence, & Heide, 2014), though the growing importance of social and digital media during crisis is undeniable and avidly studied (Heverin & Zach, 2010; Palen, Vieweg, Liu, & Hughes, 2009; Sutton, Palen, & Shlovski, 2008; Westerman, Spence, & Heide, 2014). Much of the inquiry into the effect of crises on communication originates in the growing discipline of "crisis informatics," a field that considers social media crisis communications in the context of information dissemination "within and between official and public channels and entities"(Palen, Vieweg, Liu, & Hughes, 2009, p. 469). The author takes a definition of "crisis" from this field: "large-scale emergency activity by members of the public that includes disasters but also other unexpected events" (Palen, Vieweg, Liu, & Hughes, 2009, p. 476), encompassing incidences from natural disasters (Sutton, Palen, & Shlovski, 2008) to public shootings (Heverin & Zach 2010; Palen, Vieweg, Liu, & Hughes, 2009). Individuals and organizations both contribute to—and seek information from—social media during crises, resulting in the rapid proliferation and spread of content, as well as decentralized information regulation and verification (Heverin & Zach,

2010; Huey, Nhan, & Broll, 2012). Multiple studies highlight individuals' resourcefulness in information-seeking during crises, often involving consulting multiple sources (Palen, Vieweg, Liu, & Hughes, 2009; Westerman, Spence, & Heide, 2014). Resourcefulness is also evident in information contribution, as individuals harness professionally-developed skills in distributed problem-solving and fact-checking (Huey, Nhan, & Broll, 2012; Palen, Vieweg, Liu, & Hughes, 2009; Sutton, Palen, & Shlovski, 2008).

Though past research acknowledges the risk of misinformation, insight into actual verification processes that may occur is limited. Social media are valuable during crises because real-time information might surface there before being broadcast by official channels, albeit amidst potentially misleading or malicious statements (Morris, Counts, Roseway, Hoff, & Schwarz, 2012). Consequently, further investigation is required.

A Brief Introduction to Heuristics

Individuals and organizations increasingly rely on a series of judgment shortcuts when assessing credibility online. These shortcuts, called "heuristics," rely on cues and individuals' associated beliefs—for example, that recency of publishing denotes accuracy—which in turn shape overall perceptions (Morris, Counts, Roseway, Hoff, & Schwarz, 2012; Sundar, 2008).[1] The theory supporting heuristics posits attitudes may be formed either through cognitively effortful evaluation processes involving attentive evaluation of content or through "peripheral" cues that shape perception based on existing associations (Petty & Cacioppo, 1986). Heuristics can enable hasty judgments and biases, as reliance on heuristics does not necessarily entail automatic information processing. In fact, heuristics are often enacted subconsciously or reflexively, allowing individuals to act and think quickly when seeking information online (Sundar, 2008; Metzger, Flanagin, & Medeers 2010).

Many cues—from source reputation and grammatical accuracy to website usability—may trigger heuristic judgments, though the criteria used and the effort to attentively evaluate information varies by context (Flanagin & Metzger, 2000; Sundar, 2008; Wathen & Burkell, 2002; Warnick, 2005). Technologies and media themselves may inspire heuristics given their specific affordances and capabilities (Sundar, 2008). Heuristics may not always yield desired outcomes in credibility assessment; past research has found that users were poor judges of the truthfulness of content on Twitter when relying on heuristics such as retweets or topically-related user names (Morris, Counts, Roseway, Hoff, & Schwarz, 2012). Attention to heuristics and associated cues has increased in prominence as sources of information proliferate and individuals spend less time assessing information credibility (Morris, Counts, Roseway, Hoff, & Schwarz, 2012; cf. Metzger, Flanagin, & Medders, 2010; Walthen & Burkell 2002).

Heuristic Cues Related to Credibility Assessment

People have long inferred credibility from source reputation. Individuals judge reputation by assessing a source's history of reliability, perceived level of expertise, and presence or lack of "good will" (Fallis 2008; Metzger, Flanagin, & Medders, 2010). When encountering information online, reputation assessment may rely on the name recognition of websites, the source of content on a site, or a source's credentials (Metzger, Flanagin, & Medders, 2010). Of course, reputation is not infallible and does not always engender trust in information (Tormala, Briñol, & Petty, 2006; Smith, Houwer, & Nosek, 2013). Additionally, the presentation of the message can impact a source's perceived credibility (Wathen & Burkell, 2002).

Reputation cues diminish in settings where source identity is obscured, especially those where anonymity or pseudonymity is the norm. Rains (2007), in studying anonymity in computer-mediated communication, found that anonymity can lead to diminished perceptions of a source's confidence and uncertainty regarding a source's motives, regardless of argument quality. Chesney and Su (2010) produced contradictory results, finding that identity is not considered when users assess blog credibility. Gamie (2012) argued that pseudonymity may actually be a boon in certain circumstances, such as those where communication is sensitive or subject to censor, and that in these cases a communal ethos trumps a need to assess individuals' reputation. Regardless of whether information about a source's reputation is available, users may only consult information that is immediately accessible (Fallis, 2008; Morris, Counts, Roseway, Hoff, & Schwarz, 2012). Further, users who are highly familiar with particular platforms may confer credibility to their content writ large, bypassing the evaluation of individual users (Morris, Counts, Roseway, Hoff, & Schwarz, 2012). Consequently, some believe traditional reputation cues may be outdated online (Metzger, Flanagin, & Medders, 2010; Sundar, 2008; Warnick, 2004).

Persuasive intent—the feeling that information is intended to persuade—is an intuitively negative heuristic, implying manipulation or deception (Metzger, Flanagin, & Medders, 2010). Aristotle's famous tripartite concept of "persuasive appeals" is often used in studies of persuasion in computer-mediated communications (English, Sweetser, & Ancu, 2001; Hübler & Bell, 2003; Zappen, 2005; Otterbacher, 2011). In *Poetics,* Aristotle (1961, trans.) defined three types of appeals: ethos, or persuasion through invoking character or reputation; pathos, or persuasion through appealing to the listener's emotions and sensibilities; and logos, or persuasion through logic and reasoning. Some say this scheme may limit interpretation of "appealing" rhetorical strategies, proposing alternative frameworks for evaluating persuasion online (Killingsworth, 2005; Warnick, 2005). Nonetheless, Aristotle's persuasive appeals remain a cornerstone in rhetorical analysis and a widely-accepted framework for analyzing persuasion in practice.

Overtly persuasive messaging, such as information from commercial sources, may be considered suspect given the implication of ulterior motives of the information provider (Metzger, Flanagin, & Medders, 2010). This said, individuals may not recognize all persuasive appeals. Presentation of a message, a site's usability, and a number of subtle design features may affect users' perceptions without registering as being explicitly persuasive (Fogg, 2009; Fogg, Cueller, & Danielson, 2002; Sundar 2008; Wathen & Burkell 2002).[2] Message articulation also may not be perceived as persuasive, thus generating no resistance. In a study of online reviews, Otterbacher (2011) found that the most prominent, well-received reviews were those employing the greatest number of persuasive devices. Tan, Swee, Lim, Detenber, and Alsgoff (2007) similarly found in their analysis of computer-mediated conversations that "how one 'speaks' or writes is more influential than the degree of competence ascribed to individuals by various structural features of the website" (Tan, Swee, Lim, Detenber, & Alsgoff, 2007, p. 90). Despite not recognizing message characteristics as "persuasive," individuals may consciously utilize them to persuade; Shanahan (2010) found that, in scientific discussions online, lay users employ scientific language to assert credibility and authority. One might even consider communication itself persuasive; indeed, some have grouped cues triggering multiple heuristics, treating content holistically as constituting a persuasive appeal (English, Sweetser, & Ancu, 2001; Fogg, 2009; Tormala & Clarkson, 2007).

Perception of endorsement may also play a role in establishing credibility online, particularly in social contexts. Endorsement is best defined as faith in recommendations or the use of social contacts to prioritize, filter, and evaluate information (Anderson, 1996; Metzger, Flanagin, & Medders, 2010). The logic underpinning this heuristic is that those one affiliates with or admires have correct (or at least agreeable) opinions (Metzger, Flanagin, & Medders, 2010; Sundar, 2008). Social/group credibility assessments have grown increasingly popular, as seen in the shift from traditional media gatekeepers to the "vetting" of information passed through social networks (Bruns, 2005; Metzger, Flanagin, & Medders, 2010). This is particularly observable in social networking sites or review/ratings systems where opinions of large groups can be surveyed in aggregate (Metzger, Flanagin, & Medders, 2010). In such environments, endorsement may not be so straightforward to interpret; past research indicates that social influence in collective intelligence environments may create positive ratings bubbles, artificially inflating positive endorsement and encouraging a "group think" mentality (Muchnik, Aral, & Taylor, 2013; Glenski, Johnston, & Weninger, 2015). In such cases, endorsement would lead to a rich-get-richer scenario, generating difficulties for users in interpreting endorsement as it relates to information quality.

Some heuristics may hold more or less weight during crises, as different pressures on information producers and consumers are introduced. The costs associated with the absence of information or misinformation are heightened, potentially leading users to rebroadcast information using different criteria (Gupta, Joshi, & Kumaraguru, 2012). Past research on this topic has acknowledged these differences, though consistent findings have yet to emerge. In a study of information diffusion on Twitter during the 2011 Egyptian uprising, researchers found that a large number of retweets may be an indicator of high-quality, on-the-ground information (Starbird & Palen, 2012), building upon previous work suggesting that retweets with topical keywords are more likely to be on-topic in a disaster incident than non-retweets (Starbird & Palen, 2012). Westerman, Spence, and Van Der Heide (2014), in another Twitter study, found that "the recency of updates impact[s] cognitive elaboration, which in turn impact[s]perceived credibility," hypothesizing that the characteristic immediacy of Twitter may render the platform itself a credible source in crisis events (p. 8-9). These are plausible heuristics that may be utilized during crises, but the lack of comparative data or analysis of non-crisis data in tandem in past research makes it challenging to understand how crisis plays a role.

Significance and Research Imperative

Credibility assessment is important on an individual level, but it is exponentially significant in social media environments where user activity governs information accessibility. Some platforms, such as Twitter, are biased toward recent content and rely on hashtag and keyword use to promote visibility. Other platforms, such as Facebook, utilize algorithms analyzing individual users' activity to determine what they see. Still others, such as reddit, determine visibility largely through crowd-sourced evaluation and endorsement. While the specific gatekeeping mechanisms differ from site to site, users' increased entanglement in information assessment and gatekeeping is consistent (Hinman, 2008; Singer, 2014; Westerman, Spence, & Van Der Heide, 2014). This widespread involvement in gatekeeping makes understanding credibility assessment in social media a highly interesting task; the role these platforms play in life and death situations makes it a necessary one.

Given the above, the authors ask: what cues impact the perceived credibility of content published in social media, and do the impact of these cues differ during a crisis? Developing a greater understanding of this is critical not only to furthering the state of credibility research, but also to aiding ongoing efforts of crisis responders, journalists, and everyday citizens reacting to information of unknown provenance. Knowledge of the heuristics we subconsciously rely on might allow us to see through the latest viral hoax or may prompt us to seek a second opinion in quotidian circumstances. It may also provide a valuable tool set for those scouring the Internet for crisis updates, helping them critically assess what information is accurate versus what information merely seems like it might be true.

METHODOLOGY

A common feature of contemporary credibility research is a "laboratory"-based approach, ranging from surveys to the use of custom-developed materials presented under controlled, experimental conditions and subsequent quantitative evaluation of participant responses (Flanagin & Metzger, 2000; Flanagin & Metzger, 2007; Metzger, Flanagin, & Medders, 2010; Morris, Counts, Roseway, Hoff, & Schwarz, 2012; Westerman, Spence, & Van Der Heide, 2014). This contrasts with popular approaches in crisis informatics, which typically rely on user-generated data, frequently from social media, in response to crises (Heverin & Zach, 2010; Palen, Vieweg, Liu, & Hughes, 2009; Sutton, et al., 2008). Though the data is more similar to that used in the latter field, the author's methodology is informed by both.

This study uses data from reddit, a popular social news website and frequent source of memes, scandals, and reactions to emerging events whose users are identified by pseudonyms. Though the more heavily trafficked parts of the site host message board-like group discussions, users frequently evince evidence of "shared values, norms, and understandings," utilizing site-specific language and references. Further, users may become familiar with one another in specific subsections of the site ("subreddits") or in offline gatherings, and reddit celebrities, from novelty accounts like "shitty_watercolor" to frequent contributors like "Unidan," emerge (Shelton, Lo, & Nardi, 2015). Thus, the authors consider reddit a virtual community (Ackland, 2013).

The author analyzes comments on submissions in r/news, a subsection of reddit dedicated to breaking news stories with millions of subscribers.[3] In r/news, users post links to emerging news stories from external sites, creating discussion pages where other users contribute comments. Using purposive and snowball sampling, two data sets are constructed. First, submissions between November 2013 and April 2014 covering then-emerging crises with scores over 2000 (to ensure sufficient data and visibility) were selected.[4] The author then selected complementary submissions covering non-crises with highly similar scores and times of posting.[5] The sampling methodology strategically isolates "crisis" as the primary difference between each condition, having accounted for date, audience, and relative levels of exposure (Bryman, 2012).

"Comment score," or the aggregate of "upvotes" and "downvotes," is used as a proxy for credibility, as perceptions of credibility here defy direct measurement (Rice, 1955). On reddit, the upvoting/downvoting system applies to both submissions to subreddits and comments. Each user may give one upvote or downvote per comment, generating a score reflecting overall activity. Upvotes and downvotes allow the community to elevate content due to the "value of the information in it," dependent partly on the subreddit it is within ("Frequently Asked Questions"). Consequently, implications of upvoting and downvoting differ across reddit. In the case of r/news, upvotes are intended to elevate valuable and relevant information, analysis, and commentary and downvotes to "push down" irrelevant information, opinion, or poor-quality content; this is indicated in subreddit rules and reinforced by a message that appears in r/news submissions when hovering over the downvote button that reads "This isn't a disagree button. Use selectively." The author believes that, in the context of r/news, upvotes and downvotes are strongly tethered to perceived quality and credibility of information, particularly during crisis events.

The research questions are:

RQ1: Does commenter reputation affect perceived comment credibility in pseudonymous communities?
RQ2: Does commenter reputation affect perceived comment credibility in pseudonymous communities during a crisis event?

Table 1. Variables and proxies

Variable	Proxy	Variable Type
Credibility	Comment score	Continuous
Commenter reputation	Commenter karma score (link and comment)	Continuous
Recency	Hours between time of comment posting and time of submission posting (starting at 1)	Continuous
Use of persuasive appeals	Coded scheme from Otterbacher 2011.	Categorical, Binary
Use of link (reputation cue)	*N/A*	Categorical, Binary
Visibility	Parent Comment or not	Categorical, Binary

RQ3: What characterizes the most credible comments in non-crisis and crisis news discussions in pseudonymous communities?

RQ3a: What distinguishes credible comments in non-crisis discussions from credible comments in crisis discussions?

While "commenter reputation" has been elevated to the research questions, a number of other variables are also interesting. Table 1 identifies these; when direct measurement is not possible, the author identifies appropriate proxies.[6] One set of codes—the use of persuasive appeals—requires human judgment. To enhance reliability, a coding schema from past relevant research is used (Otterbacher, 2011).

The author conducts two types of content analysis, first conducting quantitative analysis of comments within r/news submissions to analyze associations between perceived credibility and various cues. The author uses stratified random sampling, selecting 200 random comments from each submission for coding (Bryman, 2012; McMillan, 2000). Table 2 contains descriptive statistics of our continuous variables, all of which are very right skewed in both conditions.

To simplify our analysis, the author conducts logarithmic transformations on the continuous variables that are strictly positive and heavily right skewed, Link Karma and Recency (Wilkinson, Blank,

Table 2. Descriptive statistics of continuous variables, crisis, and non-crisis conditions

	Non-Crisis	Crisis
Credibility (Comment Score)	Mean: 10.962 Standard Deviation: 65.449 Range: -24 – 1652	Mean: 19.027 Standard Deviation: 126.191 Range: -196 – 2474
Reputation (Link Karma)	Mean: 2548.8 Standard Deviation: 9043.08 Range: 1 – 102486	Mean: 4048.69 Standard Deviation: 37449.8 Range: 1 – 1136795
Reputation (Comment Karma)	Mean: 15625.4 Standard Deviation: 23956.2 Range: -146 – 245499	Mean: 17540.6 Standard Deviation: 34366.1 Range: -86 – 316750
Recency (by Hour)	Mean: 11.9983 Standard Deviation: 23956.2 Range: 1 – 347	Mean: 8.582 Standard Deviation: 24.669 Range: 1 – 724

N = 1200 in both Non-Crisis and Crisis Data Sets.

& Gruber, 1996). Despite their skewed distribution, the author leaves Comment Karma and Comment Score untransformed, believing non-positive values to be important to the analysis (Osborne, 2002). Following this, the author runs multivariate regressions, building models that account for the use of individual types of appeals, as well as controlling for the use of any appeal, adjusting the interpretation of the relationships and coefficients where variables are transformed (Osborne, 2002).

The author also conducts qualitative analysis, evaluating the 200 automatically visible comments using reddit's "best" algorithm[7] in each submission. This captures the highest performing comments (plus surrounding discussion) and reflects what is most commonly immediately visible to users. The author conducts a directed content analysis using codes established in the quantitative analysis, as well as those emerging in re-evaluation as patterns in code manifestation (Cavaye, 1996; Potter & Levine-Donnerstein 1999; Hsieh & Shannon, 2005; Creswell, 2007). Through attending to emerging patterns that can only be seen within each comment's original context, as well as "manifest" content, or that which is easily observable (Potter & Levine-Donnerstein, 1999), the author develops a more complex depiction of how heuristic cues are operationalized and ascertains whether additional community or site-structural factors play a role in credibility perceptions (Diesing, 2008; Fairclough, 1992; Potter & Levine-Donnerstein, 1999).

These qualitative methods address common criticisms of quantitative content analysis, namely shortcomings in frequency-counting and subsequent statistical analysis given an inability to discern nuance in presentation (Rose, 2007). By evaluating data within its natural environment and allowing for the emergence of additional codes, the authors ensure ecological and construct validity while capturing subtleties that strictly quantitative or fixed designs might not (Robson, 2011; Grabill & Pigg, 2012).

The use of nonreactive data potentially raises ethical questions, as informed consent has not been pursued and therefore risks violating contextually assumed privacy (Enyon, Fry, & Schoeder, 2008; Janetzko, 2008; Nissenbaum, 2009). Given the nature of the data—group discussions on public forums—the author believes expectations of privacy in the analysis are not violated, and, further, doing so might disturb or alter behavior should attempts to obtain consent during an emerging news event be made. Users have been made anonymous and data was password protected.

RESULTS

Quantitative Analysis

The author constructs two multivariate regression models for each condition. Model A controls for the effects of reputation, recency, visibility, the use of a link, and the use of different types of persuasive appeals within comments. Model B, rather than measuring persuasive appeals separately, controls for the use of any appeal. The results can be seen in Table 3 and Table 4 Worth noting is that the R-Squared values for all four models are fairly low (ranging from .0577 - .0718), indicating that the models explain only a fraction of the variance in comment score. This is further addressed in our discussion section.

As Table 3 indicates, several comment characteristics appear significant in the non-crisis data set. The first of these is the karma variable. One point increase in author comment karma results in, on average, between .0003-.0004 increase in comment score. Putting this in more tangible terms, an author comment karma equivalent to the mean of the data set—15625, roughly—would, on average, be associated

Table 3. Regression results for comment credibility, non-crisis condition

	Model A	Model B
Constant	38.9505 (8.2104)	35.9197 (8.5173)
Reputation (Link Karma)	-.1134 (.696)	-.0861 (.6952)
Reputation (Comment Karma)	.0004*** (.0001)	.0003*** (.0001)
Recency (by Hour)	-17.7931*** (2.8542)	-17.621*** (2.8526)
Visibility (Parent Comment)	10.2935* (4.9124)	10.0737* (4.8134)
Use of Link	1.4862 (10.2423)	2.2176 (10.195)
Use of Logos Appeal	3.2909 (4.5710)	--
Use of Ethos Appeal	2.9066 (5.933)	--
Use of Pathos Appeal	3.195 (4.2329)	--
Use of Any Appeal	--	7.5904 (4.5751)
P > F	0.0000	0.0000
R-squared	0.0648	0.0661
Adjusted R-squared	0.0677	0.0608
No. Observations	1067	1067

Standard errors reported in parentheses. *,**, and *** indicate alphas of .05, .01, and .001 respectively.

with a comment score of approximately 45 points in Model A and approximately 41 points in Model B, holding all other variables constant.

The author also finds evidence of recency's significance. One percent increase in recency is, on average, associated with an approximate 18 point decrease in comment score. The recency variable assigns each comment a value corresponding to the number of hours between submission posting and comment posting; what this means is that comments posted closer to the time of submission are more likely to have high comment scores and that, as time goes on, newer comments are likely to have lower scores.

Finally, the author finds support for the significance of visibility; it appears parent comments have scores that are on average higher by 10 points.

There is no support for the significance of using persuasive appeals or the use of a link in the non-crisis condition, nor the significance of an author's link karma.

A very different pattern emerges from the multivariate regressions utilizing comments generated during crises, detailed in Table 4. As with the non-crisis condition, recency appears significant. The effect of recency, however, is substantially higher in the crisis data set. Here, one percent increase in recency is associated with an average decrease in comment score of approximately 23 points. Thus, as with the non-crisis data, the author finds evidence to suggest that, as time goes on, new comments are likely to

Table 4. Regression results for comment credibility, crisis condition

	Model A	Model B
Constant	24.9744 (11.4368)	28.2658 (12.1455)
Reputation (Link Karma)	2.799 (1.1791)	2.7651 (1.1862)
Reputation (Comment Karma)	-0.0001 (.0001)	-.0001 (.0001)
Recency (by Hour)	-22.5925*** (4.2642)	-23.1186*** (4.2746)
Visibility (Parent Comment)	27.6864** (8.8972)	30.6653*** (8.7382)
Use of Link	48.7656*** (13.2543)	48.8655*** (13.3067)
Use of Logos Appeal	2.8636 (8.5034)	--
Use of Ethos Appeal	42.4023*** (10.7071)	--
Use of Pathos Appeal	7.255 (7.5446)	--
Use of Any Appeal	--	10.3977 (8.0681)
P > F	0.0000	0.0000
R-squared	0.0718	0.0597
Adjusted R-squared	0.065	0.0545
No. Observations	1092	1092

Standard errors reported in parentheses. *,**, and *** indicate alphas of .05, .01, and .001 respectively.

have lower scores and comments posted closer to the time of the submission are likely to have higher scores. In a crisis, however, these effects appear to be amplified.

Visibility also again emerges as important. As occurs with recency, the relative influence of this variable is greater than in the non-crisis data set. Comment scores are, on average, roughly 28 points higher for parent comments when controlling for the use of individual types of persuasive appeals. When controlling for the use of any appeal, parent comments have comment scores that are, on average, roughly 31 points higher than child comments.

Two additional variables emerge as significant within the crisis data set. Both models indicate that the use of a link is associated with a comment score increase of, on average, roughly 49 points. The author also finds support for the significance of ethos appeals, which is associated with an average increase in comment score of approximately 42 points.

Unlike the non-crisis condition, there is no support for either measure of commenter reputation; there is also no support for the significance of logos or pathos appeals, as well as the use of appeals in general.

Qualitative Analysis

While the quantitative analysis reveals patterns occurring on a comment-by-comment basis, it does not consider the role of reddit's structure and dynamics on credibility perceptions. Further, while many of the variables have a single manifestation, such as time of posting, others appear in a variety of configurations, masked in the quantitative analysis. The author remedies these limitations with directed content analysis. The author first discusses the structure of r/news submissions and the patterns that emerge between interacting comments. The author then elaborates typical presentations of persuasive appeals within r/news and how these vary in crisis and non-crisis events. Finally, the author describes a typology of credible comments, as measured by comment score, across both non-crisis and crisis submissions.

Visibility and Structure

As mentioned in the methodology section, comment visibility on reddit is for most users governed by the "best" algorithm.[8] This ranks comments both by the percentage of upvotes versus downvotes and by the total number of votes, correcting a bias towards earlier comments in previous algorithms (reddit, "reddit's new comment sorting system"). Past research indicates that, despite this, comments on reddit are subject to "social influence bias,"; initially popular comments tend to become more popular, though there is disagreement on whether a converse effect—initially unpopular comments becoming more unpopular—occurs (Muchnik et al., 2013; Glenski, Johnston, & Weninger, 2015). This may be true to an extent; the substantial influence of comment visibility on comment score in both of the conditions, as measured by our variable "parent comment," may reinforce past findings. Yet past studies focus on comment-specific features as opposed to the ecosystem created by multiple comments, potentially overlooking equally influential environmental factors.

reddit's comment sections are structured as conversations. Parent comments provide starting points for discussion, fact-finding, and debate. One may assume the quantitative findings mean that "parent" comments will, as a rule, outperform their "children." This is not the case. Several conditions can lead to a "child" comment having a higher score than its "parent." This may occur when the function of such comments is to elaborate. Consider the following exchange in a discussion about a chain-smoking veteran; comments have been unedited and contain irregular grammar, spelling, and phraseology:

[Parent Comment], 105 points: Cigars don't carry the same risks as cigarettes, since you don't inhale the smoke.

[Elaborating Child Comment], 295 points: "Correct. They carry different risks. Namely, mouth and throat cancer. http://www.cancer.gov/cancertopics/factsheet/Tobacco/cigars.[9]

The responder refutes the initial comment, providing not only an argument but also linking to additional evidence; correspondingly, the child comment's score is higher than the parent's. A link is not needed for this effect to occur. Take below, occurring after a shooting:

[Parent Comment], 59 points: It's never good when the automated alert says "Mass Casualty Alert"...

[Elaborating Child Comment], 95 points: "Casualties" is also interchangeable with "injuries" or "wounded." Just an FYI. It doesn't necessarily mean that anyone has been killed. Keeping my fingers crossed.

While these effects are perhaps intuitive where a child comment corrects a parent comment, they are also seen in exchanges where information is provided that answers or supports the initial comment's claim. For instance, the following occurs in a thread discussing banks' unwillingness to take money from marijuana dispensaries:

[Parent Comment], 32 points: Being that Colorado does get federal monies to run their government, yes I think they would care. The Windfall over weed will not replace federal monies, not by a long shot.

[Elaborating Child Comment], 112 points: Interestingly enough, Colorado actually gets very little federal money compared to the test of the nation. In fact, Colorado ranks as the third lowest state in the nation in how much money it gets from federal programs.[10]

As mentioned before, despite their presumptive status as "corrections," such comments frequently do not link to sources or other evidence. Further, replies to elaborating comments additional information on the same topic do not necessarily benefit from this effect. An exchange illustrating this appears in a thread about a public shooting. The parent comment (comment score: 293) links to live footage of responders arriving at the scene, asking "Can anybody explain the Red, Yellow and Green tarps? is it some sort of triage system?" The following comments, each replying to the one above it, are ranked highest out of the numerous replies:

[Elaborating Child Comment 1], 429 points: Red--serious/life-threatening injury Yellow--stable but will need medical attention Green--minor injuries that don't require immediate attention

[Elaborating Child Comment 2], 251 points: Yup. There is also a Black for deceased patients. (Which I'm glad to see isn't in this picture.)

[Elaborating Child Comment 3], 185 points: Black is also for expectant casualties. As in people who aren't deceased yet but are not worth spending time trying to save. Sounds heartless but that's what you have to do during triage, if you spend time on a lost cause you might lose two reds that could have made it if they received that attention/care instead. They might not use the black tarp, but the tags usually still have that as an option.

The first comment, which provides the first "answer," receives the highest aggregate upvotes, despite not being as clearly written as the subsequent clarifications. Worth noting is that two separate responding comments to the initial question about the tarps link to the Wikipedia page explaining the system in question, though each receives substantially lower comment scores (49 and 39), suggesting that this process is not merely about providing "correct" information.

A second, equally common phenomenon associated with high comment scores for both parent and child comments is humor, an integral component of reddit's culture; reddit's structure allows users to engage in cooperative joke-making, heightening humor through replies. This is referred to colloquially as "riding the karma train" because of the boost to comment karma that each user accrues. In such situations, child comments often have higher comment scores than parent comments, increasing as jokes continue. This behavior appears throughout r/news frequently, even during crisis events. Take this multi-user exchange occurring during a school shooting, which includes participation from a user claiming to be hiding from the assailant (marked "commenter in school"):

[Commenter 1], 87 points: Stay safe!

[Commenter 2], 65 points: Stay alert!

[Commenter 3], 193 points: Stay frosty!

[Commenter in school], 459 points: Its pretty warm, actually.

[Commenter 4], 225 points: Damn. Under threat of being shot and still making jokes. Confirmed Redditor.

This is not entirely unexpected; humor is often the "central appeal" of discourse within communities that form primarily through text-based computer-mediated communications (Baym, 1995; Hübler & Bell, 2003). These comments may constitute a type of ethos appeal because effective production of contextually appropriate humor demonstrates knowledge of group norms, values, and practices (Baym, 1995; Hübler & Bell, 2003). Such exchanges need not be predicated by a humorous remark to occur. Consider the following, again occurring after a school shooting:

[Commenter 1], 141 points: The shooter told the teacher what he/she was going to do and the teacher ran off

[Commenter 2], 591 points: Caught him monologuing

[Commenter 3], 106 points: The greatest foil of any villain.

[Commenter 4], 292 points: bae caught me monologin[11]

Here, an informative statement leads to comical replies indicating pop culture knowledge (the trope of a villains revealing evil schemes). Through these culturally-informed exchanges, users help establish a sense of community (Hübler & Bell, 2003). That this is an exception to general trends identified thus far with regard to comment scores and visibility makes sense, then, given the mechanics of this social exchange.

Persuasive Appeals in Practice

Within r/news, ethos appeals frequently appear in two forms. The first is a brief note at the beginning or end of a comment contextualizing the overall remark. "I've worked disaster response for the PRC - National HQ and for the various local chapters," begins one comment regarding Typhoon Haiyan describing the Red Cross's accountability procedures. Another, discussing banks refusing money from marijuana dispensaries, starts with, "I used to be an Electronic Banking Specialist," before detailing the federal reporting obligations of financial institutions. The second form embeds the appeal within a longer comment. One commenter on Typhoon Haiyan, for instance, begins relating a typhoon experience before referencing past experiences with tornadoes. Another, regarding a shooting at LAX, begins, "Just for some context for those unfamiliar with Terminal 3 (it's the terminal I fly out of the most because of Virgin America) -- getting as far as the Burger King here is REALLY far." The element of "character" within ethos appeals varies. In some cases, users report physical location or place of origin. For instance, regarding a mall shooting, one commenter reports, "To me it sounded like a shotgun, I was on the other side of the mall though by the apple store." In other situations, users invoke professional qualifications or acquired expertise, as in the case of the first cited examples. The qualifications invoked, however, may merely imply the user's knowledge of scenarios similar to the current event. After a school shooting in Colorado, for instance, one commenter describes their experience of a shooting in Portland, while another commenter, discussing Occupy Wall Street's intention to purchase consumer debt, writes about Occupy's efforts with unrelated issues in Minneapolis.

Pathos appeals vary within r/news, engineered to elicit a range of emotions. Many present opinions without evidence. One comment about the minimum wage reads, "There's no feeling of living anymore. It's all about work." Another commenter, responding to a shooting, concludes "You want to kill yourself? That's fine. Don't kill innocent people in the process." These types of comments often evoke frustration. "Imagining working at $9.19 makes me sick to my stomach," begins another comment about minimum wage. This is not to say all pathos appeals found in r/news are melancholic; the humorous exchanges discussed earlier also constitute pathos appeals. In addition to collaborative joking, some users contribute stand-alone humor. One high-scoring comment, for example, quotes the New York Times' detailed description of a marijuana dispensary owner's security practices, car, and driving route, writing, "Well, hell, why don't they just give his license plate number too. This guy now has a thousand times more reason to be paranoid. Nice work NYT." Another example, responding to a story on Trader Joe's, is a nearly 800-word parody of a fry cook written in the style of the television show "Breaking Bad."

Logos appeals often appear in slightly longer comments attached to an ongoing discussion or debate. One example appears in a discussion of banks' decisions to not take money from marijuana dispensaries: "Pot is illegal at a Federal level, and they could still have assets seized and forfeited from the FBI or DEA, making it a risky move, and the authors all know banks don't like to take risks. Joking aside, until something changes at the Federal level, expect that Marijuana legalization efforts to be disjointed like this."[12] Another comment, left in response to a question about using birdshot in a rifle, reads, in part, "serious answer, it would depend on how far away from the muzzle you are. The weight of the projectiles or 'shot' in a load are pretty similar even in different sized shells. The issue is that bigger sized shot will travel farther, and have a lot more of an impact when it does hit... Source-been a hunter and outdoorsman for years." As implied by these examples, logos appeals may be combined with ethos or pathos appeals.

This is not, however, always the case. For instance, one response to a user bemoaning the frequency of publicized shootings reads, "There is some 10,000 + murders every year in a country of 300,000,000 million people. Obviously, that means there are 27 or so a day that happen. One of them is bound to have preliminary reports of mass shootings." Another, answering a question about whether people could purchase their own debt, replies, "The debt is bundled together and sold in large quantities, there would be no way to find your own debt after it has been combined with others. Think of it like having a box of KD[13] with your name written on it in the factory then trying to find that box at a costco, but you're only allowed to purchase KD by the crate. In the long run you'd spend more buying crates then you would paying your debt." In non-crisis scenarios, comments featuring logos appeals may link to news stories, Wikipedia pages, or reports.[14] In crises, logos comments do not usually contain links, instead typically analyzing the event itself. For instance, one response to a point regarding a man waiting for his shoes at security during a shooting at LAX starts, "Most likely he wasn't thinking straight, given the circumstances." In another discussion, stemming off one commenter's objection to a student using reddit while hiding from a school shooter, a user argues, "He's probably already texted his family telling them he's all right. And it's a bad idea to call the authorities, since they're likely already there, and what if the shooter hears him? So, after texting everyone, Reddit's a natural place to go to; especially since there's usually someone posting up-to-the-minute updates in the comments."

Many comments, of course, relay information relatively impartially. Take a comment written during a school shooting that simply reads, "Shooter is down as of 11 minutes ago." Another in the same discussion also illustrates this point, reading, "Shooter appears to be a student. Scanner just said "Shooter's locker number is ###" (not sure I should list it here)." Such comments may contain links. As is mentioned in the preceding paragraph, comments utilizing logos appeals often link to reference sites and other resources to bolster claims; the same types of sources are used in comments that contain links but lack persuasive appeals (see Appendix E for selected examples). In crisis scenarios, links predominantly appear in persuasion-free commentary and direct to primary source materials, such as police scanners or live-feeds of the event. For examples, see the following, generated during a mall shooting:

[Comment 1], 33 points: http://www.myfoxny.com/category/237002/skyfoxhd

live cam. http://www.broadcastify.com/listen/feed/14112/web

related police radio scanner.

[Comment 2], 60 points: looks like FBI just arrived http://www.myfoxny.com/category/237002/skyfoxhd

Users may also link to social media profiles of perpetrators, victims, or witnesses. Consider the following, left during the same shooting:

[Comment 1], 48 points: Bill Reiter is live tweeting: @foxsportsreiter

I was at the Virgin terminal at LAX when gunfire broke out. Many of us have run on the tarmac. I don't know what's happening but I'm fine.

A witness saw shooting in ticketing area at LAX. Now hearing three or four gunman rushed area, but that's unsubstantiated.

When gunfire broke out there was a stampede people, all of us hiding under seats the authors didn't fit under, the authors burst through the door to outside.

Hope everyone is safe - looking for more updates!!

Table 5. High credible comment typology

	Crisis Data	Non-Crisis Data	Tone	Frequency (per Submission)	Length
Common Sense	X	X	Informal	Several	Short
Insider	X	X	Informal	Several	Short
News Aggregator	X	X	Primarily formal	Typically 1-2	Long

Further examples include a user's sharing of a video taken during Typhoon Haiyan or commenters' discovery of the Instagram account of a victim in a Maryland shooting.[15]

Highly Credible Comment Typology

Across the data, a typology of highly credible comments emerges that the author terms common sense, insider, and news aggregator comments. A brief articulation of their similarities and differences appears in Table 5.

Common Sense Comments

Common Sense comments encapsulate popular viewpoints, characterized by their brevity and lack of additional or new evidence. Comments typically take the form of either logical retort or emotional response. One example of the former is a response to a story about a 107-year-old cigar-smoking, whiskey-drinking veteran, which reads:

[Commenter 1], 1650 points: Genetics plays a huge role in longevity

Another example of a Common Sense comment appeared responding to news of a school shooting:

[Commenter 1], 1003 points: Just a reminder that making these people famous[16] *does nothing to prevent a recurrence. Massive media coverage is often exactly what they want - and they get it every time.*

When Common Sense comments take emotional routes, they often reflect feelings of shock, frustration, sadness, or outrage. For instance, a commenter responding to Typhoon Haiyan states:

[Commenter 1], 157 points: I can not imagine 9.4 million of anything, let Alone 9.4 million people without water, housing, food, rx. Unfathomable.

One commenter's response to banks refusing money from the legal marijuana trade takes a sarcastic approach:

[Commenter 1], 2659 points: But terrorist money is just fine.

Regardless of approach, the lack of genuinely new information remains the same.

Insider Comments

Insider comments are purportedly from individuals directly involved in the situation. In non-crisis events, commenters assert subject matter expertise or reference relevant past experiences. News of Trader Joe's opening stores selling products past their sell-by date, for instance, draws comments from Trader Joe's employees, employees of competing grocery stores, and food bank volunteers.[17] During crises, however, successful Insider comments virtually always are purportedly from people at the event or otherwise intimately involved. One top scoring comment after a chemical spill in West Virginia, with 996 points, begins with "Resident here," before describing discovering the contamination and the concerns of other locals.[18] During a mall shooting in New Jersey, one user adds:

[Commenter 1], 350 points: Fire alarm pulled. Was in the movie theater. The place is surrounded by cops. Dont have much confirmed information. One shooter so far. By the Nordstroms.

In a similar scenario, a shooting at a Maryland mall, one top-scoring comment reads:

[Commenter 1], 1753 points: I work at the mall, the authors were hiding for almost an hour, swat team is clearing out the mall and helped us out. Edit: Thanks for the Gold although I wish it was under a different circumstance.

Insider commenters rarely provide proof of identity. There are exceptions, though, like this high-scoring Insider comment during a school shooting:

[Commenter 1], 2469 points: In the building right now as a student, it's scary as hell

Proof [link to photo] Sorry it's last year's ID, our bags are still at school along with my current ID

The user links to a photo of his student ID. This is atypical. Comments like the following, left during a mall shooting, are far more common:

[Commenter 1], 187 points: We were in the mall and by the time the authors realized what was going on, all the shops had locked up and my wife, 11 month old and I were forced to hustle through a deserted mall to go out the emergency exit.

[Commenter 2], 154 points: shit, i just got back from there not even 5 minutes ago. must have been right after I left.

[Commenter 3], 166 points: People are still calling PF Changs to see if we're open. Wow.

As these examples illustrate, Insider comments tend to offer anecdotal evidence and are characterized by individualized accounts.

News Aggregator Comments

News Aggregator comments are characterized by their relative infrequency and extremely consistent format and tone. News Aggregator comments are continually updated with incoming information, often linking or referring to external sources. These do not appear in non-crisis comments within r/news. News Aggregator comments mimic news wire reports or police scanner transmissions, though casual interjections of commentary, particularly qualifying perceived quality of information, occur. Updates are broken out chronologically, with update times prominently displayed. This format remains remarkably consistent across different users and events. To demonstrate, here is an excerpt from one such entry, written during a Maryland shooting:

[Commenter 1], 292 points: 12:51 police report a suspicious dark sedan with tinted windows fled the mall earlier and ran a few red lights.

12:57 a unit reports stopping a similar vehicle.. no additional information.

1:04 many news outlets are reporting that the 1/3 that is dead WAS the suspected killer (i still believe this is speculation and not 100% confirmed)

Compare this with a remarkably similar News Aggregator post from a New Jersey shooting:

[Commenter 1], 1343 points: 10:46pm: County officials have said that the shooter is still inside the mall. K-9 units are also there for the search, as they should be.

10:49pm: Various unconfirmed reports that police currently have the brother of the shooter on the phone at the moment. Again, it is unconfirmed.

10:50pm: "Bergen County Official: SWAT Officers doing a store by store sweep inside the Garden State Plaza Mall" - CNN

The style and format of both examples dominate the majority of News Aggregator posts. Depending on the nature of the emerging event, News Aggregator comments can become quite lengthy, sometimes officially continued in a subsequent child comment that is upvoted by the community to follow the original.

There are usually only one or two successful News Aggregator comments per submission, typically parent comments. There may be more than one comment that appears to fall within this category per submission, but excluding the most credible News Aggregator comment, these are characterized by a) "inappropriate" formatting or b) less detail, thus netting lower scores. For instance, of the two comments aggregating news in the midst of a school shooting in Colorado, the one with a higher comment score more closely mimics the style found in other submissions.[19]

DISCUSSION

Interpretation of Findings

This research investigates which factors most impact perceived credibility of information in pseudonymous environments. The analysis indicates that a variety of cues are associated with perceived credibility within r/news, and that crisis may impact which cues are most influential on perceptions.

In both conditions, parent comments have, on average, higher comment scores. The authors qualify this finding with our qualitative analysis of comment chain formations; comments that either clarify or negate the comment directly above it or else further a joke in a meaningful way often receive higher scores than comments they respond to. What our qualitative findings do not account for is the difference in coefficient size between our crisis and non-crisis data sets. A top-level parent comment will, on average, have a comment score that is approximately 10 points higher than a child comment in a non-crisis event, but will have a comment score that is, on average, between 28 and 31 points higher in a crisis scenario. This may be due to a reduction in user willingness to comb through comments during a crisis or users posting new, credible information as a new comment instead of a reply. Our results suggest that users may want to look beyond parent comments in case these are artificially inflated.

Our quantitative analysis also indicates that recency is negatively associated with perceived credibility in both non-crisis and crisis events, an effect pronounced during crises. This seemingly contradicts research indicating that recency positively impacts source credibility, though this may not be the case. As mentioned in our quantitative analysis, our variable is heavily right skewed, with the bulk of comments being posted within 24 hours. Further, users are able to modify posts without altering the time of posting recorded, a practice that our qualitative analysis reveals is not uncommon; some types of comments are even characterized by such updates, such as News Aggregator posts. Interpreting this quantitative finding is therefore complex. This may be a reflection of both commenting and upvoting tapering off as submissions age, though our data does not specify when upvotes and downvotes occur. Our finding might also be interpreted as a reinforcement of past research suggesting that earlier posts that receive endorsement permanently outpace later ones as further endorsement accrues.

No evidence was found that commenter reputation is associated with perceived credibility in crisis scenarios, though the authors find some evidence that commenter reputation, as measured by comment karma, is positively associated with perceived credibility in non-crisis events. The authors interpret this two ways. First, our qualitative analysis indicates that catering to the culture of reddit may positively impact perceived credibility. Engaging in humorous commentary or producing posts that resonate as "common sense," for instance, both result in high scores. What this could be interpreted to mean, then, is that the ability to seem like "one of the crowd" may contribute to perceived credibility in non-crisis conditions. The lack of significance of commenter reputation in crisis events may be interpreted as reinforcing past research, suggesting that the offline notion of "reputation" may be an outdated construct for online analysis in certain contexts (Gamie, 2012). What our research additionally suggests, given how comment and link karma are accrued, is that past performance is not a reliable indicator of performance in a crisis and is therefore a particularly poor barometer of the potential credibility of a comment.

The analysis of persuasive appeals suggests further differences between non-crisis and crisis evaluations. The quantitative analysis does not indicate that persuasive appeals affect credibility in non-crisis events, conflicting with past findings. The author finds, however, that ethos appeals significantly impact perceived credibility during crises. This becomes especially compelling when combined with the qualitative analysis in this chapter, which indicates that ethos appeals during crises usually take the form of individuals claiming to be involved with, or affected by, the event, the "Insider" type. Yet the qualitative analysis also reveals that Insider comments do not typically contain proof, often offering anecdotal experiences as opposed to verifiable information. This may suggest that users turn to reddit for a specific type of content during crises—firsthand reporting—and are willing to accept claims of involvement without substantial proof. Alternatively, as past research suggests, sites themselves may be the object of consideration when users assess reputation (Metzger, Flanagin, & Medders, 2010; Morris, Counts, Roseway, Hoff, & Schwarz, 2012), which may indicate that users deem reddit or r/news a trustworthy source by default and therefore are, alarmingly, more prone to simply accept claims made on the site. Whether this is the case or not, the finding that the use of ethos appeals significantly affects perceived credibility without necessarily entailing proof of involvement is troubling. Though the authors have no evidence of negative consequences in this data set, the preponderance of hoaxes perpetrated through social media suggests a need for enhanced vigilance when encountering these sorts of claims.

This is not to say that the data indicate proof is entirely unimportant. The quantitative analysis indicates that, in crisis events, comments including a link have comment scores that are, on average, higher by 49 points; during non-crisis scenarios, no such association exists. The qualitative analysis indicates that links are used differently in crises and non-crises, whereas in the latter, links point to references supporting logical arguments, comments during crises predominantly link to news stories, live camera feeds, or other sources of primary data. These links occur both in isolated comments and in News Aggregator comments, a highly stylized form of aggregated reporting that repeatedly appears as a highly credible comment across crisis events. The author combines this with the previously discussed finding regarding the use of ethos appeals to posit that different comments may satisfy different informational needs; the amount of verifiable information linked to in News Aggregator comments and other posts may compensate for the relative lack of evidence provided in more ethos-oriented Insider comments.

Additional factors also appear to impact perceived credibility, something suggested by the low amount of overall variance explained by the multivariate regressions. As the qualitative analysis indicates, the comments surrounding a comment may influence its perception. A comment meaningfully clarifying the point of another, for instance, may appear more credible than the comment it clarifies. Adopting the communication style of an external authority, as occurs in News Aggregator comments, also appears associated with perceived credibility, reinforcing past findings (Shanahan, 2010). While these observations do not point to a specific heuristic, they indicate the process of information assessment is complex and cues other than those which the author measured in the quantitative analysis may have substantial effects.

Overall, the results suggest that very different heuristics may be relevant during crises and non-crises within pseudonymous communities. During non-crises, visibility, endorsement, and the ability to produce comments that resonate culturally with the community are most strongly associated with perceived credibility. In crises, ethos appeals and the use of evidence through linking to outside sources becomes more influential, though visibility and endorsement remain significant factors. The results suggest a recalibration of information processing when consequences of misinformation are more dire; though these processes may not be perfect, they nonetheless imply different strategies and therefore different heuristics being enacted.

FUTURE RESEARCH DIRECTIONS

This study is subject to several limitations. The proxies, particularly the choice to use comment and link karma as a stand in for reputation, may come into question. The decision to transform some variables (and to not transform others) in the quantitative analysis and the choice to analyze linear relationships may also be a matter for debate. More broadly, the methodological innovativeness—using actual data generated in crisis and non-crisis scenarios to consider the role of different credibility cues—limits the scope to analyzing manifest qualities of data, thereby focusing on information characteristics instead of heuristics themselves. The use of non-reactive data collected after an event also prevents observation of dynamic processes such as content reordering. Future research might utilize experimental designs to address questions of external validity or specific proxies for various information characteristics. Alternatively, future research might attempt to capture the same type of data as it generates in order to fully monitor patterns of information interaction that may be invisible within this static, post-hoc data set. And in general, future research should investigate whether the general findings are supported by studies in other pseudonymous environments such as Tumblr or Twitter.

CONCLUSION

The issue of credibility perception and mis-appraisal is increasingly visible in popular culture, news, and scholarly research. As we more regularly rely on digital resources for critical information, we must continue to investigate the mechanics of credibility, especially in instances where mis-assessment has the harshest consequence. The research in this chapter investigates both crises and non-crises simultaneously, contributing to crisis informatics and broader credibility literature through attention to credibility in pseudonymous contexts. The use of non-reactive data and strategy for analyzing credibility cues may aid future research assessing other social media; this is a highly flexible methodology with potentially broad applications. Of course, this is not the only means of researching credibility, and research building upon or challenging this work is encouraged.

The findings have implications for users, journalists, and others browsing social media sites. The results of both the quantitative and qualitative analysis suggest that, in pseudonymous communities such as reddit, different heuristics may be operationalized when assessing information in crisis and non-crisis events. The generalized insinuations of belonging that may be effective in ordinary circumstances do not hold as much weight in a crisis, when assertions of personal involvement and linking to external sources become more important. Initially, this seems commendable because it appears that individuals may employ enhanced vigilance when the stakes of misinformation are higher. Yet, surely we ought to be critical of all information, even that about quotidian affairs. Further, while the analysis indicates that claims of being "on the ground" receive extra attention in r/news, it also reveals that users rarely provide actual proof (though the authors have no indication of instances of fabrication). And when we look to the actual content provided by such users—primarily anecdotal reporting—we must consider that unintentional misinformation even by those on the ground can still take place.

This chapter does not intend to paint a picture of social media as murky, unnavigable informational terrain. Social media and other online resources dramatically expand information options and communication opportunities, providing unprecedented access to perspectives and resources and serving as valuable tools in crisis events. The author merely advocates appropriate caution. This may entail, when available, taking advantage of the interactivity social media provides and engaging with individuals providing information to verify their claims. Simply being aware of some of the biases that affect credibility judgments may also go a long way. Journalists, news organizations, and other third parties who disseminate "official" information can contribute by publicly advocating for responsible information consumption and propagation at both the institutional and individual level; an excellent example of such an effort is *On The Media*'s 2013 Breaking News Consumer Handbook, which provides points of caution in a brief, approachable guide (Goldman, 2013). In general, the author recommends reflexively consuming information, with the understanding that when it comes to why we believe what it is we believe, there may be more than meets the eye.

REFERENCES

Ackland, R. (2013). *Web social science: Concepts, data and tools for social scientists in the digital age.* New York, NY: Sage.

Anderson, R. E. (1996). Information sifting or knowledge building on the Internet. *Social Science Computer Review, 14*(1), 81–83. doi:10.1177/089443939601400125

Aristotle, . (1961). *Aristotle's poetics* (S. H. Butcher, Trans.). New York, NY: Hill and Wang.

Baym, N. K. (1995). The performance of humor in computer-mediated communication. *Journal of Computer-Mediated Communication, 1*(2).

Blank, G. (2006). *Critics, ratings, and society: The sociology of reviews.* Washington, DC: Rowman & Littlefield Publishers.

Bruns, A. (2005). *Gatewatching: Collaborative online news production* (Vol. 26). New York, NY: Peter Lang.

Bryman, A. (2012). *Social research methods.* Cambridge, UK: Oxford University Press.

Cavaye, A. L. (1996). Case study research: A multi-faceted research approach for IS. *Information Systems Journal, 6*(3), 227–242. doi:10.1111/j.1365-2575.1996.tb00015.x

Chesney, T., & Su, D. K. (2010). The impact of anonymity on weblog credibility. *International Journal of Human-Computer Studies, 68*(10), 710–718. doi:10.1016/j.ijhcs.2010.06.001

Creswell, J. (2007). *Qualitative inquiry and research design: Choosing among five approaches.* New York, NY: Sage Publications.

D'Orazio, D. (2013) *New York Times*: Is Reddit to blame for Boston Bombing witch-hunt? *The Verge.* Retrieved from http://www.theverge.com/2013/7/25/4556380/should-reddit-be-accountable-for-boston-bombing-witch-hunt

Diesing, P. (2008). *Patterns of discovery in the social sciences.* Piscataway, NJ: Transaction Publishers.

English, K., Sweetser, K. D., & Ancu, M. (2011). YouTube-ification of political talk: An examination of persuasion appeals in viral video. *The American Behavioral Scientist, 55*(1), 733–748. doi:10.1177/0002764211398090

Enyon, R., Fry, J., & Schroeder, R. (2008). The ethics of Internet research. In N. Fielding, R. M. Lee, & G. Blank (Eds.), *The SAGE handbook of online research methods* (pp. 23–41). New York, NY: Sage Publications. doi:10.4135/9780857020055.n2

Fairclough, N. (1992). Discourse and text: Linguistic and intertextual analysis within discourse analysis. *Discourse & Society, 3*(2), 193–217. doi:10.1177/0957926592003002004

Fallis, D. (2008). Toward an epistemology of Wikipedia. *Journal of the American Society for Information Science and Technology, 59*(10), 1662–1674. doi:10.1002/asi.20870

Flanagin, A. J., & Metzger, M. J. (2000). Perceptions of Internet information credibility. *Journalism & Mass Communication Quarterly, 77*(3), 515–540. doi:10.1177/107769900007700304

Flanagin, A. J., & Metzger, M. J. (2007). The role of site features, user attributes, and information verification behaviors on the perceived credibility of web-based information. *New Media & Society, 9*(2), 319–342. doi:10.1177/1461444807075015

Fogg, B. J. (2009, April). A behavior model for persuasive design. In *Proceedings of the 4th International Conference on Persuasive Technology* (p. 40). New York, NY: ACM.

Fogg, B. J., Cuellar, G., & Danielson, D. (2002). Motivating, influencing, and persuading users. In J. Jacko (Ed.), *The human-computer interaction handbook: Fundamentals, evolving technologies, and emerging applications* (pp. 358–370). Mahwah, NJ: L. Erlbaum Associates Inc.

Frequently asked questions. (2015). reddit. Retrieved from http://www.reddit.com/wiki/faq

Gamie, S. (2012). The cyber-propelled Egyptian revolution and the de/construction of ethos. In M. Folk & S. Apostel (Eds.), *Online credibility and digital ethos: Evaluating computer-mediated communication* (pp. 316–331). Hershey, PA: IGI Global.

Glenski, M., Johnston, T. J., & Weninger, T. (2015). Random voting effects in social-digital spaces: A case study of reddit post submissions. In *Proceedings of the 26th ACM conference on hypertext & social media* (pp. 293-297). New York, NY: ACM.

Goldman, A. (2013). The breaking news consumer handbook. *On the media blog.* Retrieved from http://www.wnyc.org/story/breaking-news-consumers-handbook-pdf/

Grabill, J. T., & Pigg, S. (2012). Messy rhetoric: Identity performance as rhetorical agency in online public forums. *Rhetoric Society Quarterly, 42*(2), 99–119. doi:10.1080/02773945.2012.660369

Gupta, A., Joshi, A., & Kumaraguru, P. (2012, October). Identifying and characterizing user communities on twitter during crisis events. In *Proceedings of the 2012 workshop on data-driven user behavioral modelling and mining from social media* (pp. 23-26). New York, NY: ACM. doi:10.1145/2390131.2390142

Heverin, T., & Zach, L. (2010). Microblogging for crisis communication: Examination of Twitter use in response to a 2009 violent crisis in the Seattle-Tacoma, Washington, Area. In S. French, B. Tomaszewski, & C. Zobel (Eds.), *Defining Crisis Management 3.0* (p. 9). Seattle, WA: ISCRAM.

Hinman, L. M. (2008). Searching ethics: The role of search engines in the construction and distribution of knowledge. In A. Spink & M. Zimmer (Eds.), *Web search: Multidisciplinary perspectives* (pp. 67–76). Berlin: Springer. doi:10.1007/978-3-540-75829-7_5

Hsieh, H. F., & Shannon, S. E. (2005). Three approaches to qualitative content analysis. *Qualitative Health Research*, 15(9), 1277–1288. doi:10.1177/1049732305276687 PMID:16204405

Hübler, M. T., & Bell, D. C. (2003). Computer-mediated humor and ethos: Exploring threads of constitutive laughter in online communities. *Computers and Composition*, 20(3), 277–294. doi:10.1016/S8755-4615(03)00036-7

Huey, L., Nhan, J., & Broll, R. (2012). 'Uppity civilians' and 'cyber-vigilantes': The role of the general public in policing cybercrime. *Criminology & Criminal Justice*, 13(1), 81–97. doi:10.1177/1748895812448086

Janetzko, D. (2008). Nonreactive data collection on the Internet. In N. Fielding, R. M. Lee, & G. Blank (Eds.), *The SAGE handbook of online research methods* (pp. 161–174). New York, NY: Sage Publications. doi:10.4135/9780857020055.n9

Johnson, T. J., & Kaye, B. K. (2004). Wag the blog: How reliance on traditional media and the Internet influence credibility perceptions of weblogs among blog users. *Journalism & Mass Communication Quarterly*, 81(1), 622–642. doi:10.1177/107769900408100310

Kang, J. C. (2013). "Should Reddit Be Blamed for the Spreading of a Smear?". *The New York Times*. Retrieved from http://www.nytimes.com/2013/07/28/magazine/should-reddit-be-blamed-for-the-spreading-of-a-smear.html

Killingsworth, M. J. (2005). Rhetorical appeals: A revision. *Rhetoric Review*, 24(3), 249–263. doi:10.1207/s15327981rr2403_1

McMillan, S. J. (2000). The microscope and the moving target: The challenge of applying content analysis to the World Wide Web. *Journalism & Mass Communication Quarterly*, 77(1), 80–98. doi:10.1177/107769900007700107

Melican, D. B., & Dixon, T. L. (2008). News on the net credibility, selective exposure, and racial prejudice. *Communication Research*, 35(2), 151–168. doi:10.1177/0093650207313157

Metzger, M. J., Flanagin, A. J., Eyal, K., Lemus, D. R., & McCann, R. M. (2003). Credibility for the 21st century: Integrating perspectives on source, message, and media credibility in the contemporary media environment. *Communication Yearbook*, 27(1), 293–336. doi:10.1207/s15567419cy2701_10

Metzger, M. J., Flanagin, A. J., & Medders, R. B. (2010). Social and heuristic approaches to credibility evaluation online. *Journal of Communication*, 60(3), 413–439. doi:10.1111/j.1460-2466.2010.01488.x

Morris, M. R., Counts, S., Roseway, A., Hoff, A., & Schwarz, J. (2012, February). Tweeting is believing?: Understanding microblog credibility perceptions. From *Proceedings of the ACM 2012 conference on Computer Supported Cooperative Work* (pp. 441-450). New York, NY: ACM. doi:10.1145/2145204.2145274

Muchnik, L., Aral, S., & Taylor, S. J. (2013). Social influence bias: A randomized experiment. *Science*, *341*(6146), 647–651. doi:10.1126/science.1240466 PMID:23929980

Munroe, R. (2009, Oct. 15). *reddit's new comment sorting system*. Retrieved from http://www.redditblog. com/2009/10/reddits-new-comment-sorting-system.html

Nissenbaum, H. F. (2009). *Privacy in context: Technology, policy, and the integrity of social Life*. Palo Alto, CA: Stanford University Press.

Osborne, J. (2002). Notes on the use of data transformations. *Practical Assessment, Research & Evaluation*, *8*(6), 1–8.

Otterbacher, J. (2011). Being heard in review communities: Communication tactics and review prominence. *Journal of Computer-Mediated Communication*, *16*(3), 424–444. doi:10.1111/j.1083-6101.2011.01549.x

Palen, L., Vieweg, S., Liu, S. B., & Hughes, A. L. (2009). Crisis in a networked world features of computer-mediated communication in the April 16, 2007, Virginia Tech event. *Social Science Computer Review*, *27*(4), 467–480. doi:10.1177/0894439309332302

Petty, R. E., & Cacioppo, J. T. (1986). The elaboration likelihood model of persuasion. *Advances in Experimental Social Psychology*, *19*, 123–205. doi:10.1016/S0065-2601(08)60214-2

Potter, W. J., & Levine-Donnerstein, D. (1999). Rethinking validity and reliability in content analysis. *Journal of Applied Communication Research*, *27*(3), 258–284. doi:10.1080/00909889909365539

Rains, S. A. (2007). The impact of anonymity on perceptions of source credibility and influence in computer-mediated group communication: A test of two competing hypotheses. *Communication Research*, *34*(1), 100–125. doi:10.1177/0093650206296084

Rice, D. K. (1955). Objective indicators of subjective variables. In P. F. Lazarsfeld & M. Rosenberg (Eds.), *The Language of Social Research*. Glencoe, IL: The Free Press.

Robson, C. (2011). *Real world research* (3rd ed.). Chichester, UK: Wiley.

Rogers, K. (2015, November 16). *Paris attacks give rise to fakes and misinformation*. Retrieved from http://www.nytimes.com/2015/11/17/world/europe/paris-attacks-give-rise-to-fakes-and-misinformation. html?_r=0

Shanahan, M. C. (2010). Changing the meaning of peer-to-peer? Exploring online comment spaces as sites of negotiated expertise. *Journal of Science Communication*, *9*(1), 1–13.

Shelton, M., Lo, K., & Nardi, B. (2015) Online media forums as separate social lives: A qualitative study of disclosure within and beyond reddit. In iConference 2015 Proceedings. Newport Beach, CA: IDEALS.

Singer, J. B. (2014). User-generated visibility: Secondary gatekeeping in a shared media space. *New Media & Society*, *16*(1), 55–73. doi:10.1177/1461444813477833

Smith, C. T., De Houwer, J., & Nosek, B. A. (2013). Consider the source: Persuasion of implicit evaluations is moderated by source credibility. *Personality and Social Psychology Bulletin*, *39*(2), 193–205. doi:10.1177/0146167212472374 PMID:23386656

Starbird, K., & Palen, L. (2012, February). (How) will the revolution be retweeted?: Information diffusion and the 2011 Egyptian uprising. In *Proceedings of the ACM 2012 conference on computer supported cooperative work* (pp. 7-16). New York, NY: ACM. doi:10.1145/2145204.2145212

Sundar, S. S. (2008). The MAIN model: A heuristic approach to understanding technology effects on credibility. In M. J. Metzger & A. J. Flanagin (Eds.), *Digital media, youth, and credibility* (pp. 72–100). Cambridge, MA: The MIT Press.

Sutton, J., Palen, L., & Shklovski, I. (2008, May). Backchannels on the front lines: Emergent uses of social media in the 2007 southern California wildfires. In *Proceedings of the 5th International ISCRAM Conference* (pp. 624-632).

Tan, K. W., Swee, D., Lim, C., Detenber, B. H., & Alsagoff, L. (2007). The impact of language variety and expertise on perceptions of online political discussions. *Journal of Computer-Mediated Communication*, *13*(1), 76–99. doi:10.1111/j.1083-6101.2007.00387.x

Tormala, P. L., Briñol, P., & Petty, R. E. (2006). When credibility attacks: The reverse impact of source credibility on persuasion. *Journal of Experimental Social Psychology*, *42*(1), 684–691. doi:10.1016/j.jesp.2005.10.005

Tormala, Z. L., & Clarkson, J. J. (2007). Assimilation and contrast in persuasion: The effects of source credibility in multiple message situations. *Personality and Social Psychology Bulletin*, *33*(4), 559–571. doi:10.1177/0146167206296955 PMID:17363764

Warnick, B. (2004). Online ethos source credibility in an "authorless" environment. *The American Behavioral Scientist*, *48*(2), 256–265. doi:10.1177/0002764204267273

Warnick, B. (2005). Looking to the future: Electronic texts and the deepening interface. *Technical Communication Quarterly*, *14*(3), 327–333. doi:10.1207/s15427625tcq1403_11

Wathen, C. N., & Burkell, J. (2002). Believe it or not: Factors influencing credibility on the Web. *Journal of the American Society for Information Science and Technology*, *53*(2), 134–144. doi:10.1002/asi.10016

Westerman, D., Spence, P. R., & Van Der Heide, B. (2014). Social media as information source: Recency of updates and credibility of Information. *Journal of Computer-Mediated Communication*, *19*(2), 171–183. doi:10.1111/jcc4.12041

Wilkinson, L., Blank, G., & Gruber, C. (1996). *Desktop data analysis with SYSTAT*. Upper Saddle River, NJ: Prentice Hall.

Zappen, J. P. (2005). Digital rhetoric: Toward an integrated theory. *Technical Communication Quarterly*, *14*(3), 319–325. doi:10.1207/s15427625tcq1403_10

KEY TERMS AND DEFINITIONS

Credibility: "The capacity to elicit belief," a definition derived from the Oxford English Diction, (Blank, 2006). Credibility is a multidimensional construct applied to sources, messages, and media.

Crisis Communications: Communications made during or about crises, whether by "official" entities (such as governing bodies or NGOs), media, or members of the public.

Crisis Informatics: A field considering social media crisis communications in the context of information dissemination "within and between official and public channels and entities" (Palen, Vieweg, Liu, & Hughes, 2009, p. 469).

Crisis: Large-scale emergency activity involving or affecting members of the public. This is inclusive of natural disasters, as well as other unexpected events, such as breakouts of violence. This definition is derived from the field of Crisis Informatics.

Heuristics: Judgment shortcuts subconsciously or consciously used by individuals when assessing information that, in turn, shape overall perspectives.

Online Credibility: Credibility within or pertaining to online contexts.

Pseudonymity: The condition of being identifiable solely or primarily by a pseudonym, as opposed to one's "official" (often legal) identity.

Reddit: A popular social news website.

Social Media: Media which can be created/published by the general public, typically referring to digital platforms such as Facebook and Twitter but inclusive of digital communities (e.g., reddit) and gated digital communication environments (e.g., Whatsapp).

ENDNOTES

[1]   Note that the use of heuristics is not generated by the Internet. Instead, specific heuristics utilized in a pre-Internet age may be ineffective and cues endogenous to digital media may inspire or require new heuristics.

[2]   Much of this research has immediate consequence for user experience designers and information architects, revolving around appropriate configuration of site elements to guide users through pre-determined information experiences. These studies also illuminate subtle changes that users can make without re-architecting environments. For instance, changing a profile picture, choosing to tweet about a narrow set of subjects, or manipulating followers to following ratios are not necessarily thought of as attempts to persuade but nonetheless can dramatically increase credibility in the eyes of web users (Morris, Counts, Roseway, Hoff, & Schwarz, 2012).

[3]   The subreddit specifically forbids old stories (those more than a week old), articles about non-news events, and "slant, bias, editorial, opinion, or conjecture—whether it be left wing, right wing, green wing, or purple wing" (reddit, "/r/nNews").

[4]   Submission scores are the difference between upvotes and downvotes. It should be noted that reddit obscures raw numbers for all karma differentials, rendering it impossible to determine the actual number of users who have upvoted or downvoted any given submission or comment.

[5]   These submissions fall within 500 points of the submission score of the complimentary crisis thread and were submitted within a 72-hour window of their corresponding crisis submission. In instances where multiple submissions fulfilled this criteria, proximity to publishing time was used to isolate the most "similar" submission.

[6]   See Appendix A for full coding scheme.

[7]   The "best" algorithm sorts comments according to both comment score and sample size, calculating confidence intervals of post performance and adjusting as more feedback is received (Munroe,

2009). The best algorithm is the default algorithm for users and the most likely option selected for those who are browsing the site.

[8]   reddit's "best" algorithm is the default option for site visitors. Users may also choose to sort their comments by comment score, recency (either newest or oldest), or by controversy, elevating comments with high levels of both upvotes and downvotes. It is likely that most visitors use the "best" algorithm either because they are unaware of the other options or by preference.

[9]   This links to a fact sheet on cigar smoking by the National Cancer Institute.

[10]   The user links to a report by the Tax Foundation, a Washington, DC nonprofit.

[11]   Both commenter 3 and commenter 4, in this example, are responding to the remark made by commenter 2.

[12]   See Appendix B for full comment.

[13]   "KD" is shorthand for macaroni and cheese (ie "Kraft Dinner").

[14]   See Appendix C for examples.

[15]   See Appendix C.

[16]   This links to a blog with a more detailed version of the argument (http://thegospelcoalition.org/blogs/kevindeyoung/2013/11/26/the-punishing-sound-of-silence/).

[17]   See Appendix D for a sample of these comments.

[18]   See Appendix D.

[19]   See Appendix D.

APPENDIX A: FULL CODING SCHEME

Table 6. Variables and proxies

Variable	Proxy	Coding Scheme/Notes	Variable Type
Credibility	Comment score	N/A	Continuous
Commenter reputation	Commenter karma score (link and comment)	N/A	Continuous
Recency	Hours between time of comment posting and time of submission posting (starting at 1)	Coded as whole integers only	Continuous
Use of persuasive appeals	Coded using scheme from Otterbacher 2011; persuasive appeals concept from Aristotle's Poetics	*For each comment, coders answered yes or no to the following questions to determine whether any appeals were used and which ones to mark as in use. Appeals were not mutually exclusive; one comment could contain multiple appeals at a single time.* Ethos: "Does the reviewer attempt to convince readers of her character, experience or qualifications?" Logos: "In presenting her view of the item, does the author try to appeal to readers' sense of reason?" Pathos: "Does the reviewer try to get readers emotionally involved, by appealing to their values or sensibilities?"	Categorical, Binary
Use of link (reputation cue)	N/A	N/A	Categorical, Binary
Visibility	Parent Comment or not	N/A	Categorical, Binary

APPENDIX B: LOGOS COMMENTS

Logos Comments Containing Links

From Minimum Wage Decrease Story in November 2013

[–][Name Redacted] 60 points: *Epitome of the issue.*

World's richest woman calls for Australians to take a pay cut - 'because African workers are willing to earn just $2 a day'

    She inherited her daddies mining business and in just 5 years became the worlds richest woman due to china needed resources and shit. SHe more than doubled her inheritance and yet she bitches about the cost of labor.

    This is epitome of the problem.

    It should also be noted, that if you look, the truly self made, tend to not act like this. The oprahs and gates and such (yes gates came from a wealthy family but deny he is self made) while the kochs, reiharts and waldens tend to be selfish dicks. Science thinks it is due to a fear of losing what they inherited, since they didnt build it, they dont think they could get it back, while the self made think they can do it again. SO they worry less.

[–][**Name Redacted**] **40 points:** *Inevitably the same ignorant arguments come up from people who have taken an intro econ class and think real world scenarios play out like their oversimplified models (usually in a vacuum). Luckily the authors have real world data that the authors can rely on to easily do away with many of these common fallacies -*

Of the 23 times minimum wage was raised, the authors have data on unemployment for 20 of those raises. Of those 20 raises, 2 have been accompanied by abnormal increases in unemployment, once in 1974 and once in 2008. Again, these are likely better explained by other factors. Overall, the average unemployment change accompanying minimum wage increases is 3.95%, which is less than 1/10 of a standard deviation (22.3%) above the population average of 3.14%. Again, there is no evidence to suggest that minimum wage increases effect unemployment rates.
   Sources:

- ftp://ftp.bls.gov/pub/special.requests/cpi/cpiai.txt
- http://www.dol.gov/whd/minwage/chart.htm
- http://data.bls.gov/timeseries/LNU04000000?years_option=all_years&periods_option=specific_periods&periods=Annual+Data

From Trader Joe's Story in January 2014

[–][**Name Redacted**] **33 points:** *no, you're wrong, unfortunately... there was actually a good comment about this that i read recently: fast food is about fast food*

it's not that the poor can't afford nutritious food, it's that after working hard all day and/ or little sleep, and the pressures of child rearing, they are exhausted and can't afford the time to cook: preparation time is the real cost, not money, and is why fast food is preferred
   found it, thank's google:
   http://www.reddit.com/r/EatCheapAndHealthy/comments/1t0sw5/very_interesting_healthiest_diets_cost_about/ce3763j
   but what this really means is that there's an angle to make nutritious food available to the poor: if it can get to them with little time investment

APPENDIX C: COMMENTS WITHOUT PERSUASIVE APPEALS

Non-Crisis Examples

From Occupy Wall Street Story in November 2013

[–][**Name Redacted**] **28 points:** *Yeah - there's an example letter linked in the announcement:* http://strikedebt.org/rjupdate3/

Here's a direct link: http://strikedebt.org/wp-content/uploads/2013/11/Sample-Letter-to-Debtors.pdf

[–][**Name Redacted**] **10 points:** *References:*

1. http://rollingjubilee.org/
2. *For an entertaining story from history about purchasing randomly profitable distressed debt at low prices, check out this:* http://en.wikipedia.org/wiki/Timothy_Dexter
3. http://research.stlouisfed.org/fred2/series/CMDEBT
4. http://research.stlouisfed.org/fred2/series/HDTGPDUSQ163N
5. http://www.dawger.com/_doc_tax_implications.shtml
6. http://wizbangblog.com/content/2004/09/22/oprahs-car-give.php
7. *If it's interest-free it gets treated like a dividend for tax purposes. Nevertheless, there is a low amount and interest rate such that both the employer and the employee prefer such payment to a higher salary.*
8. http://www.irs.gov/Individuals/The-Mortgage-Forgiveness-Debt-Relief-Act-and-Debt-Cancellation-
9. http://en.wikipedia.org/wiki/Nonrecourse_debt#Tax_consequences_of_disposition_of_property_encumbered_by_non-recourse_debt
10. http://www.law.cornell.edu/uscode/text/26/6050P
11. http://www.thedailybeast.com/articles/2012/11/14/debt-and-taxes.html
12. http://blog.startfreshtoday.com/blog/bid/220069/6-Most-Common-Debts-That-Can-Be-Discharged-in-Bankruptcy
13. http://www.slate.com/blogs/moneybox/2012/11/09/rolling_jubilee_occupy_wall_street_s_bailout_of_the_people_by_the_people.html

From Drug Bust Story in December 2013

[–][**Name Redacted**] **4 points:** *As someone else has said, methamphetamine can induce something called stimulant psychosis. Whether or not this was the cause of their horrific actions, who knows. But it could definitely be a factor that will likely be examined.*

[–][**Name Redacted**] **11 points:** *Tip - vitamin c degrades amphetamines, and will help make a high shorter. If someone is going crazy a few vit c pills will make it go away faster.*

http://www.drugs.com/drug-interactions/amphetamine-with-vitamin-c-2543-0-238-3823.html

Crisis Examples

From Typhoon Haiyan Story in November 2013

[–][name redacted] 54 points: *Here's a video:*

http://video.sina.com.cn/vlist/news/zt/haiyan2013/?opsubject_id=top1#118918134
The water coming down the stairs was kind of surreal.
From Mall Shooting in Maryland in January 2014

[–][name redacted] 39 points 5 months ago: *One of the victim's instagram*

APPENDIX D: SAMPLE INSIDER COMMENTS

Comments from Trader Joe's Story in January 2014

[–][name redacted] 338 points: *I work at Trader Joe's, all of the food that is "unsellable" is donated to a local pantry. This is honestly great*

[–][name redacted] 119 points: *I work at Trader Joes as well, and the people the authors donate it to bring us doughnuts every thursday and friday.*

[–][name redacted] 41 points: *I used to volunteer at a food bank that got food from Trader Joes, they throw out so much food. Like an insane amount of food, mostly bread, but a lot of other things too. Perfectly good food that may be a couple days expired or slightly damaged packaging. I volunteered with a woman that would do pick ups 6 days a week and hand out food at a local church and send stuff over to a Mexico orphanage. She was a little crazy but dedicated to doing it for no pay.*

[–][name redacted] 191 points: *I worked at Price Chopper and the authors threw out enough food each day to feed a small village.. I've always wondered why the authors don't donate it all to food banks or homeless shelters or something like that. I mean I basically lived off of eating the stuff the authors were throwing out, mainly fruits that were deemed not suitable for display but were still perfectly fine to eat.*

[–][name redacted] 327 points: *I've always wondered why the authors don't donate it all to food banks or homeless shelters or something like that.*

I used to be a manager for a fast food cookie restaurant. The authors donated all of our leftovers to a local charity. One day someone whom this charity helped claimed that they broke a tooth on a brownie and sued us. They lost the suit, but our corporate office adopted a policy prohibition further donations.

[–][name redacted] 59 points: *I can tell you how it worked in the 90s, was my first job when I was 15.*

Wendy's made their burgers fresh so meat was constantly grilling. The job of the guy on the grill was to match the amount of meat on the grill to the demand.

Too little and customers had to wait, too much and you made chili meat (overcooked burgers) one of the metrics for performance was not making too much chili meat. So out of code is kind of not accurate, it was just any burger that was too overcooked to serve as a burger.

Comment from West Virginia Chemical Spill in January 2014

[–][name redacted] 991 points: *Resident here.*

It's not only don't drink the water, it's don't do anything with the water - meaning don't use it to cook, clean, wash clothes, brush your teeth, take a shower. The only thing the authors are supposed to do is flush the toilet. It's a real pain in the ass.

Also recently the temperature dropped drastically here so people who did not take proper precautions had their pipes bursting left and right. Bottled water was already a bit on the scarce side.

I was out and about when I heard about it yesterday so I decided to swing by Wal-Mart and grab some water. Well, there were already hundreds of people inside who had bought up all the water. The employees kept telling people there was no more water yet there was still a line of roughly 100 standing around the door where they bring out the merchandise.

I'd be willing to bet that every sheriff and officer from the neighboring town was inside that place. God forbid that anything bad really ever happen.

Also yesterday about 2 pm I was leaving my place and my mom comes knocking on my door - which is odd. Her office is nearby and when I opened the door all she said is "I'm going to shit myself! I'm going to shit myself" and apparently she went in the bathroom and shit and puked at the same time. It was later she told me that she had a cup of coffee and downed an entire cup of water right before she came by my place.

It's not only worrisome for those who are financially unable to go out and buy tons of water for every day use, but you have to think about people with formula fed babies who were drinking the water all day yesterday, and the pets that were. The local shelters need water badly, not only for hydration but to clean the cages.

Hopefully they will remedy the situation soon but it doesn't look like it. I'm going to have to go to one of the relief stations to pick up water later, so that should be fun.

Edit: The authors are being told not to boil and drink it, let alone touch it.

Edit: Press conference just notified us that yesterday during the initial contamination the level of chemicals in the water were at a 2.0. Now, over 24 hours later they are at a 1.9. Considering that the chemicals have to dissipate on its own, sounds like its going to be a long one.

EDIT for those needing water:

I just got back home and most places downtown are completely out.

WV State has tanks and short lines, just make sure you bring your own jug.

Also WV Steel in Poca is selling 6 one gallon jugs of water for $5. Of course there are other places, but those are off the top of my head.

Example of Insider Comment with Second-Hand Reporting, LAX Incident, November 2013

[–][name redacted] **1728 points:** *Holy shit. My friend's dad was there when it happened. The shooter walked by him and asked "TSA?"*

Here is his interview with Milwaukee TMJ4

They told everybody to run toward the gate, and I couldn't run because I had my shoes and my belt off. So I was trying to gather up my stuff and get going and a TSA worker walked up right behind me and started yetlling, 'get out of here get down' there so he grabbed my shoes and I just started running," Leon Saryan of Greenfield said. "And I got halfway down the hall, and I was in the hallway cowering when the guy came through. And he had a rifle in his hand and he looked at me and he said 'TSA?' and I shook my head and he just kept going."

APPENDIX D: NEWS AGGREGATOR POSTS

From Shooting at LAX in November 2013

[–][name redacted] **1680 points:** *Updating in EDT in Real Time*

Please visit /u/Acrimony87's Summary

I'd like to take a moment to thank Redditor's /u/Acrimony87, /u/StrictScrutiny, & /u/Z3R0C001 for updating Reddit on this story as well. Thanks to those who gifted me gold & silver!

Would like to point out that I saw this story break via Twitter, thus no News Sources (even via Twitter) were available to post a link too at the time. This instance highlights how fast news breaks & how slow it takes news organizations to pick up breaking stories.

Both Tory Bellici & Grant Imahara are reporting shooters at LAX.

@ToryBelleci - Heard gun shots then everyone starting running for the door. Not sure if anyone was hurt. #LAX

Photos: Evacuating & Outside on tarmac

CBS Los Angeles - LAPD Incident Reported in Terminal 3 @ LAX

Los Angeles Airport Police Friday morning confirmed an unknown incident prompted the evacuation of Terminal 3 at LAX.

Details surrounding the incident were not immediately made clear, however passengers reported being evacuated from the terminal sometime after 9 a.m.

Ariel shots from Sky2 showed buses were transporting passengers that had disembarked from planes onto the runway area.

LAPD Radio

CNN Live Video

KCBS LOCAL Live Video

UPDATE Unconfirmed - 3 Injured, One being TSA Agent. - Suspect in Custody, wound to leg.

LAX Airport Twitter - Airport officials confirm police incident began at 9:30 a.m. @ Terminal 3 at LAX. More info to come.

National Media picking up story now: CNN FOX NBC

LAX - Inbound & Outbound Traffic Shutdown

Via NBC4 SoCal:

A gunman opened fire at a security checkpoint Friday morning at Los Angeles International Airport, injuring a Transportation Security Administration employee and prompting a terminal evacuation.

A TSA spokesperson told NBC4 the shooting occurred at a security checkpoint. A traveler told NBC4 she heard gunfire in Tom Bradley Terminal, where she was preparing to board a flight to Mexico aboard Virgin America.

Details regarding the status of the gunman were not immediately available.

"The authors were just standing there and someone started shooting," witness Nick Pugh said. "I heard a total of maybe eight or 10 shots fired."

1:11pm - Unconfirmed Second suspect in custody, with weapon. NBC

1:14pm - NYPost News Feed

1:16pm - Suspect entered Terminal 3 wearing camo BDU's & open fired. Seemed to be targeting TSA Agents. Via LEO Source. NBC

1:20pm - FBI Team's arriving on scene. NBC

1:21pm - Unconfirmed - 3 Injured, One being TSA Agent. One TSA Dead. - Suspect in Custody, wound to leg.

1:22pm - Passengers are being cleared, collected & bussed off tarmac.

1:23pm - GRAPHIC: POSSIBLE KIA CASUALTY TSA Agent being wheeled away. Credit: /u/KazMux

1:24pm - Mayor & Police Chief have arrived at T3.

1:25pm - Reports that shooter was not targeting passengers. Gunman: Early 20's, caucasian, crew cut, wearing leisure workout clothes, carrying rifle. Passenger Bay NBC

1:29pm - Full ground stop in effect at LAX. via Don Lemon

1:30pm - People are still being shuttled in to a secured location. Nerves are starring to settle. Tory Belleci

1:35pm - Via /u/Eaaaaaagle -

From scanner: One suspect down in terminal. Second suspect in custody at garage. Rifle was also recovered. Also it seems that security and TSA are not to blame. They entered ticketing area at Virgin Airlines then shot their way through the security checkpoint targeting the TSA employees.

1:37pm - LAX is NOT shutdown. All upper departure levels closed. Only media allowed to park on T 1 & 2 upper departure levels. NBC

1:40pm - Via ABC - Planes are now allowed to land at LAX.

1:40pm - Suspect which was injured is now being transported to hospital via 405.

1:42pm - Offramps shutdown off of 405 to LAX.

1:42pm - No more injured have been moved to triage area since the original incident. 2 suspects currently in custody.

1:47pm - Gus Villanueva of LAPD (sp?) - At 9:30am PST, shots fired at T3, LAPD responded. One suspect in custody. 2-3 people injured. LAFD on scene.

1:49pm - Reports that [a] suspect was an off duty TSA Agent. NBC

1:50pm - LAPD is requesting that people avoid LAX area if at all possible, if you need to pass by please use 405 but be prepared for horrible traffic.

1:52pm - Live on NBC - LAX Announcement to Secure Holding Area - LAX still being cleared, search is currently being conducted. No time frame on when the airport will be secure. Please hold tight, food & water will be provided to [passengers].

2:01pm - Photo of Secure Holding Area for Passengers via Tory Balleci

2:02pm - There's an army of law enforcement from various agencies here. via Grant Imahara

2:05pm - Grant Imahara just posted photo of an object (possibly weapon) being guarded on ground outside Virgin Lounge. Look at this picture a little closer. Something on the ground. via Grant Imahara

2:07pm - News conference with Mayor of LA & LAPD Chief forthcoming. NBC

2:08pm - Via Bill Reiter: The scene on Tarmac. Fear, tears, prayers, confusion, worry.

2:13pm - Better photo of gun on ground in LAX. via AlienGurudeva sent to me by /u/suzistaxxx.

2:15pm - BREAKING. Source tells @CBSNews TSA agent who was shot at LAX has now died; the suspect is an off-duty TSA agent. Via Charlie Kaye CBS, sent to me by /u/acrimony87.

2:23pm - Press Conference with the LAPD Chief & Mayor upcoming.

2:24pm - If you're flying today please check with your departing airports as delays begin to occur around the nation.

2:26pm - Via NBCLA - Press briefing expected on LAX Shooting at 11:30 a.m. Watch live here.

2:28pm - LAPD Official Statement: Today at 9:30 am a single shooter in LAX around terminal 3 area started shooting. Multiple victims were injuried. LAX PD engaged the suspect. Suspect was taken into custody. For precautionary reasons terminal 3 and surrounding areas will be swept.

2:42pm - News Conference happening in 2 minutes. Mayor, Chief of LAPD, FBI, & Airport Police to speak.

2:44pm - NBCLA is reporting that all of those shot are TSA agents: one killed, one in critical, two in fair condition.

2:49pm - LA Time's News Conference Coverage WITH Close Captioning , sent to me by /u/acrimony87.

2:51pm - LAX gunman is NOT a current or former TSA employee, CBS reports after earlier reporting the contrary

2:51pm - One (if not two) being led away in handcuffs, walking under their own power. NBC

2:52pm - News Conference:

- *9:20am PST, shooter became actively involved in T3.*
- *Thanking LEO Community*
- *Believe to be static situation which is safe now.*
- *Working hard in ops of airport. Flights are continuing to take off, especially in Southside.*
- *If you have a flight this afternoon, please stay away due to ongoing investigation.*
- *Terminals 1 & 2 open for travelers on ground.*
- *Individual came into T3, pulled an "assault rifle" out of bag & opened fire in terminal. Proceeded into screening area, passed through screening area & moved into terminal.*
- *LEO tracked him through the terminal, & engaged him inside the terminal.*
- *At this time, the belief is that there was only one shooter involved.*
- *Tremendous amount of investigation to be done.*
- *Sweep has been completed in T3, it is safe.*

- *Multiple victims that have been shot & transported. Other injuries other than to the suspect himself.*
- *Flights are arriving in half of usual arrival rate to southside of airport.*
- *If you have flights out this afternoon, please check with your airlines and or @LAX_Official.*
- *LAFD has treated 7 patients, 6 have been transported.*
- *Natures of injuries & identity of suspect will not be released at this time.*
- *FBI is handling the investigation at this point.*
- *FBI is working hand in hand with all agencies at this time.*
- *Investigation is on-going at this time, little facts will be disseminated.*
- *Will not be talking about victims at this time.*
- *No additional threats have been identified at the airport at this time.*
- *Thanks given to first responders who were on the scene.*
- *Only ONE SHOOTER responsible at this time.*
- *Active shooter scenario was practiced three weeks ago with LAPD & other agencies.*
- *Suspect was able to penetrate Terminal 3 quite far, "towards Burger King".*

3:11pm - Just announced, law enforcement has secured the area. Slowly letting people leave this terminal. via Tory Balleci

3:12pm - Several photos from inside T3 (most likely inside Virgin's Lounge) here.

3:20pm - Upcoming news conference from UCLA Harborside Medical Center on injuries.

3:22pm - Just for some context for those unfamiliar with Terminal 3 (it's the terminal I fly out of the most because of Virgin America) - getting as far as the Burger King here is REALLY far. It's like 100 yards in from the security checkpoints and right next to all the gates and holding areas.

via /u/FreddieW

I work at T3 for Virgin America, so I can corroborate this- when I heard Burger King mentioned and saw some of the pictures, it was chilling. Those locations are WELL beyond security and at a walking pace take 2-3 minutes to access from the checkpoint.

via /u/AlexM5488

3:24pm - LAPD just said the area is still under investigation & will not be letting us leave holding area. via Tory Balleci

3:33pm - They told everybody to run toward the gate, and I couldn't run because I had my shoes and my belt off. So I was trying to gather up my stuff and get going and a TSA worker walked up right behind me and started yetlling, 'get out of here get down' there so he grabbed my shoes and I just started running," Leon Saryan of Greenfield said. "And I got halfway down the hall, and I was in the hallway cowering when the guy came through. And he had a rifle in his hand and he looked at me and he said 'TSA?' and I shook my head and he just kept going."

via /u/CorgiRawr

3:43pm - Ronald Reagan UCLA Medical News Conference
- *Level 1 Trauma Center*
- *3 Male Victims*

- ◦ *1 Patient - Critical Condition (GSW)*
- ◦ *2 Patients - Fair Condition (1 Patient GSW, 1 Patient Other)*
- ◦ *Multiple Injuries, gunshots & other types.*
- ◦ *NO DOA @ THIS HOSPITAL*
- ◦ *All adults, no children.*
- ◦ *Generally fair patients are in hospital one or two days.*

3:50pm - CNN has a large amount of photos & story updates here.

3:59pm - LA Times - Live News Feed, Including Video sent to me by /u/livingthegoodlife1

4:07pm - KTLA Live is confirming that the fatality was a TSA Agent, a male in his forties. Another TSA Agent was wounded in the stomach.

4:10pm - Almost 4 hrs since the shooting. Still here. 2000+ people. They're handing out waters & snacks. via Tory Balleci

4:29pm - NBC News is reporting shooter is 23 Year Old Paul Anthony Ciancia via /u/sgtpartydawg

4:50pm - Via the Associated Press:

- ◦ *BREAKING: Law enforcement officials identify LAX shooting suspect as 23-year-old Paul Ciancia. A law enforcement official tells The AP the shooting suspect wrote a rant about killing TSA workers. An official said the suspect, from NJ, was wearing fatigues and carrying a bag containing a note. Story*

At this time I'm going to be taking a break, the only other news conference should be from UCLA Harborside. I'll try to update if & when I get time. Please feel free to cover & update it.

[–][name redacted] 36 points: *Live audio from LAX air traffic control (North/South Tower + Helo)*

10:22am: All arrivals are being held at their destination. Aircraft that are arriving now were airborne before the ground stop went into effect.

10:25am: Currently 8 helicopters over the airport (1 Police, 7 News)

10:26am: Pilots of arriving aircraft unaware of the situation. Skywest 4480: "What's with all the helicopters?" ATC: "Shooting incident at Terminal 3."

10:30am: Departures seem to be unaffected at this time.

10:34am: PD18 (Police helicopter) is hovering between the north and south terminal complexes at 1,300ft.

10:42am: MEDEVAC helicopter inbound to LAX helipad. The MEDEVAC helicopter is in contact with emergency services on the ground.

11:00am: South complex traffic has resumed as normal. Helicopters and ground equipment still clogging up space on the north side.

11:03am: Still 7-8 helicopters over midfield and north of the complex (only 1 police helicopter, the rest are news).

11:07am: Two more news helicopters entering the area. I'm losing track of the number of helicopters. Currently 6 over midfield plus 2 on the north side.

11:09am: Ground stop has been extended until 12:00pm Pacific. Aircraft will be held at their origin airport.

[–][name redacted] 136 points: *UPDATES*

Early report - some kind of shooting.

LAPD is on tactical alert

Possible shooting in ticketing area; as many as 4 gunmen possible

LA emergency response has set up a triage area; no victims in the area yet but reports of a blood-covered TSA agent. (Source: NBA live feed located here)

LAPD confirms multi-patient incident

NBC live feed says "man with high powered rifle got past a checkpoint," conflicting with other reports, but also says they have very little information as of now.

3? victims - two shot, one sprained ankle. One shot TSA agent. (NBC live feed)

Evacuation scene

Incident began at 9:30 AM local time.

NBC confirms - 2 people shot.

NBC - no flights have taken off; all LAX appears to be shut down.

Witness said shooting occurred near checkpoint, but not past the checkpoint. NBC.

Picture of some being evacuated across tarmac.

Security at the evacuation location just said that they have caught the shooter (reports an evacuee on the phone); unconfirmed. NBC.

Four or five people have been wheeled out for treatment so far, no indication of severity. NBC

I have to go - someone pick it up for me for a bit?

From Mall Shooting in New Jersey in November 2013

[–][name redacted] 1343 points: *Might as well do this. Getting info from TV News sources (I know, not very reliable. I'll check some online sources as well.)*

All time in EST

About 9:30PM: Reports of shots fired, man with a rifle and body armor inside the Garden State Plaza mall. Along with shots fired

10:13pm: Most police are around the Nordstrom entrance, unconfirmed reports that shooter escaped.

10:15pm: Worker from a bar says he "heard shots, mall security runs in screaming at top of lungs 'GET OUT GET OUT GET OUT' and they all ran out into the parking lot." Says shooting happened outside of Nordstrom. (unconfirmed, obviously).

10:20pm: Lights are apparently shut off in the west-side of the mall. All info is coming in slowly at the moment. All the authors know so far is that a shooter is in the mall (or may have escaped) in full body armor including helmet with a rifle.

10:23pm: Caller says he heard "Two loud booms, then two more following." Caller said gunman hit 4 peopleUNCONFIRMED quite obviously. First two shots we're quick spaced out a few seconds and after the second two shots he heard no more gunshots.

10:30pm: SWAT team currently moving into the mall, there have been police in the mall but the news stations are showing the SWAT teams moving towards the mall. Weapons are at ready, aimed towards the mall while moving up.

10:33pm: Massive amount of people being let out of the mall. Seems like police are just standing around casually inside the mall from what I saw. There are currently no reports of injuries.

10:38pm: Eyewitness says shooter was wearing biker helmet, leather jacket and carrying a long gun.

10:41pm: Unconfirmed reports of about 10-20 people still locked down in Nordstroms (courtesy of /u/ ReaganxSmash).

10:42pm: No reports of injuries, no more reports of gunshots, SWAT and police have already swarmed the mall. I'll still update as I get any info whatsoever.

10:46pm: County officials have said that the shooter is still inside the mall. K-9 units are also there for the search, as they should be.

10:49pm: Various unconfirmed reports that police currently have the brother of the shooter on the phone at the moment. Again, it is unconfirmed.

10:50pm: "Bergen County Official: SWAT Officers doing a store by store sweep inside the Garden State Plaza Mall" - CNN

10:54pm: Still not many updates at the moment. Mostly just interviews with "witnesses". Apparently shooter shot into the air, not at anyone according to various witnesses.

10:57pm: According to witness the shooter said "Don't worry, I'm not here to hurt anyone." Possibly could've been a botched robbery, according to witness. Could be absolutely anything at this point.

10:59pm: If anyone is curious, here's a layout of the mall. Shooting took place around Nordstroms around 9:20pm or so.

11:02pm: Vehicle by Riverside Square mall with bullet holes found, police are either there or on there way. Not confirmed if it is connected or not. Unconfirmed

11:07pm: 2 casings were apparently found inside the mall, will be matched with the Riverside Square mall casings, if there are any.

11:08pm: Confirmed no injuries at the mall, according to sources. Lets hope that is correct.

11:09pm: According to CNN (take it with a pinch of salt): "Mayor: No injuries at mall, believes the gunman has left the garden state plaza mall." But current caller just disputed that saying police still believe gunman is still inside the mall. So pretty much; no ones knows anything.

11:11pm: According to /u/ceslek, "they're gathering people (that were in Nordstrom) at the cafe on the 2nd floor to count them and possibly evacuate them. [They're] not sure when they'll be allowed to leave. There are more than 10-20 people (employees + customers, children as well)."

11:14pm: As expected, the helicopters are doing a sweep of the roof. The police outside are very lax as of now, along with some police inside. Shows that they are not too worried.

11:16pm: Videos showing customers and employees still being evacuated.

11:17pm: User /u/ceslek says that "The people gathered and waiting at the Nordstrom cafe are only people that were/are in Nordstrom as far as I know. [They] said there are approximately 75 people."

11:19pm: Police have sent in a little robot with a camera attached to it. Helping with the search, cute little thing.

11:22pm: Unconfirmed reports of a bag and a leather jacket found in Lord and Taylor.

11:23pm: Jim Tedesco (Deputy Coordinator) says "Confirmed single shot, mall on lockdown. No one in or out without a police escort."

11:24pm: Mayor says that they "believe the shooter has left the mall, and is not apprehended at this time. It is no longer an active shooting scene. There has only been one shell casing found."

11:25pm: Mayor - "One shell casing is most likely from a long-arm rifle."

11:26pm: Various unconfirmed reports of additional shots from outside of the mall at around 11:20pm. From the police scanner. Not reports on any news sources yet. Police are also attempting to track the shooters cell phone.

11:28pm: Witness says "The man was wearing black suit with two... two balloon things on his face." Again, that is a witness. Take it with a grain of salt.

11:30pm: Police are currently treating the mall as a crime scene. Going through any evidence they can get their hands on (not much as of now, apparently). Going through any camera source they can get to as well. Surveillance, security, etc.

11:33pm: Witness says there was multiple shooters, heard shotgun shots and semi-auto shots. Witness says he is in the Navy. Apparently multiple shooters. One with shotgun one with rifle. unconfirmed. This is completely unconfirmed, from an eyewitness.

11:35pm: Previous report does not make sense with what the police and mayor has said already. Not too sure about the validity of it.

11:36pm: /u/ceslek - "[They] just told me the group was brought to Joe's restaurant in the mall and frisked, the group gathered at Nordstroms, frisked by swat team."

11:39pm: Currently the authors still do not know where the suspect is, or if there is another suspect. Police are still trying to put together an actual picture of what actually occurred. Conflicting reports on whether or not the suspect is still in the mall or not.

11:45pm: An amazing amount of conflicting reports regarding the amount of shots fired. Many sources are saying one shot, some are saying four and some are saying five shots. We'll have to see when this all calms down.

11:46pm: Police are still conducting searches of the stores, along with watching surveillance cameras. Pictures shown on news station are showing a group of people hiding in a store... all on their phones and tablets...

11:48pm: Reports of people with the shooter before he started shooting. Person reporting this (witness) claims to be from the Navy. Not sure of the validity of it. unconfirmed

11:51pm: A suicide note was found, not sure where, stating or referring to the fact that he wants to commit suicide by cop.

11:52pm: Also, according to a source (unconfirmed), Verizon was able to ping the suspects cell phone to the area of Neiman Marcus in the mall. Again, this is unconfirmed.

11:54pm: According to the scanner, the suspects phone was located (not sure if pinged or physically found) in the mall about 6 or 7 minutes ago.

12:00am: Not much new info is coming out. There may be a briefing within the next hour or so by officials, as claimed by PIX11.

12:01am: "No details at this time on who the suspect is, only one shell casing found inside the mall so far, this is still a very, very active case." - Mayor

12:02am: /u/ceslek - "SWAT people frisked everyone - women were frisking women, and men frisked men. German shepherds were also there. They were continually being told they were safe. Everyone that was frisked was interviewed and allowed to leave. [They] said Oradell cops were there as well so [they're] assuming neighboring towns were there to help."

12:04am: Phone is being pinged again to see if it has been moved. (source - scanner)

12:07am: It seems like the only news station ATM with coverage is PIX11. Please don't trust this guy with the info as of yet. Not one knows anything and he is just another eye witness. Could be bluffing just to get his 15 minutes of fame.

12:10am: "The cellphone was pinged between neiman marcus and macy's slowly clearing 2nd floor of neiman- a man was reported w/ injures nothing serious but lacerations. Uncomfirmed being taken out by helicopter."

12:12am: "FBI and SWAT are inside Neiman Marcus, clearing the building." (at about 12:06am - courtesy of/u/karmapuhlease)

12:18am: Scanner - suspect is 21 years old, 5'11" 139lbs, a Teaneck resident (also works there), and drives either a blue 2001 Honda or a black/blue Nissan. (Note: This may not be the suspect for the shooting, it could be an unrelated suspect.)

12:20am: Suspect came in, shot several shots, weapon not recovered, wearing black helmet. People still in mall/being evacuated slowly but efficiently. - According to Paramus official.

12:22am: Unconfirmed reports of someone down, at scene, unresponsive but breathing by Neiman and maybe Macys.

12:25am: Maybe be getting an official update within the next 15 minutes or so.

12:26am: Police source text to PIX11 - Found a change of clothes, along with empty and live ammo casings inside the mall.

12:30am: From /u/ceslek - Pictures - http://imgur.com/a/QAfEG

When the Nordstrom group exited the cafe on the 1st floor (not the 2nd floor like I previously said) of Nordstrom, the SWAT team was standing "in rank" outside the cafe with their guns pointed at the group and told "hands in the air, don't put your hands down" and the group then went up the escalator to the the 2nd floor and they were then frisked and told to go inside Joe's. Guns were not being pointed at the group while being frisked. The people with kids were escorted away before the guns were pointed at anyone. Police were asking for eye witnesses and anyone with knowledge was brought into rooms and interviewed. One woman said she was a witness and she was escorted to a room according to [my source]. People parked right outside Joe's were allowed to leave immediately. Others were told to stay until further notice.

12:30am: Hotels on rt 4 being checked for vehicles- this is all through the scanner and unconfirmed

12:31am: unconfirmed - Blue Nissan and a motorcycle tagged in relation with shooting- suspects possible armed.

12:35am: From a source - Seems like something is being staged by neiman marcus still- police setting up all around it on on roof not sure what really. But seems like they are not positive the mall is cleared. Makes sense since the cell phone pings were still going off there.

12:38am: Multiple police agencies are looking for an individual from Teaneck either driving a blue Honda or black motorcycle. Reports are this is the possible actor from the shooting, is possibly suicidal, and is to be regarded as dangerous. At 12:33am it was reported that the blue Honda was found and has been secured at the mall. (unconfirmed)

12:41am: Briefing should be within the next half hour or so.

12:43am: Still a sweep going on in the mall, according to the PIX11 police source.

12:52am: PIX11 Police Source - Close to 2000 officers sweeping the mall, police are still pinging the cell phone. (Which means that police do have a suspect.) The suspects family has given police his cellphone number.

12:56am: Police have identified the shooter as a Richard Shoop who is 20 and lives in Teaneck. Shoop is employed at a restaurant in Teaneck and may possibly still be in or on the mall campus as of now.

1:10am: It seems to have slowed down a bit as the police search for the suspect and get everyone out safe. I'm gonna end it here, if someone else wants to pick it up, by all means go ahead. Thank you all for the help (you know who you are) and I really appreciate the gold! First time getting it. My thoughts are with everyone effected tonight, hopefully this turd gets caught soon and doesn't hurt anyone.

Good night everyone!

From Typhoon Haiyan in November 2013

[–][name redacted] 379 points: *Edit: As of 6:00 am EST, the situation report has the following information:*

- *2,055,630 families or 9,497,847 persons were affected*
- *The number of damaged houses is currently at 19,551 (13,191 have been totally destroyed)*
- *A state of calamity has been declared in the province of Antique, as well as in Janiuay and Dumangas in the province of Iloilo*
- *Flooding, landslides, and fallen trees blocked several roads, but most are now passable thanks to ongoing clearing operations*

The Red Cross is reporting that an additional 6.5 million people in Vietnam could be affected. source
    If you are trying to find someone in the Philippines in the aftermath of the typhoon, you can try using one of these sources:

- *PeopleLocator*
- *Google PersonFinder*
- *alternate source for Google PersonFinder*
- *Red Cross request for help restoring contact*

    You can help disaster responders by working with MicroMappers and tagging tweets that are relevant to response efforts.
    MicroMappers
    If you would like to donate, here are some organizations that could use your help:

- *Red Cross Philippines via Paypal*
- *Ayala Foundation's 'Laging Handa Fund' (Always Ready), overseas donors can use this online portal for donations*
- *GlobalGiving.com. Credit and debit card donations accepted*
- *The Catholic Relief Services and Caritas Filipinas Foundation*

- *Save the Children. Save the Children has a team on the ground in Tacloban working to respond to this emergency.*
- *UNICEF*

note: I pulled the donation info from /u/hitokiri_battousai's comment here. If you have another reputable organization that is helping out, let me know and I'll add it to the list.

From School Shooting in Colorado in December 2013

[–] [name redacted] 64 points: *Shoutout to /r/Colorado.*
Update 1: Shooter is now dead. There is 1 victim in critical conditon.
Update 2: it is reported that the shooter killed himself (self-infilcted gunshot)
Update 3: Students being sent to list below -
Update 4: One student has been taken to Littleton Adventist Hospital with a gunshot would. No age, gender, or condition known.
Update 5: While there is no bomb suspected police are doing a bomb sweep of the school
Update 6: They are now looking for a subaru in the parking with the license plate 698YSW - School is slowly being cleared.

To all parents who may be affected by this police are ferrying students around to the following locations:
Nearby King Supers
Shephard of the hills church
Euclid middle school (This seems to be the primary location)
Unconfirmed The shooting started when a student entered school wanting to confront a teacher. Two students injured (one confirmed). Another student was reported injured with no reports so far on status. A second suspect was reported but it is a ongoing investigation.

[–][name redacted] 38 points 7 months ago*: *One injured unknown 15-16 year old at hospital with gun shot wound, suspect deceased self-inflicted gun shot wound.*

Update: male shooter, student at school.
Saying a second student suffered minor wound not sure if it was a gun shot wound.
Only one weapon found so far.
Apparently news conference says shooter had an issue with a particular teacher who was able to leave building in time.

From Mall Shooting in Maryland in January 2014

[–][name redacted] 558 points: *Howard County Fire and Police Scanner*

EDIT

12:02 K9 unit going to Macy's for a suspicious package

12:06 Sounds like everything happened in the Sears because that's where they're sending units. Sears is on the opposite side of the mall from the Macy's. Sears is also located right next to the food court, which is the most populated area of the mall.

12:08 Expect walking wounded who will move to the food court to receive treatment.

12:09 They're no longer sending any medical transport units to the mall, seems like they don't expect any more serious injuries.

12:15 Moving people out of the mall in groups

12:16 Having trouble keeping people warm in the staging area, bringing buses to keep people warm. Currently 26 but feels like 15.

12:25 Woman in Panera (near Macy's) just called into dispatch saying there is a suspicious man in a ski hat and black trenchcoat peeking in windows at the Macy's.

12:36 Still trying to get buses. Currently using Howard Transit buses.

Hey sorry I haven't kept up. After I contacted family and friends I turned off the scanner and got my day started. Hope everyone's family and friends are safe!

[–][name redacted] 292 points: *Columbia Mall Shooting, Updated thread: 2:00pm EST*

Continuation from above.

12:51 police report a suspicious dark sedan with tinted windows fled the mall earlier and ran a few red lights.

12:57 a unit reports stopping a similar vehicle.. no additional information.

1:04 many news outlets are reporting that the 1/3 that is dead WAS the suspected killer (i still believe this is speculation and not 100% confirmed)

1:05 police are working on clearing out JC Penny (many stores have already been cleared)

1:06 police are waiting by Lord & Taylor (this will be the next store methodically cleared out)

1:10 police are investigating a suspicious package, what looks like a bag (no further information)

1:12 police report 80% of stores have been cleared.

1:20 police are now entering Lord and Taylor with a team. (a 4 man team has already entered)

1:21 police are about to enter Macy's (this will be the next store methodically cleared out)

1:26 JC Penny employees all clear. Good news if you have family/friends that work there.

1:30 Howard County police to hold a press conference any minute now... (will update)

1:31 police are reporting 99% of stores should be cleared out by now.

1:31 press conference has started.

1:32 County executive: confirms 3 dead.

1:33 County executive: blahblahblah, no new information...

1:33 Police Chief Bill McMahon: 11:15am, 911 received reports for shots fired. Officers identified 3 victims in the mall. "one of those victims appears to be the shooter"

1:35 Police Chief Bill McMahon: "the authors don't believe at this time, that their are any more shooters in the mall"

1:36 Police Chief Bill McMahon: "the authors don't think there are any additional injuries, the authors are actively searching the mall to clear out people."

1:36 Police Chief Bill McMahon: "the authors do not have a motive of the shooting yet. the authors are still trying to secure the mall."

1:37 police scanner: waiting on somebody to open Nordstroms for them so they can clear it out.

1:38 Police Chief Bill McMahon: "the authors are very confident that it was a single shooter"

1:40 Police Chief Bill McMahon: 'our detectives are talking to people as the leave the mall to see if the authors can clear them to leave'

1:55 CNN reports that the suspect may have shot himself as bullet wounds appear to be self inflicting.

2:23 Howard County twitter: HOCO General Hospital is treating a victim from the mall who suffered a gunshot wound to the foot.

2:47 Police confirmation: the shooting took place in a skate shop called 'Zumiez' on the mall's upper level.

-== No new updates at this time ==- Press conference at 4pm EST
SPECULATION/RUMORS:
Twitter rumor: this was over a pair of Jordans??
Facebook user: asking for prayer for his friend that was shot (female) point blank with a shotgun at Columbia mall.

Chapter 11

"Don't Tell Us You're Handsome.....Post Your Great Photo and Let It Stand":
Creating and Enforcing Credibility in Online Dating

Shana Kopaczewski
Indiana State University, USA

ABSTRACT

This chapter explores the issue of credibility in online dating. 200 posts to a website called eDateReview. com were inductively analyzed. Examination of these posts revealed that online daters negotiate the potential for selective self-presentation by developing strategies for evaluating the credibility of online dating profiles which builds on established theories of self-presentation in online spaces, including the warranting principle developed by Walther and Parks (2002). These strategies include determining the credibility of the dating sites themselves, assessing the credibility of online profiles, and the demonization of dishonesty to establish norms. Implications and future research are discussed.

INTRODUCTION

I post recent photos, including full body pics. I'm not gorgeous, but I have nothing to hide. I am honest in my profile and I don't use a long list of adjectives to describe myself. No one is all of those things. Besides, if you really are compassionate, handsome, healthy, stable, honest, understanding, dependable, funny, active, handy, hard-working, loyal, secure, and a good listener—then how is it that you're divorced? Don't tell us you're handsome......post your great photo and let it stand. Don't tell me you're funny......say something funny in your profile and let the reader decide... and pleeeeeze don't post three photos of your motorcycle and one of you wearing sunglasses and a beanie. (Rebecca, personal communication, 2007)

DOI: 10.4018/978-1-5225-1072-7.ch011

Online dating continues to increase in popularity as more and more people turn to sites like Match.com to find their ideal partners. Because online dating allows people to meet and interact virtually, there has been a debate over whether one can trust the profile a person has put together to be a true representation of the self. While some researchers argue that self-presentation in online spaces is more honest, because people feel they can be their "true" selves online (Bargh, McKenna, & Fitzsimmons, 2002), others argue that the asynchronous nature of the Internet allows people to create an identity that may be quite different than their offline selves (Bailey, 2001; Hardey, 2002; Morse, 2001; Nakamura, 2001; Poster, 2006; Stone, 2001; Turkle, 2001). With the popularity of shows like MTV's *Catfish* and Dateline's *To Catch a Predator*, the question of the credibility of one's online identity has taken center stage, particularly when there is an expectation that those online interactions will transfer into offline relationships. This research builds on established theories of self-presentation in online spaces including the warranting principle developed by Walther and Parks (2002). In the context of online dating, credibility is often tied to the concept of honesty and is based on perception rather than an inherent quality within a source. For the purpose of this paper, the author defines credibility based on the concept of perceived source credibility (O'Keefe, 2002) as judgments made by a perceiver about the veracity of a communicator or communication.

The flexibility of online self-presentation is stifled by the knowledge that the presentation will ultimately need to be read as authentic in a face-to-face meeting. This approach not only shows how online daters work to decipher the credibility of information presented in profiles, but also how they create norms in the online dating community that encourage honesty by demonizing dishonesty. The purpose of this chapter is to explore "establishing and evaluating credibility" in the digital genre of online dating. This chapter will look specifically at how the discourse of Internet daters in the online dating forum eDateReview.com functions to create and enforce a perception of credibility in dating profiles. The author asserts that credibility in online dating is determined by the credibility of the online dating website and the profiles themselves, and argues that online daters actively work to establish norms of credibility by demonizing dishonesty.

BACKGROUND

With the growing ubiquity of computers and the Internet in contemporary society, the online personal ad is another move to utilize media as a resource for goal attainment in an evolving society. Online dating has become part of a cultural discourse about dating, and the implications of credibility in dating online have not been fully explored. Potential mates used to be vetted by families and communities, so that questions of credibility were managed through close social networks. Merskin and Huberlie (1996) argued that modern times have changed strategies for finding mates. Urbanization, industrialization, and the changing nature of family and religion have all contributed to a society where traditional matchmakers and arranged marriages are unworkable, influencing a cultural shift towards online dating and away from the security of having trusted persons vouch for the credibility of a potential partner. Given the current popularity of using computers to facilitate dating, research on the phenomenon is increasing, and it is important to look at the ways computer-mediated communication (CMC) and, more specifically, online dating are conceptualized and discussed by scholars. This section begins with a brief overview of relevant literature on CMC, followed by theories of online self-presentation and credibility in online dating.

Computer-Mediated Communication

Before exploring credibility in online dating, it is useful to take a closer look at the historical context of how computer technology came to hold such influence in interpersonal interaction and the general state of CMC research. Each significant new technology raises concerns about what impact it will have on communities and social relationships, and the Internet is certainly no exception (Bargh & McKenna, 2004). New technologies have always had to demonstrate their credibility to a skeptical public. The telegraph, telephone, radio, and television all went through initial phases of doubt and mistrust as people wondered what would be lost by changing how people communicate. Bargh and McKenna (2004) argued that while people speculated and feared the impact communication technologies would have on community ties and relationships, television had the greatest real impact as it allowed families to stay home for their entertainment rather than going out, and it is this actual effect of a technology on community ties that sets up a concern for the impact the Internet would have on relationships because time spent online is often not time spent with family and friends despite its usefulness in the formation and/or maintenance of relationships over long distances. As with previous technologies, the emerging ubiquity of the Internet has been met with both optimism and skepticism. According to research from the PEW Internet and American Life Project:

[A] notable share of Americans say the internet is essential to them. Among those Internet users who said it would be very hard to give up net access, most (61% of this group) said being online was essential for job-related or other reasons. Translated to the whole population, about four in ten adults (39%) feel they absolutely need to have Internet access. Among those most deeply tied to the Internet, about half as many (some 30%) said it would be hard to give up access because they simply enjoy being online. (Rainie, Fox, & Duggan, 2014, p.6)

The convenience of the Internet for facilitating tasks such as shopping, buying a home, furthering job training, and gaining information about health issues has increased the use and acceptance of the technology. There is, however, a lingering skepticism regarding the Internet's role in interpersonal relationships, particularly when it relates to meeting people online. As presented in another PEW report, research shows that a large number of people, 15% of American adults, claim they have used online dating sites/mobile apps (Smith, 2016). However, despite the large number of people going online to look for love, 45% of online daters and 60% of non-online daters agreed with the statement that going online to date was more dangerous than other ways of meeting people (Smith, 2016), and 54% of online daters felt that someone else had seriously misrepresented themselves in their dating profile (Smith & Duggan, 2013). These findings echo the arguments made by Bargh and McKenna (2004) that new developments in technology are often met by fears regarding the impact that technology will have on communities and relationships.

The Internet is a central part of modern life in schools, homes, and workplaces, but the Internet of today is different than the earliest form of the technology. The Internet began in the US Defense Department as a means of data sharing, linking computers rather than people. The technology became ever more popular as a means of interacting with others and building relationships. The technology then continued to develop to include instant messaging, discussion boards, chat rooms, multi-user dimensions, multiple-player online games, blogs, online dating sites, etc., going beyond text to allow users to communicate with sound, pictures, and video. As the technology improved and expanded, the possibilities for meeting and interacting with others online improved and expanded as well (Whitty & Carr, 2006).

Another area of CMC research that is relevant to this research is that of online advice giving. As it will be discussed later, the discourse of online daters on eDateReview.com largely represents advice giving. Research on advice giving has typically focused on spoken or face-to-face encounters such as interactions in medical encounters. Advice columns such as *Dear Abby* have also been an area of research interest that focus on the specific format of question-and-answer style advice columns. However the growing use of the Internet has inspired an increase in research on online advice giving and seeking. While some research looks very specifically at online advice columns, other research looks at advice given through discussion boards, which is much closer to the format of posts in this research. Armstrong and Powell (2009) studied the use of online discussion boards as a space for people living with long-term health conditions to both offer and seek advice, support, and information. The study found that Internet discussion boards serve as a cheap and interactive way to satisfy a need to be in contact with their peers. Given this understanding of online discussion boards as a need-fulfilling form of communicating with similar others, one could draw the conclusion that posters and visitors to online dating forums see participation as a way to connect to other online daters and to establish credibility for various online dating sites. It is also important to note here that these sites do not easily facilitate offline interactions between users. They are not trying to attract potential partners; instead, as indicated in the literature of discussion boards, they are merely trying to fulfill a need to interact online with other online daters simply for information, support, and advice. This lends a sense of authenticity to the information posted, as there would be very little benefit in creating an idealized or false presentation of self. Looking at online dating forums offers an opportunity to explore not only how people use CMC but also how people who use CMC for online dating understand issues of credibility and authenticity in the context of online dating.

Online Self-Presentation

Goffman (1959) conceptualized the presentation of one's identity to others as a performance. Individuals perform to construct their desired image of self to a specific audience. Any performance may be successful or unsuccessful in portraying the desired character to others. If a presentation is unsuccessful, the performer will likely lose face or risk being seen in way which is not desirable to the performer. The theory of hyperpersonal communication (Walther 1996) represents one explanation for how online self-presentation differs from face-to-face presentations of self. Walther (1996) expected to find that aspects of relational communication such as immediacy, affection, composure, and relaxation would be higher among face-to-face groups initially but would level out until computer-mediated groups matched face-to-face interactions on those measures. Instead, he found that computer-mediated groups rated as high as or higher than face-to-face ones from the beginning, and that in groups where the levels were similar to start, computer-mediated groups surpassed face-to-face groups over time. Walther (1996) called this phenomenon hyperpersonal communication, and posited that it may occur as compensation for the lack of immediacy in online forms of communication. Additionally, one component of hyperpersonal communication is that of optimized or selective self-presentation. Walther (1996) argued that both the reduced social cues and asynchronous nature of online interaction allow for individuals to carefully construct their presentation of self to illicit a desired effect on the audience. Because people can control and proofread their content such as the messages they send, the words and images they use, and the topics they create and interact with, they are able to create an idealized image of who they are. Other researchers have supported the idea that there is more control over what is disclosed via computer (Hancock & Dunham, 2001; Lea & Spears, 1995). Lea and Spears (1995) argued that the nature of CMC increases the users' ability to more carefully manage the impression they give. Unlike face-to-face interactions, computer-mediated interaction allows users to rework their communication until a complete and desirable presentation is achieved, all before the communication can be viewed by anyone else. The immediacy and accountability of the face-to-face interaction is altered in an online environment, which gives online interaction a more strategic quality where people purposefully choose what information is—and is not—included for a desired result. The issue of self-presentation online becomes particularly relevant in online dating contexts where relationships are initiated online but must then move into offline environments.

The movement of relational development onto the Internet has reinvigorated the exploration of theories of self-presentation as researchers try to understand what impact the online environment has on strategies of self-presentation, particularly in online dating. Hardey (2002) researched issues of embodiment in online dating sites and argued that the ability for online daters to interact separately from their bodied selves is a basis for building trust that will carry into an offline relationship, not the construction of alternate identities as some might argue. Hardey's argument presents a key issue for online daters: They must portray themselves online in ways that match their offline selves if they want to succeed in finding a partner. Researchers have increasingly investigated the unique dynamic of presenting oneself in online dating (Ellison, Heino, & Gibbs, 2006; Gibbs, Ellison, & Heino, 2006; Hancock & Toma, 2009; Hardey, 2002; Toma, Hancock, & Ellison, 2008; Whitty, 2008). Hancock and Toma (2009) discussed the tension online daters face in trying to appear as attractive as possible in their online profile without being perceived as dishonest in that profile upon meeting. This tension creates an untenable situation in which online daters have to negotiate attractiveness and honesty without any clear distinction or guidance on how much embellishment is too much. The attempts of online daters to establish ways to evaluate the credibility of online self-presentations not only allows online daters to discern credible portrayals, but also helps to define the limits of acceptable embellishment.

Credibility and Online Dating

The skepticism of using the Internet to meet people and develop offline relationships, and the unique attributes of the Internet that allow people to carefully craft their self-presentations, creates a need for online daters to develop means for determining the authenticity and credibility of the information they encounter in online dating profiles. Ellison, Hancock, and Toma (2011) described the discrepancies between online presentations and offline presence and how online daters reconcile those differences in presentation as a promise. They assert that posting a profile is essentially a promise to the viewer of who they are offline. As long as the viewer interprets the promise has been kept when the face-to-face meeting occurs, the embellishments of presentation are forgiven. If the viewer believes the promise has been broken, then the person is held accountable for those discrepancies (Ellison et al., 2011).

Online daters often turn to other online daters for advice and insight in determining the credibility of different online dating sites, and this advice often comes in the form of online reviewing. According to Sher and Lee (2009), "the use of the Internet as a channel for expressing opinions on products has become an important marketing tool to compete for consumer attention and visits" (p. 137). Chatterjee (2001) maintained that online reviews can be categorized as word-of-mouth (WOM) information on products and services. Typically WOM information is a highly influential communication channel, especially in a society where advertisements are met with increasing skepticism (Chatterjee, 2001; Sher &

Lee, 2009). However, Chatterjee also noted that because online WOM sources are relatively unknown, and the recipient of the information cannot assess similarity, expertise, and accessibility to determine credibility, online WOM information can only be regarded as weak tie information that is less convincing than strong tie information. Regardless of the strong or weak tie associated with online reviews, businesses recognize the value in providing consumers an online venue to voice their opinions and may even offer incentives for consumers who contribute (Tedeschi, 1999).

Another important theory related to online credibility is the warranting principle (Walther & Parks, 2002). Warranting proposes that when trying to assess the reliability of others' online presentations, certain kinds of information will be viewed as more representative of the offline person than others. Generally, information that is not easily manipulated or that is provided or supported by a third party is given more weight than information that is easily controlled by the person. Warranting as a theory supports the concept of credibility in online dating in a couple of key ways. First, warranting is predicated on the tension between online presentations of self and how one will be seen in a face-to-face meeting. In online dating there is real investment in being able to predict whether someone's online persona will match their offline persona. Online daters are wary of investing too much time and energy building a relationship online only to find out that the person is different than expected offline. Online daters attempt to control how they interpret another's profile through warranting, and additionally, set expectations that control how others present themselves. Second, warranting reflects the importance of not only presenting oneself honestly but also accounting for how others might interpret the presentation of self to make certain online presentation will match offline perception.

ESTABLISHING CREDIBILITY IN ONLINE DATING

For this chapter, the author collected and analyzed discourse posted to eDateReview.com, a discussion board set up for online daters to review various online dating sites like Match.com and EHarmony[1]. eDateReview.com asks posters to indicate their name, sex, location, and e-mail address. Then, they ask for a star rating of the particular dating service the person wants to review, providing a text box for a written review. Reviews are sorted by dating site and presented as discussion boards to viewers. The stated goal is not for viewers to learn more about the person posting the review, as it would be in an online personal profile, but rather to learn more about the sites that are reviewed and the experience of people who have used those sites. It is that discourse of experience with online dating sites that makes eDateReview.com an important site for exploring the concept of credibility in online dating. eDateReview lists message boards for general dating sites, Christian sites, gay sites, Jewish sites, black dating, Ivy League dating, speed dating sites, United States dating, and Canada dating. Across the message boards, eHarmony.com and Match.com were the dominant discussions with hundreds of reviews while others had typically less than 100. The author chose to focus analysis on the two most reviewed sites for this study and analyzed approximately 200 posts for eHarmony.com and Match.com, selecting the 100 most recent reviews for each of these respective dating services in which the poster contributed substantive commentary. Posts that included only a star rating were excluded. Based on the sample of 200 posts, the author determined that theoretical saturation (Strauss & Corbin, 1998) was achieved. The author used thematic analysis, facilitated by Atlas Ti, to code and analyze emergent themes in a multi-tiered process based on grounded theory methodology, which is an analytic approach based on constant comparison

(Strauss & Corbin, 1994). Thematic analysis revealed three primary discourses related to online dating credibility; 1) the credibility of the dating sites themselves, 2) the credibility of the online profiles, and 3) the demonization of dishonesty.

Credibility of Online Dating Sites

The first major theme that emerged in the discourse of online dating was the credibility of the online dating sites themselves. Perhaps this is not a surprise since eDateReview is a discussion board predicated on reviewing the services of the various online dating sites. As research on online advice-giving predicts, posters to the eDateReview forums use participation as a way to connect to other online daters and to establish credibility for various online dating sites. Posters routinely comment on various sites' ability to provide quality matches and good customer service, both of which appear to be two primary factors used to determine the overall rating of the dating site in question. Suckered (personal communication, 2013) stated, "I too was sucked in by the adds...They are all LIES!! After 3 months[2] and over a hundred dollars I have not met or even had communication with a single person. Most of the matches are hundreds of miles away." As this quote demonstrates, the poster takes issue with the amount of money spent versus the number of connections made, but it is the opening statement that truly reveals the poster's evaluation of the site's credibility. Since this research focused primarily on posts for Match.com and Eharmony, the two leading advertisers in online dating, the discourse shows that online daters have developed a sense of brand identity and expectation for these sites. When the sites fail to deliver on the promises made in the ads, users feel betrayed, scammed, lied to, and taken advantage of, which results in a loss of credibility to the consumers who pay for those promises. Ismal (personal communication, 2013) summed this up in her review which stated, "They just try to make it look like they have a deeper way to match people with their 29 dimensions of compatibility, which is a complete bunch of ridiculous psyco babble. ... Dr. Neil Clark Warren is one of the greatest scam artists of all time!" Establishing credibility in online dating is, in part, dependent on the online dating sites themselves, and whether or not they can provide a service and develop a brand that users will trust and rely on to help them be successful in their ventures, and it is clear in the discourse on eDateReview.com that online daters do use word-of-mouth reviews to establish the credibility of the various online dating services.

Credibility of Online Profiles

The second major theme that emerged in the discourse of online daters was the credibility of information presented in online profiles. The posts to eDateReview demonstrate the warranting principle, developed by Walther and Parks (2002), which proposes that when trying to assess the reliability of others' online presentations, certain kinds of information will be viewed as more representative of the offline person than others. For online daters, the question of warranting becomes paramount because the intended goal of online dating is to evaluate potential partners online in the hopes of building meaningful relationships with them offline. In an online medium, information can be carefully crafted and manipulated in ways that face-to-face interaction cannot, so online daters must find ways to determine whether what they see online is going to be an accurate portrayal of what they will find in an offline meeting. The discourse on eDateReview clearly demonstrates how online daters interpret the veracity of the information presented in dating profiles. Three main strategies emerged:

1.   Assessing photos,
2.   Searching for corroborating information online, and
3.   Analyzing the written profile.

Assessing Photos

In establishing credibility using photos, the first indicator of profile credibility is the mere presence of a photo. "I usually request communication with the women I'm matched with. The only times I don't are if there are no photos or if the profile is incomplete, as these things usually indicate someone who isn't a paying member and just took the personality test for kicks" (Ethan, personal communication, 2011). As this poster indicates, profiles that don't include photos are interpreted as being questionable, either because it may indicate that the profile belongs to someone without a membership, or it may indicate the person is trying to conceal their appearance for whatever reason, and that is viewed equally poorly as demonstrated by Stella (personal communication, 2013): "Dozens of men on this site have NO photo—who in the world would want to meet them?!"

When photos are present, the primary link to credibility is recency. Photos that might be out of date, or that represent the person when they were younger/thinner, are instantly dismissed as inauthentic, such that marking recent dates on profile photos gives credibility to the profile. Matt (personal communication, 2012) advised: "Put up accurate RECENT pics, when I see pics that have the date stamped on them from '09 I delete immediately even if they are gorgeous." Similarly, Morris (personal communication, 2013) stated: "Guys: If a photo doesn't have a date in the caption, proceed with extreme caution. I've met women who are unrecognizable in person." These posts clearly show the warranting principle in action. The date of the photo is a more important factor in assessing how well the photo represents the offline person than the image itself.

Another important factor in assessing the credibility of images is how much the pictures show of the person. If the image is only of the face, or if the profile does not include any full body pictures, that is perceived as another sign that the person is trying to create an image that does not match the offline reality. "Guys beware when all you can see is a 'shoulders up' photo. And get ready to hear all sorts of rationalizations for why she's fat" (Patrick, personal communication, 2013). Sometimes pictures can show too much, as stated by Jane (personal communication, 2012): "Some of the shirts-off photos accompanied by the match.com profile equivalent of 'Me Tarzan, you Jane' (And some idiot really made that his headline!) really tempt me to make my next headline 'ACTION FIGURES NEED NOT APPLY.'" As these and other posts indicate, what a person chooses to reveal (or not reveal) in their profile photos is as important as the photo itself in determining credibility.

Searching for Corroborating Information

The discourse on eDateReview reveals that another strategy in determining profile credibility is cross referencing the profile with other online sources. Steve (personal communication, 2013) explicitly stated, "Look up their details on Internet sites such as google, wikipedia, facebook, twitter and linkedln." This sentiment was repeated by others who recommended "Ladies, you must do your homework, google, find out where they live? Are they real? Verify where they work" (Jean personal communication, 2012); "check his profile on POF as well !!" (angl137, personal communication, 2013); and "Just check all fotos at google before you meet someone" (Melina, personal communication, 2012). Checking other online sources demonstrates, as the warranting principle predicts, that online daters seek out support-ing information, or information that is out of the person's control to determine how credible the profile information is. Where the outside information contradicts or calls into question the profile, the outside information can be trusted more than the carefully controlled profile information.

Analyzing the Written Profile

Similar to the warranting applied to photos, the credibility of the written profile is also carefully scruti-nized. Profiles that contain little or no information are often viewed with suspicion. Posters often comment that underdeveloped profiles are likely non-members, or fake profiles set up to create the appearance of more options. LadyProf (personal communication, 2012) stated, "Of course, I know now that thinly built profiles are fakes," while Brian (personal communication, 2012) asserted

… when you realize this it becomes pretty obvious. I bet ive seen the exact same phrase "I love a night out on the town but also love staying in with my man with a glass of wine" on 100 profiles over the last year. either the female gender has negative 3 creativity as a whole, or an intern at match pumps these out by the bushel.

In these posts one can see the warranting process in assessing the validity of information posted in an online dating profile. Recent pictures are more credible than older ones, full body pictures are more credible than cropped photos, contradictory information found through a web search is more real than the profile info, and demonstrating qualities in a detailed and thoughtful profile counts more than basic labels and generic platitudes given to oneself. These warranting behaviors acknowledge the ease with which one can create an identity online that is less than honest and represent a need to somehow demonstrate that people posting profiles are in fact being honest in their self-presentation. The need for online daters to police and protect the honesty in other people's online presentation of self is a reaction against a medium that people do not inherently trust so that some information becomes more credible than other information.

Demonizing Dishonesty

The last theme that emerged is the demonizing of dishonesty. Demonizing dishonesty is the attempt of posters to establish a norm of honesty by assigning some negative consequence for online daters who do not present themselves honestly. Typically this happens through the assignation of a character flaw or threat of continued dating failure. Demonizing dishonesty creates a baseline that would ostensibly allow online daters to have greater trust in the information presented in online profiles and discourage online daters from overly embellishing or presenting inaccurate material in the first place. One of the most explicit examples of this demonizing discourse states, "When evil men and women can come on a site and put up fake profiles and misleads there is much to talk about. …Men and women have come on the site claiming they have all kind of qualifications, assets and the likes hoping to impress and mislead" (Elizabeth, personal communication, 2013). In this particular quote, people who misrepresent themselves in their profiles are called "evil," which is a term that not only indicates a character flaw but also touches on a basic human archetype of good and evil, so that the connotation also carries a heavy moral judge-ment. People who misrepresent themselves are often categorized as liars and scammers, which paints a very negative image. If an online dater does not want to be seen as a liar, scammer, or even evil, the discourse here makes clear that they should think very carefully about how they present themselves.

A second tactic in demonizing dishonesty is the way the discourse ties honesty to attractiveness and success in online dating and dishonesty as unattractive and a sure way to fail. N (personal communication, 2011) stated

I think this site is more useful if you:

1. *put several pictures on that look like you (i met someone who looked NOTHING like their profile picture)*
2. *be honest about who you are and what you want on your profile (no one wants to be 'surprised', and you aren't selling a product, what you say should be you.)*
3. *be assertive and active on the site, look for people, update your profile often and don't be afraid to try to get to know people*

This quote shows how honesty is valued as a technique for success. Here N states that you should be honest in both your pictures and profile if you want the site to be "useful." Alternatively, Holly (personal communication, 2012) stated, "These men need to stop the false advertising and lying! Don't they get that deception is a major turnoff?" These quotes serve as exemplars for the way online daters make honesty a virtuous and successful strategy and dishonesty an unattractive and unsuccessful strategy. Whereas warranting behaviors represent a reactive strategy to negotiate credibility in online dating, demonizing dishonesty represents a proactive strategy to encourage honesty in the creation of profiles. Through this strategy, the burden of establishing credibility is redistributed so that both the creator and the viewer of the profile play a part in determining how credible an online profile is.

IMPLICATIONS

This study of eDateReview.com has implications for several areas of research. It contributes to bodies of literature on dating, CMC, and self-presentation in online spaces. Dating literature acknowledges that dating is a changing concept within a society impacted largely by social constraints and expectations (Bailey, 1988; Ingoldsby, 2003; Merskin & Huberlie, 1996). The advent of online dating represents a current change in the nature of dating. The discourse on eDateReview.com reflects the tension between the realities of dating in a computer driven society and the already established norms and expectations for dating that do not include the Internet. As evidenced in the posts on eDateReview.com, there is a good deal of distrust attached to online dating, perhaps as a reflection of dating norms that traditionally believed people would find dating partners through a more trusted network of friends and family.

While the Internet opens dating possibilities, at the end of the day it still just sets up a relationship that has to happen in real life. Therefore, regardless of the ability for people to present idealized versions of themselves online, they must account for those presentations at the initial face-to-face encounter. This is why the rules of online dating are more closely monitored in relation to honesty. Based on the discourse of eDateReview.com there is a perception that information about people gained online is somehow less credible than the information we gain in a face-to-face setting. Despite the fact people can lie about their personal information as easily face-to-face as they can in a profile, and they can wear a push-up bra or hairpiece to give an inaccurate picture of what they look like, there continues to be a bias against information received online that is not as prevalent when people interact in person. Perhaps this is because people think they will be able to tell when someone is lying if they can see them, or they think that it is more difficult for people to lie to someone's face. Regardless of the reasons, Goffman (1959) argued that anytime people interact, they are playing a part—crafting an image—that they wish others to accept as true. The act of self-presentation is no more real or true in one medium over another, though the bias continues. So even though some would claim that meeting people online is not "real," or that there is a danger in meeting someone who has not been properly vetted by family and friends, in actuality, meeting someone online is very similar to meeting someone at a bar while you are with friends or meeting the new guy at church. There will still be a first date, the pretenses of putting one's best foot forward will fall away eventually, and ultimately, daters will have to figure out if there is the possibility of a more serious relationship. Online dating reflects the technological changes of the current time. The technology isn't going to go away as more and more people are supplementing their face-to-face interactions with online ones. The development of warranting practices by online daters as evidenced in this study is a good sign that online daters are successfully negotiating initial distrust of online dating and are creating strategies to manage the transition from face-to-face to computer-mediated romance. The implications of these strategies on ethos have even broader appeal when one considers that online dating is only one of many ways that people are reaching out in online spaces that rely on highly visual presentations and profiles. Social media sites like Facebook, Twitter, LinkedIn, and Pinterest have shown steady increases in the number of adults who use their sites (Duggan, Ellison, Lampe, Lenhart & Madden, 2015). Like online dating sites, these social media sites are places where people meet and develop relationships based on online presentations of self. It stands to reason that social media users could use the same strategies to determine source credibility in these spaces, and that people looking to use these sites for PR and marketing purposes would benefit from knowing how credibility is perceived and information warranted by social media audiences. The research in this study shows that when faced with online presentations, audiences are skeptical and will actively engage the information to determine source credibility by assessing both the site's ethos and actual posted content; in addition, there is evidence that audiences will proactively attempt to police the veracity of existing presentations through discourse in order to craft (and attempt to enforce) an ethos in line with their initial ideals.

FUTURE RESEARCH DIRECTIONS

The results of this study show that online dating does pose unique questions of credibility not present in traditional offline dating. First, hyperpersonal communication (Walther, 1996) and the resulting idealized impressions set up a face-to-face encounter in which it may be difficult for the reality to live up to the expectation. These expectations underline a specific challenge for online daters who have two impressions to manage, the online self and the offline self, and must negotiate the transition between the two. Second, because online dating is a relatively new relational practice, there are not as many established norms to govern what is "good" or acceptable dating behavior. Online daters are in the process of determining what it means to be an online dater, and what the norms for online dating should be. As online daters work to establish these norms, this research demonstrates that they are in many ways working to reassert traditional dating norms that mirror the offline dating experience. Future research should explore how these offline norms impact online daters in this period of transition and re-constitute digital ethos and whether old norms work to establish solid ethos in this new dating culture.

Additionally, the connection between online dating and expectation violation theory (Burgoon, 1978) warrants further investigation. A central theme in the transition from online to offline interactions seems to be the expectations that are established online, and how those expectations are violated, either positively or negatively, in the face-to-face meeting. Future research should make the connection between expectation violation theory and online dating practice more explicit and provide practical advice on how online daters could better navigate the move from online to offline relationships through their own more credible profiles and the ability to manage the expectations inherent in online dating.

CONCLUSION

The Internet affords users the ability to play with their presentations of self because there is a lack of face-to-face accountability. Online daters recognize that they may be engaging with someone who is not being honest, and the discourse on eDateReview.com shows how online daters create and enforce credibility in online presentations. Online daters employ three primary strategies for creating and enforcing credibility: determining the credibility of the dating sites themselves, discerning the credibility of the online profiles, and demonizing dishonesty. These strategies represent both reactive and proactive approaches that operate to distribute the responsibility for establishing and maintaining credibility in online dating. The dating sites, creators of online profiles, and viewers of online profiles all have a vested interest in the credibility of online dating, and this chapter outlines how online daters discursively establish those interests for the parties involved. This research presents implications for current research in online self-presentation, and relational communication more generally, and calls for future research to further explore online dating norms and how relationships successfully, or unsuccessfully, transition from online to offline.

REFERENCES

Armstrong, N., & Powell, J. (2009). Patient perspectives on health advice posted on Internet discussion boards: A qualitative study. *Health Expectations*, *12*(3), 313–390. doi:10.1111/j.1369-7625.2009.00543.x PMID:19555377

Bailey, B. L. (1988). *From front porch to backseat*. Baltimore, MD: The Johns Hopkins University Press.

Bailey, C. (2001). Virtual skin: Articulating race in cyberspace. In D. Trend (Ed.), *Reading digital culture* (pp. 334–346). Malden, MA: Blackwell Publishing.

Bargh, J. A., & McKenna, K. Y. A. (2004). The Internet and social life. *Annual Review of Psychology*, *55*(1), 573–590. doi:10.1146/annurev.psych.55.090902.141922 PMID:14744227

Bargh, J. A., McKenna, K. Y. A., & Fitzsimons, G. M. (2002). Can you see the real me? Activation and expression of the ''true self'' on the internet. *The Journal of Social Issues*, *58*(1), 33–48. doi:10.1111/1540-4560.00247

Burgoon, J. K. (1978). A communication model of personal space violation: Explication and an initial test. *Human Communication Research, 4*(2), 129–142. doi:10.1111/j.1468-2958.1978.tb00603.x

Chatterjee, P. (2001). Online reviews: Do consumers use them? *Advances in Consumer Research. Association for Consumer Research (U. S.), 28*(1), 129–133.

Duggan, M., Ellison, N. B., Lampe, C., Lenhart, A., & Madden, M. (2015). *Social media update2014.* Retrieved from http://www.pewinternet.org/2015/01/09/social-media-update-2014/

Ellison, N., Heino, R., & Gibbs, J. (2006). Managing impressions online: Self-presentation processes in the online dating environment. *Journal of CMC, 11*(2), 415–441.

Ellison, N. B., Hancock, J. T., & Toma, C. L. (2011). Profile as promise: A framework for conceptualizing veracity in online dating self-presentations. *New Media & Society, 14*(1), 45–62. doi:10.1177/1461444811410395

Gibbs, J. L., Ellison, N. B., & Heino, R. D. (2006). Self-presentation in online personals: The role of anticipated future interaction, self-disclosure, and perceived success in Internet dating. *Communication Research, 33*(2), 152–177. doi:10.1177/0093650205285368

Goffman, E. (1959). *The Presentation of Self in Everyday Life.* New York: Anchor Books.

Hancock, J. T., & Dunham, P. J. (2001). Impression formation in CMC revisited: An analysis of the breadth and intensity of impressions. *Communication Research, 28*(3), 325. doi:10.1177/009365001028003004

Hancock, J. T., & Toma, C. L. (2009). Putting your best face forward: The accuracy of online dating photographs. *Journal of Communication, 59*(2), 367–386. doi:10.1111/j.1460-2466.2009.01420.x

Hardey, M. (2002). Life beyond the screen: Embodiment and identity through the internet. *The Sociological Review, 50*(4), 570–585. doi:10.1111/1467-954X.00399

Ingoldsby, B. (2003). The mate selection process in the United States. In R. R. Hammon & B. B. Ingoldsby (Eds.), *Mate selection across cultures* (pp. 3–18). Thousand Oaks, CA: Sage Publications. doi:10.4135/9781452204628.n1

Lea, M., & Spears, R. (1995). Love at first byte? Building personal relationships over computer networks. In J. T. Wood & S. Duck (Eds.), *Under-studied relationships: off the beaten track. Understanding relationship processes series* (Vol. 6, pp. 197–233). Thousand Oaks, CA: SAGE Publications.

Merskin, D. L., & Huberlie, M. (1996). Companionship in the classifieds: The adoption of personal advertisements by daily newspapers. *Journalism & Mass Communication Quarterly, 73*(1), 219–229. doi:10.1177/107769909607300119

Morse, M. (2001). Virtually female: Body and code. In D. Trend (Ed.), *Reading digital culture* (pp. 87–97). Malden, MA: Blackwell Publishing.

Nakamura, L. (2001). Race in /For cyberspace: Identity tourism and racial passing on the Internet. In D. Trend (Ed.), *Reading digital culture* (pp. 226–235). Malden, MA: Blackwell Publishing.

O'Keefe, D. J. (2002). *Persuasion: Theory & research* (2nd ed.). Thousand Oaks, CA: Sage.

Poster, M. (2006). Postmodern virtualities. In M.G. Durham & D.M. Kellner (Eds.), Media and cultural studies: Keyworks (pp. 533-548). Malden, MA: Blackwell Publishing.

Rainie, L., Fox, S., & Duggan, M. (February 27, 2014). *The web at 25 in the U.S.* Retrieved from http://www.pewinternet.org/2014/02/25/the-web-at-25-in-the-u-s

Sher, P. J., & Lee, S. H. (2009). Consumer skepticism and online reviews: An Elaboration Likelihood Model perspective. *Social Behavior & Personality: An International Journal, 37*(1), 137–143. doi:10.2224/sbp.2009.37.1.137

Smith, A. (February 11, 2016). *15% of American adults have used online dating sites or mobile dating apps*. Retrieved from http://www.pewinternet.org/2016/02/11/15-percent-of-american-adults-have-used-online-dating-sites-or-mobile-dating-apps/

Smith, A., & Duggan, M. (October 21, 2013). *Online dating and relationships*. Retrieved from http://www.pewinternet.org/Reports/2013/Online-Dating.aspx

Stone, A. R. (2001). Will the real body please stand up? Boundary stories about virtual cultures. In D. Trend (Ed.), *Reading digital culture* (pp. 185–198). Malden, MA: Blackwell Publishing.

Strauss, A., & Corbin, J. (1994). Grounded Theory Methodology. In N. K. Denzin & Y. S. Lincoln (Eds.), *Handbook of qualitative research* (pp. 217–285). Thousand Oaks, CA: Sage.

Strauss, A., & Corbin, J. (1998). *Basics of qualitative research*. Thousand Oaks, CA: Sage Publications.

Tedeschi, B. (1999). E-commerce report; Consumer products are being reviewed on more web sites, some featuring comments from anyone with an opinion. *New York Times*, 16.

Toma, C. L., Hancock, J. T., & Ellison, N. B. (2008). Separating fact from fiction: An examination of deceptive self-presentation in online dating profiles. *Personality and Social Psychology Bulletin, 34*(8), 1023–1036. doi:10.1177/0146167208318067 PMID:18593866

Turkle, S. (2001). Who am we? In D. Trend (Ed.), *Reading digital culture* (pp. 236–250). Malden, MA: Blackwell Publishers.

Walther, J. B. (1996). CMC: Impersonal, interpersonal, and hyperpersonal interaction. *Communication Research, 23*(1), 3–43. doi:10.1177/009365096023001001

Walther, J. B., & Parks, M. R. (2002). Cues filtered out, cues filtered in: CMC and relationships. In M. L. Knapp & J. A. Daly (Eds.), *Handbook of interpersonal communication* (3rd ed.; pp. 529–563). Thousand Oaks, CA: Sage.

Whitty, M., & Carr, A. (2006). *Cyberspace romance: The psychology of online dating*. New York: Palgrave MacMillan.

Whitty, M. T. (2008). Revealing the 'real' me, searching for the 'actual' you: Presentations of self on an internet dating site. *Computers in Human Behavior, 24*(4), 1707–1723. doi:10.1016/j.chb.2007.07.002

KEY TERMS AND DEFINITIONS

Computer-Mediated Communication: Any communication between people that occurs via two or more electronic devices.

Hyperpersonal Communication: A theory of computer-mediated communication which argues that due to the limited and asynchronous cues in online interaction, people tend to create idealized images of themselves and others which can lead to intensified relationships.

Online Dating: Using web-based services for the purpose of seeking out and meeting romantic partners.

Perceived Source Credibility: Judgments made by a perceiver about the veracity of a communicator or communication.

Self-Presentation: The act of managing how other people perceive one's identity.

Warranting Principle: A theory of computer-mediated communication which argues that due to the anonymous nature of the internet, people are motivated to seek out cues to judge the accuracy of a another person's profile or information.

ENDNOTES

[1]   eDateReview.com has changed format since data was collected in 2013, thereby making it difficult to access and cite the reviews used in this analysis.

[2]   In order to maintain the integrity of the text posted on eDateReview.com, quotes are copied as they appear, including any spelling or grammatical errors. Posts are cited by the username given on eDateReview.com and the year that the post appeared on the site.

Chapter 12
Revenge of Cecil the Lion:
Credibility in Third-Party Review Sites

Alison N. Novak
Rowan University, USA

ABSTRACT

Digital media has seen a proliferation of Third-Party Review Sites (TPRS) that encourage the public to comment and reflect on their interactions and experiences with a retailer, brand, or company. Sites like Yelp build massive audiences based on their credibility as authentic, accurate, external reviewers. This study looks at how the co-opting of TPRS pages by advocates and protesters influences public perceptions of credibility on these sites. Specifically, it explores the public's reaction to Yelp as a digital space of protest after the death of Cecil the Lion at the hands of a Minnesota dentist. Through focus groups, this study identifies that TPRS audiences look for consistency in reviews to determine credibility; the public sees advocacy as harming the credibility of the overall site; current events play a role in the interpretation of TPRS; and the intentions of users is key to building a reputation as credible in digital media.

INTRODUCTION

As digital spaces proliferate, representing nearly every organization and company, concerns regarding digital credibility and trustworthiness have also grown. An additional challenge originates from user-generated websites that allow the public to report on their interactions and experiences. Sites such as Yelp, Google Reviews, and Peeple serve as a type of contemporary consumer report, except this content is posted with little editing, proofing, or checking for accuracy; therefore, a current challenge in reputation management lies in what occurs in these digital spaces.

One such iteration of this online challenge occurred in August 2015 following the high-profile death of Cecil the Lion at the bow and arrow of Dr. Walter Palmer, a dentist in Bloomington, Minnesota. Following intense media coverage of the lion hunt in Hwange National Park in Zimbabwe, Yelp users took to the site to write thousands of scathing reviews of Dr. Palmer and his practice, River Bluff Dental. Rather than focus on his services and medical practice, online commenters used the platform to critique his action, behavior, and non-medical activities. Shortly after, Dr. Palmer closed his practice, citing the

DOI: 10.4018/978-1-5225-1072-7.ch012

damage to his online reputation as motivation. Eventually, Yelp released a statement asking users to turn their attention to "Yelp Talk" and leave "Yelp.com" to actual reviews of dental service.

This is one of many instances of Yelp and other Third-Party Review Sites (TPRS) being used for purposes other than actual service/product reviews. Previous scholarship has used this as evidence to question the validity and accuracy of all review websites. However, few studies have explored how events like Cecil the Lion may influence the public's perception of the helpfulness of TPRS.

This study looks at the public's views of these TPRS (such as Yelp), specifically investigating the credibility of online reviews in person-to-group communication. Through a series of focus groups, the public is asked to react to the perceived accuracy, trustworthiness, and reliability of online reviews. To achieve this, focus groups will be asked to reflect on examples, such as River Bluff Dental, as well as other (less-dramatized and mediated) cases. Based on the results, a series of criteria will be developed that reflect how the public judges the credibility of online reviews. It specifically answers: how does the public determine if an online review is credible? What factors lead to an online review being accurate, reliable, or trustworthy? This study holds implications for those studying digital credibility, reputation management, and online group communication.

Yelp is an important, yet controversial, platform for public relations because of its ability to provide potential customers with information that is perceived as objective and unbiased (Sher & Lee, 2009). By compiling and averaging reviews from previous customers, users get direct insight into the retail experience (Jensen et al., 2013). However, this means that account managers must continually monitor TPRS to ensure accuracy, clarity, and that negative information is not overwhelmingly obvious (Baek, Ahn, & Choi, 2012). Therefore, management of TPRS is one tenant of digital credibility and reputation management.

Review of Literature

TPRS are digital spaces that allow the public to give feedback and assess the success of a business, organization, individual, or brand (Talmage, 2012; Park, Gu, & Lee, 2012). Third-party reviewers are any member of the public who is not employed by the organization, which means that reviewers are often clients, customers, and members from the surrounding community. Sites are run and monitored by an external party to the entity being reviewed. Generally, TPRS offer many entities such as companies, brands, and specific retail locations to review, and the public is encouraged to provide honest, thoughtful feedback regarding recent or past experiences (Park, Gu, & Lee, 2012; Gerhards, 2015).

Previous research has identified a myriad of reasons that the public may visit or contribute a review to a TPRS (Sher & Lee, 2009; Hardey, 2010; Gerhards, 2015). Primarily, users turn to TPRS for accurate and honest reviews on products and businesses they are considering engaging, purchasing, or working with (Hardey, 2010). Hardey's (2010) work on healthcare review sites found that the public was more likely to trust the content on a TPRS than a review featured on the company's own website. Users trust the third-party information because they believe the company has less ability to manipulate, edit, or feature positive references on these TPRS (Hardey, 2010). Hardey (2010) also found that users were not only more likely to trust them, but they were also more likely to act upon the information found there, particularly when making a purchasing decision. Users were likely to make purchases or visit a company that had more positive reviews than negative ones, reflecting the ability of third-party reviews to move through the hierarchy effects model from building awareness to resulting in a purchase (Craig et al., 2010).

Reader trust of TPRS develops from the intentions of contributors. Chen and Xie (2005) noted that contributors to TPRS view their own posts as a way to benefit the larger public. Users post reviews that share information they perceive as vital to the future experiences of another customer (Chen & Xie, 2005). This is why many reviews are phrased as warnings to readers and are crafted with the hope of persuading another user to either avoid or patron a business. Adams (2010) found that users who posted their own reviews were more likely to take seriously or be influenced when reading posts on other companies or businesses. Their continued interaction with the TPRS, over time, strengthens the effectiveness and power of other reviews, as they become more important to the user's decision making process (Adams, 2010).

Shaffer and Zettelmeyer (2002) reflected that TPRS are a contemporary type of Habermasian Public Sphere. In these digital spaces, users come together with the intentions of sharing information to benefit larger society (Shaffer & Zettelmeyer, 2002). While not a perfect model (the existence of trolls and cyberbullies complicates the system, for example), the primary intention of users is to share their own stories to help others make informed decisions (Shaffer & Zettelmeyer, 2002). Furthermore, TPRS reflect the public's desire to take control of a company's image from the powerful capabilities of advertising and public relations, instead providing other members of the public with an accurate, true, or honest depiction. Kim and Kim (2011) added that in 21st century society, the public is frustrated with the all-encompassing ability of public relations and advertising to control a company's image and hide its imperfections. TPRS are one way the public has begun to challenge this power and take control in crafting or contributing to a company's reputation (Kim & Kim, 2011).

However, recent literature challenges and problematizes the ability of TPRS to provide the public with honest and accurate descriptions of a company's service. Adams (2014) found that customers are more likely to provide a review if they have had a negative or bad experience. When looking at reviews of physicians, the majority of posts discussed problems that occurred with service or healthcare (Adams, 2014). Rather than seeing the full spectrum of customer experiences, users who turned to TPRS were likely to encounter more bad reviews than good ones (Levy et al., 2013). This can have negative effects on the reputation of the company being represented, as well as the general category or industry (Lin, Lee, & Horng, 2011). If review sites primarily reflect negative traits of all companies, it is possible the public will start to view the problems shared online as inherent to all companies within that industry. Much more research needs to be conducted to understand how this effect may happen, and to what extent.

Easily the most popular TPRS is Yelp.com. Yelp is the largest and most complete database of third-party reviews, and boasts 77.3 million reviews on 2.1 million businesses (Smith, 2015). Its reviews range from commercial retailers and mom-and-pop shops to medical practices such as Dr. Palmer's River Bluff Dental. Yelp was started in 2004 by former PayPal employees who wanted to feature the ubiquity and public-centered potential of the web. Reflecting Web 2.0 principles of inclusivity, and giving users a voice, Yelp was designed as a message board that encouraged the public to share their views, experiences, and perspectives on businesses and organizations (originally in the San Francisco area). Within a year of its creation, the site's popularity soared as the public continued to add reviews of retailers and businesses around the world. By 2009, Google expressed interest in buying Yelp for a rumored one billion dollars, although no deal was ever reached. Today, Google hosts its own reviewing platform called Google Reviews. Although Google Reviews is the second most visited TPRS in the world, it still only sees half of the monthly visitors of Yelp. As of September 2015, Yelp averaged close to 200 million unique visitors each month, and added approximately 1 million posts per month. Yelp is accessible via computer, mobile device, app, and interactive kiosks located in large cities around the world. Since its creation, Yelp has also added other features such as Eat24, which allows users to order food for delivery through their site (integrating customer reviews into the ordering process); Event Finder, which helps users locate meetups and events based on their interests; and Yelp Talk, an open message board which allows users to discuss current events, issues, and topics of interest.

Pertinent to Yelp's identity and value in third-party reviews is the way the site began. The site was originally funded through crowdsourcing efforts where the public was asked to provide small donations (usually under $20) to support the growth of Yelp. This public approach to business and finances adds legitimacy to Yelp being created "by and for the people." Rather than turning to big businesses, banks, or corporations to help the startup, its origins and reputation as a public-centered site were solidified by avoiding these traditional channels.

Kuehn's (2013) work suggested that the popularity and success of Yelp is related to ideas of neoliberal citizenship. Yelp turns the public into a type of labor force, who, by posting reviews, add to the success and profitability of the site (Sperber, 2014). In return, users believe they fulfill their duties as citizen consumers, thereby helping other customers and the larger public make informed decisions (Kuehn, 2013). Users see themselves as one part of a larger unit that, when working together, improves the experiences of the larger public (Sperber, 2014; Baek, Ahn, & Choi, 2012). By also benefitting from Yelp reviews when making their own consumer decisions, the circle of neoliberal citizenship is completed (Sperber, 2014).

Despite the multitude of research conducted on TPRS, little is known regarding how these sites maintain and enhance their own credibility. While few studies have specifically looked at TPRS, the larger idea of digital credibility is even more complicated when exploring a case where the site is manipulated for other purposes than just reflecting on customer service. In the case of Dr. Palmer's River Bluff Dental, Yelps reviews turned from focusing on his dental practice to his out-of-office activities. In this case, the public co-opted the Yelp platform and the notions of neoliberal citizenship to advocate for Cecil the Lion. The public was using Yelp to fulfill their neoliberal citizen consumer ideals, but not in the way the site managers intended. While this was not the only instance of Yelp or TPRS being co-opted, it does raise into question the credibility of the space. If users can turn Yelp's River Bluff Dental page into a space of advocacy and outrage for Cecil the Lion (in effect, a review of the dentist's personal values and beliefs rather than his abilities as a dentist), what does that mean for the honesty and accuracy of other reviews and pages on Yelp?

DIGITAL CREDIBILITY

Zhu, Yin, and He (2014) noted that credibility has changed dramatically in response to the same Web 2.0 and neoliberal ideals that first made Yelp popular. The presence and growing of TPRS suggests that customers want to gain control and power over the reputation, image, and success of a retailer (Sher & Lee, 2009). TPRS give customers a platform to share experiences and gain power over the effects of advertising and public relations (Jensen et al., 2013). By posting realistic stories, consumers can combat the glossy, perfected images crafted by public relations and advertising campaigns. However, this power can only be achieved if the site and the post are deemed credible by the larger public and other readers (Lin, Lee, & Horng, 2011). Thus, the notion of digital credibility is deeply entrenched in the success of Yelp and the public's treatment of Cecil the Lion.

Credibility is defined by Rains and Karmikel (2009) as the mechanism that builds trust between a digital source and a user. For a site or posting to be credible, it needs to be perceived as honest and accurate to the reader (Rains & Karmikel, 2009). In public relations, credibility is considered one of four principles (credibility, accuracy, trustworthiness, and reliability) of message effectiveness and persuasive ability (Johnson & Martin, 2010). Traditionally, credibility is achieved by aligning a message with another credible entity, suggesting that credibility is contextual rather than an objective quality. Credibility is determined by the readers as they consider the sender, medium, and environment of a message (Holladay et al., 2013). Digital credibility is similarly determined by the audience or readers. The audience looks for visual and textual cues (such as strong design and grammar/spelling skills), as well as the overall believability of the message.

However, perhaps more importantly to Yelp, credibility is determined by the consistency of a message with the platform. As noted, Yelp is viewed as a place for honest and accurate information about a company (Fan et al., 2013). It is perceived as credible enough to enact trust and be as a base of purchasing decisions. Therefore, messages posted on Yelp are also viewed as credible because they align with the mission, style, and norms of other Yelp posts. Subramaniam et al. (2015) contended that consistency is the most important element of digital credibility, especially on TPRS. Readers are not just looking at one or two reviews, they are looking for trends among a larger set of reviews to make a decision regarding a company. One or two bad reviews when compared to hundreds of positive ones are discredited because of their inconsistency with the larger set. Further, even businesses that only have one or two posts total can have reviews discredited if the review does not follow the traditional format of a Yelp review (such as providing details of an interaction, or proper documentation of the likert-scale rating system). Therefore, a Yelp review must have consistency both within a specific page (or business) as well as across the entire platform for it to be perceived as digitally credible (Jensen et al., 2010).

The Yelp River Bluff Dental page provides an interesting point of contention for the notion of consistency as a marker of credibility. Clearly, the manipulation of the Yelp page into an advocacy page for Cecil the Lion is not consistent with the stated purpose or normal practices on Yelp. Thus, an important question remains: What effect did this have on users' perceptions of the credibility of other reviews on Yelp, as well as the larger platform itself?

Determining credibility is also a social or group labor, not one that happens within a vacuum. Users on Yelp can rate the "helpfulness" of a review. Problematically, "helpfulness" is not an operationalized term by Yelp, and some researchers have concluded that this is more likely a measure of how credible the public sees the review (Ewing, 2013). Reviews that have higher "helpfulness" (credibility) ratings are elevated to the top of the page, becoming one of the first things a user sees when they open a business's page (Baek, Ahn, & Choi, 2012). Further, digital credibility is considered a learned practice, one that is either taught in school or enacted through acculturation (French, Garry, and Mori, & 2011). Thus, to study how users make decisions about the credibility of TPRS, a method that allows for a group or social setting—such as focus groups—is necessary.

The credibility of an organization is often tied to its success and longevity in public relations research (Pang et al., 2014). Ivanov et al. (2013) found that organizations that struggle to establish themselves as credible also have difficulty introducing a new product, maintaining long-term customers/users, or controlling the use and image of its brand(s). Shortly after Cecil the Lion's media coverage, Dr. Palmer closed his dental practice, reinforcing the power a public relations crisis can have on a business. However, while it is clear that this crisis resulted in bad business for Dr. Palmer, what effect did it have on Yelp? Within hours of the thousands of Yelp reviews being posted on River Bluff Dental, Yelp locked the page and directed its users to Yelp Talk. Clearly, management was concerned that this co-opting and inconsistency of platform use may negatively impact Yelp, but it is unclear if this actually occurred. No research yet exists looking at how the co-opting of Yelp's page for social advocacy purposes influences the credibility of TPRS. This study seeks to fill this void.

Digital Reputation Management

Yelp's credibility is also challenged by other public relations efforts to manage the digital reputation of businesses. Lim and Van Der Heide (2015) found evidence of employees and owners of businesses submitting fake or false reviews of their own companies in an effort to improve their rating. While Yelp users cannot create anonymous accounts, it is relatively easy to set up a fake account by using a pseudonym and free email account (like Gmail). While suspicious reviews can be questioned and even removed by Yelp management, Lim and Van Der Heide (2015) concluded that many go unnoticed. This possibility has not escaped the attention of the public either, who note that one of their concerns when trusting Yelp lies in the possibility that the "strangers" on the other end may be in public relations or somehow actually working for the company they are reviewing (Lim & Van Der Heide, 2015).

Fake accounts are not only a problem when employees post on behalf of their own business, but also when they post false (negative) reviews on competitor pages. Bluebond (2014) argued that defamation is one of the leading concerns on TPRS. Because it is difficult to get accurate identifying information for a user, it is possible that negative reviews are fabricated, exaggerated, or manipulated with the intention of hurting a business's reputation. Gerhards (2015) added that there are few ways of challenging (either through Yelp or through the legal system) defamation that occurs on these sites. Proving defamation in court or even just deleting a bad post can take six months and legal fees.

Yelp, as the largest and most popular TPRS, has literal infinite possibilities for bored users, ex-employees, and competitors to post false or harmful reviews, thus reinforcing the need to understand how credibility is understood by readers. In the aftermath of Cecil the Lion's death, users posted thousands of "reviews" of Dr. Palmer, criticizing everything from his hunting hobbies, to his masculinity, to his physical appearance—content far outside the normal scope of Yelp reviews. While an extreme case, understanding how these reviews influence the larger credibility of Yelp may be an important component of the TPRS's future success.

METHOD

To conduct this study, a series of focus groups was conducted to learn about how instances like Cecil the Lion influence the credibility of TPRS. Dr. Walter Palmer and River Bluff Dental were selected as a focus for this study because of the widespread media coverage the lion hunt received, as well as the clear co-opting of Yelp's site. On July 1, 2015, Dr. Palmer traveled to Zimbabwe to participate in a lion hunt using bow-and-arrow hunting techniques (Matthews, 2016). Over a week-long period, Dr. Palmer and a paid hunting team lured Cecil the Lion away from the protected Hwange National Park in Zimbabwe into unprotected territory. Dr. Palmer wounded the animal with a bow strike to the abdomen approximately 40 hours before the lion was fatally wounded with a rifle (BBC, 2016). Cecil was an international attraction in Hwange National Park. He was prominently featured on park and national recreational literature and was part of an ongoing Oxford University research project looking at the traveling patterns of mature black-mane lions. Although Dr. Palmer had obtained legal permission to hunt lions in Zimbabwe, luring a lion from protected territory like Hwange National Park is illegal (Allison, 2015). Two weeks after Cecil's death, Dr. Palmer posted photos of the deceased lion on his Facebook page. Within hours, the lion was identified as Cecil and shared by social media users on Facebook, Twitter, and Tumblr more than 10,000 times. This sudden online presence prompted traditional international media (e.g., CNN, Al Jazeera, and the BBC) to investigate and add coverage. Although Dr. Palmer removed the post from his own Facebook account, he was almost instantly identified as the responsible hunter. By July 28th, international animal rights groups were demanding punishment for Dr. Palmer and were upset that the slow-moving legal process in Zimbabwe allowed the hunter to return to the United States instead of facing charges. In an effort to obtain justice for Cecil, these groups asked the public to take to the Internet to voice concern and demand justice.

The earliest posts on River Bluff Dental's Yelp page that referred to Cecil the Lion occurred on July 14, 2015, just hours after Dr. Palmer was identified by the media. Original posts were written as messages to the doctor such as "you should be ashamed of yourself" and "why did you kill Cecil?" Far from the normal use of Yelp, these posts referred to Dr. Palmer's personal life and not his dental practice or services. Further, they are written directly to the dentist, not to other readers and members of the public. By August 14, 2015 (one month later), nearly 10,000 posts were added to River Bluff Dental's page discussing his hunting of Cecil. Importantly, the majority of these posts (approximately 95%) were negative, perhaps reinforcing Adams (2010) finding that Yelp and third-party content is primarily negative in nature. On August 15, 2015, Yelp officially removed the majority of these posts, asking users to turn their attention to Yelp Talk to debate social issues and advocacy, and leave Yelp.com to official reviews of the organization. This did not, however, prevent Yelp users from continuing to post their comments on Yelp. Many users were unhappy with Yelp's policy of removing posts that referenced Cecil's death (Glaze, 2016). One user wrote on October 8, 2015, "Yelp is gonna go out of business for protecting this one bad customer of their [sic]." Users like this directly mentioned Yelp's business practices and analyzed their deletion of content as a form of protection for Dr. Palmer. Other posts similarly questioned who Yelp was trying to protect and work on behalf of: Dr. Palmer or the public? Again, such responses illustrate the bind that Yelp faced in its response to addressing what the entire site is built on—user-generated content—and reinforces the need to study how TPRS manage their own credibility during highly publicized controversies like Cecil the Lion.

Because digital credibility is often a feature of group decision-making and group learning processes, qualitative focus groups were used for this study. Focus groups allow researchers to look at group interactions surrounding a topic such as Yelp and credibility. Further, their qualitative and reflexive format allows researchers to modify and tailor questions to each group, based on their interests, previous knowledge, and points of further inquiry. For this project, a series of five focus groups were held for approximately one hour each. Each focus group contained between six and ten participants (42 participants total) who were selected based on their response to a pre-selection survey that said they used Yelp at least once in the past month (August 2015). This criterion insured that participants would be familiar with the platform and the type of content found on the site. Focus groups were held in September 2015. Participants ranged from 18 to 54 years-old; 45% male and 55% female; and 75% were residents of New Jersey, Pennsylvania, or New York. Participants were not compensated for their participation in the focus group. Focus groups were held on the campus of a large regional public university in the greater Philadelphia area. For this study, the researcher served as the focus group moderator, although an external observer was used to improve the reliability of the analysis and results. A copy of the initial schedule of questions for the focus groups is included as Appendix A. As a qualitative method, these questions evolved over time to build on the participants' previous answers.

Ultimately, these focus groups were held to identify how the public analyzes the credibility of TPRS in the wake of highly publicized co-option of the digital space. As an investigation of digital credibility, it specifically aims to answer two research questions: What guidelines or framework does the public invoke when determining the credibility of TPRS? What impact does the co-option of the site, like the posts found on River Bluff Dental's page, have on the credibility of reviews?

Focus Group Results

While the focus groups covered a myriad of topics related to TPRS, the results focus on how users understand, analyze, and interpret the site's credibility. In total, four themes emerged as the participants discussed how they understood Yelp and other TPRS digital credibility. These results include: credibility as consistency, discrediting the advocacy public, current event immediacy, and credibility in intentionality.

Credibility as Consistency

Consistency was easily the most reported means of determining credibility on Yelp and other TPRS in these focus groups. Participants reflected that they nearly always considered the larger body of reviews before determining whether one was credible. For example, one participant added, "I always look at the average reviews instead of whatever review is pushed to the top of the list so I can see what most people think. When you look at just one, it's possible that it doesn't reflect the average experience." Repeatedly, participants concluded that the average review statistics were the best means of determining the quality of an organization. One participant concluded, "look, you're probably going to have an average interaction with a company, so why not look at just the average review stats to see what that might be like." Implicit in this theme is the acknowledgment that there are extreme reviews present on TPRS. Rather than individually reviewing each post, users count on tools like the average statistics to determine the overall quality.

However, one participant challenged her group by asking what they did in situations where a company or organization only had one or two reviews. She proposed that in these cases the statistical findings were relatively worthless because readers could only average one or two data points, one or both of which could easily be an overly positive or negative reaction. Other participants agreed that in such cases they had to actually read the reviews to determine whether they were credible. For example, one participant reflected, "You've got to look at each post if there are just a few of them to see if they seem legit. You know, are they all saying the same thing. If they are, then they are probably credible and you should listen." The idea of credibility was directly tied to consistency in the reviews. Consistency, when operationalized by the participants meant asking if the general "narrative of reviews" is the same. A participant added, "Consistency means are all the posts saying the same kind of thing. Maybe not the exact words or examples, but the gist of it." Nearly uniformly, participants directly reflected on internal consistency within each company or organization. When they mention "the posts," they reference posts within one page, not the entire site. While previous research has identified that users' look at both the internal and external consistency of a post, the respondents here only supported internal checks within an organization's page (Jensen et al., 2010).

Further, the participants acknowledged the more reviews a company or organization had, the more credible the information was. One participant added, "Ok, if there is only one post, it's a lot harder to see if it's trustworthy. Like, that one post might just be one person who had a really bad day. If I say it's credible and follow it, I might miss out on something." Consistency and credibility were tied to the number of posts a company or organization received. However, when asked how many posts would qualify as enough, the focus groups struggled to find consensus. For example, many participants were quick to suggest that between five and ten reviews would be enough to check for consistency and improve credibility; however, other participants were hesitant to suggest any number at all. One participant reflected, "I think it depends on who you are reviewing. If you review a major store like Wal-Mart, than I expect to see a huge, unlimited number of reviews. If I don't, I'd be suspicious that some were deleted. But, for a small store, seeing too many posts might make me think they are fake or put up by the owners." Again, participants reflected on the subjective nature of consistency and credibility, arguing that the analysis of credibility is contextually tied to the organization and environment. This reinforces Holladay et al.'s (2013) findings that credibility is a contextual element rather than an objectively reached claim. This idea will be further analyzed in upcoming sections.

Discrediting the Advocacy Public

Building off the conversation surrounding discrediting posts, each group was asked how they identified a review that was not credible. Instantly, all groups offered examples of posts they read that were "questionable," "bad," or "clearly not credible." One participant summarized their group by adding "a review isn't credible if it seems like the person has an axe-to-grind, like if they want revenge or something." Personal examples ranged from reviews given by disgruntled former employees to clearly fabricated or exaggerated stories by angry customers. However, one participant brought up advocacy groups that "take over the page" to share their ideas and philosophies. One participant identified the South Windsor, Connecticut gun store that sold guns to Adam Lanza, the perpetrator of the Sandy Hook Elementary School shooting in 2012. In the aftermath of the violence that killed 20 children and multiple teachers, gun control advocates took to Yelp to protest the gun store and demand stronger preventative policies on gun sales. The participant reflected, "It's, like, ok if you want to be against guns and tell the world that Sandy Hook was wrong, but that's not what Yelp is for. When you take over like that, you make it harder for the customers to see if it's a good store or not. You make the whole page less credible because I can't tell who is a protester and an actual reviewer." This participant argues that the advocacy public, who use Yelp as a way to share their position and digitally protest, takes away from the credibility of the entire page (like the South Windsor Gun Store) because it is more difficult to determine who is reviewing their experience instead of pushing a social agenda. Other participants reacted to this example by adding that advocacy groups should not use Yelp because separate spaces for advocacy groups exist and should be used instead. However, when asked where these online spaces were, no participants could give a concrete answer.

Building off the discussion of advocacy groups, the participants were asked if they were familiar with Cecil the Lion and his relationship to Yelp. Only two participants said they did not previously know about it (although this number is most likely a reflection of the self-reporting bias that often occurs in social methods like focus groups); other group members were asked to describe the case to the unfamiliar participants. In each description, the advocacy groups were identified as "hunting protestors," "gun control groups," and "animal rights people" who protested Cecil's death on Yelp. While only five participants added that they had visited Dr. Palmer's Yelp page, most others noted they were familiar with the case. The moderator then asked if the advocacy posts were examples of credible reviews. Participants again struggled to find consensus in their answers.

Several participants reinforced earlier comments that advocates should take their protest to other places. One participant added, "Yelp isn't for protesting hunting. If you want to protest something, protest the guy's bad dental service. Take your protest to Facebook where it belongs." Another participant added, "Protest reviews aren't credible because they come from a place that wants to hurt the guy's business. It's not trying to help anyone, just take it out on that one dentist." Here, the participants again reinforce the desire to isolate the advocacy public from those who want to provide an "accurate" review. The intentions of the advocacy public are identified as different from the general point of a Yelp review. However, one participant challenged this by asking, "but, like, isn't the regular point of Yelp to influence somebody's business? It might not be over a social issue, but we post reviews because we want other people to shop there or avoid there- isn't that kinda the same thing?" Here, the participant questions the nature of advocacy and the difference between the advocacy appearing on River Bluff Dental and South Windsor Gun Store pages and the type of consumer advocacy that appears throughout the rest of Yelp. This is an important aspect of digital credibility, as it invokes the normal practices of TPRS. The original participant responded (to the nonverbal agreement of the group), "yeah, but, like, normally you have to have a personal experience to review on Yelp, not just a general philosophical difference."

Other participants also questioned the credibility of these advocacy posts. Several participants added that they were impressed by the use of Yelp to protest. One added, "I think it's genius. Everybody sees Yelp, and if the guy's practice was going to close, like why not use Yelp to share your message? By putting a protest in a place it doesn't belong, it's probably more effective." The advocacy public is applauded in these reflections regarding its co-option of the space, the same practice that discredited the South Windsor Gun Store. When asked if this same practice discredited the rest of Yelp reviews on River Bluff Dental's page, the participant responded, "I mean, yeah, of course, like, those statistics go right out the window, and it's probably a lot harder to find the real reviews. All of a sudden, you can't trust any of what is said because you don't know if it's coming from a protestor or a real person." The reflection on how protest may influence the credibility of the site justifies Yelp's actions on the River Bluff Dental page. By allowing advocates to protest the death of Cecil the Lion, all other reviews of Dr. Palmer are discredited--even those provided well before the controversy. In order to protect the credibility of the posts, advocacy posts had to be removed by Yelp.

Each focus group was then asked if this hurt the credibility of other pages featured on Yelp, such as other dental practices. Participants largely agreed that if advocacy continued to show up on Yelp, the credibility of the whole site might be hurt. One participant summarized the group by saying "too much protest on Yelp might hurt my trust of other reviews. Like if it happened on the dentist's page, how can I make sure that other pages haven't been attacked by protesters as well?" The participants agreed that, while somewhat innovative, the advocacy appearing on Yelp hurt the entire site's credibility. One participant added, "You've got to be aware when using Yelp. There are loads of problems with people posting fake reviews, so you have to take everything on there with a grain of salt." The presence of advocacy and fake posts puts the credibility of the entire site in jeopardy, not just the page it appears on.

When discussing the advocacy public, the notion of the neoliberal citizenship is referenced. Participants suggested that normal reviews are posted for the "good of the public" and "trying to help each other out." Reviews are designed to inform readers and help them make better decisions. Like neo-liberal citizenship, this reason for posting also references the desire to help users and the public challenge the bias appearing in public relations and advocacy. This is perhaps what causes some of the problem with advocacy and protest posts. These posts reflect a desire to promote personal ideals and philosophies by advocating for, or against, social issues. Similar to the aims and intentions of public relations and advertising, the advocacy public is in direct opposition to the goals of neoliberal citizenship. This will be further analyzed in coming sections.

CURRENT EVENT IMMEDIACY

Throughout the groups, there was an overwhelming reference to current events as a feature of the environment of determining credibility. When asked if Cecil the Lion advocacy on Yelp would influence the public's perception of the TPRS, one participant noted, "Probably for a short time, but then things can go back to normal." The notion of immediacy and current events continually occurred, noting that credibility changes overtime. Current events might influence how people assess if Yelp is credible today, but tomorrow, if the event is "forgotten," then the public might go back to trusting Yelp.

Another participant added that credibility has to be assessed daily. He added, "The day before Cecil was killed, the Dentist's page was probably pretty credible with posts from former customers. But, the day after, the page was filled with posts from protesters who never heard of the guy before that day. You never know when a current event might impact the credibility." This reinforces the need to look at credibility as an environmental concept, determined not just by the information within each post, but also what current events might dictate the content and bias appearing in posts. In essence, each review space is in constant flux (almost like the weather), and users need to constantly keep an eye out on current (and emerging) conditions to assess the credibility of reviews. When asked what other current events might influence the credibility of posts and how they view Yelp, participants mentioned "Crimes committed by the business owners and employees" (even those not related to the business) and "Awards people might win outside of work." These good and bad examples of current events were described as potentially influencing the public to provide Yelp reviews that were unrelated to actual service or experiences and more reflective of the current situation of those affiliated with the organization.

The use of the term "immediate" repeatedly occurred throughout each group, as almost all participants agreed that current events could influence the credibility of posts. However, participants were challenged to provide an actual timeline of this effect. Most participants reflected that it was likely an effect of the severity and intensity of the current event. For example, one participant concluded "It depends on what the current event is. Like the dentist's case went on for a long time, so his Yelp page was influenced for a long time. Some stories barely get one day of media coverage, so the Yelp page might go back to normal in a couple of weeks." Importantly, participants reflected that it was nearly always possible for the credibility of a page or site to make a comeback, even after particularly nasty media coverage or a negative current event. One participant noted, "Even if there are a few posts by somebody who is advocating for something, Yelp will probably take them down in a couple of days, and you can go back to trusting the content." Thus, in line once again with what Holladay et al. (2013) concluded, credibility is a contextual guideline, and non-business events are nonetheless part of a business's overall context.

Credibility in Intentionality

Intrinsic to the discussion of current events and advocacy is the reflection on the intentions of the user providing a review. Those who post advocacy messages on Yelp are viewed as less credible because of their intentions to influence the public perception of a company or organization. One participant reflected, "Credibility is all about how good a person's intentions are. Are you posting because you want to help people make a good decision about where to buy something, or are you trying to influence me to take up a social cause so that you have more support for your own beliefs?" Here, advocacy posts are discredited because the intentions of their creators are different from that of the normal use of Yelp.

Importantly, a focus on community versus personal benefit was emphasized in these reflections. Groups concluded that posts seeking to help other users make informed decisions were credible because of the intention to provide accurate information to help the Yelp community. Whether a good or bad review, users who entered Yelp with this intention were more likely to provide credible information. However, those who sought to influence the public for personal gain were discredited by readers. A frequent example discussed within groups was business owners who posted favorable reviews on their own pages or negative reviews on competitor pages. These users had personal gain intentions for providing these reviews, thus biasing their comments and preventing accurate information from being shared.

Interestingly, advocacy posts like those appearing on behalf of Cecil the Lion were also ruled as discreditable. Despite the agreement that these advocates believed they were working towards the public good, their use of the platform and emotional intentions behind the post were incongruent with the purpose of Yelp. Similar to the theme of consistency, here participants believed that the reviewer's intentions towards helping people make informed purchasing decisions on Yelp were fundamental in deciding if information was credible. The advocacy posters did not share this intention, and thus their reviews were not credible. For example, one participant added, "A credible review of the dentist should look at how he treats his patients. That would help people make a decision to go to him or not." Other group members cited the continued reviews of Dr. Palmer, even after he closed his practice, as evidence of these inconsistent intentions. One participant summarized, "If they really wanted to help people decide on a dentist visit, they wouldn't have a reason to keep posting after he closed his doors."

Further, the emotions of advocacy users were noted as a challenge to the credibility of their posts. Many participants reflected that a post written by someone who was too emotional about the death of Cecil the Lion was deemed as discreditable. One participant added, "A good post has to be unbiased and objective. If you are crying about Cecil's death when writing it, it's probably not credible." Credible posts were deemed as written with the intentions of helping other Yelp users, not as an emotional venting space. Advocacy posts were deemed too emotional and thus not credible.

DISCUSSION

The four themes, credibility as consistency, discrediting the advocacy public, current event immediacy, and credibility in intentionality demonstrate the effect that cases like Cecil the Lion can have on the credibility of a TPRS. Throughout the five focus groups, the participants reinforced the notions of neoliberal citizenship, context, and environmental considerations of credibility. The guidelines and framework invoked by users when determining the credibility of these sites is identified through the four themes emerged from the focus groups. First, credibility is a feature of consistent reviews, especially when looking internally at posts on a page. Users look at the statistical features of these sites to find consistent ratings and average out the extreme results. Participants acknowledged that extreme results, such as highly negative or positive reviews, were a norm of TPRS, but they viewed the averages as a more credible source of information. Second, credibility is a feature of the intentions of a reviewer. Reviewers with too much emotion, those seeking personal gain, or those not helping the larger community were discreditable because of the bias this may cause within their posts. Finally, credibility was a function of context and current events. Looking at what else is happening (within the media or public sphere) helps determine if a post is credible. Topics and organizations tied to current events may be less credible because reviews may be reflective of the environment rather than a specific interaction.

TPRS must maintain their credibility as a source of information for users seeking to make purchase and engagement decisions. Participants reflected that neoliberal citizenship, where contributors intend on helping other community members with these decisions, is a fundamental consideration when determining whether these sites provide credible information. Therefore, it is pertinent for those responsible with site management to create site affordances that reinforce neoliberal citizenship intentions. Thus, although users protested and were angered by the removal of advocacy posts on River Bluff Dental, according to these focus groups, it was a necessary action by Yelp administrators to help preserve the credibility of the site.

Finally, an important development from this study was the reference terms for credibility that developed. Participants used terms such "trustworthy" and "accuracy" interchangeably with credibility. These terms of reference reflect the fluid nature of credibility with other complementary concepts. As Johnson and Martin (2010) identified, credibility is one of four pillars of message effectiveness, along with accuracy, trustworthiness, and reliability. Therefore, an important area of future research would be to look at how these four pillars are further related in TPRS. It is also critical to note that a "credible post" was also rhetorically interchanged with a "good post" frequently throughout the focus groups. Good posts were considered trustworthy, accurate, and helpful to readers. While "good" was not an operationalized term in this study, future research could further look at this connection.

The focus groups were also an important area of vocabulary development. The groups frequently referred to an "advocacy public," which they identified as those members of the public who used Yelp to share their personal beliefs or advocate for Cecil the Lion. While the concept of public advocacy has been studied throughout public relations research, the term "advocacy public" is somewhat unique to these focus groups. More research exploring this group and the perceptions of how an advocacy public can shape the digital ethos of specific websites is necessary.

Finally, it is clear that the co-option of the site, such as the posts found on River Bluff Dental's page, did have an effect of the credibility of Yelp. While participants primarily examined the immediate impact, more research is necessary looking for longitudinal effects.

CONCLUSION

In the aftermath of Cecil the Lion's death, Dr. Walter Palmer and River Bluff Dental became the focus of international debate and public outrage. By co-opting Yelp, the public advocated for Cecil, dramatically changing and challenging the nature of the TPRS. Through focus groups, this study determined that events like Cecil the Lion's death influence the credibility of sites such as Yelp because Web 2.0 allows for users to bring personal agendas into public discourse and open spaces. As credibility continues to play an important role in the popularity, use, and lifetime of TPRS, more research will be necessary to determine the role of larger contexts on specific elements of credibility that may not, on the surface, appear to be related.

REFERENCES

Adams, A. K. (2014). The Third-Party notification dilemma. *The Hastings Center Report*, *44*(s3), S31–S32. doi:10.1002/hast.339 PMID:25043470

Adams, S. A. (2010). Revisiting the online health information reliability debate in the wake of "Web 2.0": An inter-disciplinary literature and website review. *International Journal of Medical Informatics, 79*(6), 391–400. doi:10.1016/j.ijmedinf.2010.01.006 PMID:20188623

Allison, S. (2015, Dec 25). Man who identified Cecil the Lion's killer vows death will not be in vain. *The Guardian.* Retrieved, January 23, 2016, from http://www.theguardian.com/environment/2015/dec/25/cecil-the-lion-zimbabwe-conservation-johnny-rodrigues

Baek, H., Ahn, J., & Choi, Y. (2012). Helpfulness of online consumer reviews: Readers' objectives and review cues. *International Journal of Electronic Commerce, 17*(2), 99–126. doi:10.2753/JEC1086-4415170204

BBC.com. (2016, Feb 1). *Lions rediscovered in Ethiopia's Alatash game park.* BBC.com. Retrieved February 22, 2016, from http://www.bbc.com/news/world-africa-35460573

Bluebond, A. (2014). When the customer is wrong: Defamation, interactive websites, and immunity. *Review of Litigation, 33*(3), 679.

Chen, Y., & Xie, J. (2005). Third-party product review and firm marketing strategy. *Marketing Science, 24*(2), 218–240. doi:10.1287/mksc.1040.0089

Craig, C. L., Bauman, A., & Reger-Nash, B. (2010). Testing the hierarchy of effects model: ParticipACTION's serial mass communication campaigns on physical activity in Canada. *Health Promotion International, 25*(1), 14–23. doi:10.1093/heapro/dap048 PMID:19875461

Ewing, L. A. (2013). Rhetorically analyzing online composition spaces. *Pedagogy, 13*(3), 554–561. doi:10.1215/15314200-2266477

Fan, Y., Miao, Y., Fang, Y., & Lin, R. (2013). Establishing the adoption of electronic word-of-mouth through consumers' perceived credibility. *International Business Research, 6*(3), 58. doi:10.5539/ibr.v6n3p58

French, L., Garry, M., & Mori, K. (2011). Relative—not absolute—judgments of credibility affect susceptibility to misinformation conveyed during discussion. *Acta Psychologica, 136*(1), 119–128. doi:10.1016/j.actpsy.2010.10.009 PMID:21112042

Gerhards, E. V. (2015). Your store is gross! how recent cases, the FTC, and state consumer protection laws can impact a franchise system's response to negative, defamatory, or fake online reviews. *Franchise Law Journal, 34*(4), 503.

Glaze, B. (2016, March 1). Victory for animal welfare campaigners after National Wildlife Crime Unit is saved. *The Mirror, UK.* Retrieved March 15, 2016, from http://www.mirror.co.uk/news/uk-news/victory-animal-welfare-campaigners-after-7469532

Hardey, M. (2010). Consuming professions: User-review websites and health services. *Journal of Consumer Culture, 10*(1), 129–149. doi:10.1177/1469540509355023

Holladay, S. J., & Coombs, W. T. (2013). Public relations literacy: Developing critical consumers of public relations. *Public Relations Inquiry, 2*(2), 125–146. doi:10.1177/2046147X13483673

Ivanov, B., Sims, J., & Parker, K. (2013). Leading the way in new product introductions: Publicity's message sequencing success with corporate credibility and image as moderators. *Journal of Public Relations Research*, 25(5), 442–466. doi:10.1080/1062726X.2013.795862

Jensen, M. L., Averbeck, J. M., Zhang, Z., & Wright, K. B. (2013). Credibility of anonymous online product reviews: A language expectancy perspective. *Journal of Management Information Systems*, 30(1), 293–324. doi:10.2753/MIS0742-1222300109

Jensen, M. L., Lowry, P. B., Burgoon, J. K., & Nunamaker, J. F. (2010). Technology dominance in complex decision making: The case of aided credibility assessment. *Journal of Management Information Systems*, 27(1), 175–202. doi:10.2753/MIS0742-1222270108

Johnson, M., & Martin, K. (2010). Digital credibility & digital dynamism in public relations blogs. *Visual Communication Quarterly*, 17(3), 162–174. doi:10.1080/15551393.2010.502475

Kim, K., & Kim, J. (2011). Third-party privacy certification as an online advertising strategy: An investigation of the factors affecting the relationship between third-party certification and initial trust. *Journal of Interactive Marketing*, 25(3), 145–158. doi:10.1016/j.intmar.2010.09.003

Kuehn, K. M. (2013). "There's got to be a review democracy": Communicative capitalism, neoliberal citizenship and the politics of participation on the consumer evaluation website yelp.com. *International Journal of Communication*, 7(1), 607–625.

Levy, S. E., Duan, W., & Boo, S. (2013). An analysis of one-star online reviews and responses in the Washington, D.C., lodging market. *Cornell Hospitality Quarterly*, 54(1), 49–63. doi:10.1177/1938965512464513

Lim, Y., & Van Der Heide, B. (2015). Evaluating the wisdom of strangers: The perceived credibility of online consumer reviews on yelp. *Journal of Computer-Mediated Communication*, 20(1), 67–82. doi:10.1111/jcc4.12093

Lin, C., Lee, S., & Horng, D. (2011). The effects of online reviews on purchasing intention: The moderating role of need for cognition. *Social Behavior and Personality*, 39(1), 71–81. doi:10.2224/sbp.2011.39.1.71

Matthews, M. (2016, Feb 4). Still upset about Cecil the Lion? Mobile group joins worldwide protest. *Alabama News*. Retrieved February 22, 2016, from http://www.al.com/news/mobile/index.ssf/2016/02/still_upset_about_cecil_the_li.html

Pang, A., Begam Binte Abul Hassan, N., & Chee Yang Chong, A. (2014). Negotiating crisis in the social media environment: Evolution of crises online, gaining credibility offline. *Corporate Communications*, 19(1), 96–118. doi:10.1108/CCIJ-09-2012-0064

Park, J., Gu, B., & Lee, H. (2012). The relationship between retailer-hosted and third-party hosted WOM sources and their influence on retailer sales. *Electronic Commerce Research and Applications*, 11(3), 253–261. doi:10.1016/j.elerap.2011.11.003

Rains, S. A., & Karmikel, C. D. (2009). Health information-seeking and perceptions of website credibility: Examining web-use orientation, message characteristics, and structural features of websites. *Computers in Human Behavior*, 25(2), 544–553. doi:10.1016/j.chb.2008.11.005

Shaffer, G., & Zettelmeyer, F. (2002). When good news about your rival is good for you: The effect of third-party information on the division of channel profits. *Marketing Science, 21*(3), 273–293. doi:10.1287/mksc.21.3.273.137

Sher, P. J., & Lee, S. (2009). Consumer skepticism and online reviews: An elaboration likelihood model perspective. *Social Behavior and Personality: An International Journal, 37*(1), 137–143. doi:10.2224/sbp.2009.37.1.137

Smith, C. (2015, May 13). 45 amazing Yelp Statistics. *Digital Marketing Research.* Retrieved September 12, 2015 from http://expandedramblings.com/index.php/yelp-statistics/

Sperber, J. (2014). Yelp and labor discipline: How the internet works for capitalism. *New Labor Forum, 23*(2), 68–74. doi:10.1177/1095796014527066

Subramaniam, M., Taylor, N. G., St. Jean, B., Follman, R., Kodama, C., & Casciotti, D. (2015). As simple as that?: Tween credibility assessment in a complex online world. *The Journal of Documentation, 71*(3), 550–571. doi:10.1108/JD-03-2014-0049

Talmage, C. (2012). Applicant quality: Exploring the differences between organizational and third-party websites. *Social Science Computer Review, 30*(2), 240–247. doi:10.1177/0894439311402147

Zhu, L., Yin, G., & He, W. (2014). is this opinion leader's review useful? Peripheral cues for online review helpfulness. *Journal of Electronic Commerce Research, 15*(4), 267–280.

APPENDIX: SCHEDULE OF QUESTIONS

Opening:

1. Informed Consent:
    a. This focus group is part of a series of focus groups looking at how people use Yelp. Your discussion will help researchers understand how review websites work.
    b. Statement of Anonymity.
2. Members introduce themselves.

Introductory Questions:

1. How do you use Yelp? For what purposes? Examples?
2. Where else can you go to find user reviews of a company, organization, or brand?
3. Can you think of a Yelp review you liked? One you didn't like? Explain the difference.
4. What would make someone want to use Yelp? What would make someone avoid Yelp?
5. What qualities would you associate with Yelp? (Prompt: Interesting, helpful, dishonest…)
6. Have you ever written a review on Yelp? Why? What type of information did you include?

Key Questions:

1. What makes a review credible? Can you provide an example?
2. When is it appropriate for Yelp to delete a review?
3. Have you heard about Cecil the Lion? (ask a member to describe what happened)
    a. Should protesters be allowed to post information about Cecil on Dr. Palmers Yelp page?
    b. Where should they post information digitally? (Prompt: what other sites should they use?)
4. Do protestors on Yelp make the site more or less credible? Why?
5. Who benefits from the information on Yelp? Why?

Conclusion:

1. Thank you for your participation. The information you provided throughout today's discussion will be incredibly helpful as I look into the credibility of review websites.
2. Is there any question I should have asked? (Prompt: anything else you would like to ask?)
3. Are there any questions I can answer about the study?

Section 4
Reconciling Individual and Group Ethos

This section examines the different impacts that individual ethos can have on how we access, assess, share, and build online information. The chapters in this section all focus on different digital sites and genres, but each one sheds light on the importance of negotiating the relationship between individual and group ethos by illustrating the specific benefits and drawbacks of acknowledging—or effacing—individual ethos in different contexts.

Chapter 13
Surf's Up:
Communicative Aspects of Online Trust–Building among Couchsurfing Hosts

Maura Cherney
University of Wisconsin – Milwaukee, USA

Daniel Cochece Davis
Illinois State University, USA

Sandra Metts
Illinois State University, USA

ABSTRACT

As human interaction increasingly shifts to on-line environments, the age-old challenge of determining communicators' credibility becomes all the more important and challenging. The absence of nonverbal behaviors adds to this challenge, though "rich media" attempt to compensate for this traditional lacuna within mediated interpersonal communication. The present study seeks to empirically understand how the ability and necessity of trust and credibility are built, maintained, and depreciated in online environments, using the on-line "Couchsurfing" travel environment as a worthy sample. In this environment, both hosts and guests must determine whether the other is a viable candidate for free housing, even though they have typically never met face-to-face, or even spoken via phone. Results show participants relying on information found in members' request messages and references, both when accepting and rejecting requests, with a lack of reliance placed on photos and other textual profile information.

INTRODUCTION

Rapidly growing sharing economy platforms (also called peer-to-peer marketplace) connect non-commercial individuals to make transactions directly (Pizam, 2014). The ability to connect through the Internet has allowed greater opportunity to innovate and collaborate with others in areas tradition-ally grounded in a commercial setting (Tapscott & Williams, 2006). Common examples of sharing

DOI: 10.4018/978-1-5225-1072-7.ch013

economy resources include providing products (e.g. *Craigslist*, group buying programs), providing services (e.g., *Airbnb*, *Zipcar*, *Uber*), and providing information (e.g., *Wikipedia*, *Tripadvisor*).

Within the scope of tourism, peer-to-peer travel includes services such as accommodations that serve as alternatives to lodging in a traditional hotel (Pizam, 2014). Services such as *Airbnb* provide individuals a platform to rent out their home to travelers at a cost. Cost savings and the ability to interact with locals add to the appeal of utilizing the sharing economy when seeking lodging, but these desires also increase reliance on the trust of other individuals (Guttentag, 2015). Hosts within the sharing economy of peer-to-peer travel face potential risks, including damage to their property or unpleasant guest behavior (Pizam, 2014).

Sharing economy marketplaces online require an added emphasis on trust-building, especially in such a high-risk situation as sharing accommodation with strangers (Guttentag, 2015). Higher levels of trust in a person can reduce the perception of risk of an interaction (Ganesan & Hess, 1997). The idea of trust has roots in ancient philosophy, particularly in Aristotle's (1932)*Rhetoric*. A major aspect of an effective argument is the ethos, or the perceived credibility of a speaker. Aristotle (1932) outlined three "sources of trust" (pp. 91-92), or aspects of ethos, that increase an audience's confidence in a speaker: intelligence, character, and goodwill. Upon reducing uncertainty by receiving information about another, a person is more willing to trust the other person's actions (Yoo, 2005). This finding created a connection between uncertainty reduction and trust. The idea of trust in digital environments was further explored in places such as Folk and Apostel's (2013) digital ethos collection and Wichowski and Kohl's (2013) specific examination of trusting information found in digital environments; moreover, new models of adapting ethos to online ethos have been developed (e.g., Frobish, 2013).

One example of a sharing economy platform involving digital ethos is *Couchsurfing*, a free accommodation service and online community allowing members to meet online before meeting face-to-face. *Couchsurfing* offers several communicative features allowing members to gain more information and reduce their uncertainty about others in order to assess whether they feel they can trust a requester before making a hosting decision, essentially determining whether the information each provides has credibility. The present study seeks to understand how trust in others is attained through credibility established via online communication in a sharing economy, and it looks specifically at interactions on *Couchsurfing* as a subset of the larger movement of the sharing economy.

BACKGROUND

Advancements in technology allow for a more collaborative, extended opportunity for the peer-to-peer travel economy than ever existed in the past (Guttentag, 2015). The hospitality exchange web community, *Couchsurfing*, puts travelers in contact with hosts in geographic areas where they plan on traveling. The website has ten million active members, representing over 200,000 cities and every country on Earth (*Couchsurfing* International, 2016a), and it includes communication with the potential to move from an online environment to face-to-face interaction.

Theoretical Framework

Uncertainty reduction theory (URT) initially addressed the role of uncertainty in initial interactions between strangers (Berger & Calabrese, 1975). In initial interactions, participants' main priority is to reduce the uncertainty they are experiencing, as uncertainty is considered to be an unpleasant cognitive state that should be avoided (Berger & Calbrese, 1975). Later, Berger and Bradac (1982) offered an expansion of the theory to include strategies interactants use to reduce uncertainty by seeking information. A passive strategy involves seeking information from observing the person, without making one's observation known. An active strategy often involves requesting more information about the other interactant from a third party source, such as asking a mutual acquaintance questions about the other person. Interactive strategies involve gathering information directly from the target, often by asking direct questions and self-disclosing.

The present chapter acknowledges the potential for risk in sharing economy platforms and considers the ability to reduce uncertainty in order to evoke trust in others. Because of the reliance on the terms "risk," "trust," and "uncertainty," clarification of these terms is required before moving on. The terms of risk, trust, and uncertainty in the present study are based on Josang and Presti's (2004) discussion of decision-making. Trust, for the purposes of the present study, is defined as, "the extent to which one party is willing to depend on somebody, or something, in a given situation with a feeling of relative security, even though negative consequences are possible" (Josang & Presti, 2004, p. 135). In a transactional interaction, the "negative consequences" within the definition of trust allude to the potential for risk; risk influences one's decision to trust. Uncertainty, then, refers to the outcome probability of a decision resulting in negative consequences (i.e., risk), or in positive consequences or gain (i.e., high reliability trust).

Although it is tempting to apply the traditionally face-to-face URT to a mediated environment, it is first important to consider the key differences between face-to-face and mediated communication. One main difference is the lack of nonverbal cues present in mediated environments when compared to the rich nonverbal communication possible in face-to-face environments, thereby forcing individuals to form impressions of one another mostly through verbal cues (Walther, 1992). Another major difference is the asynchrony of mediated communication, allowing for more time and consideration between messages, possibly contributing to selective self-presentation by the sender of the messages (Tidwell & Walther, 2002; Walther, 1996). Ramirez, Walther, Burgoon, and Sunnafrank (2002) noticed an opportunity to expand upon traditional, face-to-face information-seeking behaviors offered by Berger and Bradac (1982) because of the unique affordances of the Internet for information seeking. They proposed a fourth strategy for reducing uncertainty specific to gathering information online. An extractive strategy of reducing uncertainty involves gathering information about the target online without the target's knowledge through, for example, search engines (Ramirez et al., 2002).

Several studies have applied information-seeking and URT to a mediated environment, creating some knowledge about these concepts online. Passive uncertainty reduction strategies are used more often than the other information-seeking strategies online (Antheunis, Valkenburg & Peter, 2010). Although passive strategies are most prevalent, Antheunis et al. (2010) found that an interactive information-seeking strategy was the only strategy that significantly reduced uncertainty about other individuals online. Similarly, interactive uncertainty reduction strategies such as statements of affection, direct questions, and self-disclosure occur more often in mediated environments than in face-to-face environments (Antheunis, Schouten, Valkenburg, & Peter, 2012).

Uncertainty and Trust in a Sharing Economy

While studies using URT in mediated environments add to existing knowledge about information-seeking online, they often focus on the context of social networking site information-seeking. Although some studies have looked into marketing and reputation in sharing economy platforms, need still exists for information about information-seeking within the context of these platforms. Yannopoulou, Moufahim, and Bian (2013) found that user-generated content on sites like *Airbnb* and *Couchsurfing* contribute to forming the brand of each service. Communication through websites such as *Airbnb* can evoke trust in members through affordances such as reviewing accommodations, direct messaging between the host and guest, and including photographs and textual information in profiles (Guttentag, 2015). Many sharing economy platforms also have identity or location verification systems in place to reassure users. Yannopoulou et al. (2013) urged future research in the economy of trust in sharing economy platforms and research in how to increase the success of user-generated brands like *Couchsurfing*. The ability to look into trust through a sharing economy platform may lead to significant contributions to communication study. Because the study of trust and URT both began with face-to-face interactions, applying each of these to the study of a particular computer-mediated interaction is worthwhile.

Within the specific context of *Couchsurfing*, both members and nonmembers acknowledge the presence of risk in interactions (Tran, 2009), but the *Couchsurfing* organization uses several strategies to minimize these risks. Similar to *Airbnb* (Guttentag, 2015), several studies looking specifically at *Couchsurfing* found communicative website features often used in the decision-making process are the members' profile photos (Bialski, 2012; Germann Molz, 2012; Tran, 2009), references (Germann Molz, 2012; Rosen, Lafontaine & Hendrickson, 2011; Tran, 2009), and initial request messages (Rosen et al., 2011; Tran, 2009). Another less studied informative website feature is the textual information found in profiles. Where research is lacking, however, is in determining what members are looking for *within* the photos, references, request messages, and textual profile information that leads them to accept other members into their homes.

Of the four communicative areas of *Couchsurfing*, each fit into an information-seeking strategy identified by Ramirez et al. (2002). The present study considers focusing attention on references left by other users as a form of active information-seeking, while messaging other members directly is a form of interactive information-seeking. Past literature has applied passive and extractive information-seeking online clearly, in that passive information-seeking involves general browsing behaviors (e.g., scrolling through a newsfeed), while extractive information-seeking involves more explicit searches for information about an individual (e.g., viewing a specific profile; Wise, Alhabash, & Park, 2010). In the case of *Couchsurfing* and considering Wise et al.'s (2010) differentiation between passive and extractive information-seeking, both viewing photos and textual information on a particular member's profile would be considered extractive information-seeking. Before looking into which website feature is used most, it is necessary to gain a basic understanding of the four communicative features found often in sharing economy platforms: photos, references, direct messages, and other textual profile information.

Photos serve as communication between the owner of the profile and the online community. The *Couchsurfing* website, in particular, allows members to upload several photos onto their profile and include a caption for each photo. References serve as communication between third party sources and the online community. In *Couchsurfing*, specifically, references usually come from a person the member has met offline in the past. The references allow members to warn other members of a potentially dangerous *Couchsurfing* participant or to praise a participant after a positive experience. Direct messages, whether in the form of email, website-specific direct messaging, or instant messaging, serve as direct communication between members of the online community. In *Couchsurfing*, a common form of direct messaging is the request message, which is when one member requests accommodation from a prospective host. Aside from photos, references, and direct messages, other textual profile information may also be a source of information for the online community. The *Couchsurfing* profile allows individual members to include a wide variety of information in their profiles, which is available publically to the *Couchsurfing* community. For example, members have the opportunity to include information, such as age, location, gender (biological sex), and interests.

It is apparent that these website features are different from one another, in that they all embody different strategies of information-seeking and involve different senders and intended receivers of information. Although Antheunis et al. (2010) found that the interactive information-seeking strategy was most able to reduce uncertainty in online interactants, the study relied on social networking site data, and it is unclear if the same finding is true in a sharing economy platform like *Couchsurfing*. One factor in determining what strategy to use in information-seeking to reduce uncertainty is the technology-related factor (Ramirez et al., 2002). Interactants must determine how effective a particular source is in acquiring information needed to reduce uncertainty and, presumably, to foster trust. In the context of *Couchsurfing*, potential hosts may be suspicious of altered photos or falsely positive references. In order to determine whether a particular information source is considered more trustworthy than others, the following research question is proposed:

RQ1: What information-seeking strategy is most relied upon to trust another individual in a sharing economy web platform?

Because it is first important to gain an understanding of which of the four *Couchsurfing* website features are relied on most, the present study will attempt to determine, more specifically, what about each source of information leads others to trust.

Photos

A great deal of self-presentation takes place with the creation and management of an online profile. Goffman (1959) theorized about the self-presentation methods of people in face-to-face interactions. He explained that people put much effort into shaping how they are perceived and often portray an ideal self. Online, self-presentation can be even more selective than in face-to-face environments because of the reduced nonverbal cues and asynchrony of mediated communication (Walther, 1996). Members of online dating websites, for example, admit to presenting their ideal self, rather than their true self online (Ellison, Heino & Gibbs, 2006). In addition to theorizing about self-presentation, Goffman (1959) also discussed the evaluation of others' self-presentation attempts. He argued that within interaction, people tend to acquire information about others for practical reasons such as attempting to predict what to expect in future interactions. Individuals may judge others by appearance and fit them into expectations they possess based on previous interactions with similar people (Goffman, 1959, p. 26).

In online contexts, perceptions of others may be based on photographs in an online profile. In a trust game experiment, participants were more likely to trust attractive individuals over less attractive individuals, at least initially (Wilson & Eckel, 2006), and were also more likely to trust those who were smiling (Scharlemann, Eckel, Kacelnik & Wilson, 2001). Within the context of sharing economy platforms, Ert, Fleischer and Magen (2016) found that photographs on *Airbnb* made the transaction more personal, and were more important to forming trust than reviews on the website. Ert et al. (2016), however, urge for a better understanding of the specific features of a photograph that generate trust in another person online. Similar to *Airbnb*, existing research on *Couchsurfing* shows that members of the site use photos found on members' profiles as a communicative feature to make decisions about initiating and agreeing to interaction, but it is unknown what specific features of the photos found on profiles communicate information leading a host to trust a potential guest. These concerns lead to the present study's next research question:

RQ2: What communicative aspects of a photograph are used to increase trust in the subject of the photo?

User References

In addition to photos, references or reviews from third party sources are often present in sharing economy platforms as a potential source of information to evoke trust. *Airbnb* allows members to leave reviews after staying in a host's home, which Guttentag (2015) claimed is a key feature to establish trust. However, the reliance on these reviews is questioned in existing literature (e.g., Ert et al., 2016). The *Couchsurfing* community encourages members to write references about others they have stayed with or hosted (*Couchsurfing* International, 2016b), and leaving references is an implied norm within the *Couchsurfing* community (Germann Molz, 2012). The reference system used in the *Couchsurfing* community operates with the understanding that references about past behavior help to predict future behavior (Bialski, 2012). The reference feature allows members to rate the interaction as positive, neutral, or negative and encourages members to elaborate on their experiences with the other member. Viewing the references left about a member of a website is an example of the active information-seeking behavior in URT (Berger & Calabrese, 1975). A greater understanding can be achieved about what specifically members look for within references on a *Couchsurfing* profile, so the following research question is posed:

RQ3: What communicative aspects of online references increase trust in the subject of the references?

Direct Messages

Direct messages serve as the only interactive information-seeking strategy between individuals online before meeting face-to-face. *Airbnb*, for example, offers direct messaging between members to discuss the upcoming stay (Guttentag, 2015). Within the specific context of *Couchsurfing*, the request message is the first direct communication between the member requesting accommodation and the prospective host.

The first axiom of Berger and Calabrese's (1975) URT explained increases in verbal communication decreases the uncertainty felt among interactants. Because the original request message is asynchronous in nature, it would be considered interactive information-seeking to reduce uncertainty (Berger & Bradac, 1982). Walther (1992) explained that when constructing a message online, people have more opportunity to focus only on the verbal message sent, and not on the other aspects of interaction, allowing them to present preferable cues about themselves. Because of this, another research question is generated regarding this topic:

RQ4: What communicative aspects of request messages increase trust in the sender of the message?

Textual Profile Information

In addition to photos, references, and direct messages, interactants in sharing economy platforms have the ability to gain information about a member through other textual information found on the profile. Just as how Goffman's (1959) work on self-presentation and evaluation of others is applicable to looking into the use of photos used in online profiles, a great deal of self-presentation goes into choosing what to write in the many sections of a *Couchsurfing* profile. After viewing a social network site profile, perceptions people form about others tend to be fairly accurate (Kluemper & Rosen, 2009). People who feel confident in their ability to evaluate others based on profile information also feel comfortable meeting the person face-to-face after viewing the profile (Haferkamp & Kramer, 2010).

On *Couchsurfing*, in particular, several profile headings are provided as prompts for members to use text to explain more about themselves. The ability to gain information about a member, based on her or his profile, is an example of extractive information-seeking behavior (Berger & Calabrese, 1975; Ramirez et al., 2002; Wise et al., 2010). It needs to be understood what exactly about profile information leads hosts to trust another member. Because other profile information may have an impact on a potential host's ability to trust a member, the following research question is proposed.

RQ5: What textual profile items increase trust in the creator of an online profile?

Methods

The present study seeks to determine how uncertainty is reduced to trust others in a relationship in a sharing economy platform, having the potential to move from online to face-to-face. While the overall study looks to determine trust-building online, specific items served as an operationalization of potential information that could be found from information-seeking strategies to reduce uncertainty. In other words, the conceptual model of the present study looks to the connection between uncertainty reduction and trust, while the operational model uses items as potential information that could be obtained in order to trust enough to accept a request.

Sample

The participants were 216 *Couchsurfing* members from the United States; 65% were males, and 34% were females, with the average age being 35.43 years (1% of .participants chose not to reveal their biological sex). All participants had hosted through *Couchsurfing*, with participants having hosted an average of 34.5 guests, and 22 international guests. Many members also participated in the community as guests, with an average of 8.19 times having been a guest through *Couchsurfing*, and 4.7 times internationally. Participants were recruited through the *Couchsurfing* website using discussion boards and other online forums about *Couchsurfing*.

Procedures

Because most of the existing literature about *Couchsurfing* has been accomplished qualitatively, often with a small sample size, past findings may not be generalizable to the *Couchsurfing* community. To avoid this limitation, an online questionnaire was used to obtain data from participants.

Measurements

To study the role of online information-seeking in judgments of trust in a sharing economy platform, a survey was constructed specifically for the present study and its participants: *Couchsurfing* hosts. Several sources of information guided survey development, including previous research about *Couchsurfing* and social networking sites and aspects of URT. In addition, insight from others was collected to improve the survey, including a discussion board post posing a general question about how hosts build trust, and the think aloud protocol developed by Ericsson and Simon (1980) with two volunteers to ensure usability of the questionnaire.

The survey was presented differently to participants based on answers to the first question. The first question intended to determine which of the four major communicative website sources provide the essential information needed to trust another member by asking, "Which of these website features provide you with the information you *most* need to trust a member enough to *accept* a *Couchsurfing* member's request?" Participants rank-ordered the four features. Based on participants' answer to the first question, they were presented corresponding questions having to do with the feature they chose as the most essential, using a Likert-type response. For example, if a participant indicated that photos were most relied upon to form trust, they answered questions about how specifically they use photos. One example question states, "In the photo, the surfer appears attractive," and asks participants to indicate their level of agreement with the statement using a Likert-type response.

Analysis

To analyze data, chi-square goodness of fit tests and paired samples *t*-tests were performed. Where significant differences in means appeared, delineation points in data were determined, allowing items to be grouped into levels of essentiality. Additional paired samples *t*-tests were run to confirm the significance of grouping items. Finally, coefficient of determination (r^2) was found to determine the effect size, and whether findings were meaningful (Reinard, 2008).

RESULTS

For research question one, when accepting a request, significant deviation from chance was found in the chi-square goodness of fit test ($\chi^2(3) = 66.03$, $p < 0.001$), showing high frequencies for the request message and references and relatively lower frequencies for other textual profile information and photos. To expand on the chi-square goodness of fit test, means of rank-ordered responses were also considered, using paired samples *t*-tests. Between the references and other profile information communicative website features, a significant difference in means was found ($t = -6.872$, $p < 0.001$), with a coefficient of determination showing the difference accounting for 18% of the variance. The delineation point was

Table 1. Frequencies and paired samples t-tests of website features

Pair		Freq.	T	df
	Messages	93		
1			-0.83	215
	References	84		
2			-6.88***	215
	Other	31		
3			-1.02	215
	Photo	23		

*p<.05, **p<.01 ***p<.001.

confirmed with a significant difference between the first and third rated website features ($t = -7.49$, $p < 0.001$), with an effect size of 21% of the variance. RQ1 asked what information-seeking strategy is most relied upon to trust another individual in a sharing economy web platform, and results showed that reliance is heavily placed on direct messages and references in a profile, meaning that interactive and active information-seeking strategies are relied upon most to form trust in another in a sharing economy platform.

RQ2 asked what communicative aspects of a photograph are used to increase trust. Paired samples *t*-tests revealed significant difference ($t = 2.185$, $p = 0.038$) between the fifth and sixth highest ranked items, with 16% of the variance explained by this difference, while a significant difference between

Table 2. Paired samples t-tests photos

	Pair	t	df
1	Presence of One Photo - No photo	1.39	26
2	No photo - Photo Shows Face	0.38	27
3	Photo Shows Face - Photo Shows Personality	1.62	28
4	Photo Shows Personality - Presence of Multiple Photos	0	26
5	Presence of Multiple Photos - Photo Shows Travel	2.19*	26
6	Photo Shows Travel - Photo Attractive	0.37	27
7	Photo Attractive - Photos of Activities I like	0.51	27
8	Photos of Activities I like - Photos of Activities I Dislike	0.97	25
9	Photos of Activities I Dislike - Different Biological Sex	0.98	25
10	Different Biological Sex - Photo With Friends	-0.26	27
11	Photo With Friends - Photos Unattractive	0.34	27
12	Photos Unattractive - Same Biological Sex	0.12	27
13	Same Biological Sex - Photo Alone	0.74	26
14	Photo Alone - Different Ethnicity	0.14	25
15	Different Ethnicity - Same Ethnicity	0.44	26

*p<.05, **p<.01 ***p<.001.

any other of the top five highest ranked items was not apparent, creating a delineation point between the fifth and sixth highest ranked means. Results indicate that the presence of a photograph overall, no photograph present, a photograph showing the subject's face, the photograph showing an indication of the subject's personality, and the presence of multiple photos all significantly correspond to trust in the other individual. Other aspects of photographs were considered insignificant in forming trust.

RQ3 asked what communicative aspects of online references increase trust in the subject of the references. Significantly different pairs were found on several occasions in the rank-ordered list of responses. First, when accepting a member based on references, the item with the highest mean clearly approached statistical significance in mean difference from the next highest mean ($t = 2.0$, $p = 0.051$), but was not considered a clear delineation point. Statistical significance was found between the seventh and eighth highest means ($t = 2.59$, $p = 0.01$), with a moderate effect size ($r^2 = 0.12$). To confirm the delineation point between the seventh and eighth highest means, the top seven means were also compared to the eighth highest mean. All pairs showed significance levels of between $p < .001$ to $p = 0.01$ and effect sizes from the medium effect size of $r^2 = 0.12$ to a large effect size. These results indicate that communicative aspects of references to increase trust include the inclusion of references from past hosts, all positive references, references discussing the member's personality, references showing consistency with other profile information, references from past guests, and the presence of one or more negative references. All other aspects of online reviews are insignificant in forming trust in this context.

When accepting a request based on the request message, to consider research question four, a significant difference in means ($t = 3.09$, $p = 0.003$) with an effect size of $r^2 = 0.12$ was found using a paired samples t-test between the fourth and fifth items. To confirm the delineation point in data, all other higher means were compared to the fifth ranked item. All paired samples t-tests showed a significant difference in means among each of the highest means and the fifth-ranked mean. Effect sizes for this data ranged from $r^2 = 0.12$ to $r^2 = 0.25$. RQ4 asked what communicative aspects of request messages increase trust in the sender of the message, and results indicate that these include a personalized message, a message covering what members can teach, learn, and share with one another, a message that mentions the host's specific profile, and a message addressing why that particular host was chosen. Other aspects of direct messages were not considered to be significant in forming trust in this particular sharing economy context.

Table 3. Paired samples t-tests references

	Pair	t	df
1	Reference from Host - All Positive References	2.00	52
2	All Positive References - Discuss Personality	0.93	52
3	Discuss Personality - Ref Consistent with Other Info	0.52	52
4	Ref Consistent with Other Info - Reference from Surfer	0.00	51
5	Reference from Surfer - Cleanliness of Surfer	0.00	51
6	Cleanliness of Surfer - Presence of one or more Neg Reference	0.56	51
7	Presence of one or more Neg Reference - Activities I like	2.59*	51
8	Activities I like - Fits in With Community	0.10	52
9	Fits in With Community - Reference from Get Togethers	2.70*	52
10	Reference from Get Togethers - Activities I dislike	0.20	51

*p<.05, **p<.01 ***p<.001.

Table 4. Paired samples t-tests request message

	Pair	t	df
1	Message Personalized - Message Teach Learn Share	1.76	74
2	Message Teach Learn Share - Message Mentions My Profile	0.16	74
3	Message Mentions My Profile - Message Discusses Why Me	0.62	73
4	Message Discusses Why Me - Message Time to Prepare	3.09**	72
5	Message Time to Prepare - Message Likes Similar	0.30	73
6	Message Likes Similar - Message Free Place	1.53	71
7	Message Free Place - Message No Typo	0.42	70
8	Message No Typo - Message Negative Face	0.00	74
9	Message Negative Face - Message Positive Face	0.09	74
10	Message Positive Face - Message Sent to Multiple	0.55	73
11	Message Sent to Multiple - Message Likes Dissimilar	0.30	74
12	Message Likes Dissimilar - Message Last Minute	0.45	74
13	Message Last Minute - Message Teach Me	0.35	73

*p<.05, **p<.01 ***p<.001.

Table 5. Paired samples t-tests textual profile information

	Pair	t	df
1	Other Personal Description - Other General Info	2.41*	33
2	Other General Info - Other Philosophical Information	2.01	33
3	Other Philosophical Information - Other CS Participation	0.42	33
4	Other CS Participation - Other Interests	0.10	33
5	Other Interests - Other Teach Learn Share	0.33	33
6	Other Teach Learn Share - Other Connections	0.79	33
7	Other Connections - Other Locations	2.05**	31

*p<.05, **p<.01 ***p<.001.

The last research question deliberated what textual profile items increase trust in the creator of an online profile considering differences in means of eight items. The highest-ranked item was significantly different from the second highest mean score ($t = 2.41$, $p = 0.022$), with an effect size of $r^2 = 0.11$. This result indicates that the only significant source of information to build trust from the textual profile information is the personal description in a member's online profile.

DISCUSSION

The current study determined several noteworthy findings. Participants relied on interactive and active information-seeking, operationalized as members' request messages and references, while a lack of reliance was placed on photos and other textual profile information. Because each of the website features provides different information presented to different audiences, the affordances of each might point to some more general understandings about trust online, especially in the context of sharing economy platforms. Direct messages are used to gain compliance and are not visible to the public. Similarly, references found on a profile provide interesting insight about the member because the information comes from a third-party source. This information could be critical in determining trust because it does not rely on direct self-presentation online, but rather includes insight from an uninvolved member of the community. Conversely, photos and other textual profile information are created by the member and are put on display for the entire web community. It seems that self-presentation attempts intended for a large audience, such as photos and text found in a profile, may not be relied on heavily when determining trust of another individual.

One potential explanation for this finding is the warranting value of each feature of the website, explained in Walther and Parks' (2002) warranting theory. Warranting theory deals specifically with relationships that begin online with the possibility of moving to a face-to-face environment, and it indicates that individuals are likely to acknowledge the potential for selective self-presentation online. This acknowledgment results in greater emphasis on information online that can be corroborated or information that cannot be easily managed by the subject online. For example, Walther, Van Der Heide, Hamel, and Shulman (2009) found weak support that Facebook users tend to perceive a profile owner's personality more from indications coming from friends' posts, rather than directly from the profile owner. Of more significance was their second finding that attractiveness was most effectively conveyed through friends on a profile, rather than directly from the owner of the profile. Similarly, *TripAdvisor* reviews are of high warranting value, and users place great emphasis on these reviews, especially if reviews are written by members viewers perceive to be similar to them (Ayeh, Au, & Law, 2013). Warranting theory would be a worthy framework from which to base future research concerning uncertainty reduction or trust in sharing economy platforms.

When making decisions based on photos, the presence or absence—as well as the number—of photos seemed to be relied on most heavily when compared to other aspects of photos such as the attractiveness of the subject or the context of the photograph. References provide important information such as in what capacities the member has participated in the *Couchsurfing* community in the past and the valence of the interaction. Information of importance found in a request message includes the personalization of the message and evidence that the member had thoroughly looked over the host's profile, potentially meaning that it is perceived that the message was written for the individual, rather than a mass audience. Past research on *Couchsurfing*, in particular, has found that potential hosts respond extremely negatively to requests having been obviously sent to a mass audience (e.g., Liu, 2012; Rosen et al., 2011), and hosts much prefer individualized message. Other textual profile information deemed important was the personal description.

Implications

Although the present study looks specifically into how *Couchsurfing* members determine whether or not to trust another member, based on their information-seeking strategies, the findings in this study have implications for a much broader understanding of trust to contribute to the study of communication. Trust, a concept studied since ancient philosophers, is facing a revolution when it comes to understanding the ability to trust others in mediated contexts. Although features of a website were, for the purposes of the present study, conceptualized within the context of *Couchsurfing*, the findings about photos, references, direct messages, and textual profile information could potentially have implications for other sharing economy web platforms. Using *Couchsurfing* web features and *Couchsurfing* hosts as participants helped to contextualize a real scenario where audiences must make judgments about senders of information, especially in potentially high-risk situations, which is a situation that translates into many other sharing economy platforms that move from online to face-to-face (e.g., *Uber, Airbnb, Craigslist*). Findings about information-seeking online from the present study may not be completely generalizable, but they are applicable to other similar sharing economy platforms (e.g., *Airbnb*) and other unrelated platforms (e.g., online dating sites).

Within the broad context of sharing economy platforms, the findings from the present study have implications. Websites themselves are methods of self-presentation for companies or individuals, and businesses with a large online presence may find these results of particular interest to learn how to nurture a trusting relationship with online clients. Of particular similarity are those sharing economy websites involving modality switching from an online to face-to-face meeting. The warranting value of references, for example, might reduce uncertainty to a level individuals need to move the relationship to a face-to-face environment. Users are particularly interested in the source of the reference and the valence of the reference, so these findings might help practitioners design a web platform with affordances useful in reducing uncertainty. Aside from references, the present study also found high value in interactive information-seeking strategies such as sending direct messages. Practitioners should also be conscious of consumers' desires to interact directly with the other individual. This information could translate to online trust beyond *Couchsurfing*. For example, when choosing where to purchase an item online, it is possible that similar methods are used to determine trust in the seller of online marketplaces. It is possible that the seller's website is not as heavily relied on as direct contact with the seller or reviews from past customers.

Aside from practical implications in other sharing economy web platforms, the present study also involves theoretical implications. The overall theoretical framework of the study was URT, paying special attention to the information-seeking strategies identified by Ramirez et al. (2002) and information-seeking online. Past research has found interactive information-seeking strategies to be most effective in reducing uncertainty, and the present study further confirmed this notion with findings about the reliance on direct messaging with other members. Another valuable information-seeking strategy confirmed by the present study was active information-seeking, which for the purposes of the study was conceptualized as viewing references. Again, warranting theory (Walther & Parks, 2002) might be a better explanation for the reliance on references to reduce uncertainty. The present study found low reliance on both extractive information-seeking strategies of viewing photos and viewing textual profile information. This could be because members can selectively present themselves on their own profile, which would be considered information of low warranting value. Goffman (1959) theorized about self-presentation within a communicative lens. The present study suggests it is possible that self-presentation messages constructed for a large audience are not taken seriously in sharing economy platforms.

Limitations

Although the present study contributed significant findings to research about credibility in sharing economy platforms like *Couchsurfing*, some limitations to this study exist. First, the sample size was smaller than desired. For the present study, it would have been desirable to have at least 100 participants for each of the conditions of the online survey. However, the response rate was much lower than predicted, at 216 usable participant questionnaires. More specifically problematic, in the condition for gaining trust based on photos, data were acquired from only 23 people. Although statistical significance was achievable with this small sample, the findings may be less generalizable.

Another limitation to the present study was a technical problem resulting from participant misunderstanding that became apparent during the data analysis stage. Within the online questionnaire, the first question asked participants to rank order options on a scale of one to four to determine what feature of the website is most relied upon for information. The intention was for participants to use a unique number for each of the four items presented, with one representing the most important feature. Upon viewing data, it was apparent that some participants did not provide a unique number for each item, sometimes even repeating numbers. Although directions for the rank-ordered items could possibly have been made clearer, thereby possibly affecting statistical results, the responses were not discarded because they still provide insight into the sample's views about the website features.

FUTURE RESEARCH DIRECTIONS

The present study focused on describing how information-seeking online allowed for a decrease in uncertainty in order to build trust in others. Some findings in the present study call for more focused research in specific areas to gain a better understanding of the causes and implications of the findings. Additionally, other concepts beyond the scope of the present study are outlined as future directions for this type of research.

First, the studied sample could be expanded beyond *Couchsurfing*. The concepts in this study can be translated into a variety of online situations involving the ability to trust others online, especially sharing economy platforms that move relationships from a mediated environment to a face-to-face environment. When using the Internet to rent properties, arrange job interviews, choose babysitters, or purchase products, it should be determined how, more generally, uncertainty is reduced and trust is achieved.

Although most academic research is predictive (Bhattercherjee, 2012), it was necessary for this study to first gain a descriptive understanding of the phenomenon of trust-building on the *Couchsurfing* website. Because of this, a future direction for this type of research would be to use descriptive findings to develop a predictive study, allowing for greater insight into why and exactly how trust is achieved online (Bhattercherjee, 2012).

Although the present study collected information about particular demographics, it was beyond the scope of this study to look into the effects of demographic factors on methods used to trust others through viewing online information. Further research should determine the degree to which biological sex or age affects the information needed to trust online, especially in high trust situations. Although initial research on very young computer users suggests a digital divide in how credibility is understood in online information (e.g., Metzger, Flanagin, Medders, Pure, Markov & Hartsell, 2013), this foothold needs further research across the age spectrum, bringing in later age users with limited online experience and broad traditional ethos experience, as well as the myriad of users and their experience in-between these end points. Similarly, Flanagin and Metzger (2003) conducted exploratory work in this area, yet much remains unknown. Not only would the answers to these questions provide valuable information about trust-building on *Couchsurfing*, but they would also add to knowledge of how trust is achieved for different demographics online, in general.

CONCLUSION

Trust, a classic communication concept, needs to be considered in the context of online environments, especially through information-seeking strategies. Sharing economy platforms such as *Couchsurfing* serve as interesting sources for a variety of information to examine trust-building online. Although the *Couchsurfing* concept only covers a specific instance of trust-building online, this study can be a starting point for future research about the ability and necessity of understanding how trust is built, maintained, and depreciated in an online environment.

REFERENCES

Antheunis, M. L., Schouten, A. P., Valkenburg, P. M., & Peter, J. (2012). Interactive uncertainty reduction strategies and verbal affection in computer-mediated communication. *Communication Research*, *39*(6), 757–780. doi:10.1177/0093650211410420

Antheunis, M. L., Valkenburg, P. M., & Peter, J. (2010). Getting acquainted through social network sites: Testing a model of online uncertainty reduction and social attraction. *Computers in Human Behavior*, *26*(1), 100–109. doi:10.1016/j.chb.2009.07.005

Aristotle, . (1932). *The Rhetoric of Aristotle* (L. Cooper, Trans.). Englewood Cliffs, NJ: Prentice Hall.

Ayeh, J. K., Au, N., & Law, R. (2013). Do we believe in TripAdvisor? Examining credibility perceptions and online travelers' attitude toward using user-generated content. *Journal of Travel Research*, *52*(4), 437–452. doi:10.1177/0047287512475217

Berger, C. R., & Bradac, J. J. (1982). *Language and social knowledge: Uncertainty in interpersonal relations*. London, UK: Edward Arnold, Ltd.

Berger, C. R., & Calabrese, R. J. (1975). Some explorations in initial interaction and beyond: Toward a developmental theory of interpersonal communication. *Human Communication Research*, *1*(2), 99–112. doi:10.1111/j.1468-2958.1975.tb00258.x

Bhattercherjee, A. (2012). *Social science research: Principles, methods and practices*. Tampa Bay, FL: USF Tampa Bay Open Access Textbooks Collection.

Bialski, P. (2012). Becoming intimately mobile. In J. Wasilewski (Ed.), *Warsaw studies in culture and society* (Vol. 2). Retrieved from http://intimatetourism.files.wordpress.com/ 2012/07/paula-bialski-becomingintimatelymobile-ebook.pdf

Couchsurfing International. (2016a). *About Us*. Retrieved from http://www.*Couchsurfing*.com/about/about-us/

Couchsurfing International. (2016b). *Safety tips*. Retrieved from http://www.*Couchsurfing*.com/about/tips/

Ellison, N., Heino, R., & Gibbs, J. (2006). Managing impressions online: Self-presentation processes in the online dating environment. *Journal of Computer-Mediated Communication*, *11*(2), 415–441. doi:10.1111/j.1083-6101.2006.00020.x

Ericsson, K. A., & Simon, H. A. (1980). Verbal reports as data. *Psychological Review*, *87*(3), 215–251. doi:10.1037/0033-295X.87.3.215

Ert, E., Fleischer, A., & Magen, N. (2016). Trust and reputation in the sharing economy: The role of personal photos in Airbnb. *Tourism Management*, *55*, 62–73. doi:10.1016/j.tourman.2016.01.013

Flanagin, A. J., & Metzger, M. J. (2003). The perceived credibility of web site information as influenced by the sex of the source. *Computers in Human Behavior*, *19*(6), 683–701. doi:10.1016/S0747-5632(03)00021-9

Folk, M., & Apostel, S. (2013). *Digital ethos: Evaluating computer-mediated communication*. Hershey, PA: IGI Global.

Frobish, T. S. (2013). On pixels, perceptions, and personae: Toward a model of online ethos. In M. Folk & S. Apostel (Eds.), *Digital ethos: Evaluating computer-mediated communication* (pp. 1–23). Hershey, PA: IGI Global. doi:10.4018/978-1-4666-2663-8.ch001

Ganesan, S., & Hess, R. (1997). Dimensions and levels of trust: Implications for commitment to a relationship. *Marketing Letters*, *8*(4), 439–448. doi:10.1023/A:1007955514781

Germann Molz, J. (2012). Hospitality: The mobile conviviality of *Couchsurfing*. In J. Germann Molz (Ed.), *Travel connections: Tourism, technology, and togetherness in a mobile world* (pp. 83–110). London, UK: Routledge.

Goffman, E. (1959). *The presentation of self in everyday life*. New York, NY: Anchor Books.

Guttentag, D. (2015). Airbnb: Disruptive innovation and the rise of an informal tourism accommodation sector. *Current Issues in Tourism*, *18*(12), 1192–1217. doi:10.1080/13683500.2013.827159

Haferkamp, N., & Kramer, N. C. (2010). Creating a digital self: Impression management and impression formation on social networking sites. In K. Drotner & K. C. Schroder (Eds.), *Digital content creation: Creativity, competence, critique* (pp. 129–146). New York, NY: Peter Lang.

Josang, A., & Presti, S. L. (2004). Analysing the relationship between risk and trust. In C. Jensen, S. Poslad, & T. Dimitrakos (Eds.), *Trust Management* (pp. 135–145). Berlin, Germany: Springer. doi:10.1007/978-3-540-24747-0_11

Kluemper, D. H., & Rosen, P. A. (2009). Future employment selection methods: Evaluating social networking web sites. *Journal of Managerial Psychology*, *24*(6), 567–580. doi:10.1108/02683940910974134

Liu, J. (2012). *The intimate stranger on your couch: An analysis of motivation, presentation and trust through Couchsurfing*. Retrieved from, http://uu.diva-portal.org/smash/get/diva2:560145/FULLTEXT01.pdf

Metzger, M. J., Flanagin, A. J., Medders, R., Pure, R., Markov, A., & Hartsell, E. (2013). The special case of youth and digital information credibility. In M. Folk & S. Apostel (Eds.), *Digital ethos: Evaluating computer-mediated communication* (pp. 148–168). Hershey, PA: IGI Global. doi:10.4018/978-1-4666-2663-8.ch009

Pizam, A. (2014). Peer-to-peer travel: Blessing or blight? *International Journal of Hospitality Management*, *38*, 118–119. doi:10.1016/j.ijhm.2014.02.013

Ramirez, A., Walther, J. B., Burgoon, J. K., & Sunnafrank, M. (2002). Information-seeking strategies, uncertainty, and computer-mediated communication. *Human Communication Research*, *28*, 213–228. doi:10.1111/j.1468-2958.2002.tb00804.x

Reinard, J. C. (2008). *Introduction to communication research* (4th ed.). New York, NY: McGraw-Hill.

Rosen, D., Lafontaine, P. R., & Hendrickson, B. (2011). *Couchsurfing*: Belonging and trust in a globally cooperative online social network. *New Media & Society, 13*(6), 981–998. doi:10.1177/1461444810390341

Scharlemann, J. P. W., Eckel, C. C., Kacelnik, A., & Wilson, R. K. (2001). The value of a smile: Game theory with a human face. *Journal of Economic Psychology*, *22*(5), 617–640. doi:10.1016/S0167-4870(01)00059-9

Tapscott, D., & Williams, A. D. (2006). *Wikinomics: How mass collaboration changes everything*. New York, NY: Penguin Group.

Tidwell, L. C., & Walther, J. B. (2002). Computer-mediated communication effects on disclosure, impressions, and interpersonal evaluations: Getting to know one another a bit at a time. *Human Communication Research*, *28*(3), 317–348. doi:10.1111/j.1468-2958.2002.tb00811.x

Tran, L. D. (2009). *Trust in an online hospitality network: An interpretive study on The Couchsurfing Project*. Retrieved from https://oda.hio.no/jspui/handle/10642/877

Walther, J. B. (1992). Interpersonal effects in computer-mediated interaction: A relational perspective. *Communication Research*, *19*(1), 52–90. doi:10.1177/009365092019001003

Walther, J. B. (1996). Computer-mediated communication: Impersonal, interpersonal, and hyperpersonal interaction. *Communication Research*, *23*(1), 3–43. doi:10.1177/009365096023001001

Walther, J. B., & Parks, M. R. (2002). Cues filtered out, cues filtered in: Computer-mediated communication and relationships. In M. L. Knapp & J. A. Daly (Eds.), *Handbook of interpersonal communication* (3rd ed.; pp. 529–563). Thousand Oaks, CA: Sage.

Walther, J. B., Van Der Heide, B., Hamel, L. M., & Shulman, H. C. (2009). Self-generated versus other-generated statements and impressions in computer-mediated communication: A test of warranting theory using Facebook. *Communication Research*, *36*(2), 229–253. doi:10.1177/0093650208330251

Wichowski, D. E., & Kohl, L. E. (2013). Establishing credibility in the information jungle: Blogs, micro-blogs, and the CRAAP test. In M. Folk & S. Apostel (Eds.), *Digital ethos: Evaluating computer-mediated communication* (pp. 229–251). Hershey, PA: IGI Global. http; doi:10.4018/978-1-4666-2663-8.ch013

Wilson, R. K., & Eckel, C. C. (2006). Judging a book by its cover: Beauty and expectations in the trust game. *Political Research Quarterly*, *59*(2), 189–202. doi:10.1177/106591290605900202

Wise, K., Alhabash, S., & Park, H. (2010). Emotional responses during social information seeking on Facebook. *Cyberpsychology, Behavior, and Social Networking*, *13*(5), 555–562. doi:10.1089/cyber.2009.0365 PMID:20950180

Yannopoulou, N., Moufahim, M., & Bian, X. (2013). User-generated brands and social media: Couch-sufing and Airbnb. *Contemporary Management Research*, *9*(1), 85–90. doi:10.7903/cmr.11116

Yoo, J. (2005, May). *Why should I trust you: The path from information valence to uncertainty reduction, cognitive trust, and behavioral trust*. Paper presented at the annual meeting of the International Communication Association, New York, NY.

ADDITIONAL READING

Aubrey, J. S., & Rill, L. (2013). Investigating relations between Facebook use and social capital among college undergraduates. *Communication Quarterly*, *61*(4), 479–496. doi:10.1080/01463373.2013.801869

Berkman, R. (2004). *The skeptical business searcher: The information advisor's guide to evaluating web data, sites, and sources*. Medford, NJ: Information Today.

Bialski, P. (2011). Technologies of hospitality: How planned encounters develop between strangers. *Hospitality & Society*, *1*(3), 245–260. doi:10.1386/hosp.1.3.245_1

Brahnam, S. (2009). Building character for artificial conversational agents: Ethos, ethics, believability, and credibility. *PsychNology Journal*, *7*(1), 9–47.

Bruland, H. H. (2009). Rhetorical cues and cultural clues: An analysis of the recommendation letter in English studies. *Rhetoric Review*, *28*(4), 406–424. doi:10.1080/07350190903185064

Buchberger, S. (2011). Hospitality, secrecy and gossip in Morocco: Hosting Couchsurfers against great odds. *Hospitality & Society*, *1*(3), 299–315. doi:10.1386/hosp.1.3.299_1

Davis, D. C., Lippman, M. B., Morris, T. W., & Tougas, J. A. (2012). Face-off: Different ways identity is privileged through Facebook. In C. Cunningham (Ed.), *Social networking and impression management: Self-presentation in the digital age* (pp. 61–83). Lanham, MD: Rowman & Littlefield Publishing Group.

DeLaCruz, B. P., & Claveria, M. (2009). *ICS 691: Trust and social capital on Couchsurfing and OkCupid*. Retrieved from http://www.bjpeterdelacruz.com/files/ics691finalpaper.pdf

Flanagin, A. J., & Metzger, M. J. (2007). The role of site features, user attributes, and information verification behaviors on the perceived credibility of web-based information. *New Media & Society*, *9*, 319–342. http://doi:10.1177/1461444807075015

Flanagin, A. J., & Metzger, M. J. (2010). *Kids and credibility: An empirical examination of youth, digital media use, and information credibility*. Cambridge, MA: MIT Press.

Germann Molz, J. (2011). *Couchsurfing* and network hospitality: "It's not just about the furniture". *Hospitality & Society*, *1*(3), 215–225. doi:10.1386/hosp.1.3.215_2

Gibbs, J. L., Ellison, N. B., & Heino, R. D. (2006). Self presentation in online personals: The role of anticipated future interaction, self-disclosure, and perceived success in Internet dating. *Communication Research*, *33*(2), 152–177. doi:10.1177/0093650205285368

Gibbs, J. L., Ellison, N. B., & Lai, C. H. (2011). First comes love, then comes Google: An investigation of uncertainty reduction strategies and self-disclosure in online dating. *Communication Research, 38*(1), 70–100. doi:10.1177/0093650210377091

Haferkamp, N., Eimler, S., Papadakis, A. M., & Kruck, J. V. (2012). Men are from Mars, women are from Venus? Examining gender differences in self-presentation on social networking sites. *Cyberpsychology, Behavior, and Social Networking, 15*(2), 91–98. doi:10.1089/cyber.2011.0151 PMID:22132897

Hancock, J. T., & Toma, C. L. (2009). Putting your best face forward: The accuracy of online dating photographs. *Journal of Communication, 59*(2), 367–386. doi:10.1111/j.1460-2466.2009.01420.x

Heal, F. (1990). *Hospitality in early modern England.* Oxford, UK: Clarendon Press. doi:10.1093/acpr of:oso/9780198217633.001.0001

Lauterbach, D., Truong, H., Shah, T., & Adamic, L. (2009). Surfing a web of trust: Reputation and reciprocity on *Couchsurfing*.com. *Computing in Science & Engineering, 4,* 346–353. http://doi.org/10.1.1.184.6359

Marsh, C. (2006). Aristotelian ethos and the new orality: Implications for media literacy and media ethics. *Journal of Mass Media Ethics, 21,* 338–352. http://doi:10.1207/s15327728jmme2104_8

McCroskey, J. C., & Teven, J. J. (1999). Goodwill: A reexamination of the construct and its measurement. *Communication Monographs, 66*(1), 90–103. doi:10.1080/03637759909376464

Metzger, M. J. (2007). Making sense of credibility on the web: Models for evaluating online information and recommendations for future research. *Journal of the American Society for Information Science and Technology, 58,* 2078–2091. http://doi:10.1002/asi.20672

Metzger, M. J., Flanagin, A. J., & Medders, R. B. (2010). Social and heuristic approaches to credibility evaluation online. *The Journal of Communication, 60,* 413–439. http://doi:10.1111/j.1460-2466.2010.01488.x

Nicklin, J. M., & Roch, S. G. (2009). Letters of recommendation: Controversy and consensus from expert perspectives. *International Journal of Selection and Assessment, 17*(1), 76–91. doi:10.1111/j.1468-2389.2009.00453.x

O'Gorman, K. D. (2007). Dimensions of hospitality: Exploring ancient and classical origins. In C. Lashley, P. Lynch, & A. Morrison (Eds.), *Hospitality: A social lens* (pp. 17–32). Oxford, UK: Elsevier. doi:10.1016/B978-0-08-045093-3.50005-9

Palmieri, C., Prestano, K., Gandley, R., Overton, E., & Zhang, Q. (2012). The Facebook phenomenon: Online self-disclosure and uncertainty reduction. *China Media Research, 8*(1), 48–53.

Prentice, D. A., Miller, D. T., & Lightdale, J. R. (1994). Asymmetries in attachments to groups and to their members: Distinguishing between common-identity and common-bond groups. *Personality and Social Psychology Bulletin, 20*(5), 484–493. doi:10.1177/0146167294205005

Radford, M. L., Radford, G. P., Connaway, L. S., & DeAngelis, J. A. (2011). On virtual face-work: An ethnography of communication approach to a life chat reference interaction. *The Library Quarterly, 81*(4), 431–453. doi:10.1086/661654

Ramirez, A. Jr. (2009). Information seeking role on computer-mediated interaction. *Western Journal of Communication, 73*(3), 300–325. doi:10.1080/10570310903082040

Salimkhan, G., Manago, A., & Greenfield, P. (2010). The construction of the virtual self on MySpace. *Cyberpsychology (Brno), 4,* 1–18. Retrieved from http://www.cyberpsychology.eu/view.php?cisloclanku=2010050203

Schwammlein, E., & Wodzicki, K. (2012). What to tell about me? Self-presentation in online communities. *Journal of Computer-Mediated Communication, 17*(4), 387–407. doi:10.1111/j.1083-6101.2012.01582.x

Shulz, K., Mahabir, R. C., Song, J., & Verheyden, C. N. (2012). Evaluation of the current perspectives on letters of recommendation for residency applicants among plastic surgery program directors. *Plastic Surgery International, 1-5*. doi:10.1155/1012/728981

Siibak, A. (2009). Constructing the self through the photo selection: Visual impression management on social networking websites. *Cyberpsychology (Brno), 3,* 1–9.

Stedman, J. M., Hatch, J. P., & Schoenfeld, L. S. (2009). Letters of recommendation for the predoctoral internship in medical schools and other settings: Do they enhance decision making in the selection process? *Journal of Clinical Psychology in Medical Settings, 16*(4), 339–345. doi:10.1007/s10880-009-9170-y PMID:19688252

Steylaerts, V., & O'Dubhghaill, S. (2011). *Couchsurfing* and authenticity: Notes towards an understanding of an emerging phenomenon. *Hospitality and Society, 1*(3), 261–278. doi:10.1386/hosp.1.3.261_1

Strano, M. (2008). User descriptions and interpretations of self-presentation through Facebook profile images. *Cyberpsychology (Brno), 2*(2), 1–12.

Sullivan, J. J., Albrecht, T. L., & Taylor, S. (1990). Process, organization, relational, and personal determinants of managerial compliance-gaining communication strategies. *Journal of Business Communication, 27*(4), 331–355. doi:10.1177/002194369002700402

Tan, J. E. (2010). The leap of faith from online to offline: An exploratory study of *Couchsurfing*.org. In A. Acquisti, S. W. Smith, & A. R. Sadeghi (Eds.), *Proceedings from Trust and Trustworthy Computing Third International Conference* (pp. 367-380). Berlin, Germany: Springer. http://doi.org/ doi:10.1007/978-3-642-13869-0_27

Utz, S., & Sassenberg, K. (2002). Distributive justice in common-bond and common-identity groups. *Group Processes & Intergroup Relations, 5*(2), 151–162. doi:10.1177/1368430202005002542

Van Der Heide, B., Johnson, B. K., & Vang, M. H. (2013). The effects of product photographs and reputation systems on consumer behavior and product cost on eBay. *Computers in Human Behavior, 29*(3), 570–576. doi:10.1016/j.chb.2012.11.002

Wang, S. S., Moon, S., Kwon, K. H., Evans, C. A., & Stefanone, M. A. (2009). Face off: Implications of visual cues on initiating friendship on Facebook. *Computers in Human Behavior, 26*(2), 226–234. doi:10.1016/j.chb.2009.10.001

Warnick, B. (2004). Online ethos: Source credibility in an "authorless" environment. *The American Behavioral Scientist, 48,* 256–265. http://doi:10.1177/0002764204267273

Whitty, M. T. (2007). Manipulation of self in cyberspace. In B. H. Spitzberg & W. R. Cupach (Eds.), *The dark side of interpersonal communication* (2nd ed.; pp. 98–118). Mahwah, NJ: Lawrence Erlbaum Associates.

Wout, M., & Sanfey, A. G. (2008). Friend or foe: The effect of implicit trustworthiness judgments in social decision-making. *Cognition, 108*(3), 796–803. doi:10.1016/j.cognition.2008.07.002 PMID:18721917

Zhao, S., Grasmuck, S., & Martin, J. (2008). Identity construction on Facebook: Digital empowerment in anchored relationships. *Computers in Human Behavior, 24*(5), 1816–1836. doi:10.1016/j.chb.2008.02.012

Zwier, S., Araujo, T., Boukes, M., & Willemsen, L. (2011). Boundaries to the articulation of possible selves through social networking sites: The case of Facebook profilers' social connectedness. *Cyberpsychology, Behavior, and Social Networking, 14*(10), 571–576. doi:10.1089/cyber.2010.0612 PMID:21476838

KEY TERMS AND DEFINITIONS

AirBnB: An online community that allows people to list, find, and rent vacation homes.

Couchsurfing **Profile:** The profile each individual *Couchsurfing* member creates to present themselves to the community. The profile often includes a profile photo, text profile information, and references from other members.

Couchsurfing: An online community allowing members to meet other members online before meeting face-to-face. It is also a travel practice where individuals stay at another person's house, usually for free.

Ethos: The perceived credibility of a speaker, regardless of whether that perception is mediated or not.

Request Messages: Direct messages between *Couchsurfing* members, usually used to discuss *Couchsurfing* accommodation.

Self-Presentation: A term used to describe behavior, whether mediated or not, to display an ideal self to others.

Uncertainty Reduction Theory (URT): The theory that individuals feel uncertain during an initial interaction and use strategies to reduce uncertainty by seeking information.

Chapter 14
Modal Ethos:
Scumbag Steve and the Establishing of Ethos in Memetic Agents

Jonathan S. Carter
University of Nebraska – Lincoln, USA

ABSTRACT

Traditionally, the artistic proofs center on the individual rhetor as the locus of ethos. However, as communication becomes internetworked, rhetorical phenomena increasingly circulate independent of traditional rhetors. This absence transfers ethos onto textual assemblages that often function as agents in their own right. This transfer of ethos is particularly apparent in memes, where fragmented images constructed across divergent networked media come together to form a single agentic text. Therefore, this chapter argues that a theory of modal ethos is important to understand this artistic proof's role in a networked media ecology. Through a modal analysis of the meme Scumbag Steve, this chapter argues that the modal construction of the meme gives it a unique point of view, complete with narrative history, affective representation, and social expertise—in short, its very own ethos. This allows networked participants to evoke the meme in controversies ranging from NSA wiretapping to the Ukraine Crisis, demanding new forms of political judgment.

INTRODUCTION

The arrival of an unwanted guest at a gathering can be terrifying, particularly when that guest has a history of unsavory behavior. However, in 2011, such an individual became one of the most popular figures on the Internet. Scumbag Steve, a meme depicting a discourteous young man, became an avenue for networked participants to identify the attitudinal and behavioral traits they found least desirable. In this capacity, Steve became the embodiment of the least popular ideas on the Internet (Brad, 2015). As one of the most circulated memes on the Internet (Popular Entries, 2015), Steve has strong cultural capital amongst participants in the networked public sphere. In fact, the meme has become so popular that the subject of the photo, Blake Boston, has adopted its persona to capitalize on the preexisting networked audience (Baker, 2012).

DOI: 10.4018/978-1-5225-1072-7.ch014

More than the propositional content of individual iterations of the meme or the strength of the humor, this meme functions through social understandings of Steve's character as a disreputable and self-centered individual—a "scumbag." Because of this meme's wide circulation, Steve's *ethos* has become a powerful resource for rhetors looking to criticize undesirable rhetorics in networked public spaces. Networked participants have imbued major figures including Barack Obama, Vladimir Putin, and even Congress with the *ethos* of Steve as a method of criticizing these figures' politics. Through the participatory invention of meme users, Steve has developed an *ethos* of his own—the ultimate scumbag. To be associated with Steve via inclusion in the meme suggests a sharing of this *ethos*.

Although these memes take the form of circulated jokes, they are more than trivialities. Rather, memes exert their own form of rhetorical agency. Moreover, just because the form of the meme relies on humor does not mean that Steve's rhetoric is without political consequence. Hubler and Bell (2003) noted that humor is one of the dominant communicative modalities of networked discourse. Moreover, they contended, "Humor that conveys *ethos* pervades the rhetorical. The prerequisite knowledge and implied values of a particular style of humorous discourse have a determining influence on the structure of the community sharing the humor" (p. 277). The way that a networked public jokes about a subject, particularly its *ethos*, is constitutive of the communities that will emerge around that public. This shaping of attention then directs political action, as audiences are attuned by the meme to a particular way of viewing political events (Vie, 2014). Such influence suggests that memes have the capacity to exert rhetorical agency that does not stem from a single rhetor but is imbued in the meme itself.

Because the rhetorical force of Steve lies primarily in his *ethos* as a scumbag, he is a particularly interesting case for the evaluation of the political in networked rhetorics. Specifically, although *ethos* was traditionally considered a product of discourse, it is heavily reliant on bodies, space, and personal history—all concepts that are obscured or removed in networked contexts (Warnick, 2004). In an effort to better understand the shift of *ethos* in networked rhetorics, this chapter follows the advice of Damien Pfister (2014) to "theorize the kinds of rhetorical performances that prevail in networked media" (p. 187). Therefore, this chapter focuses on memes—and Steve in particular—because these texts are not only one of the most pervasive forms of communication native to the networked public sphere, but because their unique form offers a new model of networked *ethos*—the concept of modal *ethos*.

Borrowing from Deleuze, a modal approach to rhetorical phenomena examines form. However, it focuses on form not as a set of restrictions, but rather as a field of potentiality that is renegotiated through each subsequent iteration. Eric Jenkins (2014) argued that this approach is particularly useful for evaluating memes because they do function as traditional unitary. Instead, the assemblage of multiple iterations of the memes, the social regulation of the form of the meme, and the various cultural forces that imbue the memes all come together into a single rhetorical force, which he identifies as a mode. Scumbag Steve's *ethos* defines him as a modal assemblage. This suggests that a modal understanding of *ethos* can better explain the role of *ethos* in networked rhetorics. To develop a broader conception of modal *ethos*, this chapter unfolds in four parts. First, it offers a brief context on the communicative function of memes. Second, it explores how traditional notions of *ethos* are problematized by networked rhetorics. Next, it turns to a close reading of the mode of Scumbag Steve. The chapter concludes by exploring what insights this reading provides for networked *ethos* and the role this proof can play in fostering democratic politics.

MEMES, MODES, AND AGENCY IN NETWORKED PUBLIC ADDRESS

While much of networked rhetorical production focuses on the digital recreation of traditional media, a variety of rhetorical forms have emerged that are unique to the web (e.g. blogs, message boards, and chatrooms). Of these forms, digital memes stand out as a communicative technology that defines networked rhetorical styles, and exemplifies the conundrum behind Warnick's (2004) call to refigure *ethos* for networked environments..

Although it is easy to dismiss digital memes as communicative trivialities, networked rhetors increasingly use memes not only to make jokes in discussion threads, but to offer commentary and reframe political issues (Shifman, 2014). Memes have been demonstrated to draw attention to, and build community around, current social issues (Vie, 2014). Correspondingly, presidential candidate Ben Carson used (incorrect) information from a popular Facebook meme as a talking point in a primary debate (Feinberg, 2016). The political force of memes has become such that media outlets such as the *Washington Post* and *New York Times* often feature stories both about, and using, memes. Similarly, National Public Radio has added a recurring feature discussing the most influential memes of the week. These conversations do not frame memes as authored texts; instead, they frame them as independent agents proliferating across the web.

The understanding of digital memes as an independent force stems from their academic origins. In his influential book, *The Selfish Gene,* Richard Dawkins (1976) coined the term as part of his effort to explain cultural activities that seemed to defy biological drives to survive. In these instances, he argued that cultural drives competed with evolutionary ones. Just as genes drive natural selection, their cultural equivalent, the meme, drives cultural proliferation and selection. Dawkins selected the word meme, a truncation of the Greek work *mimema,* to identify units of cultural transaction that transmit through a process of imitation, such as songs or ideas. Three conditions define the proliferation of a meme: movement from individual to society, reproduction via imitation, and diffusion through competition and selection (Shifman, 2014).

Networked communication technologies, with their abundance of easily accessible cultural information, have become a natural home to memes. Limor Shifman (2014) noted that digital use has somewhat narrowed the conception of a meme. Digital memes are not just modes of cultural reproduction, but instead are "[groups] of digital content units sharing a common content, form, and/or stance" (Shifman, 2014, p. 188)." As audiences identify with one of these traits, they are inspired to circulate them. The capacity to circulate is enhanced if the form of the meme allows for easy remix and recirculation (Lewis, 2012). Under these capacities, memes take a variety of forms, including video remixes, rage comics, and reaction photos. However, the stock character macro is the dominant form of meme in digital environments; in colloquial usage, the term "meme" often refers to stock character macros.

Stock character macros' formal norms define the generic function of the meme. Shifman (2014) noted that these memes function through their use of a single image of a particular stock character, usually a face shot of a person or animal exhibiting some pronounced affective reaction. This genre of memes is also referred to as advice animals, as many of the early characters were animals like Courage Wolf or Socially Awkward Penguin. Each of these images is its own meme, with unique affective dimensions and implied narratives. Imposed on each macro are two lines of text in the impact font. These textual elements, colloquially known as the "topline" and "bottomline," often function, respectively, as the setup and punchline to the joke of each iteration of a meme. Meme users often police incorrect usage of particular image macros, arguing that either the textual form does not meet expectations, or that another image would offer more apt narrative or affective commentary (Vickery, 2014).

Each individual iteration of a meme is deeply embedded in a series of relations between multiple facets, including the meme's formal expectations, its users, the particular poster of an iteration, and the context of an iteration. Recognizing this litany of energies affecting the rhetorical force of a particular meme, Eric Jenkins (2014) argued that memes do not function as traditional texts, but rather as "modes." Focusing on how memes function as a larger assemblage of social forces, Jenkins defined modes as communicative forces which

Circulate across media platforms, producing a recognizable structure that enables the emergence of an open set of images subject to continual remaking. The set remains open to further adaptation and addition because the virtual mode constitutes a manner of engagement or interfacing with images shared by rhetor and audience, a seeing that circulates and thereby shapes both image production and reception. In brief, modes will be defined as manners or ways of engaging (image-) texts or, alternatively, as relational assemblages, such as the assemblage of image, medium, and viewer constituted in the processes of constructing and perceiving. (p. 443)

In understanding memes as modes, Jenkins attunes critics to the circulatory and relational elements of these networked phenomena.

Jenkins (2014) argued that modes function through their adherence to form. He is not relying on a rigid notion of form, but rather uses the term in a Burkean sense, where "form is the creation of an appetite in the mind of the auditor, and the adequate satisfying of that appetite" (Burke, 1968, p. 31). While the textual components change across specific iterations, each iteration emerges around the modal poles. The poles are those standards that dictate what content is acceptable within the assemblage of the meme. In this sense, the form gathers the iterations into a collective actor—a modal assemblage—defined by the relation between the iterations and the form. In defining the character of the meme, these formal elements provide the expectations that allow participants in the assemblage to read similar narratives and affects across iterations.

While circulation defines the life of memes, it also highlights the problem of agency in networked rhetorics. Although individual iterations of memes are deployed by individual rhetors, the ways that a particular iteration may be mobilized are largely controlled by the formal expectations. Grabill and Pigg (2012) noted that as networked texts are increasingly fragmented, remixed, and recirculated, agency becomes increasingly difficult to define. When users repost a video with a new comment, is the rhetorical action theirs, the creator of the video's, or a hybrid of the two? Moreover, many of the fragments will be anonymous in some capacity. However, the concept of the mode combines these fragments and diffuse actors into a single assemblage.

As the starting point of textual action, the mode can then be said to enact its own agency. Specifically, if agency is understood as the ability to affect change, memetic modes are able to enact this through their creation of an implied rhetor. Because the form of image macros relies on particular conceptions of affects, which are often rooted in an implied narrative, they define a meme's particular stance, as well as imply subjectivity behind the utterances. This modal construction positions the character of the meme as an independent rhetor, which can be mobilized by networked participants who deploy particular iterations of a meme. These memes are textual agencies, but lack a clearly defined body, space, or history. As *ethos* is traditionally understood as grounded in these very concepts (Carey, 2000); it must be refigured to understand its relation to modal agentic texts.

CLASSICAL *ETHOS* AND NETWORKED TEXTS

If understood simply as "credibility," *ethos* is easily reduced to the collected sum of the actions performed by a rhetor in their past. However, Holliday (2009) argued that returning to pre-modern conceptions of *ethos* provides a much richer, and more rhetorically attuned, understanding of the term. Halloran (1982) posited that the most concrete meaning for the term in the classical Greek lexicon is "a habitual gathering place" (p. 60). By focusing both on habit and dwelling, this ancient meaning of *ethos* attunes the concept to the preexisting characteristics of a rhetor (habit), within the context of current temporal practice and production (dwelling). In this tradition, many of the sophists understood *ethos* as "both a legitimating source for and a praiseworthy effect of the ethical practice of the orator's art" (Hyde, 2004, p. xiii).

Because rhetors use *ethos* to construct themselves as dwelling within a particular context and situation, a rhetor's *ethos* is intrinsically tied to community. Specifically, rhetors create a space whereby they negotiate what values identify them with a particular audience (Smith, 2004). This negotiation, an extension of *ethos*' root in habit, constructs a vision of idealized social relations.

Those who dwell within a rhetorical community acquire their character as rhetorical participants from it, as it educates and socializes them. The community does this at least in part by supplying the Aristotelian components of ethos – the judgement (phronesis), values (arête), and feelings (eunoia) that make a rhetor persuasive to other members of the community. (Miller, 2004, p. 198)

Ethos does not just constitute the subjectivity of the speaker in relation to the audience, it models ethical social behavior. Consequently, Medhurst (2004) recognized that the question of who may "dwell" within the social *ethos* constructed across political discourses is one of the most important questions of contemporary politics.

Kmetz (2011) reminded that multiple *ethoi* coexist within the civil sphere, meaning questions of politics are driven by the competition between communal *ethoi*. Interlocutors do not expect the rural citizen to have the same wisdom as the resident of the capital. Instead, each must construct a different *ethos* to maximize the force of these varied identities. Consequently, *ethos* has the potential to function akin to its Latin counterpart *persona*; different senses of *ethos* are masks that rhetors can adopt to reflect and direct the values of different audiences (Brooks, 2011). Moreover, as these performances are rooted in collective conceptions, those very collectivities themselves may adopt a sense of *ethos*; organizations, culture, and historical eras each perform their own unique *ethos* (Halloran, 1982).

Because of its performative dimension, *ethos* is intimately tied to the rhetorics of body and space. Although traditional verbal rhetoric plays a role in the construction of *ethos*, the bodily performance of that rhetoric often dictates audience acceptance.

The ethos that is constructed in a speech is a result of more than the propositional content or aural dimensions of the speech. At least in a non-mediated speaking situation, the speaker is more than a voice, rather, he or she is a presence, and how that presence is used shapes the audience perception of the speaker. (Lunceford, 2007, p. 98)

If non-verbal performance does not match audiences' expectations of the performance, no amount of verbal crafting will imbue a rhetor with a particular *ethos*. Moreover, because these standards are rooted in senses of community, the space of the performance further constrains the opportunities to construct an impactful *ethos* (Kmetz, 2011).

Rethinking *Ethos* in Networked Rhetoric

The early history of digital communication praised its potential to reinvigorate democratic expression through the ability to remain anonymous and transcend the limitations of space (Sproull & Keisler, 1991). Under these conditions, networked communication technologies offer the potential for all users to participate in deliberative practices not afforded by older forms of mediation. However, as networked communication structures replace the traditional orator with anonymous, de-spatialized, collectively authored communication, these media create problems for *ethos*—particularly because of the traditional focus of *ethos* on the presence of authorial bodies performing in discrete space. The shift to networked communication has not eliminated the utility of traditional *ethos*. Traditional *ethos* continues to operate, albeit in an updated form, in networked spaces.

Initially, much of the "anonymous" communication on the Internet retains traces of the identity of the rhetor. Crawford (2002) noted that communicative codes, gesture towards the subjectivity of online rhetors. However, even where a critic can infer or construct an authorial body, singular or collective, traditional *ethos* is less clear online. Miller (2001) argued that because prior reputation is not readily apparent in networked rhetors, online *ethos* is

Something more than an interaction between speaker and audience in the traditional sense but, rather, a complex negotiation between various versions of our online and our real selves, between our many representations of ourselves and our listeners and readers. (p. 323)

As networked technologies allow rhetors to adopt a wider range of personas and present them to a larger array of audiences, *ethos*—a force that mediates these relationships—similarly emerges as divided and multiple.

As these *ethoi* are increasingly divided, theories about networked *ethos* need to move away from the embodied rhetor as their source. Warnick (2004) argued that while networked communicators say that they engage in careful consideration of online *ethos*, in practice they rely on rapid decisions based on superficial concerns. Moreover, as information rapidly circulates across digital media, users will quickly use searches to corroborate the utility of the text. This suggests that the information verified across sources, rather than the sources themselves, becomes the foundation of credibility. Because of these forces, as well as the literal absence of identifiable authors in many cases, those traditional versions of *ethos* cannot explain networked rhetoric. Networked e*thos* resides in the text, as part of an ever-changing web of textual relations, rather than in discrete subjects and their performances.

This turn to a textual *ethos* is aided by the concept of the mode. The modal poles, in defining the form of the meme, also function as the *ethos* of the meme. Specifically, as modes manage the affective and narrative potential of the text, they imbue a particular *ethos* onto that textual mode. Moreover, as each meme implies a rhetor—often the subject of the photo—these figures become the locus of modal *ethos*. Modal *ethos* places the meme as the central source of *ethos* within particular utterances, giving each meme the agency to enact the ethical judgments intrinsic to *ethos*. To more fully evaluate this potential of a modal *ethos*, this chapter now turns to a close reading of one of the most popular stock character macros on the Internet, Scumbag Steve.

THE *ETHOS* OF SCUMBAG STEVE

Renowned across social media and web forums, Scumbag Steve—and his now infamous hat—has become a popular meme to convey an unpopular opinion (Baker, 2012). Like many memes, Steve found his origin on 4chan, a popular unmoderated web forum where users compete to create the funniest and most offensive memes. The meme reached peak popularity when a Reddit thread featuring a compilation of iterations of the meme reached the Reddit main page in January of 2011 (Brad, 2015). Since that time, the meme has been in constant circulation and has been identified as one of the 20 most popular memes by Know Your Meme—the online authority on the use and history of memes (Popular Entries, 2015). As a construction of fragments tied together by a common form, the Steve meme functions as a mode. Scumbag Steve is a particularly strong case to evaluate the modal *ethos* of memes because the meme has developed an *ethos* independent of the individual depicted in the picture. Specifically, through the implications are of Steve as a rogue youth, the ethos built around this mode is one of excessive self-interest, disreputable behavior, and indifference to social consequences—a quintessential scumbag.

The *ethos* of the meme originates in the circulating interpretations of the image behind the meme. The image at the center of the meme is a picture of Blake Boston, a young man who lives at home with his parents while aspiring to a career in rap music (Baker, 2012). Boston explained in an interview that his mother took the picture at their house in 2006 when he was 16 years old (Baker, 2012). He then posted the picture on his Myspace page, where it remained dormant for years. However, 4Chan users found the photo and transformed it into a meme, which quickly went viral under the title of Scumbag Steve. Repeated postings of different iterations of the meme then added to the character, filling out his backstory and providing additional depth. Because its status as one of the most circulated memes on the Internet (Popular Entries, 2015) allows for increasing depth, the modal construction of Steve is better able to enact its *ethos,* exerting agency independent of any one user.

The bodily and spatialized presence of Steve dominates the visual form of the mode, setting the formal conditions of its *ethos*. In the photo, Steve is framed by a door; however, the white paint and generic features of the door and molding offer little context. The styling of this architecture suggests that the location could be any suburban home —a reading bolstered by the presence of Steve, a young white male dressed in fashions associated with rap or rap-rock musical genres. The presence of the fur-lined jacket, long chain necklace, stubble-covered face, and most specifically the (mostly) backwards hat tilted at a slight angle, all work together to generate the *ethos* of the meme. Such fashion evokes images of suburban adolescents, replete with house parties and petty vandalism—setting the stage for the reading of the meme as a scumbag. Because the setting is decisively banal, the flashy fashion of Steve seems even more out of place. In the context of the meme, Steve is an unwanted outsider, separate and opposed to the collective gaze of viewers. Such positioning allows users of the meme to borrow Steve and employ him as an unwanted guest invading a comment thread or post.

Moreover, the positioning of Steve's body enhances the way the photo uses implied bodily affect to construct *ethos*. The shot of Steve positions the viewer as lower than Steve. This creates the impression that Steve is entering into a room in which the viewer has already settled. This further increases the gaze-based opposition between Steve and the viewer of the meme. Steve is invading the viewers' space as an undesirable guest. As different users draw on the fashion and its connection to lower socioeconomic classes, or youth conforming to particular images of youthful hip hop emulation, these judgments draw from classist and ageist assumptions. What party wants an economically out-of-place juvenile trying too hard to be tough to crash it? In this sense, the image of Steve evokes a narrative of an unwanted guest, positioning the textual overlay on the meme as the words of this unbearable new interlocutor.

Because the setting is non-remarkable and the photo centers on Steve's face, his facial expression is the focal point of the image. Deleuze (1986) argued that when an image focuses in on the face, removing external context, that image pushes the audience to confront the screen as a representation of a particular affect. In this capacity, the frozen visage of Steve locks the affect—and larger *ethos*—of the image into a static form. The facial expression on Steve lacks a strong emotional response. Instead, his direct but lifeless gaze, as well as his slightly slack jaw, suggests the air of indifference valued in displays of youthful hyper-masculinity (Czopp, Lasane, Sweigard, Bradshaw, & Hammer, 1998). Such a display bolsters Steve's position as an unwanted guest, as his too-cool indifference suggests he will have little regard for the consequences of his actions.

The textual poles of the mode Scumbag Steve emerged out of this visual opposition. This creates a space for users to modally construct a narrative around the figure of Steve, and by extension negotiate his *ethos*. A Reddit thread titled "I hated this guy" collected the earliest manifestations of the meme (I hated this guy, 2011). The title bolsters the frame of the juvenile, framing him as a character from the viewer's past. The title combined with the fashion sense suggests he was a regrettable acquaintance. The textual elements of respective iterations provide reasons the relationship would be undesirable. The toplines of these iterations set up a party behavior such as "borrows lighter" or "you buy the liquor I'll buy the beer." The meme then juxtaposed these lines with the rudest response to the requests, such as "steals lighter" and "case of natty lite." These textual fragments position Steve as a party crasher, lowlife, and self-centered friend. Later iterations of the meme expand the undesirable behaviors beyond the party. Notable examples of the meme include "grandpa gets surgery//steal pain meds," No bro//its spelled liberry (sic)," and "buy pot//from 12 year old" (Brad, 2015). As the meme expanded outside of party behavior, Steve became the embodiment of any undesirable conduct. Any action framed within the bottomline of the text also gains the *ethos* of Steve. The collection of iterations comes together in a mode to construct a social *ethos* of desirable behavior.

Once the modal form structured itself around the narrative and affective reactions to the unwanted guest, this condensed *ethos* allows the meme to then exert agency on other rhetorical situations. Specifically, in its circulation around the Internet, the meme imposed itself on other images in the same way that Steve imposed on parties. Further, many participants took Steve's trademark hat to function as a synecdoche for the meme writ large. Because the design of the hat is so recognizable, a pseudo hound's-tooth pattern in a color scheme reminiscent of Louis Vuitton, participants have easily transposed it onto other photos. Individuals and images, once given the hat are implied to have the same personality—and thus *ethos*—of Steve. This modal extension sets the conditions for the meme to offer commentary on a wider range of social actions than could be easily embodied by the youthful party-going Steve.

Scumbag Steve Goes to Washington

Although the creation of an *ethos* that rejects the variety of behaviors that the meme includes is certainly political onto itself, once synecdochally distilled into the hat, the mode of Scumbag Steve offers its agency to participants to be used to comment on a range of political conditions. This move into politics is hardly surprising, since as Shifman (2014) noted, with their exaggerated performance of affects and actions, stock character macros have a strong capacity to dramatize the morality of networked culture. Steve is not just able to comment on events, participants can also give his *ethos* to any other figure or issue. By enfolding these figures into the modal assemblage of the meme, they are connected to the conditions of *ethos* dictated by the meme's form. In this case, Steve's agency is intertwined with the image placed under the hat as the meme ironically proclaims the wearer of the hat a scumbag and therefore positions all of their actions as ethically suspect

The most prominent use of the Scumbag Hat is to place it on influential figures. Two of the most prolific examples across Internet discourses are Scumbag Putin and Scumbag Obama. The Scumbag Obama variant of the of mode features a picture of President Barack Obama posed in front of the capitol building, arms crossed, with a large smile. Without the imposition of the hat, the facial expression of Obama seems friendly. However, once enfolded within the Scumbag mode, with the backwards hat off-kilter on his head, the smile becomes mocking. In the *ethos* of Steve, it is the easygoing smile of someone enjoying success at the expense of another. The text of these memes supports this reread of Obama. They often suggest that the policies that Obama administration framed as victories are masks hiding the impacts of a more sinister regime. Popular versions of this meme include, "Gets our troops out of Middle East// So they can detain citizens without cause" and "Campaigns against the PATRIOT Act and NSA Phone tapping// Strengthens the programs tenfold." These iterations suggest that the stated policy accomplishments and rhetoric of the administration directly contradict its real impact. Once meme producers place President Obama in the mode, the meme agentically limits the president, constraining him within the persona of the scumbag. This modal imposition of *ethos* invites viewers to reconsider the politics and policies enfolded into the mode.

Steve gave Vladimir Putin similar memetic treatment as global protests against the invasion of Crimea and Russian anti-gay policies proliferated globally. No single picture of Putin defines the meme. Instead, iterations connect a range of pictures to the mode. In some he is smiling, in others he looks menacing, and in some he can only be described as goofy—crossed eyes and a duck face. Yet despite the range of the pictures, the text and the hat override the situated embodied *ethoi* of the photos with the mode's consistent *ethos* of hypocrisy and self-interest. The range of images seems to suggest that while President Putin may present a variety of *persone*, ranging from fun to despotic, the *ethos* of Steve—imbued via the hat—is the universal constant of his *ethos*; he will always be a scumbag. Yet this criticism seems to have a larger function than simply galvanizing the west against Putin. One iteration "wants to repair Russian space program supremacy//but only if your (sic) straight," recognizes that these policies not only violate the ethical norms implied by the meme, but also threaten the success of the Russian people. These modal frames call for a revaluation of the character of international politics. This interaction positions not only the west—the seemingly natural audience of these English language memes—but also Russian citizens as a collective unified in opposition to Putin via their recognition of the ethical judgment enabled by Steve.

Beyond targeting the policies and politics of individual politicians, connections to the mode allow participants to mobilize the meme to criticize entire ideologies by placing images that are representative of the communities and nations under the hat. Another notable meme within the Scumbag memeplex is Scumbag Christian. This iteration of the meme features the hat imposed onto an image of a smiling Kirk Cameron. Cameron, the former sitcom star turned YouTube religious educator, serves as a representative figure for a larger identity of individuals that the meme finds problematic. The meme does not label all Christians as scumbags. Rather, specific iterations proclaim, "that's in the old testament it doesn't count//hates gays" and "accuses atheists of misrepresenting Christianity//says evolution means monkeys giving birth to humans." These iterations indict those with beliefs that the meme argue are out of touch with contemporary life and biblical teachings. Specifically, the meme tends towards indicting three themes: homophobia, aversion to science, and a failure to live up to Christian ethics of love. The dual intertextual moves of using the hat, and Cameron—a figurehead of conservative Christianity who was already lambasted by networked publics—allows these two narratives to coalesce into a single assemblage, tainting the entire ideology with Steve's *ethos*.

Aside from using the hat to impose Steve's *ethos* on particular bodies and the ideologies they represent, it has also expanded to incorporate non-human symbols as representative of larger collectivities. The United States Capitol has had the hat placed over its dome and the fur-lined jacket draped over the chambers of each house of Congress. This memetic treatment transforms the grandiose architecture of the Capitol building into the arrogant posturing of the scumbag *ethos*. Most iterations suggest that Congress fails to act in the interest of citizens. Examples include, "hey bro can I borrow your rights?// never return them." In this case, the meme analogously compares rights to Steve's now infamous lighter, a gift given when needed, but lost forever because the scumbag has no concern for others. This imposition suggests that more than bodies can be enfolded into a mode: any entity that has symbolic meaning can be given this *ethos*.

Steve has also given the entirety of America the scumbag treatment. The Scumbag America meme features an American flag cut in the shape of the outline of the lower 48 states. Steve's backwards hat is perched off-kilter over Washington State, recreating the tilt of the original image. This meme continues the criticism of American wiretapping and Internet censorship– making its global costs more apparent because it frames the entire nation as complicit in the negative political action by the government. Beyond highlighting the hypocrisy of policies, the meme is also used as a more general indictment of American character: "260 year old immigrant nation//hates immigrants" and "doesn't vote for president//puts in 800 votes for American idol contestant." These textual elements, combined with the use of the American flag, indict any patriotic political display as akin to youthful bravado. Here Steve shares his *ethos* with the nation, complete with his machismo, ignorance, and destructive self-interests.

Combined, these iterations demonstrate the ways that modes exert their own *ethos*. As iterations include a wide range of actors, ideas, and communities into the form of the Steve meme, this modal construction dictates the political evaluation of all of them. Anything wearing the hat automatically gains the negative *ethos* established within the modal poles. Once reframed as a scumbag, Putin, Obama, or Congress cannot offer an opinion or policy without audiences of the memes considering them within the *ethos* of the larger meme. Consequently, the mode asserts its own agentic force by directing participants of the meme to position themselves in opposition to the policies that the meme casts as dwelling in a negative *ethos*. Recognizing this capacity of the combined iterations of networked participants to assemble into a mode that functions as an independent pseudo-agent with its own *ethos,* it is important to evaluate the implications of this unique phenomena of networked rhetorical life.

THE POTENTIALS OF MODAL *ETHOS*

Although he may have originated as a simple commentary on undesirable characters from our youth, as the modal assemblage expanded the *ethos* of the meme, Steve gained the agency to comment on a range of social and political issues. However, through the analysis of these varied iterations of the meme, it is evident that this ethical evaluation does not come solely from the verbal content of Steve, but rather from the inclusion of the issues within his modal form and the *ethos* that accompanies it. This *ethos*, which implies narrative and affective histories, positions participants in the meme based on their relation to the mode and the newly incorporated political issues. The actions of Steve are in an ethical realm that respectable members of the networked public sphere should never enter. Three functions further define the rhetorical force of modal *ethos*: reconstituting the body in networked spaces, using parody to engender democratically negotiated social *ethos,* and enacting a diffuse and ventriloquized agency.

Re-Forming the Body in Networked Space

Although networked rhetorical practice is largely defined by the removal of bodies and spaces, Scumbag Steve demonstrates how modes may virtually recreate these concepts. This move is important to the functioning of *ethos* in networked rhetorics because audiences consistently seek to recreate the embodied experiences of traditional forms of rhetoric (Goodwin, 2003). In their networked form, modes function as the forms around which the varied threads of *ethos* functioning in particular moments of networked rhetoric can re-coalesce. In the process these modes construct an implied body in a situation and with a history. Modes such as Steve can replace the traditional embodied rhetor in networked rhetorical situations. Moreover, "digital disembodied media replace rhetors with the perception of characters constructed on scene but these figures are 'an assemblage of body shots' constructed by users and participants to refigure this *ethos*" (Colacel, 2013, p. 20). Thus, the meme reconstructs any message uttered from underneath the Scumbag hat as spoken from the embodied experience of Steve, including his indifference, questionable fashion, and shady past. Scumbag Obama, Putin, or America are no longer speaking from the *ethos* of the parodied figure; they are made consubstantial with Steve. The unifying of these varied figures into one mode creates a collective *ethos* around the implied embodied performance of Steve, allowing this performance to be the dominant rhetorical agency. It bounds the force of related ideas and utterances.

Beyond replacing the bodies—literal or metaphorical—of those placed under the hat with his, Steve also replaces the bodies (and *ethos*) of the individuals posting the memes. Although Crawford (2002) asserted that linguistic practices continue to mark anonymous texts online, the particular formal expectations of the meme obfuscate these markings. Not only do uniform visual elements homogenize the posts, but the language of topline and bottomline also follow uniform patterns. Further, space constraints and memetic expectations dictate that sentences tend to be simple, direct, and laden with slang appropriate to Steve. In this capacity, utterances including words such as "bro" do not mark the poster of the meme as part of a particular subjectivity. Rather, this language is the manifestation of the linguistic norms of the modal *ethos* of Steve. This homogenization erases the agents who post particular iterations; any post could be by any networked participant, an incredibly large and diverse group of people. Without these clear actors, audiences are left to evaluate questions of *ethos* and agency only in terms of the meme.

The meme also repositions users within space. Because stock character macros predominantly focus on the face of the character, they position the meme in direct conversation with viewers (Shifman, 2014). This creates an implied proximity more akin to face-to-face encounters than digital ones. Moreover, the background of the meme enhances the mode's virtual spatialization. The doorway positions Steve as entering our dwelling space. Steve thus becomes a user of the digital space, which Fredrick (1999) noted is a collective product of all participants. This demands that Steve's unpopular opinions are rejected by those he is imposing upon. By forcing users to dwell with him, Steve demands ethical judgment. He is not just a distant text, but rather a present *ethos* whose modally manifested agency demands a response that appropriate to this direct exchange.

The bodies, each with historical narratives, created through the circulation of memes provide a space for varied vernacular rhetorics to dwell on the Internet, each offering commentary on issues that provide alternatives to dominant official narratives. Although Steve, with his dominating bodily *ethos,* provides a singular frame to read any issue or individual enfolded into his modal assemblage, his modal *ethos* gestures towards a larger potential of memes to increase the range of bodily *ethoi* functioning across network settings. Mitra and Watts (2002) argued that the possibility of a range of voices defines the larger *ethos* of networked space. The variety of memes circulating online offers modal bodies to be paired with each of these voices. Different rhetorical communities can embody the awkwardness of Bad Luck Brian, the cool calm of Good Guy Greg, the sinister glare of Pepe, etc. The plethora of memes available provides an ensemble of bodies that rhetors may deploy to provide an embodied character to previously disembodied networked voices. Not only does this range of bodies add further nuance to networked debate by increasing the range of networked rhetorical choices, it also helps to further legitimize a range of viewpoints by opening spaces for additional vernacular *ethoi*. While official discourses dictate traditional politics, vernacular voices can offer alternative *ethos* for evaluating political forces (Brooks, 2011). However, the re-spatialization and embodiment offered by these memes is essential to fostering these voices because the vernacular finds its roots in the understanding of the different ways that individuals dwell.

By providing a range of bodies that may be deployed to comment on an issue—any user may call on the Scumbag *ethos* of Steve regardless of subjectivity—users are able to impersonate the meme, and its *ethos*, for their personal politics. The move to create space for varied personal voices is an imperative in contemporary politics because the personal has become the dominant way that citizens experience government (Johnson, 2012). Consequently, by constructing a range of vernacular bodies in which participants can dwell, the memes create spaces where participants can express a variety of firsthand experiences. This increases the range of ways participants in memes can attend to politics. In allowing varied users to perform the subjectivity performed by the meme, the users also gain access to this performance (Mitra & Watts, 2002). Although such a move certainly has the potential for problematic appropriation of others' bodily *ethos*, it also allows networked communities to constantly reinvent themselves. Built on a range of modal *ethoi*, rather than just the collective *ethos* of the participants, these memes invite users to join varied embodied assemblages. In doing so, the users are also forced to renegotiate their own subjectivity. While Steve's body is positioned as oppositional to users, viewers are also positioned to ask if their attitudes could implicate them as "Scumbags."

Parodic Democratic *Ethos*

In their commentaries on political issues, varied iterations of the Scumbag Meme undeniably rely on a comedic wink to further their point. However, this parodic tone allows the *ethos* of a mode to become a site of democratic political action. As an exaggeration of normative behaviors, this modal assemblage gains its *ethos*—in part—through the recognition that Steve is a parody of the range of potentially problematic behaviors and ideas. No one individual could possibly possess all of the negative qualities of Steve; he is the comic remediation of the problematic behaviors that exist across a range of individuated performances. Consequently, it would be easy to dismiss the varied iterations of Steve as simple jokes. However, jokes are reliant on social structures that make them funny (Mulkay, 1988). Because jokes are both rooted in—and act back upon—social norms, these jokes are constitutive of community and thus intrinsically political (Hubler & Bell, 2003). We are able to laugh at Steve due to the juxtaposition of our social values against his *ethos*.

Rooting the *ethos* of Steve in this irony functions politically in two ways. Initially, by laughing at the text, we engage in what Hubler and Bell (2003) called "constitutive laughter," which is defined by "interconnected messages that function as a gravitational center for *ethos*-building humor" (p. 280). Not only does shared laughter suggest that participants share similar wisdom, virtue, and goodwill (if for no other reason than their comedic rejection of Steve's lack of these qualities), but it also intrinsically connects individuals to a larger collectivity. To laugh at the meme is to recognize that others have had a similar experience. If an audience laughs at Putin, they are joined via this identification to an anti-Putin political *ethos*. This laughter translates personal issues and experience into an intersubjective relation across networked participants. This shared relation, in constituting a community with a particular *ethos* and comic stance, then enables politics by creating new political identities.

Further, by engaging in politics through humor—rather than antagonism—Steve's modal *ethos* promotes a profoundly democratic approach to the political. Hariman (2008) asserted that since political parody punctures myths, engages in social leveling, and invites engaged spectatorship, it rejects authoritarian rhetorics and opens up space for deliberation. Placing the Scumbag Hat on important figures such as Obama or Putin reduces the aura of their celebrity, rendering their opinion only one of many that demand judgment. Similarly, Scumbag America questions the very nature of American exceptionalism. It implies that those very values that make the United States exceptional also cause the world to view it as a scumbag. Finally, as Lewis (2012) noted, because they demand remix and circulation, memes are inherently participatory. Central to their participatory nature is the drive for an ever-funnier interaction: they invite users to outdo each other. Although competitive, this one-upping extends discussion of political issues beyond news stories and dominant narratives.

However, Steve does not simply puncture the myth by offering a singular alternative; because the modal form of the meme allows for a range of iterations, participants in the meme are able to articulate a variety of competing narratives about the exact *ethos* of the issue. The memes do not force the user to judge if Obama is a good president or a scumbag; instead, they cover a range of ways that he *might* be a scumbag. This demonstrates Tønder's (2014) argument that humor provides incongruity and remediates messages to provide a multitude of different interpretations. The range of Scumbag sub-memes opens the door for debates over a variety of complex issues. Users can pass the hat around, and in the process argue that this reviled policy is the responsibility of the president, the legislators, and the American public writ large is complicit. These varied memetic interpretations create a space whereby participants can deliberate, through direct text or posting of additional memes, over who really deserves the hat. Such deliberation allows participants to democratically evaluate the *ethos* of the policies connected to the mode, rather than simply negotiate dominant political and media narratives (Tønder, 2014). Comic modal *ethos* allows the networked public sphere to democratically deliberate and reshape the very *ethos* of politics instead of simply voting for representatives and hoping they act with goodwill.

Modal *Ethos* as Ventriloquist and Ventriloquized Agency

As the combination of external rhetoric, as well as its own modal force, Steve offers a method for understanding agency in networked texts. As the possessor of this democratizing *ethos*, Steve functions as a political agent unto himself. After all, it is his *ethos* that pushes participants towards judging particular actions and ideologies as belonging to scumbags. Yet because Steve's *ethos* can only be deployed when he is circulated by individual networked participants, this agency is diffuse. In this sense, he is representative of Francois Cooren's (2006) observations about the role ventriloquism plays in the agency of constitutive texts. Cooren noted that while texts are ventriloquized by human agents who put them into motion, once put into action, the text has agentic force of its own. He uses the example of the contract to explain this concept. While human agents negotiate the terms of a contract, once in force it can exercise this agency regardless of the wishes of either participant. Similarly, as iterations define and distribute formal poles of a node, iterations are increasingly bound by them.

It is this dual nature of agency that helps Steve direct and shape politics. Certainly, the mode of Steve is comprised of the amalgamation of human authored iterations. However, once created, the meme enacts agency. Not only does a meme's *ethos* comment on issues, it disciplines aberrations from the form that do not fit within the assemblage (Vickery, 2014). When a new iteration of Steve tries to position a new figure or behavior into the meme, different users will deliberate if the iteration fits into the norms of the meme. While individual humans render judgment of these iterations, and rhetorically discipline those who violate expectations, they do so in the name of Steve and his *ethos*. In this capacity, the agency of the mode—rooted firmly in its *ethos*—becomes not merely the product of the relationship of audience and text, as in classical rhetoric (Miller, 2007), but instead that *ethos* arises from a range of human and non-human agencies coming together in a single mode. While Steve is but the force that momentarily connects these fragments into a coherent modal *ethos*, it is this capacity to connect diverse participants and direct them into a single mode that may be the most influential agency in networked rhetorics.

FUTURE RESEARCH DIRECTIONS

If we understand modes as independent actors, they also direct us to the potential of networked spaces in creating a vibrant democratic *ethos*. Specifically, in drawing attention to the ways that particular acts, figures, and ideologies might be considered "scumbags," the meme demands networked participants reconsider dominant political assumptions. Moreover, since the meme acts with a wink and a nod, audiences are able to laugh at these political proclamations. In essence, memes function as clowns in the throne room of politics. Against the stately discourse of official rhetorics they may seem trivial, but in their ability to provide comic remediation they provide an important foil to the pomposity and authority of political leaders. While less threatening, these multiple voices and participatory iterations allow networked participants' ever-growing influence to not only comment on politics, but also to redirect the affect and *ethos* surrounding those political forces. Ultimately Steve's deliberative nature and diffuse agency fractures the seemingly unified *ethos* of political rhetoricians and issues, revealing that these *ethoi* are not fixed, but subject to the negotiation of the varied participants.

Methodologically, regarding the study of memes, this evaluation of Scumbag Steve highlights the importance of considering the rhetorical force of the mode before that of individual iterations. Paulo Virno (2009) noted that particular iterations never exhaust the form. That is to say, while any one meme can demonstrate Steve in action, it cannot represent the meme's entire rhetorical potential. For example, without understanding Steve as an unruly youth entering a party unwanted, the criticisms of Putin's entrance into Crimea become both less poignant and less funny. Therefore, as future scholars engage in the study of memes, and particularly their force as conveyers of *ethos* and rhetorical agency, they ought to begin their focus with a detailed analysis of the construction of the mode. It is only in understanding memetic form as the condition of rhetorical possibility that the efficacy of individual utterances can truly be judged or understood.

Finally, the potential of modal *ethos* demands that we move beyond traditional notions of the concept. By highlighting that *ethos* is not in us, but rather "is behind us and ahead of us, and it only enters us to the extent we take it upon ourselves in the things we do" (Kenny, 2004, p. 35), modal *ethos* creates a space for humanity to care for itself. Carey (2000) argued "that as we become aware of the blurred and porous division between self and others," (p. 39) we are finally positioned to develop the interdependence of beings and shared responsibility for a more ethical life. In making *ethos* a product managed by the collective acts of varied actors, Steve's modal *ethos* demands a new politics, one where none of us are scumbags.

CONCLUSION

As the influence of memes continues to grow across varied political and social contexts, they must not simply be taken seriously as networked texts, but rather as important networked rhetorical agents in their own right. Through their modal construction they are able to develop an ethos that is greater than the sum of the iterations that make up the meme. In creating this space for the meme to dwell, memetic participants take diffuse networked fragments and aggregate them into an implied body enacting a narrative in a particular place. Simply put, once imbued with ethos, memes are able to take on the role of the traditional rhetor. Consequently, as memes and other modes are studied in the future, they ought not to be considered simply as texts employed by human agents so much so as political actors in their own right.

REFERENCES

Baker, B. (2012, November 12). Millis man savors his time as an Internet (punching) bag. *The Boston Globe*. Retrieved December 3, 2015, from https://www.bostonglobe.com/metro/2012/11/24/the-internet-favorite-punching-bag/ijnRiZeT502KmClwC8orDO/story.html

Brad. (2015, June). *Scumbag Steve*. Retrieved December 3, 2015, from *Know Your Meme*: http://knowyourmeme.com/memes/scumbag-steve#fn3

Brooks, M. P. (2011). Oppositional Ethos: Fannie Lou Hamer and the vernacular persona. *Rhetoric & Public Affairs*, *14*(3), 511–548. doi:10.1353/rap.2011.0024

Burke, K. (1968). *Counter-statement* (2nd ed.). Berkeley, CA: University of California Press.

Carey, S. (2000). Cultivating *ethos* through the body. *Human Studies*, *23*(1), 23–42. doi:10.1023/A:1005551410889

Colacel, O. (2013). The body (language) of 'The Saboteur': Obstructionism and banditry in the digital media entertainment. *Meridian Critic*, *18*(2), 13–21.

Cooren, F. (2006). The organizational world as a plenum of agencies. In *Communication as organizing: Empirical and theoretical explorations in the dynamic of text and conversation* (pp. 81–100). Mahwah, NJ: Lawrence Erlbaum.

Crawford, A. (2002). The myth of the unmarked net speaker. In G. Elmer (Ed.), *Critical perspectives on the internet* (pp. 89–104). Lanham, MD: Rowman & Littlefield.

Czopp, A. M., Lasane, T. P., Sweigard, P. N., Bradshaw, S. D., & Hammer, E. D. (1998). Masculine styles of self-presentation in the classroom: Perceptions of Joe Cool. *Journal of Social Behavior and Personality*, *13*(2), 281–294.

Dawkins, R. (1976). *The selfish gene*. New York, NY: Oxford University Press.

Deleuze, G. (1986). *Cinema 1: The movement image*. London, UK: The Althone Press.

Feinberg, A. (2016) Ben Carson's fake Stalin quote came from a right-wing Facebook meme. *Gawker*. Retrieved February 27, 2016 from http://gawker.com/ben-carsons-fake-stalin-quote-came-from-a-ring-wing-fac-1759025587

Fredrick, C. A. (1999). Feminist rhetoric in cyberspace: The *ethos* of feminist UseNet newsgroups. *The Information Society*, *15*(3), 187–197. doi:10.1080/019722499128493

Goodwin, C. A. (2003). The body in action. In J. Couplan & R. Gwyn (Eds.), *Discourse, the body, and identity* (pp. 19–42). New York, NY: Macmillan. doi:10.1057/9781403918543_2

Grabill, J. T., & Pigg, S. (2012). Messy rhetoric: Identity performance as rhetorical agency in online public forums. *The Quarterly Journal of Speech*, *42*(2), 99–119.

Halloran, S. M. (1982). Aristotle's concept of *ethos*, if not his somebody else's. *Rhetoric Review*, *1*(1), 58–63. doi:10.1080/07350198209359037

Hariman, R. (2008). Political parody and public culture. *The Quarterly Journal of Speech*, *94*(3), 247–272. doi:10.1080/00335630802210369

Holliday, J. (2009). In[ter]vention: Locating rhetoric's ethos. *Rhetoric Review*, *28*(4), 388–405. doi:10.1080/07350190903185049

Hubler, M. T., & Bell, D. C. (2003). Computer-mediated humor and *ethos*: Exploring threads of constitutive laughter in online communities. *Computers and Composition*, *20*(3), 277–294. doi:10.1016/S8755-4615(03)00036-7

Hyde, M. J. (2004). Introduction: Rhetorically we dwell. In M. J. Hyde (Ed.), *The ethos of rhetoric* (pp. xiii–xxviii). Columbia, SC: University of South Carolina Press.

I hated this guy. (2011, January 21). Retrieved December 3, 2015, from Reddit: https://www.reddit.com/r/funny/comments/f65ra/i_hated_this_dude/

Jenkins, E. (2014). The modes of visual rhetoric: Circulating memes as expressions. *The Quarterly Journal of Speech*, *100*(4), 442–446. doi:10.1080/00335630.2014.989258

Johnson, J. (2012). Twitter bites and Romney: Examining the rhetorical situation of the 2012 presidential election in 140 characters. *Journal of Contemporary Rhetoric*, *2*(3/4), 54–64.

Kenny, R. W. (2004). Truth and metaphor: Imaginative vision and the *ethos* of rhetoric. In M. J. Hyde (Ed.), *The ethos of rhetoric* (pp. 34–55). Charleston, SC: University of South Carolina Press.

Kmetz, M. (2011). 'For want of the usual manure': Rural civic *ethos* in Ciceronian Rhetoric. *Rhetoric Review, 30*(4), 333–349. doi:10.1080/07350198.2011.604607

Lewis, L. (2012). The participatory meme chronotope: Fixity of space/rupture of time. *New Media Literacies and Participatory Culture Across Borders,* 106-121.

Lunceford, B. (2007). The science of orality: Implications for rhetorical theory. *The Review of Communication, 7*(1), 83–102. doi:10.1080/15358590701211142

Medhurst, M. J. (2004). Religious rhetoric and the *ethos* of democracy: A case study of the 2000 presidential campaign. In M. J. Hyde (Ed.), *The ethos of rhetoric* (pp. 115–135). Charleston, SC: University of South Carolina Press.

Miller, C. R. (2001). Writing in a culture of simulation: Ethos online. In *The semiotics of writing: Transdisciplinary perspectives on the technology of writing* (pp. 253–279). Turnhout, Belgium: Brepols.

Miller, C. R. (2004). Expertise and agency: Transformations of *ethos* in human-computer interaction. In M. J. Hyde (Ed.), *The ethos of rhetoric* (pp. 197–218). Charleston, SC: University of South Carolina Press.

Miller, C. R. (2007). What can automation teach us about agency? *Rhetoric Society Quarterly, 37*(2), 137–157. doi:10.1080/02773940601021197

Mitra, A., & Watts, E. (2002). Theorizing cyberspace: The idea of voice applied to the internet discourse. *New Media & Society, 4*(4), 479–498. doi:10.1177/146144402321466778

Mulkay, M. (1988). *On humor: Its nature and its place in modern society.* Cambridge, MA: Basil Blackwell.

Pfister, D. (2014). *Networked media, networked rhetorics.* University Park, PA: The Pennsylvania State University Press.

Popular Entries. (2015). Retrieved December 3, 2015, from *Know Your Meme*: http://knowyourmeme.com/memes/popular

Shifman, L. (2014). *Memes in digital culture.* Cambridge, MA: The MIT Press.

Smith, C. R. (2004). *Ethos* dwells pervasively. In M. J. Hyde (Ed.), *The ethos of rhetoric* (pp. 1–19). Charleston, SC: University of South Carolina Press.

Sproull, L., & Keisler, S. (1991). *Connections: New ways of working in the networked organization.* Cambridge, MA: The MIT Press.

Tønder, L. (2014). Comic power: Another road not taken? *Theory & Event, 17*(4).

Vickery, J. R. (2014). The curious case of Confession Bear: The appropriation of online macro-image memes. *Information Communication and Society, 17*(3), 301–325. doi:10.1080/1369118X.2013.871056

Vie, S. (2014). In defense of "slacktivism": The Human Rights Campaign Facebook logo as digital activism. *First Monday, 4*(7).

Virno, P. (2009). Angels and the general intellect: Individuation in Duns Scotus and Gilbert Simondon. *Parrhesia*, *7*, 58–67.

Warnick, B. (2004). Online *ethos*: Source credibility in an 'authorless' environment. *The American Behavioral Scientist*, *48*(2), 256–265. doi:10.1177/0002764204267273

KEY TERMS AND DEFINITIONS

Agency: The ability to effect change.

Ethos: Artistic proof built around the preexisting characteristics and performed habits of a rhetor or text.

Meme: Units of cultural replication. In its most common form refers to Internet phenomena that are defined by ease of circulation, remix, common stance, and form.

Mode: A way of defining the nature of networked texts. Focuses on the way formal elements unify and direct the potential of related textual iterations.

Modal Assemblage: The sum of the combined texts, agents, materials, etc., that make up a mode. Draws attention to the capacity of modes to include preexisting texts, rhetors, and concepts.

Scumbag Steve: One of the most popular Stock Image Macros. Draws attention to violations of decorum and other "scummy" activities. Steve's hat is often used as an enthymeme for the larger meme.

Stock Image Macro: One of the most popular forms of memes. Also known as an advice animal. Defined by the topline/bottomline textual format and the use of a static image as the background.

Chapter 15
The Rise of the Modern Sports Article:
Examining the Factors that Can Influence the Credibility of Online Sports News

Sean R. Sadri
Old Dominion University, USA

ABSTRACT

The evolution of online media has brought forth a new age of fandom online for sport enthusiasts with access to hundreds of new sports articles daily. This chapter touches on the perceived credibility of the modern sports article and provides evidence from scholarly studies, including the author's own sports credibility study. The study examines how article source, medium, fan identification, and user comment tone can all impact the credibility of a sports article. Study participants were randomly assigned to read a sports article in 1 of 12 stimuli groups. The article source was indicated to have appeared on a main-stream sports website, a sports blog, a social networking site, or a wire service as well as with positive comments, negative comments, or without comments. Analysis revealed that fan identification level was an important factor in credibility ratings as highly identified fans found the article to be significantly more credible than low identification fans as a whole. The study implications and factors influencing the credibility of an online sports article are explored.

INTRODUCTION

Few aspects of American life compare to an old-fashioned sports rivalry. Nearly every fan has a favorite team, and every team has a bitter rival. Coaches and players spend all season preparing for this rivalry game they desperately want to win. For the players, it's glory on the gridiron, the field, the rink, or the court, and a chance to establish themselves under the bright lights. For the fans, these games may mean even more. Crowds pack the parking lots hours before the game to tailgate with friends and support their team. Team logos are seen on clothing, windshields, and even license plates, and it clearly establishes what side a fan is rooting for. Fans can easily spot their enemy. The attitude between opposing fans can

DOI: 10.4018/978-1-5225-1072-7.ch015

get contentious, and this all happens before the game even starts. From the opening kickoff to the final whistle, the crowd is raucous and loud as fans from both teams realize what is at stake in a rivalry. When the game is over, the fans from the winning team go home ecstatic with a year of bragging rights. This may seem like insanity, but to a sports fan, this is completely ordinary.

Whether at a live game, in front of a television, or streaming from a cell phone, millions of fans around the world have felt the highs and lows of sport, which has turned sports media into a multi-billion dollar industry. American sports programming in 2014-15 generated $8.47 billion in sales for ABC, CBS, NBC and Fox, accounting for more than one-third (37%) of those companies' overall ad revenue for that period (Crupi, 2015). In 2014, Chevrolet, AT&T, Geico, Verizon, and Budweiser each invested over $250 million in advertising during live sporting events (Crupi, 2015). While digital video recorders (DVRs) have seemingly diminished the value of television ad marketing, sports continues to guarantee a reach of millions of live viewers for hundreds of games a year. Live sports media is also no longer relegated to just television screens. For the first time ever, the National Football League broadcast a regular-season game exclusively on the Internet: October 2015 marked the first time in which audiences around the country needed a computer or mobile device to watch an NFL game (Dougherty, 2015).

Sport has become a staple of American society as millions of fans are influenced by sport every day, and more individuals are becoming interested and active in sports (Wann, Melnick, Russell, & Pease, 2001). Sports and exercise have even come to carry cultural meanings that reflect the ideologies of our wider society and have been recognized as common elements of civic engagement (Beyer & Hannah, 2000). Robbins (2004) argued that in recreational sports (such as those with friends), all players are aware of the basic rules—and the repercussions of violating those rules—and take on roles as self-officiation. Players must create order "by creating a moral code of conduct or an ethos—the spirit of the game" (p. 315). An ethos, or spirit of a culture, is a meaningful system of morals, customs, norms, or practices of a group or society, which can often influence other norms or customs (Geertz, 1973; Robbins, 2004). The inherent competition that exists within sports has also been described by scholars as the ultimate struggle of good and evil, where "winning is a sign of goodness, rightness and divine approval" (Beyer & Hannah, 2000, p. 110).

The ethos of sport is not only manifested in the athletes themselves but also by their fans. Sport fandom is associated with an individual's affinity for specific sports teams. Many fans feel connected to a sports team in ways that go beyond the games themselves and carry over into a person's daily life. Some fans are so engulfed by their relationship to a team's successes and failures that it becomes a part of their social identity (Hu & Tang, 2010). Tajfel's (1981) social identity theory asserted that maintaining memberships in significant social networks would enhance a person's social identity, which in turn results in a more positive self-concept. These significant group memberships and relationships are used in social comparisons to develop and maintain one's self-esteem. The individuals within the group typically develop a system of social norms and values, which regulate their opinions and actions (Turner, 1982). In the sports realm, fan identity is the personal commitment or emotional involvement a person has with a sports organization (Milne & McDonald, 1999).

Fan identification has been shown to predict fan consumption behavior through sport media usage as highly identified fans are more likely to watch games through media or in person, pay more for tickets, and spend more on team merchandise (Laverie & Arnett, 2000). One study found that a person residing in the environment where the team is located, such as a fan of a college football team who lives on the university's campus, may gain enduring social connections (Wann, 2006). Sport fandom has become an important aspect of social relations, and social scientists are showing more interest in understanding fan involvement online (Wann, Friedman & McHale, 2003).

The shift to online-centric media can be felt throughout the journalism industry. The Pew Research Center found that cable news viewership has dropped 8% and newspaper circulation has dropped 3% from 2013 to 2014 (Mitchell, 2015). Newspaper advertising revenue has dropped 4% to $19.9 billion in that same timeframe, but digital ad revenue increased 18% to $50.7 billion. The modern media environment has also changed how individuals receive their news. In a survey of the current state of the news media, Pew Research Center found that half of Facebook users get their news from the social media website (Mitchell, 2014). The survey also suggested that the growth of social media and mobile phones offers media organizations the opportunity to reach more people than ever before.

The gains in online readership over the years may suggest high credibility for news and sports websites, but many of these websites lack proper factual verification, analysis of content, and editorial review (Chung, Kim, & Kim, 2010). The Information Age has diminished perceptions of media credibility in the eyes of citizens because people are generally skeptical of news from the three most popular channels: television, print, and online (Kiousis, 2001). Online credibility has been questioned since the early days of Internet news by some scholars (Newhagen & Levy, 1998), but the way individuals engage with media has changed drastically in the last twenty years.

BACKGROUND

Currently, there is no concrete consensus on the elements that build online credibility, so the present study outlined in this chapter aims to provide media theorists and media professionals a blueprint for what might work for audiences across media. Several facets of online journalism are addressed, including insights on the ever-growing realm of social media. The relevance of this study is amplified by the sheer lack of research on sports journalism and sports ethos. Oates and Pauly (2007) argued that the overall principles of online and traditional media credibility are applicable to sports. The authors argued that "sportswriting fundamentally resembles other forms of reporting and that journalism should not use sports as an ethical straw man against which to defend the virtue of its serious work" (Oates & Pauly, 2007, p. 332). However, the scope of this study is not limited to sports because all facets of news credibility can be dictated by some social identity, such as political partisanship. Ultimately, the present study is meant to bring insight and clarity to the evolving discourse on online credibility and digital ethos.

Digital Ethos and Credibility in the Modern Media Environment

Since the turn of the century, the Internet has been blamed by some scholars for the decline in media credibility (Johnson & Kaye, 2000). Because both traditional media and online media are being examined, it is useful to explore literature that compares the two. Kiousis (2001) examined the perceptions of news credibility for television, newspapers, and online, and found that news consumers are generally skeptical of news from all three channels. Newspapers were rated as having the highest credibility, followed by online news, and television news finished third. The author suggests that the dissemination of new technology often shifts opinions of older media. Essentially, access to the Internet may have increased the public trust of newspapers, while simultaneously reducing the trust in television (Kiousis, 2001). Modern news consumers are potentially experiencing a similar situation with cell phone technology and social media, where news is constantly being updated every minute, but there is so much information (much of it erroneous) that people are being disillusioned sifting through the facts and hearsay.

Recent technological advancements have made the job of the journalist easier, but have changed how people get their news and what they expect from it (Meyer, Marchionni & Thorson, 2010). In a study on online credibility, Meyer, Marchionni, and Thorson (2010) determined that an online author's perceived expertise is the strongest predictor of article and organization credibility. They argue that in the Digital Age, perceived expertise is predominantly determined by the level of shared meaning by the sender (journalist, blogger, Tweeter, etc.) and receiver (audience). Apostel and Folk (2005) examined how students evaluate the credibility of websites and online sources through digital ethos. The authors found that students will verify information on one website by trying to find that information on other websites. Students will also evaluate websites based on the design and their initial "feelings" of the site based on that design (characterized as technological ethos). Additionally, students experience citation ethos when other sources link *to* their chosen website. Essentially, credibility is bestowed by the link citations a website receives rather than the links it gives.

Digital ethos and a communal identity can also influence the ways in which news consumers perceive credibility. Gamie (2013) examined digital ethos construction and the sense of shared identity that was forged on the Facebook pages of two Egyptian groups during the 2011 Egyptian Revolution. The author found that anonymity played a profound role in digital discourses and created a sense of community by legitimizing calls for activism, reform, and revolutionary work. The author asserts that activist discourse can function more positively and safely in an anonymous environment as facelessness preserves digital ethos. However, when identities are exposed, individuals can become targets of regime operatives, thus making anonymity paramount.

Digital ethos has also been used to examine the credibility of Wikipedia and its dramatic influence on the Internet, popular culture, and the production and consumption of knowledge (McGrady, 2013). Wikipedia and other Wiki sites exhibit credibility through a community ethos that acknowledges the fallibility of its individual parts. The Wikipedia community has evolved over time, and rules within this community were created to standardize, organize, and mobilize masses to help eliminate the spread of erroneous information. The credibility of each page grows as more information becomes available and statements on pages can be validated with external links.

In the same way that Wikipedia has evolved with the Internet, online newspapers have become much more than simple web-based versions of a printed newspaper. They implement a bevy of additional content (such as videos, audio, and external hyperlinks) as well as provide users up-to-the-minute updates of the day's events. A survey on web 2.0 credibility (i.e., social networking, blogs, wikis, etc.) found that journalists in countries like Portugal consider these web 2.0 news sources to be unreliable (Serra & Canavilhas, 2013). However, a disconnect exists because the majority of journalists surveyed still use these sources to discover new stories and look for new stories. The authors assert that journalists rely on both the traditional means of assessing credibility (such as interviewing and reputation) and the newer means of credibility based on group assessments and collective intelligence.

The Internet has also given rise to the online-only news site, which can offer users a different perspective on national and global news. Chung, Kim, and Kim (2010) examined online newspaper credibility and divided online news into three distinct categories: mainstream, independent, and index. Their study determined that the mainstream type of online newspapers, such as *USAToday.com*, received the highest scores on most credibility items. However, the index type of news (or an online newsfeed providing news from various sources) was rated highest in creativeness, attractiveness, and having interesting items. The authors argued that a website like *Google News* empowers users by offering them many choices of content. Online news consumers also have the freedom to subscribe to topics that interest them, such as sports news or entertainment news. The online-only independent news source had the lowest reported scores in expertise, attractiveness, and trustworthiness. Echoing these findings, Gunter (2006) determined that Internet users typically trust online news produced by established news providers more than news produced by independent online sources. The authors found that news credibility is mediated primarily by the reputation of the news supplier's brand and the relative partisanship or neutrality of news consumers on specific issues. This is analogous to sports fans who find articles disparaging of their favorite team and dismiss them for being biased, inaccurate, or untrue.

Fan Identification and the Perceived Credibility of Online Sports Articles

Social identity theory is inherently based in comparisons, so this theory can be applied to sports fans who often make comparisons between themselves and the outgroup (fans of rival teams). Wann, Dimmock, and Grove (2003) suggested that one "societal connection that may have important benefits for psychological health involves the strong ties fans often feel for their chosen sports team (i.e., those fans who are highly identified with their team)" (p. 289). Team identification has also been shown to facilitate a fan's well-being by increasing the likelihood of obtaining temporary and enduring social connections (Wann, 2006). Conversely, this beneficial relationship for fans is moderated by threats to a fan's social identity, such as a team's poor performance during the season.

The social connections established through sporting events and fan relationships are seemingly amplified through sports media. Wann and Branscombe (1992) found that the emotional responses to a sports article were different based on the level of identification with the sports team being covered. Highly identified fans experienced the most positive mood state when the article described a victory for the ingroup sports team, and whose author was an admitted loyal fan of that team. The most negative mood state was evoked when the team lost the competition and the article author was a disloyal fan of the participant's favorite team. The study also discovered that participants with low fan identification were not significantly influenced by the article author's group membership, the author's commitment to the team, or the game outcome.

Online readers have also been shown to seek out blogs that are tailored to their specific interests (Johnson & Kaye, 2004). Johnson and Kaye (2004) found that blog users judged blogs as highly credible and more credible than traditional media sources. Blog users in the study "rely on blogs because they provide more depth and more thoughtful analysis than is available in other media" (p. 633). Unbiased reporting is often considered a hallmark of traditional journalism, but the authors suggested that noticeable bias is seen as a virtue by blog users. For example, the majority of participants rated themselves as conservative, so they actively seek out conservative blogs that support their views and promote a community ethos. Sports fans will often seek out blogs that are dedicated to their favorite team but may not be objective and may refrain from being critical of that team.

For fans, the highs and lows experienced by wins and losses may even extend past the sports environment itself and validating their personal sports ethos. Van Leeuwen, Quick, and Daniel (2002) asserted that fans feel a sense of attachment to a university represented by the school's sports teams. The authors found that students at a university may feel closer to their university through sport than everyday college life, and social identity through college athletics goes well beyond on-field success. A similar study determined that college students list their parents, the talent of the players, geographical reasons (i.e., rooting for the home team), and the influence of one's friends and peers all ahead of team success as reasons they originally started following their favorite team (Wann, Tucker & Schrader, 1996). At certain universities, athletic programs also provide a sense of communal involvement within the institution, the local community, and, in some cases, an entire state (Melnick, 1993). Other scholars have found a positive relationship between identification for a university's men's basketball and football teams and a student's enjoyment and satisfaction with that university, the extent to which the university met expectations, as well as involvement and persistence at the university (Wann & Robinson, 2002).

In the field of sports broadcasting, Keene and Cummins (2009) examined the effects of a sports commentator's previous athletic experience on the perceived credibility of the broadcaster and viewer evaluations of game play. They found that athletic experience impacts perceptions of credibility, such that commentators without playing experience were viewed as least credible and participants rated their games as less enjoyable and exciting. Even a sportscaster's appearance has been shown to impact how audiences judge credibility. Scholars have found that physical attractiveness in a female sportscaster is positively correlated with competence, dynamism, expertness, and trustworthiness (Davis & Krawczyk, 2010).

The Impact of Anonymous User Comments on Credibility

The chapter author's present study also examines the impact of user comments on the perceived credibility of sports articles. The social identification/deindividuation (SIDE) model of computer-mediated communication effects is a useful tool for understanding the influence of visually anonymous peers (Reicher, Spears & Postmes, 1995). Based on previous research in this field (Lea, Spears, Watt & Rogers, 2000; Walther, DeAndrea, Kim & Anthony, 2010), this model asserts that an online reader's level of identification with online peer users can influence evaluations of credibility. Unlike Facebook wall posts from friends, the SIDE model puts primary emphasis on visual anonymity, which is essential for predicting and understanding online behavior (Lea et al., 2000). Applying the SIDE model to their study on YouTube comments, Walther et al. (2010) examined the influence of user comments on perceptions of YouTube anti-marijuana public service announcements (PSAs). The results showed that supportive or negative comments affected the study participant's evaluations of the PSAs, but did not affect a participant's attitude toward marijuana. However, the combination of user comments and the social identification of the participants to the users affected both PSA evaluations and attitudes towards marijuana positively or negatively, depending on the tone of those comments.

Scholars argue that an anonymous computer environment can give people the freedom to enact new identities and liberate themselves from the limitations brought on by reality, identity, expectations, and conventions (Turkle, 1996). Online identity is essentially a form of digital ethos in which individuals can recreate themselves into anything they imagine. Countering this argument, Postmes, Spears and Lea (1998) argued that even though a potential for identity replacement exists, people may not always want to free themselves from social constraints and look to the Internet to reinforce their real-world identities. The SIDE model suggests that an anonymous encounter in a group diverts attention from the individual level of interaction and focuses attention on the social level, which continually emphasizes social boundaries and the ingroup/outgroup dynamic (Postmes, Spears & Lea, 1998). This model is useful for examining the role of user comments in sports articles where the large majority of online users are completely anonymous. Thus, highly identified sports fans could be more likely to find an article as credible if the user comments are positive about their favorite team than if the comments are negative. Additionally, participants with low fan identification often will not waver in their credibility assessments based on the user comments.

Ultimately, there are a multitude of factors that can affect the level of credibility attributed to online sports articles. The purpose of the study in this chapter is to examine the impact of the medium and the sports news source(s) on the credibility of sports articles for fans with both high and low identification. Looking specifically at differences in online media (sports website, social networking website, and sports blog) and comparing those with a more traditional form of media (wire service), this study tested the effects of sports fan identification on the perceived credibility of a sports article. Using social identity theory, fan identification, and the SIDE model as the primary theoretical frameworks, the study also analyzed how credibility assessments of a sports article are affected by positive and negative user comments. Building off of Chung, Kim, and Kim's (2010) study on online credibility, the present study examined the influence of the website itself on credibility by comparing a mainstream sports news source (ESPN.com), an independent sports news source (a sports blog), and an index sports news source (a Facebook note) in the experiment, and compared those to a traditional wire service (*Associated Press*).

STUDY DESIGN AND METHODOLOGY

The present study was an online experiment looking primarily at online news sources, so it was designed to reflect the natural setting of reading an online article and was administered online. A convenience sample of college students was used based on availability and accessibility to a sample population at a large public academic institution in the southeastern United States. Although a convenience sample is not ideal because the findings are less generalizable, the use of a convenience sample of college students has been utilized in previous scholarly studies involving sports fans. For example, Wann and Branscombe (1992) used college students in their study on fan emotional responses to the sports page, and Pham (1992) used a sample group of undergraduate students to study the effects of fan involvement and arousal on the recognition of sponsorship stimuli at a sporting event. In the present study, the participants were recruited from undergraduate mass communication classes, and extra credit was offered as an incentive for participation in the study. The present study had a total of 376 participants, all of whom were undergraduate students at the university. The mean age was 20.45 years old, and the majority of participants were female ($N = 255$) (Table 1).

Table 1. Profile of sample population

	Total ($N = 376$)	Percentage
Gender		
Male	121	32.2
Female	255	67.8
Age		
Average	20.45	
Standard Deviation	1.757	
Fan Identification Level		
Low Identification	174	46.3
High Identification	202	53.7

Because the sample population had more female participants than male participants, a potential gender bias may have shifted the results. However, additional analysis was conducted after the data was collected, and the results showed that men and women had similar scores in nearly every scale used. Both genders had statistically similar scores on the fan identification scale ($F(1, 374) = 1.74, p = .190$), which was the basis for determining whether a participant was classified as a highly identified fan or low identification fan. Identification scores with the university ($F(1, 374) = 2.38, p = .124$) and with the anonymous users ($F(1, 250) = .82, p = .367$) were also close between the two genders. Additionally, males and females had similar evaluation ratings of the sports news sources ($F(1, 374) = 2.39, p = .123$), so the perceived gender bias did not have a profound impact on the study's results.

Additionally, threats to internal validity can impact the presumed causation between variables in an experiment (Shadish, Cook & Campbell, 2002), so a randomized-groups post-test only experimental design was used to counteract many internal validity threats. A pilot study was also run before conducting the experiment to fix any issues that could arise during the experiment. Appropriate adjustments were made to the study based on the outcome of the pilot study and recommendations of the participants. The present study was a 3 x 4 experimental design and participants were randomly assigned to one of twelve stimuli groups, each receiving the same sports article (Table 2). The article was taken from a previously published *Associated Press* article (Pells, 2012) about an NCAA Men's Basketball Tournament game involving the university being studied. The article recapped a basketball game in which the sample population's university had lost and was subsequently eliminated from the NCAA Tournament. Some minor changes to the article were made by the chapter author that did not affect the accuracy or factuality of the article itself.

During the experiment, one group of participants received the stimuli with a large ESPN.com banner at the top of the article, as well as the website's name beneath a fictional author's name. The bottom of the article had three positive user comments from users who support the university's men's basketball team, and the comments were aimed solely at the team, not at the article itself. The second group received the stimuli with a large banner for a popular sports blog that covers the university's athletic program at the top of the article, as well as the website's name beneath the fictional author's name. The bottom of the article also had three positive comments from supporters of the university's team. The third group received the stimuli as a Facebook note with the same fictional author and a large Facebook symbol at the top of the article. The note also had three positive comments at the end of the article. The large banners were all the same size and font and were designed to look nearly identical. The anonymous user comments were also identical for all three online sources.

The fourth, fifth, and sixth groups received the same initial stimuli with the same online sources as the previous three. However, these groups received a set of three negative user comments from users who support a rival university's team at the bottom of the article. The user comments would be analogous to

Table 2. 3 x 4 experimental design

ESPN.com Article	Sports Blog Article	Facebook Note	Wire Service Article
Positive User Comments (30*)	Positive User Comments (29)	Positive User Comments (33)	Positive User Comments (31)
Negative User Comments (32)	Negative User Comments (32)	Negative User Comments (32)	Negative User Comments (33)
No Comments (30)	No Comments (33)	No Comments (30)	No Comments (31)

*Note: Number denotes the number of participants that completed the study in each cell.

a Real Madrid fan posting disparaging comments on a soccer article about FC Barcelona immediately after Barcelona had been eliminated from the UEFA Champion's League tournament. The negative comments were targeted solely at the university's men's basketball team and were not disparaging of the article itself. The seventh, eighth, and ninth groups were control groups which received the article with one of the three online sources without any user comments. The comments and the fictional usernames used were all written by the chapter author, and the user comments were all reviewed in the pilot study and deemed as appropriate by the pilot study participants.

The final three groups received the stimuli as an article from a traditional wire service source, the *Associated Press*. The article had an *Associated Press* logo at the top of the article, as well as typed beneath the author's name. One group received only the article itself, while the two final groups received either positive or negative reader comments at the bottom of the page.

Because this experiment was focused on the potential impact of social identity, the manipulations of positive and negative user comment tone were measured by how positively or negatively participants identified with the anonymous users. The manipulations were analyzed after the experiment using an anonymous user comment scale, developed by Postmes, Spears, Sakhel, and de Groot (2001). Data analysis determined that the user comments with a positive tone ($M = 3.62$, $SD = 1.62$) garnered a higher identification score from participants than the user comments with a negative tone ($M = 2.19$, $SD = 1.35$). A univariate ANOVA was conducted, and it was determined that a significant difference existed between the two user comment tones ($F(1, 250) = 57.59$, $p < .001$), thereby validating the manipulations and suggesting that the user comments were appropriately constructed for this study.

The experiment began with a questionnaire that measured the participant's level of identification as a sports fan in general, as well as a fan of the university's men's basketball team. Total fan identification was measured by combining Shank and Beasley's (1998) refined sports involvement scale with Wann and Branscombe's (1993) team identification scale. The involvement scale asked participants to rate their personal feelings about sports using a $1 - 7$ bipolar scale. Participants were asked to indicate if sports are: boring/exciting, uninteresting/interesting, valuable/worthless, unappealing/appealing, useful/ useless, needed/not needed, irrelevant/relevant, and unimportant/important. For the present study, the scale was shown to be very reliable (Cronbach's $\alpha = .941$).

The team identification scale consisted of seven questions that addressed how participants feel about the university's men's basketball team (Wann & Branscombe, 1993). The questions asked participants to rate their feelings on a $1 - 8$ bipolar scale and included questions regarding how important it is that the team wins, how strongly they see themselves as a fan, how strongly their friends see them as a fan, how closely they follow the team during the season, how important being a fan is to them, how much they dislike the university's biggest rivals, and how often they display the team's name or insignia at work or at home. The team identification scale was also shown to be very reliable for this study (Cronbach's $\alpha = .931$).

These two scales were combined for the purposes of this study to define participants categorized as highly identified fans or fans with low identification. The average score of the sports involvement scale and the team identification scale were summed, and a split of the summed means determined placement into a fan identification group for this study. A mean of the combined score was determined ($M = 9.98$, $SD = 2.93$), and participants with a total above or below that score were placed in the appropriate group. A one-way ANOVA showed that there was a significant difference in mean scores between the two fan identification groups ($F(1, 374) = 763.701$, $p < .001$). Nearly all the participants were at least minimally identified as sports fans, so identification level was defined as either high or low in this study. The initial questionnaire also concluded with a set of demographic questions about participant age, gender, and field of study.

After participants completed the initial questionnaire, they were randomly assigned a sports article in one of twelve groups listed earlier (Table 2). The online experiment was programmed to randomize each group and distribute the stimuli evenly. Before seeing the article, participants received a set of on-screen instructions asking them to read everything that appeared on the following screen and informing them that they will be asked to answer questions about what they have read. The article was the same for every participant, but it was indicated as to have originated from one of the four media organizations. Additionally, unless the participant was assigned to a control scenario, the participant also saw user comments (either positive or negative) at the bottom of the page.

After reading the article, the last aspect of the experiment was a final questionnaire, although certain aspects of the questionnaire varied based on the stimulus that the participant received. The first scale in the questionnaire measured a participant's attitude toward the website the article was said to originate from or the *Associated Press* (O'Cass & Carlson, 2010). Participants were asked to rate how they feel about ESPN.com, a popular sports blog covering the team, Facebook, or the *Associated Press* on a 1 – 7 Likert scale. They were given nine statements about their mood and level of excitement when using the media source, and they were asked to indicate their feelings from "strongly disagree" to "strongly agree." O'Cass and Carlson's (2010) scale was shown to be extremely reliable for the present study (Cronbach's $\alpha = .962$).

Participants were then asked to answer nine questions developed from a scale that measures the perceived credibility of the article (Bucy, 2003). The questions determined how the participants felt about the article itself and provided two contradictory items along a 7 – point bipolar scale. The scale included ratings of how fair, interesting, clear, enjoyable, accurate, believable, informative, and in-depth it was; it also measured nicely the article flowed. The credibility scale was also shown to be highly reliable for this experiment (Cronbach's $\alpha = .89$). For participants who received the stimuli with user comments, the next scale examined a participant's attitude toward the users who posted the anonymous comments (Walther et al., 2010). Participants were given five statements about their connection and identification with that group of people, and asked to rate their feelings on a 7-point bipolar scale ranging from "not at all" to "very much." The participants that were randomly selected for the control groups were not shown this set of statements. This group identity scale was also shown to be very reliable for the present study (Cronbach's $\alpha = .962$).

Because the entire sample population was made up of undergraduate students, the final scale of the experiment was designed to measure the participant's attitude toward the university and the university's relationship to that person's social identity (Mael & Tetrick, 1992). Participants were shown ten statements and asked to mark their opinions on a 7 – point Likert scale. The statements were made to judge how closely the participants identified as a member of the university's community and how emotionally connected they were to their school. Like the other scales used for this study, the university identification scale was shown to be very reliable (Cronbach's $\alpha = .896$). After answering all the questions in the final questionnaire, the participants were shown a post-experiment debrief explaining the purpose of the experiment and the experimental procedures. Finally, participants were thanked for their time and asked not to discuss the study with others while responses were still being collected.

SPORTS ARTICLE CREDIBILITY AND DIGITAL ETHOS: EXAMINING THE STUDY FINDINGS

Online journalism can be subject to the same credibility standards of traditional media, but the around-the-clock nature of the Internet has altered the media landscape and the way news is reported to consumers. News credibility has taken a hit with the public as new (and often unreliable) websites sprout up frequently (Gunter 2006). There is reason to believe this credibility phenomenon has impacted perceptions of media coverage outside of traditional news and translated to the sports world. Sports journalism, both online and offline, is built on the same principles as traditional journalism and can oftentimes be subject to the same ethical standards and guidelines (Oates & Pauly, 2007). Because a number of factors can impact one's perception of a sports article, different aspects of the sports article were examined under the scope of digital ethos to determine what factors make these stories credible.

Influence of Medium on Credibility

In previous studies (Bucy, 2003; Kiousis, 2001; Sundar & Nass, 2001), researchers found that article medium influenced participant evaluations of credibility, so the present study sought to determine how the medium may impact the credibility of a sports article. Looking specifically at the online medium and a wire service, there was no significant difference in credibility scores between the two media ($F(1, 374) = .091, p = .763$), as both were seen as slightly credible. This lack of significance contradicts earlier studies, such as Kiousis's (2001) study on medium credibility, where print was seen as significantly more credible than other types of news media, including online and television. The results of the present study may signify a distinction between sports and news coverage, and suggest that differences exist between the modern interests of sports and news media consumers.

Moreover, the credibility of the online medium for sports media consumers may now rival traditional media based on the dedication of established news organizations providing users with up-to-the-second sports news that is continually updated throughout the day. With cell phone and tablet apps that can stream sports content live, media consumers have become accustomed to online sports access literally at their fingertips. Traditional media, such as the *Associated Press*, may have maintained a level of public trust over the years with fact-checking procedures that may not exist for less-established websites, but there is an aspect of instant gratification and digital ethos that is severely lacking in traditional media. The speed with which the Internet can provide information would seemingly enhance its credibility among consumers, but this may have been offset by the amount of false information that can spread quickly online or game results that can easily be spoiled for fans through social media.

In 2012, NBC came under fire for broadcasting the major competitions of the 2012 London Olympics on tape delay (Levy, 2012). The absence of live coverage for many of the Olympics' major events caused a social media uproar and the trending Twitter hashtag, #NBCFail, from viewers who had the competition results ruined for them online (Levy, 2012). This social media outrage, as well as the same #NBCFail hashtag, continued during the 2014 Sochi Olympics in Russia. The network edited out parts of the opening ceremony, and, just as in London, major competitions were being broadcast on tape delay (Szklarski, 2014). Less than four days after the Olympic broadcasts had begun, #NBCFail was used more than 14,000 times on social media and a petition had been started to rescind the company's broadcast and distribution rights of the Olympics (Szklarski, 2014).

Although television was not tested as a medium in this study, this phenomenon illuminates the instant gratification and digital ethos that people desire from the online medium that is notably absent from all other media platforms. Traditional media is at an even larger disadvantage because media consumers now have the online platform to broadcast their joys or frustrations to followers, and the delay for sports articles and event results does not resonate with readers. Essentially, neither medium was seen as exceedingly credible, but the limitless nature of the Internet for streaming and reporting on sports stories as they occur is an issue for sports journalists and news organizations to consider when attempting to raise the credibility of their brand.

Influence of Article Source and Fan Identification on Credibility

The present study also sought to determine which online source would be regarded as the most credible: ESPN, a sports blog, or Facebook. Despite research to the contrary (Chung, Kim & Kim, 2010; Gunter, 2006), the credibility ratings of the three online sources were not significantly different ($F(2, 278) = 2.04$, $p = .131$), which reflects this study's earlier findings about medium credibility. The overall similarity in credibility scores among the three sources may have occurred because the study participants all received the same article, which was originally published by the *Associated Press*. Because the article covered a real-life sporting event that was factually accurate and may have still been in the participants' minds, it seems logical that participants would rate the article as moderately credible.

The article also covered a sporting event in which the sample population's identified team lost. In a previous fan identification study, Wann, Dolan, McGeorge, and Allison (1994) found that highly identified fans reported greater positive emotions after a win and greater negative emotions after a loss than fans with low identification. Highly identified fans have also been shown to enhance their well-being after a win—and protect it after a loss—by using biased descriptions about the game outcome (Wann, Morriss-Shirkey, Peters & Suggs, 2002). Although the fan identification scales appeared before the article in the present study, the outcome of the game may have impacted participant responses to credibility, and sports ethos may have played a factor. In a seemingly cathartic way, both fan identification groups may have been trying to placate the negative emotions of a team loss by rating the article as less credible than they would have rated a team win. Although fans grow accustomed to reading both positive and negative game outcomes during a season, this particular article recapped a loss in the final game of the season in which the university's team was eliminated from the NCAA tournament, so the effect on credibility ratings could have been more profound.

Wann and Branscobe (1992) determined that emotional responses to a sports article differed based on degree of identification with a sports team, so the present study sought to determine whether a relationship exists between credibility and fan identification. Interestingly, highly identified fans found the article to be significantly more credible as a whole than low identification fans ($F(1, 352) = 44.89$, $p < .001$) and also in eleven out of twelve stimuli groups (Table 3). The fans of a particular team found the article about that team significantly more credible, and this may be due to familiarity with the topic. Some scholars suggest that people are more inclined to judge an article as credible if they are familiar with the subject being covered (Henkel & Mattson, 2011). Topic familiarity may create an "illusion of truth" for statements when people lack cues regarding the reliability of a source. In the present study, highly identified fans are presumably much more familiar with the topic being reported and the sources providing the information, so it seems logical they would rate the article as more credible than low identification fans. Along with familiarity, highly identified fans have a stronger level of sports ethos and attachment

Table 3. Means of credibility scores for each stimuli group separated by identification level

Stimuli Group	N	Mean*	SD
Low Identification			
ESPN Positive	14	4.79	.88
ESPN Negative	11	4.85	1.09
ESPN Control	17	4.04	.86
Blog Positive	12	4.26	1.20
Blog Negative	15	4.01	.86
Blog Control	15	4.11	.86
Facebook Positive	12	4.00	.93
Facebook Negative	20	3.96	.79
Facebook Control	17	4.03	.85
AP Positive	13	4.63	.78
AP Negative	17	4.12	1.23
AP Control	11	4.26	.86
Low Identification Total	174	4.22	.95
High Identification			
ESPN Positive	16	5.26	.80
ESPN Negative	21	4.59	1.00
ESPN Control	13	4.94	.81
Blog Positive	17	5.12	1.09
Blog Negative	17	4.97	.94
Blog Control	18	5.04	.77
Facebook Positive	21	5.01	.91
Facebook Negative	12	4.86	.97
Facebook Control	13	4.70	1.39
AP Positive	18	4.96	1.09
AP Negative	16	4.92	.89
AP Control	20	4.70	.73
High Identification Total	202	4.92	.95

*Mean values can range from 1 to 7.

to the topic being discussed. Although the article was not targeted to an audience of either team's fan base, highly identified fans may have assumed that the article was tailored more toward their own fans, thus rating the article as more credible. Ultimately, the differing level of attachment to the team and the familiarity with the topic may have caused different levels of connection to the article, which resulted in a significant disparity in perceived credibility.

The significant differences in credibility scores may also be connected to the questions that were used to assess credibility. On Bucy's (2003) perceived credibility scale, for example, participants were asked questions regarding the flow and fairness of the article, but there were also asked to assess how enjoyable and interesting it was. A fan with low identification may rate the article as very fair and having a nice flow but may not find the article as enjoyable or interesting to read as a highly identified fan. Because all of these factors have been shown to impact credibility, all of them must be taken into account when researching it. Since highly identified fans already find the articles as moderately credible, sports news websites may try to adapt their stories to the needs of low identification fans in order to gain readership and appeal to a wider audience.

The stimuli groups that garnered the highest credibility scores from each identification group were also noteworthy. The stimuli group that was rated the highest by low identification fans was the ESPN. com group with negative user comments, and for highly identified fans, it was the ESPN.com group with positive user comments. Predictably, the stimuli group that would presumably score the highest from highly identified fans was rated highest by that group. The ESPN brand is established and carries weight in the sports community, and the comments may strike a chord with those participants in the study. Conversely, low identification fans preferred the ESPN article with negative user comments. Fans with low identification were either unaffected by the comments or a lack of connection to the team made the article seem more genuine with comments that do not reflect the common opinion of a fan of the university's basketball team. In a fan identity study, Wann et al. (2001) found that ingroup favoritism and outgroup bias are most likely when individuals are highly identified with their team and their identity has been threatened. In the present study, negative comments can be viewed as a threat to social identity and sports ethos for highly identified fans, which may have caused them to rate those articles harshly. These findings support the notion that high fan identification can significantly influence how readers perceive an article and view ingroup/outgroup members, and they also support the notion that low identification has a much milder effect.

Influence of User Comments on Credibility

User comments have become ubiquitous throughout online media and continue to evolve with technological advancements (Gsell, 2009). Although the impact of anonymous comments on credibility has not been thoroughly researched, the SIDE model suggests that anonymous online interactions can polarize a person's opinions either in favor or against an issue (Lee, 2007). In the present study, it was believed that the tone of the user comments may impact the credibility assessments of highly identified fans. However, there was no significant difference between the credibility scores based on the tone of the comments ($F(2, 299) = 1.61, p = .203$). Anonymous user comments have become a staple of online news and sports articles, and, perhaps, online news readers have become desensitized to user comments over time. The impact of the user comments could have been reduced because highly identified fans may have grown to block out both positive and negative user comments, especially if they do not post regularly in the comments section. The lack of influence on credibility may have also resulted from the intended message of the comments. Sports ethos could have played a factor because the anonymous user comments were directed at the participant's identified team, either lauding or disparaging the team and its season. The comments did not, however, praise or disparage the article itself, which may explain why the credibility ratings were not significantly different for the highly identified fans or the low identification fans ($F(2, 171) = 1.95, p = .145$).

The similarity in credibility scores for both identification groups based on the user comments gives credence to the assumption that people have come to ignore or block out comments in online articles. These findings contradict earlier research on the SIDE model (Walther et al., 2010) in which user comments were shown to influence evaluations of credibility. Walther et al. (2010) found that the perceived credibility of YouTube PSAs can be influenced by the tone of anonymous user comments discussing the serious issue of marijuana use. Controversial topics (e.g., terrorism) and polarizing political news (e.g., Donald Trump's presidential candidacy) may garner a more profound ethos response from readers who see comments that greatly support or oppose their viewpoints, but most sports articles rarely elicit this type of response. Discussing newspaper websites, Gsell (2009) argued that the initial creation of user comments was designed to be a natural complement to online articles with the open culture of the Internet, but that changed when user comments "attracted spam, profanity, harassment, and unpaid advertising onto the site, creating for staff the arduous daily duty of deleting off-color comments" (p. 16). The sheer amount of irrelevant, and often disrespectful, user comments that can be posted on a single article have changed the way online sports media consumers view these comments. Even if user comments have a small impact on news stories, the results of the present study suggest that user comments do not impact the credibility of online sports articles, especially as off-color and irrelevant comments become commonplace.

CONCLUSION

Using fan identification as the primary theoretical framework, this study examined the key factors that can impact the credibility of a sports article across media. Unlike previous findings on credibility (Kiousis, 2001; Sundar & Nass, 2001), medium had little impact on the perceived credibility of the sports article. The results suggest that credibility of all media has seemingly evened out since the turn of the century, where all platforms (print, radio, television, and online) have similar credibility perceptions from news consumers, but none are rated as overly credible. Online media has seemingly come the furthest to a point where people are comfortable using it, but still do not fully trust the information they are receiving.

While there was no significant difference in the perceived credibility of the online sources overall, there was a large disparity in the credibility scores between the two identification groups. Other studies have found similar reactions from highly identified fans regarding their favorite teams, although in different sports ethos areas (Fink et al., 2009, Wann & Branscombe, 1992; Wann & Robinson, 2002). Highly identified fans found the article to be significantly more credible than fans with low identification, which is beneficial for sports media organizations who are trying to maintain readers that already visit their website or read their newspaper. However, this large credibility gap can also become a burden for media organizations who are actively trying to attract new users and engage with their audience. The pressure is now on sports media professionals to deviate from the status quo and experiment with new tactics to draw in less identified fans, such as utilizing new article layouts or new storytelling techniques.

In today's media environment, sports journalists are facing new challenges as they work to appease fans who regularly have credibility concerns and unlimited access to coverage of their favorite teams from a multitude of competing sources. Sports fans, and news consumers in general, are looking for information that is both current and credible, and modern sports journalists must look for ways to break stories as they happen without sacrificing credibility. Ultimately, this study's findings suggest that medium, source, and user comments matter less to fans when making credibility assessments than the level of connection and identity they share with their favorite team. The onus, then, falls on sports journalists to create stories that exude creativity and manage to resonate with every fan, from the most causal to the most diehard. That may mean using data visualization to make statistics easier to follow, integrating social media in a more profound way that speaks directly to readers, or incorporating elements of text, audio, pictures, and video to fully encapsulate the whole story. Technological advancements have made the possibilities endless, and sports journalists need to embrace these possibilities in order to capitalize on technological ethos (Apostel & Folk, 2005) that helps to create content whose credibility connects with a wide readership. Not only will the fans benefit, but sports journalism as a whole will benefit as we enter a new digital age.

REFERENCES

Apostel, S., & Folk, M. (2005). First phase in-formation literacy on a fourth generation Web site: An argument for a new approach to Web site evaluation criteria. *Computers & Composition Online, Spring 2005*. Retrieved March 10, 2016 from http://www2.bgsu.edu/departments/english/cconline/apostelfolk/c_and_c_online_apostel_folk/

Beyer, J. M., & Hannah, D. R. (2000). The Cultural Significance of Athletics in U.S. Higher Education. *Journal of Sport Management, 14*(2), 105.

Bucy, E. P. (2003). Media Credibility Reconsidered: Synergy Effects Between On-Air and Online News. *Journalism & Mass Communication Quarterly, 80*(2), 247–264. doi:10.1177/107769900308000202

Chung, C. J., Kim, H., & Kim, J. H. (2010). An anatomy of the credibility of online newspapers. *Online Information Review, 34*(5), 669–685. doi:10.1108/14684521011084564

Crupi, A. (2015, September 10). Sports Now Accounts for 37% of Broadcast TV Ad Spending: Big Four Nets $8.47 Billion in Ad Sales. *Advertising Age*. Retrieved November 2, 2015, from http://adage.com/article/media/sports-account-37-percent-all-tv-ad-dollars/300310/

Davis, D. C., & Krawczyk, J. (2010). Female Sportscaster Credibility: Has Appearance Taken Precedence? *Journal of Sports Media, 5*(2), 1–34. doi:10.1353/jsm.2010.0004

Dougherty, P. (2015, October 22). Sports media: Bills-Jaguars telecast on Yahoo could be sign of the future. *TimesUnion.com*. Retrieved November 2, 2015, from http://www.timesunion.com/tuplus-sports/article/Bills-Jaguars-telecast-on-Yahoo-could-be-sign-of-6585347.php

Fink, J. S., Parker, H. M., Brett, M., & Higgins, J. (2009). Off-Field Behavior of Athletes and Team Identification: Using Social Identity Theory and Balance Theory to Explain Fan Reactions. *Journal Of Sport Management, 23*(2), 142–155.

Gamie, S. (2013). The Cyber-Propelled Egyptian Revolution and the De/Construction of Ethos. In M. Folk & S. Apostel (Eds.), *Online Credibility and Digital Ethos: Evaluating Computer-Mediated Communication* (pp. 316–331). Hershey, PA: IGI Global. doi:10.4018/978-1-4666-2663-8.ch018

Geertz, C. (1973). *The interpretation of cultures: Selected essays*. New York: Basic.

Gsell, L. (2009). Comments Anonymous. *American Journalism Review, 31*(1), 16–17.

Gunter, B. (2006). Who do online news consumers trust? *Library and Information Update, 5*(9), 40–41.

Henkel, L. A., & Mattson, M. E. (2011). Reading is believing: The truth effect and source credibility. *Consciousness and Cognition, 20*(4), 1705–1721. doi:10.1016/j.concog.2011.08.018 PMID:21978908

Hu, A. W., & Tang, L. (2010). Factors Motivating Sports Broadcast Viewership with Fan Identification as a Mediator. *Social Behavior & Personality: An International Journal, 38*(5), 681–689. doi:10.2224/sbp.2010.38.5.681

Johnson, T. J., & Kaye, B. K. (2000). Using is Believing: The Influence of Reliance on the Credibility of Online Political Information Among Politically Interested Internet Users. *Journalism & Mass Communication Quarterly, 77*(4), 865–879. doi:10.1177/107769900007700409

Johnson, T. J., & Kaye, B. K. (2004). Wag the Blog: How Reliance on Traditional Media and the Internet Influence Credibility Perceptions of Weblogs Among Blog Users. *Journalism & Mass Communication Quarterly, 81*(3), 622–642. doi:10.1177/107769900408100310

Keene, J. R., & Cummins, R. G. (2009). Sports Commentators and Source Credibility: Do Those Who Can't Play. . . Commentate? *Journal of Sports Media, 4*(2), 57–83. doi:10.1353/jsm.0.0042

Kiousis, S. (2001). Public trust or mistrust? Perceptions of media credibility in the information age. *Mass Communication & Society, 4*(4), 381–403. doi:10.1207/S15327825MCS0404_4

Laverie, D. A., & Arnett, D. B. (2000). Factors affecting fan attendance: The influence of identity salience and satisfaction. *Journal of Leisure Behavior, 32*(2), 225–246.

Lea, M., Spears, R., Watt, S. E., & Rogers, P. (2000). The InSIDE story: Social psychological processes affecting on-line groups. In T. Postmes, M. Lea, R. Spears, & S. Reicher (Eds.), *SIDE issues centre stage: Recent developments in studies of de-individuation in groups* (pp. 47–62). Amsterdam: KNAW.

Lee, E. J. (2007). Deindividuation effects on group polarization in computer-mediated communication: The role of group identification, public self-awareness, and perceived argument quality. *Journal of Communication, 57*(2), 385–403. doi:10.1111/j.1460-2466.2007.00348.x

Levy, D. (2012, July 31). 2012 Olympics: NBC Finding New and Unique Ways to Fail American Viewers. *Bleacher Report*. Retrieved August 30, 2012, from http://bleacherreport.com/articles/1279506-2012-olympics-nbc-keeps-finding-new-and-unique-ways-to-fail-american-viewers

Mael, F., & Tetrick, L. (1992). Identifying Organizational Identification. *Educational and Psychological Measurement, 52*(4), 813–824. doi:10.1177/0013164492052004002

McGrady, R. (2013). Ethos [edit]: Procedural Rhetoric and the Wikipedia Project. In M. Folk & S. Apostel (Eds.), Online Credibility and Digital Ethos: Evaluating Computer-Mediated Communication (pp. 114 -130). Hershey, PA: IGI Global.

Melnick, M. J. (1993). Searching for sociability in the stands: A theory of sports spectating. *Journal of Sport Management, 7*, 44–60.

Meyer, H. K., Marchionni, D., & Thorson, E. (2010). The Journalist Behind the News: Credibility of Straight, Collaborative, Opinionated, and Blogged "News". *The American Behavioral Scientist, 54*(2), 100–119. doi:10.1177/0002764210376313

Milne, G. R., & McDonald, M. A. (1999). *Sport marketing: Managing the exchange process*. Sudbury, MA: Jones and Bartlett.

Mitchell, A. (2014, March 26). *State of the News Media 2014*. Pew Research Center. Retrieved November 15, 2015, from http://www.journalism.org/2014/03/26/state-of-the-news-media-2014-overview/

Mitchell, A. (2015, April 29). *State of the News Media 2015*. Pew Research Center. Retrieved November 16, 2015, from http://www.journalism.org/2015/04/29/state-of-the-news-media-2015/

Newhagen, J. E., & Levy, M. R. (1998). The future of journalism in a distributed communication architecture. In D. L. Borden & K. Harvey (Eds.), *The Electronic Grapevine: Rumor, Reputation, and Reporting in the New On-Line Environment* (pp. 9–21). Mahwah, NJ: Lawrence Erlbaum Associates.

O'Cass, A., & Carlson, J. (2010). Examining the effects of website-induced flow in professional sporting team websites. *Internet Research*, *20*(2), 115–134. doi:10.1108/10662241011032209

Oates, T. P., & Pauly, J. (2007). Sports Journalism as Moral and Ethical Discourse. *Journal of Mass Media Ethics*, *22*(4), 332–347. doi:10.1080/08900520701583628

Pells, E. (2012, March 25). Louisville in Final 4 with 72-68 Win over Florida. *The Associated Press*. Retrieved April 1, 2012, from http://www.lexisnexis.com

Pham, M. (1992). Effects of involvement, arousal and pleasure on recognition of sponsorship stimuli. *Advances in Consumer Research. Association for Consumer Research (U. S.)*, *19*(1), 85–93.

Postmes, T., Spears, R., & Lea, M. (1998). Breaching or building social boundaries: SIDE effects of computer-mediated communication. *Communication Research*, *25*(6), 689–715. doi:10.1177/009365098025006006

Postmes, T., Spears, R., Sakhel, K., & de Groot, D. (2001). Social influence in computer-mediated communication: The effects of anonymity on group behavior. *Personality and Social Psychology Bulletin*, *27*(10), 1243–1254. doi:10.1177/01461672012710001

Reicher, S. D., Spears, R., & Postmes, T. (1995). A social identity model of deindividuation phenomena. *European Review of Social Psychology*, *6*(1), 161–198. doi:10.1080/14792779443000049

Robbins, B. (2004). "That's Cheap." The Rational Invocation of Norms, Practices, and an Ethos in Ultimate Frisbee. *Journal of Sport and Social Issues*, *28*(3), 314–337. doi:10.1177/0193723504266992

Serra, P., & Canavilhas, J. (2013). The Credibility of Sources 2.0 in Journalism: Case Study in Portugal. In M. Folk & S. Apostel (Eds.), *Online Credibility and Digital Ethos: Evaluating Computer-Mediated Communication* (pp. 169–185). Hershey, PA: IGI Global. doi:10.4018/978-1-4666-2663-8.ch010

Shadish, W. R., Cook, T. D., & Campbell, D. T. (2002). *Experimental and quasi-experimental designs for generalized causal inference*. Boston: Houghton Mifflin.

Shank, M. D., & Beasley, F. M. (1998). Fan or fanatic: Refining a measure of sports involvement. *Journal of Sport Behavior*, *21*(4), 435.

Sundar, S. S., & Nass, C. (2001). Conceptualizing sources in online news. *Journal of Communication*, *51*(1), 52–72. doi:10.1111/j.1460-2466.2001.tb02872.x

Szklarski, C. (2014, February 10). CBC Sochi 2014 Olympics Coverage Attracts Frustrated NBC Viewers. *Huffington Post*. Retrieved December 15, 2015, from http://www.huffingtonpost.ca/2014/02/10/cbc-sochi-2014-olympics_n_4763185.html

Tajfel, H. (1981). *Human groups and social categories*. Cambridge, UK: Cambridge University Press.

Turkle, S. (1996). Parallel lives: Working on identity in virtual space. In D. Grodin & T. R. Lindlof (Eds.), *Constructing the self in a mediated world* (pp. 156–175). Thousand Oaks, CA: Sage. doi:10.4135/9781483327488.n10

Turner, J. C. (1982). Towards a cognitive redefinition of the social group. In H. Tajfel (Ed.), *Social identity and intergroup relations*. Cambridge University Press.

Van Leeuwen, L., Quick, S., & Daniel, K. (2002). The sport spectator satisfaction model: A conceptual framework for understanding the satisfaction of spectators. *Sport Management Review*, *5*(2), 99–128. doi:10.1016/S1441-3523(02)70063-6

Walther, J. B., DeAndrea, D., Kim, J., & Anthony, J. C. (2010). The Influence of Online Comments on Perceptions of Antimarijuana Public Service Announcements on YouTube. *Human Communication Research*, *36*(4), 469–492. doi:10.1111/j.1468-2958.2010.01384.x

Wann, D. L. (2006). Understanding the Positive Social Psychological Benefits of Sport Team Identification: The Team Identification–Social Psychological Health Model. *Group Dynamics*, *10*(4), 272–296. doi:10.1037/1089-2699.10.4.272

Wann, D. L., & Branscombe, N. R. (1992). Emotional Responses to the Sports Page. *Journal of Sport and Social Issues*, *16*(1), 49–64. doi:10.1177/019372359201600104

Wann, D. L., & Branscombe, N. R. (1993). Sports Fans: Measuring Degree of Identification with Their Team. *International Journal of Sport Psychology*, *24*, 1–17.

Wann, D. L., Dimmock, J., & Grove, J. R. (2003). Generalizing the Team Identification–Psychological Health Model to a Different Sport and Culture: The Case of Australian Rules Football. *Group Dynamics*, *7*(4), 289–296. doi:10.1037/1089-2699.7.4.289

Wann, D. L., Dolan, T. J., McGeorge, K. K., & Allison, J. A. (1994). Relationships between spectator identification and spectators' perceptions of influence, spectators' emotions, and competition outcome. *Journal of Sport & Exercise Psychology*, *16*, 347–364.

Wann, D. L., Friedman, K., McHale, M., & Jaffe, A. (2003). The Norelco Sport Fanatics Survey: Examining Behaviors of Sport Fans. *Psychological Reports*, *92*(3), 930–936. doi:10.2466/pr0.2003.92.3.930 PMID:12841467

Wann, D. L., Melnick, M. J., Russell, G. W., & Pease, D. G. (2001). *Sport fans: The psychology and social impact of spectators*. New York: Routledge.

Wann, D. L., Morriss-Shirkey, P. A., Peters, E., & Suggs, W. L. (2002). Highly Identified Sport Fans and Their Conflict between Expression of Sport Knowledge and Biased Assessments of Team Performance. *International Sports Journal*, *6*(1), 153.

Wann, D. L., & Robinson, I. N. (2002). The Relationship Between Sport Team Identification and Integration into and Perceptions of a University. *International Sports Journal*, 6(1), 36.

Wann, D. L., Tucker, K. B., & Schrader, M. P. (1996). An exploratory examination of the factors influencing the origination, continuation, and cessation of identification with sports teams. *Perceptual and Motor Skills*, 82(3), 995–1101. doi:10.2466/pms.1996.82.3.995

KEY TERMS AND DEFINITIONS

Associated Press: An American nonprofit news organization founded in 1846 that provides news and information to other media organizations that subscribe to its service.

ESPN: A prominent American-based global sports broadcasting network operating on cable television, satellite television, and online.

Fan Identification: The level at which a sports fan identifies with a particular sport or team.

SIDE Model: The social identity model of deindividuation effects (SIDE) is a communication studies theory developed to describe the social effects of computer-mediated communication. The model suggests that anonymous interactions online can have a profound effect on group behavior.

Social Identity Theory: A social psychological theory asserting that a person's self-concept or identity is maintained through one's group memberships. These significant group memberships and relationships are used in social comparisons to develop and maintain one's self-esteem.

Sport Blog: A web journal that is frequently updated with entries appearing in reverse chronological order and focused specifically on a sport, sports team, or sports topic.

Sports Ethos: The "spirit of the game" for athletes, competitors, and sports fans.

User Comments: Comments posted by readers at the bottom of an online article.

Chapter 16
Breastfeeding, Authority, and Genre:
Women's Ethos in Wikipedia and Blogs

Alison A. Lukowski
Christian Brothers University, USA

Erika M. Sparby
Northern Illinois University, USA

ABSTRACT

This chapter is concerned with women's mis- or underrepresentation in knowledge creation, particularly when it comes to their bodies. In this chapter, the authors examine how Wikipedia's generic regulations determine that women's often experiential ethos is unwelcome on the site. Thus, women are often unable to construct knowledge on the "Breastfeeding" entry; their epistemological methods are ignored or banned by other contributors. This chapter also examines six breastfeeding-focused mommyblogs, proposing blogs as an alternative genre that welcomes women's ethos. However, the authors also recognize that such blogs are not a perfect epistemological paradigm. The chapter closes with an examination of the implications of this work for academic collaboration across fields and for women's agency.

INTRODUCTION

Women often struggle to find a place online to express themselves and to create credible knowledge. Whether women write about issues as mundane as wedding dresses or as important as health issues, they are often harassed and silenced by a variety of strategies as overt as trolling and as opaque as editing. Previous research about breastfeeding rhetoric (Koerber, 2013; Koerber et al, 2012; Koerber, 2006) demonstrated that breastfeeding is situated in disciplinary and discursive contexts that control women's bodies, such as science, medicine, and education. One way discursive power manifests online is through controlling sources of knowledge. This chapter offers case studies of the Wikipedia "Breastfeeding" entry and six blogs written by nursing mothers, mommyblogs, to show how feminist standpoint theory (Haraway, 1988) and apparent feminism (Frost, 2015) reveal that some spaces use a guise of balance,

DOI: 10.4018/978-1-5225-1072-7.ch016

impartiality, and free speech to hinder women's processes of knowledge creation, while other spaces welcome experiential ethos. This study of knowledge production and ethos, which is grounded in the authority and credibility to create and evaluate that knowledge, reveals a reciprocal relationship between the knower and the known. The authors find that women prefer alternative *ethea* and are excluded because of cultural norms and hierarchies rather than truth or reality. Based on feminist standpoint theory and apparent feminism, this article rhetorically analyzes Wikipedia's "Breastfeeding" entry and its Talk page and six mommyblogs.

Collaborative writing has the potential to provide multiple viewpoints, but Wikipedia contributors—nearly 90% of whom are male (Simonite, 2013)—dismiss the credibility of women, even on issues of women's health. This work suggests that the design of Wikipedia's site and the culture it supports enforce a "neutral point of view" (NPOV) that excludes women's experiences because they are underrepresented in normative discourses of medicine, science, and philosophy. Wikipedia's generic conventions necessitate that contributors engage in debates about epistemology, truth, verifiability, and validity (McIntyre, 2010; Kennedy, 2009; Garfinkel, 2008). These conventions lead editors to question, challenge, or dismiss women's ethos when discussing an epistemology of their own bodies, thus silencing many female contributors. As a result of this persistent exclusion, women often avoid collaboratively curated sites like Wikipedia altogether (Hargittai & Shaw, 2015; Eckert & Steiner, 2013; Reagle & Rhue, 2011; Reagle, 2009). The consequences of these rhetorical moves have implications beyond digital spaces and contribute to society's persistent negative view of breastfeeding as something that must always happen in the margins.

In contrast, blogs provide a refreshing look at breastfeeding and women's digital ethos, giving women a forum in which to speak. However, the personal and individual nature of blogs prevents women from contributing to official narratives about their own bodies on a more public level: while their knowledge is marginalized, they continue to be ostracized for and banned from public breastfeeding despite the efforts blogs make to reverse such restrictions. The authors selected six mommyblogs—*The Breastfeeding Mother* (*TBM*), *Chronicles of a Nursing Mom* (*CoaNM*), *Paa.la*, *Unlatched*, *Dispelling Breastfeeding Myths* (*DPM*), and *Breast for the Weary* (*BftW*)—because they appeared in a list of top breastfeeding blogs and/or were top results in a Summer 2015 Google search for the keywords "breastfeeding" and "blog." The bloggers at *TBM*, *Unlatched*, and *BftW* no longer update their pages, but the information they provide therein remains relevant and sought after; *CoaNM*, *Paa.la*, and *DPM* continue to post updates. A brief note on data presentation is in order here because the authors will reference multiple posts from each blog, the date of the post will appear next to its quote or summary, but no direct links will appear in the text or references.

This chapter will examine Wikipedia and mommyblogs post-publication to determine how each site uses generic design and cultural expectations to signal to their users what kinds of ethos is welcomed. Rhetorical analysis will reveal that the epistemologies behind these culturally saturated sites mirror how our society values different forms of knowledge. Rhetorical analysis is a suitable method for this study because of the nature of this inquiry. As Koerber (2013) suggested, "[R]hetorical analysis can enrich our understanding of the manner in which expert knowledge is produced and the channels through which individuals in the public sphere receive and relate to such information" (p. 7). Likewise, Selzer (2004) explained rhetorical analysis as "studying carefully some kind of symbolic action, often after the fact of its delivery and irrespective of whether it was actually directed to you or not, so that you might understand it better and appreciate its tactics" (p. 281). This chapter also answers Novotny's (2015) call to "build and take up feminist methodologies that intervene in the designs of policies and projects that regulate female health" (p. 62). The authors examine the tensions between Wikipedia and mommy blogs to determine how women can find digital voices and create their own epistemologies. Rhetorical analysis enables the authors to recognize that because the values behind mommy blog epistemologies risk excluding others—including women of color, working-class women, and women for whom breastfeeding may not be an option—they are not a perfect paradigm. Nonetheless, opening Wikipedia and blogs to various standpoints creates more accurate and verifiable claims about breastfeeding while building a digital ethos of women writers.

BACKGROUND

This project is indebted to a long-standing tradition of work in credibility scholarship. The early 2000s saw an upswing in the debate about credibility online as more and more people adopted digital modes of publishing. The ways authors developed and used ethos becomes a central concern for digital rhetoric scholarship. The following scholars directly influenced this essay. Several scholars address credibility in the digital age: Johnson & Kaye (2004, 2010, 2011) showed how a user's demographic features and political affiliations influence his/her perceptions of credibility, and Flanagin and Metzger (2008) and Metzger (2007) illustrated that each user's perceptions of credibility depend on how the source content meets his/her unique needs and expectations. Scholars have also addressed the credibility of Wikipedia since its inception in 2001 (Chawner & Lewis, 2004; Giles, 2005; Chesney, 2006; Fallis, 2008; Garfinkel, 2008; Brooke, 2009; Brown, 2015). Gruwell (2015) argued that a critical feminist approach to Wikipedia is necessary to understand and remedy the lack of women contributors. Blogs also receive attention from credibility scholars (Johnson & Kaye, 2004; Armstrong & McAdams, 2009; Johnson & Kaye, 2010; Johnson & Kaye, 2011). Winter and Krämer (2014) concluded that female writers are more credible on topics relating to issues with which they would be expected to establish a deeper connection and thus about which they would know more, such as violence in the media (p. 450).

Credibility and epistemology have been an essential facet of feminist research for decades because all knowledge is situated within a larger cultural context (Hartsock, 1983; Rose, 1983; Haraway, 1988; Harding, 1993). Like credibility scholarship, feminist scholarship addresses the role of digital media in the early to late 2000s. Two particular strands of feminist criticism, standpoint theory and apparent feminism, shape the approach of this work. In Harding's (1993, 2003) standpoint theory, strong objectivity is reached when oppressed and marginalized perspectives are shared. Johnston, Friedman, and Peach (2011) claimed that new media technologies play a role in how women participate in knowledge generation in political blogs. Scott and White (2013) explained that standpoint theory's strength is its recognition "that we construct our knowledge by interacting with each other from our respective and situated social positions" (pp. 61-2). Apparent feminism (Frost, 2013; 2014a; 2014b; 2015) is a methodology that fights the post-feminist notion that society has moved beyond the need for feminism and shows places where women and other marginalized identities continue to face resistance and/or oppression, particularly in spaces that support a guise of neutrality or democracy. Its three goals are key to this approach: "[1] making more apparent the need for feminist interventions, [2] hailing nonfeminists as allies, and [3] demystifying the relationship between feminism and efficiency" (Frost, 2015, p. 9). Novotny (2015) employed apparent feminism by "advocating for the incorporation of diverse stakeholders" (p. 68) to engage in knowledge production.

This chapter draws on a long tradition of digital credibility, epistemology, and feminist scholarship. In doing so, the authors demonstrate an ongoing need to analyze and understand how digital genres shape knowledge about women's bodies.

DESIGN AND KNOWLEDGE/KNOWLEDGE AND DESIGN

Design and culture and the origins of knowledge are key aspects of epistemological creation on Wikipedia and blogs. The design and culture of the sites influence what kinds of actions users take and what they access, while each site has rules governing from where knowledge must come. Although this chapter isolates each aspect to discuss it separately, it is worth noting that such a construction is artificial. In reality, the design and culture and the rules that govern origins of knowledge work recursively to reinforce and construct each other. Wikipedia's encyclopedic genre dictates specific rules for the origins of knowledge (design dictates origins of knowledge), but a blog's freedom from the need for typical scholarly sources enables users to include hyperlinks to outside articles or uploads of personal photos as evidence (origins of knowledge dictate design). Thus, the reader should be aware that although this chapter addresses each phenomenon separately, each is always influenced by the other.

Design and Culture

Analyzing design is useful for discussing epistemology in Wikipedia and blogs because each space follows specific generic guidelines that govern how users can participate in the act of knowledge construction. Design choices can also reveal authorial values: the images used, page hierarchies, and font choices demonstrate how the contributors think users will engage with their content. Furthermore, the design of a site also reveals the culture it supports. For instance, Wikipedia's design privileges a polished entry page and hides the creation of that knowledge in small links to "Talk" and "History" pages; this results in an exclusive culture available only to a small percentage of page visitors. Conversely, blogs expose collaborative processes of knowledge creation by placing the entry and comments on the same page level, which results in a culture of collaboration and relevance. Rhetorical analysis of design and culture uncovers the complex relationship between knowledge and the presentation of that knowledge.

Despite its innovative use of open source and collaborative knowledge creation, Wikipedia recapitulates traditional print methods of knowledge creation because it relies on outside and verifiable sources for validation. The reliability and accessibility of its information makes Wikipedia one of the top ten sites in terms of web traffic (Brooke, 2009; Fallis, 2011; Simonite, 2013). Wikipedia differs from other reference materials such as *Encyclopedia Britannica* and *Webster's Dictionary* because its content is generated and verified by a community of volunteers rather than professional writers and researchers (Loveland & Reagle, 2013). Wikipedia's design creates a space for people to collaborate and debate the value of knowledge. As an exercise in mass-collaboration and groupthink, Wikipedia has potential to provide a voice to the marginalized. Gruwell (2015) agreed that the space could disrupt notions of single authority generated knowledges: "Wiki technology presents the potential to create a constantly evolving space that privileges collaborative writing (and meaning-making), undermining the notion that a single, unified identity is the preferred authorial position" (p. 119). Unfortunately, as Gruwell also noted, this has not been the case. Instead, Wikipedia often reflects the knowledge of the normalized majority and reenacts cultural values that minimize the contributions of women and minorities.

Furthermore, the design of Wikipedia affirms hierarchies by presenting the entry first and displaying tabs for "Talk" and "View History" secondarily; these tabs reveal how the page is constructed and who contributes to it, but they are almost invisible in the larger context of the article. As Brooke (2009) suggested, "Each entry on Wikipedia is, in fact, the tip of a much larger iceberg of activity … If a user visits Wikipedia and simply samples an entry, she or he may be missing out on a great deal of the information the site can provide" (p. 191). For instance, on the Breastfeeding "Talk" page contributors discussed whether to include a section sex and breastfeeding, during which one contributor noted that, "this article's presentation of the facts about breastfeeding does not feel encyclopedic, and most definitely does not feel comprehensive" (Breastfeeding: Talk, 2015a). In other words, readers who do not read "Talk" pages may think the entry is an objective and encyclopedic representation of breastfeeding rather than the contributions of individuals who debate the relevance and salience of each section. While every version of a page is saved and the construction of knowledge can be traced, few users actually contribute to entries or access the "Talk" and "View History" pages where the debates about truth and verifiability occur. In a single month, Wikipedia has over 370 million views worldwide and over 60 million views in North America (Wikimedia Report, 2015), yet only 70,000 users actively contribute to Wikipedia and share in creating this knowledge (Wikipedia, 2015b). While users can participate in knowledge generation, many of them do not, perhaps because the murky nature of these tabs covertly (or overtly) excludes them.

The Wikipedia interface and "Talk" and "History" pages also follow a set of editing conventions that discourage new contributors. Wikipedia acknowledges this failing: "Editors who fail to comply with Wikipedia cultural rituals, such as signing talk pages, may implicitly signal that they are Wikipedia outsiders, increasing the odds that Wikipedia insiders may target or discount their contributions" (Wikipedia, 2015b). Wikipedia even has an entry titled "Please Do Not Bite the Newcomers" that outlines a series of tools and reminders for regular editors to encourage and gently correct inexperienced contributors. Wrapped in the flag of NPOV, long-standing contributors can flag and delete edits or entries they deem unverifiable or irrelevant, which often deters newcomers from the editorial process. One editor on the Breastfeeding Talk page qualifies her meaningful contributions by pleading ignorance and using humility instead of stating that she has as much right to make changes as other contributors: "I am not a regular editor here, and I honestly don't have time to learn things like which sources are valid and how to avoid original research … I'm just someone who fixes bad spelling or syntax or throws in an episode list for a TV show I like" (Wikipedia, 2015a). Although this editor has valuable information to add to the page, she preempts an attack from the regular editors who may recognize her as an outsider. Moreover, this issue is compounded for the few women who contribute to Wikipedia because the site reflects broader cultural problems that exclude women from computing, software development, and technology in general. Gruwell (2015) suggested that women may be underrepresented on Wikipedia because the interface itself requires familiarization with basic computer coding to fully participate in the community (p. 125); historically, women have had limited access to these skills, so they may feel discouraged from participating.

In fact, we may never fully know how many women contribute to Wikipedia because the design enables users to make changes anonymously. In 2004 and 2007, Wikipedia's self-studies found that "over 80% of edits by unregistered users" are meaningful contributions. If we accept Virginia Woolf's notion that Anonymous was "often a woman," then the number of contributions women make in Wikipedia may never be quantified. And yet, if women contributors remain anonymous, we should interrogate why women choose not to identify their gender. Gruwell (2015) suggested women editors fear accusations of bias simply because they are women: one of her study participants, Sylvia, "feared that because she was a 'female writing about women,' other editors would dismiss her writing as simply the work of someone 'writing about women because they're hot.' Sylvia worried that the community would not recognize her expertise because of her embodied identity position" (p. 127). Since Wikipedia's default NPOV is heterosexual, white, and male, contributions centering on women are often trivialized. Women may not feel comfortable entering a rhetorical situation in which they are marked as outsiders; they tend to migrate to knowledge-constructing sites that contrast Wikipedia's culture of exclusion, such as blogs.

In general, blogs are designed to fit within a few generic guidelines. They operate via posts from the blog's owner, or blogger, and appear in reverse chronological order. In general, all of the different styles of blog can be boiled down to three subgenres: 1) link-driven, which compiles hyperlinks; 2) diaristic, which offers personal reflections; and 3) a hybrid that does both (Blood, 2000). The blogs examined in this chapter are largely the latter, discussing relevant breastfeeding media items and offering individual narratives to develop individual digital ethos. In particular, the benefits of this kind of knowledge include the bloggers sifting "through the mass of information packaged daily for our consumption and pick[ing] out the interesting, the important, the overlooked, and the unexpected" (Blood, 2000). Then, the blogger "may provide additional information to that which corporate media provides, expose the fallacy of an argument, perhaps reveal an inaccurate detail" (Blood, 2000). Thus, readers are able to quickly understand the issue at hand while also engaging with one or more additional perspectives.

This design creates a culture of *kairos*, or timeliness and relevance. *TBM, CoaNM, Paa.la, Unlatched, DPM,* and *BftW* offer unique opportunities for knowledge creation because each blogger responds directly to issues that are relevant to her and her readers. For example, Rachelle (*Unlatched*) and Paala (*Paa.la*) both closely follow Facebook's restrictions against posting breastfeeding photos to social media sites. Rachelle (Aug 20, 2013; Aug 27, 2013; Aug 29, 2013) and Paala (Jun 10, 2014; Jun 21, 2015; Jul 14, 2015) not only post links to external articles and websites that deal with this issue, but they also share screencaps and stories from readers and their own experiences while, most importantly, explaining why it is so important to fight back against Facebook's policies. These posts are *kairotic*; they would not have had as great an effect (or potentially any effect) had they been written months later or even preemptively months earlier. However, because they respond to the events as they are unfolding, updating the blogs' readers in real-time, they are relevant.

Another key design feature of blogs leads to a culture of collaboration: the comments section. Here, bloggers can elaborate on or defend their posts while conversing with their readers. Wikipedia editors can do so to an extent as well, but the genre necessitates that these interactions take place on a separate page. Notoriously reluctant to make extra effort, Wikipedia users must find the right link and click through to find the debates about truth and knowledge. Conversely, on blogs, the comments section is connected directly to the original blog post. Comments do not appear on the blog homepage, but each post has a unique URL that links to a separate page where the comments will appear just below it. Such placement suggests a continuity between the blogger's post and her readers' comments or her own clarifications. Because they are openly displayed with the blog post, they are held in nearly as high esteem as the main post and thus promote an interactive knowledge creation among bloggers and readers that values each other as equals.

The six breastfeeding blogs at hand display interactive knowledge creation regularly. Jenny (*CoaNM*), Paala, Teglene (*TBM*), Rachelle, and Shannon (*BftW*) all support comments from readers that provide additional information. In particular, Anne's (*DPM*) post on tongue tie (Feb 2013)—a condition resulting from a short frenulum that attaches the tongue to the lower floor of the jaw—shows her readers contributing to the information she provides in her posts. Anne explains that many doctors and other medical professionals often tell mothers whose babies have tongue tie that it either doesn't exist or doesn't affect breastfeeding; she goes on to cite advice from International Board Certified Lactation Consultants (IBCLCs) that say otherwise and points to the need for more research. Her post has received over two-dozen supportive comments, many from IBCLCs who verified that tongue-tie is often misunderstood or misdiagnosed. Several hyperlink other sources on the same topic. Taken together, the post and comments work collaboratively to provide credible knowledge about what tongue tie is and how to spot and fix it. Notably, Wikipedia's entry on "Ankyloglossia" (the medical term for tongue-tie) only includes two brief paragraphs on the condition's impact on infant feeding, and the "Breastfeeding" entry only has two sentences on it, little of it useful for a breastfeeding mother seeking information.

Although all six blogs this chapter studies enabled their comments sections, not every blog is required to do so. Such restrictions limit this valuable knowledge creation from happening on their site and, frankly, limit the authority of the blog because readers cannot offer insight that may contradict or correct the information in the posts. Sometimes bloggers may moderate their comments to restrict who leaves feedback, although it is generally considered bad blogging ethics to do so (Blood, 2000). In an interview, Rachelle admits that she moderates the comments on her blog: "I moderate my comments, so I have control over what does get published, but I don't really censor people and approve almost all comments, even if they are negative" (personal communication, June 2014). Rachelle would seem to be in the majority of mommybloggers. Typically, bloggers allow readers to comment freely on their page, in a large part because that's what many consider to be the point of a blog: to spread information collaboratively through posts and comments.

The explicit design of blogs keeps knowledge creation at the forefront. The hybridity of the link-driven and diaristic styles of blogs creates a culture that values relevance and collaboration. This is distinct from Wikipedia's two-pronged problem: women's voices *and* women's issues are often excluded. On breastfeeding blogs, women use their individual digital *ethea* to collaboratively create knowledge; however, on Wikipedia, men edit entries that should appeal to women, such as "Breastfeeding," which may misrepresent the experience and concerns of breastfeeding. Whether uninitiated Wikipedia visitors are not aware that epistemological discussions are happening just a click away or whether they do not feel welcome to join the conversation, Wikipedia's collaborative, free-access, and free-content encyclopedic genre discourages the participation of all but a select few, particularly women. However, the transparency of blogs' epistemologies provides space for women and other minorities to exercise authority in ways that Wikipedia prohibits them from doing so.

Origins of Knowledge

A second factor that influences knowledge construction on Wikipedia and blogs is how they craft their credibility and ethos. As an encyclopedic genre, Wikipedia is concerned with credibility, or the outward appearance of authority through neutrality and verifiability. As such, it maintains a NPOV and requires secondary sources to verify all knowledge claims. However, women's knowledge is often grounded in testimony and folk wisdom, which Wikipedia's generic constraints disallow; thus Wikipedia tends to silence their epistemological contributions. On the other hand, blogs are predicated on individual ethos, or identity factors—such as firsthand experience or acquired credentials—that lead to authority. Because blogs are open to multiple viewpoints and experiences, they give women and other marginalized identities a place from which to speak.

Wikipedia's "Talk" page provides a space for contributors to shape the debate about what knowledge is relevant to the entry. Wikipedia depends on the collaborative writing process for fact checking and neutrality; its entries rely on verifiable sources with citations so "that anyone using the encyclopedia can check that the information comes from a reliable source" (Wikipedia, 2015c). Many of the individuals who contribute to Wikipedia are volunteers and do not have professional or educational expertise in the pages they edit; they often have little individual ethos on most topics. For instance, one of the top editors of the breastfeeding entry is Gandydancer who also wrote significant portions of the "Gandy Dancer" and "Yodeling" entries. The "Talk" page could be a space for women to control knowledge about their bodies, but instead the generic requirements for neutrality and verifiability often silence them. On the "Breastfeeding" "Talk" page, user Fabiola Grojan requested the addition of a section entitled "breastfeeding fashion" so that mothers can "avoid the unwanted attention when breastfeeding in public without using their scarf to cover up." However, another user, SummerPhD, responded that Fabiola needs to provide "reliable sources discussing 'breastfeeding fashion' to add it to the article." The difference between the opinion of the contributor and a reliable resource seems moot here; Fabiola could easily find support from a credible source, such as an article from *The Guardian* or perhaps *Parenting*. While McIntyre (2010) argued that Wikipedia's collaborative process, verifiability, and NPOV make it verifiable and not a source of objective truth, the authors find this distinction disingenuous. Even as Wikipedia encourages contributors to cite verifiable sources such as scholarly articles and textbooks, they privilege some forms of knowledge over others, thus making them appear as objective truth. In other words, some types of sources are considered more "true" (verifiable) than others; peer-reviewed articles are more "true" than personal blogs, and any source is more "true" than personal experience or individual ethos.

But perhaps more troubling are instances when the user has direct knowledge and experience, but, by championing neutrality, Wikipedia ignores these testimonial forms of evidence. Technology futurist Jaron Lanier (2006) tried to delete parts of his own entry that called him a filmmaker because he made "one experimental short film about a decade and a half ago." However, he found himself in a battle with other Wikipedians who "corrected" the changes Lanier made. Lanier's own life experience was less important than the verifiability of his sources. For women, this bias can have devastating effects. Historically, women have been excluded from creating scholarly and verifiable research, and, in some cases, the only way to encounter the perspective of non-academic women is through experiential accounts. Cassel (2011) explained, "despite Wikipedia's stated principle of the need to maintain a neutral point of view, the reality is that it is not enough to 'know something' about friendship bracelets or 'Sex and the City.'" In her study of several regular women contributors, Gruwell (2015) shared a similar experience to Fabiola's. One study participant, Janet, explained, "'Sometimes you just can't [find citations]. Sometimes particularly for stuff you know' … 'Where do you find a source that tells you there isn't a high school in a particular suburb? I mean, I know that. I've lived there for twenty-something years'" (p. 126). While Janet's knowledge may be useful and interesting to other users, the generic requirements for citation of verifiable sources preclude any appeals to direct experience. Fabiola's and Janet's voices are silenced by a generic need for NPOV and verifiability that in turn excludes their *ethea*. Similarly, the Breastfeeding "Talk" page demonstrates how personal experience is unwelcome in Wikipedia: Gandydancer, a prolific editor, noted that her experiential ethos is not a legitimate source, but she feels the need to share it nevertheless: "From a personal POV, which I suppose I should not mention but will anyway, thinking back to my own experience, loss of interest in sex was more of my experience than feeling 'sexy' while I nursed." Regardless of her experience, Gandydancer must provide verifiable sources to justify the editorial direction of the entry.

Because they are predicated on personal ethos, blogs offer a counter-authority to Wikipedia's encyclopedic genre. For instance, Paala frequently praises pop culture figures who support breastfeeding (Jun 14, 2014) and addresses Facebook's anti-nipple policy that prohibits users from posting breastfeeding photos (Jun 10, 2014). Teglene (*TBM*) also discusses her personal experiences in relation to larger cultural norms. In one post (Sep 6, 2014), she examines the common myth that busy women should be excused from breastfeeding because it is inconvenient. She uses her own experience to claim how a mother can work breastfeeding into any schedule, particularly if she recruits help from her family. Here, Paala and Teglene both provide personal ethos to contextualize breastfeeding issues and give advice to their readers. And their readers respond positively, despite their lack of "reliable sources." Wikipedia would not allow such material because these posts and others like them express both opinions and experiences and often do not draw upon outside verifiable sources.

The value of this experiential digital ethos is that the bloggers can explain how they came to their knowledge. They can describe what happened to them and how they handled it; readers have insight into the logic that goes into the bloggers' decisions, which can help them reach their own conclusions on related issues. To illustrate, Jenny (*CoaNM*, Mar 11, 2014) advises pregnant women how to prepare for breastfeeding. She uses her experiential ethos to help women determine what is best for them. Likewise, Shannon (*BftW*, May 11, 2011) writes a lengthy post on law and justice in regard to an incident in which she was illegally ejected from a store for breastfeeding in public. She hyperlinks several outside resources, each of which pertains to the event at the store and the ensuing aftermath, including media coverage and out-of-court settlements. Although she does not cite any scholarly sources, Shannon documents her journey through this event and advises other women in similar situations on how to exercise their agency and receive restitution. In both instances, Jenny and Shannon not only share knowledge, but they also contextualize where it comes from.

Notably, this study's mommybloggers use their own credentials and outside research to boost their digital *ethea*, although the blog genre does not require them to do so. First, they are mothers who breastfeed their children, so they offer firsthand experience to substantiate their claims. In addition, several of these bloggers train in lactation and breastfeeding. Jenny has L.A.T.C.H. (Lactation, Attachment, Training, Counseling, Help) training, Anne (*DPM*) has experience as a peer supporter with her local Healthcare Trust and as a birth and postnatal doula, and Rachelle (*Unlatched*) works as a breastfeeding counselor and advocate while studying to become an IBCLC. These three women have background experience beyond their own to supplement their *ethea*. On their blogs, this *ethea* lends authority and adequately legitimizes the knowledge they produce. On Wikipedia, other contributors would reject this firsthand knowledge.

Despite the genre's freedom from the need for secondary sources, the breastfeeding bloggers still tend to draw from external materials, most frequently from sources such as *KellyMom* and *La Leche League International*, two well-reputed websites on breastfeeding and parenting. Many posts include a list of references at the end: Anne (Jul 10, 2010) hyperlinked six sources in a post about drinking alcohol while nursing (on Aug 19, 2010, her post includes a 17-item reference list), and Teglene (Dec 14, 2010) includes both hyperlinks and an APA-formatted list of references in a post about low milk production. Notably, these lists include scholarly articles and books written by healthcare professionals and breastfeeding experts with strong reputations. In the instances when the mommybloggers cite secondary sources, they demonstrate that they are well-informed readers on breastfeeding topics. All six blogs utilize some level of research, although how much and how often varies entirely by the blog post and the blogger's preferences.

Blogs show that people can have similar experiences and still learn from each other. For example, if a mother is having a hard time breastfeeding (maybe the baby isn't latching or often becomes colicky after feeding), she is certainly not the only woman who has encountered these problems. Thus, blogs lend authority to bloggers who exercise their digital *ethea*. However, because Wikipedia relies on the credibility of verifiable sources to establish authority, the "Breastfeeding" page reflects a clinical concern with how breastfeeding works. By reading on breastfeeding blogs about other women's experiences, a mother might find solutions to her problems quickly and easily without needing to spend time and money on a doctor's visit. Even though blogs are renowned for focusing on the individuals writing them, these six women have shown how the genre can balance both researched facts and personal experience in a meaningful way, something Wikipedia denies its users.

Blogs and Privileged Epistemologies

The traditional view of blogs is that they level the playing field for those who wish to write; all a person needs to do is sign up, log in, and go. Arguably, since blogs do not restrict who writes or comments, they provide marginalized voices a place from which to finally speak (Coleman, 2005). At the very least, blogs connect people all over the globe and alert each other to culturally distinct viewpoints on similar topics. At first, these six mommyblogs seem to fit with this utopian view of blogs as empowering and globally diverse: Jenny (*CoaNM*) is from the Philippines, Shannon (*BftW*) is from Canada, Anne (*DPM*) is from the United Kingdom, and Rachelle (*Unlatched*) and Paala are American; Teglene (*TBM*) does not disclose her geographical location. However, as Ratliff (2007) quoting Fraser (1992, p. 120) pointed out, "The blogosphere, like any other rhetorical situation, is 'situated in a larger societal context that is pervaded by structural relations of dominance and subordination.'" Thus, because blogs can reflect the same social strife and discrimination that exist offline, they are not always a perfect paradigm of digital credibility equality.

Gaining access to the blogosphere and having your voice heard is based on privilege, and, in our society, certain genders, races, and socioeconomic statuses still carry privilege over others. Friedman's (2010) analysis of mommyblogs revealed that women of color, queer mothers, women with disabilities, and other non-normative identities are often underrepresented on mommyblogs, in part because of marginalized identities' link to socioeconomic status. Friedman concludes that, while blogs provide opportunities for diverse experiences, "white, married, middle- or upper-class women are... perceived as not simply common, but normal" (p. 203). Indeed, not only are most of the six mommybloggers at hand racially white and apparently heterosexual-identifying, they are also all predominantly influenced by Anglo-American ideologies and narratives about breastfeeding. Although these bloggers come from diverse backgrounds, they are not representative of all breastfeeding mothers worldwide. They are not even representative of many non-normative mothers in their own countries. Their digital ethos, although valuable, has limits. And these limits have the potential to be dangerously exclusive.

Friedman (2010) examined how the "good mother" narrative in mommyblogs influences and reflects cultural norms, and the authors have noticed a similar trend in the six breastfeeding blogs. One theme ties them together: the "breast is best," or at least the "breast*milk* is best" philosophy. A quick look at some recent posts from all six bloggers reveals a bias against bottlefeeding:

- On October 18, 2014, Jenny posts a "Quick Guide to Breastfeeding Challenges," which asserts that "medical and physical reasons" should not limit a woman's ability to breastfeed.

- On September 6, 2012, Teglene tells her readers that being busy is not a valid excuse for mothers to choose not to breastfeed.
- On July 4, 2015, Paala posts photos of fellow mothers in her community breastfeeding their children. She also frequently shares breastfeeding selfies ("brelfies," as she calls them).
- On December 16, 2012, Anne asserts "birth and breastfeeding—they are connected."
- On December 12, 2012, Rachelle defends milksharing (which is when a nursing mother donates her milk to another mother so her baby can receive breastmilk).
- On April 8, 2011, Shannon tells a story about how she explained to her children (who, she makes a point to mention, were all breastfed) why they went to a nurse-in.

All of these instances may not seem significant, but together and compounded with the multifarious other times these bloggers make similar implicit and explicit assertions, they speak to a larger cultural assumption that good mothers supply their children with breastmilk. These women establish digital credibility by drawing on their credibility as "good" mothers who breastfeed.

The authors of this chapter do not intend to disparage the value of breastfeeding. Too many studies to cite here have shown that breastmilk, preferably the mother's, is healthier for babies and that formula-feeding may be risky. But because many mommyblogs refuse to consider any other viewpoints, the implication behind these "good mother" narratives is that bottlefeeding mothers are the opposite—bad mothers—and that their digital ethos is less valuable, thus depriving them of digital authority. Jenny's and Teglene's posts explicitly state that mothers do not have an excuse for not breastfeeding. Some bloggers suggest alternative options: Rachelle's post cited above offers milksharing as a substitute for breastfeeding, while Jenny (May 7, 2012) and Anne (Feb 25, 2013) propose breastpumps as another method for mothers to feed breastmilk to their children. However, these posts do not acknowledge that not all mothers have access to donor milk nor can all mothers afford expensive breastpumps. Only Anne and Paala concede that breastfeeding is not available to some mothers. Paala (Oct 23, 2015) openly addresses her breastfeeding bias while offering advice to bottlefeeding mothers. Anne (Mar 30, 2015) admits that sometimes women just cannot breastfeed even though they may want to; she emphasizes that they do not deserve scorn because of it. However, posts like Paala's and Anne's are rare. The collective ethos of the mommblogging community is reflected in posts like Jenny's and Teglene's assertions that all mothers should breastfeed or Rachelle's, Jenny's, and Anne's alternative suggestions. Such comments reveal that alternative *ethea* about breast- and bottlefeeding is not always valued in normative narratives of the "good mother." Blogs are more inclusive than Wikipedia when deciding what sources of knowledge they consider authoritative, but, as this case study of breastfeeding blogs shows, they are also culturally saturated spaces that can reinscribe cultural privilege through both implicit and explicit narratives of what it means to be a "good mother."

FUTURE RESEARCH DIRECTIONS

This chapter has provided case studies of Wikipedia and blogs to support an argument that while Wikipedia's generic constraints silence women's digital credibility and authority, blogs' generic affordances provide a space from which women use their authority to create knowledge about such important topics as health and childcare. The authors find three potential avenues for further research:

1. Digital social media may provide a different way of reaching collaborative knowledge,
2. Digital social media may still marginalize women, and
3. Wikipedia and digital social media may marginalize other identities.

Although the authors originally determined blogs to be a digital genre in which women are more likely to share information and experiences, these case studies reveal that women also use various digital social media sites (SMS) to perform these tasks. Many of the breastfeeding blogs this article examines have links to Facebook pages, Google+ accounts, and other SMS, and often the bloggers appear to use these sites more regularly than their blogs. Rachelle has not updated *Unlatched* in nearly a year, but she updates her blog's Facebook page daily (Rachelle, 2015); likewise, Anne updates *DPM* every few months, but her blog's Facebook page almost weekly (Anne, 2015b). In an interview, Rachelle explained why she uses social media more often than her blog to connect with her readers: "I use [Facebook] usually on a daily basis, whereas my blog is reserved for topics that I feel are under-covered by others. I feel that being active on social media is extremely important as a breastfeeding professional because... We need to meet moms where they are at. Facebook has given me the opportunity to connect with and help so many mothers" (personal communication, June 2014). Further research on the digital authority of women's health pages on sites like Facebook could examine if and why social media is better suited to spreading this knowledge to a larger audience.

Facebook is one of the most popular websites in the world and can certainly reach a wide audience, but what is interesting is how it limits women's expression in a way similar to Wikipedia. Paala and Rachelle both document on their blogs how Facebook deletes photos or suspends and bans accounts that violate the strict rules against showing breastfeeding photos. As a corporate entity, Facebook can control the media added by its users. Facebook (2015a) plainly states that the users own and control any content they publish to the site, but it also has equally clear Community Standards (2015b) that dictate what content is allowed to be posted and what content will be removed if published. Similarly Wikipedia (2015b) states, "Contributions remain the property of their creators," but as the "Talk" and "About" pages illustrate, content should only be published if there is communal consensus about it. These rules limit what users can publish on these corporate sites in ways that blogs typically do not. Stories that show the censorship of women on sites like Facebook and Wikipedia are troubling, and more research is needed into how the corporatization of digital social media influences how women and other marginalized identities are able to exercise digital credibility and authority in those spaces.

Finally, the authors suspect that women are not alone in their encyclopedic silencing and that race, class, and sexuality also have an impact on how knowledge is created on Wikipedia. A search for articles on these identities and Wikipedia reveals that virtually no research has been done to examine how Wikipedia excludes or empowers people of color and non-white ethnicities. Wikipedia also appears to exclude impoverished people, many of whom, as Balit (2007) found, access the Internet by mobile device only. Noam Cohen (2014) noted that less than one percent of the edits made to Wikipedia come from mobile devices, thus suggesting an implicit discrimination against people of lower socioeconomic status. Finally, only one article (Raval, 2014) touched on sexuality and Wikipedia. This may be because, although Wikipedia measures the gender, age, and nationality of its contributors (Wikipedia, 2015d), it does not measure their racial identities, socioeconomic standing, or sexuality. More research is certainly needed to explore how these factors affect editing practices on Wikipedia.

CONCLUSION

The case studies in this chapter have implications for collaborative writing in academia. There are many benefits to collaborative work (Lunsford & Ede, 2012). First, when the processes of knowledge creation are open and obvious, writers and readers on the margins can learn the rules and join the conversation. As Brooke (2009) mentioned, the final product of a Wikipedia entry is only a small representation of the epistemological activity that happens on the site. When users look at the "Talk" pages and see the debates between collaborators, they gain a better understanding of what all sides are saying about an issue and which side wins. Second, when collaboration is open and respectful to all perspectives, many standpoints may be represented, which may in turn prevent the tyranny of normativity. In particular, such valuing of multiple perspectives opens up the opportunity for alternative *ethea* when discussing knowledge.

However, there is a darker side to collaboration. Although it has the potential to open knowledge creation to multiple *ethea*, this chapter shows it does not always do so. This remains particularly true in academia, where collaboration is increasingly becoming a respected mode of authorship, not just in rhetoric and composition studies, but in many other fields. The sciences have long supported co-authored works, and fields as disparate as literature and medicine are also realizing the benefits of co-written scholarship (Kutner et al, 2006). However, a bias against experiential ethos in many fields undermines the potential value of collaboration. For instance, in 2015, evolutionary science academics Fiona Ingleby and Megan Head received a review from a peer editor who explained that their work on "gender differences in the PhD to postdoc transition" (Bernstein, 2015) was unfit for publication on the basis of the gender of the writers. The anonymous reviewer explained, "It would probably… be beneficial to find one or two male biologists to work with (or at least obtain internal peer review from, but better yet as active co-authors), to serve as a possible check against interpretations that may sometimes be drifting too far away from empirical evidence into ideologically biased assumptions" (Ingleby, 2015). This example shows that while academia has become more accepting of collaboratively written scholarship, it still does not hold alternative *ethea* equal to a normative, empirical ethos. This exclusion leads to the continued silence of women and other minority identities whose *ethea* are based in alternative epistemologies that may include experiential authority. Collaborative composition needs policing; we need more users who do not represent normative ideologies to participate in knowledge creation, lest we risk silencing valid *ethea*.

The case studies presented in this chapter also have implications for how women exercise agency over their own bodies. For instance, in 2012, Todd Akin, in a stunning display of ignorance about female anatomy, declared, "If it's a legitimate rape, the female body has ways to try to shut that whole thing down" (Eligon and Schwirtz, 2012). The authors believe that such obliviousness reveals two troubling issues. First, it speaks to the long history of physicians' and researchers' lack of consideration for women's health issues. Fausto-Sterling (2012) pointed out that research into female genetic development is decades behind research into male genetic development because of our society's implicit belief that femaleness is often defined simply as a lack of maleness. Furthermore, Fausto-Sterling explained that this gendered research disparity is slowly being rectified, but it still has a long way to go. More importantly, Fausto-Sterling's research helps explain why Akin knew so little about how female bodies work. They are deemed as less important to learn about. Society believes women's health is women's problem.

Second, Akin's comment showcases how legislators and policy makers devalue women's ethos. When women are unable to make knowledge about their own bodies, they are stripped of agency for how their bodies are controlled in public. For instance, many of the breastfeeding bloggers are also self-proclaimed lactivists who actively fight for women's rights to breastfeed in public, and they are often met with vehement resistance. Lunceford (2012) pointed to this resistance as indicative of "a strong desire to discipline and control female bodies" that arises from the internalized "belief that the breast is solely there as a sexual object" and not as a functional one (p. 51). He also explains, "[T]he cultural construction of the female breast as a sexual object... stands in the way of widespread acceptance of public breastfeeding" (Lunceford, 2012, p. 37). If women's *ethea* is accepted on a global and societal level—not just on niche blogs—their experiential knowledge could put an end to unnecessary sexualization and ignorance by informing more people about their bodies from their own perspective, which would in turn facilitate more agency when it comes to public policy and perception about issues like breastfeeding.

Above all, this case study reveals the pressing need to empower women and people of color to contribute to collaborative environments, particularly mainstream digital spaces like Wikipedia. One way to do this is to host and contribute to Wikipedia edit-a-thons and write-ins. These events are aimed at filling gaps in women's history on Wikipedia by editing, expanding, and/or creating entries. The Wikimedia Foundation often sponsors edit-a-thons in which experienced and novice editors can revise pages or create new ones. In 2012, Wikimedia Foundation community fellow Sarah Stierch "Missvain" organized an edit-a-thon at the Smithsonian to build entries about women scientists in their archives (Shen, 2012). While this is a step in the right direction, the focus on scientists implies that women are only valuable when they conform to normative discourses. However, the most famous write-in event, the Global Women Wikipedia Write-In (GWWI), does not focus solely on scientists; the GWWI solicits suggestions from the community on what needs to added or edited. Its goals are "to encourage new people to become Wikipedia editors, to provide support for new editors, and to develop best practices for rewriting Wikipedia" (Koh and Risam, 2014). Events like these empower women to exercise agency over their knowledge creation in mainstream spaces. This study also points to the need to change the rules and informal practices of collaborative environments to encourage contributors to think twice before automatically deleting entries and/or edits (a common practice on Wikipedia). Finally, the authors suggest that knowledge creators need to trust the process of open collaboration rather than thinking of themselves as gatekeepers of knowledge and truth. Only then will multiple *ethea* be considered credible and valuable, both online and off.

REFERENCES

Anne. (2015a). *Dispelling breastfeeding myths* [Blog]. Retrieved from http://mythnomore.blogspot.com/

Anne. (2015b). *Dispelling breastfeeding myths* [Facebook page]. Retrieved from https://www.facebook.com/DispellingBfMyths/

Armstrong, C. L., & McAdams, M. J. (2009). Blogs of information: How gender cues and individual motivations influence perceptions of credibility. *Journal of Computer-Mediated Communication, 14*(3), 435–456. doi:10.1111/j.1083-6101.2009.01448.x

Balit, S. (2007). Communication for isolated and marginalized groups. In *Communication and sustainable development: Selected papers from the 9th UN roundtable on communication for development* (pp. 101-122). New York: FAO UN Press.

Bernstein, R. (2015, May 1). PLOS ONE outs review, editor after sexist peer-review storm. *Science Insider*. Retrieved from http://news.sciencemag.org/scientific-community/2015/04/sexist-peer-review-elicits-furious-twitter-response

Blood, R. (2000). Weblogs: A history and perspective [Blog]. *Rebecca's Pocket*. Retrieved from http://www.rebeccablood.net/essays/weblog_history.html

Brooke, C. G. (2009). *Lingua fracta: Towards a rhetoric of new media*. Cresskill, NJ: Hampton Press.

Brown, J. (2015). *Ethical programs: Hospitality and the rhetorics of software*. Ann Arbor, MI: University of Michigan Press. doi:10.3998/dh.13474172.0001.001

Cassel, J. (2011, Feb 4). A culture of editing wars. *New York Times Online*. Retrieved from http://www.nytimes.com/roomfordebate/2011/02/02/where-are-the-women-in-wikipedia/a-culture-of-editing-wars

Chawner, B., & Lewis, P. H. (2004, October). *WikiWikiWebs: New ways of interacting in a web environment*. Paper presented at the ALA (American Library Association) LITA National Forum.

Chesney, T. (2006). An empirical examination of Wikipedia's credibility. *First Monday*, *11*(11). doi:10.5210/fm.v11i11.1413

Cohen, N. (2014, February 4). Wikipedia vs. the small screen. *New York Times Online*. Retrieved from http://www.nytimes.com/2014/02/10/technology/wikipedia-vs-the-small-screen.html?_r=0

Coleman, S. (2005). Blogs and the new politics of listening. *The Political Quarterly*, 273–280.

Eckert, S., & Steiner, L. (2013). Wikipedia's gender gap. In C. L. Armstrong (Ed.), *Media disparity: A gender battleground* (pp. 87–98). New York: Lexington Books.

Eligon, J., & Schwirtz, M. (Aug 19, 2012). Senate candidate provokes ire with "legitimate rape" comment. *The New York Times Online*. Retrieved from http://www.nytimes.com/2012/08/20/us/politics/todd-akin-provokes-ire-with-legitimate-rape-comment.html

Facebook. (2015a). *Terms*. Retrieved from https://www.facebook.com/terms.php

Facebook. (2015b). *Community Standards*. Retrieved from https://www.facebook.com/communitystandards?ref=br_tf

Fallis, D. (2011). Wikipistemology. In A. Goldman & D. Whitcomb (Eds.), *Social epistemology: Essential readings* (pp. 297–313). New York: Oxford University Press.

Fausto-Sterling, A. (2012). *Sex/Gender: Biology in a social world*. New York: Routledge.

Flanagin, A. J., & Metzger, M. J. (2008). Digital media and youth: Unparalleled opportunity and unprecedented responsibility. In M. Metzger & A. Flanagin (Eds.), *Digital media, youth, and credibility* (pp. 5–27). Cambridge, MA: MacArthur Foundation Series on Digital Media and Learning.

Fraser, N. (1992). Rethinking the public sphere: A contribution to the critique of actually existing democracy. In C. Calhoun (Ed.), *Habermas and the public sphere* (pp. 109–142). Cambridge, MA: MIT Press.

Friedman, M. (2010). On mommyblogging: Notes to a future feminist historian. *Journal of Women's History*, *22*(4), 197–208.

Frost, E. A. (2013). *Theorizing an apparent feminism in technical communication.* (Doctoral dissertation). Retrieved from ProQuest. (Order No. 3574642).

Frost, E. A. (2014a). Apparent feminist pedagogies: Interrogating technical rhetorics at Illinois State University. *Programmatic Perspectives, 6*(1), 110–131.

Frost, E. A. (2014b). An apparent feminist approach to transnational technical rhetorics: The ongoing work of Nujood Ali. *Peitho, 16*(2), 183–199.

Frost, E A. (2015). Apparent feminism as a methodology for technical communication and rhetoric. *Journal of Business and Technical Communication,* 1-26.

Garfinkel, S. L. (2008). Wikipedia and the meaning of truth. *Technology Review, 111*(6), 84–86.

Giles, J. (2005). Special report internet encyclopedias go head to head. *Nature, 439*(12), 900–901. doi:10.1038/438900a PMID:16355180

Gruwell, L. (2015). Wikipedia's politics of exclusion: Gender, epistemology, and feminist rhetorical (in) action. *Computers and Composition, 37,* 117–131. doi:10.1016/j.compcom.2015.06.009

Haraway, D. (1988). Situated knowledges: The science question in feminism and the privilege of partial perspective. *Feminist Studies, 14*(3), 575–599. doi:10.2307/3178066

Harding, S. (1993). Rethinking standpoint epistemology: What is "strong objectivity?". In L. Alcoff & E. Potter (Eds.), *Feminist Epistemologies* (pp. 49–82). New York: Routledge.

Harding, S. (Ed.). (2003). *The feminist standpoint theory reader: Intellectual and political controversies.* New York: Routledge.

Hargittai, E., & Shaw, A. (2015). Mind the skills gap: The role of Internet know-how and gender in differentiated contributions to Wikipedia. *Information Communication and Society, 18*(4), 424–442. doi: 10.1080/1369118X.2014.957711

Hartsock, N. C. M. (1983). The feminist standpoint: Developing the ground for a specifically feminist historical materialism. In S. G. Harding & M. B. Hintikka (Eds.), *Discovering reality: Feminist perspectives on epistemology, metaphysics, methodology, and philosophy of science* (pp. 283–310). Boston: D. Reidel.

Ingleby, F. (2015, April 29). *and this is a bit hypocritical given the reviewer's own ideological biases throughout the review, for example: (3/4)* [Tweet]. Retrieved from https://twitter.com/FionaIngleby/status/593408350001471489

Jenny. (2015). *Chronicles of a Nursing Mom* [Blog]. Retrieved from http://www.chroniclesofanursingmom.com/

Johnson, T.J., & Kaye, B.K. (2004). Wag the blog: How reliance on traditional media and the internet influence credibility perceptions of weblogs among blog users. *Journalism & Mass Communication Quarterly September, 81*(3), 622-642.

Johnson, T.J., & Kaye, B. K. (2010). Believing the blog of war: How blog users compare on credibility and characteristics in 2003 and 2007. *Media, War, and Conflict, 3*(3), 315–333. doi:10.1177/1750635210376591

Johnson, T. J., & Kaye, B. K. (2011). Hot diggity blog: A cluster analysis examining motivations and other factors for why people judge different types of blogs as credible. *Mass Communication & Society*, *14*(2), 236–263. doi:10.1080/15205431003687280

Johnston, A., Friedman, B., & Peach, S. (2011). Standpoint in political blogs: Voice, authority, and issues. *Women's Studies*, *40*(3), 269–298. doi:10.1080/00497878.2010.548427

Kellymom. (2015). *KellyMom* [Website]. Retrieved from http://kellymom.com/

Kennedy, K. (2009). Textual machinery: Authorial agency and bot-written texts in Wikipedia. In M. Smith & B. Warnick (Eds.), *The responsibilities of rhetoric*: Proceedings of the 2008 Rhetoric Society of America Conference. Retrieved from http://surface.syr.edu/wp/1/

Koerber, A. (2006). Rhetorical agency, resistance, and the disciplinary rhetorics of breastfeeding. *Technical Communication Quarterly*, *15*(1), 87–101. doi:10.1207/s15427625tcq1501_7

Koerber, A. (2013). *Breast or bottle? Contemporary controversies in infant-feeding policy and practice*. Columbia, SC: University of South Carolina Press.

Koerber, A., Brice, L., & Tombs, E. (2012, February). Breastfeeding and problematic integration: Results of a focus-group study. *Health Communication*, *27*(2), 124–144. doi:10.1080/10410236.2011.57 1754 PMID:21834716

Koh, A., & Risam, R. (2014). The global women Wikipedia write-in #GWWI. *Postcolonial digital humanities*. Retrieved from http://dhpoco.org/rewriting-wikipedia/the-global-women-wikipedia-write-in/

Kutner, J. S., Westfall, J. M., Morrison, E. H., Beach, M. C., Jacobs, E. A., & Rosenblatt, R. A. (2006). Facilitating collaboration among academic generalist disciplines: A call to action. *Annals of Family Medicine*, *4*(2), 172–176. doi:10.1370/afm.392 PMID:16569722

La Leche League International. (2015). *La Leche League International* [Website]. Retrieved from http://www.llli.org/

Lanier, J. (2006). Digital Maoism. *The Edge*. Retrieved from http://edge.org/conversation/digital-maoism-the-hazards-of-the-new-online-collectivism

Loveland, J., & Reagle, J. (2013). Wikipedia and encyclopedic production. *New Media & Society*, *15*(8), 1294–1311. doi:10.1177/1461444812470428

Lunceford, B. (2012). *Naked politics: Nudity, political action, and the rhetoric of the body*. Lanham, MD: Lexington Books.

Lunsford, A., & Ede, L. (2012). *Writing together: Collaboration in theory and practice, a critical sourcebook*. St. Martins.

McIntyre, A. M. C. (2010). The 'truthiness' of Wikipedia: An examination of the open content encyclopedia as a valuable vehicle in developing critical thinking in the classroom. *Access to Knowledge*, *2*(1), 2–8.

Metzger, M. J. (2007). Making sense of credibility on the Web: Models for evaluating online information and recommendations for future research. *Journal of the American Society for Information Science and Technology*, *58*(13), 2078–2091. doi:10.1002/asi.20672

Novotny, M. (2015). reVITALize gynecology: Reimagining apparent feminism's methodology in participatory health intervention projects. *Communication Design Quarterly*, *3*(4), 61–74. doi:10.1145/2826972.2826978

Paala. (2015). *Paa.la* [Blog]. Retrieved from http://paa.la/

Rachelle. (2014). *Unlatched* [Blog]. Retrieved from https://unlatched.wordpress.com/

Rachelle. (2015). *Unlatched* [Facebook page]. Retrieved from https://www.facebook.com/unlatched/

Ratliff, C. (2007). Attracting readers: Sex and audience in the blogosphere. *The Scholar and Feminist Online*, *5*(2). Retrieved from http://sfonline.barnard.edu/blogs/ratliff_03.htm

Raval, N. (2014). The encyclopedia must fail! – Notes on queering Wikipedia. *ADA: A Journal of Gender, New Media, and Technology*, *5*. Retrieved from http://adanewmedia.org/2014/07/issue5-raval/

Reagle, J. (2009). *Gender bias in Wikipedia coverage? Open communities, media, source, and standards.* Retrieved from http://reagle.org/joseph/blog/social/wikipedia/wp-eb-gender-bias-coverage

Reagle, J., & Rhue, L. (2011). Gender bias in Wikipedia and Britannica. *International Journal of Communication*, *5*, 1138–1158.

Rose, H. (1983). Hand, brain and heart: A feminist epistemology for the natural sciences. *Signs (Chicago, Ill.)*, *9*(1), 73–90. doi:10.1086/494025

Scott, K. A., & White, M. A. (2013). COMPUGIRLS' Standpoint: Culturally Responsive Computer and Its Effects on Girls of Color. *Urban Education*, *48*(5), 657–681.

Selzer, J. (2004). Rhetorical analysis: Understanding how texts persuade readers. In C. Bazerman & P. Prior (Eds.), *What writing does and how it does it* (pp. 279–308). Mahwah, NJ: Lawrence Erlbaum.

Shannon. (2011). *Breast for the Weary* [Blog]. Retrieved from http://breastfortheweary.com/

Shen, A. (Apr 4, 2012). How many women does it take to change Wikipedia? *Smithsonian Magazine.com*. Retrieved from http://www.smithsonianmag.com/smithsonian-institution/how-many-women-does-it-take-to-change-wikipedia-171400755/?no-ist

Simonite, T. (2013). The decline of Wikipedia. *The MIT Technology Review*. Retrieved from http://www.technologyreview.com/featuredstory/520446/the-decline-of-wikipedia/

Teglene. (2014). *The Breastfeeding Mother* [Blog]. Retrieved from http://thebreastfeedingmother.blogspot.com/

Wikimedia Report Card. (2015, August). Retrieved from http://reportcard.wmflabs.org/

Wikipedia. (2015a). *Breastfeeding:Talk*. Retrieved from https://en.wikipedia.org/wiki/Talk:Breastfeeding

Wikipedia. (2015b). *Wikipedia:About*. Retrieved from https://en.wikipedia.org/wiki/Wikipedia:About

Wikipedia. (2015c). *Wikipedia:Verifiability*. Retrieved from https://en.wikipedia.org/wiki/Wikipedia:Verifiability

Wikipedia. (2015d). *Wikipedia:Wikipedians*. Retrieved from https://en.wikipedia.org/wiki/Wikipedia:Wikipedians

Winter, S., & Krämer, N. C. (2014). A question of credibility – Effects of source cues and recommendations on information selection on news sites and blogs. *Communications*, *39*(4), 435–546. doi:10.1515/commun-2014-0020

KEY TERMS AND DEFINITIONS

Agency: The power a person has to act in a given situation.

Apparent Feminism: A methodology designed by Frost (2013, 2014a, 2014b, 2015) whose goal is to make apparent instances of gendered marginalization.

Collaborative Writing: A process of writing in which multiple authors, editors, and/or collaborators draft and revise a text.

Feminist Standpoint Theory: A method of knowledge creation first defined by Harding (1993, 2003) that presupposes complete objectivity can never be reached because all knowledge is culturally situated. Instead, researchers can achieve "strong objectivity" that acknowledges and includes many perspectives.

Kairos/Kairotic: The ancient Greek rhetorical concept that describes a timely response or rhetorical opportunity in a rhetorical situation that is both realist and constructivist.

Lactivism: A movement fueled by the belief that mothers should breastfeed their children. Many lactivists also believe mothers should be allowed to breastfeed in public.

Mommyblog: A genre of blog whose themes and topics pertain almost exclusively to motherhood.

Compilation of References

Aaronovitch, D. (2010). *Voodoo histories: The role of the conspiracy theory in shaping modern history*. New York, NY: Riverhead Books.

About AboveTopSecret.com. (2014). *AboveTopSecret*. Retrieved from http://www.abovetopsecret.com/about_above-topsecret.php

About Natural News. (n.d.). *Natural News*. Retrieved from http://www.naturalnews.com/About.html

About Skeptical Science. (2015). *About Skeptical Science*. Retrieved December 1, 2015, from http://www.skepticalscience.com/about.shtml

About. (2015). *Watts Up With That?* Retrieved December 1, 2015, from http://wattsupwiththat.com/about-wuwt/about2

Ackland, R. (2013). *Web social science: Concepts, data and tools for social scientists in the digital age*. New York, NY: Sage.

Adamic, L. A., & Glance, N. (2005, August). The political blogosphere and the 2004 US election: Divided they blog. In *Proceedings of the 3rd international workshop on Link discovery* (pp. 36-43). ACM. doi:10.1145/1134271.1134277

Adams, M. (2012). *Obama seizes control over all food, farms, livestock, farm equipment, fertilizer and farm production across America*. Natural News. Retrieved from http://www.naturalnews.com/035301_Obama_executive_orders_food_supply.html

Adams, A. K. (2014). The Third-Party notification dilemma. *The Hastings Center Report*, *44*(s3), S31–S32. doi:10.1002/hast.339 PMID:25043470

Adams, S. A. (2010). Revisiting the online health information reliability debate in the wake of "Web 2.0": An interdisciplinary literature and website review. *International Journal of Medical Informatics*, *79*(6), 391–400. doi:10.1016/j.ijmedinf.2010.01.006 PMID:20188623

Adams, S., & Berg, M. (2004). The nature of the Net: Constructing reliability of health information on the Web. *Information Technology & People*, *17*(2), 150–170. doi:10.1108/09593840410542484

AEI. (2015). *Charles Murray*. Retrieved December 1, 2015, from https://www.aei.org/scholar/charles-murray

Allison, S. (2015, Dec 25). Man who identified Cecil the Lion's killer vows death will not be in vain. *The Guardian*. Retrieved, January 23, 2016, from http://www.theguardian.com/environment/2015/dec/25/cecil-the-lion-zimbabwe-conservation-johnny-rodrigues

Allué, M. (2013). *El Paciente inquieto: los servicios de atención médica y la ciudadanía*. Barcelona: Edicions Bellaterra.

Al-Nakib, M. (2013, Winter). Disjunctive synthesis: Deleuze and Arab feminism. *Signs (Chicago, Ill.)*, *38*(2), 459–482. doi:10.1086/667220

Altheide, D. L., & Schneider, C. J. (2013). *Qualitative media analysis* (2nd ed.). Los Angeles, CA: Sage.

American Association of Colleges of Nursing. (2014, April 24). *Nursing shortage fact sheet*. Retrieved from http://www.aacn.nche.edu/media-relations/NrsgShortageFS.pdf

Anderson, R. E. (1996). Information sifting or knowledge building on the Internet. *Social Science Computer Review*, *14*(1), 81–83. doi:10.1177/089443939601400125

Andrejevic, M. (2004). *Reality TV: The work of being watched*. Lanham, MD: Rowman and Littlefield.

Anne. (2015a). *Dispelling breastfeeding myths* [Blog]. Retrieved from http://mythnomore.blogspot.com/

Anne. (2015b). *Dispelling breastfeeding myths* [Facebook page]. Retrieved from https://www.facebook.com/DispellingBfMyths/

Antheunis, M. L., Schouten, A. P., Valkenburg, P. M., & Peter, J. (2012). Interactive uncertainty reduction strategies and verbal affection in computer-mediated communication. *Communication Research*, *39*(6), 757–780. doi:10.1177/0093650211410420

Antheunis, M. L., Valkenburg, P. M., & Peter, J. (2010). Getting acquainted through social network sites: Testing a model of online uncertainty reduction and social attraction. *Computers in Human Behavior*, *26*(1), 100–109. doi:10.1016/j.chb.2009.07.005

Antón, A. I., Earp, J. B., He, Q., Stufflebeam, W., Bolchini, D., & Jensen, C. (2004). The lack of clarity in financial privacy policies and the need for standardization. *IEEE Security and Privacy*, *2*(2), 36–45. doi:10.1109/MSECP.2004.1281243

Apostel, S., & Folk, M. (2005). *First phase in-formation literacy on a fourth generation Web site: An argument for a new approach to Web site evaluation criteria. Computers & Composition Online, Spring 2005*. Retrieved March 10, 2016 from http://www2.bgsu.edu/departments/english/cconline/apostelfolk/c_and_c_online_apostel_folk/

Apostel, S., & Folk, M. (2008). Shifting trends in evaluating the credibility of CMC. In S. Kelsey & K. St. Amant (Eds.), *Handbook of research on computer mediated communication* (pp. 185–195). Hershey, PA: Idea Group Reference. doi:10.4018/978-1-59904-863-5.ch014

Apostel, S., & Folk, M. (Eds.). (2012). *Online Credibility and Digital Ethos: Evaluating Computer-Mediated Communication*. Hershey, PA: IGI Global.

Arab women's solidarity association. (2006, May 9). *Wayback Machine*. Retrieved from https://web.archive.org/web/20060216031423/http://www.awsa.net/

Arab women's solidarity association. (2012, September 5). *Wayback Machine*. Retrieved from https://web.archive.org/web/20110105211814/http://awsa.net/

Arduser, L. (2011). Warp and weft: Weaving the discussion threads of an online community. *Journal of Technical Writing and Communication*, *41*(1), 5–31. doi:10.2190/TW.41.1.b

Aristotle, . (1932). *The Rhetoric of Aristotle* (L. Cooper, Trans.). Englewood Cliffs, NJ: Prentice Hall.

Aristotle, . (1961). *Aristotle's poetics* (S. H. Butcher, Trans.). New York, NY: Hill and Wang.

Aristotle. (1998). Retórica. Madrid: Alianza.

Aristotle. (2001). Rhetoric. In P. Bizzell & B. Herzberg (Eds.), The rhetorical tradition: readings from classical times to the present (2nd ed.; pp. 179-240). Boston, MA: Bedford/St Martins.

Aristotle, . (2007). *On rhetoric* (G. A. Kennedy, Trans.). New York: Oxford University Press.

Aristotle, . (2007). *On rhetoric: A theory of civic discourse* (G. A. Kennedy, Trans.). Oxford, UK: Oxford UP.

Armstrong, C. L., & McAdams, M. J. (2009). Blogs of information: How gender cues and individual motivations influence perceptions of credibility. *Journal of Computer-Mediated Communication, 14*(3), 435–456. doi:10.1111/j.1083-6101.2009.01448.x

Armstrong, N., & Powell, J. (2009). Patient perspectives on health advice posted on Internet discussion boards: A qualitative study. *Health Expectations, 12*(3), 313–390. doi:10.1111/j.1369-7625.2009.00543.x PMID:19555377

Association of American Medical Colleges. (2015). *Physician supply and demand through 2025: Key findings.* Retrieved from https://www.aamc.org/download/426260/data/physiciansupplyanddemandthrough2025keyfindings.pdf

Ayeh, J. K., Au, N., & Law, R. (2013). "Do We Believe in TripAdvisor?" Examining Credibility Perceptions and Online Travelers' Attitude toward Using User-Generated Content. *Journal of Travel Research, 52*(4), 437–452. doi:10.1177/0047287512475217

Baek, H., Ahn, J., & Choi, Y. (2012). Helpfulness of online consumer reviews: Readers' objectives and review cues. *International Journal of Electronic Commerce, 17*(2), 99–126. doi:10.2753/JEC1086-4415170204

Bailey, B. L. (1988). *From front porch to backseat.* Baltimore, MD: The Johns Hopkins University Press.

Bailey, C. (2001). Virtual skin: Articulating race in cyberspace. In D. Trend (Ed.), *Reading digital culture* (pp. 334–346). Malden, MA: Blackwell Publishing.

Baker, B. (2012, November 12). Millis man savors his time as an Internet (punching) bag. *The Boston Globe.* Retrieved December 3, 2015, from https://www.bostonglobe.com/metro/2012/11/24/the-internet-favorite-punching-bag/ijnRiZeT-502KmClwC8orDO/story.html

Balit, S. (2007). Communication for isolated and marginalized groups. In *Communication and sustainable development: Selected papers from the 9th UN roundtable on communication for development* (pp. 101-122). New York: FAO UN Press.

Ball, T. (2015). *How does the IPCC explain the severe storms of history?* Retrieved December 1, 2015, from http://wattsupwiththat.com/2015/08/19/how-does-the-ipcc-explain-the-severe-storms-of- history

Balsamo, A. (1999). *Technologies of the gendered body: Reading cyborg women.* Durham, NC: Duke University Press.

Banet-Weiser, S. (2012). *Authentic: The politics of ambivalence in a brand culture.* New York: New York University Press.

Bargh, J. A., & McKenna, K. Y. A. (2004). The Internet and social life. *Annual Review of Psychology, 55*(1), 573–590. doi:10.1146/annurev.psych.55.090902.141922 PMID:14744227

Bargh, J. A., McKenna, K. Y. A., & Fitzsimons, G. M. (2002). Can you see the real me? Activation and expression of the "true self" on the internet. *The Journal of Social Issues, 58*(1), 33–48. doi:10.1111/1540-4560.00247

Baumgartner, S. E., & Hartmann, T. (2011). The role of health anxiety in online health information search. *Cyberpsychology, Behavior, and Social Networking, 14*(10), 613–617. doi:10.1089/cyber.2010.0425 PMID:21548797

Baym, N. K. (1995). The performance of humor in computer-mediated communication. *Journal of Computer-Mediated Communication, 1*(2).

Baym, N. K. (2009). What constitutes quality in qualitative internet research? In A. N. Markham & N. K. Baym (Eds.), *Internet inquiry: Conversations about method* (pp. 173–189). Los Angeles, CA: Sage Publications. doi:10.4135/9781483329086.n16

BBB offers sample privacy policy for businesses. (n.d.). Retrieved December 16, 2015, from https://www.bbb.org/dallas/for-businesses/bbb-sample-privacy-policy1/

BBC.com. (2016, Feb 1). *Lions rediscovered in Ethiopia's Alatash game park.* BBC.com. Retrieved February 22, 2016, from http://www.bbc.com/news/world-africa-35460573

Beall, J. (2015). *Potential, possible, or probable predatory scholarly open-access publishers.* Retrieved December 1, 2015, from http://scholarlyoa.com/publishers/

Bean, S. J. (2011). Emerging and continuing trends in vaccine opposition website content. *Vaccine, 29*(10), 1874–1880. doi:10.1016/j.vaccine.2011.01.003 PMID:21238571

Beck, E. (2014). Breaking up with Facebook: Untethering from the ideological freight of online surveillance. *Hybrid Pedagogy.* Retrieved January 9, 2016, from http://www.hybridpedagogy.com/journal/breaking-facebook-untethering-ideological-freight-online-surveillance/

Beck, E. (2015). The invisible digital identity: Assemblages of digital networks. *Computers and Composition, 35,* 125–140. doi:10.1016/j.compcom.2015.01.005

Becker, H. S. (1986). *Writing for social scientists.* Chicago, IL: The University of Chicago Press.

Behrens, S. J. (1994). A conceptual analysis and historical overview of Information Literacy. *College & Research Libraries, 55*(4), 309–322. doi:10.5860/crl_55_04_309

Beldad, A., de Jong, M., & Steehouder, M. (2010). How shall I trust the faceless and the intangible? A literature review on the antecedents of online trust. *Computers in Human Behavior, 26*(5), 857–869. doi:10.1016/j.chb.2010.03.013

Bell, K. E., Orbe, M. P., Drummond, D. K., & Camara, S. K. (2000). Accepting the challenge of centralizing without essentializing: Black feminist thought and African American women's communicative experiences. *Women's. Studies in Communications, 23,* 41–62.

Berg, B. L. (2009). *Qualitative research methods for the social sciences* (7th ed.). Boston, MA: Allyn & Bacon.

Berger, C. R., & Bradac, J. J. (1982). *Language and social knowledge: Uncertainty in interpersonal relations.* London, UK: Edward Arnold, Ltd.

Berger, C. R., & Calabrese, R. J. (1975). Some explorations in initial interaction and beyond: Toward a developmental theory of interpersonal communication. *Human Communication Research, 1*(2), 99–112. doi:10.1111/j.1468-2958.1975.tb00258.x

Berkeley, U. C. (2012). *Evaluating web pages: Techniques to apply & questions to ask.* Retrieved December 1, 2015, from http://www.lib.berkeley.edu/TeachingLib/Guides/Internet/Evaluate.html

Bernabeu, J. (2007). Medicina e ideología: reflexiones desde la historiografía médica española. In R. Campos, L. Montiel, & R. Huertas (Eds.), *Medicina, ideología e historia en España (siglos XVI-XXI)* (pp. 17–50). Madrid: Consejo Superior de Investigaciones Científicas.

Bernstein, R. (2015, May 1). PLOS ONE outs review, editor after sexist peer-review storm. *Science Insider.* Retrieved from http://news.sciencemag.org/scientific-community/2015/04/sexist-peer-review-elicits-furious-twitter-response

Best, J. (2001). *Damned lies and statistics: Untangling numbers from the media, politicians, and activists.* Berkeley, CA: University of California Press.

Best, J. (2004). *More damned lies and statistics: How numbers confuse public issues*. Berkeley, CA: University of California Press.

Betsch, C., & Renkewitz, F. (2009). Langfristige Auswirkungen einer Informationssuche auf impfkritischen Internetseiten. *Prävention, 32*, 125–128.

Beyer, J. M., & Hannah, D. R. (2000). The Cultural Significance of Athletics in U.S. Higher Education. *Journal of Sport Management, 14*(2), 105.

Bhattercherjee, A. (2012). *Social science research: Principles, methods and practices*. Tampa Bay, FL: USF Tampa Bay Open Access Textbooks Collection.

Bialski, P. (2012). Becoming intimately mobile. In J. Wasilewski (Ed.), *Warsaw studies in culture and society* (Vol. 2). Retrieved from http://intimatetourism.files.wordpress.com/2012/07/paula-bialski-becomingintimatelymobile-ebook.pdf

Bickham, D. S., Kavanaugh, J. R., & Rich, M. (2016). Media effects as health research: How pediatricians have changed the study of media and child development. *Journal of Children and Media, 10*(2), 191–199. doi:10.1080/17482798.2015.1127842

Blakeslee, S. (2004). The CRAAP test. *LOEX Quarterly, 31*(3), 4.

Blank, G. (2006). *Critics, ratings, and society: The sociology of reviews*. Washington, DC: Rowman & Littlefield Publishers.

Blight, M. G., Jagiello, K., & Ruppel, E. K. (2015). "Same stuff different day:" A mixed-method study of support seeking on Facebook. *Computers in Human Behavior, 53*, 366–373. doi:10.1016/j.chb.2015.07.029

Blood, R. (2000). Weblogs: A history and perspective [Blog]. *Rebecca's Pocket*. Retrieved from http://www.rebeccablood.net/essays/weblog_history.html

Bluebond, A. (2014). When the customer is wrong: Defamation, interactive websites, and immunity. *Review of Litigation, 33*(3), 679.

Bosch, X., Pericas, J. M., Hernandez, C., & Torrents, A. (2012). A comparison of authorship policies at top-ranked peer-reviewed biomedical journals. *Archives of Internal Medicine, 172*(1), 70–72. doi:10.1001/archinternmed.2011.600 PMID:22232152

boyd, d. (2013). *Where 'nothing to hide' fails as logic*. [web log]. Retrieved January 9, 2016, from http://www.zephoria.org/thoughts/archives/2013/06/10/nothing-to-hide.html

Brad. (2015, June). *Scumbag Steve*. Retrieved December 3, 2015, from *Know Your Meme*: http://knowyourmeme.com/memes/scumbag-steve#fn3

Braidotti, R. (1994). *Discontinuous becomings: Deleuze on the becoming-woman of philosophy. In Nomadic Subjects: Embodiment and Sexual Difference in Contemporary Feminist Theory* (pp. 111–123). New York, NY: Columbia University Press.

Brants, K. (2013). Trust, cynicism, and responsiveness: the uneasy situation of journalism in democracy. In C. Peters & M. Broersma (Eds.), *Rethinking journalism: Trust and participation in a transformed news landscape* (pp. 15–27). New York, NY: Routledge.

Breivik, P. S., & Jones, D. L. (1993). Information Literacy: Liberal education for the Information Age. *Liberal Education, 79*(1), 24–29.

Bridgman, K. (2014). (Re)framing the interests of English speakers: "We are all Khaled Said. In M. Ballif (Ed.), *Re/Framing Identifications* (pp. 198–204). Chicago, IL: Waveland Press.

Brock, K. (2012). Establishing ethos on proprietary and open source software websites. In M. Folk & S. Apostel (Eds.), *Online Credibility and Digital Ethos* (pp. 56–77). Hershey, PA: IGI Global.

Brockmeier, J. (2002). Remembering and forgetting: Narrative as cultural memory. *Culture and Psychology*, *8*(1), 15–43. doi:10.1177/1354067X0281002

Brooke, C. G. (2009). *Lingua fracta: Towards a rhetoric of new media*. Cresskill, NJ: Hampton Press.

Brooke, R. E. (1991). *Writing and sense of self: Identity negotiation in writing workshops*. Urbana, IL: NCTE.

Brooks, M. P. (2011). Oppositional Ethos: Fannie Lou Hamer and the vernacular persona. *Rhetoric & Public Affairs*, *14*(3), 511–548. doi:10.1353/rap.2011.0024

Brown, J. (2015). *Ethical programs: Hospitality and the rhetorics of software*. Ann Arbor, MI: University of Michigan Press. doi:10.3998/dh.13474172.0001.001

Brummett, B. (1984). Rhetorical theory as heuristic and moral: A pedagogical justification. *Communication Education*, *33*(2), 97–107. doi:10.1080/03634528409384726

Bruns, A. (2005). *Gatewatching: Collaborative online news production* (Vol. 26). Peter Lang.

Bryman, A. (2008). *Social research methods* (3rd ed.). Oxford, U.K.: Oxford University Press.

Buckingham, D. (2008). *Youth, identity and digital media*. Cambridge, MA: MIT Press.

Bucy, E. P. (2003). Media Credibility Reconsidered: Synergy Effects Between On-Air and Online News. *Journalism & Mass Communication Quarterly*, *80*(2), 247–264. doi:10.1177/107769900308000202

Buis, L. R., & Carpenter, S. (2009). Health and medical blog content and its relationships with blogger credentials and blog host. *Health Communication*, *24*(8), 703–710. doi:10.1080/10410230903264014 PMID:20183379

Burbules, N. (2001). Paradoxes of the Web: The ethical dimensions of credibility. *Library Trends*, *49*(3), 441–453.

Burgoon, J. K. (1978). A communication model of personal space violation: Explication and an initial test. *Human Communication Research*, *4*(2), 129–142. doi:10.1111/j.1468-2958.1978.tb00603.x

Burke, K. (1968). *Counter-statement* (2nd ed.). Berkeley, CA: University of California Press.

Burke, K. (1969). *A rhetoric of motives*. Berkeley, CA: University of California Press.

Burleson, B. R. (2003). Emotional support skills. In J. O. Greene & B. R. Burleson (Eds.), Handbook of communication and social interaction skills (pp. 551-594). Mahwah, NJ: Lawrence Erlbaum Associates Publishers.

Burton, F., & Nissenbaum, H. F. (2015). *Obfuscation: A user's guide for privacy and protest*. Cambridge, MA: The MIT Press.

Butler, J. (1990). *Gender trouble: feminism and the subversion of identity*. New York, NY: Routledge.

Byford, J. (2011). *Conspiracy theories: A critical introduction*. New York, NY: Palgrave-MacMillan. doi:10.1057/9780230349216

Cameron, R. E., Neal, L., & Coll, M. Á. (2005). *Historia económica mundial: desde el Paleolítico hasta el presente*. Madrid: Alianza.

Carey, S. (2000). Cultivating *ethos* through the body. *Human Studies*, *23*(1), 23–42. doi:10.1023/A:1005551410889

Carlson, J., & Kneale, R. (2011). Embedded librarianship in the research context: Navigating new waters. *College & Research Libraries News, 72*(3), 167–170.

Cassel, J. (2011, Feb 4). A culture of editing wars. *New York Times Online*. Retrieved from http://www.nytimes.com/roomfordebate/2011/02/02/where-are-the-women-in-wikipedia/a-culture-of-editing-wars

Castel, R. (1983). *La Gestión de los riesgos: de la anti-psiquiatría al post-análisis*. Barcelona: Anagrama.

Cavaye, A. L. (1996). Case study research: A multi-faceted research approach for IS. *Information Systems Journal, 6*(3), 227–242. doi:10.1111/j.1365-2575.1996.tb00015.x

Chan, M. (2014, March 5). *WHO Director-General addresses vaccine and immunization research forum (transcript)*. World Health Organization. Retrieved from http://www.who.int/dg/speeches/2014/research-uhc/en/

Chatterjee, P. (2001). Online reviews: Do consumers use them? *Advances in Consumer Research. Association for Consumer Research (U. S.), 28*(1), 129–133.

Chawner, B., & Lewis, P. H. (2004, October). *WikiWikiWebs: New ways of interacting in a web environment*. Paper presented at the ALA (American Library Association) LITA National Forum.

Chen, Y., & Xie, J. (2005). Third-party product review and firm marketing strategy. *Marketing Science, 24*(2), 218–240. doi:10.1287/mksc.1040.0089

Chesney, T. (2006). An empirical examination of Wikipedia's credibility. *First Monday, 11*(11). doi:10.5210/fm.v11i11.1413

Chesney, T., & Su, D. K. (2010). The impact of anonymity on weblog credibility. *International Journal of Human-Computer Studies, 68*(10), 710–718. doi:10.1016/j.ijhcs.2010.06.001

Children's Online Privacy Protection Rule (" COPPA "). (n.d.). Retrieved January 9, 2016, from https://www.ftc.gov/enforcement/rules/rulemaking-regulatory-reform-proceedings/childrens-online-privacy-protection-rule

Chiu, Y.-C., & Hsieh, Y.-L. (2012). Communication online with fellow cancer patients: Writing to be remembered, gain strength, and find survivors. *Journal of Health Psychology, 18*(12), 1572–1581. doi:10.1177/1359105312465915 PMID:23221492

Choi, W., & Stvilia, B. (2015). Web credibility assessment: Conceptualization, operationalization, variability and models. *Journal of the Association for Information Science and Technology, 66*(12), 2399–2414. doi:10.1002/asi.23543

Chomsky, N. (1989). *Necessary illusions: thought control in democratic societies*. Cambridge: South End Press.

Chung, C. J., Kim, H., & Kim, J. H. (2010). An anatomy of the credibility of online newspapers. *Online Information Review, 34*(5), 669–685. doi:10.1108/14684521011084564

Clesne, C. (1999). *Becoming qualitative researchers: An introduction* (2nd ed.). New York, NY: Longman.

Cohen, N. (2014, February 4). Wikipedia vs. the small screen. *New York Times Online*. Retrieved from http://www.nytimes.com/2014/02/10/technology/wikipedia-vs-the-small-screen.html?_r=0

Colacel, O. (2013). The body (language) of 'The Saboteur': Obstructionism and banditry in the digital media entertainment. *Meridian Critic, 18*(2), 13–21.

Cole, A. W., & Salek, T. A. (2014). Rhetorical voyeurism: Negotiation of literal and rhetorical audience in response to Kinsey's *Sexual Behavior in the Human Female. Journal of Communications and Media Studies, 2*(1), 22–36.

Cole, J. T., & Greer, J. D. (2013). Audience response to brand journalism: The effect of frame, source, and involvement. *Journalism & Mass Communication Quarterly, 90*(4), 673–690. doi:10.1177/1077699013503160

Coleman, S. (2005). Blogs and the new politics of listening. *The Political Quarterly*, 273–280.

Collins, P. H. (1990). *Black feminist thought: Knowledge, consciousness, and the politics of empowerment*. New York, NY: Routledge.

Coney, M. B., & Steehouder, M. (2000). Role playing on the Web: Guidelines for designing and evaluating personas online. *Technical Communication (Washington)*, *47*(3), 327–340.

Constantinides, H. (2001). The duality of scientific ethos: Deep and surface structures. *The Quarterly Journal of Speech*, *87*(1), 61–72. doi:10.1080/00335630109384318

Cook, J. (2009). *What do the 'climategate' hacked CRU emails tell us?* Retrieved December 1, 2015, from http://www.skepticalscience.com/Climategate-CRU-emails-hacked-intermediate.htm

Cooren, F. (2006). The organizational world as a plenum of agencies. In *Communication as organizing: Empirical and theoretical explorations in the dynamic of text and conversation* (pp. 81–100). Mahwah, NJ: Lawrence Erlbaum.

Cornell University. (2015). *Evaluating web pages: Questions to consider*. Retrieved December 1, 2015, from http://guides.library.cornell.edu/evaluating_Web_pages

CorruptionExposed. (2013, January 16). *Re: Vaccine Court Awards Millions to Two Children with Autism* [Online forum comment]. Retrieved from http://www.abovetopsecret.com/forum/thread918559

Cosijn, E., & Ingwersen, P. (2000). Dimensions of relevance. *Information Processing & Management*, *36*(4), 533–550. doi:10.1016/S0306-4573(99)00072-2

Costa, R. (2013). (Re)Pensar o Ofício do Investigador Qualitativo, Hoje: Metáforas, Ferramentas e Competências em CAQDAS. *Indagatio Didactica*, *5*(2), 1118–1127. Available at: http://revistas.ua.pt/index.php/ID/article/view/2513/2379

Couchsurfing International. (2016b). *Safety tips*. Retrieved from http://www.*Couchsurfing*.com/about/tips/

Couchsurfing International. (2016a). *About Us*. Retrieved from http://www.*Couchsurfing*.com/about/about-us/

Couper, M. P. (2005). Technology Trends in Survey Data Collection. *Social Science Computer Review*, (Winter): 23, 486–501. doi:10.1177/0894439305278972

Craig, C. L., Bauman, A., & Reger-Nash, B. (2010). Testing the hierarchy of effects model: ParticipACTION's serial mass communication campaigns on physical activity in Canada. *Health Promotion International*, *25*(1), 14–23. doi:10.1093/heapro/dap048 PMID:19875461

Crawford, A. (2002). The myth of the unmarked net speaker. In G. Elmer (Ed.), *Critical perspectives on the internet* (pp. 89–104). Lanham, MD: Rowman & Littlefield.

Creswell, J. (2007). *Qualitative inquiry and research design: Choosing among five approaches*. New York, NY: Sage Publications.

Creswell, J. W. (2009). *Research design: Qualitative, quantitative, and mixed method approaches*. Los Angeles, CA: SAGE Publications, Inc.

Crupi, A. (2015, September 10). Sports Now Accounts for 37% of Broadcast TV Ad Spending: Big Four Nets $8.47 Billion in Ad Sales. *Advertising Age*. Retrieved November 2, 2015, from http://adage.com/article/media/sports-account-37-percent-all-tv-ad-dollars/300310/

Czopp, A. M., Lasane, T. P., Sweigard, P. N., Bradshaw, S. D., & Hammer, E. D. (1998). Masculine styles of self-presentation in the classroom: Perceptions of Joe Cool. *Journal of Social Behavior and Personality*, *13*(2), 281–294.

D'Orazio, D. (2013) *New York Times*: Is Reddit to blame for Boston Bombing witch-hunt? *The Verge*. Retrieved from http://www.theverge.com/2013/7/25/4556380/should-reddit-be-accountable-for-boston-bombing-witch-hunt

Dalhousie University. (2015). *6 criteria for websites*. Retrieved December 1, 2015, from https://libraries.dal.ca/using_the_library/evaluating_web_resources/6_criteria_for_websites.html

Data use policy. (n.d.). Facebook. Retrieved January 2, 2016, from https://www.facebook.com/policy.php

Daugherty, T., Gangadharbatla, H., & Bright, L. (2010). Presence and persuasion. In C. Campanella Bracken & P. Skalski (Eds.), *Presence and popular media: Understanding media users' everyday experiences*. Mahwah, NJ: Lawrence Erlbaum.

Davies, C., & Eynon, R. (2013). *Teenagers and technology*. London: Routledge.

Davis, D. C., & Krawczyk, J. (2010). Female Sportscaster Credibility: Has Appearance Taken Precedence? *Journal of Sports Media*, *5*(2), 1–34. doi:10.1353/jsm.2010.0004

Dawkins, R. (1976). *The selfish gene*. New York, NY: Oxford University Press.

De Pew, K. E. (2003). *The rhetorical process of digital subjectivities: Case studies of International TAs negotiating identity with digital media*. (Unpublished doctoral dissertation). Purdue University, West Lafayette, IN.

Degli Esposti, S. (2014). When big data meets dataveillance: The hidden side of analytics. *Surveillance & Society*, *12*(2), 209–225.

Deleuze, G. (1986). *Cinema 1: The movement image*. London, UK: The Althone Press.

Demo, W. (1986). The idea of "information literacy" in the age of high-tech. Tompkins Cortland Community College. Retrieved from http://files.eric.ed.gov/fulltext/ED282537.pdf

Dennett, L., Chatterley, T., Greyson, D., & Surette, S. (2014). Research Embedded Health Librarianship: The Canadian Landscape. *Journal of the Canadian Health Libraries Association/Journal de l'Association des bibliothèques de la santé du Canada, 34*(2), 61-68.

Denscombe, M. (1998). *The good research guide for small-scale social research projects*. Buckingham, UK: Open University Press.

Denzin, N. K., & Lincoln, Y. (Eds.). (2000). *Handbook of qualitative research* (2nd ed.). Thousand Oaks, CA: Sage Publications.

Desai, T., Shariff, A., Dhingra, V., Minhas, D., Eure, M., & Kats, M. (2013). Is content really king? An objective analysis of the public's response to medical videos on Youtube. *PLoS ONE*, *8*(12), e82469. doi:10.1371/journal.pone.0082469 PMID:24367517

Diesing, P. (2008). *Patterns of discovery in the social sciences*. Piscataway, NJ: Transaction Publishers.

Directive 95/46/EC of the European Parliament and of the Council of 24 October 1995 on the protection of individuals with regard to the processing of personal data and on the free movement of such data, 1995 O.J. L 281, 23/11/1995.

Donovan, E. E., LeFebvre, L., Tardif, S., Brown, L. E., & Love, B. (2014). Patterns of social support communicated in response to expressions of uncertainty in an online community of young adults with cancer. *Journal of Applied Communication Research*, *42*(4), 432–455. doi:10.1080/00909882.2014.929725

Dougherty, P. (2015, October 22). Sports media: Bills-Jaguars telecast on Yahoo could be sign of the future. *TimesUnion.com*. Retrieved November 2, 2015, from http://www.timesunion.com/tuplus-sports/article/Bills-Jaguars-telecast-on-Yahoo-could-be-sign-of-6585347.php

Downs, J. S., Bruine de Bruin, W., & Fischoff, B. (2008). Parents' vaccination comprehension and decisions. *Vaccine*, *26*(12), 1595–1607. doi:10.1016/j.vaccine.2008.01.011 PMID:18295940

Doyle, C. S. (1994). *Information literacy in an information society: A concept for the information age.* Syracuse, NY: ERIC Clearinghouse on Information & Technology.

Dubay, E. (2010, September 22). *Re: Above Above Top Secret.com* [Online forum comment]. Retrieved from http://www. atlanteanconspiracy.com/2008/06/above-above-top-secret-com.html

Dube, E., Laberge, C., Guay, M., Bramadat, P., Roy, R., & Bettinger, J. (2013). Vaccine hesitancy: An overview. *Human Vaccines & Immunotherapeutics*, *9*(8), 1763–1773. doi:10.4161/hv.24657 PMID:23584253

Dubrofsky, R. E., & Wood, M. W. (2014). Posting racism and sexism: Authenticity, agency and self-reflexivity in social media. *Critical Studies in Media Communication*, *11*, 282–287. doi:10.1080/14791420.2014.926247

Duggan, M., Ellison, N. B., Lampe, C., Lenhart, A., & Madden, M. (2015). *Social media update2014.* Retrieved from http://www.pewinternet.org/2015/01/09/social-media-update-2014/

Earp, J. B., Antón, A. A., Aiman-Smith, L., & Stufflebeam, W. H. (2005). Examining Internet privacy policies within the context of user privacy values. *IEEE Transactions on Engineering Management*, *52*(2), 227–237. doi:10.1109/TEM.2005.844927

Eckert, S., & Steiner, L. (2013). Wikipedia's gender gap. In C. L. Armstrong (Ed.), *Media disparity: A gender battleground* (pp. 87–98). New York: Lexington Books.

Eligon, J., & Schwirtz, M. (Aug 19, 2012). Senate candidate provokes ire with "legitimate rape" comment. *The New York Times Online*. Retrieved from http://www.nytimes.com/2012/08/20/us/politics/todd-akin-provokes-ire-with-legitimate-rape-comment.html

Ellison, N. B., Hancock, J. T., & Toma, C. L. (2011). Profile as promise: A framework for conceptualizing veracity in online dating self-presentations. *New Media & Society*, *14*(1), 45–62. doi:10.1177/1461444811410395

Ellison, N., Heino, R., & Gibbs, J. (2006). Managing impressions online: Self-presentation processes in the online dating environment. *Journal of CMC*, *11*(2), 415–441.

Ellison, N., Heino, R., & Gibbs, J. (2006). Managing impressions online: Self-presentation processes in the online dating environment. *Journal of Computer-Mediated Communication*, *11*(2), 415–441. doi:10.1111/j.1083-6101.2006.00020.x

Endlich, R. W. (2013). *History falsifies climate alarmist sea level claims.* Retrieved December 1, 2015, from http://wattsupwiththat.com/2013/12/02/history-falsifies-climate-alarmist-sea-level-claims

English, K., Sweetser, K. D., & Ancu, M. (2011). YouTube-ification of political talk: An examination of persuasion appeals in viral video. *The American Behavioral Scientist*, *55*(1), 733–748. doi:10.1177/0002764211398090

Eningher, E., Benson, T. W., Ettlich, E. E., Fisher, W. R., Kerr, H. P., Larson, R. I., . . . Niles, L. A. (1971). Report of the committee on the scope of rhetoric and the place of rhetorical studies in higher education. In L. F. Bitzer & E. Black (Eds.), The prospect of rhetoric: A report of the national development project (pp. 208-219). Englewood Cliffs, NJ: Prentice-Hall, Inc.

Ericsson, K. A., Krampe, R. T., & Tesch-Römer, C. (1993). The role of deliberate practice in the acquisition of expert performance. *Psychological Review*, *100*(3), 363–406. doi:10.1037/0033-295X.100.3.363

Ericsson, K. A., & Simon, H. A. (1980). Verbal reports as data. *Psychological Review*, *87*(3), 215–251. doi:10.1037/0033-295X.87.3.215

Ert, E., Fleischer, A., & Magen, N. (2016). Trust and reputation in the sharing economy: The role of personal photos in Airbnb. *Tourism Management*, *55*, 62–73. doi:10.1016/j.tourman.2016.01.013

Eschenbach, W. (2009). *The thermostat hypothesis*. Retrieved December 1, 2015, from http://wattsupwiththat.com/2009/06/14/the-thermostat-hypothesis

Ewing, L. A. (2013). Rhetorically analyzing online composition spaces. *Pedagogy*, *13*(3), 554–561. doi:10.1215/15314200-2266477

Eynon, R., Fry, J., & Schroeder, R. (2008). The ethics of Internet research. In N. Fielding, R. M. Lee, & G. Blank, G. (Eds.), The SAGE handbook of online research methods (pp. 42-57). London, U.K.: SAGE Publications, Ltd. doi:10.4135/9780857020055.n2

Eysenbach, G. (2001). What is e-health? *Journal of Medical Internet Research*, *3*(2), e20. doi:10.2196/jmir.3.2.e20 PMID:11720962

Eysenbach, G. (2008). Medicine 2.0: Social networking, collaboration, participation, apomediation, and openness. *Journal of Medical Internet Research*, *10*(3), e22. doi:10.2196/jmir.1030 PMID:18725354

Eysenbach, G., & Köhler, C. (2002). How do consumers search for and appraise health information on the world wide web? Qualitative study using focus groups, usability tests, and in-depth interviews. *BMJ (Clinical Research Ed.)*, *324*(7337), 573–577. doi:10.1136/bmj.324.7337.573 PMID:11884321

Facebook. (2015). Data policy. *Facebook*. Retrieved December 13, 2015, from https://www.facebook.com/about/privacy

Facebook. (2015a). *Terms*. Retrieved from https://www.facebook.com/terms.php

Facebook. (2015b). *Community Standards*. Retrieved from https://www.facebook.com/communitystandards?ref=br_tf

Fairclough, N. (1992). Discourse and text: Linguistic and intertextual analysis within discourse analysis. *Discourse & Society*, *3*(2), 193–217. doi:10.1177/0957926592003002004

Fallis, D. (2008). Toward an epistemology of Wikipedia. *Journal of the American Society for Information Science and Technology*, *59*(10), 1662–1674. doi:10.1002/asi.20870

Fallis, D. (2011). Wikipistemology. In A. Goldman & D. Whitcomb (Eds.), *Social epistemology: Essential readings* (pp. 297–313). New York: Oxford University Press.

Fan, Y., Miao, Y., Fang, Y., & Lin, R. (2013). Establishing the adoption of electronic word-of-mouth through consumers' perceived credibility. *International Business Research*, *6*(3), 58. doi:10.5539/ibr.v6n3p58

Farkas, M. (2012). Participatory technologies, pedagogy 2.0 and information literacy. *Library Hi Tech*, *30*(1), 82–94. doi:10.1108/07378831211213229

Farmer, L., & Stricevic, I. (2011). Using research to promote literacy and reading in libraries: Guidelines for librarians. *IFLA Professional Report: 125*.

Fausto-Sterling, A. (2012). *Sex/Gender: Biology in a social world*. New York: Routledge.

Fayad, M. (1995, Summer). Reinscribing identity: Nation and community in Arab women's writing. *College Literature*, *22*(1), 147–160.

Federal Trade Commission. (2012, March). *Protecting consumer privacy in an era of rapid change: Recommendations for business and policymakers*. FTC Report.

Federal Trade Commission. (2016). *Internet cookies*. FTC. Retrieved January 16, 2016, from https://www.ftc.gov/site-information/privacy-policy/internet-cookies

Feinberg, A. (2016) Ben Carson's fake Stalin quote came from a right-wing Facebook meme. *Gawker*. Retrieved February 27, 2016 from http://gawker.com/ben-carsons-fake-stalin-quote-came-from-a-ring-wing-fac-1759025587

Fielding, N., Lee, R. M., & Blank, G. (Eds.). (2008). *The SAGE handbook of online research methods*. London: SAGE Publications, Ltd. doi:10.4135/9780857020055

Fink, J. S., Parker, H. M., Brett, M., & Higgins, J. (2009). Off-Field Behavior of Athletes and Team Identification: Using Social Identity Theory and Balance Theory to Explain Fan Reactions. *Journal Of Sport Management, 23*(2), 142–155.

Fischer, C. S. (1996). *Inequality by design: Cracking the bell curve myth*. Princeton, NJ: Princeton University Press.

Flanagin, A. J., & Metzger, M. J. (2000). Perceptions of internet information credibility. *Journalism & Mass Communication Quarterly, 77*(3), 515–540. doi:10.1177/107769900007700304

Flanagin, A. J., & Metzger, M. J. (2003). The perceived credibility of web site information as influenced by the sex of the source. *Computers in Human Behavior, 19*(6), 683–701. doi:10.1016/S0747-5632(03)00021-9

Flanagin, A. J., & Metzger, M. J. (2007). The role of site features, user attributes, and information verification behaviors on the perceived credibility of web-based information. *New Media & Society, 9*(2), 319–342. doi:10.1177/1461444807075015

Flanagin, A. J., & Metzger, M. J. (2008). Digital media and youth: Unparalleled opportunity and unprecedented responsibility. In M. Metzger & A. Flanagin (Eds.), *Digital media, youth, and credibility* (pp. 5–27). Cambridge, MA: MacArthur Foundation Series on Digital Media and Learning.

Flick, U. (2015). *Introducing research methodology: A beginners' guide to doing a research project* (2nd ed.). London, UK: Sage.

Fogg, B. J. (2002). *Stanford guidelines for web credibility*. Retrieved from http://credibility.stanford.edu/guidelines/#chi00

Fogg, B. J. (2003, April). *Prominence-interpretation theory: Explaining how people assess credibility online*. Paper presented at CHI 2003. Ft. Lauderdale, FL. doi:10.1145/765891.765951

Fogg, B. J., & Tseng, H. (1999). The elements of computer credibility. In Proceedings of the SIGCHI conference on Human Factors in Computing Systems (pp. 80–87). ACM. Retrieved from http://dl.acm.org/citation.cfm?id=303001

Fogg, B. J. (2003). *Persuasive technology: using computers to change what we think and do*. Amsterdam: Morgan Kaufmann Publishers.

Fogg, B. J. (2009, April). A behavior model for persuasive design. In *Proceedings of the 4th International Conference on Persuasive Technology* (p. 40). New York, NY: ACM.

Fogg, B. J., Cuellar, G., & Danielson, D. (2002). Motivating, influencing, and persuading users. In J. Jacko (Ed.), *The human-computer interaction handbook: Fundamentals, evolving technologies, and emerging applications* (pp. 358–370). Mahwah, NJ: L. Erlbaum Associates Inc.

Fogg, B., Marshall, J., Laraki, O., Osipovich, A., Varma, C., Fang, N., & Swani, P. et al. (2001). What makes web sites credible?: A report on a large quantitative study. In *Proceedings of the SIGCHI Conference on Human Factors in Computing Systems*. doi:10.1145/365024.365037

Folk, M., & Apostel, S. (2013). *Digital ethos: Evaluating computer-mediated communication*. Hershey, PA: IGI Global.

Folk, M., & Apostel, S. (2013). *Online credibility and digital ethos: Evaluating computer-mediated communication.* Hershey, PA: IGI Global. doi:10.4018/978-1-4666-2663-8

Foss, S. K. (2009). *Rhetorical criticism: Exploration and practice* (4th ed.). Long Grove, IL: Waveland Press.

Foster, D. (1997). Community and identity in the electronic village. In D. Porter (Ed.), *Internet Culture* (pp. 23–37). New York, NY: Routledge.

Foucault, M. (1979). *Discipline and punish: The birth of the prison.* New York: Vintage Books.

Fox, S., & Duggan, M. (2013). *Health online 2013.* Pew Internet. Retrieved from http://www.pewinternet.org/files/old-media/Files/Reports/PIP_HealthOnline.pdf

Fox, S., & Duggan, M. (2013). *Health Online 2013.* Washington, DC: Pew Internet and American Life Project. Retrieved from http://www.pewinternet.org/2013/01/15/health-online-2013/

Fox, S., & Duggan, M. (2013, January 15). Health online 2013: Information triage. *Pew Research Center: Internet, Science & Tech.* Retrieved from http://www.pewinternet.org/2013/01/15/information-triage/

Franklin, B., & Carlson, M. (2011). *Journalists, sources, and credibility: New perspectives.* London: Routledge.

Fraser, N. (1992). Rethinking the public sphere: A contribution to the critique of actually existing democracy. In C. Calhoun (Ed.), *Habermas and the public sphere* (pp. 109–142). Cambridge, MA: MIT Press.

Fraser, S. (Ed.). (1995). *The bell curve wars: Race, intelligence, and the future of America.* New York, NY: Basic Books.

Fredrick, C. A. (1999). Feminist rhetoric in cyberspace: The *ethos* of feminist UseNet newsgroups. *The Information Society, 15*(3), 187–197. doi:10.1080/019722499128493

Freidson, E. (1978). *La Profesión médica: un estudio de sociologia del conocimiento aplicado.* Barcelona: Península.

French, L., Garry, M., & Mori, K. (2011). Relative—not absolute—judgments of credibility affect susceptibility to misinformation conveyed during discussion. *Acta Psychologica, 136*(1), 119–128. doi:10.1016/j.actpsy.2010.10.009 PMID:21112042

French, R. P., & Raven, B. (1959). The bases of social power. In D. Cartwright (Ed.), *Studies in social power* (pp. 150–167). Ann Arbor, MI: Institutive for Social Research, University of Michigan.

Frequently asked questions about vaccine safety. (2011, February 8). *CDC.* Retrieved from http://www.cdc.gov/vaccinesafety/Vaccines/Common_questions.html

Frequently asked questions. (2015). reddit. Retrieved from http://www.reddit.com/wiki/faq

Friedman, M. (2010). On mommyblogging: Notes to a future feminist historian. *Journal of Women's History, 22*(4), 197–208.

Frobish, T. S. (2013). On Pixels, Perceptions, and Personae: Toward a Model of Online Ethos. In M. Folk & S. Apostel (Eds.), *Online Credibility and Digital Ethos: Evaluating Computer-Mediated Communication* (pp. 1–23). Hershey, PA: Information Science Reference; doi:10.4018/978-1-4666-2663-8.ch001

Frohlich, D. O., & Zmyslinski-Seelig, A. (2012). The presence of social support messages on YouTube videos about inflammatory bowel disease and ostomies. *Health Communication, 27*(5), 421–428. doi:10.1080/10410236.2011.606524 PMID:21962112

Frost, E A. (2015). Apparent feminism as a methodology for technical communication and rhetoric. *Journal of Business and Technical Communication*, 1-26.

Frost, E. A. (2013). *Theorizing an apparent feminism in technical communication.* (Doctoral dissertation). Retrieved from ProQuest. (Order No. 3574642).

Frost, E. A. (2014a). Apparent feminist pedagogies: Interrogating technical rhetorics at Illinois State University. *Programmatic Perspectives, 6*(1), 110–131.

Frost, E. A. (2014b). An apparent feminist approach to transnational technical rhetorics: The ongoing work of Nujood Ali. *Peitho, 16*(2), 183–199.

Further decline in credibility ratings for most news organizations. (2012, August 16). *People-Press.* Retrieved from http://www.people-press.org/2012/08/16/further-decline-in-credibility-ratings-for-most-news-organizations/

Gaiser, T. J., & Schreiner, A. E. (2009). *A guide to conducting online research.* London, UK: Sage. doi:10.4135/9780857029003

Gamie, S. (2012). The cyber-propelled Egyptian revolution and the de/construction of ethos. In M. Folk & S. Apostel (Eds.), *Online credibility and digital ethos: Evaluating computer-mediated communication* (pp. 316–331). Hershey, PA: IGI Global.

Gamie, S. (2013). The cyber-propelled Egyptian revolution and the de/construction of ethos. In M. Folk & S. Apostel (Eds.), *Online Credibility and Digital Ethos: Evaluating Computer-Mediated Communication* (pp. 316–330). Hershey, PA: IGI Global. doi:10.4018/978-1-4666-2663-8.ch018

Ganesan, S., & Hess, R. (1997). Dimensions and levels of trust: Implications for commitment to a relationship. *Marketing Letters, 8*(4), 439–448. doi:10.1023/A:1007955514781

Gardner, H. (1995). Cracking open the IQ box. In The bell curve wars: Race, intelligence, and the future of America (pp. 23-35). New York, NY: Basic Books.

Garfinkel, S. L. (2008). Wikipedia and the meaning of truth. *Technology Review, 111*(6), 84–86.

Garrett, R. K. (2009). Politically motivated reinforcement seeking: Reframing the selective exposure debate. *Journal of Communication, 59*(4), 676–699. doi:10.1111/j.1460-2466.2009.01452.x

Gasparyan, A. Y., Yessirkepov, M., Diyanova, S. N., & Kitas, G. D. (2015). Publishing ethics and predatory practices: A dilemma for all stakeholders of science communication. *Journal of Korean Medical Science, 30*(8), 1010–1016. doi:10.3346/jkms.2015.30.8.1010 PMID:26240476

Gasson, S., & Waters, J. (2013). Using a grounded theory approach to study online collaboration behaviors. *European Journal of Information Systems, 22*(1), 95–118. doi:10.1057/ejis.2011.24

Geertz, C. (1973). *The interpretation of cultures: Selected essays.* New York: Basic.

Geertz, C. (1999). El sentido común como sistema cultural. In *Conocimiento Local. Ensayos sobre la interpretación de las culturas* (pp. 93–116). Barcelona: Paidós Ibérica.

George, B. C., Lynch, P., & Marsnik, S. J. (2001). U.S. multinational employers: Navigating through the "safe harbor" principles to comply with the EU data privacy directive. *American Business Law Journal, 38*(4), 735–783. doi:10.1111/j.1744-1714.2001.tb00906.x

Gerhards, E. V. (2015). Your store is gross! how recent cases, the FTC, and state consumer protection laws can impact a franchise system's response to negative, defamatory, or fake online reviews. *Franchise Law Journal, 34*(4), 503.

Germann Molz, J. (2012). Hospitality: The mobile conviviality of *Couchsurfing.* In J. Germann Molz (Ed.), *Travel connections: Tourism, technology, and togetherness in a mobile world* (pp. 83–110). London, UK: Routledge.

Ghost375. (2013, February 2). *Re: Why Vaccines are Great*. [Online forum comment]. Retrieved from http://www.abovetopsecret.com/forum/thread923268

Ghostry. (2016). Tracker basics: What you need to know about trackers. *Ghostry*. Retrieved June 24, 2016, from https://www.ghostery.com/intelligence/tracker-basics/

Gibbs, J. L., Ellison, N. B., & Heino, R. D. (2006). Self-presentation in online personals: The role of anticipated future interaction, self-disclosure, and perceived success in Internet dating. *Communication Research, 33*(2), 152–177. doi:10.1177/0093650205285368

Gilbert, E., Bergstrom, T., & Karahalios, K. (2009, January). Blogs are echo chambers: Blogs are echo chambers. In *System Sciences, 2009. HICSS'09.42nd Hawaii International Conference.*

Gilbert, N. (2001). *Researching social life*. London, UK: Sage.

Giles, J. (2005). Special report internet encyclopedias go head to head. *Nature, 439*(12), 900–901. doi:10.1038/438900a PMID:16355180

Gilewicz, N., & Allard-Huver, F. (2013). Digital *parrhesia* as a counterweight to astroturfing. In M. Folk & S. Apostel (Eds.), *Online credibility and digital ethos: Evaluating computer-mediated communication* (pp. 215–228). Hershey, PA: IGI Global. doi:10.4018/978-1-4666-2663-8.ch012

Glaser, B. G. (1978). *Theoretical sensitivity: Advances in the methodology of grounded theory*. Mill Valley, CA: Sociology Press.

Glaze, B. (2016, March 1). Victory for animal welfare campaigners after National Wildlife Crime Unit is saved. *The Mirror, UK*. Retrieved March 15, 2016, from http://www.mirror.co.uk/news/uk-news/victory-animal-welfare-campaigners-after-7469532

Glenski, M., Johnston, T. J., & Weninger, T. (2015). Random voting effects in social-digital spaces: A case study of reddit post submissions. In *Proceedings of the 26th ACM conference on hypertext & social media* (pp. 293-297). New York, NY: ACM.

Goffman, E. (1959). *The presentation of self in everyday life*. New York, NY: Anchor Books.

Goffman, E. (1959). *The Presentation of Self in Everyday Life*. New York: Anchor Books.

Goldman, A. (2013). The breaking news consumer handbook. *On the media blog*. Retrieved from http://www.wnyc.org/story/breaking-news-consumers-handbook-pdf/

Goldsmith, D. J. (2004). *Communicating social support*. New York: Cambridge University Press. doi:10.1017/CBO9780511606984

Goleman, D. (1994, September 16). Richard Herrnstein, 64, dies; backed nature over nurture. *The New York Times*.

Gonzalez, J. (2000). The appended subject: Race and identity as digital assemblage. In B. E. Kolko, L. Nakamura, & G. B. Rodman (Eds.), *Race in Cyberspace* (pp. 28–50). New York, NY: Routledge.

Goodwin, C. A. (2003). The body in action. In J. Couplan & R. Gwyn (Eds.), *Discourse, the body, and identity* (pp. 19–42). New York, NY: Macmillan. doi:10.1057/9781403918543_2

Gould, S. J. (1995). Curveball. In S. Fraser (Ed.), *The bell curve wars: Race, intelligence, and the future of America* (pp. 11–22). New York, NY: Basic Books.

Grabill, J. T., & Pigg, S. (2012). Messy rhetoric: Identity performance as rhetorical agency in online public forums. *Rhetoric Society Quarterly, 42*(2), 99–119. doi:10.1080/02773945.2012.660369

Grabill, J. T., & Pigg, S. (2012). Messy rhetoric: Identity performance as rhetorical agency in online public forums. *The Quarterly Journal of Speech, 42*(2), 99–119.

Gramm-Leach-Bliley Act. (n.d.). Retrieved January 9, 2016, from https://www.ftc.gov/tips-advice/business-center/privacy-and-security/gramm-leach-bliley-act

Grant, L., Hausman, B. L., Cashion, M., Lucchesi, N., Patel, K., & Roberts, J. (2015). Vaccination persuasion online: A qualitative study of two provaccine and two vaccine-skeptical websites. *Journal of Medical Internet Research, 17*(5), e133. doi:10.2196/jmir.4153 PMID:26024907

Greenwald, G. (2013, June 6). NSA collecting phone records of millions of Verizon customers daily. *The Guardian.* Retrieved July 3, 2013, from http://www.theguardian.com/world/2013/jun/06/nsa-phone-records-verizon-court-order

Greenwald, G. (2015, December 30). *NSA cheerleaders discover value of privacy only when their own is violated.* Retrieved January 2, 2016, from https://theintercept.com/2015/12/30/spying-on-congress-and-israel-nsa-cheerleaders-discover-value-of-privacy-only-when-their-own-is-violated/

Grey, S. (1999). The statistical war on equality: Visions of American virtuosity in the bell curve. *The Quarterly Journal of Speech, 85*(3), 303–329. doi:10.1080/00335639909384263

Gross, M., & Latham, D. (2007). Attaining information literacy: An investigation of the relationship between skill level, self-estimates of skill, and library anxiety. *Library & Information Science Research, 29*(3), 332–353. doi:10.1016/j.lisr.2007.04.012

Gross, M., Latham, D., & Armstrong, B. (2012). Improving below-proficient information literacy skills: Designing an evidence-based educational intervention. *College Teaching, 60*(3), 104–111. doi:10.1080/87567555.2011.645257

Gruber, S. (2001). The rhetorics of three women activist groups on the web: Building and transforming communities. In G. Rosendale & S. Gruber (Eds.), *Alternative rhetorics: Challenges to the rhetorical tradition* (pp. 77–92). Albany, NY: State Univerity of New York Press.

Gruwell, L. (2015). Wikipedia's politics of exclusion: Gender, epistemology, and feminist rhetorical (in)action. *Computers and Composition, 37*, 117–131. doi:10.1016/j.compcom.2015.06.009

Gsell, L. (2009). Comments Anonymous. *American Journalism Review, 31*(1), 16–17.

Guan, Z., Lee, S., Cuddihy, E., & Ramey, J. (2006). The validity of the stimulated retrospective think-aloud method as measured by eye tracking. In *Proceedings of the SIGCHI conference on Human Factors in computing systems - CHI '06* (pp. 1253-1262). Montreal, Quebec, Canada: ACM Press. doi:10.1145/1124772.1124961

Guex, V. (2010). A Sociological View of the Cybertourists. In Information and Communication Technologies in Tourism 2010 (pp. 417-428). Springer. doi:10.1007/978-3-211-99407-8_35

Guèye, K. (2010, Summer). "Tyrannical femininity" in Nawal El Saadawi's *memoirs of a woman doctor. Research in African Literatures, 41*(2), 160–172. doi:10.2979/RAL.2010.41.2.160

Gunter, B. (2006). Who do online news consumers trust? *Library and Information Update, 5*(9), 40–41.

Gunther, A. C. (1992). Biased press or biased public? Attitudes toward media coverage of social groups. *Public Opinion Quarterly, 56*(2), 147–167. doi:10.1086/269308

Gupta, A., Joshi, A., & Kumaraguru, P. (2012, October). Identifying and characterizing user communities on twitter during crisis events. In *Proceedings of the 2012 workshop on data-driven user behavioral modelling and mining from social media* (pp. 23-26). New York, NY: ACM. doi:10.1145/2390131.2390142

Gurak, L. (1999). The promise and peril of social action in cyberspace: Ethos, delivery, and the protests over marketplace and the clipper chip. In P. Kollock & M. Smith (Eds.), *Communities in cyberspace* (pp. 243–263). London: Routledge.

Gurak, L. J. (1997). *Persuasion and privacy in cyberspace: The online protests over Lotus Marketplace and the Clipper Chip*. New Haven, CT: Yale University Press.

Guttentag, D. (2015). Airbnb: Disruptive innovation and the rise of an informal tourism accommodation sector. *Current Issues in Tourism*, *18*(12), 1192–1217. doi:10.1080/13683500.2013.827159

Gvirsman, S. D. (2014). It's not that we don't know, it's that we don't care: Explaining why selective exposure polarizes attitudes. *Mass Communication & Society*, *17*(1), 74–97. doi:10.1080/15205436.2013.816738

Haase, N., Betsch, C., & Renkewitz, F. (2015). Source credibility and the biasing effect of narrative information on the perception of vaccination risks. *Journal of Health Communication*, *20*(8), 920–929. doi:10.1080/10810730.2015.1018 605 PMID:26065492

Hacker, A. (1995). Caste, crime, and precocity. In S. Fraser (Ed.), *The bell curve wars: Race, intelligence, and the future of America* (pp. 97–108). New York, NY: Basic Books.

Haferkamp, N., & Kramer, N. C. (2010). Creating a digital self: Impression management and impression formation on social networking sites. In K. Drotner & K. C. Schroder (Eds.), *Digital content creation: Creativity, competence, critique* (pp. 129–146). New York, NY: Peter Lang.

Hajli, M. N., Sims, J., Featherman, M., & Love, P. E. D. (2015). Credibility of information in online communities. *Journal of Strategic Marketing*, *23*(3), 238–253. doi:10.1080/0965254X.2014.920904

Halbwachs, M. (1950). *On Collective Memory*. New York: Harper.

Halloran, S. M. (1982). Aristotle's concept of ethos, or if not his somebody else's. *Rhetoric Review*, *1*(1), 58–63. doi:10.1080/07350198209359037

Hancock, J. T., & Dunham, P. J. (2001). Impression formation in CMC revisited: An analysis of the breadth and intensity of impressions. *Communication Research*, *28*(3), 325. doi:10.1177/009365001028003004

Hancock, J. T., & Toma, C. L. (2009). Putting your best face forward: The accuracy of online dating photographs. *Journal of Communication*, *59*(2), 367–386. doi:10.1111/j.1460-2466.2009.01420.x

Hanitzsch, T. (2013). Journalism, participative media and trust in a comparative context. In C. Peters & M. Broersma (Eds.), *Rethinking journalism: Trust and participation in a transformed news landscape* (pp. 200–209). New York, NY: Routledge.

Haraway, D. (1988). Situated knowledges: The science question in feminism and the privilege of partial perspective. *Feminist Studies*, *14*(3), 575–599. doi:10.2307/3178066

Hardey, M. (2002). Life beyond the screen: Embodiment and identity through the internet. *The Sociological Review*, *50*(4), 570–585. doi:10.1111/1467-954X.00399

Hardey, M. (2010). Consuming professions: User-review websites and health services. *Journal of Consumer Culture*, *10*(1), 129–149. doi:10.1177/1469540509355023

Harding, S. (1993). Rethinking standpoint epistemology: What is "strong objectivity?". In L. Alcoff & E. Potter (Eds.), *Feminist Epistemologies* (pp. 49–82). New York: Routledge.

Harding, S. (1998). *Whose science? Whose knowledge? Thinking from women's lives*. Ithaca, NY: Cornell University Press.

Harding, S. (Ed.). (2003). *The feminist standpoint theory reader: Intellectual and political controversies*. New York: Routledge.

Hargittai, E. (2010). Digital na(t)ives? Variation in internet skills and uses among members of the 'net generation'. *Sociological Inquiry*, *80*(1), 92–113. doi:10.1111/j.1475-682X.2009.00317.x

Hargittai, E., & Shaw, A. (2015). Mind the skills gap: The role of Internet know-how and gender in differentiated contributions to Wikipedia. *Information Communication and Society*, *18*(4), 424–442. doi:10.1080/1369118X.2014.957711

Hariman, R. (2008). Political parody and public culture. *The Quarterly Journal of Speech*, *94*(3), 247–272. doi:10.1080/00335630802210369

Harris, M. (1990). *Antropología cultural*. Madrid: Alianza.

Hartsock, N. C. M. (1983). The feminist standpoint: Developing the ground for a specifically feminist historical materialism. In S. G. Harding & M. B. Hintikka (Eds.), *Discovering reality: Feminist perspectives on epistemology, metaphysics, methodology, and philosophy of science* (pp. 283–310). Boston: D. Reidel.

Hartsock, N. C. M. (1983). The feminist standpoint: Developing the ground for a specifically feminist historical materialism. In S. Harding & M. B. Hintikka (Eds.), *Discovering reality: feminist perspectives on epistemology, metaphysics, methodology, and philosophy of science* (pp. 283–310). Dordrecht, The Netherlands: D. Reidel.

Hart, W., Albarracín, D., Eagly, A. H., Brechan, I., Lindberg, M. J., & Merrill, L. (2009). Feeling validated versus being correct: A meta-analysis of selective exposure to information. *Psychological Bulletin*, *135*(4), 555–588. doi:10.1037/a0015701 PMID:19586162

Hawisher, G. E., & Sullivan, P. (1999). Fleeting images: Women visually writing the web. In G. Hawisher & C. Selfe (Eds.), *Passions, pedagogies and 21st century technologies* (pp. 268–291). Logan, UT: Utah State University Press.

Hayden, S. (1993). Chronically ill and "feeling fine": A study of communication and chronic illness. *Journal of Applied Communication Research*, *21*(3), 263–278. doi:10.1080/00909889309365371

Healy, D. (1996). Cyberspace and Place: The Internet as middle landscape on the electronic frontier. In D. Porter (Ed.), *Internet culture* (pp. 55–68). New York, NY: Routledge.

Hekman, S. (1997). Truth and method: Feminist standpoint theory revisited. *Signs (Chicago, Ill.)*, *22*(2), 341–365. doi:10.1086/495159

Henkel, L. A., & Mattson, M. E. (2011). Reading is believing: The truth effect and source credibility. *Consciousness and Cognition*, *20*(4), 1705–1721. doi:10.1016/j.concog.2011.08.018 PMID:21978908

Herrnstein, R. J., & Murray, C. (1994). *The bell curve: Intelligence and class structure in American life*. New York, NY: Free Press.

Heverin, T., & Zach, L. (2010). Microblogging for crisis communication: Examination of Twitter use in response to a 2009 violent crisis in the Seattle-Tacoma, Washington, Area. In S. French, B. Tomaszewski, & C. Zobel (Eds.), *Defining Crisis Management 3.0* (p. 9). Seattle, WA: ISCRAM.

Hewson, C., Yule, P., Laurent, D., & Vogel, C. (2003). *Internet research methods: A practical guide for the social and behavioural sciences*. London, UK: Sage Publications. doi:10.4135/9781849209298

HiddenCode. (2014, August 28). *Re: BREAKING: CDC Whistleblower Confesses to MMR Vaccine Research Fraud.* [Online forum comment]. Retrieved from: http://www.abovetopsecret.com/forum/thread1029670

Higgins, J., & Green, S. (Eds.). (2011). *Cochrane handbook for systematic reviews of interventions version* (5.1.0 ed.). The Cochrane Collaboration.

Hilligoss, B., & Rieh, S. Y. (2008). Developing a unifying framework of credibility assessment: Construct, heuristics, and interaction in context. *Information Processing & Management, 44*(4), 1467–1484. doi:10.1016/j.ipm.2007.10.001

Hinman, L. M. (2008). Searching ethics: The role of search engines in the construction and distribution of knowledge. In A. Spink & M. Zimmer (Eds.), *Web search: Multidisciplinary perspectives* (pp. 67–76). Berlin: Springer. doi:10.1007/978-3-540-75829-7_5

Hoback, C. (Director). (2013). *Terms and conditions may apply* [Motion picture].

Hoekstra, P. [peetehoekstra]. (2015, December 30). *WSJ report that NSA spied on Congress and Israel communications very disturbing. Actually outrageous. Maybe unprecedented abuse of power.* [Tweet]. Retrieved from https://twitter.com/petehoekstra/status/682007598476873728

Holbert, R., Hmielowski, J. D., & Weeks, B. E. (2012). Clarifying relationships between ideology and ideologically oriented cable TV news use: A case of suppression. *Communication Research, 39*(2), 194–216. doi:10.1177/0093650211405650

Holladay, S. J., & Coombs, W. T. (2013). Public relations literacy: Developing critical consumers of public relations. *Public Relations Inquiry, 2*(2), 125–146. doi:10.1177/2046147X13483673

Holliday, J. (2009). In[ter]vention: Locating rhetoric's ethos. *Rhetoric Review, 28*(4), 388–405. doi:10.1080/07350190903185049

hooks, b. (1989). *Yearning: Race, gender, and cultural politics.* London: Turnaround.

Hooley, T., Wellens, J., & Marriott, J. (2012). *What is online research? Using the Internet for social science research.* London, UK: Bloomsbury Academic.

Hornsey, M. J. (2008). Social identity theory and self-categorization theory: A historical review. *Social and Personality Psychology Compass, 2*(1), 204–222. doi:10.1111/j.1751-9004.2007.00066.x

Horton, D., & Wohl, R. R. (1956). Mass communication and para-social interaction. *Psychiatry, 19*, 215–229. PMID:13359569

Horton, F. W. (1983). Information literacy vs. computer literacy. *Bulletin of the American Society for Information Science, 9*, 14–18.

Hovland, C. I., Janis, I. L., & Kelley, H. H. (1963). Communication and persuasion. In Psychological studies of opinion change. New Haven, CT: Academic Press.

Howard, P. N., Duffy, A., Freelon, D., Hussain, M. M., Mari, W., & Mazaid, M. (2011). *Opening closed regimes: What was the role of social media during the Arab spring?* Available at SSRN 2595096

Hsieh, H. F., & Shannon, S. E. (2005). Three approaches to qualitative content analysis. *Qualitative Health Research, 15*(9), 1277–1288. doi:10.1177/1049732305276687 PMID:16204405

Hu, A. W., & Tang, L. (2010). Factors Motivating Sports Broadcast Viewership with Fan Identification as a Mediator. *Social Behavior & Personality: An International Journal, 38*(5), 681–689. doi:10.2224/sbp.2010.38.5.681

Hübler, M. T., & Bell, D. C. (2003). Computer-mediated humor and ethos: Exploring threads of constitutive laughter in online communities. *Computers and Composition, 20*(3), 277–294. doi:10.1016/S8755-4615(03)00036-7

Huey, L., Nhan, J., & Broll, R. (2012). 'Uppity civilians' and 'cyber-vigilantes': The role of the general public in policing cybercrime. *Criminology & Criminal Justice, 13*(1), 81–97. doi:10.1177/1748895812448086

Huff, D., & Geis, I. (1954). *How to lie with statistics.* New York, NY: W.W. Norton & Company, Inc.

Hughes, J. (Ed.). (2012). *SAGE Internet research methods.* London, UK: SAGE. doi:10.4135/9781446263327

Hunt, K. (1996). Establishing a presence on the World Wide Web: A rhetorical approach. *Technical Communication (Washington), 43*(4), 376–387.

Huvila, I. (2013). In Web search we trust? Articulation of the cognitive authorities of Web searching. Information Research, 18(1).

Hu, Y., & Haake, J. (2010). Search your way to an accurate diagnosis: Predictors of Internet-based diagnosis accuracy. *Atlantic Journal of Communication, 18*(2), 79–88. doi:10.1080/15456870903554916

Hu, Y., & Sundar, S. S. (2010). Effects of online health sources on credibility and behavioral intentions. *Communication Research, 37*(1), 105–132. doi:10.1177/0093650209351512

Hwang, H., Schmierbach, M., Paek, H. J., Gil de Zuniga, H., & Shah, D. (2006). Media sissociation, internet use, and antiwar political participation: A case study of political dissent and action against the war in Iraq. *Mass Communication & Society, 9*(4), 461–483. doi:10.1207/s15327825mcs0904_5

Hyde, M. J. (2004). Introduction: Rhetorically we dwell. In M. J. Hyde (Ed.), *The ethos of rhetoric* (pp. xiii–xxviii). Columbia, SC: University of South Carolina Press.

Hyde, M. J. (Ed.). (2004). *The ethos of rhetoric.* Columbia, SC: University of South Carolina Press.

I hated this guy. (2011, January 21). Retrieved December 3, 2015, from Reddit: https://www.reddit.com/r/funny/comments/f65ra/i_hated_this_dude/

Ingleby, F. (2015, April 29). *and this is a bit hypocritical given the reviewer's own ideological biases throughout the review, for example: (3/4)* [Tweet]. Retrieved from https://twitter.com/FionaIngleby/status/593408350001471489

Ingoldsby, B. (2003). The mate selection process in the United States. In R. R. Hammon & B. B. Ingoldsby (Eds.), *Mate selection across cultures* (pp. 3–18). Thousand Oaks, CA: Sage Publications. doi:10.4135/9781452204628.n1

Instituto Nacional de Estadística. (2012). *Survey about Household Equipement and Use of Technology 2012.* Retrieved December 13, 2013, from http://www.ine.es/jaxi/menu.do?type=pcaxis&path=%2Ft25/p450&file=inebase&L=0

International travel and health. (2014). World Health Organization. Retrieved from http://www.who.int/ith/en/

Internet Corporation for Assigned Names and Numbers (ICANN). (2015). *IANA - root zone database.* Retrieved December 1, 2015, from http://www.iana.org/domains/root/db

Internet Live Stats. (2016). Retrieved March 2, 2016 from http://www.internetlivestats.com/watch/websites/

Ito, M. (2009). *Hanging out, messing around and geeking out: Kids living and learning with new media.* Cambridge, MA: MIT Press.

Ivanov, B., Sims, J., & Parker, K. (2013). Leading the way in new product introductions: Publicity's message sequencing success with corporate credibility and image as moderators. *Journal of Public Relations Research, 25*(5), 442–466. doi:10.1080/1062726X.2013.795862

Iyengar, S., & Kyu, S. H. (2009). Red media, blue media: Evidence of ideological selectivity in media use. *Journal of Communication, 59*(1), 19–39. doi:10.1111/j.1460-2466.2008.01402.x

Jackson, R. (2008). Information literacy and its relationship to cognitive development and reflective judgment. *New Directions for Teaching and Learning, 114*(114), 47–61. doi:10.1002/tl.316

Jamieson, K. H., & Cappella, J. N. (2008). *Echo chamber: Rush Limbaugh and the conservative media establishment.* New York, NY: Oxford University Press.

Janesick, V. (1998). *Stretching exercises for qualitative researchers.* Thousand Oaks, CA: Sage Publications.

Janetzko, D. (2008). Nonreactive data collection on the Internet. In N. Fielding, R. M. Lee, & G. Blank (Eds.), *The SAGE handbook of online research methods* (pp. 161–174). New York, NY: Sage Publications. doi:10.4135/9780857020055.n9

Jenkins, E. (2014). The modes of visual rhetoric: Circulating memes as expressions. *The Quarterly Journal of Speech, 100*(4), 442–446. doi:10.1080/00335630.2014.989258

Jenny. (2015). *Chronicles of a Nursing Mom* [Blog]. Retrieved from http://www.chroniclesofanursingmom.com/

Jensen, M. L., Averbeck, J. M., Zhang, Z., & Wright, K. B. (2013). Credibility of anonymous online product reviews: A language expectancy perspective. *Journal of Management Information Systems, 30*(1), 293–324. doi:10.2753/MIS0742-1222300109

Jensen, M. L., Lowry, P. B., Burgoon, J. K., & Nunamaker, J. F. (2010). Technology dominance in complex decision making: The case of aided credibility assessment. *Journal of Management Information Systems, 27*(1), 175–202. doi:10.2753/MIS0742-1222270108

Jeon, G. Y., & Rieh, S. Y. (2014). Answers from the Crowd: How Credible are Strangers in Social Q&A? iConference 2014 Proceedings (pp. 663-668). iSchools.

Jessen, J., & Jørgensen, A. (2011). Aggregated trustworthiness: Redefining online credibility through social validation. *First Monday, 17*(1). Retrieved from http://firstmonday.org/htbin/cgiwrap/bin/ojs/index.php/fm/article/viewArticle/3731

Johnson, T.J., & Kaye, B.K. (2004). Wag the blog: How reliance on traditional media and the internet influence credibility perceptions of weblogs among blog users. *Journalism & Mass Communication Quarterly September, 81*(3), 622-642.

Johnson, J. (2010). The skeleton on the couch: The Eagleton Affair, rhetorical disability, and the stigma of mental illness. *Rhetoric Society Quarterly, 40*(5), 459–478. doi:10.1080/02773945.2010.517234

Johnson, J. (2012). Twitter bites and Romney: Examining the rhetorical situation of the 2012 presidential election in 140 characters. *Journal of Contemporary Rhetoric, 2*(3/4), 54–64.

Johnson, M., & Martin, K. (2010). Digital credibility & digital dynamism in public relations blogs. *Visual Communication Quarterly, 17*(3), 162–174. doi:10.1080/15551393.2010.502475

Johnson, T. J., & Kaye, B. K. (1998). Cruising is believing?: Comparing internet and traditional sources on media credibility measures. *Journalism & Mass Communication Quarterly, 75*(2), 325–340. doi:10.1177/107769909807500208

Johnson, T. J., & Kaye, B. K. (2000). Using is Believing: The Influence of Reliance on the Credibility of Online Political Information Among Politically Interested Internet Users. *Journalism & Mass Communication Quarterly, 77*(4), 865–879. doi:10.1177/107769900007700409

Johnson, T. J., & Kaye, B. K. (2004). Wag the blog: How reliance on traditional media and the Internet influence credibility perceptions of weblogs among blog users. *Journalism & Mass Communication Quarterly, 81*(1), 622–642. doi:10.1177/107769900408100310

Johnson, T. J., & Kaye, B. K. (2010). Believing the blog of war: How blog users compare on credibility and characteristics in 2003 and 2007. *Media, War, and Conflict, 3*(3), 315–333. doi:10.1177/1750635210376591

Johnson, T. J., & Kaye, B. K. (2011). Hot diggity blog: A cluster analysis examining motivations and other factors for why people judge different types of blogs as credible. *Mass Communication & Society, 14*(2), 236–263. doi:10.1080/15205431003687280

Johnston, A., Friedman, B., & Peach, S. (2011). Standpoint in political blogs: Voice, authority, and issues. *Women's Studies, 40*(3), 269–298. doi:10.1080/00497878.2010.548427

Jolley, D. (2013). The detrimental nature of conspiracy theories. *PsyPAG Quarterly, 88*, 35–39.

Jones, J. (1995). Back to the future with *The Bell Curve*: Jim Crow, slavery, and g. In S. Fraser (Ed.), *The bell curve wars: Race, intelligence, and the future of America* (pp. 80–93). New York, NY: Basic Books.

Jordan, J. W. (2005). A virtual death and a real dilemma: Identity, trust, and community in cyberspace. *The Southern Communication Journal, 70*(3), 200–218. doi:10.1080/10417940509373327

Josang, A., & Presti, S. L. (2004). Analysing the relationship between risk and trust. In C. Jensen, S. Poslad, & T. Dimitrakos (Eds.), *Trust Management* (pp. 135–145). Berlin, Germany: Springer. doi:10.1007/978-3-540-24747-0_11

Joseph, S. (1993). Gender and relationality among Arab families in Lebanon. *Feminist Studies, 19*(3), 465–486. doi:10.2307/3178097

Judis, J. B. (1995). Hearts of darkness. In S. Fraser (Ed.), *The bell curve wars: Race, intelligence, and the future of America* (pp. 124–129). New York, NY: Basic Books.

Kang, J. C. (2013). "Should Reddit Be Blamed for the Spreading of a Smear?". *The New York Times*. Retrieved from http://www.nytimes.com/2013/07/28/magazine/should-reddit-be-blamed-for-the-spreading-of-a-smear.html

Kapoun, J. (1998). Teaching undergrads WEB evaluation: A guide for library instruction. *College & Research Libraries News, 59*(7), 522–523.

Kareklas, I., Muehling, D., & Weber, T. J. (2015). Reexamining health messages in the digital age: A fresh look at source credibility effects. *Journal of Advertising, 44*(2), 88–104. doi:10.1080/00913367.2015.1018461

Katz, E., & Lazarsfeld, F. P. (1955). *Personal Influence*. New York, NY: Free Press.

Kaus, M. (1995). The "it-matters-little" gambit. In S. Fraser (Ed.), *The bell curve wars: Race, intelligence, and the future of America* (pp. 130–138). New York, NY: Basic Books.

Keegan, B. M. (2015). *Progressive multiple sclerosis*. Mayo Foundation for Medical Education and Research. Retrieved from http://www.mayoclinic.org/multiple-sclerosis-diagnosis/vid-20135054

Keene, J. R., & Cummins, R. G. (2009). Sports Commentators and Source Credibility: Do Those Who Can't Play. . . Commentate? *Journal of Sports Media, 4*(2), 57–83. doi:10.1353/jsm.0.0042

Ke, F., & Hoadley, C. (2009). Evaluating online learning communities. *Educational Technology Research and Development, 57*(4), 487–511. doi:10.1007/s11423-009-9120-2

Kelly, J., Fisher, D., & Smith, M. (2005). *Debate, Division, and Diversity: Political Discourse Networks in USENET Newsgroups*. Stanford Online Deliberation Conference DIAC'05.

Kellymom. (2015). *KellyMom* [Website]. Retrieved from http://kellymom.com/

Kendall, L. (2004). Studying the day-to-day meaning of email through a hybrid think-aloud protocol/In depth interview research method. In *2nd Symposium New Research for New Media*.

Kennedy, J. F. (1962). *93-Special message to the Congress on protecting the consumer interest*. Retrieved April 7, 2016, from http://www.presidency.ucsb.edu/ws/?pid=9108

Kennedy, K. (2009). Textual machinery: Authorial agency and bot-written texts in Wikipedia. In M. Smith & B. Warnick (Eds.), *The responsibilities of rhetoric*: *Proceedings of the 2008 Rhetoric Society of America Conference*. Retrieved from http://surface.syr.edu/wp/1/

Kenny, R. W. (2004). Truth and metaphor: Imaginative vision and the *ethos* of rhetoric. In M. J. Hyde (Ed.), *The ethos of rhetoric* (pp. 34–55). Charleston, SC: University of South Carolina Press.

Killi, C., Laurinen, L., & Marttunen, M. (2008). Students evaluating Internet sources: From versatile evaluators to uncritical readers. *Journal of Educational Computing Research*, *39*(1), 75–95. doi:10.2190/EC.39.1.e

Killingsworth, M. J. (2005). Rhetorical appeals: A revision. *Rhetoric Review*, *24*(3), 249–263. doi:10.1207/s15327981rr2403_1

Kim, K., & Kim, J. (2011). Third-party privacy certification as an online advertising strategy: An investigation of the factors affecting the relationship between third-party certification and initial trust. *Journal of Interactive Marketing*, *25*(3), 145–158. doi:10.1016/j.intmar.2010.09.003

Kimmel, A. J. (1988). *Ethics and values in applied social research*. Newbury Park, NJ: Sage Publications. doi:10.4135/9781412984096

Kiousis, S. (2001). Public trust or mistrust? Perceptions of media credibility in the information age. *Mass Communication & Society*, *4*(4), 381–403. doi:10.1207/S15327825MCS0404_4

Kitch, C. (2002). "A death in the American family": Myth, memory, and national values in the media mourning of John F. Kennedy Jr. *Journalism & Mass Communication Quarterly*, *79*(2), 294–309. doi:10.1177/107769900207900203

Kluemper, D. H., & Rosen, P. A. (2009). Future employment selection methods: Evaluating social networking web sites. *Journal of Managerial Psychology*, *24*(6), 567–580. doi:10.1108/02683940910974134

Kmetz, M. (2011). 'For want of the usual manure': Rural civic *ethos* in Ciceronian Rhetoric. *Rhetoric Review*, *30*(4), 333–349. doi:10.1080/07350198.2011.604607

Knadler, S. (2001). E-Racing difference in e-Space: Black female subjectivity and the web- based portfolio. *Computers and Composition*, *18*(3), 235–255. doi:10.1016/S8755-4615(01)00054-8

Knight, M. L., Knight, R. A., Goben, A., & Dobbs, A. W. (2013). Theory and Application: Using social networking to build online credibility. In M. Folk & S. Apostel (Eds.), *Online Credibility and Digital Ethos: Evaluating Computer-Mediated Communication* (pp. 285–301). Hershey, PA: IGI Global. doi:10.4018/978-1-4666-2663-8.ch016

Koerber, A. (2006). Rhetorical agency, resistance, and the disciplinary rhetorics of breastfeeding. *Technical Communication Quarterly*, *15*(1), 87–101. doi:10.1207/s15427625tcq1501_7

Koerber, A. (2013). *Breast or bottle? Contemporary controversies in infant-feeding policy and practice*. Columbia, SC: University of South Carolina Press.

Koerber, A., Brice, L., & Tombs, E. (2012, February). Breastfeeding and problematic integration: Results of a focus-group study. *Health Communication*, *27*(2), 124–144. doi:10.1080/10410236.2011.571754 PMID:21834716

Koh, A., & Risam, R. (2014). The global women Wikipedia write-in #GWWI. *Postcolonial digital humanities*. Retrieved from http://dhpoco.org/rewriting-wikipedia/the-global-women-wikipedia-write-in/

Kovach, B., & Rosenstiel, T. (2010). *Blur: How to know what's true in the age of information overload*. New York, NY: Bloomsbury.

Kruger, J., & Dunning, D. (1999). Unskilled and unaware of it: How difficulties in recognizing one's own incompetence lead to inflated self-assessments. *Journal of Personality and Social Psychology*, 77(6), 1121–1134. doi:10.1037/0022-3514.77.6.1121 PMID:10626367

Kuehn, K. M. (2013). "There's got to be a review democracy": Communicative capitalism, neoliberal citizenship and the politics of participation on the consumer evaluation website yelp.com. *International Journal of Communication*, 7(1), 607–625.

Kuhlthau, C. (2004). Seeking meaning: A process approach to library and information services (2nd ed.). Westport, CT: Libraries Unlimited.

Kuhlthau, C. (1987). Information skills: Tools for learning. *School Library Media Quarterly*, 16, 22–28.

Kuhlthau, C. C. (1999). Literacy and learning for the information age. In B. K. Stripling (Ed.), *Learning and libraries in an information age: Principles and practice*. Englewood, CO: Libraries Unlimited.

Kuiper, E., Volman, M., & Terwel, J. (2005). The Web as an information resource in K–12 education: Strategies for supporting students in searching and processing information. *Review of Educational Research*, 75(3), 285–328. doi:10.3102/00346543075003285

Kunst, H., Groot, D., Latthe, P. M., Latthe, M., & Khan, K. S. (2002). Accuracy of information on apparently credible websites: Survey of five common health topics. *BMJ: British Medical Journal*, 324(7337), 581–582. doi:10.1136/bmj.324.7337.581 PMID:11884323

Kutner, J. S., Westfall, J. M., Morrison, E. H., Beach, M. C., Jacobs, E. A., & Rosenblatt, R. A. (2006). Facilitating collaboration among academic generalist disciplines: A call to action. *Annals of Family Medicine*, 4(2), 172–176. doi:10.1370/afm.392 PMID:16569722

Kwon, J. H., Kye, S.-Y., Park, E. Y., Oh, K. H., & Park, K. (2015). What predicts the trust of online health information? *Epidemiology and Health*, 37, e2015030. doi:10.4178/epih/e2015030 PMID:26212505

La Leche League International. (2015). *La Leche League International* [Website]. Retrieved from http://www.llli.org/

Lafrance, A. (2015). How many websites are there? *The Atlantic*. Retrieved March 2, 2016, from http://www.theatlantic.com/technology/archive/2015/09/how-many-websites-are-there/408151/

Lanier, J. (2006). Digital Maoism. *The Edge*. Retrieved from http://edge.org/conversation/digital-maoism-the-hazards-of-the-new-online-collectivism

Lankes, R. D. (2008). Credibility on the internet: Shifting from authority to reliability. *The Journal of Documentation*, 64(5), 667–686. doi:10.1108/00220410810899709

Lantian, A. (2013). A review of different approaches to study belief in conspiracy theories. *PsyPAG Quarterly*, 88, 19–21.

Laverie, D. A., & Arnett, D. B. (2000). Factors affecting fan attendance: The influence of identity salience and satisfaction. *Journal of Leisure Behavior*, 32(2), 225–246.

Lea, M., & Spears, R. (1995). Love at first byte? Building personal relationships over computer networks. In J. T. Wood & S. Duck (Eds.), *Under-studied relationships: off the beaten track. Understanding relationship processes series* (Vol. 6, pp. 197–233). Thousand Oaks, CA: SAGE Publications.

Lea, M., Spears, R., Watt, S. E., & Rogers, P. (2000). The InSIDE story: Social psychological processes affecting on-line groups. In T. Postmes, M. Lea, R. Spears, & S. Reicher (Eds.), *SIDE issues centre stage: Recent developments in studies of de-individuation in groups* (pp. 47–62). Amsterdam: KNAW.

Lee, E. J. (2007). Deindividuation effects on group polarization in computer-mediated communication: The role of group identification, public self-awareness, and perceived argument quality. *Journal of Communication, 57*(2), 385–403. doi:10.1111/j.1460-2466.2007.00348.x

Lee, L. (2008). The impact of young people's Internet use on class boundaries and life trajectories. *Sociology, 42*(1), 137–153. doi:10.1177/0038038507084829

LeFevre, K. B. (1987). *Invention as a social act*. Carbondale, IL: Southern Illinois UP.

Lemann, N. (1997, January 8). *The bell curve flattened*. Slate.

Levy, D. (2012, July 31). 2012 Olympics: NBC Finding New and Unique Ways to Fail American Viewers. *Bleacher Report*. Retrieved August 30, 2012, from http://bleacherreport.com/articles/1279506-2012-olympics-nbc-keeps-finding-new-and-unique-ways-to-fail-american-viewers

Levy, S. E., Duan, W., & Boo, S. (2013). An analysis of one-star online reviews and responses in the Washington, D.C., lodging market. *Cornell Hospitality Quarterly, 54*(1), 49–63. doi:10.1177/1938965512464513

Lewis, L. (2012). The participatory meme chronotope: Fixity of space/rupture of time. *New Media Literacies and Participatory Culture Across Borders,* 106-121.

Lewis, L., & Chandley, N. (Eds.). (2012). *Philosophy for children through the secondary curriculum*. New York, NY: Continuum.

Lieu, T. A. et al.. (1994). Cost-effectiveness of a routine varicella vaccination program for U.S. children. *Journal of the American Medical Association, 271*(5), 375–381. doi:10.1001/jama.1994.03510290057037 PMID:8283587

Lim, S. (2013). Does formal authority still matter in the age of wisdom of crowds? Perceived credibility, peer and professor endorsement in relation to college students' wikipedia use for academic purposes. *Proceedings of the American Society for Information Science and Technology, 50*(1), 1–4. doi:10.1002/meet.14505001118

Lim, Y., & Van Der Heide, B. (2015). Evaluating the wisdom of strangers: The perceived credibility of online consumer reviews on yelp. *Journal of Computer-Mediated Communication, 20*(1), 67–82. doi:10.1111/jcc4.12093

Lin, C., Lee, S., & Horng, D. (2011). The effects of online reviews on purchasing intention: The moderating role of need for cognition. *Social Behavior and Personality, 39*(1), 71–81. doi:10.2224/sbp.2011.39.1.71

Lincoln, Y. S., & Guba, E. G. (2000). Paradigmatic controversies contradictions and emerging confluences. In N. K. Denzin & Y. S. Lincoln (Eds.), *The handbook of qualitative research* (pp. 163–188). Beverly Hills, CA: Sage Publications.

Lind, M. (1995). Brave new right. In S. Fraser (Ed.), *The bell curve wars: Race, intelligence, and the future of America* (pp. 172–178). New York, NY: Basic Books.

Lipman, M., Sharp, A. M., & Oscanyon, F. S. (1985). *Philosophy in the classroom*. Philadelphia, PA: Temple University Press.

Liu, J. (2012). *The intimate stranger on your couch: An analysis of motivation, presentation and trust through Couch-surfing.* Retrieved from, http://uu.diva-portal.org/smash/get/diva2:560145/FULLTEXT01.pdf

Livingstone, S., & Helsper, E. (2007). Gradations in digital inclusion: Children, young people and the digital divide. *New Media & Society, 9*(4), 671–696. doi:10.1177/1461444807080335

Lockard, J. (1996). Progressive politics, electronic individualism and the myth of virtual community. In D. Porter (Ed.), *Internet culture* (pp. 219–231). New York, NY: Routledge.

Lomanno, K. (n.d.). Savvy suffers: Website evaluation and media literacy. *AASL Learning4Life Lesson Plan Database.* Retrieved March 24, 2016, from http://www.ala.org/aasl/sites/ala.org.aasl/files/content/conferencesandevents/ecollab/lpd/SavvySurgersWebsiteEvaluationandMediaLiteracy.pdf

Loveland, J., & Reagle, J. (2013). Wikipedia and encyclopedic production. *New Media & Society, 15*(8), 1294–1311. doi:10.1177/1461444812470428

Lucassen, T., & Maarten-Schraagen, J. (2012). Propensity to trust and the influence of source and medium cues in credibility evaluation. *Journal of Information Science, 38*(6), 566–577. doi:10.1177/0165551512459921

Lunceford, B. (2007). The science of orality: Implications for rhetorical theory. *The Review of Communication, 7*(1), 83–102. doi:10.1080/15358590701211142

Lunceford, B. (2012). *Naked politics: Nudity, political action, and the rhetoric of the body.* Lanham, MD: Lexington Books.

Lunsford, A., & Ede, L. (2012). *Writing together: Collaboration in theory and practice, a critical sourcebook.* St. Martins.

Lyon, D. (2007). *Surveillance studies: An overview.* Cambridge, UK: Polity Press.

Lyotard, J. F. (1979). *The postmodern condition: A report on knowledge.* Paris: Minuit.

Mackiewicz, J. (2010). The co-construction of credibility in online product reviews. *Technical Communication Quarterly, 19*(4), 403–426. doi:10.1080/10572252.2010.502091

Mael, F., & Tetrick, L. (1992). Identifying Organizational Identification. *Educational and Psychological Measurement, 52*(4), 813–824. doi:10.1177/0013164492052004002

Mahood, Q., Van Eerd, D., & Irvin, E. (2014). Searching for grey literature for systematic reviews: Challenges and benefits. *Research Synthesis Methods, 5*(3), 221–234. doi:10.1002/jrsm.1106 PMID:26052848

Makino, T., Jung, C., & Phan, D. (2015, February 26). *Finding more mobile-friendly search results.* Retrieved May 10, 2016, from https://webmasters.googleblog.com/2015/02/finding-more-mobile-friendly-search.html

Manchikanti, L., Kaye, A. D., Boswell, M. V., & Hirsch, J. A. (2015). Medical journal peer review: Process and bias. *Pain Physician, 18*(1), E1–e14. PMID:25675064

Marshall, P. D. (2010). The promotion and presentation of the self: Celebrity as marker and presentational media. *Celebrity Studies, 1*(1), 35–48. doi:10.1080/19392390903519057

Mason, J. (2013). *The history of climate science.* Retrieved December 1, 2015, from http://www.skepticalscience.com/history-climate-science.html

Matthews, M. (2016, Feb 4). Still upset about Cecil the Lion? Mobile group joins worldwide protest. *Alabama News.* Retrieved February 22, 2016, from http://www.al.com/news/mobile/index.ssf/2016/02/still_upset_about_cecil_the_li.html

Maxwell, J. (2005). *Qualitative research design: An interactive approach* (2nd ed.). Thousand Oaks, CA: Sage Publications.

Mayo Clinic Staff. (2015, October 1). *Self-management*. Retrieved from http://www.mayoclinic.org/diseases-conditions/multiple-sclerosis/manage/ptc-20131886

Mbuagbaw, L., Thabane, M., Vanniyasingam, T., Debono, V. B., Kosa, S., Zhang, S., & Thabane, L. et al. (2014). Improvement in the quality of abstracts in major clinical journals since consort extension for abstracts: A systematic review. *Contemporary Clinical Trials, 38*(2), 245–250. doi:10.1016/j.cct.2014.05.012 PMID:24861557

McCandless, D., Evans, T., Quick, M., Hollowood, E., Miles, C., & Hampson, D. (2016). World's biggest data breaches. *Information is Beautiful*. Retrieved June 24, 2016, from http://www.informationisbeautiful.net/visualizations/worlds-biggest-data-breaches-hacks/

McClish, G., & Bacon, J. (2002). "Telling the story her own way": The role of feminist standpoint theory in rhetorical studies. *Rhetoric Society Quarterly, 32*(2), 27–55. doi:10.1080/02773940209391227

McGrady, R. (2013). Ethos [edit]: Procedural Rhetoric and the Wikipedia Project. In M. Folk & S. Apostel (Eds.), Online Credibility and Digital Ethos: Evaluating Computer-Mediated Communication (pp. 114-130). Hershey, PA: IGI Global.

McIntyre, A. M. C. (2010). The 'truthiness' of Wikipedia: An examination of the open content encyclopedia as a valuable vehicle in developing critical thinking in the classroom. *Access to Knowledge, 2*(1), 2–8.

McKeon, R. (1941). The basic works of Aristotle. *The Journal of Philosophy, 38*(20), 553. doi:10.2307/2017332

McMillan, S. J. (2000). The microscope and the moving target: The challenge of applying content analysis to the World Wide Web. *Journalism & Mass Communication Quarterly, 77*(1), 80–98. doi:10.1177/107769900007700107

Meador, J. (2009). *Does cold weather disprove global warming?* Retrieved December 1, 2015, from http://www.skepticalscience.com/global-warming-cold-weather.htm

Medhurst, M. J. (2004). Religious rhetoric and the *ethos* of democracy: A case study of the 2000 presidential campaign. In M. J. Hyde (Ed.), *The ethos of rhetoric* (pp. 115–135). Charleston, SC: University of South Carolina Press.

Melican, D. B., & Dixon, T. L. (2008). News on the net credibility, selective exposure, and racial prejudice. *Communication Research, 35*(2), 151–168. doi:10.1177/0093650207313157

Melnick, M. J. (1993). Searching for sociability in the stands: A theory of sports spectating. *Journal of Sport Management, 7*, 44–60.

Meola, M. (2004). Chucking the checklist: A contextual approach to teaching undergraduates web-site evaluation. portal. *Libraries and the Academy, 4*(3), 331–344. doi:10.1353/pla.2004.0055

Merskin, D. L., & Huberlie, M. (1996). Companionship in the classifieds: The adoption of personal advertisements by daily newspapers. *Journalism & Mass Communication Quarterly, 73*(1), 219–229. doi:10.1177/107769909607300119

Metzger, M. J. (2007). Making sense of credibility on the web: Models for evaluating online information and recommendations for future research. *Journal of the American Society for Information Science and Technology, 58*(13), 2078–2091. doi:10.1002/asi.20672

Metzger, M. J., Flanagin, A. J., Eyal, K., Lemus, D. R., & McCann, R. M. (2003). Credibility for the 21st century: Integrating perspectives on source, message, and media credibility in the contemporary media environment. *Communication Yearbook, 27*(1), 293–336. doi:10.1207/s15567419cy2701_10

Metzger, M. J., Flanagin, A. J., Medders, R., Pure, R., Markov, A., & Hartsell, E. (2013). The special case of youth and digital information credibility. In M. Folk & S. Apostel (Eds.), *Digital ethos: Evaluating computer-mediated communication* (pp. 148–168). Hershey, PA: IGI Global. doi:10.4018/978-1-4666-2663-8.ch009

Metzger, M. J., Flanagin, A., & Medders, R. B. (2010). Social and heuristic approaches to credibility evaluation online. *Journal of Communication, 60*(3), 413–439. doi:10.1111/j.1460-2466.2010.01488.x

Metzger, M. J., Hartsell, E. H., & Flanagin, A. J. (2015). Cognitive Dissonance or Credibility? A Comparison of Two Theoretical Explanations for Selective Exposure to Partisan News. *Communication Research*, 1–26.

Meyer, A. (2008). Investigating Cultural Consumers. In M. Pickering (Ed.), Research Methods for Cultural Studies (pp. 68-87). Edimburgh, UK: Edinburgh University Press.

Meyer, E. (2012, June 12). Online networking a godsend for those with rare diseases. *Chicago Tribune*. Retrieved from http://articles.chicagotribune.com/2012-06-12/news/ct-met-medical-social-networking-20120612_1_rare-diseases-social-media-social-networks

Meyer, H. K., Marchionni, D., & Thorson, E. (2010). The Journalist Behind the News: Credibility of Straight, Collaborative, Opinionated, and Blogged "News". *The American Behavioral Scientist, 54*(2), 100–119. doi:10.1177/0002764210376313

Miles, M. B., & Huberman, A. M. (1994). *Qualitative data analysis: An expanded sourcebook* (2nd ed.). Thousand Oaks, CA: Sage Publications.

Miller, C. M. (2001). Writing in a culture of simulation: ethos online. In P. Coppock (Ed.), The Semiotics of writing: Transdisciplinary perspectives on the technology of writing (pp. 253-272). Turnhout, Belguim: Brepols Publishers.

Miller, C. R. (2001). Writing in a culture of simulation: Ethos online. In *The semiotics of writing: Transdisciplinary perspectives on the technology of writing* (pp. 253–279). Turnhout, Belgium: Brepols.

Miller, C. R. (2003). The presumptions of expertise: The role of ethos in risk analysis. *Configurations, 11*(2), 163–202. doi:10.1353/con.2004.0022

Miller, C. R. (2004). Expertise and agency: Transformations of *ethos* in human-computer interaction. In M. J. Hyde (Ed.), *The ethos of rhetoric* (pp. 197–218). Charleston, SC: University of South Carolina Press.

Miller, C. R. (2007). What can automation teach us about agency? *Rhetoric Society Quarterly, 37*(2), 137–157. doi:10.1080/02773940601021197

Milne, G. R., & Culnan, M. J. (2004). Strategies for reducing online privacy risks: Why consumers read (or don't read) online privacy notices. *Journal of Interactive Marketing, 18*(3), 15–29. doi:10.1002/dir.20009

Milne, G. R., & McDonald, M. A. (1999). *Sport marketing: Managing the exchange process*. Sudbury, MA: Jones and Bartlett.

Mitchell, A. (2014, March 26). *State of the News Media 2014*. Pew Research Center. Retrieved November 15, 2015, from http://www.journalism.org/2014/03/26/state-of-the-news-media-2014-overview/

Mitchell, A. (2015, April 29). *State of the News Media 2015*. Pew Research Center. Retrieved November 16, 2015, from http://www.journalism.org/2015/04/29/state-of-the-news-media-2015/

Mitra, A., & Watts, E. (2002). Theorizing cyberspace: The idea of voice applied to the internet discourse. *New Media & Society, 4*(4), 479–498. doi:10.1177/146144402321466778

Morales, L. (2012, September 21). U.S. distrust in media hits new high. *Gallup*. Retrieved from http://www.gallup.com/poll/157589/distrust-media-hits-new-high.aspx

Morris, M. R., Counts, S., Roseway, A., Hoff, A., & Schwarz, J. (2012, February). Tweeting is believing?: Understanding microblog credibility perceptions. From *Proceedings of the ACM 2012 conference on Computer Supported Cooperative Work* (pp. 441-450). New York, NY: ACM. doi:10.1145/2145204.2145274

Morse, M. (2001). Virtually female: Body and code. In D. Trend (Ed.), *Reading digital culture* (pp. 87–97). Malden, MA: Blackwell Publishing.

Moturu, S. T., Liu, H., & Johnson, W. G. (2008). *Trust evaluation in health information on the World Wide Web.* Vancouver, BC: Engineering in Medicine and Biology Society. doi:10.1109/IEMBS.2008.4649459

Muchnik, L., Aral, S., & Taylor, S. J. (2013). Social influence bias: A randomized experiment. *Science, 341*(6146), 647–651. doi:10.1126/science.1240466 PMID:23929980

Mulkay, M. (1988). *On humor: Its nature and its place in modern society.* Cambridge, MA: Basil Blackwell.

Multiple Sclerosis (MS) Support Group. (2012). *Daily Strength.* Retrieved from http://www.dailystrength.org/c/Multiple-Sclerosis-MS/support-group

Munroe, R. (2009, Oct. 15). *reddit's new comment sorting system.* Retrieved from http://www.redditblog.com/2009/10/reddits-new-comment-sorting-system.html

Myers, G. (1986, February). Reality, consensus, and reform in the rhetoric of composition teaching. *College English, 48*(2), 154–174. doi:10.2307/377298

Naber, N. (2011). Decolonizing culture: Beyond orientalist and anti-orientalist feminisms. In Ed. R. Abdulhadi, E. Alsultany, & N. Naber (Eds.), Arab and Arab American feminisms: Gender, violence and belongings (pp. 10-28). Syracuse, NY: Syracuse University Press.

Naber, N., Desouky, E., & Baroudi, L. (2001). The forgotten '—ism': An Arab American women's perspective on zionism, racism and sexism. *The UN World Conference on Racism.* Retrieved from https://web.archive.org/web/20050306042931/http://www.awsa.net/Positionpaper.htm

Nakamura, L. (2001). Race in /For cyberspace: Identity tourism and racial passing on the Internet. In D. Trend (Ed.), *Reading digital culture* (pp. 226–235). Malden, MA: Blackwell Publishing.

Nakamura, L. (2002). *Cyber types: race, ethnicity, and identity on the Internet.* New York, NY: Routledge.

Nakamura, L. (2008). *Digitizing race: Visual cultures of the Internet.* Minneapolis, MN: University of Minnesota Press.

Naureckas, J. (1995, January 1). Racism resurgent: How media let the bell curve's pseudo-science define the agenda on race. *FAIR Extra!.*

Nelson, T. (2012). *In case you missed it, on CRU's source code: "In fact, all data between 1930 and 1994 are subject to "correction".* Retrieved December 1, 2015, from http://tomnelson.blogspot.com/2012/01/in-case-you-missed-it-on-cru-source.html

Neubaum, G., & Krämer, N. C. (2015). Let's blog about health! Exploring the persuasiveness of a personal HIV blog compared to an institutional HIV website. *Health Communication, 30*(9), 872–883. doi:10.1080/10410236.2013.8567 42 PMID:24885514

Neuman, W. L. (2011). *Social research methods: Qualitative and quantitative approaches.* Boston, MA: Pearson.

New Literacies Research Team & Internet Reading Research Group. (2006). *Results summary report from the Survey of Internet Usage and Online Reading for School District 10–C (Research Rep. No. 1).* Storrs, CT: University of Connecticut, New Literacies Research Lab.

Newhagen, J. E., & Levy, M. R. (1998). The future of journalism in a distributed communication architecture. In D. L. Borden & K. Harvey (Eds.), *The Electronic Grapevine: Rumor, Reputation, and Reporting in the New On-Line Environment* (pp. 9–21). Mahwah, NJ: Lawrence Erlbaum Associates.

NIH. (2014a). *About NIH*. Retrieved from http://nih.gov/about/

NIH. (2014b). *Biographical Sketch of Francis S. Collins, M.D., Ph.D*. Retrieved from http://nih.gov/about/director/directorbio.htm

NIH. (2014c). *Frequently Asked Questions*. Retrieved from http://nih.gov/about/FAQ.htm

NIH. (2014d). *Homepage*. Retrieved from http://nih.gov/

NIH. (2014e). *NIH Web Privacy Notice*. Retrieved from http://nih.gov/about/privacy.htm

Nisbett, R. (1995). Race, IQ, and scientism. In S. Fraser (Ed.), *The bell curve wars: Race, intelligence, and the future of America* (pp. 36–57). New York, NY: Basic Books.

Nissenbaum, H. F. (2009). *Privacy in context: Technology, policy, and the integrity of social Life*. Palo Alto, CA: Stanford University Press.

Norris, C., & Armstrong, G. (1999). *The maximum surveillance society: The rise of CCTV*. Oxford, UK: Berg.

Norris, C., McCahill, M., & Wood, D. (2004). Editorial. The growth of CCTV: A global perspective on the international diffusion of video surveillance in publicly accessible space. *Surveillance & Society, 2*(2/3), 110–135.

Norris, C., Moran, J., & Armstrong, G. (1998). Algorithmic surveillance: The future of automated visual surveillance. In C. Norris, J. Moran, & G. Armstrong (Eds.), *Surveillance, closed circuit television, and social control*. Aldershot, UK: Ashgate.

Novotny, M. (2015). reVITALize gynecology: Reimagining apparent feminism's methodology in participatory health intervention projects. *Communication Design Quarterly, 3*(4), 61–74. doi:10.1145/2826972.2826978

O'Keefe, D. J. (2002). *Persuasion: Theory & research* (2nd ed.). Thousand Oaks, CA: Sage.

Oates, T. P., & Pauly, J. (2007). Sports Journalism as Moral and Ethical Discourse. *Journal of Mass Media Ethics, 22*(4), 332–347. doi:10.1080/08900520701583628

O'Cass, A., & Carlson, J. (2010). Examining the effects of website-induced flow in professional sporting team websites. *Internet Research, 20*(2), 115–134. doi:10.1108/10662241011032209

Odom, J. (2014). Identification, consubstantiality, interval, and temporality: Luce Irigaray and the possibilities for rhetoric. In M. Ballif (Ed.), *Re/Framing identifications* (pp. 230–248). Chicago, IL: Waveland Press.

Offit, P. A. (2010). *Deadly choices: How the anti-vaccine movement threatens us all*. Basic Books.

Oftedal, K. (2014). Treating Ebola with homeopathy. *Natural News*. Retrieved from http://blogs.naturalnews.com/treating-ebola-homeopathy/

Oliver, J. E., & Wood, T. J. (2014). Conspiracy theories and the paranoid style(s) of mass opinion. *American Journal of Political Science, 58*(4), 952–966. doi:10.1111/ajps.12084

opopanax. (2013, December 19). *Re: Are all vaccines dangerous? Even Tetanus shots?* [Online forum comment]. Retrieved from http://www.abovetopsecret.com/forum/thread988907

Orwell, G. (1950). *1984: A novel*. New York: Signet Classic.

Osborne, J. (2002). Notes on the use of data transformations. *Practical Assessment, Research & Evaluation, 8*(6), 1–8.

Otterbacher, J. (2011). Being heard in review communities: Communication tactics and review prominence. *Journal of Computer-Mediated Communication*, *16*(3), 424–444. doi:10.1111/j.1083-6101.2011.01549.x

Ow, J. A. (2000). The revenge of the yellowfaced cyborg terminator. In B. E. Kolko, L. Nakamura, & G. B. Rodman (Eds.), *Race in cyberspace* (pp. 51–70). New York, NY: Routledge.

Paala. (2015). *Paa.la* [Blog]. Retrieved from http://paa.la/

Painting, R. (2007). *Positives and negatives of global warming.* Retrieved December 1, 2015, from http://www.skepticalscience.com/global-warming-positives-negatives-intermediate.htm

Palen, L., Vieweg, S., Liu, S. B., & Hughes, A. L. (2009). Crisis in a networked world features of computer-mediated communication in the April 16, 2007, Virginia Tech event. *Social Science Computer Review*, *27*(4), 467–480. doi:10.1177/0894439309332302

Palmer, B. (2014). Himalayan bath salts will not save your life. Slate. Retrieved from http://www.slate.com/articles/health_and_science/medical_examiner/2014/02/natural_news_is_a_facebook_hit_never_click_on_itsr_stories_about_cancer.html

Pang, A., Begam Binte Abul Hassan, N., & Chee Yang Chong, A. (2014). Negotiating crisis in the social media environment: Evolution of crises online, gaining credibility offline. *Corporate Communications*, *19*(1), 96–118. doi:10.1108/CCIJ-09-2012-0064

Papacharissi, Z., & Fernback, J. (2005). Online privacy and consumer protection: An analysis of portal privacy statements. *Journal of Broadcasting & Electronic Media*, *49*(3), 259–281. doi:10.1207/s15506878jobem4903_1

Pariser, E. (2011). *The filter bubble: What the Internet is hiding from you.* New York: Penguin Press.

Park, J., Gu, B., & Lee, H. (2012). The relationship between retailer-hosted and third-party hosted WOM sources and their influence on retailer sales. *Electronic Commerce Research and Applications*, *11*(3), 253–261. doi:10.1016/j.elerap.2011.11.003

Parsloe, S. M. (2015). Discourses of disability, narratives of community: Reclaiming an autistic identity online. *Journal of Applied Communication Research*, *43*(3), 336–356. doi:10.1080/00909882.2015.1052829

PatientsLikeMe. (2014a). *About Us.* Retrieved from http://www.patientslikeme.com/about

PatientsLikeMe. (2014b). *Homepage.* Retrieved from www.patientslikeme.com

PatientsLikeMe. (2014c). *Openness Philosophy.* Retrieved from http://www.patientslikeme.com/about/openness

PatientsLikeMe. (2014d). *Our Team.* Retrieved from http://www.patientslikeme.com/about/team

PatientsLikeMe. (2014e). *Privacy Policy.* Retrieved from http://www.patientslikeme.com/about/privacy

Patterson, O. (1995). For whom the bell curves. In S. Fraser (Ed.), *The bell curve wars: Race, intelligence, and the future of America* (pp. 187–214). New York, NY: Basic Books.

Patton, M. Q. (2002). *Qualitative evaluation and research methods* (3rd ed.). Thousand Oaks, CA: Sage Publications.

Pells, E. (2012, March 25). Louisville in Final 4 with 72-68 Win over Florida. *The Associated Press.* Retrieved April 1, 2012, from http://www.lexisnexis.com

Peltola, H., & Heinonen, O. P. (1986). Frequency of true adverse reactions to Measles-Mumps-Rubella vaccine: A double-blind placebo-controlled trial in twins. *Lancet*, *327*(8487), 939–942. doi:10.1016/S0140-6736(86)91044-5 PMID:2871241

Peters, C., & Broersma, M. (2013). *Rethinking Journalism: Trust and Participation in a Transformed News Landscape.* New York, NY: Routledge.

Petty, R. E., & Cacioppo, J. T. (1986). The elaboration likelihood model of persuasion. *Advances in Experimental Social Psychology, 19*, 123–205. doi:10.1016/S0065-2601(08)60214-2

Pfeifer, M. P., & Snodgrass, G. L. (1990). The continued use of retracted, invalid scientific literature. *Journal of the American Medical Association, 263*(10), 1420–1423. doi:10.1001/jama.1990.03440100140020 PMID:2406475

Pfister, D. (2014). *Networked media, networked rhetorics.* University Park, PA: The Pennsylvania State University Press.

Pham, M. (1992). Effects of involvement, arousal and pleasure on recognition of sponsorship stimuli. *Advances in Consumer Research. Association for Consumer Research (U. S.), 19*(1), 85–93.

Pizam, A. (2014). Peer-to-peer travel: Blessing or blight? *International Journal of Hospitality Management, 38*, 118–119. doi:10.1016/j.ijhm.2014.02.013

Plato. (2001). Gorgias. In P. Bizzell & B. Herzberg (Eds.), The rhetorical tradition: Readings from classical times to the present (2nd ed.; pp. 87-138). Boston, MA: Bedford/St. Martins.

Poland, G. A., & Jacobson, R. M. (2011). The age-old struggle against the antivaccinationists. *The New England Journal of Medicine, 13*(2), 97–99. doi:10.1056/NEJMp1010594 PMID:21226573

Pollach, I. (2007). What's wrong with online privacy policies? *Communications of the ACM, 50*(9), 103–108. doi:10.1145/1284621.1284627

Popular Entries. (2015). Retrieved December 3, 2015, from *Know Your Meme:* http://knowyourmeme.com/memes/popular

Poster, M. (2006). Postmodern virtualities. In M.G. Durham & D.M. Kellner (Eds.), Media and cultural studies: Keyworks (pp. 533-548). Malden, MA: Blackwell Publishing.

Postmes, T., Spears, R., & Lea, M. (1998). Breaching or building social boundaries: SIDE effects of computer-mediated communication. *Communication Research, 25*(6), 689–715. doi:10.1177/009365098025006006

Postmes, T., Spears, R., Sakhel, K., & de Groot, D. (2001). Social influence in computer-mediated communication: The effects of anonymity on group behavior. *Personality and Social Psychology Bulletin, 27*(10), 1243–1254. doi:10.1177/01461672012710001

Potter, W. J., & Levine-Donnerstein, D. (1999). Rethinking validity and reliability in content analysis. *Journal of Applied Communication Research, 27*(3), 258–284. doi:10.1080/00909889909365539

Protecting consumer privacy in an era of rapid change: Recommendations for businesses and policymakers. (2012, March 1). Retrieved January 2, 2016, from https://www.ftc.gov/sites/default/files/documents/reports/federal-trade-commission-report-protecting-consumer-privacy-era-rapid-change recommendations/120326privacyreport.pdf

Public Policy Polling. (2013, April 2). Conspiracy theory poll results.

Punch, K. F. (2014). *Introduction to social research: Quantitative and qualitative approaches* (3rd ed.). London: Sage Publications.

Punday, D. (2000). The narrative construction of cyberspace: Reading *Neuromancer*, reading cyberspace debates. *College English, 63*(2), 194–213. doi:10.2307/379040

Quackenbush, N. (2011). Speaking of—and as—stigma: Performativity and Parkinson's in the rhetoric of Michael J. Fox. *Disability Studies Quarterly, 31*(3). doi:10.18061/dsq.v31i3.1670

Queens University. (2011). *Evaluating web sources*. Retrieved December 1, 2015, from http://library.queensu.ca/inforef/tutorials/qcat/evalint.htm

Quintilian. (2001). Institutes of oratory. In P. Bizzell & B. Herzberg (Eds.), The rhetorical tradition: Readings from classical times to the present (2nd ed.; pp. 364-428). Boston, MA: Bedford/St. Martins.

Quintilian, . (2015). *Quintilian on the teaching of speaking and writing: Translations from books one, two, and ten of the Institutio Oratoria* (2nd ed.). (J. J. Murphy, Trans.). Carbondale, IL: SIU Press.

Rachelle. (2014). *Unlatched* [Blog]. Retrieved from https://unlatched.wordpress.com/

Rachelle. (2015). *Unlatched* [Facebook page]. Retrieved from https://www.facebook.com/unlatched/

Radley, A. (1990). Artefacts, memory and a sense of the past. In D. Middleton & D. Edwards (Eds.), *Collective remembering* (pp. 46–59). London: Sage.

Rainie, L., & Smith, A. (2012, March 12). *Social networking sites and politics*. Pew Internet & American Life Project. Retrieved from http://www.pewinternet.org/Reports/2012/Social-networking-and-politics.aspx

Rainie, L., Fox, S., & Duggan, M. (February 27, 2014). *The web at 25 in the U.S.* Retrieved from http://www.pewinternet.org/2014/02/25/the-web-at-25-in-the-u-s

Rains, S. A. (2007). The impact of anonymity on perceptions of source credibility and influence in computer-mediated group communication: A test of two competing hypotheses. *Communication Research*, *34*(1), 100–125. doi:10.1177/0093650206296084

Rains, S. A., & Karmikel, C. D. (2009). Health information-seeking and perceptions of website credibility: Examining web-use orientation, message characteristics, and structural features of websites. *Computers in Human Behavior*, *25*(2), 544–553. doi:10.1016/j.chb.2008.11.005

Ramirez, A., Walther, J. B., Burgoon, J. K., & Sunnafrank, M. (2002). Information-seeking strategies, uncertainty, and computer-mediated communication. *Human Communication Research*, *28*, 213–228. doi:10.1111/j.1468-2958.2002.tb00804.x

Ramos, D. (1995). Paradise miscalculated. In S. Fraser (Ed.), *The bell curve wars: Race, intelligence, and the future of America* (pp. 62–69). New York, NY: Basic Books.

Rankin, D. (2013). *U.S. politics and Generation Y: Engaging the Millenials*. Boulder, CO: Lynne Rienner.

Rapp, C. (2010). *Aristotle's rhetoric*. Stanford Encyclopedia of Philosophy. Retrieved December 1, 2015, from http://plato.stanford.edu/archives/spr2010/entries/aristotle-rhetoric/

Ratliff, C. (2007). Attracting readers: Sex and audience in the blogosphere. *The Scholar and Feminist Online*, *5*(2). Retrieved from http://sfonline.barnard.edu/blogs/ratliff_03.htm

Raval, N. (2014). The encyclopedia must fail! – Notes on queering Wikipedia. *ADA: A Journal of Gender, New Media, and Technology*, *5*. Retrieved from http://adanewmedia.org/2014/07/issue5-raval/

raymundoko. (2014, August 26). *Re: Vaccine Fraud: U.S. Mainstream Media Censors Whistleblower's Explosive Story*. [Online forum comment]. Retrieved from http://www.abovetopsecret.com/forum/thread1029262

Reagle, J. (2009). *Gender bias in Wikipedia coverage? Open communities, media, source, and standards*. Retrieved from http://reagle.org/joseph/blog/social/wikipedia/wp-eb-gender-bias-coverage

Reagle, J., & Rhue, L. (2011). Gender bias in Wikipedia and Britannica. *International Journal of Communication*, *5*, 1138–1158.

Reference and User Services Association. (2016). *American Library Association*. Retrieved from http://www.ala.org/rusa/

Reicher, S. D., Spears, R., & Postmes, T. (1995). A social identity model of deindividuation phenomena. *European Review of Social Psychology, 6*(1), 161–198. doi:10.1080/14792779443000049

Reinard, J. C. (2008). *Introduction to communication research* (4th ed.). New York, NY: McGraw-Hill.

Ren, W. H. (2000). Library instruction and college student self-efficacy in electronic information searching. *Journal of Academic Librarianship, 26*(5), 323–328. doi:10.1016/S0099-1333(00)00138-5

Reynolds, N. (1993). Ethos as location: New sites for understanding discursive authority. *Rhetoric Review, 11*(2), 325–338. doi:10.1080/07350199309389009

Rheingold, H. (2012, May 9). How to use the Internet wisely, for your health and your country's. *The Atlantic*. Retrieved from http://www.theatlantic.com/technology/archive/2012/05/how-to-use-the-internet-wisely-for-your-health-and-your-countrys/256898/

Rice, D. K. (1955). Objective indicators of subjective variables. In P. F. Lazarsfeld & M. Rosenberg (Eds.), *The Language of Social Research*. Glencoe, IL: The Free Press.

Rich, A. (1986). *Notes toward a politics of location. In Blood, read, and poetry: selected prose 1979-1985* (pp. 210–231). New York, NY: Norton.

Ricker, J. (n.d.). *Evaluating websites. AASL Learning4Life Lesson Plan Database*. Retrieved March 24, 2016, from http://www.ala.org/aasl/sites/ala.org.aasl/files/content/conferencesandevents/ecollab/lpd/EvaluatingWebsites.pdf

Robbins, B. (2004). "That's Cheap." The Rational Invocation of Norms, Practices, and an Ethos in Ultimate Frisbee. *Journal of Sport and Social Issues, 28*(3), 314–337. doi:10.1177/0193723504266992

Robson, C. (2011). *Real world research* (3rd ed.). Chichester, UK: Wiley.

Rodriguez, N. J. (2015). *Toward a better understanding of vaccine-hesitant discourse*. (Unpublished doctoral dissertation). University of Kansas, Lawrence, KS.

Rogers, K. (2015, November 16). *Paris attacks give rise to fakes and misinformation*. Retrieved from http://www.nytimes.com/2015/11/17/world/europe/paris-attacks-give-rise-to-fakes-and-misinformation.html?_r=0

Ronald, K. (1990). A reexamination of personal and public discourse in classical rhetoric. *Rhetoric Review, 9*(1), 36–48. doi:10.1080/07350199009388911

Rose, H. (1983). Hand, brain and heart: A feminist epistemology for the natural sciences. *Signs (Chicago, Ill.), 9*(1), 73–90. doi:10.1086/494025

Rosen, J. (2006, June 27). *The people formerly known as the audience*. Retrieved from: http://archive.pressthink.org/2006/06/27/ppl_frmr.html

Rosen, D., Lafontaine, P. R., & Hendrickson, B. (2011). *Couchsurfing*: Belonging and trust in a globally cooperative online social network. *New Media & Society, 13*(6), 981–998. doi:10.1177/1461444810390341

Rosen, G. (1985). *De la policía médica a la medicina social: Ensayos sobre la historia de la atención a la salud*. México: Siglo XXI.

Rosen, J., & Lane, C. (1995). The sources of *The Bell Curve*. In S. Fraser (Ed.), *The bell curve wars: Race, intelligence, and the future of America* (pp. 58–61). New York, NY: Basic Books.

Rubin, A. M., & Rubin, R. B. (1985). Interface of personal and mediated communication: A research agenda. *Critical Studies in Mass Communication, 2*(1), 36–53. doi:10.1080/15295038509360060

Rubin, R. B., & McHugh, M. P. (1987). Development of parasocial interaction relationships. *Journal of Broadcasting & Electronic Media, 31*(3), 279–292. doi:10.1080/08838158709386664

Ruiz, J. B., & Bell, R. A. (2014). Understanding vaccination resistance: Vaccine search term selection bias and the valence of retrieved information. *Vaccine, 32*(44), 5776–5780. doi:10.1016/j.vaccine.2014.08.042 PMID:25176640

Saint, S., Christakis, D. A., Saha, S., Elmore, J. G., Welsh, D. E., Baker, P., & Koepsell, T. D. (2000). Journal reading habits of internists. *Journal of General Internal Medicine, 15*(12), 881–884. doi:10.1046/j.1525-1497.2000.00202.x PMID:11119185

Salek, T. A. (2014). Faith turns political on the 2012 campaign trail: Mitt Romney, Franklin Graham, and the stigma of nontraditional religions in American politics. *Communication Studies, 65*(2), 174–188. doi:10.1080/10510974.2013.851097

Salek, T. A. (2015). Controversy trending: The rhetorical form of Mia and Ronan Farrow's online firestorm against #WoodyAllen. *Communication, Culture & Critique.* doi:10.1111/cccr.12123

Salmons, J. (2010). *Online interviews in real time.* London, UK: Sage.

Sanders, G. D., & Taira, A. V. (2003). Cost effectiveness of a potential vaccine for *human papillomavirus. Emerging Infectious Diseases, 9*(1), 37–48. doi:10.3201/eid0901.020168 PMID:12533280

Saracevic, T. (1975). Relevance: A review of and a framework for the thinking on the notion in information science. *Journal of the American Society for Information Science, 26*(6), 321–343. doi:10.1002/asi.4630260604

Saracevic, T. (1996). Relevance reconsidered. In *Proceedings of the Second Conference on Conceptions of Library and Information Science.*

Sardar, Z. (1996). alt. civilizations.faq cyberspace as the darker side of the west. In J. R. Ravetz & Sardar, Z. (Eds.), Cyberfutures: culture and politics on the information superhighway (pp. 14-41). New York, NY: Routledge.

Savolainen, R. (2007). Media credibility and cognitive authority. The case of seeking orienting information. *Information Research, 12*(3).

Savolainen, R. (1995). Everyday Life Information Seeking : Approaching Information Seeking in the Context of «Way of Life». *Library & Information Science Research, 0*(17), 259–294. doi:10.1016/0740-8188(95)90048-9

Scharlemann, J. P. W., Eckel, C. C., Kacelnik, A., & Wilson, R. K. (2001). The value of a smile: Game theory with a human face. *Journal of Economic Psychology, 22*(5), 617–640. doi:10.1016/S0167-4870(01)00059-9

Schiappa, E., Gregg, P. B., & Hewes, D. E. (2005). The parasocial contact hypothesis. *Communication Monographs, 72*(1), 92–115. doi:10.1080/0363775052000342544

Schmertz, J. (1999). Constructing essences: Ethos and the postmodern subject of feminism. *Rhetoric Review, 18*(1), 82–91. doi:10.1080/07350199909359257

Schmidt, G. A. (2007, January). The physics of climate modeling. *Physics Today, 60*(1), 72–73. doi:10.1063/1.2709569

Schofferman, J., Wetzel, F. T., & Bono, C. (2015). Ghost and guest authors: You can't always trust who you read. *Pain Medicine, 16*(3), 416–420. doi:10.1111/pme.12579 PMID:25338945

Scholz-Crane, A. (1998). Evaluating the future: A preliminary study of the process of how undergraduate students evaluate web sources.RSR: Reference Services Review, 26, 53-60.

Schostak, J. (2006). *Interviewing and representation in qualitative research*. Glasgow, UK: Open University Press.

Schuplin, M. [Mallery Schuplin]. (2014a, April 21). *Multiple Sclerosis Monday—Being JCV Positive Tysabri* [Video file]. Retrieved from https://youtu.be/QMvplQmlDU4

Schuplin, M. [Mallery Schuplin]. (2014b, April 28). *Multiple sclerosis Monday – the early symptoms* [Video file]. Retrieved from https://youtu.be/4DGoxl0lDAs

Schuplin, M. [Mallery Schuplin]. (2014c, May 5). *Multiple sclerosis Monday – the scariest day of my life* [Video file]. Retrieved from https://youtu.be/aykvwXMgZ_I

Scott, K. A., & White, M. A. (2013). COMPUGIRLS' Standpoint: Culturally Responsive Computer and Its Effects on Girls of Color. *Urban Education*, *48*(5), 657–681.

Seitz-Wald, A. (2013, May 2). Alex Jones: Conspiracy Inc. *Salon*. Retrieved from http://www.salon.com/2013/05/02/alex_jones_conspiracy_inc/

Selegean, J. C., Thomas, M. L., & Richman, M. L. (1983). Long-range effectiveness of library use instruction. *College & Research Libraries*, *44*(6), 476–480. doi:10.5860/crl_44_06_476

Self-regulation and privacy online: A report to Congress. (1999, July 1). FTC. Retrieved January 2, 2016, from https://www.ftc.gov/system/files/documents/reports/self-regulation-privacy-onlinea-federal-trade-commission-report-congress/1999self-regulationreport.pdf

Selzer, J. (2004). Rhetorical analysis: Understanding how texts persuade readers. In C. Bazerman & P. Prior (Eds.), *What writing does and how it does it* (pp. 279–308). Mahwah, NJ: Lawrence Erlbaum.

Serra, P., & Canavilhas, J. (2013). The Credibility of Sources 2.0 in Journalism: Case Study in Portugal. In M. Folk & S. Apostel (Eds.), *Online Credibility and Digital Ethos: Evaluating Computer-Mediated Communication* (pp. 169–185). Hershey, PA: IGI Global. doi:10.4018/978-1-4666-2663-8.ch010

Shadish, W. R., Cook, T. D., & Campbell, D. T. (2002). *Experimental and quasi-experimental designs for generalized causal inference*. Boston: Houghton Mifflin.

Shaffer, G. (2002). The power of EU collective action: The impact of EU data privacy regulation on US business practice. *European Law Journal*, *5*(4), 419–437. doi:10.1111/1468-0386.00089

Shaffer, G., & Zettelmeyer, F. (2002). When good news about your rival is good for you: The effect of third-party information on the division of channel profits. *Marketing Science*, *21*(3), 273–293. doi:10.1287/mksc.21.3.273.137

Shanahan, M. C. (2010). Changing the meaning of peer-to-peer? Exploring online comment spaces as sites of negotiated expertise. *Journal of Science Communication*, *9*(1), 1–13.

Shank, M. D., & Beasley, F. M. (1998). Fan or fanatic: Refining a measure of sports involvement. *Journal of Sport Behavior*, *21*(4), 435.

Shannon. (2011). *Breast for the Weary* [Blog]. Retrieved from http://breastfortheweary.com/

Shapiro, A. L. (1995, July3). Street corners in cyberspace. *Nation (New York, N.Y.)*, *261*(1), 10–14.

Shelton, M., Lo, K., & Nardi, B. (2015) Online media forums as separate social lives: A qualitative study of disclosure within and beyond reddit. In iConference 2015 Proceedings. Newport Beach, CA: IDEALS.

Shen, A. (Apr 4, 2012). How many women does it take to change Wikipedia? *Smithsonian Magazine.com.* Retrieved from http://www.smithsonianmag.com/smithsonian-institution/how-many-women-does-it-take-to-change-wikipedia-171400755/?no-ist

Sher, P. J., & Lee, S. H. (2009). Consumer skepticism and online reviews: An Elaboration Likelihood Model perspective. *Social Behavior & Personality: An International Journal, 37*(1), 137–143. doi:10.2224/sbp.2009.37.1.137

Shifman, L. (2014). *Memes in digital culture.* Cambridge, MA: The MIT Press.

Shumaker, D. (2012). *The embedded librarian: Innovative strategies for taking knowledge where it's needed.* Medford, NJ: Information Today, Inc.

Sillence, E., & Briggs, P. (2015). Trust and engagement in online health: A timeline approach. In S. S. Sundar (Ed.), *The Handbook of the Psychology of Communication Technology* (pp. 469–487). Chichester, UK: Wiley Blackwell. doi:10.1002/9781118426456.ch21

Simonite, T. (2013). The decline of Wikipedia. *The MIT Technology Review.* Retrieved from http://www.technologyreview.com/featuredstory/520446/the-decline-of-wikipedia/

Singer, J. B. (2014). User-generated visibility: Secondary gatekeeping in a shared media space. *New Media & Society, 16*(1), 55–73. doi:10.1177/1461444813477833

Skalli, L. (2006). Communicating gender in the public sphere: Women and information Technologiesin MENA. *Journal of Middle East Women's Studies, 2*(2), 35–59.

Smith, A. (February 11, 2016). *15% of American adults have used online dating sites or mobile dating apps.* Retrieved from http://www.pewinternet.org/2016/02/11/15-percent-of-american-adults-have-used-online-dating-sites-or-mobile-dating-apps/

Smith, A., & Duggan, M. (October 21, 2013). *Online dating and relationships.* Retrieved from http://www.pewinternet.org/Reports/2013/Online-Dating.aspx

Smith, C. (2015, May 13). 45 amazing Yelp Statistics. *Digital Marketing Research.* Retrieved September 12, 2015 from http://expandedramblings.com/index.php/yelp-statistics/

Smith, C. R. (2004). *Ethos* dwells pervasively. In M. J. Hyde (Ed.), *The ethos of rhetoric* (pp. 1–19). Charleston, SC: University of South Carolina Press.

Smith, C. T., De Houwer, J., & Nosek, B. A. (2013). Consider the source: Persuasion of implicit evaluations is moderated by source credibility. *Personality and Social Psychology Bulletin, 39*(2), 193–205. doi:10.1177/0146167212472374 PMID:23386656

Smith, E., & Williams-Jones, B. (2012). Authorship and responsibility in health sciences research: A review of procedures for fairly allocating authorship in multi-author studies. *Science and Engineering Ethics, 18*(2), 199–212. doi:10.1007/s11948-011-9263-5 PMID:21312000

Smith, V. (1998). *Not just race, not just gender: Black feminist readings.* New York, NY: Routledge.

Solove, D. (2007). I've got nothing to hide' and other misunderstandings of privacy. *The San Diego Law Review, 44.* Available http://papers.ssrn.com/sol3/papers.cfm?abstract_id=998565

Solove, D. J. (2007). *The future of reputation: Gossip, rumor, and privacy on the Internet.* Binghamton, NY: Vail-Ballou Press.

Sowell, T. (1995). Ethnicity and IQ. In S. Fraser (Ed.), *The bell curve wars: Race, intelligence, and the future of America* (pp. 70–79). New York, NY: Basic Books.

SpearMint. (2013, February 2). *Re: Why Vaccines are Great.* [Online forum comment]. Retrieved from http://www.abovetopsecret.com/forum/thread923268

Sperber, J. (2014). Yelp and labor discipline: How the internet works for capitalism. *New Labor Forum, 23*(2), 68–74. doi:10.1177/1095796014527066

Špiranec, S., & Zorica, M. B. (2010). Information Literacy 2.0: Hype or discourse refinement? *The Journal of Documentation, 66*(1), 140–153. doi:10.1108/00220411011016407

Spivak, G. (1990). *The postcolonial critic: Interviews, strategies, dialogues* (S. Harasym, Ed.). New York, NY: Routledge.

Spoel, P. (2008). Communicating values, valuing community through health-care websites: Midwifery's online ethos and public communication in Ontario. *Technical Communication Quarterly, 17*(3), 264–288. doi:10.1080/10572250802100360

Sproull, L., & Keisler, S. (1991). *Connections: New ways of working in the networked organization.* Cambridge, MA: The MIT Press.

Stalder, F. (2002). Opinion. Privacy is not the antidote to surveillance. *Surveillance & Society, 1*(1).

Starbird, K., & Palen, L. (2012, February). (How) will the revolution be retweeted?: Information diffusion and the 2011 Egyptian uprising. In *Proceedings of the ACM 2012 conference on computer supported cooperative work* (pp. 7-16). New York, NY: ACM. doi:10.1145/2145204.2145212

Steinhauser, C. (n.d.). *Web evaluation. AASL Learning4Life Lesson Plan Database.* Retrieved March 24, 2016, from http://www.ala.org/aasl/sites/ala.org.aasl/files/content/conferencesandevents/ecollab/lpd/WebEvaluation.pdf

Steinmetz, K. F. (2012). Message received: Virtual ethnography in online message boards. *International Journal of Qualitative Methods, 11*(1), 26–39.

Stephan, R. (2013). Creating solidarity in cyberspace: The case of Arab Women's Solidarity Association United. *Journal of Middle East Women's Studies, 9*(1), 81–109. doi:10.2979/jmiddeastwomstud.9.1.81

Stone, A. M. (2013). Dilemmas of communicating about Alzheimer's disease: Professional caregivers, social support, and illness uncertainty. *Journal of Applied Communication Research, 41*(1), 1–17. doi:10.1080/00909882.2012.738426

Stone, A. R. (1992). Will the real body please stand up? Boundary stories about virtual cultures. In M. Benedikt (Ed.), *Cyberspace: First steps* (pp. 81–118). Cambridge, MA: MIT Press.

Stone, A. R. (2001). Will the real body please stand up? Boundary stories about virtual cultures. In D. Trend (Ed.), *Reading digital culture* (pp. 185–198). Malden, MA: Blackwell Publishing.

Strauss, A., & Corbin, J. (1994). Grounded Theory Methodology. In N. K. Denzin & Y. S. Lincoln (Eds.), *Handbook of qualitative research* (pp. 217–285). Thousand Oaks, CA: Sage.

Strauss, A., & Corbin, J. (1998). *Basics of qualitative research.* Thousand Oaks, CA: Sage Publications.

Street, J. M., Rogers, W. A., Israel, M., & Braunack-Mayer, A. J. (2010). Credit where credit is due? Regulation, research integrity and the attribution of authorship in the health sciences. *Social Science & Medicine, 70*(9), 1458–1465. doi:10.1016/j.socscimed.2010.01.013 PMID:20172638

Strudler, A. (2009). Deception and trust. In C. Martin (Ed.), *The philosophy of deception* (pp. 139–152). Oxford, UK: Oxford University Press. doi:10.1093/acprof:oso/9780195327939.003.0009

Subramaniam, M., Taylor, N. G., St. Jean, B., Follman, R., Kodama, C., & Casciotti, D. (2015). As simple as that?: Tween credibility assessment in a complex online world. *The Journal of Documentation, 71*(3), 550–571. doi:10.1108/JD-03-2014-0049

Sundar, S. S. (2008). The MAIN model: A heuristic approach to understanding technology effects on credibility. In M. J. Metzger & A. J. Flanagin (Eds.), *Digital media, youth, and credibility* (pp. 72–100). Cambridge, MA: The MIT Press.

Sundar, S. S., & Nass, C. (2001). Conceptualizing sources in online news. *Journal of Communication, 51*(1), 52–72. doi:10.1111/j.1460-2466.2001.tb02872.x

Sunstein, C. R. (2009). *Going to extremes: How like minds unite and divide.* New York: Oxford University Press.

Sunstein, C. R., & Vermeule, A. (2009). Conspiracy theories: Causes and cures. *Journal of Political Philosophy, 17*(2), 202–227. doi:10.1111/j.1467-9760.2008.00325.x

Surface Stations. (2009). *About.* Retrieved December 1, 2015, from http://surfacestations.org/about.htm

Surowiecki, J. (2004). *The wisdom of crowds.* New York: Anchor Books.

Survey: One third of American parents mistakenly link vaccines to autism. (2014). National Consumers League. Retrieved from http://www.nclnet.org/survey_one_third_of_american_parents_mistakenly_link_vaccines_to_autism

Sutton, J., Palen, L., & Shklovski, I. (2008, May). Backchannels on the front lines: Emergent uses of social media in the 2007 southern California wildfires. In *Proceedings of the 5th International ISCRAM Conference* (pp. 624-632).

Swan, M. (2009). Emerging patient-driven health care models: An examination of health social networks, consumer personalized medicine and quantified self-tracking. *International Journal of Environmental Research and Public Health, 6*(2), 492–525. doi:10.3390/ijerph6020492 PMID:19440396

Swenson, J., Constantinides, H., & Gurak, L. J. (2002). Audience-driven Web design: An application to medical Web sites. *Technical Communication (Washington), 49*(3).

Swift, A. (2013). Honesty and ethics rating of clergy slides to new low: Nurses again top list; lobbyists are worst. *Gallup.* Retrieved from: http://www.gallup.com/poll/166298/honesty-ethics-rating-clergy-slides-new-low.aspx

Szklarski, C. (2014, February 10). CBC Sochi 2014 Olympics Coverage Attracts Frustrated NBC Viewers. *Huffington Post.* Retrieved December 15, 2015, from http://www.huffingtonpost.ca/2014/02/10/cbc-sochi-2014-olympics_n_4763185.html

Sztompka, P. (1999). *Trust: A sociological theory.* Cambridge, UK: Cambridge University Press.

Tai, Z., & Zhang, Y. (2013). Online identity formation and digital ethos building in the Chinese blogosphere. In M. Folk & S. Apostel (Eds.), *Online Credibility and Digital Ethos: Evaluating Computer-Mediated Communication* (pp. 269–284). Hershey, PA: IGI Global. doi:10.4018/978-1-4666-2663-8.ch015

Tajfel, H. (1981). *Human groups and social categories.* Cambridge, UK: Cambridge University Press.

Tajfel, H., Billig, M., Bundy, R. P., & Flament, C. (1971). Social categorization and intergroup behaviour. *European Journal of Social Psychology, 1*(2), 149–178. doi:10.1002/ejsp.2420010202

Takayoshi, P. (1999). No boys allowed: The World Wide Web as a clubhouse for girls. *Computers and Composition, 16*(1), 89–106. doi:10.1016/S8755-4615(99)80007-3

Tal, K. (1996). *The unbearable whiteness of being: African American critical theory and cyberculture.* Retrieved from http://gse.buffalo.edu/fas/bromley/classes/socprac/readings/Kali-Tal-unbearable.htm

Talmage, C. (2012). Applicant quality: Exploring the differences between organizational and third-party websites. *Social Science Computer Review, 30*(2), 240–247. doi:10.1177/0894439311402147

Tan, K. W., Swee, D., Lim, C., Detenber, B. H., & Alsagoff, L. (2007). The impact of language variety and expertise on perceptions of online political discussions. *Journal of Computer-Mediated Communication, 13*(1), 76–99. doi:10.1111/j.1083-6101.2007.00387.x

Tapscott, D., & Williams, A. D. (2008). *Wikinomics: How mass collaboration changes everything.* Penguin.

Tatarchevskiy, T. (2011). The "popular" culture of Internet activism. *New Media & Society, 13*(2), 297–313. doi:10.1177/1461444810372785

Taylor, A., & Dalal, H. A. (2014). Information literacy standards and the world wide web: Results from a student survey on evaluation of internet information sources. *Information Research: An International Electronic Journal, 19*(4), 1–33.

Taylor, J. (2015). An examination of how student journalists seek information and evaluate online sources during the newsgathering process. *New Media & Society, 17*(8), 1277–1298. doi:10.1177/1461444814523079

Tedeschi, B. (1999). E-commerce report; Consumer products are being reviewed on more web sites, some featuring comments from anyone with an opinion. *New York Times*, 16.

Teglene. (2014). *The Breastfeeding Mother* [Blog]. Retrieved from http://thebreastfeedingmother.blogspot.com/

Terms of Service. Didn't Read. (n.d.). Retrieved December 7, 2015, from https://tosdr.org/index.html#services

Terras, M. M., & Ramsay, J. (2012). The five central psychological challenges facing effective mobile learning. *British Journal of Educational Technology, 43*(5), 820–832. doi:10.1111/j.1467-8535.2012.01362.x

Test, D. W., Kemp-Inman, A., Diegelmann, K., Hitt, S. B., & Bethune, L. (2015). Are online sources for identifying evidence-based practices trustworthy? An evaluation. *Exceptional Children, 82*(1), 58–80. doi:10.1177/0014402915585477

Tewksbury, D. (2006). Exposure to the newer media in a Presidential primary campaign. *Political Communication, 23*(3), 313–332. doi:10.1080/10584600600808877

The University of British Columbia. (2015). *Evaluating information sources.* Retrieved December 1, 2015, from http://help.library.ubc.ca/evaluating-and-citing-sources/evaluating-information-sources/

Thoits, P. A. (2011). Mechanisms linking social ties and support to physical and mental health. *Journal of Health and Social Behavior, 52*(2), 145–161. doi:10.1177/0022146510395592 PMID:21673143

Thomas, N. P. (2004). *Information Literacy and information skills instruction: Applying research to practice in the school library media center.* Westport, CT: Libraries Unlimited.

Thomson, R., Ito, N., Suda, H., Lin, F., Liu, Y., Hayasaka, R., & Wang, Z. et al. (2012). Trusting tweets: The fukushima disaster and information source credibility on twitter. In *Proceedings of the 9th International ISCRAM Conference.*

Tidwell, L. C., & Walther, J. B. (2002). Computer-mediated communication effects on disclosure, impressions, and interpersonal evaluations: Getting to know one another a bit at a time. *Human Communication Research, 28*(3), 317–348. doi:10.1111/j.1468-2958.2002.tb00811.x

Toma, C. L., Hancock, J. T., & Ellison, N. B. (2008). Separating fact from fiction: An examination of deceptive self-presentation in online dating profiles. *Personality and Social Psychology Bulletin, 34*(8), 1023–1036. doi:10.1177/0146167208318067 PMID:18593866

Tønder, L. (2014). Comic power: Another road not taken? *Theory & Event, 17*(4).

Top 15 Most Popular Health Websites. (2014, September). Retrieved from http://www.ebizmba.com/articles/health-websites

Tormala, P. L., Briñol, P., & Petty, R. E. (2006). When credibility attacks: The reverse impact of source credibility on persuasion. *Journal of Experimental Social Psychology*, *42*(1), 684–691. doi:10.1016/j.jesp.2005.10.005

Tormala, Z. L., & Clarkson, J. J. (2007). Assimilation and contrast in persuasion: The effects of source credibility in multiple message situations. *Personality and Social Psychology Bulletin*, *33*(4), 559–571. doi:10.1177/0146167206296955 PMID:17363764

Tracy, C. (2012). *The newsphere: Understanding the news and information environment*. New York: Peter Lang.

Tran, L. D. (2009). *Trust in an online hospitality network: An interpretive study on The Couchsurfing Project*. Retrieved from https://oda.hio.no/jspui/handle/10642/877

Tsfati, Y., & Cappella, J. N. (2003). Do people watch what they do not trust? Exploring the association between news media skepticism and exposure. *Communication Research*, *30*(5), 1–26. doi:10.1177/0093650203253371

Turkle, S. (1996). Parallel lives: Working on identity in virtual space. In D. Grodin & T. R. Lindlof (Eds.), *Constructing the self in a mediated world* (pp. 156–175). Thousand Oaks, CA: Sage. doi:10.4135/9781483327488.n10

Turkle, S. (2001). Who am we? In D. Trend (Ed.), *Reading digital culture* (pp. 236–250). Malden, MA: Blackwell Publishers.

Turner, J. C. (1982). Towards a cognitive redefinition of the social group. In H. Tajfel (Ed.), *Social identity and intergroup relations*. Cambridge University Press.

Ulmer, G. (1994). *Heuristics: The logic of invention*. Baltimore, MD: Johns Hopkins University Press.

University of Pittsburgh. (2015). *Evaluating web resources*. Retrieved December 1, 2015, from http://www.library.pitt.edu/evaluating-web-resources

Vallone, R. P., Ross, L., & Lepper, M. R. (1985). The hostile media phenomenon: Biased perception and perceptions of media bias in coverage of the "Beirut Massacre.". *Journal of Personality and Social Psychology*, *49*(3), 577–585. doi:10.1037/0022-3514.49.3.577 PMID:4045697

Van Cuilenburg, J. (1999). On competition, access and diversity in media, old and new. *New Media & Society*, *1*(2), 183–207. doi:10.1177/14614449922225555

Van Leeuwen, L., Quick, S., & Daniel, K. (2002). The sport spectator satisfaction model: A conceptual framework for understanding the satisfaction of spectators. *Sport Management Review*, *5*(2), 99–128. doi:10.1016/S1441-3523(02)70063-6

Vassilakaki, E., & Moniarou-Papaconstantinou, V. (2015). A systematic literature review informing library and information professionals' emerging roles. *New Library World*, *116*(1/2), 37–66. doi:10.1108/NLW-05-2014-0060

Vickery, J. R. (2014). The curious case of Confession Bear: The appropriation of online macro-image memes. *Information Communication and Society*, *17*(3), 301–325. doi:10.1080/1369118X.2013.871056

Vie, S. (2014). 'You are how you play': Privacy policies and data mining in social networking games. In J. deWinter & R. Moeller (Eds.), *Computer Games and Technical Communication: Critical Methods and Applications at the Intersection*. Ashgate.

Vie, S. (2014). In defense of "slacktivism": The Human Rights Campaign Facebook logo as digital activism. *First Monday*, *4*(7).

Virno, P. (2009). Angels and the general intellect: Individuation in Duns Scotus and Gilbert Simondon. *Parrhesia*, *7*, 58–67.

Vogt, C., & Chen, P. (2001, September). Feminisms and the Internet. *Peace Review*, *13*(3), 371–374. doi:10.1080/13668800120079072

Wager, E., & Williams, P. (2011). Why and how do journals retract articles? An analysis of Medline retractions 1988–2008. *Journal of Medical Ethics*, *37*(9), 567–570. doi:10.1136/jme.2010.040964 PMID:21486985

Walters, F. D. (1995, November). Writing teachers writing and the politics of dissent. *College English*, *57*(7), 822–839. doi:10.2307/378405

Walther, J. B. (1992). Interpersonal effects in computer-mediated interaction: A relational perspective. *Communication Research*, *19*(1), 52–90. doi:10.1177/009365092019001003

Walther, J. B. (1996). CMC: Impersonal, interpersonal, and hyperpersonal interaction. *Communication Research*, *23*(1), 3–43. doi:10.1177/009365096023001001

Walther, J. B., DeAndrea, D., Kim, J., & Anthony, J. C. (2010). The Influence of Online Comments on Perceptions of Antimarijuana Public Service Announcements on YouTube. *Human Communication Research*, *36*(4), 469–492. doi:10.1111/j.1468-2958.2010.01384.x

Walther, J. B., & Parks, M. R. (2002). Cues filtered out, cues filtered in: CMC and relationships. In M. L. Knapp & J. A. Daly (Eds.), *Handbook of interpersonal communication* (3rd ed.; pp. 529–563). Thousand Oaks, CA: Sage.

Walther, J. B., & Parks, M. R. (2002). Cues filtered out, cues filtered in: Computer-mediated communication and relationships. In M. L. Knapp & J. A. Daly (Eds.), *Handbook of interpersonal communication* (3rd ed.; pp. 529–563). Thousand Oaks, CA: Sage.

Walther, J. B., Van Der Heide, B., Hamel, L. M., & Shulman, H. C. (2009). Self-generated versus other-generated statements and impressions in computer-mediated communication: A test of warranting theory using Facebook. *Communication Research*, *36*(2), 229–253. doi:10.1177/0093650208330251

Wang, R. (2006). The lasting impact of a library credit course. *Libraries and the Academy*, *6*(1), 79–92. doi:10.1353/pla.2006.0013

Wang, Y. D., & Emurian, H. H. (2005). An overview of online trust: Concepts, elements, and implications. *Computers in Human Behavior*, *21*(1), 105–125. doi:10.1016/j.chb.2003.11.008

Wann, D. L. (2006). Understanding the Positive Social Psychological Benefits of Sport Team Identification: The Team Identification–Social Psychological Health Model. *Group Dynamics*, *10*(4), 272–296. doi:10.1037/1089-2699.10.4.272

Wann, D. L., & Branscombe, N. R. (1992). Emotional Responses to the Sports Page. *Journal of Sport and Social Issues*, *16*(1), 49–64. doi:10.1177/019372359201600104

Wann, D. L., & Branscombe, N. R. (1993). Sports Fans: Measuring Degree of Identification with Their Team. *International Journal of Sport Psychology*, *24*, 1–17.

Wann, D. L., Dimmock, J., & Grove, J. R. (2003). Generalizing the Team Identification–Psychological Health Model to a Different Sport and Culture: The Case of Australian Rules Football. *Group Dynamics*, *7*(4), 289–296. doi:10.1037/1089-2699.7.4.289

Wann, D. L., Dolan, T. J., McGeorge, K. K., & Allison, J. A. (1994). Relationships between spectator identification and spectators' perceptions of influence, spectators' emotions, and competition outcome. *Journal of Sport & Exercise Psychology*, *16*, 347–364.

Wann, D. L., Friedman, K., McHale, M., & Jaffe, A. (2003). The Norelco Sport Fanatics Survey: Examining Behaviors of Sport Fans. *Psychological Reports*, *92*(3), 930–936. doi:10.2466/pr0.2003.92.3.930 PMID:12841467

Wann, D. L., Melnick, M. J., Russell, G. W., & Pease, D. G. (2001). *Sport fans: The psychology and social impact of spectators*. New York: Routledge.

Wann, D. L., Morriss-Shirkey, P. A., Peters, E., & Suggs, W. L. (2002). Highly Identified Sport Fans and Their Conflict between Expression of Sport Knowledge and Biased Assessments of Team Performance. *International Sports Journal*, *6*(1), 153.

Wann, D. L., & Robinson, I. N. (2002). The Relationship Between Sport Team Identification and Integration into and Perceptions of a University. *International Sports Journal*, *6*(1), 36.

Wann, D. L., Tucker, K. B., & Schrader, M. P. (1996). An exploratory examination of the factors influencing the origination, continuation, and cessation of identification with sports teams. *Perceptual and Motor Skills*, *82*(3), 995–1101. doi:10.2466/pms.1996.82.3.995

Warner, B. R. (2010). Segmenting the electorate: The effects of exposure to political extremism online. *Communication Studies*, *61*(4), 430–444. doi:10.1080/10510974.2010.497069

Warnick, B. (2004). Online ethos: Source credibility in an "authorless" environment. *The American Behavioral Scientist*, *48*(2), 256–265. doi:10.1177/0002764204267273

Warnick, B. (2005). Looking to the future: Electronic texts and the deepening interface. *Technical Communication Quarterly*, *14*(3), 327–333. doi:10.1207/s15427625tcq1403_11

Warnick, B. (2007). *Rhetoric online: Persuasion and politics on the World Wide Web* (Vol. 12). New York, NY: Peter Lang.

Wartenberg, T. E. (2014). *Big ideas for little kids: Teaching philosophy through children's literature* (2nd ed.). New York, NY: Rowman & Littlefield.

Wathen, C. N., & Burkell, J. (2002). Believe it or not: Factors influencing credibility on the web. *Journal of the American Society for Information Science and Technology*, *53*(2), 134–144. doi:10.1002/asi.10016

Watts, A. (2010). *Earth hour in North Korea a stunning success*. Retrieved December 1, 2015, from http://wattsupwiththat.com/2010/03/27/earth-hour-in-north-korea-a-stunning-success

Watts, A. (2011). *Breaking news – CERN experiment confirms cosmic rays influence cloud seeds*. Retrieved December 1, 2015, from http://wattsupwiththat.com/2011/08/24/breaking-news-cern-experiment-confirms-cosmic-rays-influence-climate-change

Watts, A. (2012). *Over 250 noteworthy climategate 2.0 emails*. Retrieved December 1, 2015, from http://wattsupwiththat.com/2012/01/06/250-plus-noteworthy-climategate-2-0-emails

Watts, A. (2015a). *#AGU15 religion and climate change addressed*. Retrieved December 15, 2015 from, http://wattsupwiththat.com/2015/12/15/agu15-religion-and-climate-change-addressed

Watts, A. (2015b). *Green war on jobs: Britain's last deep coal-mine closes*. Retrieved December 21, 2015, from http://wattsupwiththat.com/2015/12/21/green-war-on-jobs-britains-last-deep-coal-mine-closes

Watts, A. (2015c). *Press release – Watts at #AGU the quality of temperature station siting matters for temperature trends*. Retrieved December 15, 2015, from http://wattsupwiththat.com/2015/12/17/press-release-agu15-the-quality-of-temperature-station-siting-matters-for-temperature-trends

Watts, A. (2015d). *Study: Current climate models misrepresent El Niño*. Retrieved December 15, 2015, from http://wattsupwiththat.com/2015/12/15/study-current-climate-models-misrepresent-el-nino

Wayne, G. P. (2007). *How reliable are climate models?* Retrieved December 1, 2015, from http://www.skepticalscience.com/climate-models.htm

Web M. D. LLC. (2015). *Multiple sclerosis health center.* Retrieved from http://www.webmd.com/multiple-sclerosis

WebMD (2014c). *Privacy Policy.* Retrieved from http://www.webmd.com/about-webmd-policies/about-privacy-policy?ss=ftr

WebMD (2014d). *Who We Are.* Retrieved from http://www.webmd.com/about-webmd-policies/about-who-we-are

WebMD. (2014a). *About WebMD.* Retrieved from http://www.webmd.com/about-webmd-policies/default.htm?ss=ftr

WebMD. (2014b). *Homepage.* Retrieved from http://www.webmd.com/

Westerman, D., Spence, P. R., & Van Der Heide, B. (2014). Social media as information source: Recency of updates and credibility of Information. *Journal of Computer-Mediated Communication, 19*(2), 171–183. doi:10.1111/jcc4.12041

What does past climate change tell us about global warming ? (2015). Skeptical Science. Retrieved December 1, 2015, from http://www.skepticalscience.com/climate-change-little-ice-age- medieval-warm-period.htm

What Internet users know about technology and the web. (2014, November 25). Retrieved January 2, 2016, from http://www.pewinternet.org/2014/11/25/web-iq/

Whitty, M. T. (2008). Revealing the 'real' me, searching for the 'actual' you: Presentations of self on an internet dating site. *Computers in Human Behavior, 24*(4), 1707–1723. doi:10.1016/j.chb.2007.07.002

Whitty, M., & Carr, A. (2006). *Cyberspace romance: The psychology of online dating.* New York: Palgrave MacMillan.

Wichowski, D. E., & Kohl, L. E. (2013). Establishing credibility in the information jungle: Blogs, microblogs, and the CRAAP test. In M. Folk & S. Apostel (Eds.), *Online Credibility and Digital Ethos: Evaluating Computer-Mediated Communication* (pp. 229–251). Hershey, PA: IGI Global.

Wichowski, D. W., & Kohl, L. E. (2013). Establishing credibility in the information jungle: Blogs, microblogs, and the CRAAP test. In M. Folk & S. Apostel (Eds.), *Online credibility and digital ethos: Evaluating computer-mediated communication* (pp. 229–251). Hershey, PA: IGI Global. doi:10.4018/978-1-4666-2663-8.ch013

Wikimedia Report Card. (2015, August). Retrieved from http://reportcard.wmflabs.org/

Wikipedia. (2015a). *Breastfeeding:Talk.* Retrieved from https://en.wikipedia.org/wiki/Talk:Breastfeeding

Wikipedia. (2015b). *Wikipedia:About.* Retrieved from https://en.wikipedia.org/wiki/Wikipedia:About

Wikipedia. (2015c). *Wikipedia:Verifiability.* Retrieved from https://en.wikipedia.org/wiki/Wikipedia:Verifiability

Wikipedia. (2015d). *Wikipedia:Wikipedians.* Retrieved from https://en.wikipedia.org/wiki/Wikipedia:Wikipedians

Wilkinson, L., Blank, G., & Gruber, C. (1996). *Desktop data analysis with SYSTAT.* Upper Saddle River, NJ: Prentice Hall.

Williams, R. (2003). *Television.* London: Routledge.

Wilson, P. (1983). *Second-hand knowledge: An inquiry into cognitive authority.* Greenwood Press Westport.

Wilson, R. K., & Eckel, C. C. (2006). Judging a book by its cover: Beauty and expectations in the trust game. *Political Research Quarterly, 59*(2), 189–202. doi:10.1177/106591290605900202

Wimmer, R. D., Dader, J. L., & Dominick, J. R. (1996). *La Investigación científica de los medios de comunicación: una introducción a sus métodos.* Barcelona: Bosch.

Winter, S., & Krämer, N. C. (2014). A question of credibility – Effects of source cues and recommendations on information selection on news sites and blogs. *Communications*, *39*(4), 435–546. doi:10.1515/commun-2014-0020

Wise, K., Alhabash, S., & Park, H. (2010). Emotional responses during social information seeking on Facebook. *Cyberpsychology, Behavior, and Social Networking*, *13*(5), 555–562. doi:10.1089/cyber.2009.0365 PMID:20950180

Witte, K., & Allen, M. (2000). A meta-analysis of fear appeals: Implications for effective public health campaigns. *Health Education & Behavior*, *27*(5), 591–615. doi:10.1177/109019810002700506 PMID:11009129

Wojcieszak, M. (2010). "Don't talk to me": Effects of ideologically homogeneous online groups and politically dissimilar offline ties on extremism. *New Media & Society*, *12*(4), 637–655. doi:10.1177/1461444809342775

Wood, J. (1997). *Communication theories in action: An introduction*. Belmont, NY: Wadsworth.

Wood, M. (2013). Has the Internet been good for conspiracy theorizing? *PsyPAG Quarterly: Special Issue: The Psychology of Conspiracy Theories*, *88*, 31–34.

World Health Organization. (2001). *The World Health Report 2001. Mental health: new understanding, new hope*. Retrieved from http://jama.jamanetwork.com/article.aspx?articleid=194394

Wright, C. (2014). Lemon: The quintessential cancer destroyer and all-around health tonic. *Natural News*. Retrieved from http://www.naturalnews.com/043671_lemon_rind_cancer_cures.html

Xu, H., Dinev, T., Smith, J., & Hart, P. (2011). Information privacy concerns: Linking individual perceptions with institutional privacy assurances. *Journal of the Association for Information Systems*, *12*(12), 798–824.

Xu, Q. (2013). Social recommendation, source credibility, and recency: Effects of news cues in a social bookmarking website. *Journalism & Mass Communication Quarterly*, *90*(4), 757–775. doi:10.1177/1077699013503158

Yannopoulou, N., Moufahim, M., & Bian, X. (2013). User-generated brands and social media: Couchsufing and Airbnb. *Contemporary Management Research*, *9*(1), 85–90. doi:10.7903/cmr.11116

Yoo, J. (2005, May). *Why should I trust you: The path from information valence to uncertainty reduction, cognitive trust, and behavioral trust*. Paper presented at the annual meeting of the International Communication Association, New York, NY.

Young, I. M. (1990). The ideal community and the politics of difference. In L. Nicholson (Ed.), *Feminism/Postmodernism* (pp. 300–323). New York, NY: Routledge.

Zaitchik, A. (2011, March 2). Meet Alex Jones. *Rolling Stone*. Retrieved from http://www.rollingstone.com/politics/news/talk-radios-alex-jones-the-most-paranoid-man-in-america-20110302

Zappen, J. P. (2005). Digital rhetoric: Toward an integrated theory. *Technical Communication Quarterly*, *14*(3), 319–325. doi:10.1207/s15427625tcq1403_10

Zelizer, B. (1992). *Covering the body: The Kennedy assassination, the media, and the shaping of collective memory*. Chicago: University of Chicago.

Zhou, W. (2003). Surveillance for safety after immunization: Vaccine Adverse Event Reporting System (VAERS) --- United States, 1991-2001. *MMWR. Surveillance Summaries*, *52*(1), 1–24. PMID:12825543

Zhu, L., Yin, G., & He, W. (2014). is this opinion leader's review useful? Peripheral cues for online review helpfulness. *Journal of Electronic Commerce Research*, *15*(4), 267–280.

Zurkowski, P. G. (1974). *The information service environment relationships and priorities*. Washington, DC: National Commission on Libraries and Information Science. Retrieved from http://files.eric.ed.gov/fulltext/ED100391.pdf

About the Contributors

Abigail Bakke is an Assistant Professor of Technical Communication at Minnesota State University, Mankato.

Estee Beck is an assistant professor of technical and professional writing/digital humanities in the Department of English at The University of Texas at Arlington.

Kristine L. Blair is Professor of English and Dean of the College of Liberal Arts and Social Sciences at Youngstown State University. The author or co-author of numerous publications on gender and technology, the politics of distance learning, electronic portfolios, and feminist pedagogies, Blair currently serves as editor of both the international print journal *Computers and Composition* and its separate companion journal *Computers and Composition Online*. She is also a recipient of the Conference on College Composition and Communication's Technology Innovator Award and the Computers and Composition Charles Moran Award for Distinguished Contributions to the Field.

Jonathan S. Carter is a Ph.D. candidate at the University of Nebraska. His research focus how emerging technologies, especially the digital, afford and constrain the rhetorical production of new politics and social identifies.

Maura R. Cherney is a current Ph.D. candidate in the Department of Communication at the University of Wisconsin – Milwaukee. Her research focuses mainly on communication technologies and interpersonal communication.

Andrew W. Cole received his PhD in Communication from the University of Wisconsin-Milwaukee in 2014. He is currently a Communication Instructor at Waukesha County Technical College. His research focuses on communication and technology, particularly at intersections of health and education.

Rosalina Pisco Costa is a sociologist and assistant professor at the University of Évora, where she has been teaching social research methodologies for over fifteen years. She is also a researcher affiliated at the Research Centre for the Study of Population, Economy and Society (CEPESE, Portugal). She works mainly in the Sociology of the Family, Childhood, Everyday Life and Consumption Studies, while crosswise exploring different methodologies. Her current research interests cover family, gender and personal life; social time and ages of life; ritualization, memory and familiar aesthetic; everyday life, consumption and mobilities; history and institutionalization of Sociology in Portugal; ethics in social sciences; QDA software, qualitative, sensory and creative social research methodologies.

Daniel Cochece Davis is an Assistant Professor in Illinois State University's School of Communication. His research focuses on the intersection of organizational, leadership and intercultural communication, especially those dimensions containing a neurological/physiological basis. He is coauthor of the upcoming "Communicate Bond Belong Theory" of human relationships in the journal of Communication Theory.

Samaa Gamie received her BA in English language and literature from the University of Alexandria, Egypt in 1995. She received her MA in Professional Writing from the University of Massachusetts at Dartmouth in 2003 and her Ph.D. in English with concentration in Rhetoric and Composition from the University of Rhode Island in 2009. She is currently an Associate Professor of English at The Lincoln University, PA. She is also the Director of the Writing and Reading Center and the Assistant Director of the Writing Proficiency Program. She has published poems, reviews, and essays in AEE, EAPSU, MLS, JCW, and has book chapters published by IGI Global, Columbia University Press, and Syracuse University Press and has other forthcoming publications by NYU Press and IGI Global.

Jill R. Kavanaugh, MLIS, is a solo embedded Librarian at the Center on Media and Child Health, in the Division of Adolescent and Young Adult Medicine at Boston Children's Hospital. Jill provides research support, assists in creating content for the Center's various tools, co-authors papers and publications, and monitors research related to youth, media, technology, and health.

Shana Kopaczewski is currently an Assistant Professor at Indiana State University. She holds a PhD in Interpersonal Communication from the University of Iowa. Her research is centered mainly on intersections between interpersonal communication and new media, particularly online dating, stigma in online spaces, and discourses of the body in online environments.

Candice Lanius is a PhD Candidate in the Department of Communication and Media at Rensselaer Polytechnic Institute. As a data sociologist, she studies how big social data and ubiquitous data collection are changing daily life. She is co-chair of the Research Data Alliance's interest group on Ethics and Social Aspects of Data and a member of the Big Data, Ethics, and Society Network.

Sarah Lefkowith is an American researcher and creative professional based in London. She holds an MSc (Distinction) in the Social Science of the Internet from the University of Oxford and a BA in Media, Technology, and Social Action from New York University's Gallatin School of Individualized Study.

Bartlomiej A. Lenart, Ph.D., is a Lecturer in the Department of Philosophy at the University of Alberta. His research interests are at the intersection of Philosophy, Health Care Ethics, and Information Science. He is also currently pursuing an MLIS.

Lluïsa Llamero, PhD (ORCID number: 0000-0001-5150-3343), is an active member of the research group Digilab: Media, Strategy and Regulation, School of Communication and International Relations Blanquerna-Ramon Llull University. Her research focus are on the field of New Media reception, with a particular interest in the cognitive processes of credibility assessment. She is also exploring interdisciplinary dialogue in fields like health communication, economy and tourism. She collaborates with the research institute Incom-UAB (Autonomous University of Barcelona) and the Medical Anthropology Research Center-Universitat Rovira i Virgili.

Alison Lukowski is an Assistant Professor of Rhetoric and Writing at Christian Brothers University in Memphis, TN. Her research interests include digital rhetoric, the history of rhetoric, and professional writing. She is currently developing a book manuscript about the rhetoric of revolution in new media discourse.

Sandra Metts is a professor emeritus in the School of Communication at Illinois State University, Normal, IL. She served as president of the Central States Communication Association and was recently inducted into the CSCA Hall of Fame. She has been the editor of Communication Reports and associate editor of Journal of Social and Personal Relationships. Her research interests include emotions in families and close relationships, face theory, and sexual communication. Recent publications include "The experience and expression of stepchildren's emotions at critical events in stepfamily life" in the Journal of Divorce and Remarriage and "Logging on, hooking up: The changing nature of romantic relationship initiation and romantic relating" in Human bonding: The Science of Affectional Ties.

Alison N. Novak is an Assistant Professor of Public Relations and Advertising at Rowan University in Glassboro, New Jersey. She received her Ph.D. from Drexel University's doctoral program in Communication, Culture, and Media. Her work explores youth engagement in digital media, online credibility, and political engagement. She is the author of "Millennials, Media, and Politics," and the co-editor of "Defining Identity and the Changing Scope of Culture in the Digital Age."

Nathan Rodriguez, Ph.D., is an Assistant Professor at the University of Wisconsin-Stevens Point.

Sean R. Sadri, Ph.D., is an Assistant Professor at Old Dominion University teaching courses in journalism and media studies. He is a California native who has attended UC Davis and Syracuse University as well as received a Doctorate of Philosophy in Mass Communication from the University of Florida.

Thomas A. Salek received his Ph.D. in Rhetoric and Public Culture from the University of Wisconsin-Milwaukee. He is currently an Assistant Professor at the University of Wisconsin-Stevens Point.

Erika M. Sparby is a PhD candidate in English at Northern Illinois University, specializing in digital, feminist, and visual rhetoric. In particular, she is interested in the rhetorical function of memes and trolling in digital spaces. Her dissertation examines how users create and maintain collective identities in digital social media spaces such as 4chan, Reddit, Facebook, and Twitter.

Index

A

C

D

E

Become an IRMA Member

Members of the **Information Resources Management Association (IRMA)** understand the importance of community within their field of study. The Information Resources Management Association is an ideal venue through which professionals, students, and academicians can convene and share the latest industry innovations and scholarly research that is changing the field of information science and technology. Become a member today and enjoy the benefits of membership as well as the opportunity to collaborate and network with fellow experts in the field.

IRMA Membership Benefits:

- **One FREE Journal Subscription**

- **30% Off Additional Journal Subscriptions**

- **20% Off Book Purchases**

- Updates on the latest events and research on Information Resources Management through the IRMA-L listserv.

- Updates on new open access and downloadable content added to Research IRM.

- A copy of the Information Technology Management Newsletter twice a year.

- A certificate of membership.

IRMA Membership $195

Scan code to visit irma-international.org and begin by selecting your free journal subscription.

Membership is good for one full year.